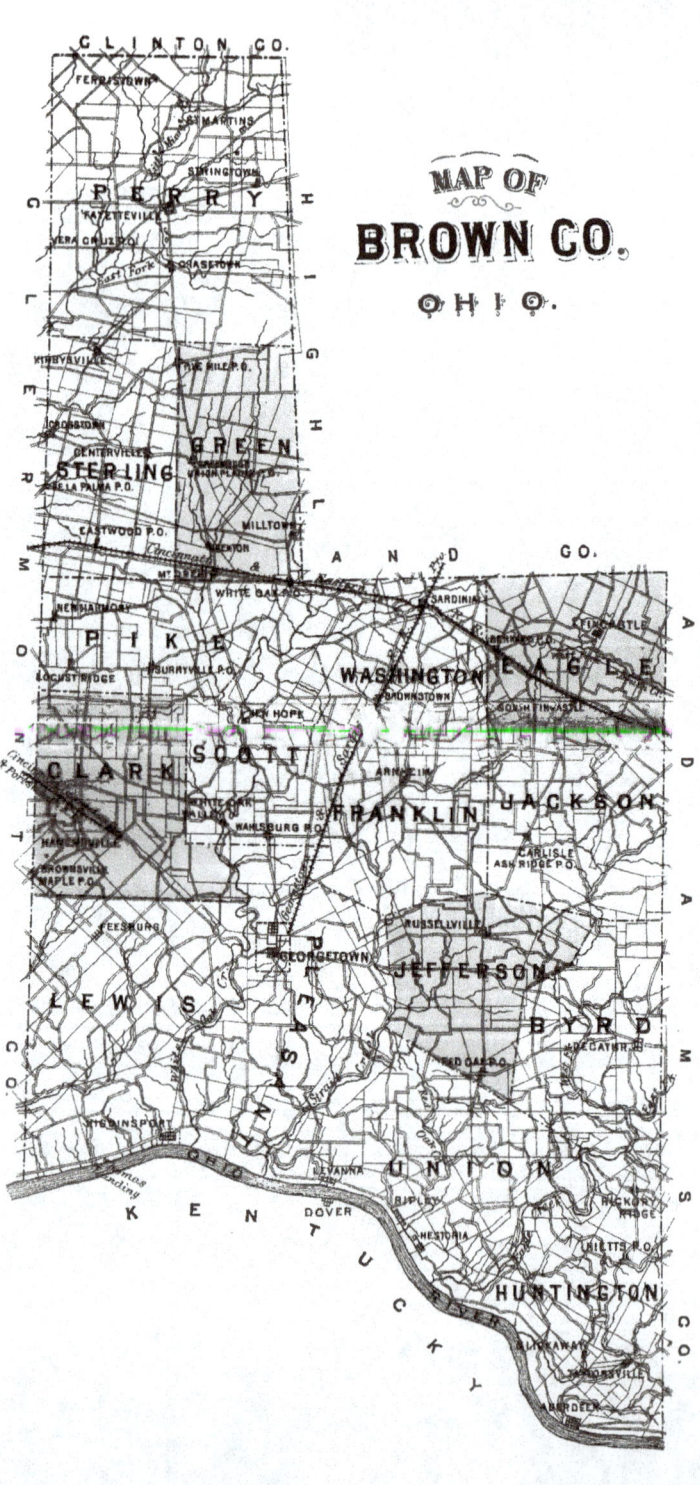

THE HISTORY
of
BROWN COUNTY
OHIO

— Containing —

A History of the County; Its Townships, Towns, Churches, Schools, Etc.; General and Local Statistics; Portraits of Early Settlers and Prominent Men; History of the Northwest Territory; History of Ohio; Map of Brown County; Constitution of the United States, Miscellaneous Matters, Etc., Etc.

[Part III and Part IV from the Original]

W. H. Beers & Co.

HERITAGE BOOKS
2013

HERITAGE BOOKS
AN IMPRINT OF HERITAGE BOOKS, INC.

Books, CDs, and more—Worldwide

For our listing of thousands of titles see our website
at
www.HeritageBooks.com

A Facsimile Reprint
Published 2013 by
HERITAGE BOOKS, INC.
Publishing Division
5810 Ruatan Street
Berwyn Heights, Md. 20740

Copyright © 1995 Heritage Books, Inc.

Originally published Chicago: W. H. Beers & Co., 1883

— Publisher's Notice —
In reprints such as this, it is often not possible to remove blemishes from the original. We feel the contents of this book warrant its reissue despite these blemishes and hope you will agree and read it with pleasure.

International Standard Book Numbers
Paperbound: 978-0-7884-0271-5
Clothbound: 978-0-7884-6866-7

PREFACE.

THE generation of hardy men who first settled the region comprising Brown County has nearly all passed away. The names and deeds of those who encountered the perils of Indian warfare, endured the privations of pioneer life and, with rifles by their sides, cleared away the giants of the forest, rescuing from savages and wild beasts the lands the present generation possesses in peace, should not be forgotten. It is the purpose of this volume to give the history of their achievements, and to record the growth and development of this county, that the present and future generations may know something of what it cost to give them this fair land, and who were the brave men and noble women who converted a wilderness into the smiling region we now behold.

The volume has been prepared in strict accordance with the announcements made in the prospectus of the work. Brief histories of the Northwest Territory and the State of Ohio are first given. The outline history of the county contained in Part III was prepared by Josiah Morrow, the author of the history of Warren County, recently published. Mr. Morrow has devoted much attention for several years past to the history of the Miami Valley. In collecting materials for this work, he has examined the records of the county, explored the earlier history of the original counties from which Brown was formed, and searched out every book, pamphlet and manuscript relating to the history of the Virginia Military District in the State Library at Columbus; the Library of the Ohio Historical and Philosophical Society; the Young Men's Mercantile Library and the Public Library at Cincinnati.

The township histories contained in Part IV are designed to chronicle the annals of each neighborhood, thus rescuing from oblivion much interesting and valuable local history that would otherwise be lost through the death of early settlers and the ravages of time. Interest in local annals has much increased in recent years. The joint resolution of Congress in 1876, recommending the preparation of a sketch of the history of each town and county to be preserved in the Library of Congress, gave an impetus to local historical studies. In addition to the writers of the township histories, whose names are placed at the head of their articles, grateful acknowledgments are due to Dr. I. M. Beck, of Sardinia, and Peter L. Wilson, Esq., of Georgetown, for valuable assistance and suggestions.

The biographical sketches in Part V were prepared for the most part by the soliciting agents of the publishers. The personal and family histories given in these sketches may be found in succeeding years to possess an interest and value, which will cause the book to be much sought after by explorers in genealogies and pedigrees. The study of family history is not for the purpose of ministering to an aristocratic pride; it is perfectly consistent with democratic simplicity and Christian humility. It is not necessary to have noble blood in our veins to give us an intelligent interest in our ancestral relations. It is desirable that the genealogical story of at least every old and long-settled family in each county should be recorded in a form both permanent and readily accessible.

The writers have faithfully aimed at accuracy, but he who expects to find the work entirely free from errors or defects has little knowledge of the difficulties attending the preparation of a work of this kind. To procure its materials, its compilers have explored many hundred pages of manuscripts and written records. In some cases, it was necessary to reconcile contradictory statements. Some errors are unavoidable. The publishers trust that the book will be received in that generous spirit which is gratified at honest efforts, and not in that captious spirit which refuses to be satisfied short of unattainable perfection.

To the county officers, town and township officers, editors, members of the bar, and many intelligent citizens of Brown County, the publishers are indebted for favors and generous assistance. **THE PUBLISHERS.**

CONTENTS.

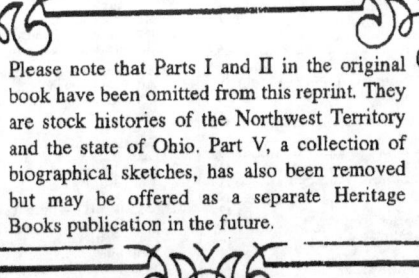

Please note that Parts I and II in the original book have been omitted from this reprint. They are stock histories of the Northwest Territory and the state of Ohio. Part V, a collection of biographical sketches, has also been removed but may be offered as a separate Heritage Books publication in the future.

PART III.
HISTORY OF BROWN COUNTY.

CHAPTER I—
   Physical Features and Pre-historic Remains........ 215
   Antiquities 217

CHAPTER II—
   The Indian Owners.. 220
   Indian Mode of Life... 223
   Character of the Indians 224
   Extinguishment of Indian Titles........................ 224

CHAPTER III—
   Adventures and Conflicts with the Indians......... 226
   Simon Kenton taken Prisoner in Brown County.. 226
   Logan's Expedition and Logan's Gap................. 230
   Killing of Amos and William Wood.................... 231
   Neil Washburn and his Adventures.................... 231
   A Battle with the Indians on East Fork............. 232

CHAPTER IV—
   Virginia Military Titles—Titles—Surveys............ 236
   The Claim of Virginia... 236
   The Cession and Reservation of Virginia............. 239
   Entry and Survey of Land Warrants................... 240
   Adventures of the Early Surveying Parties........ 241
   Want of System in the Surveys 244

CHAPTER V—
   Pioneer History... 249
   First Settlement in the Virginia Military District 250
   Progress of Settlements....................................... 251
   A Journey through the County in 1797............. 254
   A Pioneer's Experience in 1800. 256
   A Visit in 1808 259
   Pioneer Life 260
   Character of the Pioneers................................... 263
   The Primitive Forests.. 265
   Wild Animals.. 266

CHAPTER VI—
   The Great Kentucky Revival and Shakerism in Brown County 270

CHAPTER VII—
   Civil Organization 275
   Early Courts and Commissioners' Proceedings... 280
   Territorial Elections.. 282
   The County Seat Contest................................... 284

CHAPTER VIII—
   General Progress of the County—County Buildings... 290
   Roads 291
   Turnpikes 292
   Ohio River Navigation... 292
   Railways 293
   Churches 294
   The Legal Profession... 299
   The Medical Profession....................................... 302
   Agriculture 303
   Horses.. 304
   Cattle... 305
   Swine 305
   Tobacco 306
   Brown County Agricultural Society and Fairs.... 309
   Growth of Wealth and Population..................... 310
   Population of Brown County.............................. 311
   Political History 311
   Anti-slavery Settlements..................................... 313
   Vote of Brown County at Various Periods.......... 316

CHAPTER IX—
   The Catholic Church of Brown County............. 318
   St. Martin's Church.. 318
   Theological Seminary 324
   The Ursuline Convent... 324
   St. Patrick's Church, Fayetteville...................... 326
   St. Patrick's Academy, Fayetteville................... 330
   Church of the Holy Ghost, Vera Cruz............... 330
   St. Michael's Church, Ripley.............................. 331
   St. Mary's Church, Arnheim.............................. 332

CHAPTER X—
   Military History—The War of 1812.................... 334
   The Mexican War.. 335
   The Civil War 335

CHAPTER XI—
   Sketches of Distinguished Citizens—Gen. Thomas L. Hamer... 343
   Elder Matthew Gardner 352
   Dr. Alexander Campbell..................................... 354
   James Loudon 355
   Nathaniel Beasley 359
   Abraham Shepherd.. 360

CHAPTER XII—
   List of Officers.. 361-366

CONTENTS.

PART IV.
TOWNSHIP HISTORIES.

CHAPTER I.—PLEASANT TOWNSHIP. PAGE.
Early Settlers 371
Mills 380
Cemeteries 381
Roads 381
Schools 382
Churches 382
Villages 384
Georgetown 385
Incorporation and Mayors 393
Grant's Boyhood 393
Morgan's Raid 394
The Press 394
Schools 399
Churches 400
Societies 406
Hotels 406
Business Interests 409
Postmasters 409

CHAPTER II.—UNION TOWNSHIP 411
Early Settlements 412
Ripley 415
Levanna 416
Hestoria 419
Churches 420
The Press of Ripley 422
The Schools, Early Teachers, etc. 425
Steamboat Building at Ripley 429
Societies 430
The Floods in the Ohio River 434
Politics 439
Pork Packing 441
The Horse Trade 442
Statistics 443
Fossil Remains and Other Curiosities 445
Cemeteries 445
Banks in Ripley 446
Underground Railroad 449
The War of the Rebellion 449
Ripley Fair 451
Ripley Gas Light and Coke Company 452
Ripley Buildings and Savings Association 452
Trades and Professions 453

CHAPTER III.—LEWIS TOWNSHIP.
Pioneer Settlements 455
Schools 463
Schools of Higginsport 464
Churches 464
Early Roads 469
Cemeteries 469
Township Treasurers 470
Early Incidents, Manners, etc. 470
Mills 471
Tanneries 471
Saw-mills 471
Higginsport 472
Feesburg 472
Societies 473

CHAPTER IV.—PERRY TOWNSHIP.
Pre-historic Remains 475
Geology 475
Pioneers 476
Political History 484
Mills 485
Cemeteries 486
Churches 486
Education 489
Fayetteville 491
Societies 492

CHAPTER V.—HUNTINGTON TOWNSHIP.
Streams 493
Timber 494
Pioneers 494
Schools 500
Churches 501
The Great Storm of 1860 502
Cemeteries 504
Mills 505
Turnpike Roads 509
Prominent Men of the Township 509

PAGE.
Military 511
Villages 513
Lodges 515
General 515

CHAPTER VI.—CLARK TOWNSHIP.
Political 519
Justices of the Peace 521
Settlement 521
Pioneer Biographies 521
Schools 525
Churches 525
Mills 526
Roads and Railroads 526
Hamersville 529

CHAPTER VII.—FRANKLIN TOWNSHIP 530
Early Settlement 531
Arnheim 544
Mills 545
Churches 546
Cemeteries 549
Schools 549
Franklin Grange 550
Township Officers 550

CHAPTER VIII.—PIKE TOWNSHIP.
Improvements 554
Early Settlers 555
Religious 562
Schools 563
Secret Societies 564
Post Offices 564
Justices of the Peace 565
Soldiers of the Late War 566
Township Officers 571

CHAPTER IX.—EAGLE TOWNSHIP 574
Early Settlers 575
Township Officials 579
Marriages, Early 581
Mills 581
Schools 583
The Sub-School Districts 584
Churches 585
Cemeteries 586
The Fincastle Cemetery 589
Roads 589
The Cincinnati & Eastern Railway 591
The Colored Settlement 591
Fincastle 592
The Fincastle Fairs 593
Vanceburg 594
Bernard 594
John Morgan's Raid 594
Tornado 595
Ancient Remains 595

CHAPTER X.—JEFFERSON TOWNSHIP 599
Roads 600
Saw-Mills 601
Officers 601
Early Settlers 602
Churches 610
Cemeteries 614
Schools 615
War Record 616
Societies 619
The First Fair 619
Russellville 620

CHAPTER XI.—SCOTT TOWNSHIP 622-642

CHAPTER XII.—GREEN TOWNSHIP.
Early Settlement 643
Churches 645
Schools 649
Villages 649
Industries 650
Justices of the Peace 651
Green in the War of the Rebellion 651

CHAPTER XIII.—JACKSON TOWNSHIP.
Officers 655
Justices of the Peace 659

CONTENTS.

	PAGE.
Statistics	659
Pioneers	659
Churches	662
Schools	662
Carlisle	663

CHAPTER XIV.—WASHINGTON TOWNSHIP.

Early Settlement	664
Justices of the Peace	669
Township Officials	669
Churches	672
Graveyards	675
Schools	675
Mills	678
Villages	678
Tornado	680

CHAPTER XV.—STERLING TOWNSHIP.

Land Surveys	681
Pioneer Settlers	682

	PAGE.
Township Organization	686
Property Holders of 1838	687
Churches and Graveyards	688
Schools	691
Post Offices	692
Industries	692

CHAPTER XVI.—BYRD TOWNSHIP.

Early Settlers	693
Early Times and Customs	694
Roads	696
First Mill	697
Cemeteries	698
Schools	698
Churches	699
Societies	701
Politics	701
The War Record	702
Neal	702
Decatur	702

PART III.

HISTORY OF BROWN COUNTY.

BY JOSIAH MORROW.

HISTORY OF BROWN COUNTY.

CHAPTER I.

PHYSICAL FEATURES AND PRE-HISTORIC REMAINS.

BROWN COUNTY borders on the majestic Ohio, and may properly be termed an Ohio River County; but in the division of the State of Ohio into hydrographic basins it has usually been placed in the Miami Valley. It lies nearly midway between the Little Miami and the Scioto; a small portion of the county is drained by East Fork into the Little Miami; no part of the drainage reaches the Scioto. Nearly all of the surface is drained directly into the Ohio by White Oak, Straight and Eagle Creeks and smaller streams.

The county contains 470 square miles, and is bounded on the north by Clinton, on the east by Highland and Adams, on the west by Clermont, and on the south by the Ohio River. Although not the largest in the State, a longer line can be drawn in it than in any other county in Ohio, the diagonal from the southeast to the northwest corners being about forty-five miles. The county has a different shape from that of any other in the State, about one-fourth of its area forming what is popularly called "the boot leg," being from seven to eight miles in width and fifteen in length.

Perhaps no county in Ohio has a more diversified topography or contains a greater variety of soil. Within it are hills so steep and high that they may be called mountains, and large tracts of land marvelously level; extensive areas drained by nature in the most perfect manner, and swamps of vast extent; farms on steep hill-sides, and farms all "wet lands;" black swamps, white swamps and limestone hills; beech lands and oak lands. The county has some of the richest and some of the poorest soil in the State.

The county may be considered as an extensive plain, originally level, and elevated above the Ohio from four hundred to five hundred feet, and having only a slight inclination toward the south. The streams rising in the highest lands have a rapid fall in reaching the Ohio, and have cut for themselves deep channels. Hills as high and steep as those along the Ohio extend some distance up the principal streams which drain the county. The deep channels of these streams are serious impediments in the construction of roads and railways. On account of their rapid descent, the roar of the waters of White Oak Creek is much greater than that of the Miamis.

Picturesque scenery may be found in the county along the Ohio and the streams which flow into it. The hills along the Ohio are said, perhaps with truth, to be unsurpassed in beauty on the globe. The roads leading from the river to reach the high table-lands pass along the beds of the streams between beautifully undulating hills, now denuded of their forest covering, and furnishing valuable and productive farms for tobacco growing. On the turnpike between Ripley and Georgetown, is an extended view of hilly and broken land. A singularly formed elevation near Georgetown, called Bald Point, commands a beautiful view of the wide and deep-cut channel of the White Oak. This narrow and high ridge is in the bend of the stream; has nearly precipitous sides, and on either hand from its crest can be seen the bed of the stream three hundred feet below. The Cincinnati road formerly passed over this ridge, but the way, being both difficult and dangerous for vehicles, was abandoned. The ascent is, however, comparatively easy for the foot passenger, who finds his path strewn with numerous fossils of many species.

The northern portion of the county constitutes a part of an extended flat-lying tract, which takes in portions of Warren, Clermont, Clinton, Brown and Highland, the surface of which is almost a dead level, and was long popularly known as "the swamps." These swamps have mostly been drained, but the descent from them is so slight that there are extensive localities in which the water can be taken with nearly equal facility in different directions. In the early settlement of the county, these wet lands were considered worthless; they were called slashes, and were covered with water more than half the summer. A change has taken place in public opinion concerning their value. As the lands have been reclaimed, the soil, which at first was stubborn and intractable, has been found under a wise management to be rich in agricultural possibilities. These swamps, however, long delayed the settlement and improvement of a considerable portion of the county. They long remained covered with the dense original forests, which shut out the sun's rays from the surface of ground, and, lying about the sources of the streams, they furnished a constant supply of water for the tributaries of the Ohio which flow through the county.

The soils of the county are of two classes, having distinct origins, viz., native and foreign. The native soil consists of clays and sands formed by the disintegration of the native limestone rocks, or those immediately underlying the soil. It is chiefly found on the slopes of the hills along the Ohio and its tributary streams, and constitutes a considerable proportion of the southern half of the county. This soil is of great strength and fertility, and is well adapted to the growth of Indian corn and wheat. The famous tobacco lands of this county belong to this class. The foreign soil consists of drift or materials of foreign origin, and is made up of yellow, white and black clays, and alluvium. These different soils were characterized by different kinds of forest growths. The indigenous trees were the best evidence to the early settler of the character, capacity and fertility of the soil. Although there is usually much difference between native and foreign soils, yet as the underlying rock is limestone, and the gravels and sands of the drift are largely composed of the same kind of rock, the foreign soils in this region are largely calcareous.

Geologically, the stratified rocks of the county belong to the Cincinnati Group, the Hudson River Period, the Lower Silurian Age and the Paleozoic Era. On the Ohio River, near the western boundary of the county, may be found rocks which underlie those exposed at Cincinnati. The Point Pleasant beds of Clermont County are the oldest rocks of Ohio. The latest formed strata of the Cincinnati Group may be found in the highlands of Eagle Township. From Point Pleasant, in Clermont County, to the northeastern corner of Brown County, may be found the entire series of strata of the Lower Silurian of Ohio, having a vertical scale of over seven hundred feet. The Niagara formation, or Upper Silurian, of Adams County extends over the western boundary of that county, and embraces the highest lands in the eastern portion of Eagle Township.

The blue limestone strata form the floor of the county as well as Southwestern Ohio. The name indicates the color of the rocks. The bluish tinge is due to the presence of an oxide of iron. Exposure frequently changes the color to a light gray or drab. Many of stratified rocks of Brown are popularly termed gray limestone. Geologically, however, they all belong to the strata called by Prof. Orton the Cincinnati and Lebanon beds of the blue limestone, and are characterized by precisely the same fossils.

The drift beds are spread over almost the entire county. They consist of clays, sands, gravels, bowlders, and buried vegetable remains, all of which have been transported by glacial action, or by glaciers and icebergs, a greater or less distance from the places of their origin. These beds vary much in depth, in the materials of which they are composed and in the order in which the layers of different materials are arranged. Fragments of wood are frequently found deeply buried in the drift.

Bowlders are scattered irregularly over the county as well as other portions of the Miami country, and constitute an interesting feature of the surface geology. They are termed erratic rocks, hardheads or grayheads. They are universally recognized as of northern origin. They are composed of rocks foreign not only to the county but to Ohio. All geologists agree that many of them were brought from the Lake Superior region and the Canadian highlands, and that far the largest number have been brought from beyond the great lakes. Prof. J. S. Newberry, late Chief Geologist of Ohio, believes that these bowlders were deposited at a later date than the most recent stratified beds of drift, and that they were floated to their present resting places by icebergs, just as icebergs are now known to transport great quantities of rocks, gravel and sand, sometimes, in the case of a single iceberg, amounting to 100,000 tons.

There are few bowlders of very large size in the county. One of the largest is found in the immediate neighborhood of Fayetteville. The large masses of cliffs which attract the attention of the traveler on the Ohio River hills above Higginsport are not bowlders, but examples of the Drift Conglomerate, and formed of the gravels of the drift cemented through the agency of lime water.

Fossiliferous remains of great beauty and variety are found in abundance throughout the county. Perhaps no locality in Ohio furnishes superior facilities for the study of the ancient living forms inhabiting the seas, at the bottom of which the upper beds of the Lower Silurian were formed. They occur in such numbers and are so perfectly preserved that the most careless observers have their attention directed to them in the stones by the wayside and in the village pavements. They are ofttimes so crowded together as to constitute the chief substance of the rocks. The higher or Lebanon beds especially are very fossiliferous, and consequently less valuable for building purposes.

ANTIQUITIES.

The ancient remains of Brown County are chiefly mounds, inclosures and cists. It cannot be said that any law governing the arrangement or distribution of these works has been discovered. They are, perhaps, most numerous in the valleys near the Ohio, but they are found on the flat lands in the north of the county, and also on the most inaccessible places. A small mound is situated on the summit of the hill called Bald Point, near Georgetown. Two mounds near the Ohio, not far from Aberdeen, are the largest in the county. The purpose for which the mounds were built is unknown. They may have been surmounted with houses and appproachable only with ladders, or foundations for watch towers and signal stations, or places of worship and sacrifice. A more common view is that the mounds were places of sepulture and memorials raised over the dead, the largest mounds being erected in honor of distinguished personages. The notion that they contain the remains of vast heaps of dead fallen in great battles is wholly unsupported by the facts obtained from excavations and examinations. But one or two skeletons are usually found in these mounds, and where many are found, it is probable that the later Indians, and, in some cases, Europeans, have buried their dead in them. The new American Cyclopedia assumes, from facts and circumstances deemed sufficient to enable us to arrive at approximate conclusions concerning the antiquity of the Mound-Builders' records, that we may infer, for most of these monuments in the Mississippi Valley, an age of not less than 2,000 years. "By whom built, whether their authors migrated to remote lands under the combined attractions of a more fertile soil and more genial clime, or whether they disappeared beneath the victorious arms of an alien race, or were swept out of existence by some direful epidemic or universal famine, are questions probably beyond the power of human investigations to answer. History is silent concerning them, and their very name is lost to tradition itself." The inclosures, which seem to have been works of defense, and are commonly called ancient forts, in Brown County are not numerous or important.

There are several pre-historic cemeteries in this county, and in some of them a number of skeletons have been found, and frequently implements in connection with the skeletons. The bodies were usually placed in shallow graves, on the sides and ends of which were placed stones on edge, forming a stone box or cist. It has been doubted by some whether these graves are as ancient as the mounds. They were found both in the northern and southern part of the county, but they attracted most attention at the mouth of Eagle Creek. James Finley, Postmaster at West Union, on February 1, 1809, wrote: "Graves are found in different parts of the county. The bodies are deposited in sepulchers made by digging the grave about three feet wide and walling it up with flat stones. The small bones crumble to dust when touched; the large ones are yet sound. Several of these graves are on the bank of the Ohio just above Eagle Creek. The bank has fallen away, and they appear like the end of a conduit made for the conveyance of water."

The archæological remains of Brown County are not so numerous or extensive as those of Ross, Pickaway and Warren Counties; yet here, as in almost the whole of the Ohio Valley, are found traces of a numerous and busy ancient and now extinct race, not of nomadic tribes, but tillers of the soil, workers in copper mines and builders of extensive towns and works of defense—a people with fixed laws, customs and religious rites. Many of the pre-historic works of the county have been obliterated by the cultivation of the soil, and few of them have been accurately surveyed and described. The ancient remains of other counties in Southern Ohio have attracted more attention from writers on American antiquities than any in Brown. In Adams County is an earthwork representing an enormous serpent 1,000 feet in length, which seems about to swallow an egg-shaped figure 164 feet in length. On the summit of Fort Hill, in Highland County, is an ancient work over half a mile in length, a full description and drawing of which are given by Dr. John Locke in the First Geological Report of Ohio. Fort Ancient, in Warren County, one of the largest and most important of the pre-historic works of defense in the Ohio Valley, has been frequently described.

Among the most interesting archæological relics are the utensils, implements, weapons and personal ornaments of pre-historic times. It should be borne in mind that, while most writers on American antiquities make a distinction between the Mound-Builders and the tribes the whites found in possession of the country, such a line of demarkation cannot well be drawn with accuracy with respect to the stone, flint and copper relics. Some of these relics may belong to a pre-historic race of the distant past, some to the earliest Indian tribes inhabiting the country, and others to later Indians, whose mechanical arts may have been modified by contact and trade with the whites. It is, therefore, impossible to separate the relics of the Mound-Builders from those of the later races. We cannot refer the copper implements to any particular epoch, nor can we determine when the stone age began or ended. Stone implements have been found associated with the remains of animals long since extinct, yet these implements are not different from those known to have been in use among the savage tribes when first seen by the whites.

The relics now under consideration have been found in as great quantities in this county, perhaps, as in any county in Ohio. With respect to the purposes for which they were designed, they may be divided into utensils for domestic use, implements for handicraft, weapons and ornaments. With respect to the materials from which they were fabricated, they are stone, flint, slate, copper, pottery, bone, horn and shell.

The most common relics are the flint arrow-heads, spear-heads and daggers. Thousands of arrow and spear heads have been picked up in the county. Other flint implements, such as knives and cutting tools, scrapers and borers, have been found. Of stone relics, the most common are axes and hammers, grooved so that a forked branch or split stick could be fastened for a handle; balls more or less round, probably used as hand hammers; pestles for crushing grain, and many ornaments—among them flat perforated tubes of highly polished slate, and various forms of flat stones, polished and perforated. Stone pipes are found of various sizes and construction. Specimens of ancient pottery have not been often found in the county.

Charles Rau, the author of several valuable papers on American antiquities, has shown that there was an extensive trade or traffic among the pre-historic races of America. This is rendered evident from the fact that their manufactured articles consist of materials which must have been obtained from sources in far distant localities. The materials of which many relics found in the Miami country are composed, can only be found at a distance of hundreds of miles. The term "flint," used to describe the material of which various chipped implements are manufactured, is used to include various kinds of hard and silicious stones, such as hornstone, jasper, chalcedony, and different kinds of quartz. There have been found in the United States, places where the manufacture of flint implements was carried on. There was a great demand for arrow-heads among the primitive tribes, and, in places where the proper kind of material could be found, there were workshops for their manufacture. An important locality to which the aborigines resorted in Ohio for quarrying flint is now called Flint Ridge, and extends through Muskingum and Licking Counties. Dr. Hildreth says of this ancient flint quarry:

"The compact, silicious material of which this ridge is made up seems to have attracted the notice of the aborigines, who have manufactured it largely into arrow and spear heads, if we may be allowed to judge from the numerous circular excavations which have been made in mining the rock, and the piles of chipped quartz lying on the surface. How extensively it has been worked for those purposes may be imagined from the countless number of the pits, experience having taught them that the rock recently dug from the earth could be split with more freedom than that which had lain exposed to the weather. These excavations are found the whole length of the outcrop, but more abundantly at Flint Ridge, where it is more compact and diversified with rich colors."

The greenish, striped slate, of which variously shaped tablets are made, is believed to occur in no part of the Union except the Atlantic Coast District, and to have been transported, either in a rough or worked condition, from that region to the different parts of the Mississippi Valley, in which the relics are found. The copper used by the aboriginal tribes was probably obtained chiefly from the northern part of Michigan.

CHAPTER II.

THE INDIAN OWNERS.

THE territory composing Brown County was uninhabited on its discovery and exploration by white men. So far as is known, no tribe of Indians ever lived upon its soil. There is no historic proof that any people ever had permanent habitations within its limits after the pre-historic race, the Mound-Builders, had passed away, until the English-speaking white men took possession of the land, and began the work of clearing away the forests which had been growing for centuries over the earthworks of a people whose history is enveloped in obscurity. When the Ohio Valley was first explored by white men, the Miami Indians laid claim to nearly all of Western Ohio, and a vast region extending through Indiana to Illinois and northward to the Maumee. This powerful tribe, or rather confederacy of tribes, had villages on the Scioto, the head-waters of the Miamis, the Maumee and the Wabash. But of their vast territory, much that was then the most beautiful and is now the most valuable, was entirely unoccupied. The Ohio, from the mouth of the Scioto, was without evidences of human habitations on either side. The region of the two Miamis, from their union with the Ohio well up to their sources, was an unbroken solitude. Why a region so inviting as Kentucky and Southwestern Ohio should have remained uninhabited for so long a period, while the inhospitable regions of the lakes were peopled, has, perhaps, not been satisfactorily explained. The theory that Kentucky was a common hunting-ground, and purposely kept bare of inhabitants, has been advanced. That it was a disputed ground and battle-field between the tribes of the South and those of the Northwest has been suggested. Perhaps the lack of human inhabitants may be explained with the simple fact that sufficient time had not elapsed since the advent of the Indian races upon the continent to people the whole territory; and that savage tribes, as well as civilized races, are not always successful in first selecting and occupying the best and most pleasing regions. But whatever may be the explanation, the fact that the region referred to was destitute of all traces of recent settlement is established by the testimony of the first explorers and emigrants. Mr. Butler, in his history of Kentucky, says that "no Indian towns within recent times were known to exist within this territory, either in Kentucky or the Lower Tennessee." Gen. Harrison, whose long acquaintance with the Miami Valley before its settlement by white men, and his familiarity with Indian history and traditions, entitle his opinion to the greatest weight, was emphatic in denying the occupation of the country for centuries before its discovery by the Europeans, although he thought there was evidence, from the remains of pottery, pipes, stone hatchets and other articles of inferior workmanship to those of the Mound-Builders, of its being inhabited by some race inferior to that people.

At the threshold of this history, then, we are to conceive of the territory of Brown County during the generations preceding the approach of white men, not as thickly populated with dusky braves, whose villages dotted the shores of its streams, but as a wilderness inhabited only by the beasts of the forest. There was not a town or settlement upon its soil. The smoke curled up from no scattered wigwams; no council fires were lighted; no fields of maize were tilled by the squaws within its limits. The Ohio rolled "his amber tide" along the southern boundary of the county through an unbroken solitude. James Kirke Paulding, in his poem, "The Backwoodsman," describes the scene which met the eyes of the voyagers down the Ohio before the commencement of the wars between the white and the red men.

> "As down Ohio's ever ebbing tide,
> Oarless and sailless, silently they glide,
> How still the scene, how lifeless, yet how fair
> Was the lone land that met the stranger there!
> No smiling villages or curling smoke,
> The busy haunts of men bespoke;
> No solitary haunts the banks along.
> Sent forth blithe labor's homely, rustic song;
> No urchin gambol'd on the smooth, white sand,
> Or hurled the skipping-stone with playful hand.
> Where now are seen, along the river side,
> Young, busy towns, in buxom, painted pride,
> And fleets of gliding boats, with riches crowned,
> To distant Orleans or St. Louis bound,
> Nothing appeared but nature unsubdued
> One endless, noiseless, woodland solitude."

But, while there were no Indian residents, there were Indian owners. We have said that the Miami Indians claimed the territory. They were, doubtless, the rightful owners of the soil when the first white men visited the Miami Rivers. This tribe had important towns on the head-waters of the Great Miami in 1751. It was then probably the most powerful of the North American tribes. Little Turtle, the famous Miami chief, a few days before he agreed to the treaty at Greenville, and ceded his right to these lands, spoke with pride and yet with sadness, of the former greatness and dominion of his tribe. His words are preserved in the American State Papers:

I hope you will pay attention to what I now say to you. You have pointed out to us the boundary line between the Indians and the United States; but I now take the liberty to inform you, that that line cuts off from the Indians a large portion of country which has been enjoyed by my forefathers time immemorial, without molestation or dispute. The prints of my ancestors' houses are everywhere to be seen in this portion. It is well known to all my brothers present, that my forefather kindled the first fire at Detroit; from thence he extended his lines to the head-waters of Scioto; from thence to its mouth; from thence down the Ohio to the mouth of the Wabash; from thence to Chicago on Lake Michigan. At this place, I first saw my elder brothers, the Shawnees. I have now informed you of the boundaries of the Miami nation, where the Great Spirit placed my forefather a long time ago, and charged him not to sell or part with his lands, but to preserve them for his posterity. This charge has been handed down to me. I was surprised to find my other brothers differed so much from me on this subject; for their conduct would lead one to suppose that the Great Spirit and their forefathers had not given them the charge that was given to me, but on the contrary had directed them to sell their lands to any white man who wore a hat, as soon as he should ask it of them.

Little Turtle took pride in the antiquity of his race, as well as in the extent of territory controlled by his ancestors. In 1797, this Miami chief met Volney in Philadelphia. The French philosopher explained to the savage orator the theory that the Indian race had descended from the dark-skinned Tartars, and by a map showed the supposed communication between Asia and America. Little Turtle replied: "Why should not these Tartars, who resemble us, have descended from the Indians?"

The tribes which in Ohio resisted the encroachments of the whites were the Wyandots, Delawares, Shawnees, Chippewas, Ottawas, Pottawatomies, Miamis, Weas and Eel Rivers. The last three were in fact but one tribe, but, at the treaty of Greenville, Gen. Wayne recognized this division, so as to allow them a larger share of the money which was stipulated to be paid by the United States. Gen. Wayne thought it just that the Miami Indians should receive more of the annuities promised by the Government than they would be entitled to as a single tribe, because he recognized the fact that the country ceded by the treaty was in reality their property. It was the opinion of Gen. Harrison that all the Indian tribes of Indiana and Ohio which were united in the war against the whites could not at any time during the ten years which preceded the treaty of peace in 1795 have brought into the field more than 3,000 warriors, although a few years before the Miamis alone could have furnished more than that number. The ravages of the small-pox were the principal cause of the great decrease in their numbers. They composed, however, a body of the finest light infantry troops in the world. They delayed the settlement of the country now forming Brown County and adjoining counties for more than seven years, and, if they had been under an efficient system of discipline, their conqueror at Tippecanoe admits that the settlement of the country might have been attended with much greater difficulty.

While the Miami Indians were the rightful owners of the soil when the Miami country was first visited by white men, they were not the only nor the principal tribe which resisted the settlement of the country by the white men. About ten years before the beginning of the Revolutionary war, the Miami tribes abandoned their towns on the Great Miami and removed to the region of the Maumee. The Shawnees, a warlike and numerous tribe, then established themselves on the head-waters of the two Miami Rivers. It was the Shawnees that the first settlers of the Miami country most frequently came in contact with. They came from the South, and first appeared in Ohio under the protection of the Miamis. Before the removal of the Miamis to the northward, the boundary line between the hunting grounds of the Shawnees and the Miamis appears to have passed through Brown County, the former holding sway over the Scioto Valley, the latter over the Miami Valley. After the settlements in Kentucky had been commenced, the Shawnees held dominion over the whole region now included in Brown and adjoining counties north of the Ohio.

The Indians frequently encamped and hunted within the limits of Brown County. They also often crossed the Ohio near the present sites of Aberdeen and Ripley, for the purpose of stealing horses and annoying the settlements in Kentucky. Tecumseh, in his youthful days, was often in this region. He was born at an Indian village in what is now Clark County, Ohio, and when only about seventeen years of age, or about the year 1785, manifested signal prowess in an attack on some boats on the Ohio near the site of Aberdeen. The boats were captured and all in them killed, except one person, who was burnt alive. The youthful Tecumseh was a silent spectator of the cruel punishment, never having before witnessed the burning of a prisoner, and after it was over he expressed in strong terms his abhorrence of the act, and by his eloquence endeavored to persuade his party never again to burn a captive. Seven years later, Tecumseh was the leader of a party of Indians in a severe engagement with the whites on East Fork, an account of which is given on a subsequent page.

Col. Harmar, in a letter to the Secretary of War, dated May 14, 1787, speaks of having recently seen a party of Shawnees with six or seven prisoners encamped on the Ohio opposite Limestone, Ky., and waiting to exchange their prisoners for an equal number of Indians taken in Col. Logan's expedition. The Indians were commanded by a chief named Wolf. Col. Harmar went over the river and remonstrated with the chief against the frequent murders in Kentucky by the Indians, and told him that the thirteen Great Fires would be provoked to such a degree that they would send their young warriors and destroy all their nations. The chief's answer was in the usual style, that none of the Shawnees committed these murders, but they were done by banditti, countenanced by none of the tribes.

The Shawnees who roamed over the territory now forming Brown County

HISTORY OF BROWN COUNTY. 223

lived in villages on the Scioto and its branches, and the upper waters of the two Miamis. The important towns nearest to Brown County were situated on the North Fork of Paint Creek, near the site of Frankfort, in Ross County, and three miles north of the site of Xenia, in Greene County. The former was called Chillicothe; the latter Old Chillicothe. There were several Indian towns in Ohio called Chillicothe, which appears to have been a favorite name for towns with them. Besides those named, there was one on the Scioto at the site of Westfall, in Pickaway County, and another near the site of Piqua, in Miami County.

INDIAN MODE OF LIFE.

Long before the first settlement of the Miami country by the whites, the habits of the Indians had been modified by their contact with the Europeans. The French and English traders had supplied them with fire-arms, scalping-knives and tomahawks. They had iron pots and brass kettles for cooking and sugar-making. They had learned to love strong drink, and were given to great excesses in eating and drinking. Some of their own arts showed great skill and ingenuity. According to James Smith, a captive among the Delawares in Ohio, the Indian squaws in the sugar-making season of 1756 made vessels for collecting sugar-water in a very curious manner, from freshly peeled elm bark. The manner of construction he does not describe. They raised gourds, and used them for cups and dishes.

Their huts were generally built of small, round logs, and covered with bark or skins. Old Chillicothe was built somewhat after the manner of a Kentucky station—that is, a hollow square. A long council house extended the entire length of the town, in which embassies were received and the chiefs met to consult on grave questions. Some of the houses are said to have been covered with shingles or clapboards. Many Indian huts were made by setting up a pole on forks and placing bark against it; there being no chimney, the smoke passed through an opening at the top.

The agriculture of the Indians was confined chiefly to the growing of corn and beans, to which potatoes were afterward added. The extent of their cornfields was much greater than is generally supposed. A journal of Wayne's campaign, kept by George Will, under date of August 8, 1794, says: "We have marched for four or five miles through corn-fields down the Auglaize, and there are not less than 1,000 acres of corn around the town." The same journal describes the immense corn-fields, numerous vegetable patches and old apple trees found along the banks of the Maumee from its mouth to Fort Wayne. It also discloses the fact that the army obtained its bread and vegetables for eight days, while building Fort Defiance, from the surrounding corn and potato fields. Four years before, Gen. Harmar, in his expedition, burnt and destroyed at least 20,000 bushels of corn. In the cultivation of these large fields, nearly all the work was performed by the women. In addition to field work, the Indian women procured water and firewood, dressed skins, made garments and moccasins, and were little more than mere slaves of the men. The men went to war, procured game, manufactured such arms and implements as were not obtained from the whites, and kept them in repair. They disdained ordinary labor, except upon an object of such dignity and importance as a canoe or a dwelling. Their hunting grounds were often a great distance from their villages. Thus, while the Indian squaw was cultivating these fields or gathering the corn, her warrior lord may have been hunting on the banks of the White Oak or Eagle Creek, and have shot the arrow whose flint head the Brown County farmer of to-day turns up with his plow.

CHARACTER OF THE INDIANS.

Gen. William Henry Harrison thus speaks of the intellectual and moral qualities of the Indians who roamed over this region, in his discourse before the Historical and Philosophical Society of Ohio, on the aborigines of the Ohio Valley.

"The Wyandots, Delawares, Shawnees and Miamis were much superior to the other members of the confederacy. The Little Turtle of the Miami tribe was one of this description, as was Blue Jacket, a Shawnee chief. I think it probable that Tecumseh possessed more integrity than any other of the chiefs who attained to much distinction; but he violated a solemn engagement which he had freely contracted, and there are strong suspicions of his having formed a treacherous design, which an accident only prevented him from accomplishing. Similar instances are, however, to be found in the conduct of great men in the history of almost all civilized nations. But these instances are more than counterbalanced by the number of individuals of high moral character which were to be found amongst the principal and secondary chiefs of the four tribes above mentioned. This was particularly the case with Tarhe, or the Crane, the great sachem of the Wyandots, and Black Hoof, the chief of the Shawnees. Many instances might be adduced to show the possession on the part of these men of an uncommon degree of disinterestedness and magnanimity, and strict performance of their engagements under circumstances which would be considered by many as justifying evasion.

"By many they are supposed to be stoics, who willingly encounter deprivations. The very reverse is the fact. If they belong to either of the classes of philosophers which prevailed in the declining ages of Greece and Rome, it is to that of the Epicureans. For no Indian will forego an enjoyment or suffer an inconvenience if he can avoid it, but under peculiar circumstances, when, for instance, he is stimulated by some strong passion. But even the gratification of this he is ready to postpone whenever its accomplishment is attended with unlooked-for danger or unexpected hardships. Hence their military operations were always feeble, their expeditions few and far between, and much the greater number abandoned without an efficient stroke, from whim, caprice, or an aversion to encounter difficulties." He adds: " When, however, evil comes which he cannot avoid, then he will call up all the spirit of the man and meet his fate, however hard, like the best Roman of them all."

EXTINGUISHMENT OF INDIAN TITLES.

The Indian titles to the lands in Brown County were extinguished by the treaties of Fort McIntosh in 1785, Fort Harmar in 1789, and Greenville in 1795. The first stipulated for the distribution of goods among the different tribes for their use and comfort, but their value is not specified. The last provided that the United States should deliver to the tribes goods to the value of $20,000, and for a perpetual annuity of $9,500, payable in goods reckoned at first cost in the city or place where they should be procured. By these three treaties, the Indians relinquished forever all their claims to two-thirds of the State of Ohio. The great councils of the Northwestern tribes, however, refused to recognize the validity of the two former treaties, because they were made with only a few of the tribes, and had not been sanctioned by the united voice of the Indian confederacy. The Indians could have obtained a much larger sum for these lands had they accepted the offers of the United States Government made previous to Wayne's victorious campaign against them. In 1793, President Washington instructed the Commissioners appointed by him to negotiate a treaty of peace with the Northwestern Indians to use every effort to obtain a confirmation of the boundary line established at Fort Harmar, and to offer in payment $50,000 in hand, and an annuity of $10,000 forever. The Indians refused the money, claiming that the treaties already made were void because not sanctioned by all the tribes, demanded that the Ohio River should be considered the boundary, and that every white settlement should be removed from the Northwest Territory. The Commissioners explained to them that the United States Government had sold large tracts of land northwest of the Ohio, and that the white settlements and improvements were numerous, and had cost much money and labor, and could not be given up; but the Government was willing to pay a larger sum in money and goods than had been given at any one time for Indian lands since the whites first set their feet on this continent. The Indians gave as their final reply:

"Money is of no value to us, and to most of us unknown. As no consideration whatever can induce us to sell the lands on which we get sustenance for our women and children, we hope we may be allowed to point out a mode by which your settlers may be easily removed, and peace thereby obtained.

"We know these settlers are poor, or they never would have ventured to live in a country which has been in continual trouble since they crossed the Ohio. Divide, therefore, this large sum of money which you have offered to us among these people. Give to each, also, a proportion of what you say you will give to us annually over and above this large sum of money, and, we are persuaded, they will most readily accept it in lieu of the land you sold them. If you add, also, the great sums you must expend in raising and paying armies with a view to force us to yield you our country, you will certainly have more than sufficient for the purpose of repaying these settlers for all their labor and their improvements.

"We shall be persuaded that you mean to do us justice, if you agree that the Ohio shall remain the boundary line between us. If you will not consent thereto, our further meeting will be altogether unnecessary."

The Commissioners on the part of the Government said: "That they had already explicitly declared to them that it was now impossible to make the Ohio River the line between their lands and the lands of the United States. Your answer amounts to a declaration that you will agree to no other boundary than the Ohio. The negotiation is therefore at an end."

Nothing remained for the Government but a vigorous prosecution of the war. The Indians were defeated by Gen. Wayne in August, 1794, and in August, 1795, a treaty of peace was ratified by all the tribes.

Who was in the wrong in the long and bloody war which attended the early settlement of Ohio? Are we placed in the dilemma of believing either that our pioneer fathers were rapacious invaders of the lands of the Indians, or that the red men were regardless of their solemn engagements? Fortunately, we are not compelled to adopt either alternative. Enough has already been said to show that the war was not one in which all the wrong was on one side and all the right on the other. An honest effort was made by the Government of the United States to observe good faith toward the Indians, and to prevent their lands from being taken from them without their consent in treaties duly ratified, but in the earlier treaties for the purchase of lands in Ohio, all the tribes who had just claims were not represented.

CHAPTER III.

ADVENTURES AND CONFLICTS WITH THE INDIANS.

THE pioneer hunters and woodsmen of Kentucky often passed over the Ohio into the territory now forming Brown County in pursuit of marauding parties of Indians. This county was the scene of some adventures of thrilling interest during the times of tumult and suffering through which the Northwest Territory passed. Daniel Boone, Simon Kenton, Neil Washburn and other noted hunters and scouts passed over the hills and through the swamps of Brown County long before there was a white settler within its limits.

In 1778, Daniel Boone was a prisoner among the Indians of Ohio for several months. He probably passed through the county in making his flight homeward, when he made the marvelous journey of 160 miles, from Old Chillicothe to Boonesboro, in less than five days, during which he had but one meal.

About the 1st of August of the same year, Boone and Kenton were in a small party formed for the purpose of surprising the Indians at the small Shawnee town on Paint Creek. Before reaching the town, it was learned that the Indian warriors had left it, and were marching against Boonesboro. Boone thereupon, with most of his men, returned to Kentucky to assist in defending the station. Simon Kenton and his companion, Montgomery, determined to proceed alone and capture some horses as a recompense for the trouble of their journey. Reaching the Indian village, they approached it with the stealthy pace of the cat or the panther, and took their stations in the corn-field, supposing the Indians would enter it as usual to get roasting ears. They remained all day and did not see a single Indian, and heard only the voices of some children who were playing near them. At night, they entered the town, and, capturing four of the best horses they could find, they made a rapid night march for the Ohio, which they crossed in safety, and, on the second day afterward, reached Logan's Fort with their booty.

SIMON KENTON TAKEN PRISONER IN BROWN COUNTY.

About the 1st of September, 1778, Simon Kenton, becoming tired of the quiet of a life in the stations of Kentucky, planned a raid against the Indian town on the North Fork of Paint Creek, in what is now Ross County. He was joined by Alexander Montgomery and George Clark. The party set off from Boone's Station with the avowed purpose of taking horses from the Indians, the Kentucky settlements having lost many horses by Indian raids. They crossed the Ohio and proceeded cautiously to Chillicothe, and arrived at the Indian town without meeting any adventures. Kenton's biographer, John McDonald, says:

"In the night, they fell in with a drove of horses that were feeding in the rich prairies. They were prepared with salt and halters. They had much difficulty to catch the horses; however, at length they succeeded, and, as soon as the horses were haltered, they dashed off with seven—a pretty good haul. They traveled with all the speed they could to the Ohio. They came to the Ohio near the mouth of Eagle Creek, now in Brown County. When they came to the river, the wind blew almost a hurricane. The waves ran so high that the horses were frightened, and could not be induced to take the water. It

was late in the evening. They then rode back into the hills some distance from the river, hobbled and turned their horses loose to graze, while they turned back some distance and watched the trail they had come, to discover whether or no they were pursued. Here they remained till the following day, when the wind subsided. As soon as the wind fell, they caught their horses and went again to the river; but their horses were so frightened with the waves the day before that all their efforts could not induce them to take the water. This was a sore disappointment to our adventurers. They were satisfied that they were pursued by the enemy; they therefore determined to lose no more time in useless efforts to cross the Ohio; they concluded to select three of the best horses, and make their way to the Falls of the Ohio, where Gen. Clark had left some men stationed. Each made choice of a horse, and the other horses were turned loose to shift for themselves. After the spare horses had been loosed and permitted to ramble off, avarice whispered to them, and why not take all the horses. The loose horses had by this time scattered and straggled out of sight. Our party now separated to hunt up the horses they had turned loose. Kenton went toward the river, and had not gone far before he heard a whoop in the direction where they had been trying to force the horses into the water. He got off his horse and tied him, and then crept, with the stealthy tread of a cat, to make observations in the direction he heard the whoop. Just as he reached the high bank of the river, he met the Indians on horseback. Being unperceived by them, but so nigh that it was impossible for him to retreat without being discovered, he concluded the boldest course to be the safest, and very deliberately took aim at the foremost Indian. His gun flashed in the pan. He then retreated. The Indians pursued on horseback. In his retreat, he passed through a piece of land where a storm had torn up a great part of the timber. The fallen trees afforded him some advantage of the Indians in the race, as they were on horseback and he on foot. The Indian force divided; some rode on one side of the fallen timber, and some on the other. Just as he emerged from the fallen timber at the foot of the hill, one of the Indians met him on horseback, and boldly rode up to him, jumped off his horse and rushed at him with his tomahawk. Kenton, concluding a gun-barrel as good a weapon of defense as a tomahawk, drew back his gun to strike the Indian before him. At that instant, another Indian, who, unperceived by Kenton, had slipped up behind him, clasped him in his arms. Being now overpowered by numbers, further resistance was useless—he surrendered. While the Indians were binding Kenton with tugs, Montgomery came in view, and fired at the Indians, but missed his mark. Montgomery fled on foot. Some of the Indians pursued, shot at, and missed him; a second fire was made, and Montgomery fell. The Indians soon returned to Kenton, shaking at him Montgomery's bloody scalp. George Clark, Kenton's other companion, made his escape, crossed the Ohio and arrived safe at Logan's Station.

"The Indians encamped that night on the bank of the Ohio. The next morning, they prepared their horses for a return to their towns, with the unfortunate and unhappy prisoner. Nothing but death in the most appalling form presented itself to his view. When they were ready to set off, they caught the wildest horse in the company and placed Kenton on his back. The horse being very restive, it took several of them to hold him, while the others lashed the prisoner on the horse. They first took a tug, or rope, and fastened his legs and feet together under the horse. They took another and fastened his arms. They took another and tied around his neck, and fastened one end of it around the horse's neck; the other end of the same rope was fastened to the horse's tail, to answer in place of a crupper. They had a great deal of amusement to themselves, as they were preparing Kenton and his horse for fun and

B

frolic. They would yell and scream around him, and ask him if he wished to steal more horses. Another rope was fastened around his thighs, and lashed around the body of his horse; a pair of moccasins was drawn over his hands, to prevent him from defending his face from the brush. Thus accoutered and fastened, the horse was turned loose to the woods. He reared and plunged, ran through the woods for some time, to the infinite amusement of the Indians. After the horse had run about, plunging, rearing and kicking for some time and found that he could not shake off or kick off his rider, he very quietly submitted himself to his situation, and followed the cavalcade as quiet and peaceable as his rider. The Indians moved toward Chillicothe, and in three days reached the town."

LOGAN'S EXPEDITION AND LOGAN'S GAP.

The most important army which passed through this county in the campaigns against the Indians was that commanded by Col. Benjamin Logan, in the autumn of 1786, and which destroyed the Mack-a-Cheek towns, in what is now Logan County, Ohio. In the autumn of this year, Gen. George Rogers Clark raised forces for an expedition against the Indians on the Wabash, and ordered Col. Logan to raise a force and march against the Indian towns on the head-waters of the Great Miami. Logan succeeded in raising four or five hundred mounted riflemen, with whom he crossed the Ohio near where Maysville, Ky., now stands, and passed northward, and would have succeeded in surprising the Indian towns had not one of his men deserted to the enemy and given notice of his approach. He succeeded, however, in destroying the towns and numerous corn-fields, killing about twenty Indians and taking seventy or eighty prisoners. He returned by the same route and crossed the Ohio near Limestone, after an absence of about two weeks.

Daniel Boone, Simon Kenton, Col. Robert Patterson and other noted woodsmen were in this expedition, as was also Gen. William Lytle, then only sixteen years old, and, being too young to come within the requisition of the law, offered himself as a volunteer. Among the prisoners taken by Col. Logan back to Kentucky were an Indian woman, known as the "grenadier squaw," who was a sister of Cornstalk, and upward of six feet high, and an interesting Indian lad about sixteen years old, who was adopted by Col. Logan as a member of his family, and was afterward known as Capt. Logan.

The route of Col. Logan through Brown and Clinton Counties was well known to the early surveyors of the Virginia Military District. The place from which the deserter left the army was on Todd's Fork, in Clinton County, about three miles northeast of Wilmington, and since known as "the Deserted Camp." This also was a well-known locality to the early surveyors.

A few miles below Aberdeen, on the north side of the Ohio, is an opening through the river hills to which the attention of travelers on steamboats is often directed, and which is known as Logan's Gap. Through this gap the valley of Eagle Creek is easily reached. Tradition has assigned different reasons for the origin of this name. It is probable that Logan's army passed through this gap, and that thus it received its name.

So numerous were the depredations of the savages during the year 1789 that an expedition was planned against the Indians, who had frequently harassed boats on the Ohio from a lofty rock near the mouth of the Scioto. The Kentuckians being aroused, Gen. Charles Scott, with 230 volunteers, crossed the Ohio at Limestone, and was joined by Gen. Harmar with 100 regulars of the United States, and, on the 18th of April, 1790, marched for the Scioto. The plan adopted was to strike the Scioto some distance from the Ohio, with the hope of intercepting the Indians. The Indians, however, had abandoned their camp, and there was no general action. On the route, a small Indian trail was discovered; thirteen men were detached to follow it; they came upon four Indians in camp, all of whom were killed at the first fire. No official report of this abortive expedition appears ever to have been made to the War Department.

KILLING OF AMOS AND WILLIAM WOOD.

Amos Wood was an early settler on the Kentucky side of the river, near the site of Dover. Mr. Wood, in company with his son William, and Thomas Watts, crossed the Ohio and passed back on a ridge to a deer-lick, for the purpose of procuring venison. Having killed a deer, they were engaged in dressing the meat, when Indians were seen approaching them. Leaving the venison, they fled, and were pursued by the savages to the Ohio. Unfortunately, they failed to reach the river, where they had left their boat. Amos plunged into the river, and was shot and killed. His body was afterward found near Cincinnati. William was overtaken and killed with a tomahawk on the bank of the river. Thomas Watts was engaged in a close encounter with one of the savages. The Indian threw his tomahawk at him and missed him; Watts gained possession of the weapon, and it served him a useful purpose in his own defense. He reached the boat and crossed the river in safety, with the Indian's tomahawk as a trophy. This tragedy of the killing of Amos Wood and his son was witnessed by their friends from the Kentucky shore. The date of the occurrence is not now attainable. The widow of Amos Wood afterward resided at Cincinnati, in a cabin made of papaw poles, and, at a later period, on Mad River.

NEIL WASHBURN AND HIS ADVENTURES.

This celebrated hunter, trapper and scout killed his first Indian in Brown County, and afterward was for some time a resident of this county. Some account of him is appropriate in this place. Cornelius Washburn was a native of New Jersey, was born about the year 1774, and was the son of Jeremiah Washburn. When Neil was six years old, his father moved to the Red Stone country, in Pennsylvania, and, nine years later, to the vicinity of Maysville, Ky. Thomas McDonald, an early pioneer of Ohio, furnished the following account of Neil for Henry Howe, when he was compiling his historical collections:

"In the year 1790, I first became acquainted with Neil Washburn, then a lad of sixteen, living on the Kentucky side of the Ohio, six miles below Maysville. From his early years, he showed a disposition to follow the woods. When only nine or ten, he passed his time in setting snares for pheasants and wild animals. Shortly after, his father purchased for him a shotgun, in the use of which he soon became unexcelled. In the summer of 1790, his father, being out of fresh provisions, crossed the Ohio with him in a canoe to shoot deer at a lick near the mouth of Eagle Creek. On entering the creek, their attention was arrested by a singular hacking noise some distance up the bank. Neil landed, and, with gun in hand, cautiously crawling up the river bank, discovered an Indian, about twenty feet up a hickory tree, busily engaged in cutting around the bark, to make a canoe, in which he probably anticipated the gratification of crossing the river and committing depredations upon the Kentuckians. However this may have been, his meditations and work were soon brought to a close, for the intrepid boy no sooner saw the dusky form of the savage than he brought his gun to a level with his eye and fired; the Indian fell dead to the earth, with a heavy sound. He hastily retreated to the canoe, from fear of the presence of other Indians, and recrossed the Ohio. Early the next morning, a party of men, guided by Neil, visited the spot, and found the body of the Indian at the foot of the tree. Neil secured the scalp, and the same day showed it, much elated, to myself and others, in the town of Washington, in Mason. Several persons in the village made him presents, as testimonials of their opinion of his bravery.

"In the next year, he was employed as a spy between Maysville and the mouth of the Little Miami, to watch for Indians who were accustomed to cross the Ohio into Kentucky to steal and murder. While so engaged, he had some encounters with them, in which his unerring rifle dealt death to several of their number. One of these was at the mouth of Bullskin, on the Ohio side.

"In 1792, the Indians committed such great depredations upon the Ohio, between the Great Kanawha and Maysville, that Gen. Lee, the Government agent in employing spies, endeavored to get some of them to go up the Ohio, above Kanawha, and warn all single boats not to descend the river. None were sufficiently daring to go but Neil. Furnished with an elegant horse and well armed, he started on his perilous mission. He met with no adventures until after crossing the Big Sandy. This he swam on his horse, and had reached about half a mile beyond, when he was suddenly fired upon by a party of Indians in ambush. His horse fell dead, and the Indians gave a yell of triumph; but Neil was unhurt. Springing to his feet, he bounded back like a deer, and swam across the Big Sandy, holding his rifle and ammunition above his head. Panting from exertion, he rested upon the opposite bank to regain his strength, when the Indians, whooping and yelling, appeared on the other side, in full pursuit. Neil drew up, shot one of their number, and then continued his retreat down the Ohio, but, meeting and exchanging shots with others, he saw it was impossible to keep the river valley in safety, and, striking his course more inland, to evade his enemies, arrived safely at Maysville.

"In the fall of the same year, he was in the action with Kenton and others against Tecumseh, in what is now Brown County. Washburn continued as a spy throughout the war, adding the sagacity of the lion to the cunning of the fox. He was with Wayne in his campaign, and at the battle of the Fallen Timbers manifested his usual prowess.

"Neil Washburn was in person near six feet in height, with broad shoulders, small feet, and tapered beautifully from his chest down. He was both powerful and active. His eyes were blue, his hair light and his complexion fair. A prominent Roman nose alone marred the symmetry of his personal appearance."

After peace with the Indians was restored, Washburn spent most of his time in hunting and trapping until the war of 1812, in which he served as a ranger. He owned land in Brown County, about six miles east of the site of Georgetown, and resided there for some time. In 1813, he sold his land in Brown County. The records of this county show that this noted scout, like many others of his time whose lives were spent in the woods, was unable to write his name, and there are records of several documents, in signing which both he and his wife made their marks. In 1815, he moved to Williamsburg, Clermont County, which was his home for several years, but most of his time was spent in hunting and trapping in the Southwest. It is believed that he was killed by the Indians in 1833, while trapping on the Yellowstone.

A BATTLE WITH THE INDIANS ON EAST FORK.

In the month of March, 1792, some horses were stolen by the Indians from the settlements in Mason County, Ky. A party of whites to the number of thirty-six was immediately raised for the purpose of pursuing them. It embraced Simon Kenton, Cornelius Washburn, Benjamin Whiteman, McIntyre,

Calvin, Downing, Ward and other experienced woodsmen. The trail of the Indians being taken, it was found that they had crossed the Ohio where Ripley now stands. The pursuing party reached the Ohio the first evening, prepared rafts, crossed over and encamped for the night. Simon Kenton was placed in command. Early the next morning, the trail was again taken, and followed in a north course, the weather being bad and the ground wet.

When fairly in the Indian country, a portion of the party became dissatisfied; a difference of opinion as to the best plan to pursue was found to exist, and twelve of the men were granted liberty to return. The remaining twenty-four continued the pursuit until a bell was heard, which they supposed indicated their approach to the Indian camp. A halt was called, and all useless baggage and clothing laid aside. Whiteman and two others were sent forward as spies in different directions, each followed by a detachment of the party. After moving forward some distance, it was found that the bell was approaching them. A solitary Indian came riding toward them. When within 150 yards, he was shot and killed. Kenton directed the spies to proceed, being satisfied that the Indian camp was near at hand. They pushed on rapidly and found the Indians encamped on East Fork. The indications of a considerable body of Indians were so strong that the expediency of an attack at that hour was doubted by Kenton.

A hurried council was held, in which it was determined to retire, if it could be done without discovery, and lie concealed until night, and then assault the camp. This plan was carried into execution. Two of the spies were left to watch the camp and ascertain whether the pursuing party had been discovered. The others retreated, and took a commanding position on a ridge. The spies watched until night, and then reported that they had not been discovered by the enemy. The men, being wet and cold, were now marched down into a hollow, where they kindled fires, dried their clothes and put their rifles in order. The party was then divided into three detachments, Kenton commanding the right, McIntyre the center, and Downing the left. By agreement, the three divisions were to move toward the camp simultaneously, and, when they had approached as near as possible without giving an alarm, were to be guided in the commencement of the attack by the fire from Kenton's party. When Downing and his detachment had approached close to the camp, an Indian rose upon his feet and began to stir up the fire, which was but dimly burning. Fearing a discovery, Downing's party instantly shot him down. This was followed by a general fire from the three detachments upon the Indians, who were sleeping under some marquees and bark tents, close upon the margin of the stream. But unfortunately, as it proved in the sequel, Kenton's party had taken "Boone" as their watchword. This name, happening to be as familiar to the enemy as themselves, led to some confusion in the course of the engagement. When fired upon, the Indians, instead of retreating across the stream, as had been anticipated, boldly stood to their arms, returned the fire of the assailants and rushed upon them. They were re-enforced, moreover, from a camp on the opposite side of the river, which, until then, had been unperceived by the whites. In a few minutes, the Indians and the Kentuckians were blended with each other, and the cry of " Boone " and " Che Boone " arose simultaneously from each party.

It was after midnight when the attack was made, and, there being no moon, it was very dark. Kenton, perceiving that his men were likely to be overpowered, ordered a retreat, after the attack had lasted for a few minutes; this was continued through the remainder of the night and part of the next day, the Indians pursuing them, but without killing more than one of the retreating party. The Kentuckians lost but two men—Alexander McIntyre and John

Barr. The loss of the Indians was much greater, according to the statements of some prisoners, who, after the peace of 1795, were released, and returned to Kentucky. They related that fourteen Indians were killed and seventeen wounded. They stated further that there were in the camp about one hundred warriors, among them several chiefs of note, including Tecumseh, Battise, Black Snake, Wolf and Chinskau; and that the party had been formed for the purpose of annoying the settlements in Kentucky, and attacking boats descending the Ohio River. Kenton and his party were three days in reaching Limestone, during two of which they were without food, and destitute of sufficient clothing to protect them from the cold winds and rains of March. The foregoing particulars of this expedition are taken form the narrative of Gen. Benjamin Whiteman, one of the early and gallant pioneers of Kentucky, afterward a resident of Greene County, Ohio. His statement was followed in the account of the battle given in Drake's Life of Tecumseh.

Stephen Ruddle, who had been captured by the Indians when quite young, and had adopted their habits, was with Tecumseh in this engagement. His Indian name was Sinnamatha. His account of the engagement differs somewhat from that before given. He says but two Indians were killed, and that their force was less than that of the whites. Ruddell states that, at the commencement of the attack, Tecumseh was lying by the fire, outside of the tents. When the first gun was heard, he sprang to his feet, and, calling upon Sinnamatha to follow his example and charge, he rushed forward and killed one of the whites [John Barr] with his war-club. The other Indians, raising the war-whoop, seized their arms, and, rushing upon Kenton and his party, compelled them, after a severe contest of a few minutes, to retreat. One of the Indians, in the midst of the engagement, fell into the river, and, in the effort to get out of the water, made so much noise that it created a belief in the minds of the whites that a re-enforcement was crossing the stream to aid Tecumseh. This is supposed to have hastened the order from Kenton for his men to retreat. The afternoon prior to the battle, one of Kenton's men, by the name of McIntyre, succeeded in catching an Indian horse, which he tied in the rear of the camp, and, when a retreat was ordered, he mounted and rode off. Early in the morning, Tecumseh and four of his men set off in pursuit of the retreating party. Having fallen upon the trail of McIntyre, they pursued it for some distance, and at length overtook him. He had struck a fire and was cooking some meat. When McIntyre discovered his pursuers, he instantly fled at full speed. Tecumseh and two others followed, and were fast gaining on him, when he turned and raised his gun. Two of the Indians, who happened to be in advance of Tecumseh, sprang behind trees, but he rushed upon McIntyre and made him prisoner. He was tied and taken back to the battle-ground. Upon reaching it, Tecumseh deemed it pru ent to draw off his men, lest the whites should rally and renew the attack. He requested some of the Indians to catch the horses, but, they hesitating, he undertook to do it himself, assisted by one of the party. When he returned to camp with the horses, he found that his men had killed McIntyre. At this act of cruelty to a prisoner, he was exceedingly indignant, declaring that it was a cowardly act to kill a man when tied and a prisoner. The conduct of Tecumseh in this engagement, and in the events of the following morning, is creditable alike to his courage and humanity. Resolutely brave in battle, his arm was never uplifted against a prisoner, nor did he suffer violence to be inflicted upon a captive without promptly rebuking it.

It is a singular fact that two brothers named Ward were in this engagement, and on opposing sides. John Ward had been captured by the Indians in 1758, when he was three years old, had been adopted as a member of the

Shawnee tribe, and had married an Indian woman, by whom he had several children. He, with his wife and children, was in the camp at the time of the attack by the whites. Capt. Charles Ward, of Mason County, Ky., then a mere lad, was with the party under Kenton, and afterward informed the author of "Western Adventures" that, just before firing began, while he stood within rifle shot of the camp, an Indian girl, apparently about fifteen years old, attracted his attention. Not recognizing her sex, he raised his gun and was on the point of firing, when her open bosom betrayed her sex, and her light complexion caused him to doubt whether she could be an Indian by birth. He afterward learned that she was his brother's child. John Ward was killed in an engagement with the whites one year later, another brother, Capt. James Ward, Simon Kenton and about thirty others, being in the engagement.

Several accounts of the battle on East Fork have been published. There is some difference in the accounts respecting its exact locality. Howe's Historical Collections places it at Salt Licks, Perry Township, Brown County. The history of Clermont County says the camp of the red men when they were attacked was "on the southeast side of the East Fork of the Little Miami River, in Jackson Township, Clermont County, at Limekiln Ford, near the mouth of Grassy Run, and on what are now (1880) the lands of Thomas Goldtrap, J. G. Hutchinson, Samuel Bicking's heirs, about two miles south of Marathon and five miles northeast of Williamsburg." The writer of the account in the Clermont County history claims that Cornelius Washburn, who for some time made his home in the immediate vicinity of the battle, often pointed out the battle-ground and located it as just described. "Western Adventures" says the engagement took place on the Little Miami, which is evidently an error for East Fork of the Little Miami. The account given by Benjamin Whiteman says the Indians were encamped "on the southeast side of the East Fork of the Little Miami, a few miles above the place where the town of Williamsburg has since been built." Solomon Claypool, one of the very earliest settlers in Perry Township, and who was acquainted with both Washburn and Ruddell, located the battle above the mouth of Grassy Run, in Perry Township. It would not be easy, even for those who participated in the struggle, to point out its exact locality after the lapse of many years, and all that can now be said with certainty is that the engagement was on the southeast side of East Fork, and not far from the boundary line between Clermont and Brown Counties.

McDonald, in speaking of this action, says:

"The celebrated Tecumseh commanded the Indians. His cautious and fearless intrepidity made him a host wherever he went. In military tactics, night attacks are not allowable, except in cases like this, when the assailing party are far inferior in numbers. Sometimes, in night attacks, panics and confusion are created in the attacked party, which may render them a prey to inferior numbers. Kenton trusted to something like this on the present occasion, but was disappointed; for, when Tecumseh was present, his influence over the minds of his followers infused that confidence in his tact and intrepidity that they could only be defeated by force of numbers."

CHAPTER IV.
VIRGINIA MILITARY LANDS—TITLES—SURVEYS.

BROWN COUNTY lies within the district known as the Virginia Military Lands, sometimes called the Virginia Military Reservation. These lands are bounded on the south by the Ohio, on the east and north by the Scioto, and on the west by the Little Miami, and a line drawn from the source of the Little Miami to the source of the Scioto. They include the whole of Adams, Brown, Clermont, Clinton, Fayette, Highland, Madison and Union Counties; one half of Franklin, Hardin and Logan; one-fourth of Champaign; one-sixth of Clark; three-fourths of Greene; two-fifths of Warren and Scioto; three-fifths of Pike; two-thirds of Ross and Pickaway; one-fifth of Delaware and Marion; Anderson Township in Hamilton County; and part of Goshen Township in Auglaize County.

At the time of the Revolution, the charters of some of the States embraced large portions of Western unappropriated lands, and each of them, on becoming sovereign and independent, claimed the right of soil and jurisdiction over the whole region embraced within its charter. Some of the States which had no such charters urged that the Western lands ought to be appropriated for the benefit of all the States, as the title to them had been secured by the common blood and treasure. After much contention, these lands were ceded to the United States. Virginia, in March, 1784, ceded to the General Government the right of soil and jurisdiction to the country embraced in her charter situated northwest of the Ohio, reserving the lands between the Little Miami and the Scioto for the payment of the land warrants of her troops in the Revolution, in case they should be needed for that purpose.

THE CLAIM OF VIRGINIA.

The foundation of the claim of Virginia to this region rests upon what is called the Virginia charter of 1609. This was not, strictly speaking, as the name now given to it and that by which it is called in the act of cession would seem to imply, a charter to Virginia, or to the colony of Virginia, or to the people of Virginia, but it was a charter by James, in 1609, to a company of gentlemen residing principally in and about the city of London, and who, by that charter, were organized into a corporation under the name and style of "The Treasurer and Company of Adventurers and Planters of the City of London for the First Colony of Virginia." By this charter, the King, in the first place, authorized this company, which was anciently called "the London Company," with his license to purchase and hold "any manner of lands, tenements and hereditaments, goods and chattels, within our realm of England and dominion of Wales." He, in the next place, grants to the corporation, their successors and assigns, "all those lands, countries and territories situate, lying and being in that part of America called Virginia, from the point of land called Cape or Point Comfort, all along the seacoast to the northward 200 miles, and from the said point of Cape Comfort all along the seacoast to the southward 200 miles, and all that space and circuit of land lying from the seacoast of the precinct aforesaid up into the land throughout, from sea to sea, west and northwest; and, also, all the islands lying within 100 miles along the coast of both seas of the precinct aforesaid."

HISTORY OF BROWN COUNTY.

The following account of the origin of the claim of Virginia to this region is abridged chiefly from a full discussion of the subject by Hon. Samuel F. Vinton, in his argument delivered before the General Court of Virginia at its December term, 1845, for the defendants in the case of the Commonwealth of Virginia versus Peter M. Garner and others for alleged abduction of certain slaves. The pamphlet containing Mr. Vinton's argument is now out of print.

By the words "from sea to sea," the Atlantic and Pacific are supposed to be meant. The grant begins by drawing a base line of 400 miles in length along the Atlantic coast, of which Point Comfort is the center, the northern extreme of which would be at or near Cape May, in New Jersey, and the southern termination at or near Cape Fear, in North Carolina. From one of these terminations a line was to be drawn west, and from the other northwest, back into the land "from sea to sea;" but from which extremity the west and from which the northwest line is to be run, the grant does not specify. If the west line be drawn from the northern termination of the coast line, and the northwest from its southern termination at Cape Fear, it would leave the State of Ohio west of and beyond the grant; but as these two lines would come together before reaching the sea, the Virginia construction always has been that the west line must be drawn from the southern termination on the coast, and the northwest line from the other extremity of the coast line. If the lines be drawn in this way, the west line would strike the Pacific in the Gulf of California, some eight degrees of latitude south of the present boundary line between the United States and Mexico. The other, or northwest line, would cross into Canada somewhere between Lakes Erie and Ontario, and strike the Pacific in the Arctic Circle, somewhere north of Behring's Straits, embracing a portion of the continent that would make not less than forty-five or fifty States of equal extent of territory with the present State of Virginia.

While the magnitude of this grant to a small colony is calculated to strike us with amazement, it should be remembered that at that time the northwest coast of America was wholly unknown, the interior of the continent had never been penetrated from either ocean, and, except the line of coast along its Atlantic border, the vast region of country embraced within the limits of this grant was a sealed book to the world, of whose contents all civilized men were profoundly ignorant. Sir Francis Drake, not long before, from the top of a mountain in the Isthmus of Darien, had seen both oceans. This naturally led to the inference that the continent was a long and narrow strip of country. Smith, in his History of Virginia, relates a fact which shows that, at that time, it was the belief in England that the South Sea, as the Pacific was then called, was but a short distance from the Atlantic. He states that, in the year 1608, the year before the date of the charter, "they fitted up, in England, a barge for Capt. Newton, who was afterward a Deputy Governor of Virginia, under the charter, which, for convenience of carriage, might be taken into five pieces, and with which he and his company were instructed to go up James River as far as the falls thereof (where the city of Richmond now is), to discover the country of the Monakins; and from thence they were to proceed, carrying their barge beyond the falls, to convey them to the South Sea, being ordered not to return without a lump of gold or a certainty of the said sea." It thus appears that the ignorance of the geography of North America which existed in England in the early part of the seventeenth century has affected the titles to the lands of a vast portion of Ohio.

THE CESSION AND RESERVATION OF VIRGINIA.

The history of the times of the Revolution shows that nothing, except the war itself, so deeply agitated the whole country as the question to whom properly belonged the vast Western domain, and no question subjected the Union to a greater peril. All the States were greatly straitened for the means of bearing their respective proportions of the expenses of the war. All attached a very great and probably undue importance to these lands, as a source of revenue, or as a fund on which to obtain credit by their hypothecation. Two sets of opinions, or two parties, sprang up about the right to them. One maintained that the States, respectively, had succeeded to the crown lands within their limits. The other, that the confederacy, or nation at large, had succeeded to the rights and property of the crown, as a common fund. Many very distinguished men arrayed themselves on different sides of this question. Mr. Hamilton, for example, held the latter opinion, and Mr. Madison the former. Those States whose colonial limits embraced any considerable amount of these lands claimed that they were the property of the State, and that the right of the crown, by the Declaration of Independence, had passed to the State sovereignties, where the lands happened to be. Those, on the contrary, who had none of these lands within their limits, claimed that all the crown lands and crown property had passed to the nation, on the principle that what was acquired and conquered by the common effort, blood and treasure was, by the law of nations and of justice, the common property of all. Seven States, embracing within their limits large bodies of these lands, insisted on the right of the State sovereignty; the other six strenuously insisted on the right of the nation, and thus the controversy forthwith found its way into the Congress of the Confederation.

In January, 1781, Virginia passed an act yielding to Congress all her right and claim to the country northwest of the Ohio, but this surrender was clogged with various conditions, of which one was that the United States should guarantee to her all of her remaining territory on the southeast side of the river, which included the present States of Tennessee and Kentucky. The acceptance of this act of cession was urged upon Congress for more than two years by the Virginia delegation in Congress, with great perseverance, when, in May, 1783, it was finally refused by Congress.

The act of cession which was accepted by Congress was passed by the General Assembly of Virginia October 20, 1783, and accepted by act of Congress passed March 1, 1784. The latter date is the date of the deed of cession. The following is the reservation in the deed of cession of the lands in Ohio known as the Virginia Military Lands:

That in case the quantity of good lands on the southeast side of the Ohio, upon the waters of the Cumberland River and between the Green River and Tennessee River, which have been reserved by law for the Virginia troops upon Continental establishment, should, from the North Carolina line bearing in further upon the Cumberland lands than was expected, prove insufficient for their legal bounties, the deficiency should be made up to the said troops, in good lands, to be laid off between the Rivers Scioto and Little Miami, on the northwest side of the River Ohio, in such proportions as have been engaged to them by the laws of Virginia.

The titles to the lands in this district rest upon land warrants issued by Virginia for services in the Revolutionary war. A number of acts were passed by the State of Virginia promising bounties to her troops. An act passed in October, 1779, fixed the quantity to be granted at the end of the war as follows: A private was to receive 200 acres; a non-commissioned officer, 400 acres; a subaltern 2,000 acres; a Captain, 3,000 acres; a Major, 4,000 acres; a Lieutenant Colonel, 4,500 acres; a Colonel, 5,000 acres; a Brigadier General, 10,000 acres; a Major General, 15,000 acres.

ENTRY AND SURVEY OF LAND WARRANTS.

The lands were entered, located and surveyed under the laws of Virginia.

HISTORY OF BROWN COUNTY. 241

Gen. Richard C. Anderson was appointed principal surveyor, and he opened an office for the reception and location of surveys at Louisville, Ky., August 1, 1784. The lands on the Kentucky and Tennessee were to be first surveyed. The deficiency, if any, was to be made up in the lands between the Little Miami and Scioto. Before the close of the year 1786, it became evident that the lands south of the Ohio would not be sufficient to satisfy the warrants, and attention was directed to the reservation north of the Ohio.

An office for the location and survey of the lands between the Little Miami and Scioto was opened by Gen. R. C. Anderson August 1, 1787. Before this, and as early as the winter and spring of 1787, John O'Bannon and Arthur Fox, two enterprising surveyors from Kentucky, explored the district. Their object was to obtain a knowledge of the region for the purpose of making choice locations of warrants as soon as the office for entries was opened. They explored the whole extent of country along the Ohio, and passed some distance up the Scioto and Little Miami, and some of the smaller streams which flow into these rivers. It was probably from his exploration that O'Bannon Creek received its name. A white-oak tree at the mouth of this creek was marked "O'B. Cr." as early as 1787, as is shown by the record of the land entries.

It is said by a writer in the *American Pioneer* that the first location of lands in the Virginia Military District was made for Mace Clements, being 1,000 acres at the mouth of Eagle Creek, and was recorded August 1, 1787.

John O'Bannon was the first to make surveys in the district, and also the first to make a survey within the present limits of Brown County. The first survey in the whole district is said to be that on which the town of Neville, in Clermont County, and on the Ohio, is now situated, which was surveyed by O'Bannon November 13, 1787. On the next day, he made two surveys in Clermont County, one of which includes the present town of Moscow. On the third day, November 15, 1787, O'Bannon made the first survey in Brown, being that opposite Maysville (No. 396)—1,000 acres, entered by Phillip Slaughter.

On the 17th, he surveyed 1,000 acres at the mouth of Eagle Creek (No. 386), entered for Mace Clements.

Seven different surveys were made by O'Bannon within the limits of Brown County before the close of the year 1787, as well as large quantities of land in Clermont County. At this early period, notwithstanding the winter season and the dangers from the Indians, in a single day he surveyed, in Clermont County, 3,400 acres, in several different tracts, some of them miles apart. John O'Bannon is the name of the only surveyor who returned a survey of lands in Brown County before the close of the year 1788.

On July 17, 1788, Congress, by resolution, declared that all locations and surveys between the Little Miami and the Scioto invalid, for the reason that it had not been officially ascertained that there was a deficiency of good lands in the reservation south of the Ohio. This resolution was repealed by an act of Congress passed August 10, 1790, which declared that the lands on the south of the Ohio were insufficient for the purpose for which they had been reserved.

ADVENTURES OF THE EARLY SURVEYING PARTIES.

After the removal of obstructions by Congress, the surveys proceeded rapidly. The principal deputy surveyors under Gen. R. C. Anderson, who made surveys in Brown County prior to the close of the year 1800, were John O'Bannon, Nathaniel Massie, William Lytle, Arthur Fox, John Beasley and Joseph Kerr. Among those whose names appear as chain-carriers or markers in the returns of surveys in Brown County are Duncan McArthur, afterward a surveyor, and General and Governor of Ohio; John McDonald, author of "McDonald's

Sketches," whose biographies of Massie and McArthur give much interesting information concerning the dangers and hardships of the early surveyors of this district; and a large number of names familiar to the early settlers of Brown County, and prominent among whom were the Washburns and the Beasleys.

We condense from John McDonald's Life of Gen. Nathaniel Massie some interesting facts concerning the early surveys:

A Virginia statute, fixing the fees of the surveyors, provided that they should be paid in tobacco. The fee for surveying and platting 1,000 acres was 320 pounds of tobacco. However, as the risk of making entries was great, and as it was desirable to possess the best land, the owners of warrants, in most cases, made liberal contracts with the surveyors. One-fourth, one-third, and sometimes as much as one-half, acquired by the entry of good lands were given by the proprietors to the surveyors. If the owners preferred paying money, the usual terms were £10, Virginia currency, for each 1,000 acres entered and surveyed, exclusive of chainmen's expenses. These terms cannot appear extravagant when we consider that, at that time, the danger encountered was great, the exposure during the winter severe, and that the price of first-rate land in the West was low, and an immense quantity in market.

The locations of land warrants in the Virginia Military District between the Scioto and the Little Miami, prior to 1790, were made by stealth. Every creek which was explored, every line that was run, was at the risk of life from the savage Indians, whose courage and perseverance were only equaled by the perseverance of the whites to push forward their settlements. The winters were selected as the season most secure for the surveys, the Indians then being in winter quarters.

After Gen. Nathaniel Massie had made the first settlement in the district at Manchester, in the winter of 1790, he became the most extensive surveyor and land speculator in Ohio at that time. When seventeen years old, he had been in the Revolutionary war. He then studied surveying, and in 1785, when he was twenty years old, left for Kentucky to seek his fortune.

"Young Massie soon became an expert surveyor, and it was a matter of astonishment (as he was raised in the dense population east of the mountains) how soon he acquired the science and habits of the backwoodsmen. Although he never practiced the art of hunting, he was admitted, by all who knew his qualifications as a woodsman, to be of the first order. He could steer his course truly in clear or cloudy weather, and compute distances more correctly than most of the old hunters. He could endure fatigue and hunger with more composure than most of those persons who were inured to want on the frontier. He could live upon meat without bread, and bread without meat, and was perfectly cheerful and contented with his fare. In all the perilous situations in which he was placed, he was always conspicuous for his good feeling and the happy temperament of his mind. His courage was of a cool and dispassionate character, which, added to great circumspection in times of danger, gave him a complete ascendancy over his companions, who were always willing to follow when Massie led the way."

In his surveys, he usually had, besides himself, three assistant surveyors, and six men with each surveyor. The parties all moved with great caution. First went the hunter, looking for game and on the watch for the Indians; next, the surveyor, two chainmen and marker; then the packhorse man with baggage, and, two or three hundred yards in the rear, a watchman, on the trail, to guard against an attack from behind. When night came, four fires were made for cooking—that is, one for each mess. Around these fires, till sleeping time arrived, the company spent their time in the most social glee, singing songs and telling stories. When danger was not apparent or immediate, they were as merry a set of men as ever assembled. Resting time arriving, Massie always gave the signal, and the whole party would then leave their comfortable fires, carrying with them their blankets, their firearms and their little baggage, walking in perfect silence two or three hundred yards from their fires. They would then scrape away the snow and huddle down together for the night. Each mess formed one bed; they would spread down on the ground one-half of the blankets, reserving the other half for covering. The covering blankets were fastened together by skewers, to prevent them from slipping apart. Thus prepared, the whole party crouched down together, with their rifles in their arms, and their pouches under their heads for pillows; lying spoon fashion, with three heads one way and four the other, their feet extending to about the middle of their bodies. When one turned, the whole mess turned, or else the close range would be broken and the cold let in. In this way they lay till broad daylight, no noise and scarce a whisper being uttered during the night. When it was perfectly light, Massie would call up two of the men in whom he had most confidence, and send them to reconnoiter and make a circuit around the fires, lest an ambuscade might be formed by the Indians to destroy the party as they returned to the fires. This was an invariable custom in every variety of weather. Self-preservation required this circumspection.

During one of his expeditions, which set out from Manchester in the winter of 1794-95, with Nathaniel Beasley, John Beasley and Peter Lee as assistant surveyors, and took the route of Logan's trace to the Deserted Camp, the ground was covered with a sheet of snow from six to ten inches deep. During the tour, which continued upward of thirty days, the party had no bread. For the first two weeks, a pint of flour was distributed to each mess once a day, to mix with the soup in which meat had been boiled.

After the defeat of the Indians by Wayne, the surveyors were not interrupted by the Indians; but on one of their excursions, still remembered as "the starving tour," the whole party, consisting of twenty-eight men, suffered extremely in a driving snow-storm for about four days. They were in a wilderness, exposed to this severe storm, without hut, tent or covering, and, what was still more appalling, without provision, and without any road or even track to retreat on, and were nearly one hundred miles from any place of shelter. On the third day of the storm, they luckily killed two wild turkeys, which were boiled and divided into twenty-eight parts, and devoured with great avidity, heads, feet, entrails and all.

Gen. William Lytle was one of the most extensive surveyors and land-dealers in Clermont and Brown Counties. When only seventeen years old, he passed through Brown County, a volunteer in Col. Logan's expedition against the Indians. He was born in Cumberland, Penn., and, in 1799, his family emigrated to Kentucky, where his boyhood was mostly passed. When a young man, he began to make surveys and locate land warrants in the Virginia Military District. This business he followed for the greater portion of his life. Before the treaty of Greenville, he was exposed to incessant dangers, suffered great privations, and was sometimes attacked by the Indians. About 1796, he laid out the town of Williamsburg, which at first was known as Lytlestown. Lytle became the first Clerk of Court of Clermont under the Territorial government. In 1810, Gen. Lytle removed from Williamsburg to Cincinnati, where he died in 1810.

While the early surveys were in progress in Brown and adjoining counties, the Indian depredations upon boats on the Ohio and into the settlements of Kentucky were so numerous and destructive that scouts or spies were engaged to range along the river from Maysville to the mouth of the Big Sandy River, and also, for a part of the time at least, between Maysville and the mouth of the Little Miami. In the spring of 1792, the four scouts who ranged between Maysville and the mouth of the Big Sandy, as their names appear in the account given in McDonald's Sketches, were Samuel Davis, Duncan McArthur (afterward Governor of Ohio), Nathaniel Beasley (afterward a prominent citizen of Brown County) and Samuel McDowell. Benjamin Beasley, a brother of Nathaniel, and afterward an early settler of Brown County, although not named by McDonald, was also for a time a scout along the Ohio. "These men," says McDonald, "upon every occasion, proved themselves worthy of the confidence placed in them by their countrymen. Nothing which could reasonably be expected of men but was done by them. Two and two they went together. They made their tours once a week to the mouth of Big Sandy River. On Monday morning, two of them would leave Limestone, and reach Sandy by Wednesday evening. On Thursday morning, the other two would leave Limestone for the mouth of Sandy. Thus they would meet or pass each other about opposite the mouth of Scioto River; and by this constant vigilance, the two sets of spies would pass the mouth of Scioto, in going and returning, four times each week. This incessant vigilance would be continued till late in November, or the first of December, when hostilities generally ceased, in the later years of the Indian wars. Sometimes the spies would go up and down the Ohio in canoes. In such cases, one of them would push the canoe and the other would go on foot, through the woods, keeping about a mile in advance of the canoe, the footman keeping a sharp lookout for ambuscade or other Indian sign."

WANT OF SYSTEM IN THE SURVEYS.

In the Virginia Military District, lands to satisfy the military warrants were located in various geometrical figures, and with boundary lines running in every direction. The tract was never laid out into regular townships or sections. The owner of a Virginia military warrant was permitted to locate it in such shape and in whatever place in the district it pleased him, provided the land had not been previously located. The only limitation of the shape of the location was that of a Virginia statute which required the breadth of each survey to be at least one-third of its length in every part, unless the breadth was restricted by mountains, water-courses or previous locations. In consequence of this want of system, there were interferences and encroachments of one land entry upon another, and great difficulty is to-day experienced in tracing titles in this district.

In addition to the troubles resulting from the overlapping of one survey upon another, sometimes, when a tract was intended to adjoin another, the surveyors failed to run along the lines of the tract already surveyed, thus leaving a strip of unappropriated land to become the subject of controversy and litigation. A case went to the Supreme Court from Brown County in 1846, in which forty-one and one-fourth acres between two surveys long before located were in controversy. In this case, John Joliffe, Hamer & Johnston and J. H. Johnson were the attorneys. The Supreme Court in this case decided that the survey limits the grant to the calls of the survey, and that, where a discrepancy exists in the calls, the line actually run is to be found by having recourse to the more certain, fixed and natural objects called for in the boundary.

The early settlers, in their haste to locate upon the lands they had bought, and reclaim them from the woods, were often careless about their titles, and frequently were grossly imposed upon. The records and traditions give accounts of some who were compelled to pay twice for their lands; some who paid over again a portion of what they had paid years before; and others who lost their lands entirely, and were compelled to leave their farms, already partly cleared and improved.

In consequence of the want of system in the original surveys, the irregularities in the locations of the warrants, the large size of the tracts located, and their remaining in the possession of non-residents for two or more generations, it is believed that more than double the litigation has arisen concerning titles and boundaries in the Virginia Military District than in any other portion of Ohio of equal extent. Time and the statute of limitations, however, have cured most defects of title and settled most questions of disputed boundaries.

The following, from the pen of Hon. Reader W. Clarke, on the subject of land titles in this district, we find in the history of Clermont County, page 49:

"Most persons holding the Virginia land warrants never saw the land upon which they were laid, as surveyors took them to locate, and generally for a share of the land, more or less, as they could drive the bargain. Large tracts of a thousand acres or more were often thus located; the surveyor getting for his pay the larger half, and, being upon the ground, was enabled to secure the best portion. Some of the surveys are large, calling for several thousand acres, and invariably overrunning the quantity named. Breckenridge's Survey, upon which Bethel is situated, called for 4,000 acres, while in fact it contains over six thousand; and thus the Government was cheated out of the surplus of the survey. It was not unfrequently the case that holders of warrants could have them laid upon well-chosen lands by competent surveyors for the surplus, and it often happened in such cases that the surveyor would get the most land. About the year 1835, a land speculator got a small warrant, calling for about one hundred acres, located by a surveyor who was a preacher of the Gospel, and who was to make the location for the surplus; and he did his work well; but the surplus was larger than the quantity called for in the patent. By this method of locating large tracts, to remain in the hands of non-residents, living far away from the lands, and often descending by death to heirs, and the title becoming tangled and difficult to be gathered up into a perfect legal conveyance; and, furthermore, by the very bad practice of speculators selling lands to emigrants upon mere bond for title, without themselves having perfected their right to such lands, or, indeed, often without intending ever to do so, the broad foundation for future trouble was laid. Land was sold very cheap, even so low as $1 per acre for choice selections, and for sometimes 50 cents, 25 cents, and less, if more could not be had; but, cheap as it appeared to the unsuspecting purchaser, it often proved his ruin. He would go upon his land, build his cabin, clear out his fields, and, just as he was beginning to realize some of the fruits of his hard labor, a claimant with a better title would call upon him, and he would have to surrender up all, without a return of his purchase money or pay for improvements. Sometimes the occupants would hold on to their shadow of a title and risk the chances of a law suit; but of course the better title prevailed, and they lost not only their land, but, as before narrated, were harassed by lawyers' fees and cost bills, which, in many cases, finished up the administration of the poor man's worldly effects, and left him almost as naked as when he came into the world. Many bought their farms a second and even a third time before they were quieted in their titles.

"Few men contributed more to this ruinous state of things than Gen. Lytle, who was extensively engaged in locating land warrants and selling lands, and had many and influential friends, and all adventurers into the county who wanted land were recommended to Lytle. He was a man of easy and affable address, not difficult to trade with, and of course the all-confiding purchaser desired nothing but the word and bond of Gen. Lytle for a deed, and felt secure that all was right, and in his faith paid his money and expended his labor to improve his possessions. Old pioneers say that any person wishing land had only to call on Gen. Lytle, name the quantity and location, and he would at once close the bargain, take the money and give his bond for a deed, although he had no particle of title whatever, or right to sell, but probably he intended to get in the title—a thing not difficult for him, but not always done—and of course the consequence was the poor, confiding settler lost his land and all his labor bestowed upon it, as well as the purchase money; for our information is, very few were ever fully indemnified by Lytle for their losses. Tradition says Gen. Lytle made most of his surveys on horseback, and the well-known historical fact that his surveys, more than those of any other early surveyors, overran in quantity, is to be attributed to this circumstance; for in the saddle he was not able, on account of the thickets, ravines, underbrush and other obstructions, to get around, but stopped short or went beyond the required points to make his surveying accurate; and, as land was cheap as a song, and there was never an expectation that it would all be taken up and farmed, Lytle was not particular, but surveyed his tracts in wanton disregard of the great future trouble and litigation to subsequent owners and occupants."

CHAPTER V.

PIONEER HISTORY.

THE question who was the first white settler in Brown County is an interesting one, but it is one which can now never receive a satisfactory answer. It is very probable that the first white men who built their cabins within the limits of the county were intruders upon the lands of the Government of the United States. Tradition gives accounts of such intruders on the fertile valleys near the Ohio in this county, and official reports of military officers directed to drive off persons attempting to settle on the lands of the United States, without mentioning this region as one which was intruded upon, render the tradition probable. As early as January 24, 1785, the Commissioner of Indian Affairs instructed Col. Harmar "to employ such force as he may judge necessary in driving off persons attempting to settle on the lands of the United States."

From the correspondence published in the St. Clair papers, it appears that the number of persons who had established themselves northwest of the Ohio before the settlement at Marietta was much larger than is usually supposed. John Emerson, on March 12, 1785, took upon himself the authority to issue a proclamation for elections by the inhabitants of the west side of the Ohio for the choosing of members of a convention for forming a constitution—the elections to take place on April 10, 1785, one at the mouth of the Miami, one at the mouth of the Scioto, one on the Muskingum and one at the house of Jonas Menzons. Ensign John Armstrong reported early in 1785 to Col. Harmar that, from the best information he could obtain, there were 1,500 persons on the Miami and Scioto, and upward of 300 families on the Hockhocking and the Muskingum, and down the Ohio for a great distance, there was scarcely one bottom without one or more families. These intruders were all dispossessed by the Government authorities. There are traditions of some of these early adventurers intruding themselves into what is now Huntington Township, in the vicinity of Aberdeen, but the details of the history of the attempted settlement there are lost.

The location of the best lands and the most fertile valleys had become known to the whites by means of the expeditions of Kentuckians against the Indians, passing from Limestone northward and northeastward through the County; the explorations of the agents of the owners of Virginia military land warrants, and the excursions of hunters and adventurers. Daniel Boone, Simon Kenton and other early adventurers had passed through the county in different directions long before the first surveys were made.

Limestone, now Maysville, was the chief landing place of the early emigrants to Kentucky, who descended the Ohio in their journey to their new homes. So numerous were the flat-boats that descended the Ohio and stopped at this place that they were scarcely of any value, and were frequently sent adrift in order to make room for others. Gen. Harmar, in building Fort Washington, at Cincinnati, which was one of the most substantial and solid wooden fortresses in the whole territory, obtained the planks for its construction from the flat-boats brought to Limestone.

January 14, 1790, he wrote the War Department that he had contracted at Limestone for forty or fifty flat-boats at the moderate price of $1 or $2 each.

Gen. Harmar wrote to the Secretary of War from Fort Harmar, May 14, 1787, concerning the number of emigrants passing down the Ohio: "Curiosity prompted me to order the officer of the day to take an account of the number of boats which passed the garrison. From the 10th of October, 1786, until the 12th of May, 1787, 127 boats, 2,689 souls, 1,333 horses, 756 cattle and 102 wagons have passed Muskingum bound for Limestone and the Rapids."

Indian hostilities delayed the settlement of Brown County for several years after the first lands were legally granted to the owners of warrants. More than seven years elapsed from the time the first entry was surveyed and located before it was safe to attempt a settlement in any part of the Virginia Military District without the protection of a fortified station.

FIRST SETTLEMENT IN THE VIRGINIA MILITARY DISTRICT.

The first permanent settlement between the Little Miami and the Scioto was made by Gen. Nathaniel Massie, at Manchester, in Adams County, five miles east of the Brown County line. At this place several of the earliest pioneers of Brown County located themselves until it became safe to settle upon their lands, and from it as a base of operations for the early surveying parties were large tracts of land in this and adjoining counties surveyed. John McDonald, in his interesting volume of biographical sketches, says:

"Massie, in the winter of the year 1790, determined to make a settlement that he might be in the midst of his surveying operations and secure his party from danger and exposure. In order to effect this, he gave general notice in Kentucky of his intention, and offered each of the first twenty-five families, as a donation, one inlot, one outlot and 100 acres of land, provided they would settle in a town he intended to lay off at his settlement. His proffered terms were soon closed in with, and upward of thirty families joined him. After various consultations with his friends, the bottom on the Ohio River, opposite the lower of the Three Islands, was selected as the most eligible spot. Here he fixed his station, and laid off into lots a town, now called Manchester, at this time a small place, about twelve miles above Maysville (formerly Limestone), Ky. This little confederacy, with Massie at the helm (who was the soul of it), went to work with spirit. Cabins were raised, and, by the middle of March, 1791, the whole town was inclosed with strong pickets, firmly fixed in the ground, with block-houses at each angle for defense.

"Thus was the first settlement in the Virginia Military District, and the fourth settlement in the bounds of the State of Ohio, effected. Although this settlement was commenced in the hottest Indian war, it suffered less from depredation, and even interruptions, from the Indians, than any settlement previously made on the Ohio River. This was no doubt owing to the watchful band of brave spirits who guarded the place--men who were reared in the midst of danger and inured to perils and as watchful as hawks. Here were the Beasleys, the Stouts, the Washburns, the Ledoms, the Edgingtons, the Denings, the Ellisons, the Utts, the McKenzies, the Wades and others, who were equal to the Indians in all the arts and stratagems of border war.

"As soon as Massie had completely prepared his station for defense, the whole population went to work, and cleared the lower of the Three Islands, and planted it in corn. The island was very rich and produced heavy crops. The woods, with a little industry, supplied a choice variety of game. Deer, elk, buffalo, bears and turkeys were abundant, while the river furnished a variety of excellent fish. The wants of the inhabitants, under these circumstances, were few and easily gratified.

"When this station was made, the nearest neighbors northwest of the Ohio

HISTORY OF BROWN COUNTY.   251

were the inhabitants at Columbia, a settlement below the mouth of the Little Miami, five miles above Cincinnati, and at Gallipolis, a French settlement, near the mouth of the Great Kanawha."

The following contract between Massie and his associates in establishing this settlement illustrates the dangers which were apprehended and the necessity of offering rewards to those who were willing to face the dangers:

Articles of agreement between Nathaniel Massie, of one part, and the several persons that have hereunto subscribed, of the other part, witnesseth : That the subscribers hereunto doth oblige themselves to settle in the town laid off on the northwest side of the Ohio, opposite the lower part of the Two Islands ; and make said town or the neighborhood on the northwest side of the Ohio their permanent seat of residence for the two years from the date hereof. No subscriber shall absent himself more than two months at a time, and during such absence shall furnish a strong able-bodied man sufficient to bear arms at least equal to himself. No subscriber shall absent himself the time above mentioned in case of actual danger ; nor shall such absence be but once a year. No subscriber shall absent himself in case of actual danger ; or, if absent, shall return immediately. Each of the subscribers doth oblige themselves to comply with the rules and regulations that shall be agreed upon by a majority thereof for the support of the settlement.

In consideration whereof, Nathaniel Massie doth bind and oblige himself, his heirs, &c., to make over and convey to such of the subscribers as comply with the above conditions, at the expiration of two years, a good and sufficient title unto one in-lot in said town, containing five poles in front and eleven back ; one out-lot of four acres convenient to said town in the bottom, which the said Massie is to put them in immediate possession of ; also 100 hundred acres of land, which the said Massie has shown to a part of said subscribers, the conveyance to be made to each of the subscribers, their heirs or assignees.

In witness whereof each of the parties have hereunto set their hands and seals this 1st day of December, 1790.

Nathaniel Massie,
John Lindsey,
William Wade,
John Block,
Samuel † Smith,
Jesse † Wethington,
Josiah Wade,
John Clark,
Robert Ellison,
Zephaniah Wade,

John Ellison,
Ellen Simmeral,
John † McCutcheon,
Andrew † Anderson,
Matthew † Hart,
Henry † Nelson,
John Peter Christopher Shanks,
John Allison,
Thomas Stout,
George † Wade.

Done in presence of—
John Beasly,
James Jittle.

PROGRESS OF SETTLEMENTS.

There were no fortified stations or block-houses for defense against the Indians within the limits of Brown County. The long war which ended with Wayne's treaty at Greenville was a cruel one. The Miami country was known as the "Miami Slaughter House." Early in the spring of 1794, a committee of the citizens of the settlements protected by Fort Washington and the block-houses at Columbia published a notice in the *Centinel of the Northwest Territory*, offering premiums for the scalps of Indians killed in the Miami country. The premiums offered were from $95 to $136 for each scalp "having the right ear appendant" of an Indian killed within the limits of the district described in the proclamation issued by the committee. The survey of lands and the marking of trees by the surveyors, indicating an intention of permanently occupying the hunting grounds of the Indians, had greatly incensed the savages and increased their cruelty.

Wayne's victory over the Indians was achieved August 20, 1794. It did not at once reduce the savages to absolute submission. Six months after the victory, there were occasional reports of white men murdered by Indians. The treaty of peace at Greenville, ratified August 3, 1795, put an end to these murders.

It would seem improbable that there could have been any permanent settlements in Brown County much before the ratification of the treaty at Greenville, although some of the more daring woodsmen may have ventured to build their huts north of the Ohio without the protection of a fortified station soon after Wayne's victory. If so, they were willing not only to brave dangers from savage foes, but to endure privations of a lonely life in the wilderness.

Family traditions concerning the early settlements sometimes confound the date of the first visit of a pioneer to his lands, or the date of his purchase, with that of his settlement. Many of the pioneers had purchased their lands long before it was safe to settle upon them. They may have made frequent visits to their lands, and perhaps begun the work of clearing and making improvements, before becoming permanent residents thereon. Many of the early settlers had selected choice tracts of land in Brown County for their future homes, and remained in Kentucky, anxiously waiting the subjugation of the savages to render it safe to remove north of the Ohio. Doubtless in some cases crops of corn were raised north of the river by those who still lived in the more secure settlements of Kentucky.

It has been claimed that Belteshazzar Dragoo built the first cabin and was the first permanent settler on Eagle Creek. In the Atlas of Brown County, published in 1876, it states that "the first settlement within the limits of the county, of which any definite account can be obtained, was made by Belteshazzar Dragoo, who settled on Eagle Creek, about three miles from Ripley, in 1794. He had a family of twelve children, of whom only one (Benjamin) is now living, he being the youngest of the family. He is supposed to have built the first house, a log cabin, in the county." The question whether this was the first settlement in the county must be left an open one. It is certain, however, that Dragoo had his attention directed to the lands on Eagle Creek at a very early period, as is shown by a title bond which was among the first documents recorded in the land records of Adams County, Ohio. In the bond, which was dated August 24, 1791, Alexander McIntyre, of the State of Virginia and District of Kentucky, bound himself in the penal sum of £200 lawful currency to make unto Belteshazzar Dragoo, whose residence is not stated, "a good and sufficient deed for 450 acres of first-rate land lying on both sides of and on the waters of Eagle Creek, where it shall be convenient for a mill seat, with four feet head and fall; the said deed to be made as soon as it can be obtained from the office, and the said lands to lie within ten miles of the river."

The details of the early settlements belong to the histories of the townships. Leaving the questions of the date of the first settlement in the county and the name of the first settler as unsettled, and now impossible to be determined, we may safely assume from known facts that there were few, if any, families within the limits of the county prior to Wayne's treaty of peace and no considerable immigration to the county until the succeeding spring.

The earliest settlers usually established themselves on the Ohio or the streams flowing into that river. It is certain that in the year 1799, there was a considerable population on Eagle, Red Oak, Straight and White Oak Creeks It was in the spring of 1796 that the full tide of emigration to the Northwest Territory began to flow in, and, within a few years from that time, most of the fertile tracts in the southern portion of this county were picked out and occupied by actual settlers.

The first town within the limits of the county was St. Clairville, laid out by Basil Duke and John Coburn, August 1, 1801. The name was about fifteen years later changed by the Legislature to Decatur.

In August, 1803, a census was taken of the white male inhabitants twenty-one years old and upward of the new State of Ohio. The number reported in Adams County was 906; the number in Clermont County, 755. Assuming that the territory now forming Brown County contained one-third of the aggregate population of these two counties, there were in Brown County, the first year of the existence of Ohio as a State, 550 white adult males, or a total population of about 2,200. This is a smaller population than was then found in Butler, Warren or Ross, but larger than that in Montgomery or Greene, and about double that of Scioto.

A large portion of the land in Brown and Clermont Counties was regarded as an interminable swamp, and was settled slowly. These flat lands were covered with water more than half the year, and were called slashes. Much of this land was regarded as worthless. As late as 1828, large tracts of these wet lands lying along the water-shed between White Oak and East Fork had not been surveyed or located.

George Sample, writing in the *American Pioneer* in 1842, says that in the year 1797 he rode from Manchester to Wood's Mill, on the Little Miami, below Deerfield, and there was then but one house on the trace from Manchester to the Little Miami; that house was situated about seven miles from the site of New Market. As late as 1809, James Finley, writing from West Union, said of Adams County, which then included a large portion of Brown, that the country did not improve very rapidly; that he knew of but one brick or stone building in the country, and that one was unfinished.

The Virginia Military Reservation was not settled and improved as rapidly as many other parts of the State. The Virginians who owned the original surveys were indisposed to settle upon them because of the prohibition of slavery in the ordinance of 1787. At the first session of the Legislature of the Northwest Territory, in 1799, petitions were presented from Virginians who owned lands between the Little Miami and the Scioto, asking for a temporary suspension of the provision of the ordinance which prevented them from removing with their slaves to their lands. The Legislature at once decided that they had no authority to grant the prayer of the petitioners.

There were other causes of a slower increase in the population of this district—first, the large surveys in which the land was generally divided, which prevented persons of small means from seeking farms here; second, the difficulty emigrants experienced in finding the real owners of the surveys, who generally resided in Kentucky or Virginia and frequently had no agents in the district to subdivide, sell or show the lands; and third, the frequent interference of different entries and surveys with each other, rendering titles insecure and giving rise to litigation. Although only a small portion of the lands of Brown County were subject to this last difficulty, yet it cannot be doubted that many persons were thereby deterred from purchasing lands here and settling upon them.

For some years after the whites made their homes in the county, small parties of Indians encamped occasionally near the settlements. It is believed that no white man was killed by an Indian in this region after the Greenville treaty of peace. The Indians continued to steal horses from the whites long after that treaty. In a note book of Samuel B. Walker, an early surveyor, it is stated that his horse was stolen by the Indians in the neighborhood of Williamsburg, on the night of May 22, 1799, and Robert Dickey's horse was stolen the same night. In the autumn of the same year, both horses were returned to their owners; and Walker in his lifetime stated that they were returned in response to a proclamation of the Territorial governmental authorities, offering rewards for the return of horses stolen by the Indians. In 1796, Judge John Cleves Symmes wrote that he wished Congress would make it a penal offense for a white man to buy a horse from an Indian, as the Indian would steal another to take the place of the one sold—no Indian being willing to walk if he could stoal a horse. Oxen were sometimes used by the early pioneers, being much less likely to be run off. There is reason to believe that roving bands of Indians were not so numerous in the settlements of Brown County as they were between the Miami Rivers. An early pioneer used to say that he removed from Columbia to Brown County in order to get out of the way of the Indians.

The following old petitions, preserved by their publication in Cist's "Cincinnati Miscellany," in 1845, give the names of some of the earliest settlers in the central portion of Brown County:

January 10, 1799.

To the Honorable Arthur St. Clair, Esq., Governor of the Northwestern Territory:

DEAR SIR—We, a number of inhabitants situated in the aforesaid territory and county of Hamilton, between the waters of Eagle and Straight Creeks, and thereabouts, being at a great distance from a Magistrate, or Justice of the Peace—a grievance which we consider ourselves to labor under—we therefore have thought proper to petition your Honor for Alexander Martin to be commissioned in such an office, as we look upon him to be an honest, well-meaning man, and a citizen here amongst us, whom we have selected for that purpose. This, dear sir, being our grievance, a removal of which, we, your petitioners, humbly pray:

Matthew Davidson,
Thos. M'Connell,
Joseph Lacock,
Isaac Ellis,
Wm. M'Kinney,
Wm. Forbes,
Geo. M'Kinney,
Jacob Miller,
John Mefford,
John Caryon,
Wm. Lewis,
Fergus M'Clain,
Richard Robison,
Henry Rogers,
Thomas Ark,
Valentine M'Daniel,

Wm. Woodruff,
Geo. J. Jennings,
Ichabod Tweed,
Amos Ellis,
James Henry,
Wm. Moore,
Isaac Prickett,
Tom Rogers,
Wm. Long,
Joseph Moore,
Benjamin Evans,
Jacob Nagle,
Lewis Sheek,
John Phillips,
James Prickett,
James Young,

Uriah Springer.

January 10, 1799.

To the Honorable Arthur St. Clair, Governor of the Northwestern Territory:

DEAR SIR—We, a number of inhabitants situated between the waters of Eagle and Straight Creeks, and thereabouts, in the aforesaid territory and county of Hamilton, being destitute of militia officers, such as Captain, Lieutenant and Ensign, we therefore have thought proper to petition your Honor for such, and have selected Thomas McConnell for Captain, John Mefford, Lieutenant, and Amos Ellis, Ensign, if your Honor shall think proper to commission them in that office. This, dear sir, being the desires for which we, your petitioners, do humbly pray:

Abel Martin,
George M'Kinney,
William M'Kinney,
Forgy M'Clure,
Henry Rogers,
N. McDaniel,
Jno. Henry,
Thomas Dougherty,
John Redmon,
William Forbes;
Jas. Prickett,
John Caryon,

Thomas Rogers,
Tom Ash,
Wm. Moore;
Isaac Ellis,
Jacob Nagle,
Geo. J. Jennings,
Uriah Springer,
Joseph Jacobs,
Samuel Tweed,
William Lewcas,
Jacob Miller,
Walter Wall.

A JOURNEY THROUGH THE COUNTY IN 1797.

In October, 1797, Rev. James Smith, then of Powhatan County, Va., made a journey from his native State through Kentucky to the Northwest Territory. As he rode northward through Mason County, Ky., the first lands north of the Ohio he saw were the hills of Brown County. He afterward rode through the wilderness in the northern part of this county. The following are extracts from his manuscript journal:

"Monday, 2d October, 1797.—Brother McCormick, Brother Teal, Mr. Sewell and myself set out for the Ohio. We traveled about thirty miles and reached a little village called Germantown, about 8 o'clock in the evening, and took up with a Mr. Black.

"Tuesday, 3d.—We pursued our journey and reached a little town on the bank of the Ohio, about 11 o'clock. From a high eminence, we had a view of that beautiful country beyond the river, and were charmed with its appearance. I longed to be there. We took some refreshment at Augusta, then took boat, and, about 1 o'clock, made the opposite shore. The Ohio River, of all that I ever saw, is the most beautiful stream. It flows in a deep and gentle current; it is from one-half to three-quarters of a mile in width; it is confined in high banks, which it seldom, if ever, overflows. The adjoining hills are lofty, from which a charming view of the river and lower lands presents itself. How delightful will be the scene when these banks shall be covered with towns, these hills with houses and the noble stream with the produce of these fertile and fruitful countries! We rode down the river three or four miles, to the mouth of the Bullskin Creek; then left the river and passed northwardly through a rich and beautiful country. The land after leaving the river lies high and is very level. The trees, which are mostly white and red oak, are the largest and most beautiful timber I ever beheld. The soil appears deep, clear of stone, and wild peavines are abundant. It was very pleasant to see the deer skipping over the bushes and the face of the country clad in a livery of green. We crossed the waters of Bear Creek, Big Indian and arrived at Dunham's Town, on the waters of Poplar Fork of the East Fork. Dunham's Town, or Plainfield, is about twelve miles and a half from the Ohio. Here we saw the fruits of honest industry. Mr. Dunham is a Baptist minister, who left Kentucky on account of its being a land of oppression. He arrived here last April, and since then has reared several houses, cleared a small plantation, has a fine field of corn growing, a number of vines and garden vegetables, an excellent field of wheat and a meadow already green with the rising timothy. The old man seems to possess both grace and talents, with a spirit greatly opposed to slavery. He thinks that God will withdraw His spirit from such countries and persons as having the light resist it. *   *   *   *   *

"Monday, 16th.—Brother McCormick, Brother Howard, Mr. Sewell and myself started for the Scioto. We traveled up the East Fork of the Little Miami about twelve miles and encamped in the woods. The lands on East Fork are very rich, lie well, and are of a soft, light nature when cleared, and easy to cultivate.

"Tuesday, 17th.—We rose a little before day, fed our horses, and, as soon as it began to be light, pursued our journey. We arrived about 8 o'clock at a little town called Williamsburg, settled last spring by eight or nine families. Here we got breakfast, then set forward, pursuing a course north 75 degrees east, through an amazingly level and sometimes swampy country. It lies about midway between the Miami and the Scioto, on the waters of a creek called White Oak. The growth is mostly gum, maple, white oak, etc. After leaving the waters of White Oak, we fell in upon the waters of the Rocky Fork of Paint Creek. Here night took us and we encamped.

"Wednesday, 18th.—We started as soon as we could see, and about 1 o'clock reached a house on the banks of Paint Creek. This house is the first we have seen for upward of forty miles. Here we stopped and got a little refreshment. Paint Creek is a clear, pure stream, and at this place is about one hundred yards wide. It seems to be a fine stream for fish, as we stood on the bank and saw a fine shoal of them near the opposite shore, which, from the distance we saw them, must have been very large.

"At this house, I saw a curiosity. It was the under part of the beak of a fowl called a pelican. It was about eighteen inches long and nine inches broad. Underneath this was a natural bag, which, when the bird was killed, held about a peck. The whole together seemed to bear a near resemblance to a fisherman's skimming net, and, this bird being one that feeds on fish, it is more than probable that this net is used in catching them.

"On the bank of Paint Creek I saw cut in the bark of a beech tree the letters 'T. L. & T. D., 1750.' From this circumstance, it is evident that some white man had been here as long as forty-seven years ago; but whether English or French, white trader or prisoner, we cannot now determine. We rode down Paint Creek about twenty miles, and, for beauty and fertility, it exceeds anything that ever my eyes beheld. Here we traveled over ancient walls, ditches, monuments, etc., etc., at the sight of which a considerate mind feels lost in silent contemplation. We arrived a little after dark at Chillicothe, and took up at Umpston's tavern.

"Saturday, 21st.— * * * Having now traveled between three and four hundred miles through the country, I think I can form a tolerable judgment concerning the same, and will, as concisely as possible, give a general description of the same before leaving it. The land naturally claims the first place. Bordering on the rivers, the land exceeds description. Leaving the rivers, a high hill skirts the low ground; reaching the top of this hill, another level presents itself. There is generally but little stone. Quarries of free stone are plenty on the Scioto, and limestone in many places. Indian corn grows to great perfection. Grass of the meadow kind grows all over the country, and white clover and blue grass grow spontaneously wherever the land is cleared. A country so favored for grass must, of course, be excellent for all kinds of stock. Here I saw the finest beef and mutton I ever saw fed on grass. Hogs also increase and fatten in the woods in a most surpassing manner. Incredible numbers of bees have found their way to this delightful region, and in vast quantities deposit their honey in the trees of the wood, so that it is not uncommon for the people to take their wagon and team and return loaded with honey."

A PIONEER'S EXPERIENCE IN 1800.

The father of Elder Matthew Gardner emigrated from Stephentown, N. Y., and settled in Brown County in 1800. Elder Gardner, in his autobiography, says:

"It was on a beautiful morning on the 1st of September, A. D. 1800, when we started. I was in my tenth year when we left Stephentown, and well do I remember the scenes of my childhood. We had but one small wagon with three horses, and other means correspondingly limited. We pursued our way patiently, but perseveringly. The mountains were difficult to climb, the streams were dangerous to ford, the undertaking was hazardous and the journey was long; the weather was pleasant, and the journey was as prosperous as we could expect. We reached Pittsburgh by the 1st of October, just one month from the time of starting. We waited two weeks before we found a boat going down the river. Then we embarked on a flat-boat—the boats then used—with four other families, furniture, wagons, horses and all crowded on one small flat-boat. The river was low; the progress was slow; sometimes we floated rapidly and sometimes we were long aground. We were four weeks coming down to Limestone—a little village on the Kentucky side of the river. It had but few houses then. Limestone is now called Maysville. Here Henry Hughs, a

HISTORY OF BROWN COUNTY. 259

land trader, came to the boat to sell us land in Ohio. Father went with him to see the land. He liked it and traded him two horses for 100 acres. We then proceeded on with the boat down the river about twelve miles till we came opposite our land, at a landing two miles below where Ripley now stands. We landed within a few miles of our land, and soon reached our future home, where everything seemed new and strange. We were all in good health, except one brother and sister, who had slight attacks of fever and ague, which soon disappeared. My father rented a little cabin to move into, while he and my two older brothers built a cabin on our land. It was now about the last of November, the most pleasant and delightful autumn I have ever known before or since. This fine weather continued until after Christmas. My father and brother having completed our new home house, we moved into it about the 1st of January, 1801. The fine weather continued that year all winter, there being no weather to prevent out-door work.

"There were but two cabins within some two or three miles of us. There was no ground to rent. Provisions were scarce and only to be procured at any price from a great distance. Our money was about all expended. Our land was covered with a heavy forest, principally of beech and poplar, which must immediately be cleared for crops to prevent starvation the coming year. All who were large enough commenced work. By spring, we had nearly five acres cleared, which we planted in corn and potatoes, which sustained us the coming year. One of our greatest difficulties was to procure those things which the land would not produce. Salt cost from $3 to $4 for a bushel of fifty pounds; other merchandise was proportionately high. We were forced to study economy and compelled to practice it. Wild beasts were plenty. There were birds in abundance. Bears, deer and wild turkeys supplied our table with meat till we reared domestic animals. Sheep and wool were not to be had; our clothing was of flax and hemp. Suits of these served for all seasons, summer and winter alike. Father and the boys prepared the materials, and my mother and sisters manufactured the cloth and made the garments. We wore no shoes, but moccasins, made of dressed deer skins, for we could get no leather. The deer skin, being spongy, absorbed the water from the ground and snow, so that our feet were often wet. Yet we were all stout and healthy. We needed no doctors, which was well, as none were to be had. We did not eat the wheat, because it was called 'sick wheat,' making those sick who ate it. Our swine refused it. We tried other stock, but all animals rejected it. We preferred the corn. It fell to my lot to take care of the cattle. We had no fenced fields, and while they roamed in the forest for food, it was my care to seek them and keep them from straying far away and being lost. Sometimes in cloudy weather I would get lost, and finding the cattle by the tinkling of the bell, they would then pilot me home.'

A VISIT IN 1808.

The following is an extract from "Sketches of a Tour in the Western Country," by F. Cuming:

"Thursday, Friday and Saturday (August 7, 8 and 9, 1808), I was employed in rambling about the woods, exploring and examining a tract of land of 1,000 acres, in the State of Ohio, which I had purchased when in Europe last year, and which had been the principal cause of my present tour. As it was only six miles from Maysville, I crossed the Ohio and went to it on foot. I had expected to have found a mere wilderness, as soon as I should quit the high road, but, to my agreeable surprise, I found my land surrounded on every side by fine farms, some of them ten years settled, and the land itself, both in quality and situation, not exceeded by any in this fine country. The population was also astonishing for the time of the settlement, which a muster of militia while I was there gave me an opportunity of knowing—there being reviewed a battalion of upward of 500 effective men, most expert in the use of the rifle, belonging to the district of ten miles square. And now I experienced among these honest and friendly farmers real hospitality, for they vied with each other in lodging me at their houses, and in giving me a hearty and generous welcome to their best fare. Robert Simpson, from New Hampshire, and Daniel Ker and Thomas Gibson, from Pennsylvania, shall ever be entitled to my grateful remembrance. I had no letters of introduction—I had no claims on their hospitality, other than what any stranger ought to have. But they were farmers, and had not contracted habits which I have observed to prevail very generally amongst the traders in this part of the world.

"On Saturday, I returned to Ellis Ferry, opposite Maysville. On the bank of the Ohio I found Squire Ellis seated on a bench under the shade of two locust trees, with a table, pen and ink and several papers, holding a Justice's court, which he does every Saturday. Seven or eight men were sitting on the bench with him, awaiting his awards in their several cases. When he had finished, which was soon after I had taken a seat under the same shade, one of the men invited the Squire to drink with them, which he consented to do; some whisky was provided from Landlord Powers, in which all parties made a libation to peace and justice. There was something in the scene so primitive and so simple that I could not help enjoying it with much satisfaction.

"I took up my quarters for the night at Powers', who is an Irishman from Ballibay, in the county of Monaghan. He pays Squire Ellis $800 per annum for his tavern, fine farm and ferry. He and his wife were very civil, attentive and reasonable in their charges, and he insisted much on lending me a horse to carry me the first six miles over a hilly part of the road to Robinson's tavern, but I declined his kindness, and, on Sunday morning, the 9th of August, after taking a delightful bath in the Ohio, I quit its banks. I walked on toward the northeast, along the main post and stage road, seventeen miles to West Union. The road was generally well settled, and the woods between the settlements were alive with squirrels and all the varieties of woodpeckers with their beautiful plumage, which in one species is little inferior to that of the bird of paradise, so much admired in the East Indies."

PIONEER LIFE.

A truthful account of the mode of life among the early settlers of the Ohio forests cannot fail to interest and instruct. As the backwoods period recedes, its interest increases. It is to be regretted that more of the traditions of the pioneers, giving homely but faithful pictures of the everyday life of the early settlers, have not been preserved. Their recollections of their journeys from the older States over the Alleghany Mountains, the flat-boat voyage down the Ohio, the clearing in the wilderness, the first winter in the rude cabin and the scanty stores of provisions, the cultivation of corn among the roots and stumps, the cabin raisings and log rollings, the home manufacturing of furniture and clothing, the hunting parties and corn huskings, their social customs and the thousand scenes and novel incidents of life in the woods, would form a more entertaining and instructive chapter than their wars with the Indians or their government annals. Far different was the life of the settler on the Ohio from that of the frontiersman of to-day. The railroad, the telegraph and the daily newspaper did not then bring the comforts and luxuries of civilization to the cabin door of the settler; nor was the farm marked out with a furrow and made ready for cultivation by turning over the sod.

The labor of opening a farm in a forest of large oaks, maples and beech was very great, and the difficulty was increased by the thick growing bushes. Not only were the trees to be cut down; the branches were to be cut off from the trunk, and, with the undergrowth of bushes, gathered together for burning. The trunks of the large trees were to be divided and rolled into heaps and reduced to ashes. With hard labor the unaided settler could clear and burn an acre of land in three weeks. It usually required six or seven years for the pioneer to open a small farm and build a better house than this first cabin of round logs. The boys had work to do in gathering brush into heaps. A common mode of clearing was to cut down all the trees of the diameter of eighteen inches or less, clear off the undergrowth and deaden the larger trees by girdling them with the ax and allowing them to stand until they decayed and fell. This method delayed the final clearing of the land for eight or ten years, but when the trunks fell they were usually dry enough to be burned into such lengths as to be rolled together.

The first dwellings of the settlers were cabins made of round logs notched at the ends, the spaces between the logs filled in with sticks of wood and daubed with clay. The roof was of clapboards, held to their places by poles reaching across the roof called weight-poles. The floor was of puncheons, or planks split from logs, two or three inches in thickness, hewed on the upper side. The fire-place was made of logs lined with clay or with undressed stone, and was at least six feet wide. The chimney was often made of split sticks plastered with clay. The door was of clapboards hung on wooden hinges and fastened with a wooden latch. The opening for the window was not infrequently covered with paper made more translucent with oil or lard. Such a house was built by a neighborhood gathering, with no tools but the ax and the frow, and often was finished in a single day. The raising and the log rolling were labors of the settlers, in which the assistance of neighbors was considered essential and cheerfully given. When a large cabin was to be raised, preparations would be made before the appointed day; the trees would be cut down, the logs dragged in and the foundation laid and the skids and forks made ready. Early in the morning of the day fixed, the neighbors gathered for miles around; the captain and corner men were selected, and the work went on with boisterous hilarity until the walls were up and the roof weighted down.

The cabin of round logs was generally succeeded by a hewed log house, more elegant in appearance and more comfortable. Indeed, houses could be made of logs as comfortable as any other kind of building, and were erected in such manner as to conform to the tastes and means of all descriptions of persons. For large families, a double cabin was common; that is, two houses, ten or twelve feet apart, with one roof covering the whole, the space between serving as a hall for various uses. Henry Clay, in an early speech on the public lands, referred to the different kinds of dwellings sometimes to be seen standing together, as a gratifying evidence of the progress of the new States "I have," said he, "often witnessed this gratifying progress. On the same farm, you may sometimes behold, standing together, the first rude cabin of round and unhewn logs, and wooden chimneys; the hewed log house, chinked and shingled, with stone or brick chimneys; and lastly, the comfortable stone or brick dwelling, each denoting the different occupants of the farm or the several stages of the condition of the same occupant. What other nation can boast of such an outlet for its increasing population, such bountiful means of promoting their prosperity and securing their independence?"

The furniture of the first rude dwellings was made of puncheons. Clapboards, seats and tables were thus made by the settler himself. Over the door was placed the trusty flint-lock rifle, next to the ax in usefulness to the pioneer, and near it the powder horn and bullet pouch. Almost every family had its little spinning-wheel for flax and big spinning-wheel for wool. The cooking utensils were few and simple, and the cooking was all done at the fireplace. The long winter evenings were spent in contentment, but not in idleness. There was corn to shell and tow to spin at home, and the corn huskings to attend at the neighbors. There were a few books to read, but newspapers were rare. The buckeye log, because of its incombustibility, was valuable as a back log, and hickory bark cast into the fire place threw a pleasing light over a scene of domestic industry and contentment.

The wearing apparel was chiefly of home manufacture. The flax and wool necessary for clothing were prepared and spun in the family, cotton being comparatively scarce. Carding wool by hand was common. Weaving, spinning, dyeing, tailoring for the family were not infrequently all carried on in the household. Not a few of the early settlers made their own shoes. Wool dyed with walnut bark received the name of butternut. Cloth made of mixed linen and wool, called linsey, or linsey-woolsey, of a light indigo blue color, was common for men's wear. A full suit of buckskin with moccasins was sometimes worn by a hunter, but it was not common. A uniform, much worn in the war of 1812, is described as consisting of a light blue linsey hunting-shirt with a cape, the whole fringed and coming half way down the thigh, a leather belt, shot-pouch, powder-horn, a large knife and tomahawk, or hatchet, in the belt, and rifle at the shoulder. The author of the history of Miami County says he has seen Return J. Meigs, Governor of Ohio, and Jeremiah Morrow, United States Senator, and other high officials, wear this hunting-shirt while on frontier duty during that war.

With the early settlers, almost the only modes of locomotion were on foot and on horseback. The farmer took his corn and wheat to mill on horseback; the wife went to market or visited her distant friends on horseback. Salt, hardware and merchandise were brought to the new settlements on packhorses. The immigrant came to his new home not infrequently with provisions, cooking utensils and beds packed on a horse, his wife and small children on another horse. Lawyers made the circuit of their courts, doctors visited their patients and preachers attended their preaching stations on horseback. The want of ferries and bridges made the art of swimming a necessary quality in a saddle-horse. "Is he a good swimmer?" was a common question in buying a horse for the saddle. Francis Dunlavy, as President Judge of a district embracing ten counties, made the circuit of his courts on horseback, never missing a court and frequently swimming his horse over the Miamis rather than fail of being present.

In 1803, when Jeremiah Morrow was called to the National Capital as the first Representative in Congress from Ohio, he made the journey on horseback, taking with him his wife and their two children, aged, respectively, three years and eighteen months, to the residence of Mrs. Morrow's parents in the old Redstone country in Pennsylvania. Leaving his wife and children at the home of her parents until the close of the session, he continued his journey over the mountains to Washington. For sixteen successive years did Mr. Morrow make this annual horseback ride from his home on the Little Miami to attend the sessions of Congress. The journey was more trying to the strength and endurance of the horse than the rider. Especially was the return homeward in the spring slow and difficult. The forests kept the roads moist longer than they now remain, and in the fresh condition of the soil they often became almost impassable. With one favorite and hardy horse, Mr. Morrow made twelve trips over the Alleghanies. But this was exceptional. With no other horse he owned was it deemed advisable to attempt a third journey.

The country was infested with horse-thieves. The unsettled condition of the country made the recovery of stolen horses very difficult. The horse-stealing proclivity of the Indians was one of the chief causes of the hatred of the early settlers toward the red men; but, after all depredations by the Indians had ceased, the farmers continued to suffer much from horse-thieves, who were believed to be often organized into gangs. The great value of the horse and the difficulty of recovering one when run away caused the pioneer to look with malignant hatred upon the horse-thief. The early Legislatures were composed almost entirely of farmers, and they endeavored to break up this kind of larceny by laws inflicting severe penalties—corporal punishment, fines, imprisonment and even mutilation. The following is the penalty for horse-stealing prescribed in an act passed in 1809: "The person so offending shall, on conviction thereof, for the first offense, be whipped not exceeding one hundred and not less than fifty stripes on his naked back, and on conviction of each succeeding offense of a like nature shall be whipped not exceeding two hundred nor less than one hundred stripes on his naked back; for the third offense shall have both ears cropped, and in either case shall restore to the owner the property stolen or repay him the value thereof, with damages, in either case, and be imprisoned not exceeding two years, and fined not exceeding $1,000 at the discretion of the court, and be ever after the first offense rendered incapable of holding any office of trust, being a juror or giving testimony in any court in this State."

Ear-cropping was prescribed for no other offense, and, as it was the penalty for the third offense of the horse-stealer, it is doubtful whether it was ever actually inflicted in Ohio. The railroad and the telegraph, by affording the means for the more certain detection of the criminal and the recovery of the stolen property, did more to put down this crime than the most severe penalties.

The little copper distillery was to be found in most neighborhoods throughout the county. Rye and corn whisky was a common drink. It was kept in the cupboard or on the shelf of almost every family, and sold at all the licensed taverns, both in the town and country. The early merchants advertised that good rye whisky, at 40 cents a gallon, would be taken in exchange for goods; houses and lots were offered for sale, flour or whisky taken in full payment. It was a part of hospitality to offer the bottle to the visitor. Whisky in a tin cup was passed around at the house-raising, the log-rolling and in the harvest field. It is a mooted question not easily settled whether intemperance was more common then than now. That the spirituous liquors of those days were purer is admitted, but the notion that they were less intoxicating seems not to have been well founded. Excess in drinking then as now brought poverty, want and death. The early settler with the purest of liquors could drink himself to death.

CHARACTER OF THE PIONEERS.

The early emigrants to Brown County may be described as a bold and resolute, rather than a cultivated people. It has been laid down as a general truth that a population made up of immigrants will contain the hardy and vigorous elements of character in a far greater proportion than the same number of persons born upon the soil and accustomed to tread in the footsteps of their fathers. It required enterprise and resolution to sever the ties which bound them to the place of their birth, and, upon their arrival in the new country, the stern face of nature and the necessities of their condition made them bold and energetic. Individuality was fostered by the absence of old familiar customs, family alliances and the restraints of old social organizations. The early settlers of Brown County were plain men and women of good sense, without the refinements which luxury brings, and with great contempt for all shams and mere pretense.

A majority of the early settlers belonged to the middle class. Few were, by affluence, placed above the necessity of labor with their hands, and few were so poor that they could not become the owners of small farms. The mass of the settlers were the owners in fee simple of at least a small farm.

Perhaps a majority of the pioneers were opposed to slavery. Although the larger proportion of them had emigrated from slaveholding States, they had fled from the evils of slavery and were opponents of the slave system. As a consequence, that form of pride which looks upon labor as degrading never had a foothold in the county. Rev. James Smith, whose journal is elsewhere quoted, noted this fact. He had been reared in Virginia, but had a great abhorrence for every form of human bondage. Speaking of the inhabitants of the Northwest Territory, he says:

"Here the industrious farmer cultivates his farm with his own hands, eats the bread of cheerfulness and rests contented on his pillow at night. The mother instructs her daughters in the useful and pleasing accomplishments of the distaff and the needle, with all things else necessary to constitute them provident mothers and good housewives. The young man, instead of the cowskin, or some other instrument of torture, takes hold of an ax or follows the plow. The ruddy damsel thinks it no disgrace to wash her clothes or milk her cows or dress the food of the family. In a word, it is here no disgrace to engage in any of the honest occupations of life, and the consequence is the people live free from want, free from the perplexity and free from the guilt of keeping slaves."

The backwoods age was not a golden age. However pleasing it may be to contemplate the industry and frugality, the hospitality and general sociability of the pioneer times, it would be improper to overlook the less pleasing features of the picture. Hard toil made men old before their time. The means of culture and intellectual improvement were inferior. In the absence of the refinement of literature, music and the drama, men engaged in rude, coarse and sometimes brutal amusements. Public gatherings were often marred by scenes of drunken disorder and fighting. The dockets of the courts show a large proportion of cases of assault and battery and affray. While some of the settlers had books and studied them, the mass of the people had little time for study. Post roads and post offices were few, and the scattered inhabitants rarely saw a newspaper or read a letter from their former homes. Their knowledge of politics was obtained from the bitter discussions of opposing aspirants for office. The traveling preacher was their most cultivated teacher. The tourist from a foreign country or from one of the older States was compelled to admit that life in the backwoods was not favorable to amenity of manners. One of these travelers wrote of the Western people in 1802: "Their Generals distill whisky, their Colonels keep tavern and their statesmen feed pigs."

Josiah Espy, author of "Memoranda of a Tour in Ohio and Kentucky in 1805," traveled through the Virginia Military District. In passing from Limestone, Ky., to Chillicothe, Ohio, he traveled over the new State road and over a very rugged and thinly populated portion of the district, and formed an unfavorable opinion of the region. He thus recorded in his journal his impressions of the people of Ohio:

"The emigration to the State of Ohio at this time is truly astonishing. From my own personal observations, compared with the opinion of some gentlemen I have consulted, I have good reason to conclude that, during the present year, from twenty to thirty thousand souls have entered that State for the purpose of making it their future residence. They are chiefly from Pennsylvania, Virginia, New Jersey, Maryland, Kentucky and Tennessee, but, on inquiry, you will find some from every State in the Union, including many foreigners. The inhabitants of the State of Ohio, being so lately collected from all the States, have, as yet, obtained no National character. The state of society, however, for some years to come, cannot be very pleasant—the great body of the people being not only poor, but rather illiterate. Their necessities will, however, give them habits of industry and labor, and have a tendency to increase the morals of the rising generation. This, with that respect for the Christian religion which generally prevails among that class of people now emigrating to the State, will lay the best foundation for their future National character. It is to be regretted, however, that at present few of them have a rational and expanded view of the beauty, excellence and order of that Christian system, the essence of which is divine wisdom. The great body of the people will, therefore, it is to be feared, be a party for some years to priestcraft, fanaticism and religious enthusiasm."

Gov. St. Clair, in a letter to Paul Fearing, dated at Chillicothe, December 25, 1801, argued that the people of the Territory were not prepared for self-government. The following is an extract:

"Where is the information necessary for the formation of a constitution for so extended a country, inhabited by people whose manners are so different, and where are the means to support it? Our people are all so poor (a few excepted about this place, who have suddenly raised great fortunes by speculations in lands and many of those not the most honorable), that they can barely live in a very wretched manner; but, of the few towns, there is scarcely a habitation to be seen better than Indian wigwams. The greatest part of the people are new-comers, and you well know that it requires a long time to subdue a country all in forests, and much labor and expense, so that had we even many men of talents and information, as we certainly have some, they have no leisure from the calls to provide for their future welfare, to employ their thought on abstruse questions of government and policy." In an earlier letter to Senator James Ross, Gov. St. Clair said: "A multitude of indigent and ignorant people are but ill-qualified to form a constitution and government for themselves."

THE PRIMITIVE FORESTS.

It is not easy to describe the forests of Ohio as they appeared in their primitive luxuriance to the eyes of the pioneers. No woodland to-day, even in the most unfrequented spot, wears the rich and exuberant garb which nature gave it. Under the transforming power of civiliziation, the earth assumes a new aspect. Even the woods and the streams are changed. Herbage and shrubs which once grew luxuriantly in our forests have been eaten out by cattle until they can only be found in the most secluded and inaccessible places. Trees cut down are succeeded by others of a different growth.

The general face of the country exhibited to the pioneer a wild luxuriance, which cannot well be described. The native forests covered the whole surface of the county, unrelieved by those open plains or natural meadows so common fifty or seventy-five miles north. Even without the savage war-whoop, it was a wild country. There stood the forests, not, as now, by their contrast with the sunny fields and dusty roads, inviting the traveler and laborer to repose in their shade, but every tree seemed an enemy to be slaughtered by the woodman's steel. Now the grove is the attractive spot; then the clearing which let in the sunlight seemed only inviting.

One hundred and three species of trees and herbaceous plants, native of the Miami woods, were catalogued by Dr. Daniel Drake at the beginning of this century, thirty of which rise to the height of sixty feet or more. There is no dividing line in nature between a tree and a shrub, but most botanists have agreed arbitrarily upon thirty feet as a minimum height of a species entitled to be called a tree. The richness of the Miami woods will be seen when it is stated that in all Germany, embracing the whole of Central Europe, there are but sixty species of trees. In France, the number is given by some at thirty; by others, as thirty-four. In Great Britain, there are but twenty-nine species above thirty feet high, and of these, botanists describe but fifteen as large or moderately high.

The white oak here obtained a remarkable development of size, if it did not quite reach the same strength attained in West Virginia. This noble tree, at the first settlement, was found wherever there was a good clay soil, three or four feet in diameter and three or four hundred years old, but still green and flourishing. Five or six varieties of the oak were found in Brown County. The wild cherry, so valuable to the cabinet-worker, was scattered throughout the county, and, in some localities, was abundant. Now it is rarely found. Large black walnut trees were cut down and reduced to ashes, a single one of which could now be sold as it stood upon the ground for more than an acre of cultivated land in some parts of the county. Along the margins of the streams were seen the giant sycamores and elms; near by, on the alluvial bottoms, the camp of sugar-maples, with its undergrowth of papaw, indicative of a rich soil; on higher grounds, the poplars, hickories and white walnuts grew to a stately height. In some places, the beech had almost exclusive possession.

The age of the gigantic denizens of our forests has probably been overstated. Some writers have spoken of them as of many centuries' growth. There are probably very few trees now standing in the Miami Valley which had begun to grow before the discovery of America, in 1492. The greatest portion of even our largest trees are probably less than three hundred years old. Our hardwood species probably attain a diameter of thirty inches in two and a half centuries.

There was beauty, as well as magnificence, in the primeval forests. Under the branches of the giant trees grew shrubs and flowers, as perfect as if they had been cultivated by the skillful florist. There were wild lilies and roses. In the early spring were seen the bright green of the buckeye leaves, the pure, white blossoms of the dogwood, the purple hue of the red-bud, and on the ground the many hues of more than a hundred species of wild flowers. A tall weed covered the fertile bottoms of the streams, growing thick as hemp and overtopping horse and rider.

WILD ANIMALS.

The buffalo and elk, probably never numerous in this vicinity, had disappeared before the approach of the white man, but the bear, the deer, the wolf, the panther, the wild cat, the otter, the beaver, the porcupine, the wild turkey, the rattlesnake, racer, moccasin and copperhead of the fauna, which have now disappeared, remained in greater or less numbers for some years after the occupancy by the whites. The streams were infested with leeches. Swine were the chief means of the destruction of poisonous snakes, from which the county has been almost entirely free for fifty years.

Wolves were so numerous and destructive to sheep that several acts were passed by the Territorial and State Legislatures providing premiums for killing them. Considerable sums were allowed by the Commissioners of Adams and Clermont Counties for wolf-scalps, the bounty varying at different times

from $2 to $2.50 for each wolf killed over six months old, and half these sums for those under six months. The wolf-killer, before receiving his bounty, was required by law to produce the scalp of each wolf killed, with the ears entire. The first law required the whole head of the wolf, with the ears entire, to be produced. He was also required to take an oath, which, in 1799, was of the following form:

I do solemnly swear (or affirm) that the head now produced by me is the head of a wild wolf, taken and killed by me in the county of ———, within six miles of some one of the settlements within the same to the best of my knowledge, and that I have not wittingly or willingly spared the life of any bitch wolf, in my power to kill, with the design of increasing the breed. So help me God.

Premiums for killing panthers were also provided for by the law, but panther scalps were rarely presented to the Commissioners of the two counties from which Brown was formed. The records of the Commissioners of Clermont County show the payment of only four premiums for the killing of panthers; three of these were in the year 1804 and one in 1810. On the other hand, $28 were allowed for killing wolves at a single session of the Commissioners of the same county. The last panther killed in this region is said to have been a huge one, measuring eight feet in length, and killed by the celebrated hunter, Adam Bricker, in the forests not far from Williamsburg. Bricker had been imitating the cries of the fawn to decoy the doe, but instead of the deer, he was confronted with the ferocious panther. It required quick work to save himself from being torn to pieces. Fortunately, at his first fire the panther fell dead.

Countless numbers of squirrels were to be found in the woods, and unceasing vigilance was required on the part of the settler to protect his cornfields from their ravages. They sometimes passed over the country in droves, traveling in the same direction. These animals were a nuisance, and were too common to be regarded as valuable for food. The Legislature, in 1809, passed a singular act, having the double object in view of destroying squirrels and providing the people with a currency. It was entitled "An Act to Encourage the Killing of Squirrels," passed and bearing date December 24, 1807. Its first section provided "that each and every person within this State, who is subject to a county tax, shall, in addition thereto, produce to the Clerk of the township in which he may reside such number of squirrels' scalps as the Trustees, at their annual meeting, apportion to the currency levies, provided that it does not exceed one hundred nor less than ten. Each taxpayer, at the time his property was listed for taxation, was to be furnished with a list of the scalps he would be required to furnish. On failure or neglect to furnish the required scalps, the taxpayer was required to pay into the treasury of the township 3 cents for every scalp he was in default; and every person producing to the Township Clerk an excess of scalps over and above the number apportioned to him was to receive from the Township Clerk a certificate of the number of scalps, which certificate was a warrant on the Township Treasurer, each scalp being valued at 2 cents. These certificates were for the purpose of furnishing the people with a currency. They were secured by the faith of the township, and were received by the merchant for goods and the mechanic for work.

Other kinds of game were abundant. For some years, the red deer were as numerous as cattle to-day. Wild turkeys could be shot or entrapped in great numbers. When mast was abundant, a drove of more than one hundred wild turkeys, all large and fat, might be found in the near vicinity of the settlements, and when mast was scarce large numbers would sometimes come to the barn-yards for grain.

CHAPTER VI.

THE GREAT KENTUCKY REVIVAL AND SHAKERISM IN BROWN COUNTY.

THE great revival at the beginning of the present century, which spread from Kentucky into the territory now forming Brown and Adams Counties, was a remarkable event in the religious history of the region. This memorable religious excitment began in Kentucky about 1800, and soon spread into Tennessee, North Carolina, West Virginia and the territory north of the Ohio. It originated in the Cumberland country under the preaching of Rev. James McGready, a Presbyterian clergyman, who is described as a homely man, with sandy hair and rugged features, so terrific in holding forth the terrors of hell that he was called a son of thunder. He pictured out "the furnace of hell with its red-hot coals of God's wrath as large as mountains;" he endeavored to open to the sinner's view "the burning lake of hell, to see its fiery billows rolling, and to hear the yells and groans of the damned ghosts roaring under the burning wrath of an angry God." Under his preaching, several persons fell down with a loud cry, and lay powerless, groaning, praying and crying to God for mercy. The excitement spread. Great camp-meetings were held—the first in the United States. Large numbers fell down and swooned, with every appearance of life suspended. Families came to these meetings a distance of fifty or a hundred miles. The camp-meetings continued three or four days and nights. Those from a distance slept in their wagons, in tents or temporary structures. At Cane Ridge, Bourbon Co., Ky., in August, 1801, it was estimated that 20,000 persons were present, many of whom were from the north side of the Ohio. It was estimated at this meeting that 3,000 persons fell to the ground under the unnatural excitement. There were at these meetings other strange physical manifestations, which increased the excitement and deeply moved the multitude. There were nervous affections, which produced horrible convulsions of the body and contortions of the countenance. The more shocking bodily exercises caused a division among the clergy as to the work. But opposition was compelled too often to succumb to the cry, "It is God's work." At Concord, in May, 1801, seven Presbyterian ministers were present, four of whom opposed the work until the fourth day, when they, too, succumbed, and all professed to be convinced that it was the work of God.

The effects of the great awakening began to be felt in what is now Brown County during the year 1801. The movement, both in Kentucky and Ohio, prevailed chiefly among the Presbyterian and Methodist Churches; the Baptists were little affected by it. The first camp-meeting in Northern Kentucky near the Ohio was held at Cabin Creek, beginning May 22, 1801, and continuing four days and three nights. Rev. Richard McNemar, then pastor of the Presbyterian Church at Cabin Creek, was the leading spirit of the meeting. He says there were persons at the meeting from Cane Ridge, Concord, Eagle Creek and other congregations, who partook of the spirit of the work and caused it to be spread abroad. "The scene," he continues, "was awful beyond description; the falling, crying out, praying, exhorting, singing, shouting, etc., exhibited such new and striking evidences of a supernatural power, that few, if any, could escape without being affected."

The first large camp-meeting north of the Ohio was held at Eagle Creek;

it began June 5, 1801, and continued four days and three nights. Rev. John Dunlavy was pastor of the Eagle Creek Presbyterian Church, and Rev. Mr. McNemar and probably other ministers were present at the camp-meeting. McNemar says of the Eagle Creek meeting: "The number of people there was not so great, as the country was new; but the work was equally powerful according to the number. At this meeting, the principal and leading characters at that place fully embraced the spirit of the work, which laid a foundation for its continuance and spread in that quarter."

Rev. John Dunlavy, who was a conspicuous figure in forwarding the great revival, was the son of a Presbyterian emigrant from Ireland, and a brother of the first President Judge of the Court of Common Pleas of the First District of Ohio. He came from Western Pennsylvania to Kentucky, where he taught school for some time. Becoming a Presbyterian minister, he was in 1797 ordained over the congregations at Lee's Creek, Big Bracken and North Bracken. Not long after, he removed to Ohio, and was settled as pastor of Eagle Creek congregation, between the sites of Ripley and West Union. Dr. Davidson, in his History of the Presbyterian Church in Kentucky, thus describes him with an unfriendly hand: "He was one of the most gloomy, reserved and saturnine men that ever lived; his soul seemed to be in harmony with no one lively or social feeling, and the groans he continually uttered drove away all pleasure in his company. He was above the middle stature and well proportioned, but of a swarthy complexion and dark, forbidding countenance. His manners were coarse, rough and repulsive. His talents were not above mediocrity; his knowledge was superficial; he was never regarded as a leading or influential man, nor was he a popular preacher. His favorite topics were those of terror, not consolation."

The singular bodily exercises and convulsions which accompanied this revival on both sides of the Ohio, wherever there was undue excitement, have often been described by eye-witnesses of unimpeachable veracity, and their accounts agree so substantially that all suspicion of exaggeration is dispelled. There are still living a few old persons, who, in early life, saw some of this remarkable work. Mr. McNemar published a brief history of the revival. Peter Cartwright, the pioneer Methodist preacher, in his autobiography gives an account of what he himself saw of the work in Kentucky; and A. H. Dunlavy has published a brief sketch of the revival work at Turtle Creek. With such authorities before us, we feel confidence in the substantial accuracy of the description of the physical manifestations we shall now give.

It was not uncommon in large meetings for large numbers to fall in a short time, and to lie unconscious, with hardly any signs of breathing or beating of the pulse. Some would lie for a short time only; others for hours. Almost all the adult persons in a large congregation sometimes fell in this manner.

The *jerks* was the popular name for convulsions, which caused a rapid and spasmodic motion of the head, and sometimes affected the limbs and the whole body. The head would fly backward and forward, or from side to side, with such rapidity that the features could not be recognized. The looker-on would fear a dislocation of the neck, but no such injury is known to have ensued. "I have seen," says Rev. Peter Cartwright, "more than five hundred persons jerking at one time in my large congregations. To see those proud, well-dressed gentlemen and ladies take the jerks would often excite my risibilities. The first jerk or so, you would see their fine bonnets, caps and combs fly; and so sudden would be the jerking that their long, loose hair would crack almost as loud as a wagoner's whip." The disease was sometimes communicated to those who had no serious impressions, and mocked at the revival. There were recurring fits of the strange disorder seven or eight years after the revival, and, indeed, sporadic cases at a much later period. The most graphic description of the jerks is that given by Richard McNemar. He says:

"Nothing in nature could better represent this strange and unaccountable operation than for one to goad another alternately on every side with a piece of red-hot iron. The exercise commonly began in the head, which would fly backward and forward, and from side to side, with a quick jolt, which the person would naturally labor to suppress, but in vain, and the more anyone labored to stay himself and be sober, the more he staggered, and the more his twitches increased. He must necessarily go as he was inclined, whether with a violent dash on the ground and bounce from place to place like a foot-ball, or hop round, with head, limbs and trunk twitching and jolting in every direction, as if they must inevitably fly asunder. And how such could escape without injury was no small wonder among spectators. By this strange operation, the human frame was commonly so transformed and disfigured as to lose every trace of its natural appearance. Sometimes the head would be twitched right and left to a half round, with such velocity that not a feature could be discovered, but the face appeared as much behind as before; and in the quick, progressive jerk, it would seem as if the persons were transmuted into some other species of creature. Head-dresses were of little account among the female jerkers. Even handkerchiefs bound tight round the head would be flirted off almost with the first twitch, and the hair put into the utmost confusion; this was a very great inconvenience, to redress which the generality were shorn, although directly contrary to their confession of faith. Such as were seized with jerks were wrested at once, not only from under their own government, but that of every one else, so that it was dangerous to attempt confining them or touching them in any manner, to whatever danger they were exposed, yet few were hurt, except it were such as rebelled against the operation, through wilful and deliberate enmity, and refused to comply with the injunctions which it came to enforce."

There were other exercises which were not so common, and are sufficiently described by their names, viz., rolling, running, dancing and the holy laugh. There were instances of spinning around on the foot after the manner of the whirling dervishes of the East. The most disgusting of all the exercises was called the "barks" in which the subject not only imitated the bark of the dog, but sometimes ran upon all fours, growling, snarling and foaming at the mouth. That there were cases of this kind of brutish action cannot be doubted, but to the credit of human nature it is to be recorded that they were rare. It is noteworthy here that among the *Convulsionists* of France, seventy years before, there were persons similarly affected, some being called barkers and some mewers.

The subjects of these strange disorders were sincere men and women, who could give no rational account of their movements, and would only say they could not help it. In persons of peculiar nervous organization, over-excitement may result in actions which seem to be wholly involuntary, when there is really a hidden volition of their own, and they are influenced by sympathy with and imitation of what they have seen or heard of others doing under like circumstances. Psychological diseases always have been more or less epidemic and contagious. Emotions which do not seriously affect us when alone may become overpowering when many are affected. Thus, sympathy, "that wonderful instinct that links man to man in a social whole," in the wild excesses of popular feeling becomes a dangerous power that seizes upon all it can reach, and sweeps them round and round until they are drawn into the devouring vortex. Hysterical symptoms in times of great religious excitement should be promptly repressed, or they may become epidemic. There is evidence that where the excesses we have described were most encouraged by the clergy and others in authority, they were most common; where they were discouraged, they were kept in check. It is narrated that a Baptist clergyman, who did not believe that convulsions were the work of the Holy Spirit, seeing symptoms of the jerks appearing under his own preaching, exclaimed in a loud voice, "I command all unclean spirits to depart hence," and thus completely stayed the disorder.

Soon there were visions, prophecies and revelations among the revivalists. Their sons and daughters prophesied, their young men saw visions and their old men dreamed dreams. The new light which dawned upon them, or the internal manifestations of a Divine wisdom, was such a favorite phrase with them, that for several years the revival party were called New Lights. In 1803, at the meeting of the Presbyterian Synod of Kentucky, it was proposed to enter upon a trial of some of the revivalists for unsoundness in doctrine; five ministers of the revival party, including Dunlavy, seceded from the Synod and formed a separate Presbytery. On the 28th of June, 1804, the ministers of the revival party, three north and three south of the Ohio, members of the Independent Presbytery, becoming convinced that all Presbyteries were unauthorized human devices, dissolved that body by writing its *will* and subscribing their names as witnesses. The witnesses of the last will and testament of the Springfield Presbytery, as it was called, say that from its first existence the body was knit together in love, lived in peace and concord and died a voluntary and happy death. Before the close of the year 1804, the New Lights, or revivalists, reported seven societies in Southwest Ohio, viz., Trutle Creek, Eagle Creek, Springdale, Orangedale, Clear Creek, Beaver Creek and Salem. They repudiated all creeds and confessions of faith except the Bible. They soon gave up the doctrine of the Trinity, and became immersionists. They declined to be called New Lights, and adopted the name of Christians, and are to-day a distinct and respectable body. The New Light revival swept all the Presbyterian churches in Southwestern Ohio, except those at Duck Creek and Round Bottom. The church at Cincinnati was largely tainted with the new doctrines and methods.

The public meetings of the revivalists were often scenes of tumult and confusion. There would be singing, praying and exhorting at the same time. They invented what was termed the "praying match," which is stated to have had for its object the determination of "the brightest, boldest and loudest gift of prayer." According to McNemar, it was a custom, when one would begin to preach or exhort and was deemed uninteresting, that he would presently be confronted with a prayer by some one else, and whichever manifested the greatest warmth and awakened the liveliest sensations, gained the victory and secured the general shout on his side. The Turtle Creek pastor approvingly represents his flock as "praying, shouting, jerking, barking or rolling, dreaming, prophesying, and looking as through a glass at the infinite glories of Zion." The whole congregation, also, sometimes prayed together with such power and volume of sound that, if the pastor does not exaggerate, "the doubtful footsteps of those in search of the meeting might be directed sometimes to the distance of miles around." Some time in the year 1804, they began to encourage one another to praise God in the dance.

Twenty years before, there had died in the wilds of New York an illiterate woman, who had been the wife of a blacksmith until her religion had taught her to abandon the marriage relation. During her whole life, she endured great tribulations, saw visions, had frequent communications with the world of spirits, and was believed to be mad. A native of England, she had been imprisoned at Manchester for raising a tumult by street preaching. She believed that the Savior appeared to her in her prison cell and, in some mysterious manner, became united to her, and through her Heaven set up a church which is never to be destroyed. She gathered around her a little knot of followers, who called her "Mother Ann," and styled themselves "Believers in Christ's Second Appearing," but they were usually known as Shakers, an appellation at which they took no offense. Coming to America in 1774, a band of eight persons, they made a settlement near Albany, and continued few in numbers until a great revival in 1779 occurred at New Lebanon, N. Y., which was attended with physical manifestations, not altogether unlike those just described. A number of the subjects of this revival visited Mother Ann, and found the key to their religious experience. Thus did the Shakers receive their first considerable accession to their numbers.

The Shakers at New Lebanon, N. Y., heard of the remarkable religious work in the forests of Kentucky and Ohio, and resolved to send missionaries to proclaim to the subjects of the revival the mystical creed in which they had found peace. On the 1st day of January, 1805, John Meacham, Benjamin S. Youngs and Issacher Bates set out from New York, and made the journey to Kentucky and Ohio for the most part on foot. They wore broad-brimmed hats and a fashion of dress much like that of the followers of George Fox. They passed through Kentucky and arrived in Southwestern Ohio about the 20th of March. They visited the different societies of the revivalists, and taught the doctrines of Ann Lee. Their first converts in the West were at Turtle Creek, in Warren County, where the largest Shaker society in the West still exists.

The Shakers obtained their first converts among the revivalists of Brown County at Eagle Creek in June, 1805. In the following month, Rev. John Dunlavy espoused the new faith, and was thenceforward a leading light in the Society of United Believers. He wrote "The Manifesto," which has been regarded by the Shakers as one of the strongest arguments ever published in favor of their doctrines. Within two years, twenty-five or thirty families at Eagle Creek embraced Shakerism. Husbands and wives abandoned the family relation, and consecrated all their property, personal and real, to the sacred use of the church. Some of the best men in the new settlements, honest, conscientious and benevolent, joined the community under the conviction that they were seeking salvation by renouncing the world and all its temptations. Their sincerity no one can question. The society established several communities in Kentucky and Ohio, all among the subjects of the great revival. Four of the ministers who had been foremost in the revival work became converts, and died in the Shaker faith, having passed in four years from the creed of Calvin to that of Ann Lee. The Shakers never established a village at Eagle Creek, but lived in scattered houses, meeting on Sunday in the open air for worship by singing, dancing and preaching. They were all removed from Brown County about 1809 or 1810. A large proportion of them established themselves at the society called West Union or Buseron, on the Wabash, in Indiana. When that community was abandoned on account of the unhealthiness of the location, most of them then moved to Union Village, near Lebanon, Warren Co., Ohio. Among the converts at Eagle Creek was Belteshazzer Dragoo, believed by many to have been the first permanent settler in Brown County; he died in the faith at Union Village.

CHAPTER VII.
CIVIL ORGANIZATION.

THE territory comprising Brown County was a part of Clermont and Adams Counties from the organization of the Government of the State of Ohio until March 1, 1818. Prior to the formation of the State Government, the territory had belonged, in whole or in part, to Hamilton, Adams and Clermont Counties.

Hamilton was the second county formed by the proclamation of Gov. St. Clair. As originally organized, it did not include any part of Brown. It was organized January 2, 1790, and was at first bounded on the south by the Ohio, on the east by the Little Miami, on the west by the Great Miami, and on the north by a line drawn due east from the Standing Stone Fork, or branch of the Great Miami. The Standing Stone Fork is supposed to have been Loramie's Branch, which flows into the Great Miami near the northern boundary of Miami County.

On August 15, 1796, in a proclamation forming Wayne County, Gov. St. Clair declared that the eastern boundary of Hamilton County is "a due north line from the lower Shawnees' town upon the Scioto River." From this date until the organization of Adams County, the whole of Brown County was a part of the large county of Hamilton.

Adams, the fourth county of the territory northwest of the Ohio, dates from July 10, 1797. Its original boundaries were as follows:

"Beginning upon the Ohio River at the upper boundary of that tract of 24,000 acres granted unto the French inhabitants of Gallipolis, by an act of Congress of the United States, bearing date the 3d of March, 1795; thence down the said Ohio River to the mouth of Elk River (generally known by the name of Eagle Creek), and up with the principal water of the said Elk River, or Eagle Creek, to its source or head; thence by a due north line to the southern boundary of Wayne County; and easterly along said boundary so far that a due south line shall meet the interior point of the upper boundary of the aforesaid tract of 24,000 acres, and with said boundary to the place of beginning."

On the 20th of August, 1798, a proclamation was issued, to take effect September 1, 1798, changing the western boundary of Adams, and attaching a part of Hamilton to Adams, as follows:

"To begin on the bank of the Ohio where Elk River, or Eagle Creek, empties into the same, and run from thence due north until it intersects the southern boundary of the county of Ross; and all and singular the lands lying between the said north line and Elk River, or Eagle Creek, shall, after the said 1st day of September next, be separated from the county of Hamilton, and added to the county of Adams."

"The first court in Adams County was held in Manchester. Winthrop Sargent, the Secretary of the Territory, acting in the absence of the Governor, appointed Commissioners, who located the county seat at an out-of-the-way place, a few miles above the mouth of Brush Creek, which they called Adamsville. The locality was soon named, in derision, *Scant*. At the next session of the court, its members became divided, and part sat in Manchester and part at Adamsville. The Governor, on his return to the Territory, finding the people in great confusion, and much bickering among them, removed the seat of justice to the mouth of Brush Creek, where the first court was held in 1798. Here a town was laid out by Noble Grimes, under the name of Washington. A large log court house was built, with a jail in the lower story, and the Governor appointed two more of the Scant party Judges, which gave them a majority. In 1800, Charles Willing Byrd, Secretary of the Territory, in the absence of the Governor, appointed two more of the Manchester party Judges, which balanced the parties, and the contest was maintained until West Union became the county seat."

Clermont County was formed by proclamation December 6, 1800, with the following boundaries:

"Beginning at the mouth of Nine-Mile or Muddy Creek where it discharges itself into the Ohio, and running from thence with a straight line to the mouth of the East Branch of the Little Miami River to the mouth of O'Bannon's Creek; thence with a due east line until it shall intersect a line drawn north from the mouth of Elk River, or Eagle Creek; thence with that line south to the mouth of the said Elk River or Eagle Creek; and from thence with the Ohio to the place of beginning."

The county seat of Clermont, from its organization until the formation of Brown County, was at Williamsburg—a very convenient location for the county as originally organized. Bethel was the principal contestant against Williamsburg for the seat of justice.

At the time of the organization of Clermont, there was a protracted dispute between Gov. St. Clair and the Territorial Legislature as to whom belonged the power of creating new counties. The Governor claimed that this power was legally invested in himself alone, and he placed his absolute veto on all acts of the Legislature establishing new counties. It is an interesting fact that, among the acts vetoed by Gov. St Clair, was one passed at Cincinnati at the first session of the Territorial Legislature, which was organized September 27, 1799, creating a county to be called Henry, and which embraced a portion of the present county of Brown. The act was entitled, "An act to establish a new county on the Ohio between the Little Miami River and Adams County." Denhamstown (Bethel) was made the temporary seat of justice, and the following persons were named in the act as Commissioners for the purpose of fixing on the most eligible place in the said county of Henry for the permanent seat of justice, some of whom resided within the present limits of Brown: Richard Allison, Samuel C. Vance. William Buckhannon, Robert Higgins, Hezekiah Conn, Alexander Martin, William Perry and Peter Light.

It thus appears that all that portion of Brown County between its present western boundary and a line drawn due north from the mouth of Eagle Creek formed a part of Hamilton County, with its seat of justice at Cincinnati from August 15, 1796, until December 6, 1800, and from the latter date until March 1, 1818, a part of Clermont, with its seat of justice at Williamsburg. That portion lying between Eagle Creek and a line drawn due north from the mouth of Eagle Creek was a part of Hamilton from August 15, 1796, until September 1, 1798, and from the latter date a part of Adams until the organization of Brown County. And all that portion lying between Eagle Creek and the eastern boundary of Brown was a part of Hamilton from August 15, 1796, until July 10, 1797, when it became a part of Adams, and so remained until the organization of Brown.

But at still earlier dates, this territory had been made a part of political divisions called counties. During the Revolution, this region would have been marked on the map of the North American colonies as a part of Virginia, whose extensive domain, making her the mother of States, as well as of Presidents,

Joseph Cachran

reached to the Mississippi. Out of this broad territory, vast counties were formed. The county of Kentucky included the whole of the present State of that name. In October, 1778, Virginia, by statute, declared that: "All the citizens of the Commonwealth of Virginia, who are already settled or who shall hereafter settle on the western side of the Ohio, shall be included in a distinct county, which shall be called Illinois County." This territory, then, once formed a part of the vast western county of Virginia called Illinois.

But, going back a few years further, we find this region included in a county of still more vast extent. South of the Natural Bridge, between the Blue Ridge and the Alleghanies, and intersected by the James River, is a county of Virginia, with Fincastle for its seat of justice, named Botetourt, in honor of Norborne Berkeley, Lord Botetourt, a conspicuous actor in American colonial history, and Governor of Virginia. That county was established in 1769, and originally included our county within its limits. It was bounded on the east by the Blue Ridge, on the west by the Mississippi, and comprised Western Virginia, Ohio, Indiana, Illinois, Michigan, Wisconsin and Minnesota. Fincastle then, as now, was the county seat.

The following curious provision is found in the act of Virginia creating Botetourt County:

"And whereas, the people situated on the Mississippi, in the said county of Botetourt, will be very remote from the court house, and must necessarily become a separate county as soon as their numbers are sufficient—which probably will happen in a short time: Be it therefore enacted by the authority aforesaid (House of Burgesses), that the inhabitants of that part of the said county of Botetourt which lies on the said waters shall be exempted from the payment of any levies to be laid by the said County Court, for the purpose of building a court house and prison for said county."

AN ACT TO ERECT THE COUNTY OF BROWN.

SECTION 1. *Be it enacted by the General Assembly of the State of Ohio*, That so much of the counties of Adams and Clermont as comes within the following boundaries, be, and the same is, hereby erected into a separate and distinct county, which shall be known by the name of Brown, *to wit*: Beginning at a point eight miles due west from the court house, in the town of West Union, in the county of Adams; thence running due north to Highland County line; thence west with Highland County line to Clermont County line; thence north with Clermont County line to Clinton County line; thence west with Clinton County line so far that a line running south will strike the Ohio River two miles above the mouth of Bulskin Creek; thence up the Ohio River, and with the same so far that a line running due north will intersect the point of beginning.

SEC. 2. *Be it further enacted*, That all suits or actions whether of a civil or criminal nature which shall be pending; and all crimes which shall have been committed within the limits of those parts of Adams and Clermont Counties, so to be set off and erected into a separate county previous to the organizing of the said county of Brown, shall be prosecuted to final judgment and execution, within the said counties of Adams and Clermont, in the same manner as they would have been if the county of Brown had not been erected; and the Sheriffs, Coroners and Constables of the counties of Adams and Clermont, shall execute all such process as shall be necessary to carry into effect such suits, prosecutions and judgments, and all the collectors of taxes for said counties of Adams and Clermont, shall collect all such taxes as shall have been levied and unpaid within those parts of the aforesaid counties previous to the taking effect of this act.

SEC. 3. *Be it further enacted*, That all Justices of the Peace within those parts of the counties of Adams and Clermont, which by this act shall be erected into a new county, shall continue to exercise the duties of their offices, until their term of service expires, in the same manner as if they had been commissioned for the county of Brown.

SEC. 4. *Be it further enacted*, That the electors within the fractional townships which may be occasioned by the erection of the county of Brown, shall elect in the next adjoining townships.

SEC. 5. *Be it further enacted*, That on the first Monday of April next, the legal voters residing within the county of Brown, shall assemble in their respective townships at the usual places of holding elections, and shall proceed to elect their several county officers who shall hold their office until the next annual election.

SEC. 6. *And be it further enacted,* That the courts of the said county of Brown shall be holden at the house of Alexander Campbell in the town of Ripley, until the permanent seat of Justice shall be established for the said county of Brown.

This act to take effect and to be in force from and after the first day of March next.

DUNCAN M'ARTHUR, *Speaker of the House of Representatives,*
December 27, 1817.   ABRAHAM SHEPARD, *Speaker of the Senate.*

The county was named in honor of Gen. Jacob Brown, who had distinguished himself in the late war with England. He was born in Bucks County, Penn., May 9, 1775, and died in Washington City February 24, 1828. He was an early surveyor in the public lands of Ohio; entered the army in 1812 as a Brigadier General, and had distinguished himself at the battles of Chippewa and Niagara Falls and the siege of Fort Erie. At the time of the organization of this county, he was a Major General in the regular army, and, three years later, succeeded to the supreme command.

The curious reader will be interested in knowing the origin of the six lines forming the boundaries of Brown, some of which had been described in statutes long before the organization of the county.

The northern boundary of Perry Township, which is also the northern boundary of the "boot-leg" of the county, is part of a line drawn due east from the mouth of O'Bannon's Creek, which empties into the Little Miami at Loveland. This line is first mentioned in a proclamation of Gov. St. Clair, dated December 6, 1800, and was the original northern boundary of Clermont.

The county line forming the northern boundary of Washington and Eagle Townships is part of the southern boundary of Highland County, and is first described in the act creating that county, passed February 18, 1805. It is an east and west line, drawn past the Twenty-Mile Tree, in the original boundary between Adams and Clermont, which was a due north line from the mouth of Eagle Creek.

The eastern boundary of the "boot-leg" is the western boundary of Highland, and is a due north line drawn from a point on the North Fork of White Oak Creek, where that fork is intersected by the southern boundary of Highland, just described.

The eastern boundary of Brown is a due north and south line drawn through a point eight miles west of the court house in West Union. A special act of the Legislature provided that this line should be run by the compass without making any allowance for the variation of the needle.

The western boundary is a due north line drawn from the Ohio River at a point two miles above the mouth of Bullskin Creek.

The southern boundary of the county is the State southern boundary, which has been judicially determined to be the low-water mark on the northern side of the Ohio, and not the middle of that stream—a fact which is explained by the cession of the lands forming Ohio in 1784 by Virginia, which cession is described in the deed accepted by Congress as "lands northwest of the Ohio."

The line drawn due north from the mouth of Eagle Creek is frequently mentioned in the proclamations of Gov. St. Clair, and in the acts of the Territorial and early State Legislatures.

Gov. St. Clair at one time suggested this line as a suitable west boundary for the eastern State to be formed out of the territory northwest of the Ohio. An act of the Territorial Legislature passed January 23, 1802, provided that this line should be run and completed before the 1st day of May following. All traces of the line in Brown County seem to have disappeared.

EARLY COURTS AND COMMISSIONERS' PROCEEDINGS.

The judiciary under the Government of the Northwest Territory consisted of the Courts of General Quarter Sessions of the Peace and of the Common

HISTORY OF BROWN COUNTY.

Pleas. The law provided that the Court of General Quarter Sessions should be held four times a year in each county. A competent number of Justices of the Peace were commissioned by the Governor in every county, and these Justices, or any three of them, constituted Judges of the Court of Quarter Sessions. Usually the magistrates composing the Court of Quarter Sessions were the same as those composing the Court of Common Pleas. The law establishing these courts was adopted from the statutes of Pennsylvania, and was framed and published at Cincinnati June 1, 1795. Corporal punishment, even for light offenses, was the usual penalty, and an old statute of the Northwestern Territory was entitled, "An act directing the building and establishing of a court house, county jail, pillory, whipping post and stocks in every county." Among the names of the early Judges and Jurors of the Territorial courts of Adams and Clermont Counties, some will be recognized as early pioneers of Brown County.

The first court of Adams County was that of the Quarter Sessions, held at Manchester in September, 1797. The Judges of the court were Nathaniel Massie, John Beasley, John Belli, Thomas Wetherington, Hugh Cochran, Benjamin Goodin, Thomas Scott and Thomas Kirker; Sheriff, David Edie; Coroner, Andrew Ellison; Crier, Job Denning. The first Grand Jury of the county consisted of James January, foreman; Thomas Massie, John Barrett, John Ellison, Duncan McKenzie, Jesse Eastburn, Elisha Waldron, John Lodwick, Stephen Bayless, Robert Ellison, William McIntyre, Nathaniel Washburn, Zephaniah Wade, James Naylor and Jacob Piatt.

At this session of the court, the county was divided into six townships, named, respectively, Cedar Hill, Manchester, Iron Ridge, Union, Scioto and Upper. The first-named township was the only one which included any portion of the present county of Brown. The boundaries of Cedar Hill Township began at the mouth of Eagle Creek, and extended up the Ohio to a point opposite the mouth of Cabin Creek, in Kentucky, at Lawson's Ferry, thence north to the northern boundary of the county, thence west to the west line of the county, thence with the west line of the county to the place of beginning. William Rains was Collector of Cedar Hill Township in 1798. The townships of Adams County were re-organized by the County Commissioners in 1806.

The first court ever held in Clermont County was that of the General Quarter Sessions, convened at Williamsburg on the fourth Tuesday in February, 1801, with the following magistrates as Judges: Owen Todd, Presiding Jusice; William Hunter, Amos Ellis, William Buchanon, Philip Gatch, Robert Higgins and Jasper Shotwell. The court was organized with William Lytle as Prothonotary, and William Perry, Sheriff. The following persons were impaneled as a Grand Jury—the first in Clermont: Amos Smith, John Charles, John Trout, John Boothby, Henry Willis, Samuel Brown, Joshua Lambert, Jonathan Clark, John Kain, John Cotteral, John Anderson, Samuel Nelson, Benjamin Frazee, John Colthar, Kally Burke, Harmon Pearson, Ebenezer Osborn and Absalom Day. This Grand Jury of staid men, appointed to inquire into crimes and misdemeanors committed in their county, reported that they found no indictments, as did also the Grand Jury at the next session—a good report of the people of that day. Thomas Morris, who had recently removed from Columbia to Williamsburg, entered into a contract with the Judges to furnish a suitable house for the meetings of the court, with tables, benches, fuel, etc., for the term of four years, at $20 per year. In addition to the Judges of this court, the names of the following persons appear in the minutes of subsequent Territorial courts of Clermont as magistrates who sat upon the bench, viz.: Peter Light, Houghton Clark, Alexander Martin and John Hunter.

The foremen of the Grand Juries of Clermont County during the Territorial stage of government were as follows: Ephraim McAdams, May 26, 1801; John Boude, August 25, 1801; May 25, 1802, Bernard Thompson; August 25, 1802, Jonathan Hunt; November, 1802, Jeremiah Beck.

The Justices' Court of the General Quarter Sessions of Clermont County, at its first term, February 25, 1801, divided the new county, Clermont into five townships—Williamsburg, Ohio, Washington, O'Bannon (a year or two later changed to Miami) and Pleasant (now in Brown); but the records of the court, so far as they can now be found, fail to give the boundaries of these townships. We, however, may date the existence of Pleasant Township from February 25, 1801.

Lewis Township was formed by the Commissioners of Clermont County June 2, 1807. A number of the inhabitants of the east end of Washington Township having petitioned for the formation of a new township, the prayer was granted and the new township was named Lewis. It extended from the east end of Washington Township (the Adams County line) down the Ohio to Bullskin Creek, and northward to the Denhamstown road.

Clark Township was created by the Commissioners of Clermont County October 18, 1808, with the following boundaries: "Beginning where the State road from Denhamstown to West Union crosses White Oak; thence running with the State road to the Adams County line; thence north with said line to Highland County; thence with said county line to the corner of Highland, and continuing west so far as to include Aaron Leonard and Moses Moss; thence south to Lewis Township line; thence with the same to the place of beginning."

Perry, the last of the townships within the limits of Brown formed by the Commissioners of Clermont, dates its existence from June 6, 1815. Its original boundaries were as follows: "Beginning on the Clermont County line at the corner of Warren and Clinton Counties; thence a straight course to Samuel Ashton's old place on Anderson State road; thence east by south to the line between Clermont and Highland Counties; thence north with Clermont County line to the Clinton County line; thence with Clermont and Clinton County line to the place of beginning."

At the first session of the Clermont County Commissioners at Williamsburg, beginning on the first Monday in June, 1804, Edward Hall was allowed $5 for services as Supervisor of Highways in Pleasant Township. Thomas McFarland was granted $1.50 for killing one old wolf. January 22, 1804. On July 23, 1804, Henry Chapman was allowed $1 for returning the poll book of Pleasant Township. In 1804, the name of William White appears as Lister of Taxable Property in Pleasant Township.

In June, 1805, the rates for tavern licenses were established as follows: In Williamsburg, $8; in Bethel, $6; in White Haven (Higginsport), $4; in Staunton (Ripley), $4; all other taverns, $4. Ferry licenses were priced as follows: At Staunton (Ripley), $2; at Waters' Ferry, $4; at Samuel Ellis', above the mouth of White Oak, $1.50; at White Haven, $4; at Boude's and Bolander's, $4 each; at the mouth of Bullskin, $5; at or within one mile of Twelve Mile Creek, $3; at all other ferries that may be established across the Ohio, $2.

TERRITORIAL ELECTIONS.

The first elections for Representatives in the Territorial Legislature were held at the seats of justice of the respective counties. There was so little of democracy in the government established by the celebrated ordinance of 1787 that the settlers were seldom called on to exercise the right of suffrage. Under that ordinance, no one could vote unless he was the owner of fifty acres of land. All the officers of the Territory were required to be residents for specified periods, and all to be land-owners—the Governor to own 1,000 acres; the Secretary and Judges, 500 acres each; the members of the Legislative Council, 500 acres each; the members of the House of Representatives, 200 acres each, The first election for Representatives was held on the third Monday of December, 1798. At this time, the greater portion of Brown County was included in Hamilton County.

In October, 1880, an election was held for Representatives in the second Territorial Legislature. This election was held under a law, passed by the first Territorial Legislature, which required the polls to be open in each county at the court house on the second Tuesday in October, 1800, between the hours of 10 and 11 in the forenoon, and to be kept open until 5 o'clock in the afternoon, and again opened the next day from 10 until 5 o'clock, and then finally closed, unless some candidate or the Judges desired the election to be continued, in which case the poll was to be open the third day from 10 until 3 oclock. The election at Cincinnati continued three days. The vote was taken *viva voce*. There were seven Representatives to elect from Hamilton County, and the following is the vote of the successful candidates: M. Miller, 284; J. Smith, 273; F. Dunlavy, 229; J. Morrow, 212; D. Reeder, 204; J. Ludlow, 187; J. White, 162. On the same day, William Lytle was elected for the ensuing session in place of Aaron Cadwell, who had removed from the Territory. The vote stood: William Lytle, 153; F. Dunlavy, 140. Thirty-five persons had been announced by their friends in the columns of the *Western Spy* as candidates, and at least twenty-four of them received votes. The total number of votes cast at this election cannot now be ascertained. In both the first and second Territorial Legislatures, Nathaniel Massie and Joseph Darlington were the Representatives from Adams County.

At the election for members of the convention to form a State constitution, held in October, 1802, the electors of Clermont County voted at Williamsburg. The delegates chosen from Clermont County were Philip Gatch, a Methodist minister, who had been a member of an abolition society in his native State; and James Sargent, who had freed his slaves in Maryland before removing to the Western country. It is said that both were elected because they were anti-slavery men. Joseph Darlington, Israel Donalson and Thomas Kirker were elected Delegates from Adams County.

This election was attended with great excitement. It was the first election north of the Ohio in which entered questions of national party politics. One of the questions before the people was, whether a State Government at all should at that time be formed. The enabling act of Congress, under which the election was held, provided that, after the members of the convention had assembled, they should first determine, by a majority of the whole number elected, whether it was or was not expedient to form a constitution and State Government at that time. The friends of Gov. Arthur St. Clair and the Federalists generally were opposed to the formation of a State Government; the Republicans generally favored an immediate admission of the Territory into the Union as a State. At the last session of the Territorial Legislature, the opponents of a State Government had been largely in the majority, and, under the lead of Jacob Burnet, of Cincinnati, had passed an act having for its object the division of the Territory into two future States, a measure which, had it received the sanction of Congress, would long have delayed the admission of both into the Union. The act passed the Council unanimously, and the House by a large majority. A minority of seven Representatives entered their solemn protest against it, and began an appeal to the people and to Congress with a fixed determination to defeat the division of the Territory and to secure an early State Government. They were successful. Congress not only refused to divide the Territory, but passed an act to enable the people to form a State Government. The canvass which preceded the election of members of the convention was one of great bitterness; fast friends became enemies for life. The increasing unpopularity of Gov. St. Clair, who was accused of a tyrannical and arbitrary exercise of the powers of his office, and the declining fortunes of the Federalists in the States, intensified the popular excitement. A large majority of the people of Adams and Clermont Counties at this time were anti-Federalists.

THE COUNTY SEAT CONTEST.

The contest for the seat of justice of Brown County was a heated one, and continued for several years. The contest was between the advocates of Ripley and the advocates of a central location. Ripley was the largest and most important town in the county, but it was thirty-five miles distant from the northwest corner of the new county. The act creating the county designated the house of Alexander Campbell, in Ripley, as the place of holding the courts until the permanent seat of justice should be established.

On January 29, 1818, one month after the passage of the act creating the county, the Legislature, by joint resolution, appointed Gen. Isaac Cook and William McFarland, of Ross, and Philip Good, of Green, Commissioners to locate the seat of justice in Brown. Their duties were defined by a general law. They were required to give twenty days' notice of the time and place of their meeting, and, after taking an oath to discharge their duties faithfully, "to proceed to examine and select the most proper place as the seat of justice, as near the center of the county as possible, paying regard to population and quality of land, together with the general convenience and interest of the inhabitants." They were required to make a report of their proceedings to the next Court of Common Pleas held in the county.

The three Commissioners met, and, after examination, made a report, on March 27, 1818, in favor of a place on Straight Creek, since known as Bridgewater, or the "Old County Seat." On July 23, 1818, George Edwards was appointed by the court a Director to purchase the land at the place selected, lay out a town and sell lots for the erection of county buildings.

The friends of Ripley were much dissatisfied with the selection made, and used every means in their power to prevent the seat of justice from being established at Bridgewater. It was claimed that the title of the land selected was imperfect. A majority of the Judges of the court were opposed to the location made, and, after much controversy, decided to reject the report of the Commissioners, and ordered them to return to the county and select another place. In the meantime, the Legislature passed the following act, which shows that the report of the Commissioners was not regarded as a final settlement of the question:

AN ACT TO AMEND THE ACT ENTITLED "AN ACT TO ERECT THE COUNTY OF BROWN."

SECTION 1. *Be it enacted by the General Assembly of the State of Ohio,* That from and after the first day of June next the courts of the county of Brown shall be holden at the place fixed upon as the seat of justice by the Commissioners appointed by the General Assembly at its last session, until a permanent seat of justice shall be established for said county, and that so much of the act to which this is an amendment, as refers to holding the courts of said county at the house of Alexander Campbell, in the town of Ripley, be and the same is hereby repealed.

This act to take effect and be in force from and after the passage thereof.

JOSEPH RICHARDSON, *Speaker of the House of Representatives,*
ROBERT LUCAS, *Speaker of the Senate.*

February 8, A. D. 1819.

The Commissioners appointed by the Legislature were induced to meet again and make a new selection, and this time Ripley came off victorious. The following is their report to the Court of Common Pleas:

We, the undersigned commissioners, appointed by the General Assembly of the State of Ohio, for fixing the seat of justice for the county of Brown, did proceed to examine the various sites in said county, and made report on the 27th of March, 1818, in favor of one on the east side of Straight Creek, near where the State road from West Union to Cincinnati crosses said creek, on the land of James Poage and John Abbott; and, whereas the Court of Common Pleas of said county of Brown gave official notice to us that the title to said land was incomplete, we again met in said county, and, after further examination and consideration, have fixed on the town of Ripley, on the banks of the Ohio, for the permanent seat of justice for the county of Brown.

Witness our hands this 8th day of April, 1820.

WM. MCFARLAND,
ISAAC COOK.

The County Commissioners, on June 7, 1820, let the contract for the erection of a court house at Ripley to George Poage for $2,999. The citizens of Ripley and vicinity had subscribed $7,488 for the erection of county buildings, the subscriptions being conditioned on the location of the county seat at that place.

The question now arose, Where should the courts of the county be held? —at Bridgewater, in accordance with the act of February 8, 1819, given above, or at Ripley, under the proceedings of the Commissioners in their second report of April 8, 1820. The contest, of course, was carried into the Legislature at its next session. A bill was introduced and passed the House of Representatives by a vote of forty-six yeas to sixteen nays, declaring that "the permanent seat of justice of Brown County be, and the same is hereby, declared to have been legally established on the east side of Straight Creek, near where the State road from West Union to Cincinnati crosses said creek, on the lands of James Poage and John Abbott, as fixed by the Commissioners appointed for that purpose by the General Assembly." The Representatives from Brown, Adams and Clermont all voted in the affirmative. When the bill came up in the Senate, an amendment by way of a substitute was proposed, which provided for "submitting all the papers, etc., in relation to the establishment of a seat of justice in Brown County to the Supreme Court for judicial investigation and determination whether any seat of justice has been fixed in said county, and if any, where it is." The vote on the substitute stood, yeas, eighteen; nays, fourteen, Mr. Pollock, of Clermont; Mr. Russell, of Adams; and Mr. Nathaniel Beasley, of Brown, voting in the negative. The proposed amendment was then, on leave, withdrawn, and a substitute by way of amendment was, on motion of Mr. Beasley, agreed to, appointing new Commissioners to fix the seat of justice. The act, as it finally passed both Houses, is as follows:

AN ACT TO ESTABLISH A PERMANENT SEAT OF JUSTICE IN THE COUNTY OF BROWN.

SECTION 1. *Be it enacted by the General Assembly of the State of Ohio*, That there shall be three commissioners appointed by a joint resolution of both Houses of the present General Assembly, whose duty it shall be to fix on a place for the permanent seat of justice for the county of Brown, who, in discharge of their duty, shall be governed in all respects by the provisions of the act, entitled "An act to establish seats of justice," and the place fixed upon by said commissioners shall be the permanent seat of justice for said county, any place heretofore selected by commissioners for the seat of justice to the contrary notwithstanding.

SEC. 2. *Be it further enacted*, That the County Commissioners of said county shall not make any further contract for the erection or completion of any public buildings in the county of Brown until the commissioners to be appointed to fix the permanent seat of justice in said county shall have performed that duty.

SEC. 3. *And be it further enacted*, That no exception shall ever be taken against the proceedings of the Court of Common Pleas for the County of Brown, on account of said court having been holden in the town of Ripley, and the several courts for said county shall continue to be holden in said town of Ripley until the first day of June next, and until said commissioners shall have fixed on a permanent seat of justice of said county, after which time the courts of said county shall be holden at the place selected by the commissioners appointed by virtue of this act.

JOSEPH RICHARDSON, *Speaker of the House of Representatives*,
ALLEN TRIMBLE, *Speaker of the Senate*.

January 19, 1821.

On January 29, 1821, the General Assembly, by joint resolution, appointed John Pinkerton, of Preble County; Francis Dunlavy, of Warren County; and Henry Weaver, of Butler County, Commissioners under the provisions of the foregoing act. The following is their report:

To the Honorable the Judges of the Court of Common Pleas in and for the county of Brown.

We, the undersigned, having been appointed Commissioners by the General Assembly of the State of Ohio, by virtue of an act entitled, "An act to establish a permanent seat of justice in the county of Brown," passed January 19, 1821, beg leave to report: That, having assembled at the present place of holding courts for said county, in the town of Ripley, on Thursday the 10th of the present instant, according to a previous notice duly published, and having taken the oath prescribed by law, we proceeded to examine said county as the law directs, and are unanimously of opinion that Georgetown previously laid out and duly recorded, is the most proper place for the seat of justice in said county, and that we have accordingly selected the said town of Georgetown for the permanent seat of justice for said county of Brown. And we, the Commissioners aforesaid, further report to your Honors that a certain tract of land containing fifty acres adjoining said town of Georgetown can be procured for the price of $5 per acre, and which we are of the opinion is a reasonable price, and which we, therefore, limit to the price of $5 per acre as aforesaid, all of which will more fully appear by certain documents herewith enclosed, and which are numbered.

We, the Commissioners aforesaid, beg leave also to refer to your Honors certain documents proposing certain benefits, privileges and facilities for the advantage of said county of Brown, and the inhabitants thereof, which last mentioned are also herewith enclosed and numbered 2, 3, 4, 5, 6, all which is most respectfully submitted by

FRANCIS DUNLAVY,
HENRY WEAVER,
JOHN PINKERTON.

RIPLEY, Ohio, May 13, A. D. 1821.

The courts had been held at Ripley, except one or two terms which were held in a log structure at Bridgewater. The Court of Common Pleas was in session at Ripley when the foregoing report was presented. On the second day of the term, the Judges proceeded to Georgetown, which has ever since been the seat of justice. The agitation of the county seat question, however, was continued for some years later. The propriety of a law submitting the question to a vote of the people was discussed. The continued agitation of the subject is shown by the following editorial from the *Benefactor and Georgetown Advocate*, of the date October 1, 1824, a paper then edited by Thomas L. Hamer:

"The settlement of the county seat has been again brought up as a pivot on which the election is to turn. This hobby has been prodigiously useful to the politicians of this county. The people have been duped once or twice by it, and it is to be hoped they will not be again. The candidates who expect to be elected by declaring their determination to support the law for fixing it by vote do not believe such a law can be passed. They are men of too good sense. It is impossible in the nature of things it should be passed. Whoever brings in a bill and petitions to that effect before the Legislature will feel a sensation they never experienced before. They will be laughed out of countenance. Their sensibility will be wounded, and they will feel ashamed of the project and of themselves.

"No county in the State (except, perhaps, Clermont) has had so much done for it by the Legislature as this one. We have been listened to; our

grievances redressed; our claims investigated; and everything granted us consistent with justice and good policy. We may rest assured the Legislature will not listen to complaints and petitions such as are now talked of. They cannot with propriety do so. Suppose they should pass such a law as Gen. Cochran and Capt. Brackenridge are in favor of—what would be the consequence? Have they any assurance that we will be satisfied with the result of one election? What security have we to give them against future applications for relief? None; none at all. Our former proceedings are proof against us that we will not be satisfied. If a majority of one vote should fix the county seat at Ripley or Georgetown or Bridgewater, is it probable that the minority would be satisfied? Would not the malcontent parties unite and crowd their claims before the Legislature again? Have they not done so heretofore in this county? Have they not done it in Clermont, and in every county where there are two parties? They have; and if a majority is to govern in this way, then we have no stability, no security—no prospect of any. Whenever that part of the county which has lost the seat of justice (say by one vote) gets a half-dozen more voters in it, they will be able to show a majority of petitions and voters, and then huzza for Republican principles; away goes the county seat again to some other part of the county. This simple consideration is sufficient to show the fallacy of the project, and to convince every unprejudiced man that no reasonable Legislator would ever vote for a law of that kind."

E

CHAPTER VIII.

GENERAL PROGRESS OF THE COUNTY.

COUNTY BUILDINGS.

THE first court house was built at Ripley; work on its construction was commenced in 1820. By a special act of the Legislature, the contractor, George Poage, was allowed $3,350, with interest thereon from the time the building was accepted by the County Commissioners. This building, after the location of the seat of justice at Georgetown, was sold at public auction for a small sum.

The contract for the erection of the first court house at Georgetown was let by the Commissioners on August 1, 1823. The contractors were Thomas L. Hamer, William White, Michael Weaver, William Butt and David Johnson. The sum agreed upon for the construction was $3,999.99, which was to be paid out of the proceeds of the sale of lots donated to the county by James Woods, Abel Reese and Henry Newkirk. This building was accepted by the Commissioners August 2, 1824, and, for twenty-five years, was the court house of Brown County. A representation of this quaint old building, as it appeared a few years before it was taken down, may be found in Howe's Historical Collections of Ohio.

The first jail was erected at the expense of parties who were interested in having the seat of justice at Georgetown. The date of its completion cannot be ascertained from the records. It stood on the site of the present jail, and was constructed of stone. Before the erection of the first jail, a defendant was committed on a writ of capias to the custody of the Sheriff. There being no prison, the defendant escaped. The plaintiff in the case brought suit against the Sheriff for damages sustained by reason of the escape, and obtained judgment. The Sheriff, William Butt, paid the judgment, and brought suit against the County Commissioners for the amount he had paid. The case of William Butt against the Commissioners of Brown County was finally decided in the Supreme Court. The Supreme Court was divided in their opinions, but a majority of the Judges held that, where an escape happens in consequence of the want of a jail, the Sheriff is liable to the party sustaining damages, and the Commissioners, in their official capacity, liable to the Sheriff, who has been compelled to pay damages thus resulting.

April 18, 1827, the Commissioners contracted with John Walker for the erection of Auditor's and Clerk's offices, at $390. Thomas L. Hamer and Jesse R. Grant were the sureties of Walker for the faithful performance of his contract. The rooms were completed and accepted by the Commissioners on the 4th of December following. On January 14, 1828, the Commissioners sold the old Clerk's office to the highest bidder for $3.50.

The Commissioners, on January 15, 1828, authorized the Auditor to advertise for the purchase of land and proposals for building a poor house. On January 16, 1829, the Commissioners purchased of Michael Weaver a farm for the use of the county, for which they paid $522. On the same day, Job Egbert, Edward Thompson and Noah Ellis were appointed the first Poor House Directors.

On March 18, 1835, the Commissioners contracted with David Johnston

HISTORY OF BROWN COUNTY.

for building a new jail, at the sum of $2,389. This jail stood on the southwest corner of Cherry and Pleasant streets, and the building is now used as a residence.

March 7, 1849, the Commissioners, being of the opinion that the old court house was insufficient, employed Hubbard Baker to prepare a draft of a plan for a new court house, and at the same time rented, for the use of the county, the basement of the Methodist Church, at an annual rental of $100. The contracts for the erection of the new court house were let May 22, 1849. The building, which has served the purpose for which it was erected until the present time, was completed and accepted by the county in 1851.

The contracts for the erection of the present substantial stone jail were let on August 13, 1868. It was completed in 1870, at a total cost of $34,314.57. On May 18, 1870, the old jail was sold.

ROADS.

The first roads in Brown County were mere traces or paths for horses. The public highways located by the authorities of Adams and Clermont Counties were for several years little more than tracks through the woods, cleared of timber, without bridges, and, in the fresh condition of the soil, became almost impassable in the wet seasons. Wagoning, however, was an important business, and it was common for several wagons to travel together for the mutual aid to be derived from combining teams when a wagon stuck fast in the mud.

Zane's trace, the most important thoroughfare of the Northwest Territory, struck the Ohio River at the site of Aberdeen. In May, 1796, Congress passed an act authorizing Ebenezer Zane to open a road from Wheeling, Va., to Limestone, Ky., and, in the following year, Mr. Zane, accompanied by his brother, Jonathan Zane, and his son-in-law, John McIntyre, all experienced woodsmen, proceeded to mark out the new road, which was afterward cut out by the two latter. The cutting, however, was a very hasty work, nothing more being attempted than to make the road passable for horsemen. As a compensation for opening this road, Congress granted to Ebenezer Zane the privilege of locating military warrants upon three sections of land, not to exceed one mile square each; the first of these, at the crossing of his road at the Muskingum; the second, at the Hockhocking; and the third, at the Scioto. One of the conditions annexed to the grant to Mr. Zane was that he should keep ferries across these three rivers during the pleasure of Congress. Zane's trace was a great route of travel for forty years of Ohio's history. In 1798, the first overland mail in Ohio was carried over this route, the mail from Wheeling meeting that from Limestone at Zanesville.

After the admission of Ohio into the Union, Congress applied 3 per cent of the proceeds of the public lands sold within the State to the construction of roads. This 3 per cent fund was appropriated for the purposes intended by the Legislature, and the roads thus established were known as State roads. The first appropriation of money for a State road extending into Brown County was made February 18, 1804, when $1,200 were appropriated "for opening and making a road from Chillicothe by West Union, in the county of Adams, to the River Ohio, where it may intersect the same in the most convenient and proper route to Limestone, in the State of Kentucky." Under this somewhat unintelligible expression of the law, a State road was constructed, which was elsewhere described as "the road from Chillicothe by West Union to Limestone." Josiah Espy, in his "Tour in Ohio and Kentucky," under the date of October 16, 1805, writes: "In passing from Limestone to Chillicothe, I took what is called the new State road, which passes through a poor, hilly country, almost uninhabited. This circumstance (aided, no doubt, by my indisposition) led me to think very unfavorably of the soil of Ohio, compared with Kentucky, which I had left with most favorable impressions." The poor and hilly portions of the country over which he passed were chiefly in Adams County.

An appropriation was also made in 1804 for a State road from Chillicothe to Cincinnati. The road passed through Perry Township; it was opened about 1806, and, being surveyed by Col. Richard C. Anderson, was usually known as the Anderson State road. The first appropriation for this road was $1,650.

The first Legislature which met after the organization of Brown County appropriated $1,000 for the benefit of roads in the county, and appointed Commissioners, under whose direction the money was to be expended, as follows:

On the State road leading from Ripley to Hillsboro, $430—Commissioner, William Dunlap; on the State road leading from West Union to the mouth of Clough Creek, $420—Commissioner, Abram Evans; on the part of the State road leading from Limestone to West Union which lies within the county of Brown, $50—Commissioner, Evan Campbell; on the part of the road leading from Hillsboro to Williamsburg which lies within the county of Brown, $100 —Commissioner, Thomas Ross.

TURNPIKES.

The first turnpikes in Ohio were completed in the decade from 1835 to 1845. The Milford & Chillicothe Turnpike Company was chartered February 11, 1832, and constructed an important road, seventy-eight miles in length, less than half of which was macadamized in 1839. The road did much for the development of the northern part of Brown County. Gov. Allen Trimble, of Hillsboro, was long the President of the company. Its capital stock was $344,000, held in equal portions by the State and individuals. For the year ending November 15, 1849, its receipts were $10,498.60, and its expenditures $4,115.72, leaving profits of over $6,000 to be divided between the State and individual stockholders.

The Ripley & Hillsboro Turnpike Company was chartered February 19, 1833, to construct a macadamized road thirty-five miles and twenty-six poles in length. The officers reported in 1839 that five and one-fourth miles near Ripley were completed, and ten miles on the northern end were under construction. At that time, A. Liggett was President, and William V. Barr, Engineer.

The Zanesville & Maysville Turnpike Company was chartered to construct a road 126 miles in length, of which eighty miles were reported as completed in 1839. The pike follows the general direction and route of Zane's trace. Although this turnpike passes over one of the most hilly regions in Ohio, the report of its engineer shows the remarkable fact that 104 miles were graded with an elevation of but two degrees with the horizon; fifteen miles, with from two to three degrees; four miles, with from three to four degrees; and only three miles with an elevation of four degrees—the maximum allowed.

Since 1866, a large number of free pikes have been constructed in Brown County, and most of the toll pikes have been made free. In 1880, the county had thirty-four pikes, with an aggregate length of 215 miles. Only two of these, with an aggregate length eight miles, belonged to incorporated companies.

OHIO RIVER NAVIGATION.

The navigation of the Ohio River has always been a matter of vast importance to Brown County. The first boats employed on its waters were canoes and flatboats, the latter made of stout and heavy green oak plank. In

HISTORY OF BROWN COUNTY.   293

January, 1794, a line of keelboats was established between Cincinnati and Pittsburgh, each boat making a trip in four weeks. These boats were covered so as to be protected against rifle and musket balls, and had port-holes to fire from; each boat was armed with six cannon, carrying pound balls, and a number of muskets, and well supplied with ammunition, as a protection against the Indians. There were separate cabins for ladies and gentlemen. The proprietor of the line, Jacob Myers, announced in the *Western Spy* that " a table of the exact time of the arrival and departure to and from the different places on the Ohio between Cincinnati and Pittsburgh may be seen on board each boat. Passengers will be supplied with provisions and liquors of all kinds, of the finest quality, at the most reasonable rates possible. Persons desiring to work their passage will be admitted on finding themselves, subject, however, to the same order and directions from the Master of the boat as the rest of the working hands of the boat's crew."

The first steamboat which made a voyage down the Ohio left Pittsburgh in October, 1811, and, in four days, arrived at Louisville. This boat was called the New Orleans, and was intended to ply between Natchez and New Orleans. On the voyage down the Ohio, no freight or passengers were carried. The novel appearance of the vessel, and the rapidity with which it made its way over the waters, excited a mixture of terror and surprise among many settlers along the banks, whom the rumor of such an invention had never reached. Several smaller steamboats were constructed at Pittsburgh, Brownsville and Wheeling within the succeeding five years, but it was not until the successful voyages of the Washington between Louisville and New Orleans, in 1817, that the public were convinced that steamboat navigation of the Western waters would succeed. The General Pike, built at Cincinnati in 1818, to ply between Louisville, Cincinnati and Maysville, is said to have been the first steamboat on the Western waters for the exclusive convenience of passengers. This vessel measured 100 feet keel, twenty-five feet beam, and drew three feet three inches of water. At one end were six and at the other eight state-rooms. The cabin was forty feet long and twenty-five feet broad. She was described as having ample accommodations, spacious and superb apartments and perfectly safe machinery.

RAILWAYS.

Many years elapsed after the completion of the first railroads to Cincinnati before it was thought practicable to construct a railway through a river county situated as is Brown. The Cincinnati & Eastern Railway Company was organized at Batavia January 10, 1876. It was called at first, and for a short time only, the Cincinnati, Batavia & Williamsburg Railroad Company. In May, 1876, it was resolved to extend the line from Williamsburg to Portsmouth. The road was completed as a three-feet gauge road from its junction with the Little Miami Railroad to Batavia, October 18, 1876; to Williamsburg, March 1, 1877; to Mt. Oreb. April 19, 1877; to Sardinia, June 4, 1877; to Winchester, in September, 1877. This was the first railroad running east and west through the central portions of Clermont County, and the first of any kind to reach Brown and Adams Counties.

The Cincinnati & Portsmouth Railroad Company was incorporated March 1, 1873, for the purpose of constructing a narrow-gauge railway through the counties of Hamilton, Clermont, Brown, Adams and Scioto. The work of construction did not begin until three years after the organization of the company. In July, 1880, the road was in running order from Columbia to Cleveland's, one mile east of Amelia. The road was completed to Hamersville in December, 1881. The great cost of the long and high bridge necessary for the crossing of White Oak Creek has delayed the completion of the road to Georgetown.

The Georgetown & Sardinia Railroad dates from May 9, 1879, when the Legislature passed an act authorizing the village of Georgetown, after an affirmative vote of its electors, to construct a railroad. The people of Georgetown having given their approval, bonds for the construction of the road to the amount of about $17,000 were issued by the municipal authorities. Three Trustees having charge of the construction were appointed by the Court of Common Pleas. Nearly all the grading of the road-bed was completed in the autumn of 1882, and the road was then leased to the Columbus & Ohio River Railroad Company. The right of way was donated by the land-owners along the line of road. The line of the road passes over a level country, and it has between the towns it connects but two variations from a straight course, and each of these is only one degree.

CHURCHES.

The pioneer preachers were mounted rangers. The Methodist preachers were circuit-riders, and their circuits extended a hundred miles. The Presbyterian and Baptist ministers had several congregations or preaching stations under their charge, which were often at a great distance apart. All were expected to seek out and preach to the scattered members of their fold over a large territory. They traveled on horseback, with their capacious saddle-bags under them; but these seldom contained manuscript sermons; a sermon written out and read to a congregation would have been received with little favor.

The first preaching in a community was almost always at a private house. The first churches were made of logs, hewed inside and outside. They were larger and built with more care than the schoolhouses, and, when the spaces between the logs were properly filled in with mortar, they proved to be comfortable rooms, cool in summer and warm in winter.

The itinerant clergy were important teachers among the early settlers. They lodged in their cabins and conversed with their families. Newspapers and periodicals of every kind were rare. Religious newspapers were then unknown. The preacher was usually a welcome guest.

The Baptists established the first church in Southwestern Ohio at Columbia, in 1790. The Miami Baptist Association, organized in 1799, was the earliest institution of the kind in Ohio. The earliest Baptist Churches of Clermont and Brown Counties were members of this association. The minutes of the Miami Baptist Association, which are still in existence, and have been carefully examined by the writer, give more authentic information concerning the Baptist Churches of the Northwest Territory than any other source. The first Baptist Church within the present limits of Brown County of which we have any account was the Straight Creek Church, which was admitted into the Miami Association at a meeting at Columbia in September, 1799. The Straight Creek Church then reported twenty-one members. William Lacock was the first messenger of this church to the association. In 1813, a new association was formed, embracing the churches of Brown and some of the adjoining territory, which was called the Straight Creek Association.

A large proportion of the early pioneers of Brown County were Presbyterians. The territory, on the first preaching of the Gospel by Presbyterian ministers, belonged to the Transylvania Presbytery of Kentucky. The minutes of this body show that, at a meeting held April 1, 1798, at Cabin Creek, north of Maysville, "a settlement of people living on Eagle Creek, Straight Creek and Red Oak Creek asked to be taken under the care of Presbytery, and to be known as the congregation of Gilboa." In October, 1798, the territory of Brown County was placed in a new Presbytery, called Washington Presbytery, from the town of Washington, Mason Co., Ky. The church of Red Oak was the first Presbyterian Church organized in Brown County. Its first log meeting-house was probably erected in 1799. Rev. John Finley, a member of the Washington Presbytery, was pastor of the church near the close of the last century.

The Methodists of Brown County, at the time of the first organization of churches of that denomination in Southern Ohio, were included in the Miami Circuit. Rev. John Kobler was the first regularly ordained minister of the Methodist Episcopal Church in the Miami Valley. Henry Smith was the first minister in charge of the Miami Circuit in 1799. Early in the present century, there were several local preachers in this large circuit. They went everywhere preaching the Word. They preached not only on Sundays, but on other days. They held two-days' meetings, and kept up a system of quarterly meetings, which, by this time, were attended by large numbers. Men and women would walk twenty and sometimes thirty miles to attend them. At night, the men would be quartered in barns and out-houses; the women, in the cabins. In 1802, Elisha W. Bowman, then a beardless youth, was sent to the Miami Circuit. In 1803, John Sale and Joseph Oglesby were the preachers for this large circuit. Francis McCormick, Phillip Gatch and John Collins all resided within the present bounds of Clermont County. In 1808, the White Oak Circuit was formed, with David Young as the first minister in charge. In 1810, there were in this circuit 766 white members and one colored member. The Straight Creek Circuit was formed in 1820, William P. Finley being the first minister in charge of it.

The Christian denomination originated in the West, in the revival known as the Great Kentucky Revival, at the commencement of the present century. No churches of this denomination were organized within the limits of Brown County for several years after the close of the revival. In 1810, a Christian Church was organized by Archibald Alexander, and a good stone meeting-house was built for the society on the east bank of the West Fork of Eagle Creek. This was the first church erected by the Christian denomination in Brown County. Elder Matthew Gardner says that it was "the first erected by the Christians in Southern Ohio." The Union Church, two miles from Higginsport, was organized in 1818 : the Bethlehem Church, in Huntington Township, in 1820; Georgetown Church, in 1822–23; Pisgah, about 1824; and Russelville, about 1826. The Southern Ohio Christian Conference was organized at the forks of Brush Creek, in Adams County, October 20, 1820.

Religious statistics and materials for a history of the progress of religion are not readily accessible in a country where there is no State church or governmental support of religion. The State of Ohio requires full statistical reports to be made annually of the condition and growth of the schools maintained by public taxation, but the chief matters pertaining to religion which have been noticed by the State or national statisticians are the number of church organizations and church edifices, the amount of church sittings or accommodations for public worship, and the value of church property; and our information concerning these is derived chiefly from the census returns of the United States since 1850.

According to the census of 1850, there were in Brown County sixty-one churches, valued at $66,740. In 1870, the churches had increased to seventy-nine, and were valued at $279,850. It thus appears that, in twenty years, the cost of churches increased much more rapidly than their number. The aggregate church accommodations or sittings in the county had not increased from 1850 to 1870, being returned in both years at about twenty-six thousand. Comparing this number with the population of the county at the same dates, and making but a slight deduction from the population for infants, the sick and the infirm, it appears that at both periods there were seats in the churches for more than the entire population of the county who could attend public worship.

The statistics of churches given in census returns do not in all cases agree with the statements put forth by the denominational organs of the various sects. The census superintendents have their own point of view, and apply tests different from those known to the compilers of religious year books and registers. It should be borne in mind, too, that reports of the number of church edifices, their accommodations and value, are not always true measures of the religious activity of a community. A strong denomination with numerous churches may often strengthen itself by suffering a weak church to cease to exist when it becomes unable to support itself. There are churches which find a place on the rolls of a denomination, and may be enumerated in census returns, which, having a legal title to an edifice, and maintaining some kind of an organization, have ceased to gather congregations or support a minister.

Great changes have taken place in the mode of public worship since the first rude churches of hewed logs sprang up beside the green fields. In the former days, sermons were from an hour and a half to two hours in length, while the other services were protracted by long prayers and commentaries on the chapter read from the Scriptures, to a length that would now be thought unendurable. Often there were two services, separated by an intermission of fifteen minutes. During both services, horses, in the absence of a society for the prevention of cruelty to animals stood, without food or water, haltered to trees, from which they gnawed the bark. The autumn sun was low in the horizon before the benediction was pronounced and the worshipers departed, some to distant homes. The singing was not artistic. The innovation of singing hymns without lining them out caused many a difficulty in the older churches. Sometimes there was a compromise between the opposing parties, and one hymn each Sunday was sung without being read line by line, and the others in the old way. A new tune, which all could not sing, caused some to grieve. The introduction of a choir or of a musical instrument caused serious dissension. Instrumental music was not common in the rural churches until after the introduction of the cabinet organ. The sin of wearing elegant attires and adornment with broidered hair, or gold, or pearls, or costly array, was a favorite topic in the pulpit. Flowers on the sacred desk would have been considered as ministering to a worldly vanity. The most beautiful comedies and the sublimest tragedies to be seen on the stage were declared unfit for Christian eyes. Many pastimes and divertisements which scatter sunshine and sweetness over the cares and hardships of life were regarded as inconsistent with the seriousness, gravity and godly fear which the Gospel calls for.

It cannot be doubted that there was less harmony among the different denominations formerly than now. The religious men of former generations were sincerely and intensely sectarian. They believed that they had "thus saith the Lord" for their distinctive tenets. They believed themselves to be, and were determined to remain, rigidly "orthodox"—a term which, according to Dean Stanley, "implies, to a certain extent, narrowness, fixedness, perhaps even hardness of intellect and deadness of feeling, at times, rancorous animosity." Sermons were more controversial and doctrinal than now. It can hardly be doubted that, with the increase of culture and refinement in the clergy and laity, have come a larger religious sympathy and a higher and broader view, which would break down the party wall of sectarianism and sweep away the petty restrictions on thought and opinion.

The early Presbyterian and Baptist Churches were severely Calvinistic, and their pulpits dwelt more frequently and more strenuously than their modern successors on the five points of their creed—predestination, particular redemption, total depravity, effectual calling and the certain perseverance of the saints. The terrors of the eternal torment of the wicked were more frequently and more vividly portrayed than in the modern days. The belief in a material fire in hell for the future and endless punishment of the unregenerate was common in all the churches. The doctrine of a literal fire in hell was preached by Rev. J. B. Findlay and other early Methodist preachers, in which they followed the explicit teachings of the sermons of John Wesley. It is doubtful if a person known to be a disbeliever in eternal punishment would have been suffered to remain a member of any of the early orthodox churches. To-day, a belief in the final holiness and happiness of all mankind is not an insurmountable bar to a place among the laity of the evangelical denominations.

But let us not judge the religious men of former days harshly. They were noble men, and the county owes them a debt of gratitude. We cannot believe in all things as they believed, but we cannot fail to recognize their virtues and their worth.

Most of the changes in the religious beliefs and modes of worship that have taken place since the establishment of the pioneer churches are not such as result in modifications of creeds and articles of faith. They are the result of inevitable tendencies, and are brought about, not so much by theological discussions as by the changes in human modes of thinking, feeling and believing, which, taken together, we call the spirit of the age. The advance of the refinements of civilization may render the religious doctrines of good men in one age repugnant to those of the text.

THE LEGAL PROFESSION.

Biographies of some of the most distinguished members of the legal profession in Brown County will be found elsewhere in this work. It is proposed in this place to narrate, with some regard to chronological order, some facts concerning the bar of the county not elsewhere recorded. The sketch must necessarily be imperfect.

The legal business of the early pioneers of Brown County, before the organization of a State Government, was transacted at Cincinnati and various towns in Kentucky. In 1796, there were nine practicing attorneys at Cincinnati, all of whom, except two, became confirmed drunkards, and descended to premature graves. Several of the early lawyers in Cincinnati and the towns in Northern Kentucky attended the courts of Clermont and Adams Counties until the organization of Brown County. Judge Jacob Burnet says:

"It was always my opinion that there was a fair proportion of genius and talent among the early members of the bar. Some of them, it is true, were uneducated, and had to acquire their legal knowledge after they assumed the profession. These were not numerous, but were noisy and officious, and, for some time, were able to procure a considerable amount of practice. This may be accounted for, in part, by the fact that the docket contained a large number of actions for slander, and assault and battery, and indictments for larceny, libels and the like."

It is worthy of note that Francis Dunlavy, the first President Judge of the circuit which embraced Cincinnati and the southwestern third of the State, was not a regularly educated lawyer, nor was he admitted to the bar until after his retirement from the bench. He was, however, a classical scholar, and had served as a member of the convention which formed the State constitution, and of the Territorial and State Legislatures. He practiced law for some years after his retirement from the bench, in 1817. His home was at Lebanon.

The attorney who prosecuted pleas in behalf of the State was appointed by the Supreme Court, and was frequently a non-resident of the county. In the earlier courts, the sum of $20 was the usual allowance for the services of a Prosecuting Attorney at a single term. Aaron Goforth, of Cincinnati; Arthur St. Clair, Jr., of Cincinnati; Joshua Collett, of Lebanon, were appointed attorneys for the State at different terms of the courts of Clermont County from 1803 until 1809. Arthur St. Clair was a son of the Territorial Governor. He is said to have appeared in court with a sword and a cocked hat. Joshua Collett was the first resident lawyer in Warren County, and practiced in the courts of Southwestern Ohio until he became President Judge. He presided at the first court in Brown County.

Jacob Burnet, of Cincinnati, afterward a Judge of the Supreme Court of Ohio, and a United States Senator, had a large practice in this portion of the circuit over which he traveled.

John McLean, of Lebanon, who afterward presided on the bench in Brown County as a Supreme Judge of Ohio, and was afterward a Justice of the Supreme Court of the United States, was known to the pioneers of this region as an able young lawyer.

Martin Marshall, of Augusta, Ky., was regular in attendance at the courts of Brown County. He was a profound lawyer and a successful advocate.

Owen T. Fishback, of Clermont County, admitted to the bar in 1815, was for more than forty years a distinguished practitioner, and seven years a President Judge of the Court of Common Pleas. "Half a century an ornament to the bar, of strong opinions, which he was accustomed to strongly express at all proper times, he was a man who left a decided impress on the history of his time and county."

Thomas Morris, although he was never a resident of Brown County, was so long and prominently identified with the practice of law in the region now composing the county, both before and after its organization, that he should receive here more than a passing notice. He was born in Pennsylvania January 3, 1776, and died at his homestead, near Bethel, Ohio, December 7, 1844. The son of a Baptist minister of Welsh descent, his early life was passed in the wilds of West Virginia, where he had few advantages of schools. Excepting three months at a common school, his entire education was received in his log cabin home, where his mother taught him to read before he was six years old. In 1795, he removed to Columbia, in the Northwest Territory, where he clerked in the store of Rev. John Smith, one of the first Senators from Ohio in Congress. In 1797, he married Rachel Davis. In 1800, he removed to Williamsburg, and, in 1804, to Bethel, which was his home for most of his active life. In 1802, without the assistance of friends, without pecuniary means, without a preceptor, with a growing family and with but few books, he commenced the study of law. Early and late he was at his law books. After the hard labors of the day, night found him reading Blackstone by the light of hickory bark or a clapboard, at his cabin, and often by a brick-kiln which he was burning for the support of his family. Completing two years of study, in 1804 he was admitted to the bar. With a resolute purpose and an iron will, he pushed his onward way; he soon took a leading position at the bar; reputation and business rapidly accumulated, and for forty years he maintained his position among the able and successful lawyers of Ohio. He was among the ablest of the early lawyers of Clermont, many of his clients being from the region now forming Brown County. At the organization of Brown County, he was in the full tide of successful practice, and for years he had an extensive practice both in the courts of Clermont and Brown. Before a jury there were few who surpassed him in power and effect. Indomitable energy was one of his marked characteristics. His son and biographer relates that " in a case of great importance before the court of Brown County, he desired a continuance of his case, a principal witness being absent on account of high waters. The court refused the motion. Mr. Morris procured a horse, swam the stream, and, with his witness behind him, returned and replunged into the swollen stream, entered the court and gained his case." He was often elected to the General Assembly, where he served on the most important committees, frequently being Chairman of the Judiciary Committee. In 1809, he was elected a Judge of the Supreme Court of Ohio; but, by an act of the Legislature called "the sweeping act," he was prevented from taking his seat on the bench. In 1832, he was elected United States Senator, and served six years. In the Senate he distinguished himself as an opponent of slavery. In 1844, the Liberty party nominated him a candidate for Vice President. On his monument in the cemetery at Bethel is the following inscription:

Thomas Morris,
Born January 3, 1776,   Died December 7, 1844,
Aged 69 years.
Unawed by power and uninfluenced by flattery,
He was, throughout life, the fearless advocate
of
Human Liberty.

John S. Wills, who was admitted to the bar in Virginia in 1797, came from Columbus, Ohio, to Ripley, the temporary seat of justice of Brown County, about the time of the organization of the county, and was among the first resident practicing attorneys of Ripley. He afterward removed to Georgetown, and was engaged in the practice of his profession until his death, in 1829.

George W. King, the first resident Prosecuting Attorney of Brown County, came from his native State of Pennsylvania, where he was admitted to the bar in November, 1817, to visit his brothers in this county. He arrived in the county in December of the same year, and, after the formation of the county, began the practice of his profession at Ripley. It is believed that Wills and King were the only resident lawyers of the county when the first courts were held at Ripley.

Thomas L. Hamer commenced the practice of law at Georgetown in August, 1821; Archibald Liggett, at Ripley, in 1825; David G. Devore, at Georgetown, in 1833; Andrew Ellison, at Georgetown, in 1835; Chambers Baird, at Ripley, in 1837; Hanson L. Penn, at Georgetown, in 1837; and John G. Marshall, in 1846.

For twenty years after the organization of the county, only four or five lawyers residing in the county were engaged in active practice at any one time. Attorneys and physicians were then subject to a tax of a few mills on each dollar of their annual income, and the records of the County Commissioners contain lists of the practicing attorneys in the county for a number of years following 1831. The list for 1831 is: Thomas L. Hamer, Archibald Liggett, George W. King, John J. Higgins and Daniel F. Barney. Of these, Messrs. Higgins and Barney were not long engaged in the practice. In 1833, 1834 and 1835, only four lawyers were taxed on their incomes.

In 1840, there were six practicing attorneys resident in the county, viz.: Thomas L. Hamer, David G. Devore, Chambers Baird, Hanson L. Penn, Thomas H. Linch and Josiah Q. Gallup. Although the lawyers were few in numbers, it was not until about this time that the income of any one of them was estimated as high as $1,000, and in most cases it was only about one-half that sum.

In 1850, there were twenty practicing attorneys in the county—one at Aberdeen, one at Higginsport, two at Fayetteville, two at Ripley and fourteen at Georgetown. In 1880, the number of practicing attorneys in the county was thirty-five.

Riding the circuit was the uniform custom of the early lawyers, whether they were old in the profession and had an established practice, or were young, briefless, and perhaps penniless, members, in search of business. They traveled on horseback, with their saddle-bags under them, an overcoat and umbrella strapped behind the saddle, and leggings well spattered with mud, tied with strings below the knees. Traveling the circuit became less common in the decade between 1830 and 1840, and finally ceased. Subsequent to 1840, it was continued only by the older lawyers, who had established a practice in the different counties of the circuit which made the toilsome journey, which took them away from their homes a considerable portion of the year, a remunerative one.

Lawyers' fees were low in the early practice in Ohio. A charge of hundreds of dollars was rare; a fee of thousands of dollars for services in a single case was almost unknown. Ejectment suits, which frequently arose from the disputed boundaries and titles of the Virginia Military Lands, were, perhaps, the most profitable part of the early lawyers' practice. It may be safely assumed that, for thirty years after the organization of the State of Ohio, $750, which was for a part of that time the salary of the Judge of the Court of Common Pleas, was above rather than below the average annual income of a lawyer in full practice at Williamsburg, Batavia and Georgetown. The salary of the Judge of the Court of Common Pleas was fixed, in 1803, at $750; in 1816, at $1,000; in 1837, at $1,200; in 1852, at $1,500; and in 1867, at $2,500.

THE MEDICAL PROFESSION.

There are in existence no records from which we can learn the names of the physicians who practiced in the region now forming Brown County, previous to the organization of the county, and for several years subsequent there to. The Legislature passed various acts to regulate the practice of medicine and surgery. The first of these was passed in 1811, when the whole State was divided into five districts. Among the censors named in early acts authorized to grant licenses to practice medicine and surgery in the districts which included the region of Brown County were Dr. Alexander Campbell, of Ripley; Dr. Levi Rogers, of Clermont County; Dr. J. D. Keith; and Dr. Edward Tiffin, the first Governor of Ohio.

The medical system of the noted New England empiric, Samuel Thompson, was introduced into this county about 1826. It was termed the Botanic system, or Thompsonian system. Steaming a patient for the purpose of producing perspiration was such an important branch of the practice that the followers were frequently called steam doctors. They were also popularly termed herb or root doctors. The practitioners purchased Dr. Thompson's " New Guide to Health, or Botanic Family Physician, containing a complete system of practice upon a plan entirely new," with a patent right to the system, and, without any previous course of study, they were prepared for the practice of medicine. The system was extensively introduced in Ohio between the years 1825 and 1835. Dr. Thompson's book and patent right to the system were sold at $20, and the publishers of the book at Columbus, Ohio, put forth the statement that Thompson's agents disposed of 4,319 copies in three and a half years preceding 1832, and that Dr. Thompson's share of the proceeds of his Western agency for that time was $17,500. The most important article used in Dr. Thompson's practice was lobelia, which he called the emetic herb, and the medicinal virtues of which he claimed to have discovered. The following extract from the "Botanic Physician" gives the Doctor's prescription of a stock of medicines for a family: "One ounce of the emetic herb, two ounces of cayenne, one-half pound bayberry root bark in powder, one pound poplar bark, one pint of the rheumatic drops This stock will be sufficient for a family for one year, with such articles as they can easily procure themselves when wanted, and will enable them to cure any disease which a family of common size may be afflicted with during that time. The expenses will be small and much better than to employ a doctor, and have his extravagant bill to pay." It is impossible to learn, at this time, how many of the practitioners of this system were to be found in this county. They were probably most numerous in Ohio about 1832.

The following is the list of physicians taxed on their income in Brown County in 1831: Greenleaf Norton, Alfred Beasley, Phillip J. Buckner, Samuel W. Penn, Enoch M. Ellsberry, George B. Bailey, Adam Wylie, Joseph Matthews, Thomas S. Williamson, Alexander Campbell, Samuel P. Anthony, T. M. Brown, Isaac M. Beck, Peter Williams.

The following is the list for 1841: Alfred Beasley, Simon L. Bearce, Isaac M. Beck, George B. Bailey, P. J. Buckner, Clinton Campbell, Henry Courtney, V. M. Diball, Enoch M. Ellsberry, A. B. Heterick, William Herbert, Dr. Kincade, William B. McCormack, Peter Marshall, Thomas M. Moore, James B. McConnell, Edward Newton, Daniel Porter, Nathan Scofield, John Thompson, William B. Thompson.

In 1831, $550 was the highest income upon which any physician in the county was taxed, and in 1841, the income of only one was placed as high as $1,000.

AGRICULTURE.

The great embarrassment under which the pioneer farmer labored was the difficulty of getting the products of his soil to a market. In spite of roots and stumps, sprouts and bushes, the newly cleared land brought forth bountiful harvests; but the wagon roads were imperfect, canals and railroads unthought of, and the distance by the Ohio River to the principal markets so great, the navigation so difficult, tedious and hazardous, that the early farmer had little encouragement to increase the products of his fields beyond the wants of his family and the supply of the limited home market created by the wants of the inhabitants of the neighboring towns and the newly arrived emigrants. The average time required for a journey by a flatboat propelled by oars and poles, from Cincinnati to New Orleans and return, was six months. The cargoes taken in these boats were necessarily light, the boats could not be easily brought back, and were generally abandoned at New Orleans, and the crew returned by land, generally on foot, through a wilderness of hundreds of miles. A large part of the proceeds of the cargo was necessarily consumed in the cost of taking it to market. Beeswax, skins and feathers were the principal articles that could profitably be transported by wagons to distant markets. Hogs and cattle were driven afoot, over the mountains, and, after a journey of a month or six weeks, found an uncertain market in Baltimore. Corn rarely commanded more than 10 or 12 cents per bushel; wheat, 30 or 40 cents; hay was from $3 to $4 per ton; flour, from $1.50 to $2 per hundred; pork, from $1 to $2 per hundred; the average price of good beef was $1.50 per hundred, while oats, potatoes, butter and eggs scarcely had a market value, and the sale of cabbage and turnips was almost unheard of. But the early farmers supplied their homes liberally with the comforts of pioneer life; they lived independently, and, perhaps, were as happy and contented as those who have the luxuries brought by wealth and commerce.

The proximity of a spring, rather than the claims of taste or sanitary considerations, usually determined the location of the first residence of the pioneer farmer; and the log stable and the corn-crib, made of rails or poles, were apt to be in close proximity to the residence. The first fences, both for the fields and the door-yard, were made of rails in the form of the Virginia, or worm, fence. This, in a new country, where timber, readily split with the wedge and maul, was abundant, was the cheapest and most durable fence. Unsightly as it is, it is yet superseded to a limited extent only by post and rail, board or wire fences, or hedges.

Agricultural implements were at an early period necessarily few in number and rude and simple in construction. The plow first used was of rude contruction—often made on the farm with the assistance of the neighboring blacksmith. It had a wooden mold-board and a clumsy iron share. It took a strong man to hold it, and twice the strength of team now requisite for the same amount of work. The cast-iron plow was slowly introduced. The early harrows were made of bars of wood and wooden teeth, and were rude and homely in construction. Sometimes, in place of the harrow, a brush, weighted down with a piece of timber, was dragged over the ground. The sickle was in universal use for harvesting grain until about 1825, when it was gradually superseded by the cradle. The sickle is one of the most ancient of farming implements, but reaping with the sickle was always slow and laborious. For the twenty years succeeding 1830, there were few farmers who did not know how to swing the cradle and scythe, but during the next twenty years, reapers and mowers, drawn by horses, became almost the only harvesters of grain and grass. The first reaping machines merely cut the grain; a raker was necessary to gather the grain into sheaves ready for the binders. Self-raking reaping machines soon followed, and, about 1878, self-binding machines were introduced. Of the two old-fashioned methods of separating the grain from the straw—the flail and tramping with horses—the latter was the most common in this county. To-day, instead of this slow and wasteful method, a horse or steam-power thresher not only separates the grain, but winnows it and carries the straw to the stack, all at the same time.

HORSES.

The capital invested in domestic animals constitutes a large item in the wealth of the county. Improvements in breeds of all the farm animals have kept pace with the improvements in agricultural implements and methods of tilling the soil. After the land had been generally cleared of the forests, the necessity of oxen ceased, and interest in the improvement of the horse commenced. The possession of good horses—elegant, strong and speedy—became a matter of pride with the farmer. Speed was not considered of special value in the horse until the improvements in the public roads rendered possible the use of the modern light carriage. The improvements in the horse are doubtless largely due to the infusion of the blood of the thoroughbred, which was early introduced into Southern Ohio. The Morgan, the Cadmus, the Bellfounder, the C. M. Clay and the Hambletonian stock were also common at different periods; but whatever breed has been introduced, the tendency has always been to amalgamate it with the stocks already in use. The strains of blood have not, therefore, been kept distinct. The farm horse, or horses for general purposes, found throughout the county are of a most uncertain blood, but it is certain that they have been greatly improved within thirty years in style, action, form, temper and endurance.

CATTLE.

The cattle of the early settlers were introduced from various quarters, immigrants from Pennsylvania, Virginia and Kentucky bringing many with them, and it is believed by some that cattle raised by the Indians previous to the first settlements by the whites were an element in the original or common herds in the West. Of course, they were a heterogeneous collection, yet, in process of time, the stock was assimilated to the locality, acquiring local characteristics, by which the experienced cattle-dealer determined, from their general appearance, the region in which they were reared. The early farmers suffered their cattle to wander through the woods and uncultivated grounds, browsing for their living, and thus some of the native grasses and shrubs were extirpated by being cropped off early in the spring before their flowers and seeds were formed. In winter, the cows were not housed nor sheltered, but found their subsistence at a stack of wheat straw, or in the cornfield after husking time; or, at best, were fed twice a day in an open lot, with fodder and unhusked corn. The practice, which is still common, of securing the corn before it is fully matured, by cutting off the stalks near the ground and stacking it in the field, is said to have originated with the cattle-feeders of Virginia.

The Patton stock of English cattle, imported into Kentucky early in this century, doubtless found their way across the Ohio and were crossed with the common cattle. Excellent Short-Horn cattle were introduced from time to time, until there is scarcely a neighborhood in the county in which more or less of their cross is not found. Of late years, the Jersey cows are coming into favor, especially in the towns and on farms adjoining the towns.

SWINE.

The raising of hogs has proved so well adapted to the agriculture of the county that on almost every farm it has been carried on, and the animal has been made to serve both as a popular and cheap article of food, and a means of condensing for the market a large part of the extensive crops of Indian corn. Of all domestic animals, the hog comes to maturity quickest, requires least skill and care to handle, and has been most generally relied on in the regions around Cincinnati for domestic consumption and for profit. Ripley was at one time an important pork market.

Several breeds of hogs have been introduced into Southwestern Ohio, and have found their way into Brown County. The swine of the early settlers were long and slim, coarse, large-boned and long-legged, with erect bristles on the neck and back. They were active and healthy, and capable of making heavy hogs, but two years or more were required for them to mature. Until a short time before being butchered or driven to market, they were suffered to run at large in the woods, subsisting as foragers. They were sometimes known as "razor-backs."

The Big China hogs, from which originated the celebrated Poland-China hogs, were introduced into Warren County in 1816. In that year, John Wallace, then a Trustee of the Shaker society, visited Philadelphia on business, and was shown what were called the Big China hogs. He was pleased with them, and purchased four hogs, and brought them the same season to Union Village. These four hogs were entirely white, except one, upon which were some sandy spots, in which appeared small black spots, They were represented to be either imported or the immediate descendants of imported stock, and are believed to have been the first China hogs in Southwestern Ohio. Subsequently, other China hogs were introduced.

They were extensively raised and crossed with the best breeds then existing, and the product of these crosses constituted a breed of fine qualities, which was generally known as the "Warren County hog," sometimes as the "Shaker hog."

The Berkshires were introduced in 1835 or 1836, by Mr. Munson Beach, who operated in connection with his brother, Louis Beach, then a prominent merchant in the city of New York. The Berkshires introduced by the Messrs. Beach were generally black, with occasional marks of white, either on the feet, the tip of the tail or in the face. They were muscular, active and round-bodied hogs, and, in most cases, had sharp-pointed, upright ears. Some families, however, were large in size, deep in their bodies, with ears that lopped.

The Irish Grazier breed of hogs was imported direct into Southwestern Ohio by William Neff, Esq., of Cincinnati, about 1839. The Graziers were white, with only occasional sandy spots, which appeared about the eyes. These three breeds—the Big China, the Berkshires and Irish Graziers—were extensively used in making crosses by the best breeders in Southwestern Ohio. The stock thus produced has resulted in what is known as the Poland-China hog.

The first part of this name, however, is a misnomer, as the best authorities agree that there never was a breed of hogs known as the Poland in the Miami Valley, and no Poland cross entered into the formation of the breed. The first part of the name is believed to have originated from the fact that a Polander residing in Hamilton County, having purchased some of the Shaker or Warren County hogs many years ago, disposed of them to purchasers, who named them Poland, or Polander, hogs. The National Convention of Swine Breeders of 1872 retained this misnomer for the reason that the great mass of breeders so called the breed, and to change a name generally used is difficult.

In recent years, pure-blooded Berkshires have been brought into Brown County, and these, with the Poland-China, are the principal breeds raised in the county.

TOBACCO.

Tobacco early became an important crop in Brown County. For some years previous to 1850, it ranked second in importance to corn only. The crop at that time was estimated at some fourteen hundred hogsheads, the average yield per acre being about one thousand pounds. The price varied with the quality, from 3 to 8 cents per pound. The crop was sold at Ripley, Higginsport and other places on the Ohio, where it was pressed into hogsheads and shipped to New Orleans.

Some of the agriculturists of Brown County foresaw the importance of the tobacco-growing interest. Previous to the civil war, Gen. James Loudon offered, at a meeting of the State Board of Agriculture, a resolution granting a premium on the best crop of tobacco grown upon an acre of ground in the State, but the proposition was ridiculed and voted down, the majority believing that the growth of tobacco should not be encouraged. In 1863, Gen. Loudon, at a meeting of the same board, renewed his proposition, and stated that the production of tobacco was found to be the greatest and most profitable industry on the limestone lands of the Ohio River counties—the most profitable crop in Southern Ohio. He called attention to the fact that the hillsides of Brown County had been advertised for sale a few years before, and nobody would bid over 62½ cents per acre for them; then, the same land was worth $50 per acre. The Germans, by their skill and industry, had made these steep hillsides the best producing land in Ohio. It had been asserted that Ohio

could never compete with Kentucky in raising tobacco; but at that time, he said, the best tobacco sold in the Cincinnati market, at 40 cents per pound, as Mason County, Ky., tobacco, had been raised in Brown County, Ohio.

For more than twenty years past, tobacco-growing has been the most important industry of the county. In 1840, Brown stood tenth among the counties of Ohio in the amount of tobacco grown; in 1850 and 1860, fifth; since the civil war, Brown has been second to Montgomery only in the number of acres planted and number of pounds grown. While Montgomery County far exceeds Brown in the amount of tobacco grown, the quality of the leaf in Brown is far superior, and brings in the market a much higher price than that grown in Montgomery.

The growth of tobacco culture in Brown County is exhibited in the following table. The figures for the years 1840, 1850 and 1860 were obtained from the United States Census returns; those for the succeeding years, from the Ohio Statistical Reports:

For the year 1840, 63,260 pounds; 1850, 1,279,510 pounds; 1860, 1,-898,846 pounds; 1863, 3,594 acres, 2,684,503 pounds; 1866, 3,093 acres, 2,-760,739 pounds; 1871, 3,251 acres, 2,828,422 pounds; 1873, 4,514 acres, 4,-085,755 pounds; 1876, 4,261 acres, 3,420,120 pounds; 1879, 4,847 acres, 3,-721,793 pounds; 1880, 5,004 acres, 4,156,921 pounds.

The White Burley variety, so celebrated and highly prized for the manufacture of chewing tobacco, both fine-cut and plug, originated in Brown County. The story of its origin generally accepted is this: About the time of the civil war, a tobacco-grower named Joseph Fore, residing on the farm of Capt. Kautz, on White Oak, between Georgetown and Higginsport, observed in his tobacco bed some plants of a remarkably white color. The color of both stems and leaves of these plants was similar to that of chance stocks of corn called "sick corn." The seed sown in the tobacco bed was of the Little Burley variety. One or two stalks of the new and strange variety, although unpromising in appearance, were permitted to mature, and the seed they produced was saved. The plants grown from the seed, though not so large, thrifty and hardy as other varieties, were found to consist of an excellent fiber, to cure of a bright color, to be free from gum, and to possess all the qualities desirable for cutting purposes. The seed from the new variety was gradually spread over Brown, and portions of adjoining counties in Ohio and Kentucky. It soon became the most desirable tobacco in the Cincinnati market, and commanded the highest prices. It is now almost the only variety grown in the Brown County, Ohio, and the Mason County, Ky., districts, and its culture has extended to other portions of the country. The growing crops of this variety during the first years of its culture were white, as if covered with hoar-frost. In later years, the white color is less marked, and a tendency toward a reversion to the original Burley tobacco, from which it sprang, has been observed.

BROWN COUNTY AGRICULTURAL SOCIETY AND FAIRS.

The Brown County Agricultural Society was organized on the 17th day of January, 1850, agreeably to the laws of Ohio. The following were the first officers: Samuel Kerr, Decatur, President; Alexander Campbell, Ripley, Vice President; Reason Shepherd, Ripley, Secretary; John Glaze, Russellville, Treasurer; George W. Brown, Elhannan W. Devore, James Tweed, Samuel G. Moore and Daniel Gilmer, Managers.

The first fair of the society was held at Russellville, on the 16th of October, 1850. The exhibition, though not large, was considered a respectable one, and the officers, in their annual report, stated that the number of animals and articles offered for exhibition and the competition for premiums were far greater than they had anticipated. No admission fee to the fair was charged. The following is the first report of the Treasurer of the society:

Amount received from members of the society	$158 00
Amount received from the County Treasurer	119 00
Total amount received	$277 00
Amount paid out in premiums	$116 00
Amount paid for printing and incidental expenses	20 35
	$136 35
Balance on hand	$140 65

The officers elected January 17. 1851, were: Alexander Campbell, Ripley, President; Philip Jolly, Ripley, Vice President; Reason Shepherd, Ripley, Secretary; John Glaze, Russelville, Treasurer; John Williamson, Russelville; Absalom King, Georgetown; David Dixon, Ripley; and James Tweed, Ripley, Managers. The second annual fair was held at Ripley on the 2d and 3d days of October, 1851. The attendance was larger, and the number of articles and animals on exhibition greater, than at the first fair. The Treasurer's report shows that the total expenditures of the fair were $492.85, of which $409.75 were for premiums. At the annual meeting of the board, premiums on crops were awarded as follows: To George Snedaker, on corn, 120 bushels per acre; to the same, on wheat, twenty-eight bushels per acre; to Alexander Campbell, on oats, sixty-four and three-fourths bushels per acre; to Reason Shepherd, on buckwheat, twenty-four bushels per acre; to Samuel G. Moore, on hay, two and a half tons per acre; to Russell Shaw, on onions, fifty-four and one-fourth bushels, raised on forty-two poles of ground.

A change having been made in the constitution of the society, the third annual election for officers was held on the second Tuesday of November, 1851. The election was held at Georgetown, and the following officers were chosen: H. L. Penn, Georgetown, President; E. B. Fee, New Hope, Vice President; Newton A. Devore, Secretary (declined); Abraham King, Georgetown; John Markley, Georgetown; James Loudon, Georgetown; Charles Richards, Georgetown; Henry Young, New Hope, Managers. The fair was permanently established at Georgetown; grounds were there purchased, upon which the exhibitions of the society have since been annually held.

In 1855, the society reported its total receipts at $893.60, and its expenditures at $727.34. In 1870, there were 556 members; the total receipts, $2,100; the total expenditures, $1,891. In 1876, the total receipts were $2,054.72. In 1880, there were 540 members; the total receipts were $2,490. The society has sixteen acres of ground, which, with the improvements thereon, is valued at $3,000.

A few years ago, the Directors of the society abolished horse-racing at the annual fairs, and since that time no premiums for speed horses have been offered. This measure, which was looked upon by many as a hazardous experiment, has resulted beneficially to the financial condition of the society. The fair for 1882 was the most successful in the history of the society.

GROWTH OF WEALTH AND POPULATION.

The assessment of property under the laws for the collection of taxes affords an imperfect means of comparing the wealth of the county at different periods. It gives by no means the market value, being generally much below the selling price. It is, however, the best means at our command to show the growth of the wealth of the county. Subjoined are the statistics for several years, giving the total value of all real estate, both in the towns and in the country:

YEAR.	Value of Lands.	Average Value per Acre of Farming Lands.	Value of Real Property in Towns.	Total Value of Real Property.
1825	$830,292	$3.23	$ 96,411	$926,603
1835	713,007	2.56	142,584	924,766
1840	1,287,157	3.83	192,229	1,391,623
1846	3,771,255	12.65	517,826	4,074,628
1853	5,567,276	17.88	724,713	6,291,989
1859	6,804,229	....	778,838	7,088,067
1870	6,891,743	22.62	1,002,111	7,843,749
1880	6,064,875	20.03	1,253,521	7,318,396

A change in the mode of assessing property was adopted in 1846, after which the valuation approached much nearer the true value than in the preceding years. This accounts for the great rise in values between 1841 and 1846. Prior to 1826, real estate in Ohio was put upon the duplicate for taxation for State purposes only. All lands in the State were divided, for the purposes of taxation, into three grades, called first quality, second quality and third quality, and a uniform rate of taxation was fixed by the Legislature for all lands of the same grade. For six years succeeding the organization of the State, the rate of taxation on lands of the first quality did not exceed 1 cent per acre, and at no time prior to 1826 did it reach 4 cents per acre. There were revaluations of the real property of Ohio in the years indicated in the table.

POPULATION OF BROWN COUNTY BY TOWNSHIPS IN 1850, 1860, 1870 AND 1880.

TOWNSHIPS.	1850.	1860.	1870.	1880.	TOWNSHIPS.	1850.	1860.	1870.	1880.
Byrd	1,642	1,283	1,251	1,299	Higginsport*	535	507	530	762
Clark	1,450	1,371	1,691	1,761	Perry	2,781	2,810	3,016	2,868
Eagle	1,279	1,364	1,166	1,249	Fayetteville*	317	399	397	890
Franklin	1,169	1,172	1,225	1,165	Pike	1,022	1,211	1,314	1,339
Green	669	1,172	1,490	1,916	Pleasant	2,074	2,331	2,605	2,940
Mt. Oreb*	....	....	....	242	Georgetown*	618	723	1,037	1,293
Huntington	2,684	2,854	3,020	3,085	Scott	1,036	1,162	1,070	1,224
Aberdeen*	808	836	871	885	Sterling	981	1,209	1,394	1,662
Jackson	1,256	1,081	995	963	Union	4,378	5,650	5,899	5,776
Jefferson	....	1,311	1,267	1,300	Ripley*	1,780	2,725	2,323	2,546
Russellville*	386	465	359	478	Washington	1,185	1,229	1,082	1,206
Lewis	2,720	2,748	2,817	3,188					

* Villages.

The following unincorporated villages have been returned separately to the census department in 1880. The population is only approximated, as the limits of the places are not sharply defined:

Arnheim, 98; Benton, 20; Brownstown, 49; Carlisle, 63; Chasetown, 51; Decatur, 258; Fincastle, 118; Feesburg, 179; Greenbush, 49; Hamersville, 231; Hestoria, 376; Kirbyville, 35; Levanna, 294; Locust Ridge, 42; New Harmony, 43; New Hope, 138; St. Martin's, 50; Sardinia, 283; Taylorsville, 77; Wahlsburg, 19; White Oak Valley, 48.

POLITICAL HISTORY.

The political history of Brown County may be summed up in the statement that a majority of her voters were at first Anti-Federalists or Jeffersonian Republicans, and in later years Democrats. The first presidential election in which the voters of Brown participated after the organization of the county was in 1820, when party lines were obliterated, and James Monroe was reelected President with the electoral vote of every State in the Union. This was "the era of good feeling in politics." In 1824, the Republicans or Anti-Federalists, who had before been united in the support of Jefferson, Madison and Monroe, were somewhat divided in their choice for President. There were four candidates for President, three of them having electoral tickets in Ohio. Many old Republicans supported J. Q. Adams; others Andrew Jackson, but Henry Clay carried the State of Ohio. Early in the canvass, it became evident that a large majority of the people of Brown were in favor of Gen. Jackson. This was shown by the votes taken at militia musters. Many newspapers in Ohio were neutral with respect to the opposing candidates, and contented themselves with the publication of communications from the friends of all the aspirants. Young Thomas L. Hamer, who then edited the *Benefactor* at Georgetown, was an outspoken advocate of the election of Jackson. The following is from his paper of the date of October 25, 1824: "Awake, citizens of Ohio! Come forward and give your voice to the man who has done more for the welfare of your country than all the other candidates put together. Andrew Jackson deserves your suffrages if Washington deserved the offices conferred on him. Whilst Clay, Crawford and Adams were lolling on beds of down and feasting on the delicacies of both hemispheres, he was wading through swamps, sleeping on the cold ground and living upon acorns." Jackson received in the county nearly twice as many votes as were cast for both Clay and Adams. The full vote of the county by townships is not before us, but it is believed that Jackson received a plurality in every township in the county. At the October election this year, questions of national politics had little effect on the vote for the various candidates. The friends of Jackson, Clay and Adams in Brown united in supporting Jeremiah Morrow for Governor, and J. W. Campbell for Congress. There were this year four candidates for Representative in the Legislature; six candidates for County Commissioner; six candidates for Auditor, and three candidates for Coroner.

In 1828, party lines were closely drawn between the Adams men and Jackson men. Rallying committees were appointed in the various townships for the purpose of getting out a full vote at the election for President. At that time, and for many succeeding years, one of the most hotly contested questions at issue was which was the old Republican party. Both parties claimed to be the old Jeffersonian Republicans. Federalist, the name of the party to which Washington and Hamilton belonged, had long before become a term of reproach. At the October election in 1828, John W. Campbell, the Jackson candidate for Governor, resided in Brown County. He had for ten years been a Representative in Congress, during which time he was a resident of Adams County. In 1826, he removed to Brown County, and settled on a farm on Straight Creek, which he improved with care and built upon it a large and convenient residence, which he named "Solitude." Mr. Campbell was a native of Augusta County, Va., and studied law at Morgantown, Va., and was admitted to the bar at West Union, Ohio, in 1808. In the canvass for Governor in 1828, he was defeated by Allen Trimble, and was afterward appointed a Judge of the United States District Court; he then removed to Columbus, Ohio, where he resided until his death, in 1831. His literary papers were published in a volume by his widow. Judge J. W. Campbell was a brother of Joseph N. Campbell, of Ripley, one of the first Associate Judges of Brown County, who died of cholera July 13, 1833, aged fifty years.

In the early history of the county, candidates were generally placed before the people without the intervention of a party caucus, a political convention or primary election. The names of candidates for county offices and members of

HISTORY OF BROWN COUNTY. 313

the Legislature were usually announced by themselves or their friends in the newspapers of the county several weeks prior to the election. Sometimes there were seven or eight candidates for a single office; usually there were but two or three. The personal popularity of a candidate and his fitness for the office were of more importance than his views on national politics. The county seat contest for several years was an important factor in the selection of officers, especially members of the Legislature. On July 14, 1824, a meeting was held at Georgetown, which resolved that it was expedient "that the friends of the center interest delegate one or more persons from each township in the county to meet at Georgetown on the first day of the next official muster to select candidates for the next October election."

In 1832, a call signed by more than two hundred supporters of the administration of Andrew Jackson was published, recommending the voters of the Jackson Democratic party in Brown County to meet on Saturday, August 11, at the usual place of holding elections in each township, and appoint five persons from each township to represent them in a convention to be held at Georgetown on August 25, 1832, for the purpose of selecting a ticket for the State Legislature and nominating committees of vigilance and correspondence, and transacting such other business as may be deemed necessary. At the county convention only eight out of fourteen townships were represented. The convention nominated candidates for Representative in the Legislature, and resolved that it was inexpedient to nominate candidates for county offices. Daniel F. Barney, Thomas L. Hamer and Jesse R. Grant were appointed a committee to prepare an address to the Democratic voters of the county.

It was not long until the custom was fixed of making party nominations for candidates, both for the Legislature and for county offices.

In the early exciting contests the county was often flooded with handbills and circulars gotten up by the opposing candidates and their friends. Mr. Hamer, both when a candidate for the Legislature and for Congress, found it advisable to issue circulars explaining his views and replying to the charges made by his opponents. When he became a candidate for Congress the first time, he authorized the announcement of his candidacy in a Georgetown newspaper dated July 31, 1832, and at the same time authorized the editor to say that Mr. Hamer, "as soon as professional avocations will permit, will publish an address to the electors, announcing his political principles. This measure is deemed necessary, not only because the people have a right to know the sentiments of candidates for popular favor, but also to relieve other gentlemen from the trouble of circulating and explaining his sentiments for him—a work which has been in progress, as he understands, for some time past."

Mr. Hamer's address "To the voters of the Fifth Congressional District of Ohio" was dated August 15, 1832, and consisted of an eight-page circular. It gave a full and frank expression of views on nullification, the tariff, the United States Bank and internal improvements by the General Government. On some of these subjects he differed with his best personal and political friends. A circular was soon issued and widely circulated by the friends of Thomas Morris, in which Mr. Hamer was accused of having deserted the Jackson party, and abandoned his Democratic principles. To this Mr. Hamer replied in a circular of equal length with his first address. Other circulars and handbills were issued on both sides in this memorable contest in the Brown, Adams and Clermont District.

ANTI-SLAVERY SENTIMENTS.

The doctrines of the Abolitionists were very unpopular in this county, and those who maintained them were subjected to much odium and abuse. There was, however, a small minority of the people who never flinched from avowing their deep-seated and uncompromising opposition to every form of human bondage. Leicester King, the Abolition candidate for Governor in 1842, received 108 votes in the county, the total number of votes being 3,792. In 1846, Samuel Lewis, the Liberty candidate, received 208 votes, and in 1853 the same man, as the Free Soil candidate, received 593 votes in the county. The greater portion of the Abolitionists of the county were in and about Ripley, Sardinia, Russellville, the Red Oak neighborhood and some other localities.

Among the prominent leaders of the anti-slavery cause were Rev. John Rankin, of Ripley; Rev. James Gilliland, of Red Oak; Rev. Jesse Lockhart, of Russelville; Dr. Bearce, of Decatur; Rev. Robert B. Dobbins, of the Sardinia Presbyterian Church; Dr. Isaac M. Beck, of Sardinia; Rev. John B. Mahan and John Moore, of Washington Township; Dr. Alexander Campbell, of Ripley, and others whose names apppear in other parts of this work.

Many fugitives from bondage passed through the county on their way to Canada, and found friends to assist them on their way to liberty. A common route followed by escaping slaves was from Ripley through the neighborhoods of Red Oak and Russellville to Sardinia; thence to the Quaker settlements in Clinton County. John W. Hudson, a colored man, did much service in piloting the fugitives.

The operation of the Underground Railroad through Brown County awakened the most bitter animosity on the part of the Kentuckians against those who were believed to assist the slaves in their flight. At an anti-slavery meeting of the citizens of Sardinia and vicinity, held on November 21, 1838, a committee of respectable citizens presented a report, accompanied with affidavits in support of its declarations, stating that for more than a year past there had been an unusual degree of hatred manifested by the slave-hunters and slaveholders toward the Abolitionists of Brown County, and that rewards varying from $500 to $2,500 had been repeatedly offered by different persons for the abduction or assassination of Rev. John B. Mahon, and rewards had also been offered for Amos Pettijohn, William A. Frazier and Dr. Isaac M. Beck, of Sardinia, Rev. John Rankin and Dr. Alexander Campbell, of Ripley, William McCoy, of Russellville, and citizens of Adams County.

The trial of Rev. John B. Mahan, of Brown County, Ohio, in the Circuit Court of Mason County, Ky., for felony in aiding certain slaves to escape from their master, was a celebrated case in the history of anti-slavery agitation. Mahan was a local preacher and kept a tavern on temperance principles in Sardinia. He was indicted in Mason County, Ky., on the charge of "aiding and assisting certain slaves, the property of Wiliam Greathouse, to make their escape from the possession of the said William Greathouse, out of and beyond the State of Kentucky." Mahan claimed that he had never seen one of the two slaves of Greathouse which had escaped; that the other had stopped at his tavern, but had not been secreted by him, and that he had no agency whatever in causing or assisting the escape of either of the slaves; nor had he been in Mason County or any adjoining county for nearly twenty years. After his indictment, the Governor of Kentucky sent a requisition to the Governor of Ohio for his delivery to the authorities of the former State. Joseph Vance, Governor of Ohio, on the 6th of September, 1838, issued a warrant for the arrest of Mahan, and his delivery to the custody of the Sheriff of Mason County, Ky.

On Mahan's arrest, several of his friends accompanied him to Georgetown for the purpose of securing his release on a writ of habeas corpus. The writ was obtained, but it was directed to the Sheriff of Brown County, Ohio, and Mahan was already in the custody of the Sheriff of Mason County, Ky., who was on his way with the prisoner to Kentucky, and refused to regard the command of the writ. Mahan remained in prison until his trial, which commenced on November 13, and continued six days. He was absent from his home in all nearly ten weeks. He was acquitted by the jury, under the charge of Judge Walker Reid, that the court had no jurisdiction of the case, if the jury should find that the prisoner was a citizen of Ohio, and had not been in the State of Kentucky until brought there by legal process.

Although he was granted a fair trial and was acquitted, the surrender of Mahan to the authorities of another State was justly regarded as a great hardship. His defense cost him a large sum of money. A civil suit was brought against him for damages for the loss of the two slaves he was accused of helping to escape. The case directed public attention to the extradition laws of Ohio as they then existed, and which certainly needed revision for the protection of the personal liberty of its citizens. The Governor of Ohio, in his annual message, referred at length to the case as one which had caused much political excitement, and defended his conduct in surrendering Mahan as a high duty of an executive officer under the requirement of the National Constitution, but he expressed the hope that the Legislature would take such steps as would best secure the peace and tranquility of our border population. The conduct of Gov. Vance in the case was severely censured by many citizens of Ohio.

This case occurred fourteen years before the passage of the Fugitive Slave Law, two years before the organization of the Liberty party, and in the first year of the publication of the *Philanthropist*, the organ of the Ohio State Antislavery Society, edited by Gamiliel Bailey, Jr., and printed at Cincinnati. The Mahan case occupied considerable space in the columns of the *Philanthropist* and other anti-slavery journals for several successive numbers. The report of the trial was published in a pamphlet, and anti-slavery societies were called on to assist in spreading it far and wide, as it would do much for the cause of Abolition. The White Oak Anti-Slavery Society, at a meeting held at Sardinia, adopted resolutions in relation to the Mahan case, as did the anti-slavery citizens of Sardinia at a public meeting. One of the resolutions adopted at the later meeting severely condemned Hon. T. L. Hamer for refusing his services as attorney in the habeas corpus case for the benefit of Mahan.

One year later, John B. Mahan, Joseph Pettijohn and Amos Pettijohn were tried at Georgetown on an indictment for riot in rescuing a negro from the hands of a Constable. David G. Devore, Prosecuting Attorney; W. C. Marshall and T. L. Hamer appeared on the side of the prosecution. Thomas Morris and Messrs. Jolliffe and Fishback for the defendants. Mahan and Joseph Pettijohn were found guilty, and were sentenced each to pay a fine of $50, to be imprisoned in the dungeon of the jail of Brown County for ten days, and to be fed on bread and water only during the term of imprisonment. The case was taken to the Supreme Court, and the execution of the sentence was suspended until the decision of the higher tribunal. In pronouncing sentence upon Mahan, the court reminded him that it had been proved on the trial that he was a minister of the gospel of peace; that the riot had taken place on the Sabbath day; that instead of attending to the duties of his sacred calling he had been found traversing the country on horseback in company with armed men, violating the laws of his country and resisting a ministerial officer in the regular discharge of his duties. He "advised him that his present situation should be a warning to him, and that he should not allow his excessive philanthropy to lead him into similar aggressions in the future." The sentence was reversed by the Supreme Court for error in empanneling the jury.

The following from the pen of Rev. John B. Mahan is here given in justice to him, and as reflecting not only his own sentiments, but probably those of the great majority of his cotemporary Abolitionists:

"However much every good man desires that slavery should have an end, and however much Abolitionists are willing to hazard and sacrifice for this oppressed, degraded and despised portion of our fellow men, I am confident that few, if any, for various reasons, would invade the jurisdiction of another State to give aid or encouragement to slaves to escape from their owners. But it ought not to be concealed that a very great majority of Northern people, as well as those that are not Abolitionists as well as those that are Abolitionists (however much human nature has been marred by sin), are not capable of violating the sympathies of their nature or the dictates of their common humanity so far as to be able to drive from their doors the unsheltered, unprotected stranger, or send away unfed, unclothed, unprovided-for the outcasts or wandering poor."

VOTE OF BROWN COUNTY AT VARIOUS PERIODS.

1818—Vote for Governor: Ethan Allen Brown, 438; James Dunlap, 229; total vote, 667.

1820—Vote for Governor: Ethan Allen Brown, 998; *William Henry Harrison, 337; *Jeremiah Morrow, 115; total vote, 1,450.

1822—Vote for Governor: Allen Trimble (Republican) 1,153; Jeremiah Morrow (Republican), 554; William W. Irvin (Republican), 40; total vote, 1,747.

1824—Vote for Governor: Jeremiah Morrow (Republican), 1,080; Allen Trimble (Republican), 597; total vote, 1,677.

1826—Vote for Governor: Alexander Campbell (Republican), 1,222; Allen Trimble (Republican), 447; John Bigger (Republican), 88; Benjamin Tappan (Republican), 36; total vote, 1,793.

1828—Vote for Governor: John W. Campbell (Jackson), 1,573; Allen Trimble (Adams), 524; total, 2,097.

1829—Vote for President: Andrew Jackson, 1,630; John Quincy Adams, 703; total, 2,333.

1830—Vote for Governor: Robert Lucas (Democrat), 1,206; Duncan McArthur (National Republican), 863; total vote, 2,069.

1832—Vote for President: Andrew Jackson (Democrat), 1,597; Henry Clay (National Republican), 847; William Wirt (Anti-Mason), 3; total vote, 2,447.

1834—Vote for Governor: Robert Lucas (Democrat), 1,251; James Findlay (Whig), 841; total vote, 2,092.

1836—Vote for President: Martin Van Buren (Democrat), 1,675; William Henry Harrison (Whig), 1,223; total vote, 2,898.

1838—Vote for Governor: Wilson Shannon (Democrat), 1,547; Joseph Vance (Whig), 1,190; total vote, 2,737.

1840—Vote for Governor: Wilson Shannon (Democrat), 2,010; Thomas Corwin (Whig), 1,840; total vote, 3,850.

1842—Vote for Governor: Wilson Shannon (Democrat), 1,994; Thomas Corwin (Whig), 1,690; Leicester King (Abolition), 108; total vote, 3,792.

1844—Vote for Governor: David Tod (Democrat), 2,315; Mordecai Bartley (Whig), 1,706; Leicester King (Abolition), 172; total vote, 4,193.

1846—Vote for Governor: David Tod (Democrat), 2,117; William Bebb (Whig), 1,343; Samuel Lewis (Abolition), 208; total vote, 3,668.

1848—Vote for Governor: John B. Weller (Democrat), 2,330; Seabury Ford (Whig), 1,871; total vote, 4,201.

---

*Neither Gen. Harrison nor Senator Morrow had consented to be a candidate in opposition to the re-election of Gov. Brown.

HISTORY OF BROWN COUNTY.

1850—Vote for Governor: Reuben Wood (Democrat), 1,844; William Johnston (Whig), 1,503; Edward Smith (Free Soil), 37; total vote, 3,384.

1851—Vote for Governor under new constitution: Reuben Wood (Democrat), 1,807; Samuel F. Vinton (Whig), 1,081; Samuel Lewis (Free Soil), 165; total vote, 3,053.

1853—Vote for Governor: William Medill (Democrat), 1,925; Nelson Barrere (Whig), 1,008; Samuel Lewis (Free Soil), 593; total vote, 3,526.

1855—Vote for Governor: William Medill (Democrat), 1,843; Salmon P. Chase (Republican), 1,571; Allen Trimble (American), 286; total vote, 3,700.

1857—Vote for Governor: Henry B. Payne (Democrat), 2,099; Salmon P. Chase (Republican), 1,583; Philip Van Trump (American), 84; total vote, 3,766.

1859—Vote for Governor: Rufus P. Ranney (Democrat), 2,275; William Dennison (Republican), 1,657; total vote, 3,932.

1861—Vote for Governor: Hugh J. Jewett (Democrat), 2,509; David Tod (Republican), 2,052; total vote, 4,561.

1863—Vote for Governor: C. L. Vallandigham (Democrat), 2,744; John Brough (Republican), 3,018; total vote, 5,762.

1865—Vote for Governor: George W. Morgan (Democrat), 2,879; Jacob D. Cox (Republican), 2,610; total vote, 5,489.

1868—Vote for President: Horatio Seymour (Democrat), 3,238; U. S. Grant (Republican), 2,715; total vote, 6,053.

1872—Vote for President: Horace Greeley (Liberal), 3,337; U. S. Grant (Republican), 2,593; total vote, 5,930.

1880—Vote for President: Winfield S. Hancock (Democrat), 4,324; James A. Garfield (Republican), 3,184; total vote, 7,516.

CHAPTER IX.
THE CATHOLIC CHURCH OF BROWN COUNTY.*

WHEN war, ambition and avarice fail, religion pushes onward and succeeds. In the discovery of the New World, wherever man's aggrandizement was the paramount aim, failure was sure to follow; but when this gave way, the followers of the Cross came upon the field, and the result was success. Years before the Pilgrims anchored their bark on the cheerless shores of Cape Cod, "the Roman Catholic Church had been planted, by missionaries from France, in the eastern moiety of Maine; and Le Caron, an ambitious Franciscan, the companion of Champlain, had passed into the hunting-grounds of the Wyandots, and, bound by the vows of his life, had, on foot or paddling a bark canoe, gone onward, taking alms of the savages, until he reached the rivers of Lake Huron." Through the religious zeal of Catholic missionaries for the salvation of souls, the rivers and lakes of the Great Northwest were discovered and explored, and as long as time shall last, the history of those sainted missionaries will be honored and revered.

The Jesuit and Franciscan fathers were the pioneers in this holy work, and the names of Fathers Mesnard, Dreuillettes, Gareau, Allouez, Dablon, Marquette and others are enrolled high upon the imperishable records of religious conquest. Later on came the order of St. Sulpice, with the immortal La Salle at the head of this devoted band of priests. Subsequently, he secured the services of Fathers Hennepin, Ribourde, Membre and others, whose names are familiar to every school-boy in the land. These devoted servants of Christ spread themselves over the then unknown Western territory, preaching the Gospel of their Master to the red savages of the forest, and often yielding up their lives at the hands of those they came to save; yet the "Black Gown" was soon a favorite among the Indians, his coming hailed with joy, and his words listened to with respect and veneration. If one fell by hunger, cold, or a more terrible death, others stood ready to take up the Master's work, and, if need be, to give their lives at the martyr's stake, and receive a martyr's crown.

ST. MARTIN'S CHURCH.

The history of Catholicism in Brown County, Ohio, begins with the donation of a tract of 200 acres of land in 1823, for the purpose of Catholic education, by Gen. William Lytle, who was at that time Government Surveyor of the Virginia Military District. He was a man of noble character, as generous as he was brave, and fought the Indians, side by side with Boone in Kentucky, and Kenton and Washburn throughout Ohio. His name is one of the most illustrious in the annals of Indian warfare. Another tract of 100 acres, adjoining that of Lytle's, was donated by Michael Scott, for a similar purpose, these grants constituting the present site and property of the Ursuline Convent at St. Martin's. About the same time, a tract of 100 acres was given by William Bamber, for the purpose of erecting a church in the southwestern part of Perry Township. A log house was accordingly built, and, soon after its completion, the few faithful Catholics then in the settlement were made happy by the presence of a priest in their midst.

---
*The history of the Catholic Churches and schools of Perry Township was prepared by Dr. T. M. Reade, while the whole chapter on Catholicism was corrected and revised by R. C. Brown.

J. B. Purcell
Aby. Cin.

This was the Rev. Father Hill, an English missionary, who was traveling from Lancaster, Ohio, to Cincinnati. He administered the sacrament of baptism to Elizabeth, infant daughter of Edward and Mary Boyle (Mrs. Hugh Breslin); also to Edward, son of William Boyle, these being the first children of Catholic parentage born in Perry Township. He celebrated the first mass in the little log church, devoutly assisted by the families of William and Edward Boyle and William Bamber—all there were in the vicinity at that time. After attending to the spiritual wants of the little flock, Father Hill departed on his mission.

Three years afterward, in 1826, Rev. Father Mullen visited the settlement and celebrated mass in the old schoolhouse of John H. O'Connor. From time to time, a missionary would appear and offer up the sacrifice of the mass at this point, thus keeping alive the spark of Catholic faith in the hearts of these sturdy pioneers of the church, but no regular pastor was appointed until 1830, in which year the Rev. Martin Kundig was sent to take charge of this mission, by the Rt. Rev. Edward Fenwick, Bishop of Cincinnati. He was the first priest who volunteered to undertake the arduous task of laying the foundation of the church in the new settlement.

He was a young man of extraordinary zeal and indomitable courage. Although a stranger in a strange land, with nothing to aid him but that spirit of self-sacrifice characteristic of the pioneer priests whose footprints mark the onward march of civilization and Christianity, and a firm reliance on the providence of God, he chose from among the few scattering missionary stations then in Ohio the most unauspicious and uninviting—that of Brown County. Father Martin Kundig was a native of Luzerne, Switzerland. He founded the first Catholic Church in Brown County in the fall of 1830, and dedicated it in honor of his patron, St. Martin. He was transferred, in 1832, to Milwaukee, Wis., and at the time of his death, in 1876, he was Vicar General of that diocese. A few years previous to his death, he wrote a letter to one of his old friends at St. Martin's, in which he tells the simple story of his early struggles. A few extracts will serve to throw light upon the character of the man and the times in which he lived.

He says: "When I visited your present neighborhood in the year 1830, I found within ten miles about eight families, poor, forlorn and isolated in their little log houses. There were 100 acres of woodland at Bamber's, and, four miles from it, 300 acres more, all covered with woods, as the property of the church. No sooner was I there than I heard a voice—'To this neighborhood you have come; stay here and lay the foundation.' Bishop Fenwick laughed at my proposition, and compared me to a young horse without a bridle. He considered the proposition foolish, so I had to drop it. When, however, the Vicar General came from Europe, I renewed to him my plan, and he forthwith removed every obstacle. So, asking a few articles from the ladies, such as some plates, a knife and fork, two pans, a kettle, a blanket and a mattress, I set out for Brown County, without money or expecting a congregation to support me. After living six months in a log cabin without a window, I succeeded in furnishing my residence.

"It took me six weeks to bring my first palace into order. It was about ten by twelve feet, where I had my study, parlor, kitchen, bedroom and cellar altogether, with a window of six panes of glass. Very often I love to go back to the days which I spent in my little hermitage in St. Martin's, where I lived in solitude and apostolic poverty. It was a school where I learned to live without expense, for I had nothing to spend. I built eleven houses, without nail or board, for I could not buy them without money, and I cooked my meals without flour, fat or butter, for I had them not.".

The first mass in the log cabin church of St. Martin's was an event in the lives of the pioneers never to be forgotten. They were for the most part Irish Catholics, who, having bravely struggled through the rigors of religious persecution in Ireland; after the perilous voyage of thousands of miles over ocean, river and mountain; after years of the trials and hardships incident to pioneer life; after many vain efforts, were finally successful in the realization of their fondest hopes. A new era was dawning upon them. Their children were to be educated in the faith of their fathers. The dark night of persecution had passed away forever, and they beheld with grateful hearts the bright future of peace and good will which was to follow under the benign influence of civil and religious liberty. So the pastor and his little flock gathered at their first mass, in the rude cabin in the wilderness. The bell was rung and the candles were lighted on the altar. The giant oaks of the forest re-echoed for the first time the sound of sacred song. The people bowed down in adoration, and, as their prayers ascended like incense to the Throne of Grace, the green sod upon which they knelt was moistened with their tears.

Thus it was that the seed was sown at St. Martin's, which, after the lapse of half a century, has borne fruit a thousand fold. The eight families mentioned by Father Kundig were those of William Boyle, William Bamber, John Scanlan, John Savage, Sr., Edward Boyle, Hugh McDonald, Edward Brannan, Edward McCaffrey. The choir was composed of two Indian boys; also two men, John Ballard and John Mueller, and two girls, Margaret McCaffrey and Betsy Bamber.

Of Catholics who were in this vicinity at that time, or soon afterward, we might mention the following well-remembered names, some of whom assisted in erecting the log church where the convent stands: Patrick Savage, Thomas Ballard, Thomas Bamber, Sr., Peter Rock, Michael Barnes, Nicholas Halpin, Mrs. Crosson, James Murray, Michael O'Connor, John Rogers, Nicholas Breason, Thomas Kelly, William Shaysgreen, Michael Crone, Mr. McGroty, Mr. Neill, Barney Kelly and James Hughes, of Highland County, the two latter of whom helped to build the log cabin church spoken of previously.

How changed the scene to-day! The little log church has passed away, and upon the site of its ruin stands, in stately magnificence, the far-famed Ursuline Convent. All is changed. The congregation and its pastor have gone to receive their reward. The woods have disappeared, and the wilderness has been transformed into an agricultural garden. Of the choir who chanted for the first time the sacred anthems which have never ceased since that date, all but one have passed away. Margaret McCaffrey alone remains, and she is

"Only waiting till the shadows
Are a little longer grown;
Only waiting till the glimmer
Of the day's last beam has flown.

"Till the night of earth has faded
From the heart once full of day ;
Till the stars of heaven are breaking
Through the twilight soft and gray."

Rev. James Reed succeeded Father Kundig in 1832, remaining in charge of the parish for a few years. During this time, he organized and conducted a day and boarding school for the benefit of the children of the surrounding country, and replaced the log church, which stood on the convent grounds, by a brick structure. He was followed by Father Masquelette, who remained until 1839, in which year Fathers Gacon and Cheymol were appointed by Bishop Purcell to take charge of this and five adjoining counties.

The labors, trials and difficulties of these devoted servants of God cannot be recounted here. Always ready for the call of duty, they traveled through the unfrequented woods, sometimes making sick calls fifty miles distant from their humble residence at St. Martin's, where, like their venerable predecessors, they lived in apostolic poverty. They sought neither wealth nor fame. The former they never possessed. The latter can add nothing to their merits. It formed no part of the object of their lives. But, as long as the church which they labored to establish holds her place in Ohio, the names of Father Gacon and Father Cheymol will be revered and honored by her devoted children. Rev. Claude Gacon and Rev. William Cheymol, natives of Bas Auvergne, Department of Clermont, France, were life-long companions until the death of Father Gacon, which occurred in 1865. Father Cheymol is still in the performance of his duty as Chaplain of the Ursuline Convent. After forty-three years of unremitting labor, he bids fair to remain many years in the future to guide and direct his devoted children.

In 1865, Rev. F. X. Dutton was appointed parish priest of St. Martin's. Soon after his arrival, he undertook the erection of a new church, which he carried to a successful completion. It is a handsome brick structure, modern in style and finish, and the interior will compare favorably with city churches. Father Dutton is an earnest, zealous pastor, who has done much toward building up God's kingdom on earth since his ordination to the priesthood, and the beautiful edifice of St. Martin's will ever stand as a monument of his faithful stewardship in this parish. The congregation at present is in a prosperous condition, and embraces a membership of 750 souls. Close to the church is a cemetery, with many handsome headstones marking the last resting-place of those who are asleep in the Lord.

In connection with the history of Catholicism and Catholic institutions in Brown County, we deem it appropriate to give a brief sketch of the Most Rev. John B. Purcell, the venerable Archbishop, who, having devoted his whole life to God, is now spending his few remaining days at the beautiful retreat of St. Martin's. He was born at Mallon, in the county of Cork, Ireland, February 26, 1800, and is a son of Edmund and Johanna Purcell, natives of that land. His early years were passed under the care of pious parents and in the service of his parish church, receiving as good an education as could be obtained in his native place. His hopes of a collegiate course at Maynooth were unexpectedly blasted, and, at the age of eighteen, he emigrated to the United States. Soon after reaching Baltimore, he applied for and received a teacher's certificate from the faculty of Asbury College. He began his duties as tutor in a private family, who were living on the eastern shore of Maryland, where he remained two years, at the end of which time he entered, as a student, Mt. St. Mary's College, near Emmitsburg, in the same State.

In 1824, he went to Paris, France, in company with the Rev. Father Brute, subsequently Bishop of Vincennes, Ind., to complete his studies at the Seminary of St. Sulpice. On the 21st of May, 1826, he was ordained priest by Archbishop De Quelen, in the cathedral of Notre Dame, Paris. Upon his return to America, he was appointed Professor of Philosophy in Mt. St. Mary's College, Emmitsburg, Md. His learning and ability soon attracted the attention of his superiors, and, on the death of the Rt. Rev. Edward Fenwick, Bishop of Cincinnati, who was stricken down by cholera in 1832, Rev. John B. Purcell was selected by the Pope to fill the vacancy, and, October 13, 1833, was consecrated Bishop of the Cincinnati Diocese. This ceremony took place at the Cathedral of Baltimore, Md., and was performed by Archbishop R. Whitfield. The week following his consecration, he took part in the Second Provincial Council of Baltimore, after which he set out for Cincinnati, the seat of his bishopric. The diocese then comprised the whole State of Ohio, and contained sixteen small churches, while Cincinnati possessed but one. In 1847, the diocese of Cleveland was erected, and in 1868, that of Columbus.

In 1850, Bishop Purcell was appointed Archbishop, receiving the Pallium from the Pope's hands the following year. It will not be out of place to here give the names of the religious, educational and charitable institutions that this venerable prelate established or founded during his administrative career. Under his direct administration came into life the following institutions, viz.: The Theological Seminary at Mt. St. Mary's of the West; St. Xavier's College; the Passionist Monastery, Mt. Adams; the Catholic Gymnasium of St. Francis Assisium; St. Joseph's Academy; St. Mary's Institute; six literary institutes for young ladies, three of which are conducted by the Sisters of Notre Dame, the others by the Ladies of the Sacred Heart, Sisters of Charity and Ursuline nuns; six convents; the Foundling Hospital and Lying-In Hospital of St. Vincent de Paul; the Protectory for Boys; St. Mary's Hospital and the Hospital of the Good Samaritan; St. Peter's, St. Joseph's and St. Aloysius' Orphan Asylum; besides parochial schools in every parish throughout his diocese where such could be supported.

In 1862, Archbishop Purcell visited Rome for the fourth time, at the invitation of the immortal Pope Pius the Ninth. In 1867, he repaired once more to the "Eternal City," and again in 1869, to take part in the great Ecumenical Council of the Vatican, whose voice was heard throughout the world. The fifty-sixth anniversary of his elevation to the priesthood was celebrated at St. Martin's on the 21st of May, 1882, while the forty-ninth of his consecration as Bishop occurred October 13 of the same year. He has been twenty-two years Archbishop, and has always been loved and venerated by his priests and people, as well as by those outside of the Catholic Church. His standing as an able theologian and scholar is far-famed, while his gentleness and humility of spirit are emblematic of the worthy servant of God.

THEOLOGICAL SEMINARY.

The Brown County Theological Seminary was established on the Lytle Grant in 1840, by the Rt. Rev. John B. Purcell, with Rev. Joseph O'Malley as its first President and Superior. The object of the institution was the education of young men for the priesthood. Father O'Malley was succeeded by Father Borlando, Superior of the Lazarists, who served as its President about three years. In 1845, it was abandoned and turned over to the Ursuline Sisters, Bishop Purcell providing a place for the students at the Athenæum, near St. Xavier's, Cincinnati, and subsequently at Mt. St. Mary's Seminary. Among the students were Rt. Rev. John H. Luers, who was consecrated first Bishop of Fort Wayne, Ind., January 10, 1858; Revs. Cornelius Daly, Thomas Boulger, Patrick O'Malley, J. V. Conlon, William McCallian, James Kearney and James Cahill.

THE URSULINE CONVENT.

This well-known institution is beautifully situated on a large farm about forty-five miles from Cincinnati, and has convenient railroad and telegraphic communication with all parts of the country. It was founded in 1845 by a colony of French nuns from the convents of Boulogne Sur Mer and Beaulieu, presided over by Mother Julia Chatfield, an English lady and convert to the Catholic faith, who had entered the community of Boulogne.

Archbishop Purcell had invited the Ursulines to his diocese, and, on their arrival, he gave them a fatherly welcome with the choice of locating in Chillicothe, Ohio, or on the 300 acres of land in Brown County, Ohio, that had been deeded to him by Gen. Lytle for educational purposes. Their choice fell upon the latter, and, on the 21st of July, 1845, the daughters of St. Ursula arrived in the parish of St. Martin's, three miles from Fayetteville, where they were kindly received by the Reverend Fathers Gacon and Cheymol, and the modest buildings previously used as a seminary for the training of young men for the priesthood of the newly formed diocese of Cincinnati were vacated to give the nuns a temporary home.

School opened the following September, and the small brick building and adjacent frame house gave but scant accommodation for thirteen pupils and the religious; accordingly, with the assistance of the mother-house, in France, and under the supervision of the Reverend Fathers Gacon and Cheymol, the present main building was erected and opened as an academy, in the year 1847.

In this early period, the Rev. Superior, Father Gacon, by his saintly counsels, sustained and encouraged the young community, amid the hardships inseparable from missionary life, and, when death removed him from the scene of his labors, he was replaced by his life-long friend, Father Cheymol, the present chaplain of the convent, who, for nearly half a century, has devoted himself entirely to the spiritual and temporal interests of the community.

Soon the fame of the "Brown County Convent" spread beyond the limits of the neighborhood, as could be seen on Commencement Day, when, to accommodate the visitors, who came from near and far, a large tent was erected, and the grand old woods resounded with the voice of song, while from every village of the surrounding country the people thronged to make it a gala day.

But the inconvenience attending open-air commencements made it necessary to have a permanent commencement hall. To meet this exigency, the chapel building, as it is called, was erected in 1859, and it was not long before Mother Julia and her industrious co-laborers received a palpable proof of the popularity of their institution in the increased number of pupils that flocked from all parts of the Union. Still fresh in the memory of many are those days in which Mother Julia gave such abundant proofs of her excellent administrative ability, and few, if any, who knew her, can forget the charming grace and sincere piety of Mother Stanislaus, who was, for so many years, the cherished and trusty assistant of good Mother Julia.

The academy was chartered in 1846, with the privilege of conferring graduating degrees. A well-selected library, cabinet of physics and natural history were added, the curriculum of studies brought up to the highest standard, offering to young ladies the advantages of a thorough English and French education, including training in music, the fine arts and the modern languages. Owing to the continued increase of patronage, the music hall was built in 1867. Here the musical department receives the most exact attention. A monthly examination, in presence of teachers and pupils, forms an interesting feature in this academy, and the proficiency of the pupils on organ, piano, harp and guitar, in vocal music and the elements of thorough base, bears evidence of a high musical standard.

The sequestered situation of this lovely spot removes young ladies from the allurements and distractions of city life, while the extensive and pure country air render it still more favorable to the pursuits of study. Careful cultivation and natural wildness have been interestingly mingled in the laying out of the convent grounds, and whether the pupils ramble in the wood, where at day-dawn the song of birds announces the rising sun, gather wild flowers by the creek or lake, stroll down the dear old graveyard walk, or pause to pray at the shrine of the Sacred Heart, everywhere they are made sensible of the beauty and tranquility which distinguish this home of learning and religion.

In a little volume entitled "Snatches of Song," dedicated by its gifted authoress "to my friends at St. Martin's, Ohio, whose care and valued lessons are pleasantly remembered," Mary A. McMullen (Una) thus lovingly refers to the scenes of her girlhood at this school:

> "Sweet, happy spot, where holy peace forever,
> A pure, bright spirit, sits with folded wings,
> Where virtue's radiant, ever-blooming flowers
> Are watered by religion's crystal springs,
> Thou seemest in thy tranquil, placid beauty,
> From earth's wild strifes and sins and sorrows free;
> Thou sittest throned amid thy broad, green woodlands,
> A sunny island in an emerald sea.
>
> "Apart from all the gay world's gilded pleasures,
> Brave, patient spirits in thy walls abide,
> In toil and prayer and self-denial, treading
> The hidden pathway of the crucified;
> And many young hearts nurtured by their kindness,
> Will think of them and thee when distant far,
> And look back to thy altar lamps' pale shining,
> As once the shepherds looked to Bethlehem's star.
>
> "Some of the brightest days that I can number,
> Within thy groves like sunny steams went by,
> And to my heart thou shalt be linked forever,
> By memories that cannot fade or die.
> God's blessing rests on thine and thee forever,
> Fair dwelling-place of purity and truth;
> As now, mayst thou remain through coming ages—
> The home of virtue and the guide of youth."

ST. PATRICK'S CHURCH, FAYETTEVILLE.

This church was founded by Rev. Joseph O'Malley in 1841. Father O'Malley was one of the most energetic and successful of the pioneer priests of Ohio, having founded churches and schools in various parts of the State. He remained but a short time in charge of the new congregation, and was succeeded by Rev. Thomas Butler, who was transferred here from Hamilton, Ohio He had previously occupied the eminent position of President of Mount St. Mary's Seminary, at Emmittsburg, Md.

Father Butler was a good scholar and a brilliant orator. He encountered great difficulties on account of the rude and lawless state of society which existed at that time, but he bore opposition and poverty with Christian fortitude and heroic devotion to his sacred calling. He was appointed Vicar General of the diocese of Covington, Ky., in 1849, and occupied that position until the time of his death.

Rev. Cornelius Daly succeeded Father Butler in 1849. He was born in the County of Cork, Ireland, came to this country at an early age and received his education at St. Mary's of the Barrens, Missouri, and at the theological seminary, Brown County. His first mission was in Perry County, Ohio, where he spent six years, established a congregation and from thence was removed to Fayetteville. He built St. Mary's Church, Hillsboro, Ohio, in 1856, and established several missions in this and adjoining counties. In 1860, he founded St. Patrick's Academy, and established the Sisters of Charity in Fayetteville. His death, which occurred at his residence adjoining the church in Fayetteville, on the 24th of January, 1876, was regarded as a public calamity by the entire community, and his funeral was attended by thousands of people of every creed and denomination.

The life and character of Father Daly, is so indelibly engraven upon the hearts and minds of the people of this community, that it would be vain to attempt to speak of him in a manner that would meet the expectations of those who, during his lifetime, had never ceased to honor and to love him; but, when

Rev. William Cheymol.

the generations who followed him in the paths of duty, and learned the word of God from his sainted lips shall have passed away forever, let their children read in the words of the poet the character of Father Daly:

> " A man he was to all the country dear,
> And passing rich with forty pounds a year;
> Remote from towns he ran his godly race,
> Nor e'er had changed nor wish'd to change his place
> Unskillful he to fawn, or seek for power,
> By doctrines fashioned to the varying hour
> For other aims his heart had learned to prize.
> More bent to raise the wretched than to rise,
> His house was known to all the vagrant train:
> He chid their wanderings, but relieved their pain.
> The long remembered beggar was his guest,
> Whose beard descending swept his aged breast.
> The ruined spendthrift, now no longer proud,
> Claim'd kindred there, and had his claims allow'd.
> The broken soldier, kindly bade to stay,
> Sat by his fire and talked the night away;
> Wept o'er his wounds or tales of sorrow done,
> Shoulder'd his crutch and shew'd how fields were won.
> Pleased with his guests, the good man learned to glow,
> And quite forgot their vices in their woe:
> Careless their merits or their faults to scan,
> His pity gave ere charity began.
> Thus to relieve the wretched was his pride,
> And e'en his failings lean'd to virtue's side:
> But in his duty prompt at every call
> He watch'd and wept, he prayed and felt for all;
> And, as a bird, each fond endearment tries
> To tempt its new-fledged offspring to the skies,
> He tried each art, reproved each dull delay,
> Allured to brighter worlds and led the way.
> Beside the bed where parting life was laid,
> And sorrow, guilt and pain by turns dismay'd,
> The reverend champion stood. At his control
> Despair and anguish fled the struggling soul;
> Comfort came down the trembling wretch to raise,
> And his last faltering accents whisper'd praise.
> At church, with meek and unaffected grace,
> His looks adorned the venerable place;
> Truth from his lips prevailed with double sway,
> And fools who came to scoff remained to pray.
> The service past, around the pious man
> With steady zeal, each honest rustic ran;
> E'en children followed with endearing wile,
> And pluck'd his gown to share the good man's smile.
> His ready smile a parents warmth expressed,
> Their welfare pleased him, and their cares distressed;
> To them his heart, his love, his griefs were given,
> But all his serious thought, had rest in heaven.
> As some tall cliff that lifts its awful form
> Swells from the vale and midway leaves the storm,
> Though round its breast the rolling clouds are spread,
> Eternal sunshine settles on its head."

As an illustration of his high standing throughout the county, we give verbatim the notice of his death as published in the *Brown County News* of January 26, 1876: " Rev. Cornelius Daly, of Fayetteville, this county, died on last Monday morning, after several weeks' illness, of a pulmonary disease. Father Daly was one of the best and most gentlemanly men we ever knew. He had charge of the Catholic Church at Fayetteville for over a quarter of a century, and was sincerely loved by his parishioners and by all who knew him. He always had a kind word for every one, and especially for the afflicted and the needy poor. In life and conduct he exemplified the true character of his high calling. The people of that neighborhood have sustained a severe loss in the death of Father Daly." Thus passed away one of God's chosen ones, who lived and died faithful to his Lord and Master.

Rev. Francis Mallon was appointed pastor of St. Patrick's in 1876, where he remained until 1878, when he resigned his charge and is now residing in Cincinnati.

Rev. John Bowe, the present pastor, succeeded Father Mallon. In 1879, he was instrumental in having a monument erected to the memory of Father Daly. In 1880, he established the Fayetteville Total Abstinence Society, and continues to labor earnestly in the cause of temperance. Father Bowe has served many years as a priest of God, and has always labored zealously in behalf of Christ and His church. The present membership of St. Patrick's is about 1,500, and the church is a substantial brick structure, nicely painted and frescoed within. The pastor's residence adjoins the church on the rear. A cemetery lies to the right of the church in the same lot, and the whole is well shaded with forest trees.

ST. PATRICK'S ACADEMY, FAYETTEVILLE.

The object of this school is to provide for boys between the ages of five and twelve years a place where they may enjoy all the comforts of home and care of parents, together with the benefits of salutary discipline and careful teaching in the usual English branches. In addition to the boarding-school, a parish school is maintained, under the efficient management of the Sisters of Charity. This institution was founded in 1860 by Rev. Father Daly. A new building is now being constructed outside of Fayetteville, on the Georgetown road, occupying a beautiful site, upon which the academy is to be located in the future. The growth and progress of this school will compare favorably with like institutions throughout the State, and in it the Catholics of Perry Township have one of the strongest evidences that education and religion should go hand in hand. In their liberal support of this institution, they are carrying out and obeying the precepts of their church, as well as forwarding the true principles of civilization.

CHURCH OF THE HOLY GHOST, VERA CRUZ.

This church was founded by the Rev. Father Stehle, of Cincinnati, and dedicated by Archbishop Purcell in 1863. Andrew McQuaillan donated two acres of ground for the church, and Patrick McConn a like amount for a cemetery. The following pastors have served this congregation since its organization: Revs. Father Schmidt, Father McMahon, Francis Mallon, Bernard Roesner, Thomas Boulger and Henry Kiffmeyer, the present pastor.

Father Kiffmeyer was educated at Mt. St. Mary's Seminary, and ordained in 1868, by Archbishop Purcell. His first mission was at St. Philomena's Church, where he remained several years, and was then transferred to St. Rose's Church, where he labored until 1880, when he took charge of the Church of the Holy Ghost. The congregation numbers about 500, and their church is a beautiful brick edifice in keeping with the age and progress of the country. There are few, if any, townships in Ohio, where Catholicism has taken such deep root as in that of Perry. Their churches and schools are all in a flourishing condition, and from the mustard-seed of faith planted here nearly sixty years ago, the tree has grown until its spreading branches cover hundreds of faithful Catholics, who are imbued with a firm faith and ardent love for the church of the early fathers.

HISTORY OF BROWN COUNTY.

ST. MICHAEL'S CHURCH, RIPLEY.

Some time between the period of 1833 and 1836, several Catholic families settled in and near the village of Ripley. Prominent among them were Michael Waters, Joseph Helbling and Jacob Bellinger, of whom the last two were Germans. Mass was occasionally celebrated at the houses of Messrs. Waters and Helbling by visiting and traveling priests. In the summer of 1840, an effort was made by these few devout Catholics to erect a house of worship, which they succeeded in doing that year, and the little frame building still standing on the east side of the Ripley and Hillsboro pike, within the corporate limits of the village, is the monument of their enterprise. This church was erected upon ground given for the purpose by Michael Waters, who, it is said, was mainly instrumental in its construction, which fact seems quite evident from the following: On a sandstone in the foundation of the building is this inscription: "Michael Waters, Ripley, Ohio, September 22, 1840." It is said that the church was built by the contributions of six families, the bulk of the money being given by Mr. Waters, who was partially reimbursed by future Sabbath collections. This building was dedicated to the service of God by the Most Rev. Archbishop Purcell.

Among later members of St. Michael's Church were Frank Chevalier, Jacob Ernst, John Schwallie, John Greiner, Jacob Lauth, Ignatius Spiller, Joseph Tamme, Joseph Sertel, Andrew Lang, Sebastian Rubenecker, John Fichter, Frank Vogel, Conrad Ebensteiner, Fred Fleig, George Finnin and the Brisbois brothers—Michael, Andrew and Joseph. After the completion of the church, the congregation was occasionally visited by the parish priests of the city of Portsmouth, who administered to their spiritual wants, christened and baptized their children and performed marriage ceremonies. In the absence of records, the names of the many visiting priests who came to this congregation to preach God's word to the faithful few cannot be given. However, among the number were Fathers Thienpont and Herzog. From 1840 until 1849, the priests were from Portsmouth. During the latter year, a visit was made to this people by Rev. Tobbe, then the parish priest at New Richmond, now Bishop of Covington, Ky. He subsequently visited this congregation and fixed his visitations at every fifth Sabbath, and thus continued from December, 1854, until November, 1856. His successor was Father Fuchs, whose visits were during the year beginning in November or December, 1856.

The year 1858 marked a new era in Catholicism in Ripley, for it was then that the first resident priest came here to dwell. This was the Rev. Father H. Bocker, who, as parish priest, served the congregation until some time in the spring of 1861. He subsequently died at Aviston, Ill., at the age of forty-six years. The second pastor of St. Michael's Church was the Rev. Father Casperus Wiese, who was born in Callenhardt, Kreiss Lippstadt, Westphalia, in 1801, ordained priest at Padaerborn in 1830, and died at St. Elizabeth's Hospital, Covington, Ky., July 1, 1881.

The successor of Father Wiese was Rev. J. D. Kress, who assumed the pastorate in the spring of 1864. Father Kress is a native of this country. He served the congregation until 1867. His successor was the Rev. Father Lewis J. Schreiber, who resigned the pastorate of the church on account of ill health, after a stay of a few months, and died in St. Mary's Hospital, Cincinnati, in the summer of 1868. After the resignation of Father Schreiber, the church was without a pastor until the latter part of the year 1868, when Father Bartholomew Schmitz was placed in its care, and remained until the close of 1870. He was a native of Luxembourg. The Rev. Father Geyer, a native of the city of Dayton, this State, succeeded Father Schmitz, and entered upon the church work here in May, 1871, and, in the summer of 1873, while bathing in the Ohio

River, he was drowned. Father Geyer was ordained to the priesthood in the city of Rome, Italy. The Rev. Father Lawrence Klawitter succeeded Father Geyer, commencing his labors with the church December 24, 1873, and served the congregation until November 22, 1878. His ordination took place in Cincinnati in 1868, and he was first stationed at St. Stephen's Church, Columbia. The next and last pastor of St. Michael's is the Rev. Father Andrew Fabian, who succeeded Father Klawitter. Father Fabian was born at Alsace, March 27, 1828, and was ordained priest in Strasburg in 1853, and, in 1874, came to America.

The congregation continued to worship in the frame building before described until the increasing membership made it necessary to build a more commodious structure, and, in 1864, the one-story brick house, now occupied by them, located on the north side of Fourth street, near Market, was erected at a cost of about $5,000. The interior of the building comprises one large audience room, with a seating capacity of about four hundred persons. The room is supplied with a reed organ and the walls are decorated with scriptural paintings representing the different stations of the cross. The altars, three in number, are of modest design, the lesser ones being those of St. Mary and St. Michael. The dedication of this church took place January 6, 1865, the Right Rev. Sylvester H. Rosecrans officiating. The congregation has been from the beginning almost entirely a German one, and now is composed of about one hundred and twenty families.

A new church building is now in process of construction just west of the present one. It is to be of brick, in size 90x45 feet, with a tower 120 feet high, in which is to be suspended a chime of bells. The edifice will cost about $12,000, and will be an ornament to the village and a credit to the congregation. The architect is George Brink, of Cincinnati. One of the oldest and most devout members of the church, who, for nearly fifty years, was a faithful worker in the church at Ripley, and one of the most respected citizens of the place, was Joseph Helbling, who died April 20, 1882, in his eighty-second year.

The first Catholic school was taught in a frame building, which stood on the present site of the new Methodist Episcopal Church, by a Mr. Trapp, whose given name is supposed to be Christian. Subsequently, a Catholic school was conducted in a little brick building, which stood several hundred yards south of the old frame church on the Ripley and Hillsboro pike. A Mr. Cruikencamp and John Rutland were among the early teachers. In 1864, the present schoolhouse, a two-story brick building, situated next to the church, was erected, at a cost of about $3,000, in which the youth of the congregation have since been instructed. There is one teacher employed, and the average attendance is eighty. The common branches only are taught. The pastor of the congregation is furnished with a neat little house situated in the rear of the church, and the teacher of the school resides on the second floor of the school building.

ST. MARY'S CHURCH, ARNHEIM.

Among the first Catholics who settled in Franklin Township were Wendall Klein, John Ernst, John Lauth, Peter Gabberdenn, George Klockner, John Ernst, Jr., Jacob Lauth, Frederick Keller, Balthazer Yecko, Joseph Wegman, Joseph Weber, John Berger and John Schwallie. Previous to 1837, they were visited twice or three times a year by missionary priests who said mass at the house of Wendall Klein. In 1837, Wendall Klein, who then owned the farm which is now the property of Louis Schwalm, donated half an acre of ground for a cemetery and church, on which the above-named settlers, together with

HISTORY OF BROWN COUNTY.

Frederick Kerwald, John Ferdinand and John Goodin, who were then living in Georgetown, erected a log building, 22x30 feet. It was located one-half mile north of the present village of Arnheim, and received the name of St. Wendall's Church, in honor of the donor. In 1844, this building was weatherboarded and the interior plastered; also a sacristy added to the church.

Here divine services were held from 1837 to 1848, by priests located at Fayetteville and Cincinnati; from 1848 to 1851, by those at Stone Lick, and from the latter date up to 1858, the priests of New Richmond had charge of this congregation. In 1856, Rev. M. A. Tobbe received subscriptions toward the erection of a new church, which was accordingly built in the village of Arnheim in 1858. It is a brick building, 40x60 feet, and was dedicated as St. Mary's Church. The ground on which the building stands was purchased from Jacob Arnby by John Weisbrodt, and donated for church purposes. The old church was abandoned, and, in 1874, sold to Peter Forthoffer, who moved to Arnheim, and now uses it as a wagon factory.

The following is a list of the priests who have had charge of the congregation from 1836 to the present, viz.: 1836-39, Rev. William Cheymol; 1839-41, Rev. Claude Gacon; 1842, Rev. Joseph O'Malley; 1843, Rev. G. Schonat; 1844, Rev. Michael Heiss, now Archbishop of Milwaukee; 1844, Rev. M. Bobst; 1845, Rev. J. B. Jaconet; 1846-47, Rev. B. Henghold; 1848, Rev. J; F. Patchowski; 1848-49, Rev. J. B. Baumgarten; 1850, Rev. L. Navarronn. 1851, Rev. L. Kupfer and W. Brummer; 1851-52-53, Rev. M. St. Herzog; 1854-55, Rev. B. Henghold; 1855-56, Rev. M. A. Tobbe the present Bishop of Covington, Ky.; 1857, Rev. F. Fuchs; 1858-59-60-61, Rev. H. Bocker, who celebrated the first mass in the new church; 1861-62-63, Rev. C. Wiese; 1864-65-66-67, Rev. J. D. Kress; 1867, Rev. L. J. Schreiber; 1868, Rev. H. Thien; 1869-70, Rev. Bartholomew Schmitz; 1871-72-73, Rev. Peter Geyer, who was drowned in the latter year while bathing in the Ohio River. He noticed his brother struggling in the water, and, going to his assistance, both lost their lives. From 1873 to 1878, Rev. L. M. Klawitter; 1878-79-80-81-82, Rev. A. Fabian.

The present pastor, Rev. F. Mesner, is the first resident priest of Arnheim, and to him we are indebted for the history of St. Mary's Church. Prior to 1882, service was held but once a month. August 1 of that year, Bishop Elder formed a parish from the mission of Arnheim, embracing the central townships of Brown County, southwest townships of Highland and northeastern portion of Adams County. This parish contains sixty familes, or three hundred members, who attend divine service at Arnheim.

In reviewing the history of Catholicism in Brown County, the reader will be forcibly reminded of its steady, healthy growth. In comparing the present condition of the church with what it was fifty years ago, he will discover a fair illustration of the Gospel parable of the mustard seed. The three handsome churches in Perry Township, with a membership of 2,750 souls, the church at Ripley, with 600 members, and the Arnheim Church, with 300, is surely a showing that the Catholics of Brown County may well be proud of; but when we add to these the parish schools, St. Patrick's Academy and the far-famed Ursuline Convent, we may safely conclude that God has blessed the labors of His servants in this field, and crowned them with the diadem of success.

CHAPTER X.

MILITARY HISTORY.

THE WAR OF 1812.

IT is impossible, at this day, to learn the number of men from the region now forming Brown County who served their country in the last war with England. A list even of the commissioned officers from the county cannot be obtained. There are on file in the Adjutant General's office at Columbus only nine of the muster rolls of the war of 1812. As the terms of service for which the men were called out were generally short, not exceeding six months, the number of persons who served at some time during the war was quite large, and the names of the commissioned officers would form an extended list. The military system under which the war was carried on would by no means have answered the purposes of the Government in the great war of the rebellion. In many cases, the raw militiamen had scarcely learned to drill as soldiers when their terms of service expired, and they were succeeded by fresh, untrained recruits. But in every vicissitude of the conflict, the conduct of the people of the county was patriotic and honorable. They volunteered with alacrity, and endured the hardships of the campaigns in the Northwest with patience and cheerfulness.

A company of riflemen, commanded by Capt. Jacob Boerstler, went from the vicinity of Williamsburg, and formed a part of the Third Ohio Regiment of Volunteers, and, in the march to Detroit, was attached to Col. Cass' regiment, of the First Brigade, of the First Division. The period of service of this company was six months—from April 24 to October 24, 1812. This company was engaged in the battle of Brownstown, in which the Captain and three privates were killed.

Another company, raised in Clermont County, was commanded by Capt. Stephen Smith, of Williamsburg. This company, after the battle of the Thames, in October, 1813, was ordered to take charge of about four hundred British prisoners captured by the American army, and conduct them through the swamps of Northwestern Ohio to Newport, Ky. The Black Swamp, as it was called, was nearly covered with water, and extended for many miles through a dreary wilderness. The commissioned officers becoming sick, the command devolved on William H. Raper, afterward a distinguished Methodist preacher. In their march, the guides became bewildered and lost their way, and the company, with the prisoners, were three days and nights in the swamp without food.

In the first year of the war, Allen Trimble, of Highland County, was appointed Colonel of one of the regiments raised in Southern Ohio, and in 1813, a regiment was raised from Highland and Adams Counties, of which Trimble was Major. This regiment marched to Upper Sandusky.

George Edwards was Colonel of the Second Ohio Regiment, which was discharged at Sandusky in 1814.

Col. Mills Stephenson, one of the earliest pioneers of Union Township, who had served in the Indian wars, was an officer in the war of 1812. Fort Stephenson, at the site of Fremont, Ohio, then known as Upper Sandusky, was named in his honor.

HISTORY OF BROWN COUNTY.

Capt. Elijah Martin, of the vicinity of Aberdeen, recruited, in 1812, a rifle company, and commanded it during the period of its service—one year.

A company of mounted volunteers, raised chiefly in what was then Clermont County, for the relief of Fort Meigs and Fort Stephenson, was commanded by Capt. Robert Haines, and served from July 27 until August 13, 1813—a period of sixteen days.

Lebanon and Chillicothe were the chief places of rendezvous for the troops raised in Clermont and Adams Counties.

THE MEXICAN WAR.

Perhaps no county in the State of Ohio exhibited more promptness and alacrity in meeting the call for volunteers for the war with Mexico. While some of the counties of Southern Ohio sent scarcely a dozen soldiers into the field during the whole of that war, Brown raised one of the first companies of volunteers, and more men proffered their services than could be accepted. This was largely due to the influence of Thomas L. Hamer, who zealously maintained the justice and necessity of the war measures of the national administration, by his eloquence roused the patriotism of his fellow-citizens, and himself volunteered. "His example became contagious; his law partner, S. W. Johnston, volunteered; two of their law students volunteered; a bound boy of Mr. Hamer's volunteered; and finally the young son of Hamer pressed forward to join the patriotic throng, but his father kindly stayed his steps." The Brown County volunteers, on the organization of volunteers at Camp Washington, Cincinnati, became Company G, First Ohio Regiment. Its first officers were: Sanders W. Johnston, Captain; James P. Fyffe, First Lieutenant; W. P. Stewart and Carr B. White, Second Lieutenants. After the death of Gen. Hamer, Capt. Johnston resigned and returned home. Carr B. White was then elected Captain. This company was soon called to see the stern realities of war in the storming of Monterey, and Gen. Taylor, in his official dispatches, called attention to the good conduct of Capt. Johnston at that hard-fought battle.

The term of enlistment was one year. On the 1st of Septembr, 1847, about twenty-two men from Brown County, under Lieut. James P. Fyffe, enlisted, and, uniting with forty-two men from Clermont County, formed Company C, Second (re-organized) Ohio Regiment of Volunteers. Of this company John W. Lowe was Captain; James P. Fyffe, First Lieutenant; and Milton Jameson and William Howard, Second Lieutenants.

William Wall served in the war against Mexico as Major of the Second Ohio Regiment. Educated at West Point, he excelled in the science of mathematics. He taught school in this county, and afterward occupied the chair of mathematics in the Ohio University at Athens. He was thoroughly versed in military science, was a member of the bar, and, for a short time, editor of a newspaper published at Georgetown. He died November 17, 1856, aged sixty years five months and twenty-two days, and was buried at Georgetown.

Ulysses S. Grant, who, three years before, had graduated at West Point, to which institution he was sent a cadet from Brown County, served in the regular army in the Mexican war, with the rank of Lieutenant.

August V. Kautz, afterward Major General of Volunteers, when but eighteen years of age volunteered as a private in the first company from Brown County in this war.

THE CIVIL WAR.

The record of Brown County in the war of the rebellion is one which will ever be contemplated with pride by her people. Though a majority of her citizens were decided opponents of the election of Lincoln, yet, when the national flag was fired upon, the county was prompt and thorough in response to the call to arms, and the great mass of her people exhibited alacrity and patriotism in bearing their share of the burdens of the momentous struggle.

Until fire opened upon Fort Sumter, the mass of the people did not apprehend civil war. Even after the inauguration of President Lincoln, with Jefferson Davis ruling at Montgomery—two Presidents with their Cabinets, two Governments standing face to face—the people still seemed incredulous as to the imminence of a clash of arms. While a minority of the people of the county were willing to see a civil strife begun as a means for the destruction of slavery, the great majority hoped for a happy and peaceful issue from the national complications. Probably a majority were disposed to favor such measures of conciliation as the repeal of the personal liberty bills in the Northern States which interfered with the enforcement of the fugitive slave law, and to give assurance that slavery should never be interfered with in any of the States where it then existed.

Immediately after the proclamations of President Lincoln and Gov. Dennison, calling for volunteers, were received, the following call for a meeting was issued, signed by J. G. Marshall, D. W. C. Loudon, Maj. C. B. White, Lieut. T. T. Taylor, Capt. R. H. Higgins, W. H. Sly, Alfred Jacobs and fifty-six others:

UNION MEETING.

We, the undersigned, citizens of Brown County, Ohio, in compliance with the call of Abraham Lincoln, President of the United States, through Gov. Dennison, hereby present to the citizens of said county the following call for a meeting to be held at the court house of said county, on Saturday, the 20th of April, A. D. 1861, for the purpose of taking into consideration the formation of a volunteer company to aid in the enforcement of the laws and in quelling the rebellion now progressing in our Union.

Believing that the present hour is the darkest and most dangerous ever experienced by our Confederacy, and that our liberty and Union will be endangered, if not absolutely destroyed, by the success of said revolution, we trust all Union-loving and law-abiding citizens will once more rally round the Stars and Stripes, and adopt measures that will secure the prompt compliance with the call of our Chief Magistrate, the President of the United States.

The meeting was held at the appointed time and place, and was called to order at 2 o'clock P. M. The meeting was large, and was marked by a general and enthusiastic approval of armed measures for the suppression of the rebellion. G. W. King, Esq., was called to the chair. Earnest and patriotic addresses were made by the President of the meeting, Hon. C. A. White, John G. Marshall, D. W. C. Loudon and D. Murphy. Democrats and Republicans forgot their differences and resolved to stand together in support of the constitution and the Union. Whatever spirit of conciliation and concession had before existed, there was now no more talk of coaxing or pleading with traitors, who had dared to aim their cannon at the national flag. At the close of the meeting, volunteers were called for to form a company to leave at once for the service of their country, and some thirty men were enrolled, who proceeded to ballot for officers. The following were elected: Captain, Dr. Carr B. White; First Lieutenant, William Hays; Second Lieutenant, T. T. Taylor, then Prosecuting Attorney. Among the volunteers were five physicians and five attorneys. The company was soon made up, and, on the following Wednesday, left for Camp Chase. The sight of real soldiers was new to most of the people, and the marching to camp of a company for the three-months service made more ado than was afterward occasioned by the departure of a regiment for the three-years service. The ladies of Higginsport prepared a bountiful supper for the volunteers, which was spread upon a long table in the public square. At Cincinnati, the company was entertained at the Broadway Hotel

HISTORY OF BROWN COUNTY. 339

free of expense. The company bore with them a war-worn flag under which Capt. White had fought in the Mexican war.

The first company which left the county under the telegraphic call was the Ripley company, which left on Tuesday, April 23. Its first Captain was Jacob Ammen, a graduate of West Point, who volunteered two days after the firing on Fort Sumter, and reported at Columbus with his company on April 24. The next year, he became a Brigadier General.

On April 20, the Town Council of Ripley, in behalf of the people of that place, adopted resolutions declaring that, while they were prepared and determined to defend themselves against invasions, attacks or unlawful interference from any quarter, they contemplated no hostilities against their neighbors of Kentucky, and that they would not countenance any movements hostile to them, and proposed to the authorities of Maysville, Dover and Augusta that they take measures to co-operate with the authorities of Ripley in preserving the peace along the border and protecting the citizens on both sides of the Ohio. These resolutions met with favorable and friendly responses from Augusta, Dover and Maysville.

The war spirit was soon aroused throughout the county. The national flag was seen floating from stores, workshops and residences. The whole country was filled with the noise and excitement of military preparation.

The women of the county were earnest in their ministrations to the soldiers. From the beginning until the close of the war, they were constant in their efforts to supply those comforts and delicacies needed in the field, and still more in the hospital, and which no government does or can supply.

On May 3, the President issued his first call for men to serve three years or during the war. Then began the serious work of enlistment. Early in the war, there was appointed in each county of the State a standing military committee, which had the charge and direction of the military matters of the county. The raising of funds for bounties, enlisting recruits and looking after the families of those who were absent in the army, and many other duties, devolved upon the committee. The Governor consulted with this committee before commissioning military officers. The war called for so large a proportion of the entire male population that the quota of the county was not in all cases filled without difficulty. Drafts and the offer of large bounties to volunteers were found necessary. Liberal provisions were made for the support of the families of soldiers and marines in active service. Of the men who filled the quota of Brown County, all, except an inconsiderable fraction, were volunteers. Within eighteen months after the first call for three-years' men, the county, with a total militia enrollment of 5,127, sent into the service 1,753 men, of whom only 129 were drafted.

Most of the recruits, on being mustered into the service, received a considerable bounty. Under the last calls of the President, the local bounties were unusually large, amounting to upward of $500, while still larger sums were paid to acceptable substitutes. In this way an enormous sum was expended. The money for this purpose was raised in part by taxation, under the authority of law, but more largely by the voluntary contributions of the stay-at-home citizens. The large bounties were a great incentive to desertion, and it was estimated that of the recruits enlisted to fill the quota of Ohio under the call of July, 1864, more than ten thousand deserted. The deserters would present themselves at a new recruiting station, or, with a change of name, to the same station, be again mustered in, receive a second large bounty, and again desert. To put a stop to this "bounty-jumping," the plan was adopted of withholding the bounty until the recruit had reached his regiment.

The raid of Col. John Morgan through Southern Ohio occurred in July,

1863. The excitement and apprehension throughout the region within twenty miles of the line of march of the raiding party was unprecedented in the history of the State. The farmers, with prudent forethought, drove off their horses and cattle and concealed them in the most unfrequented woods. Morgan's men, following the example of the Union raiding forces in the South, took horses and provisions wherever they could find them, if they were needed. They made few attempts at wholesale destruction of property, but frequently carried off small articles, some of which were utterly useless to the raiders, and were soon thrown away. The militia in the southwestern counties was called out by Gov. Tod on the 12th of July, the militia of Brown being ordered to report at Camp Dennison. Col. John Morgan encamped at Williamsburg on the evening of July 14, after having marched more than ninety miles in about thirty-five hours—the greatest march ever made, even by Morgan. "The column could be tracked by the slaver dropped from the horses' mouths. It was a terrible, trying march. Strong men fell out of the saddles, and at every halt the officers were compelled to move continually about in their respective companies, and pull and haul the men, who would drop asleep in the road. It was the only way to keep them awake. Quite a number crept off into the fields and slept until they were awakened by the enemy." [Duke's History of Morgan's Cavalry.]

On the next day, July 15, the main body of the raiders passed through the northern portion of Brown, being closely pressed by the Union troops following them. About two or three hundred of the rebels, under the command of Col. Dick Morgan, passed through Georgetown, Russelville and Decatur.

In 1864, the Legislature ordered the appointment of a Board of Commissioners to examine and pass upon the claims for damages to property during the Morgan raid. This commission largely reduced the claims, and classified them into damages done by the rebels, by the United States troops, and by the State militia, respectively. The following are the figures for the amounts claimed and passed upon for Brown County:

Claims for damages by the rebels, $28,992.51; claims for damages by Union forces under United States officers, $8,967.35; claims for damages by Union forces not under United States officers, ———; total amount claimed, $37,959.86. Amount allowed for damages done by rebels, $25,556; amount allowed for damages by Union forces under United States officers, $7,228; amount allowed for damages by Union forces not under United States officers, ———; total amount allowed, $32,784.

The following list of the commissioned officers from Brown County in the war of the rebellion was prepared by Capt. C. F. King, of the Adjutant General's office:

Twelfth Ohio Volunteer Infantry—Col. C. B. White, Maj. E. M. Carey, Capt. W. W. Liggett, Lieut. A. M. Ridgway, Lieut. F. M. Slade, Lieut. J. H. Palmer, Lieut. E. C. Devore.

Thirteenth Ohio Volunteer Infantry—Capt. Thomas J. Loudon.

Twenty-fourth Ohio Volunteer Infantry—Col. Jacob Ammen (appointed Brigadier General of Volunteers).

Thirty-fourth Ohio Volunteer Infantry—Maj. C. W. Boyd, Capt. O. P. Evans, Lieut. F. G. Shaw, Lieut. I. N. Anderson.

Forty-sixth Ohio Volunteer Infantry—Col. Thomas T. Taylor, Lieut. G. W. Reeves.

Fifty-ninth Ohio Volunteer Infantry—Col. James P. Fyffe, Capt. Lewis J. Egbert, Capt. R. H. Higgins, Capt. C. F. King, Capt. F. R. Kautz, Capt. O. J. Hopkins, Lieut. H. F. Liggett, Lieut. William H. Lawrence, Lieut. W. T. Trout, Lieut. G. P. Tyler, Lieut. James Jennings, Lieut. Hamer J. Higgins, Lieut. John O'Conner, Lieut. Michael Sells, Lieut. Michael Lynch, Lieut. W. W. McColgin, Lieut. J. P. Purden, Lieut. J. W. Shinn, Lieut. R. C. Drake, Lieut. G. H. Dunham, Assistant Surgeon S. C. Gordon.

Sixtieth Ohio Volunteer Infantry—Lieut. Bowen Dunham.

Seventieth Ohio Volunteer Infantry—Col. D. W. C. Loudon, Lieut. Col. W. B. Brown, Capt. Joseph Blackburn, Capt. F. G. Sloane, Capt. John Campbell, Capt. Marquis de La Fayette Hare, Capt. John J. T. Brady, Lieut. W. R. Harmon, Lieut. Alfred Loudon, Lieut. Amos F. Ellis, Lieut. R. C. Menaugh, Lieut. James Brown, Lieut. Lewis Love, Chaplain John M. Sullivan.

Eighty-ninth Ohio Volunteer Infantry—Col. John G. Marshall, Maj. William Hays, Capt. J. H. Jolley, Capt. D. V. Pearson, Capt. T. H. B. Norris, Capt. John S. Lakin, Capt. C. E. Harrison, Capt. G. H. De Bolt, Lieut. J. W. King, Lieut. Dudley King, Lieut. F. M. Creekbaum.

Ninety-seventh Ohio Volunteer Infantry—Surgeon Thomas W. Gordon.

One Hundred and Ninety-fifth Ohio Volunteer Infantry—Lieut. H. C. Loudon.

One Hundred and Eighty-ninth Ohio Volunteer Infantry—Capt. A. J. Applegate, Lieut. J. H. Sellers, Lieut. F. M. Fowler.

Second Ohio Volunteer Cavalry—Col. A. V. Kautz.

Seventh Ohio Volunteer Cavalry—Maj. James McIntyre, Capt. R. C. Rankin, Capt. John McColgin, Lieut. Samuel Dryden, Lieut. John V. Srofe, Lieut. B. F. Powers, Lieut. William McKnight.

Eleventh Ohio Volunteer Cavalry—Maj. Wesley Love, Lieut. C. W. Waters.

First Regiment Ohio Volunteer Light Artillery—Maj. D. T. Cockerill, Capt. G. A. Cockerill, Lieut. S. M. Espy, Lieut. Norval Osborn.

Fourth Ohio Independent Cavalry Company—Capt. J. S. Foster, Capt. J. L. King, Lieut. W. H. Hannah, Lieut. Thomas J. Thompson, Lieut. J. F. Thomas, Lieut. S. D. Porter, Lieut. Thomas C. Yates.

The private soldiers of Brown County were scattered through so large a portion of the United States army, and in so many regiments and branches of the service, that the record of the county can only be given in the record of Ohio in the rebellion. Such a record, to be complete, should exhibit the military history of every soldier and officer—name, age, rank; when, where and by whom enrolled; when, where and by whom mustered into service; the nature and date of every promotion; date of death, discharge, muster out, transfer or desertion—in short, everything pertaining to the soldier's military career. The military records in the Adjutant General's office at Columbus are now being transcribed, and it is hoped that the completed work will supply the information necessary for the full war record of every soldier in an Ohio regiment during the rebellion.

Brown County claims her full share of the glory in the achievements of Ohio soldiers in quelling the rebellion. Whitelaw Reid, in his "Ohio in the War," says:

"Ohio soldiers fought on well nigh every battle-field of the war. Within forty-eight hours after the telegraphic call, two Ohio regiments were on their way to the rescue of the imperiled capital in the spring of 1861. An Ohio brigade, in good order, covered the retreat from the first Bull Run. Ohio troops formed the bulk of the army that saved West Virginia; the bulk of the army that saved Kentucky; a large share of the army that took Fort Donelson; a part of the army at Island No. 10; a great part of the army that, from Stone River, and Chickamauga, and Mission Ridge, and Kenesaw, and Atlanta, swept down to the sea, and back through the Carolinas to the Old Dominion. They fought at Pea Ridge; they charged at Wagner; they campaigned against the Indians at the base of the Rocky Mountains; they helped to redeem North Carolina; they were in the siege of Vicksburg, the siege of Charleston, the siege of Richmond, the siege of Mobile. At Pittsburg Landing, at Antietam, at Gettysburg, at Corinth, in the Wilderness, before Nashville, at Five Forks, at Appomattox Court House—their bones, reposing on the fields they won, are a perpetual binding pledge that no flag shall ever wave over these graves of our soldiers but the flag they fought to maintain."

CHAPTER XI.

SKETCHES OF DISTINGUISHED CITIZENS.

[The biography of Thomas L. Hamer here presented is the first one given to the public of this distinguished lawyer, statesman and soldier. The materials for the sketch of Matthew Gardner were obtained from his autobiography. These sketches, with others of deceased citizens who were honored with high official positions and were prominent actors in the early history of the county, it is thought may appropriately form a chapter in this part of the work.]

GEN. THOMAS L. HAMER.

Thomas Lyon Hamer was born in Northumberland County, Penn., in the month of July, 1800, and died near Monterey, Mexico, December 2, 1846. His father was a farmer of moderate means, who, about the year 1812, removed his family to the State of New York and resided for a short time in the vicinity of Lake Champlain. While there, it was the lot of Thomas L., then a youth of fourteen years, to be an eye-witness of the naval action fought by the heroic McDonough, and that thrilling scene, with its triumphant result, gave him, as he often declared, an inclination toward warlike achievements, which adhered to him through life. In 1817, the elder Hamer removed with his family to Ohio, and purchased a farm near Oxford, Butler County, where he resided until his death. Young Thomas accompanied the family until they reached the mouth of Nine Mile Creek, a stream of Clermont County which empties into the Ohio at the western boundary of the county. Here he bade his parents adieu, resolved no longer to be a charge upon their slender resources, and here, at the age of seventeen, with no money save only "one and sixpence," in his pocket, with no property except the homespun clothing he wore, without friends or acquaintances, a stranger in a strange land, he began his career. He had received a tolerable English education, and in the immediate vicinity of the place where he landed, he taught a school for about four months. He borrowed while there, from a noted Magistrate named Lindsey, an old and worm-eaten copy of "Espinasse's Nisi Prius," which he read during his spare hours, reciting his first lessons in the law to the learned Justice of the Peace. He continued the business of teaching at Withamsville, where he had access to the library of Dr. William Porter. Subsequently, he took charge of a school at Bethel, where he boarded in the family of Thomas Morris, the pioneer lawyer of Clermont County, who superintended his legal studies until his admission to the bar. From a subscription paper, dated at Bethel, October 16, 1820, still in existence, it appears that the price of tuition in Mr. Hamer's school at that time was $2 per quarter; the regular branches to be taught were reading, writing and arithmetic; grammar would be taught, if requested, at $3 per quarter; the number of pupils subscribed was seventeen, the subscribers agreeing to furnish a schoolroom and fuel.

In the spring of 1821, Mr. Hamer was admitted to the bar by the Supreme Court at Williamsburg, Thomas Morris and Thomas Porter recommending his admission. It is said that up to this time, he had never, at any time, been within the walls of a court house, and was a modest, diffident and unassuming young man. On the 4th of July succeeding his admission to the bar, he delivered an oration at Withamsville, which was printed in the *Farmer's Friend*, a newspaper published at Williamsburg. This address indicates literary taste, is carefully written, and must have added to the reputation of the youthful member of the legal profession, who was just reaching his majority.

In the month of August, 1821, he moved to Georgetown, which, three months before, had been made a seat of justice, and then was a marshy piece of ground covered with a dense forest, with stakes driven into the ground to mark the corners of the lots into which it had been laid out. Here, in a new town and a newly formed county, at the age of twenty-one, he commenced the practice of law, and here was his home until his lamented death. Soon after establishing himself at Georgetown, he married Lydia Bruce Higgins, daughter of Col. Robert Higgins, a prominent citizen of Brown County.

The young lawyer soon became a favorite in the community. He was intelligent and talented; his manners were attractive, his conversation fascinating; he won for himself both esteem and affection. As is usual with young lawyers, his practice did not occupy all his time, but his spare hours were not passed in idleness. His tastes were literary and scholarly, and he read extensively. He accepted the office of Justice of the Peace of Pleasant Township, and, on the removal of the *Benefactor*, the first newspaper of Brown County, to Georgetown, in January, 1824, he became its editor and so continued for two years. For a while, he was lawyer, Magistrate and editor. His practice in writing, combined with his literary studies, gave him the power—not less valuable than oratory—of expressing his thoughts on paper in a style easy, clear and forcible. His practice at the bar increased and became lucrative. He rapidly rose to distinction in his profession, especially as a jury lawyer. His success in his profession arose more from his great knowledge of human nature and his "artless and spirit-stirring eloquence" than for any fondness for the intricacies and technicalities of the science of law and the common-law pleading. He came in contact with able and distinguished lawyers, who traveled the judicial circuit, but in ability to sway a jury, there were none superior to young Hamer.

Mr. Hamer early evinced a warm interest in politics. In 1824, his newspaper advocated the election of Andrew Jackson, and the same year he was proposed for the Legislature, but he declined to be a candidate. In 1825, he was first elected a Representative in the General Assembly. In 1828, he was a Presidential elector on the Jackson ticket, and was again elected a Representative in the Legislature, and was re-elected in 1829. At the organization of the House of Representatives, in December, 1829, he was unanimously elected its Speaker, a station he was admirably qualified to fill by reason of his acquaintance with parliamentary law, his courteous deportment and singular self-possession. Among the distinguished members of this Legislature were Gen. Duncan McArthur and Robert Lucas, in the Senate, who became the opposing candidates for Governor at the next election, and in the House, ex-Gov. Morrow and Thomas Corwin. Between Corwin and Hamer a friendship was formed, and was long continued, notwithstanding their differences in politics.

As a member of the Legislature and Speaker, Mr. Hamer's course was marked by impartiality and independence, rather than a narrow partisan spirit. Indeed, he was accused by some of the hot-headed members of his own party of a lack of zeal in promoting the interests of the Jackson party. The body over which he presided was composed of thirty-seven Jackson and thirty-five Adams men. In appointing the fifteen standing committees, he appointed a majority of Jackson men on eight and a majority of Adams men on seven committees. In appointing select committees on local questions, he wholly disregarded political differences. In a caucus of the Jackson men of both Houses, held in January, 1830, a motion was made that the members pledge themselves to vote in the Legislature for the candidate for any office selected by a majority of the caucus. Mr. Hamer opposed the motion in two or three speeches, and gave several reasons why he could not abide by the rule if adopted. The Legislature then elected Supreme Judges and President Judges. Mr. Hamer said that a majority of the caucus was composed of farmers, mechanics and merchants, who were not versed in the law, and that if they should, with honest motives, select a candidate for Judge of the Supreme Court whom he personally knew to be not qualified, he could not go into the Legislature and vote for him. At the election of Judges, Mr. Hamer voted against two of the nominees of the Jackson caucus, one for Supreme Judge and one for President Judge. In defending himself against the charge of having been unfaithful to the interests of his party, Mr. Hamer afterward said:

"The business of legislating for the people of Ohio, generally speaking, has no sort of connection with party politics; it is impossible to bring them together. None but men of narrow minds and strong party prejudices ever did or ever will discover any such connection. In voting for State officers, however, all admit that the question should have its influence. How far that influence is to extend, is a different consideration. I have never believed that a man who goes to the Legislature and takes an oath to discharge all his duties according to the best of his judgment and ability, as every member does, would be justifiable in voting for a candidate for Judge or any other office, whom he knew was unfit for the station. Does he not violate his oath if he gives such a vote? He swears to vote according to the dictates of his judgment; his judgment tells him the candidate is not qualified, but he still votes for the man because he is a Jacksonian, and has been taken up by the Jackson party. Is this honest? Is it a faithful discharge of the duty he owes his constituents? Is it not a violation of his oath? I think so, and if any other man thinks otherwise, let him act accordingly. I never have and never will obey the dictates of party principles or party caucuses, when by so doing I must violate my oath as Representative, betray my constituents or injure my country."

In 1832, Mr. Hamer was first elected to the Congress of the United States from the district composed of the counties of Brown, Clermont and Adams. He appeared before the people as an Independent Democratic candidate; the opposing candidates were Thomas Morris, of Clermont, who claimed to be the nominee of the Democratic party; Owen T. Fishback, of Clermont, the Whig candidate, and William Russell, of Adams, then a member of Congress, who also appeared as an anti-Jackson candidate. The election for Governor that year was hotly contested, and party lines were closely drawn; the great excitement in the Fifth District, however, was the race for Congress, and this contest aroused the whole people. The three principal candidates, Morris, Fishback and Hamer, were all strong men; all three were lawyers of ability and had had experience in the Legislature. Morris lived at Bethel, Fishback at Batavia, Hamer at Georgetown, and Russell at West Union. The canvass could not well have been carried on without some bitterness, and there was perhaps more between the supporters of Morris and Hamer than of the other candidates. Hamer was successful, the aggregate vote of all the candidates being as follows: Hamer, 2,171; Fishback, 2,069; Morris, 2,028; Russell, 403. Morris carried his own county, receiving 1,319 to 1,186 for Fishback, 409 for Hamer and 19 for Russell, but the eloquence of young Hamer carried captive the Democratic yeomanry of Brown and Adams, and their majorities bore him triumphant to Congress.

It is remarkable that Thomas Morris, so distinguished in the political history of Ohio, when first a candidate for Congress, was defeated by the young man whose law studies he had directed. Two months after his defeat, he was elected by the Legislature a United States Senator, and Thomas Morris and Thomas L. Hamer took their seats as members of the Congress of the United States at the same time, and each served just six years, one in the Upper, the other in the Lower House. Both were elected as members of the same political party, and though differing widely, especially as to slavery agitation, both became distinguished and honored men. After the death of Hamer in Mexico, a member-elect of Congress, a son of Senator Morris, was, without opposition, elected to fill the seat in Congress vacated by his death, and upon that son, Jonathan D. Morris, devolved the duty of pronouncing in the House of Representatives a eulogy upon Gen. Hamer.

In 1834 and 1836, Mr. Hamer was re-elected to Congress from the Fifth District by large majorities, the party favoring the administration of Gen. Jackson being largely in the ascendency in each of the three counties of the district. Mr. Hamer took his seat on December 2, 1833, at the beginning of the session of the Twenty-third Congress. This session has been commonly called the "Panic Session," on account of the state of the country following the President's veto of the United States Bank-Charter Bill and the removal of the deposits of the public money from that bank. The sessions of this Congress were the most eventful and exciting the country had known, and abounded with the men of high talents. From Ohio in the Senate were Thomas Ewing, Sr., and Thomas Morris; in the House were three young men who subsequently rose to distinction—Thomas Corwin, William Allen and Thomas L. Hamer, the last named being one of the youngest members of the Congress. One of the first votes Mr. Hamer cast in the House was in favor of a series of resolutions offered by James K. Polk, declaring that the Bank of the United States ought not to be rechartered, and that the public deposits ought not to be restored to the Bank of the United States. These resolutions were long and vehemently debated, but finally were adopted by large majorities.

The second Congress in which Mr. Hamer served was memorable for the exciting scenes which arose when the agitation of the slavery question was first carried into the halls of Congress, and John Quincy Adams, with a small minority, stood up boldly for the sacred right of petition. Mr. Hamer was a member of the select committee to which was referred every paper or proposition in relation to slavery offered in the House. This committee reported that for the purpose of arresting agitation and restoring tranquility to the public mind, they recommended "that all petitions, memorials, resolutions, propositions, or papers relating in any way to the subject of slavery, or the abolition of slavery, shall, without being either printed or referred, be laid upon the table; and that no further action whatever be had upon them." This report, though strongly opposed by John Quincy Adams, was adopted by a large majority. Mr. Adams himself was strongly opposed to the objects of the Abolitionists, and was governed by a sense of the sacredness of the right of petition, and what he deemed the most effectual way of putting an end to an agitation which he sincerely deprecated.

While a member of the House of Representatives, Mr. Hamer was industrious and faithful to the trust reposed in him by his constituents. Ready and able as he was in debate, his appearance in the discussions of the House was rare; set speeches from him were still rarer. Among his more important speeches found in the Congressional Globe, are his remarks on the bill fixing the northern boundary of Ohio, a speech in favor of the appropriation for an exploring expedition to the South Seas, and a speech on the admission of the

States of Michigan and Arkansas into the Union. The constitutions of these States having been formed without the previous assent of Congress, and some aliens having participated in their adoption, Mr. Hamer, in favoring the admission of the States, discussed, in a philosophical manner, the right of aliens to vote before being naturalized, and argued that the right of suffrage is not inseparably connected with citizenship, but that the privileges are totally distinct—the Federal Government having the sole power to regulate naturalization, the State Governments the sole right to regulate suffrage.

The slavery clause of the constitution of Arkansas was a subject of controversy, and Mr. Hamer concluded his speech with an eloquent allusion to the distractions of the country which had prevailed during the controversy over the admission of Missouri, a congratulation upon their disappearance by the adoption of the Missouri Compromise, and an earnest exhortation to harmony and the preservation of good feeling by the speedy admission of the two States. Copious extracts from this speech are given in Benton's "Thirty Years' View," and the conclusion of the speech is perhaps the best specimen of his eloquence which has been preserved and is accessible to the general reader.

Having declined a re-election to Congress, Mr. Hamer, in 1839, retired to the management of his private business, and devoted himself to the practice of his profession with distinguished success. He continued, however, to mingle freely in the discussion of political questions. He had become widely known as a most effective popular political speaker, and his power to sway the masses caused his services to be in great demand in every important political contest. As a popular orator, he occupied much the same position in the Democratic party of Ohio as his distinguished cotemporary Tom Corwin did in the Whig party. The announcement of the name of Hamer was sufficient to insure a large political meeting. As a stump speaker, he was the favorite among the Democrats of the State. His wit and keen satire and ready repartee irresistably drew the masses to him. For years his "red-head" was the center of attraction in mass meetings. The red hair of Hamer and the dark skin of Corwin were familiar subjects of remark. Each orator found occasions to make playful allusions to his own complexion for the amusement of his hearers. Large open-air meetings, which had been dispersed into lounging and talking groups by the solemn and wise discussions of able but tedious statesmen were brought into a compact mass as soon as Hamer took the stand. The people seemed never to weary of hearing him. They would sit or stand for hours, entranced by the magic of his voice and his manner. Old and young would press about him and lean forward to catch every utterance.

Mr. Hamer at various times wrote articles for the newspapers on public questions. He also carried on an extensive correspondence with many of the most distinguished public men among his cotemporaries. Among those with whom he most frequently corresponded were James K. Polk, John McLean, Lewis Cass and Thomas Corwin. The fact that he did not confine his studies to law and politics is illustrated by the following extract from a private letter written by him to Rev. Alexander Campbell, the distinguished religious reformer, and dated at Georgetown, October 31, 1837:

"Although a young man, and for twelve or fourteen years past immersed in professional avocations and politics, still I have found time to read a good deal upon the subject of theology. Among other works, yours have not escaped me, and I have read with interest, and, I trust, not without profit, a number of your productions. In my examination of the ancient religious systems of India, Egypt, Persia and Palestine, I have found much to perplex me, as every one must, who attempts to thread the maze of this interesting subject. But passing by all other difficulties, I am desirous to obtain information upon one point connected with the Holy Scriptures. The question is this: Is there any external evidence that the Pentateuch was ever committed to writing previous to the Babylonish captivity? If you have in the course of your extensive reading met with any proof upon this point, you will confer a peculiar favor upon me by directing my attention to the place where it may be found."

The letter from which this is an extract called forth from the distinguished theologian a long, learned and able reply, which reached Mr. Hamer at Washington City.

President Polk, in a letter dated October 3, 1845, tendered Mr. Hamer the office of Commissioner of Indian Affairs, which he declined. The next year he manifested a willingness to return to public life, and early in the summer of 1846, he was nominated as the Democratic candidate for Congress in the district composed of Brown, Clermont and Highland Counties.

When Congress authorized the President to accept the services of 50,000 volunteers to carry on the war which was declared already to exist with Mexico, Mr. Hamer rode over his district, addressed meetings, and, by his fervid eloquence, aroused the war spirit of his countrymen. He volunteered as a private soldier. At the organization of the First Ohio Regiment, at Camp Washington, he was elected Major. He was almost immediately appointed a Brigadier General of volunteers, and notified of his appointment by the following letter:

WASHINGTON CITY, June 29, 1846.

My Dear Sir: I have this day nominated you to the Senate of the United States as a Brigadier General, to command the Brigade of Volunteers called into the service from Ohio. I have only time to say that I have never performed any public duty with more pleasure than in conferring upon you this important command. That you will discharge your duty gallantly, and satisfactorily to the brave men you are called to command, as well as to the country, I have the greatest confidence,

I am, Very Truly, Your Friend, JAMES K. POLK.
GEN. THOS. L. HAMER, of Ohio.

This letter of the President was directed to Gen. Hamer at Cincinnati; thence it was forwarded to New Orleans, and thence to Point Isabel. The appointment was accepted in a letter to the President from Matamoras, dated July 24. Gen. Hamer's commission reached him at Camp Belknap, Texas, on the 1st day of August.

Gen. Taylor was at this time preparing for an attack on Monterey, which occupied a strong position by nature, was well fortified by art and occupied by the Mexican General Ampudia, with 10,000 regular troops. "Whilst at Camargo," says Rufus P. Spalding, in his eulogy on Gen. Hamer, "the General-in-Chief resolved to proceed to the assault of Monterey with none but regular troops and Southern volunteers. The course pursued by Gen. Hamer on this occasion, would, in the days of yore, have secured to him a hecatomb. He declared in a council of war, that if a conquest of territory was to be made in the Mexican Empire, the citizen-soldiers from the Free States, and especially those from the Free States of the West, would claim the privilege, not only of taking part in the contest of arms, but also in the civil contest that would ensue as to the government and laws of the subjugated territory. His timely remonstrance produced the desired effect; the order of march was changed, and Gen. Hamer's Brigade, led on by their brave chieftain, performed prodigies of valor and won immortal renown at the storming of Monterey."

The capture of Monterey is justly regarded as one of the most brilliant achievements in the history of modern warfare. Gen. Hamer commanded the First Brigade of the Third or Volunteer Division. The Brigade consisted of the First Ohio and First Kentucky Regiments. Gen. William O. Butler commanded the division. In storming the city, a part of Gen. Hamer's Brigade was left to support the mortars and howitzers, while Gen. Butler entered the edge of the city with the First Ohio. One of the forts of the city was called El Diablo. Gen. Butler advanced toward this fort under a severe fire, and was preparing to storm it when he received a severe wound and was compelled to retire. His command then was surrendered to Gen. Hamer, who moved the regiment to a new position and within sustaining distance of the American batteries, which already occupied another of the forts. While these efforts were being made to carry the advance works, several demonstrations were made by the Mexican cavalry, one of which was repulsed by the First Ohio, aided by a part of the Mississippi Regiment. "For six long hours the contest in the lower part of the city continued, and the streets were slippery with the blood of the assailants. It was truly a scene of havoc and slaughter." One stronghold after another was captured, the Mexicans contesting desperately every foot of ground until nothing remained in their possession but the citadel. On the 23d of September, Gen. Ampudia capitulated.

On the second Tuesday of October, 1846, Gen. Hamer was, without opposition, elected a Representative in Congress. But how unstable is the enjoyment of earthly renown!

A letter from a private soldier from Georgetown, Ohio, serving in Gen. Hamer's Brigade, dated at Camp, near Monterey, Thursday, December 3, 1846, says:

"Gen. Hamer died last night between 9 and 10 o'clock. I have not heard the name of his disease. He had been unwell since he landed in Mexico, and dangerously ill for about a week. Every attention was paid to him by his physicians, who used every effort to stop the progress of his disease, but all in vain. By this dispensation of Providence, not only our company and regiment, but the whole brigade, have met with an irreparable loss, and the Nation is left to mourn one whose services in her councils were worth far more than all the country in dispute for which he so gallantly sacrificed his life. On the march from Comargo to this place, he was scarcely able to sit on his horse. But he said: 'While I am able to ride, I will go at the head of my brigade.' He went at our head and led us into Monterey. He went at the head of the Ohio Regiment, which carried the first stars and stripes that ever waved in the streets of that city. The whole camp to-day is shrouded in gloom. All seem to feel the greatness of their loss. By his firmness and courage, he had won the respect of the officers, both in the regular and volunteer corps. To me it seems I have almost lost a father. To him I could always go with confidence, for advice and assistance."

Maj. Gen. Taylor, in announcing the death of Gen. Hamer, said: "In counsel, I found him clear and judicious, and in the administration of his command, though kind, yet always impartial and just. He was an active participant in the operations before Monterey, and since had commanded the volunteer division. His loss to the army at this time cannot be supplied."

The body of the dead soldier was interred with honors to which his rank entitled him in a cemetery about a mile from the quarters he had occupied in his last sickness. His remains were afterward removed to his adopted State and buried in the cemetery at Georgetown in the presence of thousands of sorrowing spectators: Fitting eulogies were pronounced upon him in the Congress of which he was a member-elect by his successor, J. D. Morris, and others; before the two Houses of the General Assembly of Ohio by Rufus P. Spalding, and at his burial by Hon. David T. Disney.

Thus passed away in the prime of life and in the midst of his usefulness one of the most talented men of his time. Perhaps no man in the whole history of Ohio had more warm admirers. His prospects for the highest office in the nation were considered bright.

Thomas L. Hamer was of medium stature; his hair was very red, and, to a stranger, his personal appearance was not at first prepossessing; he had great vivacity and cheerfulness and boundless kindness of heart. He was generous and hospitable, and treated the humblest with unaffected friendliness. He was neat in his attire and careful as to his personal appearance. While a member of Congress, his face was shaved every day. He was a delightful companion, and held his friends to him as with hooks of steel. Many of his political opponents were his warm personal friends. His portrait was placed in the capitol at Columbus by Gov. R. B. Hayes.

ELDER MATTHEW GARDNER.

This pioneer preacher and remarkable man was born in Rensselaer County, N. Y., near the Massachusetts State line, December 5, 1790. His father, a small farmer and carpenter, was of Quaker descent. When Matthew was ten years old, his father moved to the Northwest Territory, and settled in what is now Brown County, Ohio, in the autumn of 1800. There were no schools in the region in which he first lived in Ohio, and Matthew's education was limited and obtained by his own industry. The first money he obtained was 25 cents for a raccoon skin; this he expended for a copy of Webster's Spelling-Book. He was then about fourteen years old, and had so far forgotten what he had learned in New York that he could scarcely read. His spare hours at night he now applied to study, and, by diligence, he soon learned to read and write. When seventeen years old, he made a flat-boat voyage from Cincinnati to New Orleans, and was absent from home about six months. In his twentieth year, he went to school twenty-seven days, which comprised all his school education, except that received in New York when he was six or seven years old. In these twenty-seven days, he acquired all the knowledge of arithmetic absolutely necessary for ordinary business purposes, and was able to solve almost any practical problem in arithmetic. In 1810, he joined the Christian Church, and was baptized in the West Fork of Eagle Creek by Elder Archibald Campbell, and, about the same time, began to exercise his gifts in public speaking and exhortation. In 1812, he received his letter as a preacher of the Christian Church, and traveled and preached in various parts of Kentucky and Ohio as an associate of Barton W. Stone, William Kinkade and others. He, however, supported himself by work as a carpenter and on a farm which he purchased. He continued his studies, and, having procured a copy of Lindley Murray's Grammar, he studied it diligently, frequently continuing his studies until midnight, after working hard all day. As he became able, he procured other books. He was ordained to the Gospel ministry by the Kentucky Christian Conference March 2, 1818.

Soon after his ordination, he organized Union Church, two miles from Higginsport, and, in 1819 or 1820, he organized a Christian Church at Bethel, Ohio; later in 1820, he formed a regular circuit in Brown and Clermont Counties, with two appointments for each day, several miles apart. This circuit required a two weeks' journey. As a pioneer preacher, he was remarkably successful. He was six feet one inch high, and weighed over two hundred pounds. He had a strong, clear voice, and as he led the singing in an outdoor meeting he was told that his voice was sometimes heard and recognized at a distance of a mile and a half. In his personal appearance, he bore a striking resemblance to Joshua R. Giddings. His manner in preaching was dignified and attractive, and his congregations were large. He continued to preach in groves and churches and to organize new societies for sixty-three years. The churches he first organized were poor and unable to pay a preacher. He believed he could support himself and his family by laboring one-half of his time, and resolved to devote the other half to the work of a Gospel minister. Near the close of his life, he computed that he had organized twenty-two churches, and that 6,100 persons had embraced religion under his ministry.

He says: "When my ministry began, there were no Christian Churches to support ministers. I therefore received little compensation for many years. When the churches grew, my conscience compelled me to decline putting a price on my preaching the Gospel. I could find no 'thus saith the Lord' for it. I do not reprove those who do, however. I therefore left this to the churches to say how much they would give. This was commonly a mere trifle, about $50 or $60 a year for monthly preaching. The Bethlehem Church possessing a good deal of wealth, proposed to give me $100 a year, and, in 1866, they gave me $200 a year for semi-monthly preaching on Saturday and Sabbath, and attending their communion and protracted meetings, etc. This was by far the largest salary, if it may be so called, I ever received, and this was paid for only one or two years out of forty-five."

Beginning life in poverty, Elder Gardner was compelled to practice rigid economy and frugality, which became habitual with him and was continued after he became a man of wealth. He had but four pairs of shoes in twenty years, although he wore shoes all the time, summer and winter. He wore one overcoat twenty years. His clothing of all kinds, including shoes, did not cost him to exceed $10 or $12 a year. He carried one small two-bladed pocket-knife thirty-five years, and an umbrella twenty-five years. It was by this rigid economy that he was enabled, he said, without salary from the churches and dependent on his own resources in a new country, to spend one-half his time in traveling and preaching, to support his family, to give many hundreds of dollars to aid in building Christian chapels and to sustain the the cause of religion in Southern Ohio, to give $1,100 for the endowment of Union Christian College, and to divide $60,000 among his eleven children, while he had nearly that amount left in his old age.

Elder Gardner was of a combative disposition, and, while he had many devoted friends, he had many bitter enemies. He was engaged in several public debates with ministers of other denominations, and was a party to some vexatious law-suits and ecclesiastical trials, an account of which he narrates in his autobiography. He was a strong opponent of secret societies.

In October, 1867, Elder Gardner closed his pastoral labors with the Bethlehem Church, after a pastorate of forty-five years. He had been re-elected by a unanimous vote each year, except one, and then the brother who objected soon gave up his objection and became the pastor's friend. The church was large and had lived in peace. Nearly fifteen hundred members had been received into the church during the pastorate of Elder Gardner. Four other churches had been organized from its members, and still it was the largest church in the conference. The Elder thus describes his farewell with this people:

"Elder Pangburn preached an excellent sermon. Then I felt constrained to speak. if only a few words. I referred to my visits among them nearly fifty years before. Then the country was wild; now it is cultivated. Then the roads were by the mountain paths and the meandering valley brooks. Then they lived in log cabins, where now they have fine residences. I threaded my way over the hills and through the hollows, boldly fording the mountain streams and searching out their rudest homes. Then the people had little culture, where now they are educated. Then they were without hope and without God in the world. I took them by the hand and led them to God. I was inexperienced, but earnest. I preached in their rudest cabins. I led them in prayer at their fireside altars. I baptized in their woodland streams. I kneeled at the dying pillows of their parents, and preached the funerals of their children. God blessed my labors, and changed the lion to the lamb, the raven to the dove, and made the desert to blossom as the rose. My eyes could see but few present who were living in the country at the beginning of my ministry there. Then I was young and strong, but now I am old and feeble—too old to serve them, and they to whom I then preached are gone. I tried to say that this was the last day of my pastorate, but I could not. I tried to say farewell, but there was so much weeping that utterance was choked and tears blinded my eyes. Some kind brother started a farewell hymn, and, while singing, they gave me the parting hand."

He died October 10, 1873, in the eighty-third year of his age, and was buried at Union Christian Church, in Brown County, the first church he organized. The autobiography of Matthew Gardner, edited by N. Summerbell, D. D., was published by the Christian Publishing Association, at Dayton, Ohio, in 1874. Dr. Summerbell says of Elder Gardner: " His opponents will concede that he was great in the things they dislike, and successful in the things they disapprove, and his friends will indorse the rest. Without excusing his defects or magnifying his virtues, his friends contend that his life gives its own lessons, and that he was a great thinker, a great worker, a great economist, a great friend, a great antagonist, a great preacher, a great debater, a great farmer and a great financier."

DR. ALEXANDER CAMPBELL.

The subject of this sketch was the only resident of Brown County who reached the high position of United States Senator. He was a native of Greenbrier County, Va., and was born in the year 1779. When he was quite young, his parents moved to East Tennessee, where they remained five or six years, and then, in company with several families, removed to Crab Orchard, Ky., the removal being effected by traveling on horseback the distance of 170 miles. The Campbell family located at Morrison's Station for a few months, and then settled about one mile from the station. Here they built a cabin, cleared a few acres of land and planted it in corn. The father, Alexander Campbell, Sr., a few months after his settlement, was called back to East Tennessee on important business; while on his way, he was taken sick, and died on the ninth day after leaving home. His wife was now left a widow in a land almost a wilderness, with a family of eight small children. Young Alexander had not up to this time attended school, there being none in the new country in which his young days had been passed. As soon as a school was established, he was sent to it. His mother purchased a small farm of ten acres in Woodford County, Ky., and removed with her children to it. Here the children attended school in winter, and as soon as the spring approached, resumed work upon the little farm. A school having been established at Pisgah Meeting-House, two miles distant, at which Latin and Greek were taught, Alexander urgently solicited his mother to permit him to attend it. Her embarrassed circumstances were such that he not only agreed to work in the morning and evening, but also to refund to his brothers and sisters the cost of his tuition. Having studied at the school, he went to Lexington, and studied medicine with Drs. Ridgely and Brown. Having pursued the study of medicine two years, in 1801, he commenced the practice of his profession in Cynthiana, Ky. Here he married Nancy, daughter of Col. Alexander Dunlap. While at Cynthiana, he was elected a member of the Kentucky Legislature. In 1804, he removed north of the Ohio and settled in what is now Brown, then Adams, County. In

1807, he was elected a Representative in the Legislature from Adams County; in 1808, he was re-elected, and was chosen Speaker of the House of Representatives; in 1809, he was re-elected and was again chosen Speaker.

While serving as Speaker, he was, on December 12, 1809, elected a United States Senator to succeed Hon. Edward Tiffin, resigned. His principal competitor for this high office was Richard S. Thomas, a lawyer then residing at Lebanon. Campbell received thirty-eight votes and Thomas twenty-nine. Dr. Campbell served in the United States Senate four years. He voted against the declaration of war with Great Britain in 1812, and also against the renewal of the charter of the United States Bank. On the expiration of his term, he returned to his home and resumed the practice of medicine and also engaged in mercantile pursuits. As a physician, he took a high rank, and more than once was appointed by the Legislature a member of the medical society which was authorized to grant licenses for the practice of medicine. After the organization of Brown County, he was elected to the Legislature, serving in the Senate in 1822 and in 1823, and in the House in 1832. In 1820, he was elected a Presidential elector on the James Monroe ticket, and, in 1836, on the William Henry Harrison ticket. In 1826, he was one of four candidates for Governor of Ohio; the people in Brown County gave him a large majority over the combined vote of his three competitors, but Allen Trimble was elected. He was a man of uncompromising anti-slavery principles. He died at Ripley in 1857.

JAMES LOUDON.

The subject of this sketch was born in Henry County, Ky., October 21, 1796, and was the oldest of three children whose parents were John and Dorcas (Masterson) Loudon. His father, a native of Washington County, Penn., followed agricultural pursuits through life, and was a participant, under Gen. Wayne, in the battle of Fallen Timbers. He died in Henry County, Ky., where he had settled in 1794. His paternal grandfather was actively engaged in association with the patriots during the Revolutionary struggle. His maternal grandfather, John Masterson, was one of the body guards of Gen. Washington, and was intimately identified with colonial measures and efforts. His mother was a native of Washington County, and one of a family whose male members were prominent throughout the Revolutionary period. In 1806, Gen. Loudon removed with his mother to this county, settling at a point about six miles east of Georgetown, on the farm of Neil Washburn, whence, at the expiration of four years, he and family removed to Arnheim, where a farm was rented and a residence maintained for a period of about two years. His mother was then again married, to Joshua Jordan, one of the earliest pioneer settlers of the country, whereupon the family removed to River Hill, on the Ohio River, a short distance below Ripley. Here he made his home during the ensuing fourteen years, employed in laboring on the farm, and during the summer months of five or six of those years in clerking in dry goods stores, which with river occupations consumed his time during the winters.

His first boating was on the Ohio River, in the old keel-boat line. In the fall of 1813, he made a trip to the salt works on the Kanawha River; the next fall he made a trip from Cincinnati to Pittsburgh, and attempted to go to the head of navigation on the Alleghany River, but, after getting up about sixty miles, found there was not water enough to allow the boat to pass over the shoals; so the boat had to wait for a rise in the river, and the men went back to Pittsburgh. Here he found his old boat loaded with iron and ready to descend the river. He took a situation on the boat as a hand; arriving at Cincinnati, the freight for that port was discharged and preparations made to descend to Louisville. The Captain desired very much to have him continue on the boat, and offered him a clerkship; so he continued to the port aforesaid, and, after "keeping boat" a few weeks, was discharged. Thus ended his keel-boating, and at the date of his death, he firmly believed himself the last of that strong, hardy, daring race of men who carried on the commerce of the Ohio Valley in keel-boats, propelled against the current by long poles, with heavy iron sockets on the lower end and a round, smooth knob, turned from the root of the laurel, to fit the shoulder on the top end. In the fall of 1818, and also in 1819, he made trips to New Orleans in flat-boats. On both these occasions, he had to work his way home on foot through the wilderness and two savage nations of Indians. He made many other trips to that Southern center in the same class of boats, and was always lucky enough to find a steamboat to return in.

In 1820, he associated himself with William Butt and Daniel Ammen, in the printing of a newspaper at Levanna, two miles below Ripley, on the Ohio River, and, in July of that year, the *Benefactor* made its appearance. This was the pioneer newspaper of Brown County. His connection with the paper continued one year; he then sold his interest to one of his partners, and the paper was removed to Georgetown, where its publication was continued for many years. Although his early education had been quite limited, in both degree and kind, his reading and study and one year's drilling with the composing stick at the type case, together with his keen power of observation, counterbalanced to a considerable degree the lack of primary training. In 1822, he taught a country school with more satisfaction to his employers than to himself. In the fall of this year, his friends elected him to the office of Coroner of the county. In 1824, he was re-elected to the same office. In 1826, he was elected Sheriff of Brown County, and re-elected to the same position in 1828, thus serving his county as Coroner and Sheriff eight years. He was married, July 11, 1826, to Elizabeth Chapman, a native of this county, and a daughter of Henry Chapman, one of the early pioneers of the country, who came from Kentucky in 1800. He was a native of Pennsylvania, and an active participant in the war of 1812.

In 1831, Gen. Loudon was employed in a dry goods store in Georgetown. In the spring of 1832, he left Georgetown, and settled on his farm, about four miles south of the village, and engaged in general agriculture, taking a hand in any branch incident to the business. In 1834, many of his friends urged him to be a candidate for the Lower House of the Ohio Legislature; he finally consented to stand a poll and was elected. In 1835, he was re-elected to the same place. This year trouble arose between the authorities of the State of Ohio and those of the Territory of Michigan, in regard to the northern boundary of Ohio (known in Michigan history as the Toledo war). A long and threatening correspondence was kept up between Gov. Lucas and the Department of State at Washington. Gov. Lucas called an extra session of the Legislature of Ohio, which met in June of that year. At this session, Gen. Loudon took a very active part in support of the claim of Ohio and indorsed the course of her Governor.

In 1836, Gen. Loudon was again elected to the Lower House of the General Assembly. At this session he took an active part, and probably did more than any one else in electing his friend William Allen to the United States Senate. March 2, 1837, having been previously elected to the Legislature, he was formally commissioned Major General by Gov. Vance, and was given command of the Eighth Division of the Ohio Militia. In 1842, he was elected to fill a vacancy in the Ohio Senate, occasioned by the resignation of Senator Foos, of Clinton County. In 1843, he was re-elected to the same position, and served two terms, during 1843-44-45-46. In 1849, he was elected a delegate

from Brown County to the Constitutional Convention; was made Chairman of the Committee of Finance and Taxation, and successfully carried through the twelfth article, and it became a part of the constitution. He addressed the people in every township in his district, and urged them to vote for the adoption of the constitution.

When his labors terminated with that deliberative body, he returned to his farm, intending never again to mingle in the arena of politics; nor would he, had it not been for the terrible rebellion that came upon the country. On the arrival of the news that Fort Sumter was fired upon, and that the wicked war had begun, he declared his ardent love for the "Old Star Spangled Banner," and, like his political godfather, "Old Hickory," swore "By the eternal, the constitution must be preserved." From that time he was outspoken in his denunciations of the rebel spirit, South or North, doing all in his power to encourage the patriotic sentiment of the country. In 1863, the Republicans and Union men of his district held a convention to select a candidate for State Senate, and in his absence gave him a unanimous vote for that position. On being notified of the action of the convention, he accepted the nomination and took early steps for a vigorous canvass. Although he had to encounter a Democratic majority of some 1,500 votes, he was elected. He took his seat in January after the election, and for two years gave his best efforts to the cause of his country.

After the close of his official career, he lived in peaceful retirement at his Georgetown home until his death. For more than fifty years, he was a working member of the Masonic fraternity. He was a believer in the Christian religion, but not a member of any religious sect. He was a positive man, whose word was respected alike by friend and foe, even in the most bitter political contests. His life was a useful one. He lived more than eighty years, and died November 14, 1876.

NATHANIEL BEASLEY.

Gen. Beasley was born in Spottsylvania County, Va., May 19, 1774. When he was about fourteen years old, his father with a large family of children emigrated to Limestone, Ky., or that vicinity. The Beasley brothers became noted as sagacious pioneers, hunters and scouts, and were the associates and assistants of Gen. Nathaniel Massie in the early survey and settlement of the Virginia Military District. Previous to Wayne's victory, Nathaniel and Benjamin were employed by Simon Kenton to serve as spies or scouts along the Ohio for the protection of the Kentucky settlements. These scouts, of whom there were several, ranged up and down the Ohio in pairs from Limestone to the mouth of the Big Sandy, alternately performing tours of service of from two to four weeks' duration. They were especially charged to give information to Kenton, who lived at Washington, near Limestone, of Indians who had crossed the Ohio or were about to cross over into Kentucky. Among those who served in the capacity of scouts were Samuel Davis, Samuel McDowell, Duncan McArthur, afterward Governor of Ohio, Benjamin and Nathaniel Beasley. Some of the adventures of these scouts with the Indians were recorded in McDonald's sketches, and Otway Curry wrote an account of others, which he obtained from Samuel Davis and published in the year 1838 in the *Hesperian*, printed at Cincinnati. The account given by McDonald and quoted at length in Howe's Historical Collections of Ohio, of an adventure two of the scouts had with the Indians near the mouth of the Scioto, is in one particular erroneous, as Curry learned from the lips of Davis himself. It was Benjamin Beasley and not Duncan McArthur who accompanied Davis on that occasion.

John, Benjamin and Nathaniel Beasley were assistant surveyors under Massie in the Virginia Military District, and their privations and dangers are elsewhere described in this volume. Nathaniel became an extensive dealer in the lands of what is now Brown County. He settled upon a farm near Decatur, which was his home until his death. He served as a Major in the war of 1812, and in the militia he rose to the rank of Major General. In 1814, he was elected a Representative in the Legislature, and a Senator in 1818; he was again a Senator in 1820 and 1821. On February 25, 1824, he was appointed a member of the State Board of Canal Commissioners by joint resolution of the General Assembly. In the capacity of Canal Commissioner, he accompanied Gov. De Witt Clinton, of New York, and Gov. Morrow, of Ohio, at the ceremony of breaking ground in 1825 for the construction of the two State canals, at Licking Summit and Middletown. Gen. Beasley was married to Sarah Sutton, who died August 19, 1841, aged sixty-one years. He died March 27, 1835, aged sixty years, ten months and eight days, and was buried at Decatur.

ABRAHAM SHEPHERD.

Mr. Shepherd was born August 13, 1776, at or near Shepherdtown, Va., a town laid out by his grandfather. He received what was then regarded as a good education. When he was nineteen years old, his father left Eastern Virginia, crossed the mountains and settled in West Virginia. In early manhood Abraham engaged in the business of surveying. About 1798, he was for a time in the vicinity of Mayslick, Ky., and not long after crossed the Ohio and made his home in what is now Brown County. He married Margaret Moore in 1799. On the north side of the Ohio he first lived near where the Red Oak Presbyterian Church stands, and afterward built a brick house about two miles from the site of Russellville, and operated the mills afterward known as Pilson's. In the war of 1812, he raised a company and served as Captain. In 1817, he moved to Ripley, and operated the mills on Red Oak, about one mile from the town. In 1825, he added steam power to these mills. In connection with others, he built the mill one mile farther up Red Oak.

In 1803, he was elected a Representative in the Legislature, and served as a member of the Lower House, in all, six years. In 1815, he was first elected to the State Senate, and served in that body six years. He was Speaker of the House in 1806 and Speaker of the Senate in 1816, 1817 and 1826. His name is signed as President of the Senate to the act organizing Brown County. In 1818, he resigned his position as Senator, and became the first Clerk of the Common Pleas and Supreme Courts of Brown County, a position he occupied until 1824.

In 1816, he was a Presidential Elector on the James Monroe ticket. After the organization of the Whig party, he became a Whig and was a great friend and admirer of Henry Clay and his American system, and was consequently in the minority in Brown County. In religion, he was a Presbyterian, and long held the office of Ruling Elder in that church. In 1834, he moved to Putnam County, Ill., where he died in 1846, in the seventy-first year of his age.

CHAPTER XII.
LIST OF OFFICERS.
AUDITORS.

THE duties of this office were discharged by the Commissioner's Clerk until 1821. William Middleton, the first Auditor, served from 1821 to 1827; William Butts, 1827 to 1829; Benjamin Evans, 1829 to 1831; Samuel Glaze, 1831 to 1838; Hezekiah Lindsey, 1838 to 1841, but left before his term expired, and Peter L. Wilson was appointed to fill the vacancy, six months; James J. Smith, 1841 to 1845; Stephen T. Brunson, 1845 to 1849; John McColgin, 1849 to 1853; Lewis J. Egbert, 1853 to 1855; P. Ellis, 1855 to 1857; John W. Purdom, 1857 to 1861; J. W. Heterick, 1861 to 1863; William W. Elsberry, 1863 to 1865; James A. Stevenson, 1865 to 1867; Alonzo G. Quinlan, 1867 to 1871; William W. Elsberry, 1871 to 1875; Enoch E. Roney, 1875 to 1880; William J. Jacobs, 1880———.

TREASURERS.

William Humphreys, part of 1818; George King, 1818 to 1820; William Humphreys, 1820 to 1822; Amos Ellis, 1822 to 1829; William Middleton, 1829 to 1836; Thomas Middleton, 1836 to 1846; John D. White, 1846 to 1854; Reason J. Bennett, 1854 to 1856; Benjamin W. Whiteman, 1856 to 1858; John McColgins, 1858 to 1862; John P. Louiso, 1862 to 1866; William Norris, 1866 to 1870; Alfred J. Parker, 1870 to March, 1874; Peter L. Wilson, March, 1874, to September, 1874; George W. Drake, 1874 to 1878; Enos B. Fee, 1878.

CLERKS OF COURT.

Abraham Shepherd, 1818 to 1824; William Shepherd, 1824 to 1830; James Finley, November term, 1830, to 1833; George W. King, 1833 to August term, 1841; A. C. Stewart, pro tem., August term, 1841; John H. Blair, pro tem., October term, 1841, and until 1849; Gideon Dunham, 1849 to 1855; Hervey McKibben, 1855 to 1858; R. H. Higgins, 1858 to November term, 1864; R. C. Mitchell, 1864 to 1867; R. H. Higgins, 1867 to 1876; John Lafabre, 1876 to 1882; C. C. Blair, 1882 ———.

PROSECUTING ATTORNEYS.

Thomas Morris, March, 1818, to July, 1818; George W. King, 1818 to 1826; Alexander Gilliland, 1826 to 1835; A. Liggitt, 1835 to 1836; Thomas H. Linch, 1836 to 1838; David G. Devore, 1838 to 1840; Andrew Ellison, 1840 to 1843; C. F. Campbell, 1843 to 1845; William Boyle, 1845 to 1849; C. W. Blair, 1849 to 1852; C. A. White, 1852 to 1855; John G. Marshall, 1855 to 1856; William H. Sly, 1856 to 1858; William F. Wylie, 1858 to 1860; Thomas T. Taylor, 1860 to 1863; E. C. Devore, 1863 to 1867; J. W. Bailey, 1867 to 1870; W. J. Thompson, 1870 to 1875; C. A. Linn, 1875 to 1877; W. W. McKnight, 1877 to 1879; John R. Moore, 1879 to 1883.

SHERIFFS.

William Butt, 1818 to 1823; Robert Allen, 1823 to 1827; James Loudon, 1827 to 1831; Jeremiah Purdum, 1831 to 1835; John H. Blair, 1835 to 1839;

John J. Higgins, 1839 to 1843; William Shields, 1843 to 1847; Thomas Middleton, 1847 to 1849; William P. Allen, 1849 to 1853; Henry Young, 1853 to 1855; John S. Foster, 1855 to 1857; Charles Oursler, 1857 to 1861; Alfred Jacobs, 1861 to 1865; William C. Howard, 1865, part of a year; George R. Shields, October, 1865, to 1866; William C. Howard, 1866 to 1867; George R. Shields, 1867 to 1871; John Dillen, 1871 to 1875; John T. Brady, 1875 to 1877; John Carrigan, Sr., 1877 to 1881; J. P. Helbling, 1881 ——.

RECORDERS.

Amos Ellis, 1819 to 1822; David Ammen, 1831 to 1834; Charles White, 1834 to 1837; David Crawford, 1837 to 1843; Thomas M. Barker, 1843, gave up the office July, 1847; David Ferrier, July, 1847, died May 28, 1850; James T. Morgan, May 28, 1850, to 1853; John P. Biehn, 1853 to 1856; John H. Dugan, 1856, died August, 1857; Robert H. Higgins, August to October, 1857; James T. Morgan, 1857 to 1863; Amos T. Ellis, 1863 to 1866; John F. Black, 1866 to 1869; John W. Evans, 1869 to 1875; Grandison Pinckard, 1875 to 1881; George Ellis, October, 1881 ——.

COUNTY SURVEYORS.

James Pilson, 1818 to 1824; William Wall, 1824 to 1828; Jephtha Beasley, 1828 to 1836; John D. White, 1836 to 1844; Abraham Sallee, 1844 to 1847; William Tatman, 1848 to 1854; Abraham Sallee, 1854; William Hays, 1854 to 1857; O. P. Ralston, 1857 to 1864; J. R. C. Brown, 1864 to 1867; James M. Stivers, 1867 to 1872; Jacob H. Bower, 1872 to 1878; H. L. P. Vance, 1878 to 1881; G. L. McKibben, 1881 ——.

COMMISSIONERS.

James Wells, 1818 to 1820; John Lindsey and William White, part of 1818; Walter Wall, 1818 to 1824; John Evans, 1818 to 1826; William W. Clark, 1820 to 1822; Robert Breckenridge, 1822 to 1824; William Humphreys, 1824 to 1830; John Lindsey, 1824 to 1825; William Leggitt, 1825 to 1830; Robert Allen, 1826 to 1829; Henry Chapman, 1829 to 1835; Joseph Stableton, 1830 to 1833; James McCall, 1830 to 1833; John Lindsey, 1833 to 1837; William Parker, 1833 to 1834; J. D. McCarty, 1834 to 1835; Jephtha Beasley, 1835 to 1836; Noah Ellis, 1835 to 1841; Samuel Kerr, 1837 to 1843; Samuel Ross, 1836 to 1839; Richard W. Ditto, 1839 to 1845; Michael Pindell, 1841 to 1844; Joseph Dugan, 1843 to 1846; William Norris, 1844 to 1848; William P. Allen, 1845 to 1846; Robert W. McClain, 1846 to 1853; James F. Thompson, 1846 to February 29, 1848, resigned, and Peter L. Wilson appointed to fill vacancy; Charles W. Reed, 1848 to 1852; John Wright, 1850 to 1856; Shary Moore, 1852 to 1855; Joseph Briant, 1853 to 1855; Thomas Hunter, 1855 to April, 1857, removed from county, and Samuel M. Blair, who was appointed to fill vacancy, served until 1861; William F. Pickrell, 1855 to February, 1856, resigned, Shary Moore, appointed; David Keithler, 1856 to 1857; William B. Logan, 1857 to 1864; John Brady, 1856 to 1863; James Campbell, 1861 to 1864; James F. Davis, 1863 to 1866; Huston Bare, 1864 to 1868; Samuel McNown, 1866 to 1869; C. A. Linn, 1867 to 1870; James Campbell, 1868 to 1871; William Fulton, 1869 to 1875; William Vance, 1870 to 1873; Peter L. Wilson, 1871 to 1874; John Wright, 1874 to 1879; James L. Burger, 1874 to 1877; W. B. West, 1875 to 1881; Daniel McConn, 1877 to 1880; Jefferson Fite, 1879 to 1882; Farmer Thornton, six months, 1879; N. W. Neal, 1880; John A. Jennings, 1881; Ross Wise, 1882.

HISTORY OF BROWN COUNTY.

JUDGES OF THE COURT OF COMMON PLEAS.

The President Judges under the old constitution who presided in the courts of the circuits which embraced Adams and Clermont Counties, before the organization of Brown, were Francis Dunlavy, of Warren; John Thompson, of Fayette; and Joseph H. Crane, of Butler. On the organization of Brown County, it was first placed in the Seventh Circuit, along with Butler, Warren and Hamilton. Joshua Collett, of Warren, was President Judge from 1818 to 1820; John Thompson, of Fayette, 1820 to 1824; Joshua Collett, of Warren, 1824 to 1826; George P. Torrence, of Hamilton, 1826 to 1833; and John M. Goodenow, of Hamilton, 1833 to 1834. In 1834, the circuit consisted of Brown, Clermont and Hamilton, and John W. Price was Judge from 1834 to 1841; Owen T. Fishback, of Clermont, 1841 to 1848; George Collins, of Adams, 1848 to 1851; Shepherd F. Norris, appointed to fill the vacancy caused by the resignation of Collins, 1851 to 1852.

Under the present constitution, the Judges of the Court of Common Pleas in the First Subdivision of the Seventh Judicial District, embracing the counties of Brown, Adams and Clermont, have been:

Shepherd F. Norris, of Clermont, 1852 to 1861; Thomas M. Lewis, of Clermont, February to October, 1861; Thomas Q. Ashburn, of Clermont, 1861 to 1876; David Tarbell, of Brown, 1872 to 1882; Allen T. Cowen, of Clermont, 1878 to 1883; D. W. C. Loudon, elected in 1881.

ASSOCIATE JUDGES.

Joseph N. Campbell, 1818 to 1823; James Moore, 1818 to 1825; William Anderson, 1818 to 1832; William White, 1823 to 1824; James Finley, 1824 to 1831; Robert Breckenridge, 1825 to 1836; David Johnson, 1831 to 1845; Hugh B. Payne, 1832 to 1838; Benjamin Evans, 1836 to 1840; Henry Martin, 1838 to 1852; Micah Wood, 1840 to 1847; John Kay, 1845 to 1851; Isaac Carey, 1847 to 1852; Benjamin Sells, 1851 to 1852.

PROBATE JUDGES.

John J. Higgins, 1852 to 1855; John W. King, 1855 to 1857 (resigned); James H. King, 1857 to 1858; D. W. C. Loudon, 1858 (resigned); J. H. Marshall, 1858 to 1859, James P. Fyffe, 1859 to 1861 (resigned); Charles F. Campbell, 1861 to 1862; William P. Allen, 1862 to 1864; Charles F. Campbell, 1864 (died); George W. King, 1864; David Tarbell, 1864 to 1870; S. H. Stevenson, 1870 to 1876; J. P. Biehn, 1876 to 1882; George P. Tyler, 1882.

MEMBERS OF THE GENERAL ASSEMBLY.

Before the organization of Brown County, Adams and Clermont Counties were represented in the Legislature by the following-named persons, several of whom resided within the present limits of Brown County.

The Senators from Adams were Joseph Darlington, 1803; Thomas Kirker, 1804 to 1814; Abraham Shepherd, from 1815 to 1817; Nathaniel Beasley, 1818.

The Representatives from Adams were Thomas Kirker, Joseph Lucas, William Russel, 1803; Abraham Shepherd, Thomas Waller, Phillip Lewis, Jr., 1804; Abraham Shepherd, Phillip Lewis, Jr., 1805; Abraham Shepherd, Phillip Lewis, Jr., James Scott, 1806; Phillip Lewis, Jr., Alexander Campbell, Andrew Ellison, 1807; Alexander Campbell, Andrew Ellison, 1808; Alexander Campbell, Abraham Shepherd, William Russell, 1809; Abraham Shepherd, John W. Campbell, 1810; John Ellison, Jr., William Russell, 1811–12; John Ellison, Jr.. John W. Campbell, 1813; Nathaniel Beasley, John Ellison, Jr., 1814; John W. Campbell, Josiah Lockhart, 1815; Thomas Kirker, John

Ellison, 1816; William Middleton, Robert Morrison, 1817; Robert Morrison, G. R. Fitzgerald, 1818.

The Senators from Clermont were William Buchanan, 1803; James Sargent, 1804, 1805 and 1806; David C. Bryan, 1807, 1808 and 1809; William Fee, 1810; Levi Rogers, 1811 and 1812; Thomas Morris, 1813 and 1814; John Boggess, 1815 and 1816; John Pollock, 1817, 1818 and 1819.

The Representatives from Clermont were R. Walter Waring, Amos Ellis, 1803; Robert Higgins, 1804; Jonathan Taylor, 1805; Thomas Morris, 1806; John Pollock, 1807; Thomas Morris, William Fee, 1808; John Pollock, Amos Ellis, 1809; John Pollock, Thomas Morris, 1810, 1811; John Pollock, George C. Light, 1812; John Pollock, John Boggess, 1813, 1814; John Pollock, 1815; Henry Chapman, Gideon Minor, 1816; Henry Chapman, John Denman, 1817; Henry Chapman, J. Shaw, 1818.

The following is the list of the Senators and Representatives of Brown County since its organization:

1820—Senator, Nathaniel Beasley; Representative, George Edwards.
1821—Senator, Nathaniel Beasley; Representative, George Edwards.
1822—Senator, Alexander Campbell; Representative, George Edwards.
1823—Senator, Alexander Campbell; Representative, George Edwards.
1824—Senator, Thomas Kirker, district, Brown and Adams; Representatives, George Edwards and John Cochran.
1825—Senator, Abraham Shepherd, district, Brown and Adams; Representative, Thomas L. Hamer.
1826—Senator, Abraham Shepherd, district, Brown and Adams; Representative, John Cochran.
1827—Senator, John Fisher, district, Brown and Adams; Representatives, John Cochran and George Edwards.
1828—Senator, John Fisher, district, Brown and Adams; Representatives, John Cochran and Thomas L. Hamer.
1829—Senator, John Cochran, district, Brown and Adams; Representative, Thomas L. Hamer.
1830—Senator, John Cochran, district, Brown and Adams; Representatives, George Edwards and Nathan Ellis.
1831—Senator, Joseph Riggs, district, Brown and Adams; Representative, James Pilson.
1832—Senator, Joseph Riggs, district, Brown and Adams; Representatives, George Edwards and Alexander Campbell.
1833—Senator, James Pilson, district, Brown and Adams; Representative, James Loudon.
1834—Senator, James Pilson, district, Brown and Adams; Representatives, James Loudon and Nathan Ellis.
1835—Senator, John Patterson, district, Brown and Adams; Representative, Joseph Stableton.
1836—Senator, John Patterson, district, Brown, Adams and Scioto; Representatives, John Glover, James Loudon, district, Brown, Adams and Scioto.
1837—Senator, Charles White, district, Brown, Adams and Scioto; Representatives, William Kendall, Nelson Barrere, district, Brown, Adams and Scioto.
1838—Senator, Charles White, district, Brown, Adams and Scioto; Representatives, Joseph Leedom and John H. Blair, district, Brown, Adams and Scioto.
1839—Senator, John Glover, district, Brown, Adams and Scioto; Representatives, Joseph Leedom and John H. Blair, district, Brown, Adams and Scioto.
1840—Senator, John Glover, district, Brown, Adams and Scioto; Repre-

sentatives, R. B. Harlan, R. W. Clarke and Gideon W. Dunham, district, Brown, Clermont and Clinton.

1841—Senator, Griffith Foos, Jr., district, Brown, Clermont and Clinton; Representatives, Stephen Evans, Reader W. Clark and Gideon Dunham, district, Brown, Clermont and Clinton.

1842—Senator, James Loudon, district, Brown, Clermont and Clinton; Representatives, David Fisher, Thomas Ross, Moses Rees and John D. White, district, Brown, Clermont and Clinton.

1843—Senators, William H. Baldwin and James Loudon, district, Brown, Clermont and Clinton; Representatives, William Roudebush, James F. Sargeant and John D. White, district, Brown, Clermont and Clinton.

1844—Senators, James Loudon and William H. Baldwin, district, Brown, Clermont and Clinton; Representative, John J. Higgins.

1845—Senator, Douty Utter, district, Brown and Clermont; Representative, John J. Higgins.

1846—Senator, Douty Utter, district, Brown and Clermont; Representative, Andrew Ellison.

1847—Senator, Benjamin Evans, district, Brown and Clermont; Representative, James H. Smith.

1848—Senator, Benjamin Evans, district, Brown and Clermont; Representative, James H. Smith.

1849—Senator, William Howard, district, Brown and Clermont; Representative, Enos B. Fee.

1850—Senator, William Howard, district, Brown and Clermont; Representative, Enos B. Fee.

Under the constitution of 1851, Brown and Clermont constituted District No. 4.

1852—Senator, Sanders W. Johnston; Representative, John McClanahan.
1854—Senator, Michael H. Davis; Representative, William P. Allen.
1856—Senator, Chambers Baird; Representatives, John T. Games, James F Thompson.
1858—Senator, William P. Kincaid; Representatives, J. S. West, J. T. Richardson.
1860—Senator, Chilton A. White; Representative, Newton A. Devore.
1862—Senator, John Johnston; Representative, E. B. Fee.
1864—Senator, James Loudon; Representative, Andrew Evans.
1866—Senator, S. F. Dowdney; Representative, Elijah M. Fitch.
1868—Senator, S. F. Dowdney; Representative, Elijah M. Fitch.
1870—Senator, Learner B. Leeds; Representatives, John G. Marshall, John C. Waldron.
1872—Senator, Learner B. Leeds; Representative, John C. Waldron.
1874—Senator, H. V. Kerr; Representative, Eli B. Parker.
1876—Senator, H. V. Kerr; Representative, E. Flaugher.
1878—Senator, George P. Tyler; Representative, Eli B. Parker.
1880—Senator, George P. Tyler; Representative, Robert Cochran.

MEMBERS OF CONSTITUTIONAL CONVENTIONS.

Convention of 1850—James Loudon and John H. Blair.
Convention of 1873—Chilton A. White.

REPRESENTATIVES IN CONGRESS.

From the organization of the State Government in 1803 until 1813, Ohio had but one Representative in the Lower House of Congress—Jeremiah Morrow, of Warren County.

From 1813 to 1823, the State consisted of six Congressional districts. The Second District consisted of Clermont, Adams, Highland, Clinton, Fayette and Green Counties, of which John Alexander, of Green, was the Representative from 1813 to 1817, and John W. Campbell, of Adams, from 1817 to 1823.

From 1823 to 1833, the Fifth District consisted of Brown, Adams, Clinton and Highland, the Representatives of which were John W. Campbell, of Adams, from 1823 to 1827, and William Russell, of Adams, from 1827 to 1833.

From 1833 to 1843, the Fifth District consisted of Brown, Clermont and Adams, the Representatives of which were Thomas L. Hamer, of Brown, from 1833 to 1839, and William Doane, of Clermont, from 1839 to 1843.

From 1843 to 1853, the Seventh District consisted of Brown, Clermont and Highland, the Representatives of which were Joseph J. McDowell, of Highland, from 1843 to 1847; Jonathan D. Morris, of Clermont, from 1847 to 1851; and Nelson Barrere, of Adams, from 1851 to 1853. In the autumn of 1846, Thomas L. Hamer was elected from this district, but he died before taking his seat.

From 1853 to 1863, the Sixth District consisted of Brown, Clermont, Adams and Highland, the Representatives of which were Andrew Ellison, of Brown, from 1853 to 1855; Jonas R. Emrie, of Highland, from 1855 to 1857; Joseph R. Cockerill, of Adams, from 1857 to 1859; William Howard, of Clermont, from 1859 to 1861; Chilton A. White, of Brown, from 1861 to 1863.

From 1863 to 1873, the Sixth District consisted of Brown, Clermont, Highland, Clinton and Fayette, the Representatives of which were Chilton A. White, of Brown, from 1863 to 1865; Reader W. Clarke, of Clermont, from 1865 to 1869; and John A. Smith, of Highland, from 1869 to 1873.

From 1873 to 1879, the Seventh District was composed of Brown, Highland, Adams, Pike and Ross, the Representatives of which were Lawrence T. Neal, of Ross, from 1873 to 1877; and Henry L. Dickey, of Highland, from 1877 to 1879.

From 1879 to 1881, the Eleventh District consisted of Brown, Clermont, Adams, Highland and Clinton, the Representative of which was Henry L. Dickey, of Highland.

On February 26, 1880, the Legislature restored the apportionment of 1872. The Representative of the Seventh District from 1881 to 1883 is John P. Leedom, of Adams.

Truly yours
Andrew Evans.
(DECEASED.)

PART IV.

TOWNSHIP HISTORIES.

TOWNSHIP HISTORIES.

CHAPTER I.

PLEASANT TOWNSHIP.

Pleasant Township was one of the original five into which Clermont County was divided at the first term of the Justices' Court of General Quarter Sessions, February 25, 1801. The other four were Williamsburg, Ohio, Washington and O'Bannon. The records do not reveal its original boundaries or extent, but it is certain that it included much more territory than it contains at present. Washington Township seems to have intervened between it and the river, extending to the old Adams County line, and Lewis Township formed from the eastern end of Washington in 1807, included a part of what is now Pleasant. By the successive formation of neighboring townships, Pleasant has been reduced to its present limits. Its location is in the south central part of the county. Lewis and Clark Townships bound it on the west, Scott and Franklin on the north, and Jefferson and Union on the east; the Ohio forms its southern boundary. Its outlines are irregular. The meandering waters of White Oak Creek encompass it on the west, and the greater part of its eastern line is marked by the channel of Straight Creek, which is straight only in name. In size, it is third in the county. Perry exceeds it considerably, and Lewis slightly. Its area is 23,153 acres. Topographically, it exhibits all the varieties of surface, from almost perfectly flat and level farms to the deepest and most precipitous gorges found in this region. From the narrow valley that lines the Ohio, the hills rise to an altitude of several hundred feet, but break away within a few miles into rolling land, which, toward the northern part of the township, becomes level. The little runs that drain the township into White Oak and Straight Creeks have cut their way through the limestone strata to a great depth, forming ravines so steep that they are scarcely approachable in places. The soil is usually argillaceous. Along the hills, the limestone, which enters into its composition, yields it the strength which makes it most excellent tobacco land. On the ridges in the southern part of the township, it possesses great fertility, but becomes more shallow and less productive toward the north. Ash, walnut, maple, sugar, linn and other varieties of timber grow luxuriantly in the southern portion, but toward the north, save in the bottom lands of the streams, the prevailing types were poplar, beech, hickory and oak. Tobacco is extensively raised, and may be considered the leading crop, though corn and wheat are also produced in considerable quantity. Much land in the northern part is used for hay and grass.

EARLY SETTLERS.

Foremost among the pioneer settlers of Pleasant Township were the Ellises. By general assent, they are regarded as the first white men to make a permanent settlement in the township. Five brothers—Samuel, James, Hezekiah, Jeremiah and Nathan Ellis—in 1796, floated down the Ohio in a keelboat from Virginia, in quest of Western homes. Nathan landed at the site of Aberdeen, and subsequently became its founder, and a prominent citizen. Jeremiah and Hezekiah both settled on Eagle Creek, while James and Samuel continued on down the river in the boat until they reached a point one and a half miles above the mouth of White Oak Creek. Here they stopped and agreed to locate. They retained possession of the boat, using it for a residence until they had erected log cabins. The cabin of James was built farther down, within half a mile of the White Oak Creek bridge. James here kept one of the earliest distilleries in the county. He raised a family of children, but none of them or their posterity now live in that vicinity. Samuel soon puchased the land he settled on, and rose to opulence and prominence. He was tall in stature, possessed a vigorous constitution and indomitable energy. He died in his ninety-third year. At his request, he was interred on the spot where he first pitched his tent on landing in the Northwest Territory in 1796, but so close was it to the shore of the river that subsequently it became necessary to remove the remains to another portion of the farm. His children were James, Noah, Abram, Samuel, Matilda, Mary, Christina, India Ann, Nancy and Rebecca.

William Lyon was among the noted pioneers of Pleasant Township. He was born in Ireland, of Scotch-Irish parentage, his ancestors having settled in Ireland under Cromwell. In early life, William left his well-to-do parents and crossed the ocean. So deeply was he attached to them, however, that he three times visited them across the briny deep. He worked at a furnace in Philadelphia awhile, then wandered westward, and became a chain-carrier for Duncan McArthur in the surveys of Southwestern Ohio. During this time, he made his home in Mason County, Ky. From his earnings as surveyor he purchased several tracts of land, and spent a portion of his time on them. He was married to Anna Brown, in Kentucky, several years prior to 1800, and immediately emigrated to his land in the southern part of this township. He had made a little clearing and planted it in corn the spring previous, but, while away, Samuel Ellis' cattle broke in and totally destroyed the crop. While preparing the ground and planting the corn, he slept in a hollow log, returning to Kentucky once a week for provisions. Mrs. Lyon possessed the characteristics of a true pioneer woman. She was reared amidst the dangers of Indian warfare in Kentucky, and the training she received developed the qualities of self-reliance and energy in a high degree. For a number of years after he came to this township, Lyon would boat his farm products to Cincinnati. He was once detained longer than he had expected to be, when the harvest season was at hand. The wheat ripened and must be reaped, but laborers would not work without money wages, and of this rare article Mrs. Lyon did not then possess a dollar. Engaging hands, however, when the cutting could be delayed no longer, and her husband had not yet appeared, she promised that they should be paid, and, ripping open all her beds, she packed the feathers and conveyed them on horseback to Cincinnati, where she sold them and returned in time with the money. Mr. Lyon was a genuine Irishman. He inherited the relish of his countrymen for the flowing bowl, and in early life indulged freely, but afterward became a total abstainer. He was whole-souled and generous-hearted, and, in consequence of bailing his neighbors and paying their debts, as he seemed destined almost invariably to do, his finances were often seriously embarrassed. He possessed the art of coining wealth from his business enterprises, but it melted away under his liberality and the obligations he assumed for his acquaintances. His old age was passed, however, in comfortable circumstances, and he died in 1837. His wife survived him many years. His family consisted of only two children—Mary and Robert. Mary left no posterity, but the descendants of Robert still till the soil of their pioneer ancestor.

Capt. Daniel Feagins was noted not only for being among the earliest settlers in the county, but as well for his prowess as a hunter and Indian scout. He was a native of Virginia, and served through the whole of the Revolutionary war as Captain. About 1786, he emigrated from Loudoun County, Va., to

PLEASANT TOWNSHIP.

Kentucky, descending the Ohio in a boat with several other families, and intending to proceed as far as Salt River. On their way down, they landed at Limestone, now Maysville, Ky., and Capt. Feagins there met Simon Kenton, with whom he was acquainted in early life. Kenton protested against their going farther down the river, declaring that it was almost certain the boat would be attacked by the Indians at a certain point farther down. At his solicitation, Feagins landed, and moved his family and effects out to Kenton's Station, near where Washington now is; the balance of the boat continued down the river, and, as Kenton had predicted, they were attacked by the savages, and all aboard massacred. Feagins remained at Kenton's Station several years, and located a large quantity of land in what is now Bracken County, Ky., but, by some mishap, he afterward lost nearly all of it. In about 1796, he moved to within sight of what is now Georgetown, locating just south of the corporation, on the farm adjoining the fair grounds. He had a family of nineteen children. Several of them settled around him, among them Daniel, Fielding and Susan. The last was the sixth child of this large and noted family, and was born May 25, 1780. She was married, April 20, 1803, to Edward Thompson, and lived near Georgetown. Her death occurred in 1855. Capt. Feagins, after opening his farm here, with his sons and their families moved to Paint Creek, in Fayette County, Ohio. So accustomed had he become to the perils and freedom of the extreme frontiersman's life that he was only content when living remote from other human habitations, surrounded only by the wildnesses and solitude of the Virginia forests. He died of "cold plague," in July, 1815, while on a visit to his old home near Georgetown. His wife, Violet, survived him many years, and lived to be a centenarian. Daniel and Fielding, their eldest children, both settled near Georgetown. While in Kentucky, they were trained in Indian warfare by Simon Kenton, and both participated in many of the expeditions against the savages; they served as spies on the river to watch the hostile movements of the red men in times of apprehended danger from attack. While Fielding was once hunting deer with his brother-in-law, Absalom Craig, near Augusta, Ky., they were fired upon by a party of Indians, and Craig was killed just as he was stooping to drink from a spring of water. Fielding, abandoning his horse and venison, with difficulty made his escape. His hatred against the Indians was ever afterward bitter and intense. The body of Craig was recovered, and found to be horribly mutilated. While Fielding Feagins was living near Georgetown, two roving Indians made their appearance at his cabin and asked for food. Fielding recognized on one of them the shot-pouch that Absalom Craig had worn when he was killed. Instantly, the deep slumbering animosity against them was aroused to a high pitch, and, following them when they departed from the cabin, he raised his unerring rifle and shot one, instantly killing him. The other Indian escaped. This occurred on the west bank of White Oak, about a mile west from Georgetown, between the upper mill and the county infirmary. Fielding buried his victim on the banks of the stream, and threw his rifle into the water. He kept the matter a secret until after the flood of 1832, when the skeleton of the savage was washed out. While on a visit to his sister, Mrs. Thompson, he narrated the circumstance. The residence of Daniel Feagins, Jr., stood about where the Georgetown Presbyterian Church now is. Capt. Feagins had obtained a patent for a large amount of land in the Lawson Survey, February 23, 1807, and the following deeds are found, bearing subsequent dates, from himself and Violet, his wife: March 27, 1807, 100 acres to William White; September 24, 1807, to James Roney, Jr., and John Roney; October 13, 1807, to Joseph Van Meter's executors, 541 acres in the southeast corner of the Lawson Survey, " for and in consideration of the sum of five pepper corns to them the said Daniel Feagins and Violet, his wife, in hand paid;" May 30, 1808, to Allen Woods, 200 acres in the Lawson Survey, adjoining lands previously sold to John Roney; October 17, 1808, also to Allen Woods, fifty acres in addition to his first purchase. Robert Lawson's Survey, No. 2,523, was entered on Military Warrant No. 1,921.

In 1798, Walter Wall settled on the Heath Survey of 1,000 acres in the south central part of the township. He was from Western Pennsylvania, where he had been engaged in farming, but, for a few years prior to his emigration here, he had been occupied largely in trading and boating between Pittsburgh and Cincinnati, it then being an incident of a farmer's life to seek a market for his products. He also operated a heavy distillery in Pennsylvania, and supplied Cincinnati with a fair share of its early popular beverage. He descended the Ohio in a flat-boat, bringing with him his family, a few farm implements, a team and several cows, and landed at the mouth of Straight Creek. Thence he followed an Indian trail northward to his purchase. He had bought the entire Heath Survey, the southern half for himself, and the northern half for the heirs of his deceased brother. They came years after and settled on it. Mr. Wall was accompanied here by two Yankees, names unknown, who were only sight-seeing in the then great West, and by John Davis, his brother-in-law, who settled just east of Wall's place, and who was drowned a few years later in Kentucky. The flat-boat that conveyed them down the Ohio was taken apart by Mr. Wall, hauled to his land and converted into a camp, which served them for shelter for a week or two, until his log cabin was completed. His two New England acquaintances remained with him till he was safely domiciled in his new home, and then returned East. Mr. Wall and his wife, whose maiden name was Elizabeth Applegate, reared a large family of children here, all of whom, except the eldest four, were born in this township. Hester was married to George Vanemon, and removed to near Dayton, Ohio; Abigail remained at home; Sarah died in girlhood; James remained a resident of the farm until his death; Aseneth, the wife of James Young, went to Illinois; Daniel became a citizen of Clermont County; Mary was the wife of Henry Pierce, of this township; John resided in the northwest part of the county; Elizabeth, wife of John Pierce, resided in Clermont County; William still occupies, the old place; and Ann was the wife of Griffith Leming, of Clark Township. Mr. Wall died about 1857, at the age of eighty-three years; his wife survived him several years. In the rude, pioneer times, he was Justice of the Peace for many years.

The elections of Pleasant Township were held for awhile at Mr. Wall's house, but were discontinued there at the request of Mrs. Wall. Certain citizens, it seems, were accustomed to take a good supply of whisky on the day of election to the house, and sell it to the voters there assembled. As election day was regarded as a holiday, the consequence was that a large number of the citizens became so intoxicated that they were unable to get away at nightfall, and remained in a semi-conscious or totally unconscious state upon the premises. The compassionate housewife was loath to leave them to the mercy of the elements without, and provided them with sleeping room in the cabin, but the discomfort arising from this became unbearable, and the elections were held elsewhere.

Jacob Berry and Thomas Berry, two brothers, were living on the Ohio, near the mouth of White Oak, prior to 1798. They were of Irish descent, and born in Pennsylvania, powerful in physique, but without any considerable means. Jacob Berry, in 1798, married Elizabeth Shick, the daughter of Lewis Shick, a German, who had settled just across the line of Pleasant in Scott Township, and he and his brother Thomas took a lease on Walter Wall's land, where they remained about fifteen years. At the expiration of the lease, Jacob purchased a farm near the northwest corner of the township, and spent the remainder of his life there. He had a family of eleven children, the only survivor of whom is Samuel, the second child. He lives on the old place, at the advanced age of eighty-one years. Thomas Berry bought a farm, after he quit the Wall place, just north of Georgetown, but died there soon after. A Mr. Crab had settled on the Jacob Berry place temporarily very early, built a cabin and made some little improvements, but he remained but a short time, and went nobody knows whither.

In the history of Clark Township, by O. P. Ralston, mention is found of Christian Smith, a native of Holland, and a man educated for the Catholic priesthood but subsequently leaving the church, who is said to have came to the site of Georgetown in 1797 or 1798, with Feagins, Ayres, Roney and others, and located on land in the Robert Lawson Survey, No. 2,523. He had settled at Washington, Ky., in 1790. Mr. Ralston states that Daniel Feagins built a "still-house" on the branch, a short distance below Smith's house, a few years after their arrival, and that Smith, in consequence, traded his farm to William Still for 100 acres of land in what is now Clark Township, and removed to the latter in 1804. Smith was an accomplished scholar, and, after his removal to Clark, held numerous offices of trust. He was often importuned to teach school, but would never consent to do so, although he would generously impart such information as he could to those in search of knowledge. He died in Clark Township in 1832, aged eighty-four years. He is said to have owned the first sheep ever brought to this part of the country.

In 1801, Robert Curry settled on the James Curry Survey of 1,000 acres just south of Georgetown. Maj. James Curry was an officer in the Revolutionary war, and this survey was made on his warrant for military services, but, not caring to tempt the wilds of the far West himself, he disposed of the tract to his nephew, Robert, who, in 1799, left his home in Rockingham County, Va., with his wife, Phœbe, and several small children, and with his young brother, John, for the seat of their purchase. They remained two years in Bourbon County, Ky., where John was accidentally killed, and, in 1801, arrived at their future home. Mr. Curry built his cabin in the southern portion of the survey, across the road but not far from the present residence of Mrs. Parker. Until this time, there had been no white occupant on this survey. He spent four years in clearing and improving the place, but had accomplished comparatively little when he was cut off by a sudden attack of fever, leaving his wife with a family of helpless children to struggle on in the wilderness as best she could. Mrs. Curry survived until July, 1822. They had six children—Abigail married William Florer and moved to Kentucky; Mary became the wife of William Moore, of this township; Lucinda married Elijah Evans, and died on the home farm in 1860; William moved to Clermont County; Rebecca married Andrew Moore, and Phœbe, Samuel Colvin, both of Pleasant Township.

Henry Ralston, a relative of Mrs. Curry, came about the time the Currys did, settling just east of them, where John T. Brady now lives. He was originally from Rockingham County, Va., but, like most of the settlers, had lived awhile in Kentucky before coming here. He arrived here so late in the spring that the neighbors, who had finished their spring work, "turned in" and helped him clear a piece for corn. He had a family of six children—John, Robert, Jesse, James, Mrs. Abbie Derough and Mrs. Phœbe Jolly.

His brother, James Ralston, settled in the western part of the township, on the V. M. Loudon place.

Issachar Davis was originally from Pennsylvania, directly from Kentucky.

In 1802, he settled in the western part of the township, where his grandson, A. W. Davis, now lives. He was a cabinet-maker by trade, and, besides farming, he worked at carpentering, millwrighting and the undertaking business. He lived here over thirty years and died. Seven sons grew to maturity and married—John, Isaac, William, Issachar, Thomas, Solomon and Samuel. One or two daughters died young.

Jonathan Moore was living on the J. McMichael place, north of Davis, in 1801. He was for a long time Elder in the Presbyterian Church. Joseph Foor, John T. Parker and Stephen Calvin were also early settlers in this vicinity. Mr. Moore was one of the first settlers to possess a team, and took great pride in having a good one. He raised a family in the township, then sold his farm and moved West.

Three brothers, George, John and Daniel Evans, became residents of the township about the close of the last century. They hailed from Jessamine County, Ky., and came separately. George landed on the site of Ripley, where he remained a year and cleared off a portion of the land that now forms the town. He then made a purchase on the Tibbs Survey, two and a half miles southeast from Georgetown, and removed there with his wife, Jane, and two children, John and Anne. He at once made a clearing for his crops, but, when the survey of his purchase was made, learned, to his dismay, that the clearing was not on his land. A second purchase was made, which included the improved ground. Mr. Evans remained here during life. He was twice married, and raised a large family of children. Daniel settled in this neighborhood, but John bought 250 acres off the O'Bannon tract, four miles southwest from Georgetown, where he died in 1828 or 1829, leaving a family of nineteen, whose descendants still own land here.

James Woods was born in Ireland, and emigrated with his family to Washington County, Penn. He afterward removed to Kentucky, and, very soon after, 1800, to Pleasant Township, settling on what is now the William Pangburn farm, about four miles below Georgetown. He possessed deep religious convictions, and was an earnest, God-fearing man. His children were Allen, Nathaniel, Samuel and Anna. Samuel lived in Lewis Township; Allen, on the site of Georgetown; Nathaniel, on the home farm, below Georgetown. Nathaniel, when not engaged in farming, boated a great deal on the river, trading produce, pork, flour, etc., at different points on the Ohio and Mississippi, often extending his trip as far south as New Orleans, and then walking back overland to his home. He was married, in Pennsylvania, to Jane Stewart, and raised his family on the farm, where he died about 1837. His wife survived him many years.

Abel Rees was from Kentucky. He settled, at a very early date, just east of Georgetown, on the farm now owned by H. L. Penn. Though he had little or no education, he was a man of mark in his community. In connection with his farm duties, he labored at the forge and anvil, and wrought out many axes for his neighbors. He was a hearty Methodist—one of the few who devoted themselves heart and soul to its welfare. Preaching was often held at his cabin, and his generous hospitality would never permit those who had gathered there from long distances for the purpose of hearing the word of God preached to return home without first dining at his table.

James Parker was an early settler on the Potterfield Survey, near the river. He came to the place a young married man, and remained the rest of his life. His nationality was purely Irish.

Hugh Maklem and his son John, a youth of about eighteen years, settled on a place of 150 acres in the southern part of the Tibbs Survey, now owned by L. Heizer, in 1802 or 1803. Hugh was a native born Scotchman, who left his

Benj. F. Dyer

home a widower and crossed the ocean with his only child, John. They tarried in Virginia a short time, then came westward to Kentucky, and, after sojourning there for a year or two, crossed the river and settled here. He was a mill-wright by trade, but tilled the soil here. For a few years, he and John kept bachelor's hall, but John probably tired of this mode of living, for, in 1809, he took unto himself a wife, Martha Parker, and raised a large family. He spent his life in this township, and died July 4, 1875, aged ninety years.

John Roney was one of the pioneers, though the exact date of his arrival is not known. He was a native born Irishman, and emigrated to America about 1790. Remaining on James River, Virginia, a few years, he found his way to Limestone, now Maysville, Ky., and lived there and at Washington, Ky., for some time, then settled just east of Georgetown. He afterward bought the place he settled on from Mr. Fagins. He was a millwright, but gave his entire attention, after his removal to this township, to developing his farm. His children were James, John, Frank, Rosa and Andrew. James settled on White Oak, in Lewis Township, and became a miller; John remained on the home place, where his son, John, still lives; Frank and Rosa settled six miles north of Georgetown; and Andrew died a young man, from the effects of a rattlesnake bite.

Israel Jennings brought his wife, Charity, and family of twelve children to Brown County from Bardstown, Nelson Co., Ky., in 1802 or 1803. His father's family was farming on Long Island during the Revolutionary war, and, when the British took possession, was given the alternative of swearing allegiance to the King or losing the property. Preferring the latter, the family moved to Chatham, N. H., and, subsequently, Israel came West. He lived a year in Union Township, then purchased 200 acres off the north part of the Rhea Survey, about two miles east of Georgetown, and moved to it. No clearing had been made on the place, but the deserted cabin of some previous squatter was found, and Mr. Jennings made it his habitation for eighteen months, when he built himself a substantial log cabin. He had been a house carpenter, but devoted himself here exclusively to farm pursuits, and died at the home place at a good old age. William Jennings, the youngest child, still lives on the site of the old cabin, at the advanced age of eighty-two years.

His neighbors, who came shortly before or very soon after him, were Stephen Colvin, who lived north on the S. Huey place; Jacob Slack, on Camp Sun; John Sharp; John Dye and James, his son, on the Rhea Survey; Thomas Scott, on Straight Creek; and John Day, on the Rhea Survey. The latter came in 1804, and died in 1857.

Other early pioneers, who settled on what is now the Ripley pike, were James and Francis Thompson, two brothers. They were from Pennsylvania; were Presbyterians; good, steady citizens; raised families and removed to Indiana. James taught several terms of school in this township. James Hamilton came very early in the century; married a daughter of James Woods, but, after awhile, moved farther west. Gideon Dunham settled about two miles south of Georgetown. He made the first improvements on the William Frost place; was from Pennsylvania, and removed from this township to Perry Township, becoming a pioneer there. Francis Daugherty settled on what is now the W. B. Frost farm. He emigrated from Pennsylvania, and, after remaining in Pleasant Township a number of years, continued westward to Illinois. He was a stone mason, and built most of the rude stone chimneys for the pioneers in his vicinity. He had two sons—Mayberry and James. Andrew Kirkpatrick was a pioneer squatter. He made a clearing a short distance east of Olive Chapel, but changed his habitation frequently. When last heard from, he was in Indiana. James Calvin occupied the Joseph Shepard place.

He belonged to a family of "great fighters" in pioneer times, and, when the country in this vicinity became settled, he removed West. James Kilpatrick was one of the earliest shoemakers. He was a tall, spare individual, and, when not at work at his bench, engaged in agriculture. He afterward removed his family to Illinois.

Levi White, a native of Pennsylvania, emigrated to Kentucky, and there, near Dover, married Elizabeth, daughter of Amos Wood, and, not a great while later, removed to this township, buying and settling on a little farm where Jesse Printy now lives, on "Free-Soil" Ridge. Both he and his eldest son, Amos, were under arms in the war of 1812, in Capt. Shumalt's company. Soon after, he sold his place and removed to Indiana, but, not liking that country, he returned to this county and spent the remainder of his life here. He died about 1819, and his widow survived him about forty years. They had eleven children, only two of whom are now living.

It would be impossible to mention all the early settlers of the township within the limits of this work, even if their names and history could be learned. Each succeeding year, after the emigration once began, brought more and more citizens into the township, until it was fully occupied. Many of those who came first, becoming habituated to the free and independent life of pioneer backwoodsmen, felt the restraint of the increasing settlement around them, and again sought more Western homes, probably continuing to ride on the advance wave of civilization until overtaken by death. As has doubtless been noticed, the earliest settlers, almost without exception, lived awhile in Kentucky, and a greater part of them had emigrated thither from Virginia and Pennsylvania.

Among the settlers who came somewhat later than most of the above, may be mentioned Moses Hicks, John T. Parker, Jacob, Aaron and Valentine Burgett, James Colvin, Robert Sample, Samuel Ross, Edward Hall, Robert Wright, Robert King, Fielding Martin, James McKinney, John Liggett, John Mefford, Joshua Jordon, Thomas Rodgers, Abram Sells, Archibald Tweed, John Forsyth, Robert Forsythe, the McKees, the Dugans, Amos Mitchell and Edward Thompson.

MILLS.

The earliest pioneers were obliged at first to convey their corn to mills across the river; but, as time advanced, little horse mills, then water mills, were started in different localities in the county. The two streams that confine Pleasant Township on the east and west each had a number of mills on their banks, but the greater number of them were built on the other sides of the streams, and do not belong properly to this township. On Straight Creek, William Huggins built a mill in Pleasant Township in an early day, in the northern part of the Merriweather Survey. It contained two run of buhrs, and was resorted to very generally for a long time. Besides a large overshot wheel, which communicated the water-power, a tread-wheel was attached and made available during low water, so that the mill was in operation during the greater part of the year. Besides milling, Mr. Huggins gave his attention to farming, blacksmithing and wagon-making. He disposed of the mill to William Barnes. It afterward passed through a number of hands, and was finally abandoned, owing to the diminution of the water supply and the introduction of steam mills.

Another early mill on this stream was built on the now Charles Abbott farm, by John Thompson. After his death, it was purchased by John Abbott, who operated it for awhile, then, in 1832 or 1833, rebuilt it, and afterward sold it to his son, Lewis Abbott. It still grinds a little corn occasionally. Mr. Abbott also built a saw-mill here about 1820, and for many years after converted logs into building lumber.

On White Oak, Henry Pierce built a mill and put it in operation in May, 1842. A fulling and saw mill had previously occupied this site, built by his father. Three run of buhrs were attached to the mill—two for wheat and one for corn. Mr. Pierce not only did custom work, but bought large quantities of wheat, made flour of it, and shipped the flour down the Ohio. He died in 1881. During the last few years, little grinding has been done, and the mill has been practically abandoned.

The Thompson Mills, on White Oak, just west of Georgetown, were at one time the most important in the county. They are three in number, within a quarter of a mile of each, two in this township, the upper one in Lewis. About 1843, Edward Thompson built the upper and lower mills, and purchased the middle mill, which was built at an early time by John Davidson. It was owned successively by a number of millers before reaching Mr. Thompson's possession, among the proprietors being Samuel Horne and James Sidwell. Mr. Thompson gave each of his three boys a mill, the upper to James, the middle one to John and the lower one to William. The lower one, known as the Tunnel Mill, cost in its erection $2,500. Its water supply is received through a long tunnel, excavated at an immense expense through a hill. It is now owned by Frederick Shuster, and is run by both water and steam power, and does an important business. These three mills bought a vast amount of grain at one time, extending their purchases even into Highland County. The flour made from it was shipped down the river.

CEMETERIES.

Public cemeteries were unknown for awhile after the first settlers arrived, and, as the members of a family died, they were usually interred in a secluded spot selected on the place. Family burial-grounds thus became common, and are found on almost all of the first-settled farms in the township. One may be seen on the Pangburn farm, another on the Berry place. The Ellises, Dugans, Lyons, Heizers, and many others, each buried their dead in this way. On Wall's farm, adjoining the old Straight Creek Presbyterian Church, is a large cemetery, where rest the remains of many of the old pioneers. Another is adjacent to Hilman's Church.

ROADS.

Within Pleasant Township may be found some of the best roads in the county, and here also are some which in point of roughness, it would seem difficult to surpass. These latter, however, are not public thoroughfares, but roads opened mainly for the convenience of farmers in getting to the better roads. In the southern part of the township, several descend to the rocky bed of some little run, down a precipitous and rock-jutting hill, and follow its meanderings over exceedingly stony beds to the river. Four well-graveled pikes lead from Georgetown in the four directions of the compass, affording excellent means of ingress and egress to any part of the county. In very early times, a State road from West Union to Cincinnati passed through the northern part of the township, entering from the east, on the Charles Abbott place, and crossing the township a little north of Georgetown. It was traveled very extensively, being the main road from Cincinnati eastward. Along its route were scattered public inns at no great distance apart. One of these was in Pleasant Township, on the old J. Roney place, in the extreme northeast part of the township. It was kept by Amos Moore, and was a noted rendezvous for settlers in early times. General musterings and various other kinds of gatherings assembled here. Indians frequently passed over the road from 1807 to 1810. Soon after Georgetown was laid out, the road was vacated for the most part, and the road passing east and west through Georgetown substituted for it by the County Commissioners.

SCHOOLS.

Where the first school in Pleasant Township was held, who taught and who attended it, can never be known. The oldest residents in the township are the youngest members of the second generation of settlers, and their memories are all the light we have in ascertaining something of the early schools, and their remembrance does not and cannot extend back to the period when schools were probably introduced, in their most rudimentary form, it is true, in the pioneer settlement. A Mr. Holmes and Mr. Bartlett, the latter a New Englander, were among the first pedagogues who swayed the ferule and held in subjection the untamed youngsters of this township. Robert McCurdy taught in a schoolhouse about 1818, that stood in the woods near Hilman's Church. He lived in that vicinity, and afterward moved West. School was held in the same house for a few years, and then in a schoolhouse where now stands the church. Alexander Innis was another pioneer teacher, teaching in various localities as opportunity offered. He was from Pennsylvania; married a Miss Kilpatrick here, and moved West. One of his schools was on the Pangburn farm about 1820; another, on the William Wall place, taught probably in 1819. The first schools were held in deserted cabins, stables, or any kind of building that could be obtained; but in a few years, most neighborhoods built houses for school purposes, the rude character of which has been made familiar to all. A blacksmith shop, owned by William Boles, on the Wall tract of land, was utilized for educational purposes very early. Another early schoolhouse stood on John Roney's farm, just below Georgetown. At present, there are nine subdistricts in this township.

CHURCHES.

The earliest preaching in Pleasant Township of which any knowledge is had consisted of a series of Shaker religious meetings at John Sharp's house, in the northeastern part of the township, on Camp Run. H. Steigler now owns the farm where they were held. William Jennings remembers distinctly that he could hear the wild shouting and dancing in the meetings from his father's cabin, a half-mile or more distant. Mr. Sharp and his entire family, except one son, Benjamin, joined the community, and removed with it to Warren County. One of the boys, Nathan, rose to an important office of trust in the sect, and disappeared with a large amount of money in his possession. The meetings were very successful, for quite a number of families became members of the community. They were mostly, however, from the upper waters of Straight Creek, beyond the limits of this township.

From the best authority available, it is believed that the Presbyterian Church was next to organize a society within the bounds of Pleasant Township as now constituted. Soon after the earliest settlements in the county were made, a Presbyterian congregation was organized in Union Township, on Straight Creek, near the place where the Georgetown & Ripley pike crosses that stream. In a few years, however, it was discovered that most of its members lived way to the west of the church in Pleasant Township, and, for their convenience, the place of worship was changed to a more central location. A spot was selected adjacent Wall's Cemetery, near the center of the Heath Survey, about three miles south of Georgetown. Here a log church was built, about 30x30 in size. The exact date of its erection is not known, as the church records cannot be found, and old members differ somewhat regarding it, but it is thought to have been about 1810. As the membership increased, the building became too contracted in its limits for the comfort of the congregation, and an extension was built to it. Among its prominent early members were George, John and Daniel Evans, John Wiley, James and Francis Thompson, Jonathan Moore, John and James Parker, Walter Wall and John Maklem. When the old double log church became dilapidated, one was built farther to the west, near the road, and near the present "Free-Soil" Church, occupied by a Methodist society. During all this time, the church retained its original name, Straight Creek, though removed several miles from that stream. Rev. James Gilliland was an early minister. Other names cannot be obtained. The Presbyterians who settled in Georgetown, as that town began to grow, joined the Straight Creek Church, and finally became a preponderating element in it. About 1829, the name was changed to Georgetown Presbyterian Church, and the place of holding services removed there, though preaching was jointly held at the old church for a number of years. The subsequent history of the church is given under the mention made of the Georgetown churches.

The Free Presbyterian Church of Straight Creek was organized at the residence of Samuel Martin, October 25, 1848. Its organization was due to a division in Georgetown Church on the question of slavery, which, about that time, produced a disruption of the Presbyterian Church very extensively. Application for dismissal from the Georgetown Church was made by Samuel Martin, William J. Evans and others, for the purpose of organizing a "Free" Presbyterian Church. The application was not granted, and the applicants for dismissal withdrew informally. The records of the Georgetown Church for December 9, 1848, contain a resolution, striking the following names from the roll of membership for withdrawing and organizing a Free Church: Samuel Martin, Elizabeth Martin, John G. Martin, William J. Evans, Louisa Evans, Sarah Evans, Thomas Salisbury, Martha Salisbury, Rachel A. Salisbury and Mary Ferris. Others who united with these to organize the new church were Absalom King, Mary King, Victor M. King, Alexander Salisbury, Margaret Salisbury, Isaiah Salisbury, Elizabeth Salisbury, John Salisbury and John Parker. In 1850, Rev. D. M. Moore was the regularly installed minister. Rev. A. B. Frazier succeeded, serving from 1852 to 1854. Following him the pastors have been A. Thompson, 1855-56; James W. West, 1857-65; Joseph Swindt, 1866-67; and W. J. Rogers, 1868. Immediately after the organization, measures were taken to build a church. Six leading members subscribed $50 each, and $200 more was raised by general subscription, and a modest frame structure, about 36x48, still standing, was speedily reared. The congregation, small at first, attained a numerical strength of seventy-five. A flourishing Sabbath school was maintained. In 1869, the church consolidated with the Georgetown Church, though for some time afterward services were regularly conducted at the "Free-Soil" Church.

The Elders of the church were Absalom King, D. E. Parker, Samuel Martin, William Evans, William Matthews, James Cumberland and Newton Parker. In the records of the session, the following appears: "July 15, 1863 —In consequence of the Morgan raid, it was impossible to have a meeting of the session at the time appointed."

About three miles southeast from Georgetown, in the northeastern part of J. Tibbs' Survey, stands Hilman's Church. This has been one of the oldest Methodist preaching-places in the county. The first structure on the spot that was used exclusively for religious services was a hewed-log meeting-house, of goodly dimensions for those days, erected as early as 1812. Joseph Hilman donated the land on which it stands, and the church has ever since been known by his name. He was a very zealous Methodist, though his education was meager in the extreme. His faculty for accumulating property was well developed, and his good deeds to the church took the shape of substantial offerings, rather than speech-making. The work of constructing the building was performed by him, Abel Rees, Israel Jennings, Isaac Waters and several others. Besides these mentioned, Arter Boxwell, John Dye and perhaps a few more were the first members. Rev. Chinneth, William Finley, John Finley and Rev. Dobbins conducted services here among the earliest. In after years, the old church was torn down and its materials used in building a schoolhouse on an adjacent to. Meetings were continued here regularly for a number of years, then for a few years they were partially discontinued; but about thirty years ago, under the ministry of Rev. Zachariah Wharton, the old-time fervor was restored, and has been kept glowing ever since.

Services have been conducted in the schoolhouse once in two weeks by the Georgetown ministers. In December, 1881, Rev. Jonathan Verity opened a protracted meeting, which resulted in greatly swelling the membership of the class. About the 1st of April last, this people determined to erect a house of worship. A subscription paper was circulated, and as a result a neat frame edifice, 32x44, costing in all about $1,500, was dedicated June 8, 1882. The membership is now forty-nine; the Class-Leaders, John Jennings and William Brady. A successful Sabbath school has been held during summer months for a number of years.

What is known as Straight Creek Methodist Church, several miles south of Georgetown, was organized by Rev. Henry Miller, during his two years' pastorate at Georgetown, from 1876 to 1878. Rev. Edward McHugh succeeded him for two years, and the two years' period of labor of Rev. Jonathan Verity has just closed. Services are held in the old Presbyterian Church. Warren C. Rees was the first Class-Leader, succeeded by Joseph Foor. The present membership is forty-two. A flourishing Sabbath school is maintained. The society is a branch of the Georgetown Church, and has services each alternate Sunday.

Olive Chapel, a neat, modest meeting-house, on the Ripley pike, about three miles south of Georgetown, is the home of a Christian or New-Light congregation, which was organized at Woods' Schoolhouse March 12, 1871, by Elder C. W. Garoutte, assisted by Elders T. W. Graybill and Walker Mefford, with a membership of nine, viz., Josiah Perry, Isaac Purdum, Hannah Purdum, Robert Cochran, Sallie Cochran, Nancy Wallace, Nelson Tucker, Lewis Jones and John Heiser. The church was built the same year. Elder J. W. Mefford was the first pastor. Those succeeding him have been J. P. Daugherty, Rufus McDaniel, G. C. Hill, Jacob Hawk, William Pangburn, William Bagley and J. Bowman. The membership increased rapidly, and soon reached several hundred. During the last several years, however, the effectiveness of the church has been seriously impaired by church dissensions. A Sunday school is conducted during the summer.

A small society of the African Methodist Episcopal Church worships in a schoolhouse several miles east of Georgetown, on Straight Creek. Revs. Dillon, Alfred March and Robert Davis have been recent ministers.

VILLAGES.

Unfortunately, the records of Pleasant Township have been lost or destroyed, and its official history, consequently, cannot be noticed. Georgetown is the only village within its limits, though one or two attempts to establish towns in other portions of its territory have been made. The site originally selected for the county seat of Brown County lay partly within this township and partly in Jefferson. The Pleasant Township portion was just south of where Straight Creek enters the township, on the Charles Abbott place. Bridgewater was the name given to the embryo city, comprising 100 acres of land, forested, but platted and staked. A term of court was held here in the soli-

PLEASANT TOWNSHIP. 385

tude, in a hewed-log house; a deserted cabin, which had stood on the Fielding Martin place, a half-mile to the westward, had been hastily torn down and removed to the seat of justice one Saturday, roofed on Sunday, and, the following morning, was in readiness for the tribunal that issued its mandates of law from the midst of most dismal surroundings. But one term of court is said to have been held here, as narrated elsewhere in this volume, and the virgin forests, preserved intact, bore no evidence that this locality had once been the seat of justice of a populous and wealthy county.

Another attempt at town making was made by Amos Mitchel shortly before Georgetown was laid out. The spot he hoped would attain great municipal power and renown he dubbed Monroe, in honor of the then President. It was located on his farm, two miles below Georgetown, on the Ripley pike, now occupied by Mrs. Frost. A plat of forty-six lots was laid out, surrounded and intersected with all the necessary streets and alleys, but it came to naught. It is not known that a single house was erected there, save the cabin of its proprietor.

GEORGETOWN.

December 10, 1819, Allen Woods appeared before Henry Chapman, a Justice of the Peace in and for Brown County, and acknowledged a plat of Georgetown, containing twenty-two lots and two outlots, including nine acres and forty-two poles, located on a part of Robert Lawson's Survey, No. 2,523, and described as follows on the record: "The land contained in the above plat begins at a post near a white oak; thence west sixty-five poles to a walnut post; thence north twenty-two poles and eight-tenths to a walnut post; thence east sixty-five poles to a walnut stake, near a branch; thence south twenty-two poles and eight-tenths to the place of beginning." Lots 2 to 10, 20 to 24, and 26 to 38, inclusive, were four poles wide and eight poles deep; Lot 11, same depth, and one and nine-tenths rods front; Lots 12 to 19, five rods front and six rods deep; Lot 25, two and eight-tenths poles front and eight poles deep. Main street, running north and south, was three poles wide and twenty-two and eight-tenths long; Apple street, same length, two poles wide; North street, one and eight-tenths poles wide, twelve long; Main alley, one pole wide and eight long. Lots 29 and 30 contained respectively 200 and 281 square poles.

May 15, 1820, Henry Newkirk and James Woods made large additions, increasing the whole number of lots to 138, extending Main street and laying out Main Cross street three poles wide. The public square, containing 144 square poles, is in Newkirk's Addition, which was much the larger of the two. An outlot of four acres south of Main Cross street, at its eastern terminus, was occupied at the time by a tanyard. Lots 31 and 138, at the west side of the Newkirk Addition, were donated "for the use of a public school and a meeting-house for public worship."

James Woods' Second Addition was laid out September 27, 1821, "beginning at a stake in the line dividing the lands of Abel Rees and myself," etc.

Henry Newkirk's Second Addition was platted on the following day—September 28, 1821—on the south side of his former addition, extending the existing streets and alleys. He says, in his deed of the property, "All the streets and alleys herein described is set apart as public ground, with an exception of the privilege to citizens of the town to make walk pavements on the borders of the streets, not to exceed seven feet, to and of which I hereby relinquish all my right, title and interest for the purposes before and herein expressed."

Abel Rees made an addition September 27, 1821; Andrew Donaldson,

July 30, 1822; Thomas Jennings, May 19, 1842; John G. Marshall, February 28, 1867; C. A. White, April 19, 1867; and John Wills, date not given, made the latest addition, at some time within the past three or four years.

The following are copies of papers which accompanied the report of the Commissioners appointed to locate the seat of justice of Brown County. The report will be found elsewhere in this volume, together with a full account of the county seat contest:

No. 1.—I do oblige myself to make sufficient title to the within bounded fifty acres of land, provided the seat of justice be fixed at Georgetown, for the county of Brown, for the sum of $5 per acre, to be paid me out of the proceeds of the sale of the lots, as witness my hand this 12th day of May, 1821.

Attest: J. EGBERT,
JAMES BAKER.
HENRY NEWKIRK.

No. 2.—I do oblige myself to give a donation to the county of Brown, the lot No. 50, or 51, for the purpose of a jail, whichever the Director, when appointed, may see best, provided the Commissioners may select Georgetown for the permanent seat of justice.

Attest: WILLIAM B. JOHNSON,
J. EGBERT.
HENRY NEWKIRK.

No. 3.—I do hereby oblige myself to make a good title to the within bounded lot of land, being ten acres and one-half of the donation, provided the seat of justice is placed at Georgetown, reserving one-half acre to surround my house that is on said land. As witness my hand this 12th day of May, 1821.

Attest: J. EGBERT,
ALLEN WOOD.
JAMES WOOD.

No. —.—I do obligate myself to make a sufficient title to the within bounded forty acres of land, should the seat of justice for Brown County be placed at Georgetown, and this forty acres be received, in preference to the thirteen acres proposed, for the sum of $7 per acre, to be paid out of the proceeds of the sale of the lots, the choice of the two lots to be left to the Commissioners.

Attest: J. EGBERT,
JAMES BAKER.
ABLE REESE.

No. 4.—I do hereby oblige myself to make a sufficient title for the within bounded thirteen and a half acres of land, for the sum of $7 per acre, provided the seat of justice for Brown County be placed at Georgetown, to be paid out of the proceeds of the sale of lots. As witness my hand this 12th day of May, 1821.

Attest: J. EGBERT,
JAMES BROWN.
ABLE REESE.

No. 5.—I do obligate myself to furnish the county of Brown with a suitable house to hold the court in until one can be built for that purpose, provided the Commissioners do select Georgetown for the seat of justice for said county.

WILLIAM B. JOHNSTON.

The condition of this obligation is such that we, the undersigned, being the persons to whom the donations for the public buildings for the county of Brown, provided the seat of justice for said county be established at Georgetown, were made payable, do obligate ourselves, our heirs, executors, administrators and assigns, and every of them, to the county of Brown, should the present Commissioners establish the seat of justice at Georgetown, to build a stone jail, thirty-six feet by twenty-two feet, containing two good fire-places; two stories high, each story to be eight feet in the clear, the first story three feet thick, the second two and one-half; the foundation sunk two feet under ground, with eighteen-inch thick floor of stone, all to be laid in lime and sand, and each floor to be laid with timber ten by twelve inches thick, set on edge close together and covered with plank two inches thick, spiked down, and to be ceiled with the same with four rows of spikes in each wall, and ceiled overhead in the same manner. There is to be a stone partition through the middle, from top to bottom, two feet thick, ceiled with two-inch plank and spiked in the same manner as aforesaid, and a partition to cut off five feet for an entry off of one end, leaving a room at the same end for a dungeon, seven by fifteen feet in the clear. Said partition is to be of stone, two feet thick, ceiled as the other walls, and a pair of stairs to raise from the entry, giving convenience by two doors to the rooms above; the outer door to come in at the entry and two other doors to give convenience to the two rooms below; the upper doors to be made double, of oak, and well united; the lower doors to be of oak plank, double, well ironed with sheet iron and riveted, with sufficient lock to each door, and four windows of twelve lights in front, and three of six each, well grated with iron. The whole to be under a good joint shingle roof, all of which is to be done in a sufficient workmanlike manner. And we further obligate ourselves to furnish 200,000 brick for the court house, delivered in said town in the kiln. In testimony whereof

Respectfully
E. Flaugher.

PLEASANT TOWNSHIP.

we have hereunto set our hands this 9th day of May, one thousand eight hundred and twenty-one.

Attest: J. EGBERT,
WILLIAM B. JOHNSTON.

HENRY NEWKIRK,
JOHN CAMPBELL,
JOHN WALKER,
JAMES BAKER,
JAMES McKINNY.

In the issue of the *Benefactor* (published at Levanna, or, as the name is often spelled, Levana) for June 7, 1821, the following notice appeared:

Take Notice, that on Thursday, the 7th day of June next, there will be a public sale of lots in Georgetown, the seat of justice for the county of Brown, Ohio. Those wishing to purchase can probably then suit themselves better than at any other future sale, as the lots intended to be offered are situated near the public square. Terms will be made known at the commencement of the sale by the proprietor.

May 21, 1821.
HENRY NEWKIRK.

It seems, from the paragraph which here follows, that Mr. Newkirk's death occurred within a short time after the publication of this notice. The notice appeared the last time on the day of sale, having been published three weeks. The paper in which it appeared was subsequently removed to Georgetown, and its name lengthened to the *Benefactor and Georgetown Advocate*, and, at the latter place, was edited by Thomas L. Hamer, who subsequently won fame in the National Congress and on the fields of Mexico, his career being cut short by the hand of death before the Mexican war had ended. He is mentioned at length elsewhere in this volume.

By an act of the Legislature of Ohio, passed January 1, 1822, Thomas Morris and William Middleton were appointed Trustees for the town of Georgetown, "with authority to receive conveyances from James Woods, Abel Rees, and the administrators of Henry Newkirk, for their several tracts of land adjoining Georgetown, which lands are given by said Woods, Rees and Newkirk for the use and benefit of the county of Brown, in the State of Ohio; and by the act aforesaid, the said Thomas Morris and William Middleton were empowered to sell and dispose of all lots by them laid off on said land, for the best price that could be had for the same, either at public or private sale, and to convey any lot or lots laid off on said land to any purchaser, and that the deed thus made should vest in the purchaser all the title of the said James Woods and Abel Rees, and the title vested in the said Henry Newkirk at the time of his death." The Trustees appointed accepted the trust reposed in them, and gave bond for the faithful performance of their duty, receiving deeds of warranty from Woods, Rees, and the administrators of Newkirk, on the 21st day of August, 1823. They subsequently made many deeds to purchasers, in each of which the facts concerning their appointment, etc., were fully set forth.

Gen. Robert Lawson, who owned the 2,000-acre survey on which Georgetown stands, and two of 1,000 acres each in what is now Lewis Township, was a veteran of the Revolution; although he never settled here, he was in the vicinity often, and was wont to linger around the numerous still-houses and dram shops which abounded, and is said to have been in a state of intoxication a great portion of the time. When in that condition, he was often induced to make bargains for the sale of portions of his land, which he probably would never have done if he had been sober. He had no family, and it is not now known what became of him. At one time, in the vicinity of Georgetown, there were twenty-four distilleries. This statement is made on the authority of Peter L. Wilson. Esq., who says that one of them, which was located near his present home in Pleasant Township, east of Georgetown, was kept by John Hall, and was a well-known rendezvous for military men during the war of 1812. They met at the place and held many a carousal, and perhaps some of them fought harder and with greater zeal in settling some private difficulty at the distillery than they ever did in the cause of their country. Besides this distillery, Hall was also proprietor of a small store, and had a small "horse-mill" for grinding corn.

Albert Woods, a native of Ireland, came to America when small, and located in the State of Pennsylvania. Upon arriving at maturity, he was married in that State, and removed to Georgetown, Ky., where he resided several years. Soon after Ohio was admitted into the Union, he came to it and located on the site of Georgetown; this was probably in 1803 or 1804. His son, Allen Woods, Jr., now a retired physician of Clermont County, was born here in October, 1805, and a daughter, now the wife of Peter L. Wilson, Esq., was born on the old place in 1808. In the latter year, Mr. Woods purchased 200 acres of land of Daniel Feagins, in Robert Lawson's Survey, No. 2.523, and it was upon a portion of this purchase that he laid out the original town in 1819, probably naming it from his former residence, Georgetown, Ky. His home at Georgetown, Ohio, was at the lower end of the village. He has been numbered among the dead for many years. His son, James Woods, who laid out an addition to the town in 1820, settled here with his father, and there were several other children.

When Peter L. Wilson came to Georgetown, in the winter of 1821-22, there was not a finished building in the place. Two or three brick houses were up, but their gable ends were open, and a frame house stood where the city bakery now is, having in it timber enough for two ordinary structures. There were then but five or six houses in the town in the aggregate. A frame building stood opposite the northeast corner of the court house square, where McKibben now is, but it was never finished. The boys were accustomed to playing ball against its walls. It was intended for a two-story edifice, but was finally demolished. Very few people had their homes in Georgetown at that day. Others were coming and going, but the attractions of the place were not yet sufficient to induce new-comers to locate. James Woods lived in a small log cabin on Outlot 21, in the northwest part of town. Allen Woods lived at that time in a log house which stood near the northwest corner of Main and Main Cross streets, a little in the rear of the brick building which he put up on the corner, and which constitutes a part of the old American Hotel. Mr. Wilson subsequently removed the log building. William Butt was living here at the same time, in a small, unfinished frame house where the Methodist Episcopal Church now stands. He published the first newspaper in the place, and held several responsible offices—Sheriff, Auditor, etc.

The following items are taken from numbers of the early Georgetown papers which have been placed at our disposal:

The *Benefactor and Georgetown Advocate*, edited by T. L. Hamer, and printed and published by James J. Smith, in its issue of February 23, 1824, besides giving some account of the county seat controversy, contained numerous advertisements. Victor Larimer advertised a quantity of "Kanhaway" salt for sale, offering to take cash, hides, wheat or pork for pay, the wheat to be delivered at Lemon's mill, and the pork at his house. "The pork must weigh at least 150 pounds to the hog." A notice to the creditors of the estate of Joseph Reynolds, deceased, late of Jackson Township, ordered them to bring in their accounts for settlement. Philip D. Brumbaugh announced that he had commenced the "tailoring business in Georgetown, at the house lately occupied by John Campbell as a tavern, corner of Main and Cherry streets, where all orders in the line of his profession will be duly attended to." John A. Smith, under date of February 5, 1824, advertised that he had "commenced the hatting business in Georgetown, in the brick building north of Allen

Woods' tavern, on Main street." Several petitions for divorce were published in this number, and the proprietors of the paper were in want of an apprentice to the printing business.

In the issue of the same paper for March 3, 1824, William Butt or David Johnson offered for sale Lots 95 and 96 in Georgetown, and S. H. Stitt "respectfully informs the public that he now keeps and intends keeping private entertainment in Georgetown, where his stables are good and well-furnished, and everything else necessary for the accommodation of man and horse in as good order as the nature of the country will admit. The terms as reasonable as can be expected."

June 14, 1824, the paper contained several new advertisements, among others that of a new pressing machine, "applicable to the pressing of apples, tobacco, oil, cotton, cheese, cloth, hay, the packing of flour, etc." Franklin Shaler was the patentee, and T. L. Hamer was agent in Georgetown. The cheese presses could be obtained of James Firriers, near Georgetown. The following " regimental order " was promulgated: "The commissioned officers of the Second Regiment, Fourth Brigade and Eighth Division of Ohio Militia, whose commissions are not recorded as the law directs, are hereby ordered to forward the dates to the Adjutant for that purpose, on or before the 20th of June inst. Commandants of companies will forthwith give notice to the commandant of the regiment of all vacancies there may be in their respective commands, that orders for elections to fill the same may be issued. By order of the Colonel. James Loudon, Adjutant."

August 9, 1824, under the heading, " Union Inn," Jonathan Vandike "Respectfully informs his friends and the public generally that he has opened a house of public entertainment in Georgetown, in the large frame house formerly occupied by D. Johnson & Co., and lately by F. White & Co., as a store. His house is large and convenient, his beds are new and good, and his table shall be furnished with the best the country affords and the nature of the times will admit. His stabling is entirely new, large and convenient, and shall be constantly supplied with good hay, corn and oats, and shall be attended by an experienced ostler, and he is determined to spare no pains to give general satisfaction to all those who may favor him with their custom. His charges shall be proportioned to the present pressure of the times." The marriage notice was published of Charles White, of Georgetown, and Miss Amanda Morris, of Bethel, Clermont County, the ceremony occurring August 1, 1824.

August 19, 1824, T. L. Hamer advertised that he wanted a good distiller, single man preferred, to commence business in October following. The publishers of the paper, in September, offered to take wheat on subscription, and were at the same time paying $2\frac{1}{2}$ and 3 cents per pound for clean cotton and linen rags.

October 1, 1824, William Butt, Postmaster at Georgetown, advertised the following list of letters lying unclaimed in the office: John Archer, Charles Black, John Burton, John Bartley, James Baker, Benjamin Bowman, James H. Bowler, Lewis Coon, William Chrozan, John Derrough, Edwin Dyer, Alexander Goodwin, Elisha Gilbreath, Rees Hughes, John Hirons, David Henderson, Amos Hook, Thomas Jolly, Thomas Johnston, James Knight, William King. Margaret King, John Lany, Henry Lyman, M. C. Mount, Charles S. Mount, John McBeth or Christopher Day, Josiah Pricket, Samuel Ross, Lazarus Ross, Abel Sturdevant, Robert Stewart, Aaron Wilson, James H. Wall, Joseph Waddle, Thomas Williams, James Wall.

In the *Castigator* for July 31, 1832, published at Georgetown, the following parties advertise their business in that place: Dr. George B. Bailey, new stock of drugs and medicines; office in the "brick building on the corner, south of the court house, and adjoining Mr. White's tavern." James Ferrier, Colonel Second Regiment, Fourth Brigade, Eighth Division, Ohio Militia, ordered commissioned and staff officers of the regiment to meet on the public square at Georgetown, August 30, armed and equipped, for the purpose of officer drill. Thomas Paskins, blacksmith, shop "fronting the northeast part of the public square, opposite to Col. James Ferrier." D. Johnson & Co., new goods. Clark, Higgins & Co., new goods, first quality Muskingum salt, by the barrel. John Walker, saddler and harness-maker, returned to Georgetown and opened a shop on south side of public square, "one door west of Charles White's tavern, and adjoining Dr. Bailey's apothecary shop."

The next issue of this paper contained orders from the commanding officers of the First Rifle Battalion, Fourth Brigade, Sixth Division, and the Third Regiment, Fourth Brigade, Eighth Division, Ohio Militia, to the commissioned and staff officers, to meet on the public square at Georgetown, August 30, for officer drill. A meeting was also appointed of the citizens favorable to an amendment of the militia law. William K. Burt had opened a tin shop southwest of the court house, in the building previously occupied by Jonathan German as a wagon shop.

In the *Democratic Standard* of Georgetown for October 31, 1839, appeared the following: "Notice is hereby given that a Brigade Court of Inquiry, for the assessment of fines on delinquent commissioned and staff officers of the Second Brigade, Eighth Division, Ohio Militia, will convene at Georgetown on Friday, the 29th day of November next, at 10 o'clock A. M. of said day. By order of the commandant of the brigade. C. F. Campbell, Inspector, Second Brigade, Eighth Division, Ohio Militia."

The advertisers at that time in Georgetown were: T. Myers and B. C. Baker, dry goods; Jacob Fowler, cabinet-maker, formerly of Cincinnati; J. M. Blair, cabinet-maker; S. Horn, general dealer—"inks and ink powders for sale;" Martin Marshall and Hanson L. Penn, law firm; D. Johnson & Co., general; J. & C. Kay, hatters; T. M. Kay, chair shop, "a short distance north of the public square;" A. C. Stewart, "Conemaugh salt;" David Crawford, groceries; Dr. George B. Bailey, office east of court house; Dr. S. W. Penn, office in second door of D. J. & A. C. Stewart's store; Hamer & Devore, law firm; Benjamin Sells, gunsmith; John Ralston wanted wheat on account; S. C. Snider, tailor, "shop on Main street, near the Georgetown Inn;" James Jacobs, wool-carding.

In the issue of July 6, 1841, David Ferrier announced that he had commenced the hatting business in Georgetown—shop on west side of Main street, three doors south of David Crawford's grocery store. J. Dorsey, "jeweler, and watch and clock maker," also had an advertisement.

May 28, 1842, J. B. Davis, proprietor of the West Union & Cincinnati Mail Stage, had an advertisement in the paper. The stage route lay from Cincinnati through Madison, Milford, Perin's Mills, Batavia, Bantam, Bethel, Hamersville, Georgetown, Russellville and Decatur, to West Union, in Adams County. The stage office at Georgetown was at William Downey's.

On Saturday evening, February 14, 1852, a meeting was held in the Methodist Church at Georgetown, and a society organized called the "Friends of Hungary," for the purpose of raising funds for Louis Kossuth, who was then in the United States, to take back for the relief of his country. The association met again on the 17th, adopted a constitution and chose the following officers: D. G. Devore, President; John McColgin, Vice President; Gideon Dunham, Treasurer; John Martin, Secretary; John J. Higgins, R. A. Bower, W. P. Allen, Directors. At this meeting the sum of $75 was raised. Kossuth had addressed a large audience at Cincinnati a few evenings before. The

PLEASANT TOWNSHIP.   393

association continued but a short time, and but little aid was rendered in the county, except at Georgetown, where subscriptions were raised amounting to over $100.

Col. Robert Higgins, a Revolutionary veteran, and the first settler where Higginsport now is, removed from the latter place to Georgetown a few years before his death, which occurred here in 1825. His oldest son, John J. Higgins, who was born at Higginsport, settled at Georgetown in 1822, and read and practiced law. He was subsequently engaged in mercantile business; served two terms as Sheriff of Brown County (elected first time in 1838); was elected to the Legislature in 1841; became the first Judge of Probate for the county in 1851, and died at Georgetown in 1857. His son, Capt. Robert H. Higgins, became an honored, prominent and respected citizen of the place, and has had a brilliant career.

Joseph Stableton lived within the present limits of the corporation, in the northeast part, years before the town was laid out. He moved from Winchester, Va., to Mason County, Ky., when a child, with his father. He was there married to Mary Purdum, formerly of Greene County, Penn., and, in 1809, came to what has since become known as Georgetown. He was a stone mason by trade, but directed his attention largely to farming. He was Justice of the Peace for Pleasant Township for about eighteen years, and his house was the scene of many an early trial. In the agitation concerning the location of the county seat, Mr. Stableton worked strenuously for Georgetown. In 1835-36, he served as State Representative, and, for many years, Infirmary Director. He raised a large family, and died in 1854, in the seventieth year of his age.

INCORPORATION AND MAYORS.

Georgetown was incorporated by act of the State Legislature February 8, 1832. The following is a nearly complete list of its Mayors to the present time: S. Glaze, 1832; John J. Higgins, 1833-35; Michael N. Ammen, 1835-36; George K. Snyder, 1836-37; Jesse R. Grant, 1837-39; J. T. Smiley, 1839-40; W. T. Galbreath, 1843-44; John T. Smiley, 1846-48; John Donaldson, 1848-50; Thomas G. Penn, 1850, died in office; unexpired term filled by John G. Marshall, who was also elected in 1851; John Martin, 1852, resigned and succeeded by J. W. King; 1854-55, Chilton A. White; 1855-56, D. A. Pomeroy; 1856-59, John Allen; 1859-60, George Kerans; 1860-61, W. J. Omsler; 1861-62, William Hays; 1862-63, D. V. Pearson; 1863-65, William H. Sly; 1865-67, William N. Pickerill; 1867-68, George W. Reeves; 1868-70, William P. Allen; 1870-72, James Wilson; 1872-78, George Kerans; 1878, J. T. Stephenson, died—Charles Fee appointed successor; 1880-82, Charles B. Fee; 1882-84, E. B. Parker.

GRANT'S BOYHOOD.

Jesse R. Grant, on the 23d of August, 1823, purchased Lot No. 18 in the Georgetown plat, for $50, of Alexander McGaffick. It had first been sold by Allen Woods to Matthew Kelly, who sold it to McGaffick. The deed to Mr. Grant was acknowledged before Thomas L. Hamer, Justice of the Peace. Mr. Grant was at that time a citizen of Brown County, having removed to Georgetown the same year, from Clermont County. October 16, 1824, he purchased Lot No. 147, for $40, of Thomas Morris and William Middleton, who had been appointed by the Legislature as Trustees for the sale of lots in the village. On the same date, he purchased Lot No. 119, for $16, of the same parties, and subsequently became a considerable landholder in the vicinity. He sold Lot 18 to Zachariah Riley February 20, 1824.

The house he lived in for many years stood on Lot 264, at the northwest corner of Main Cross and Water streets. His tannery was across Main Cross street, on Outlot 14, where Single's grist-mill now stands. Ulysses S. was but a year old when his father came to Georgetown, and his boyhood and youth were spent here until he received his appointment to West Point in 1839. He assisted his father at the tannery, but was particularly fond of horses, and was usually employed in teaming. His father was a contractor, and Ulysses hauled the stone for many of the old substantially erected buildings, among them the jail on Pleasant street, and the old market house. A prominent attorney of Georgetown recollects that, at a circus exhibiting east of the square, where Judge Biehn's residence now stands, the trick mule was produced, and the boys invited to ride it. Several young men attempted the feat, but were one after another ingloriously landed on the ground. Finally, Ulysses ventured forth, and, mounting the beast, stayed there, notwithstanding the frisky animal's attempts to unseat him. He often showed his skill in horsemanship by riding a horse at full speed, standing perfectly erect, sometimes on one foot, to the envy and astonishment of his companions. His school days were passed in the little brick schoolhouse on South Water street. He is remembered as a lively, companionable boy, frank, generous and open-hearted, a leader and favorite among the Georgetown boys, who, at that time, were not very numerous, and "hung together" well. He was studious and faithful in the performance of whatever he undertook. He was regarded as an ordinary, practical boy, of good common sense, without any special marks of genius. Jesse R. Grant was a local politician of considerable note, but so blunt and uncompromising in his nature that he provoked hostility on the part of those whose aims were not the same as Grant's. The appointment to the cadetship was secured through Gen. Hamer, then representing this district in Congress. The young cadet, when visiting his old home during vacations, and long afterward, always sought his old acquaintances. His social feelings forbade him slighting any whom he had known in early life, and many an old resident, who had perhaps almost forgotten him, was traced up and greeted with a hearty hand-shake and pleasant word.

MORGAN'S RAID.

Wednesday, July 15, 1863, was a day which will not soon be forgotten by the citizens of Georgetown. It was the occasion of the visit of Morgan's raiders, 200 or 300 strong, under the command of Col. Dick Morgan, brother of John Morgan, the famous rebel guerrilla chieftain. The detachment arrived over the Georgetown & New Hope road, about half past 9 o'clock in the morning of the day given, and remained three hours, picketing their horses around the court house square. Several loyal citizens of the town were shot at, among them Lieut. William Hannah, who was at home on a furlough from Vicksburg; no one was hit, although some received close calls from the leaden messengers. The raiders stole a number of horses in and around Georgetown, robbed the post office and took goods from various parties to the estimated value of $3,-105, as follows: C. Theis, groceries, $500; H. Stigler, groceries and three watches, $200; P. Stigler, groceries, $60; H. Brunner, boots, shoes, watch and breast-pin, $50; H. McKibben, dry goods, $30; C. Newkirk, dry goods, $1,500; Evans & Woodward, dry goods, $3050; Adam Shane, clothing, $150; C. Zaumseil, jewelry, $200; Rieves & Taylor, drugs, $50; Louis Weaver, saddlery, $60; C. Hurst, grocer, $5. About 12:30 P. M., the rebels left for Russelville, which they also raided, and proceeded thence to Decatur. The main body had passed through the northern portion of the county via Mt. Oreb and Sardinia.

THE PRESS.

The history of the press of Georgetown has been carefully prepared by Dr. T. W. Gordon, and to him are we indebted for the following, published in the Brown County Atlas: The first printing establishment brought to this county was purchased by Louden, Butt & Co., of Morgan, Lodge & Co., in Cincinnati, and a newspaper was published on it in Levanna in June, 1820, called the *Benefactor*. It continued one year at that place, when a dissolution took place between the owners, and Mr. Louden sold his interest to William Middleton, of Ripley. At that time, a man who was a silent partner is said to have entered the office, and to have taken possession of and carried away a large portion of the material, including the main screw of the press and the platten. These he hid amongst the "dog-fennel" and "Jamestown weeds," then growing abundantly in and about Levanna. No paper was issued from June, 1821, until November of the same year, when the owners tried to collect the materials thus scattered by a writ of replevin, but failed in their efforts. They, however, gathered up what they could find of the material left, and, adding new material to it, the *Benefactor* again made its appearance, conducted by Butt & Middleton; but, with the partial change of owners, it made a complete change of location, and, leaving the banks of the Ohio, it found a home at Georgetown. Its publication was continued here by Butt & Middleton until May 16, 1822, when Middleton sold his interest to Hon. Thomas Morris, of Bethel. The *Benefactor* made its appearance under the management of Butt & Morris until January, 1824, when Hon. Thomas L. Hamer became the editor, and James J. Smith the publisher. The publication was continued by these gentlemen until 1825, when it was discontinued. For a time prior to its final suspension, it was called the *Benefactor and Georgetown Advocate*. The size of the paper was 17x22 inches, four pages of four columns each, filled almost exclusively with foreign and political news and local advertisements. In 1824, it advocated the election of Gen. Jackson to the Presidency. The subscription price was $2 per annum, if paid in advance.

In August, 1826, the *Castigator*, a paper which had been published in Ripley for two years, was removed to Georgetown. Its publisher was David Ammen. It at first rather favored the election of John Q. Adams to the Presidency, but, after another paper was started in the county, which came out in July for Mr. Adams, the *Castigator* ceased to support or even favor his election, and, at a later period, became an active partisan in favor of the election of Gen. Jackson, and, on his retirement, it hoisted the name of Martin Van Buren, and fought manfully for his election. In May, 1836, Mr. Ammen sold the paper to Benjamin Morris, of Clermont County, who, on July 10 following, resold it to Mr. Ammen, losing nearly one-half the price of the establishment in the speculation. Mr. Ammen admitted his son, Michael Ammen, into partnership with him, and they published the paper until March 27, 1837, when it was purchased by a purse raised for the purpose. Its politics were changed to Whig, and John Duffy and Thomas H. Lynch continued its publication until June 21, 1837, when its name was changed to the *Political Examiner*. After the issue of a few numbers, Duffy & Pollock managed the paper, and continued its publication until after the returns of the election in 1838, when it was discontinued. At this time, Preston Sellers owned a share in the press, and he resumed its publication and continued it until August, 1839, when Mr. Lynch sold the material to C. Edwards, of Ripley, and it was removed by him to that village and used in the publication of the Ripley *Telegraph*. Mr. Sellers then procured new material, and the *Examiner* was revived by him. He continued at its head, but, in August, 1843, sold out to Isaac N. Walters, who removed the press and fixtures to Clark County. Sellers then purchased, at Xenia, the printing material from which the *Free Press* had been there published, and, removing it to Georgetown, once more had the *Examiner* in process of publication. In

March, 1845, it was removed to Ripley, and there published until August following, when the material was transferred by the Sheriff to Messrs. Shaw, and the Ripley *Bee* brought into existence.

The *Western Philanthropist* was a short-lived newspaper, that dated its existence from December 1, 1825. It was published by Daniel F. Barney, of Georgetown, and continued for a few weeks only.

The first number of the *Western Ægis* was issued June 13, 1827, by A. & J. Butt. Some time in 1828, the office and material were consumed by fire, but new material was purchased and the paper started again. In December of the same year, however, the owners removed it to Waverly, Pike Co., Ohio.

The *Democrat and People's Advocate* was published at Georgetown by Isaac N. Morris, the first number making its appearance November 12, 1833. Six months later, the proprietor sold the material to C. F. Campbell, who moved it to Ripley, and there published the *Ohio Whig*.

The next Georgetown paper was the *Democratic Standard*. Its first issue was made July 4, 1837, by Amos Derrough, who continued the publication until January 9, 1838, when he sold the establishment to L. B. Leeds and Francis M. Allen. They published it until October 12 of the same year, when Mr. Allen retired, and left Mr. Leeds in sole charge. He, in January, 1839, re-conveyed it to Mr. Derrough, who published it for one year, or until January, 1840. The *Standard* was revived August 1, 1840, by D. F. Palmer, who published it until February, 1845. Will Tomlinson then became proprietor, and published it until 1847. In that year, J. H. Smith and C. W. Blair were issuing the paper, and in 1848 J. H. Smith and T. Q. Blair. The year following, D. W. C. Johnson came into possession, and changed its name to the Georgetown *Standard*. In a short time, Mr. Johnson resold it to Will Tomlinson, who published it until 1850, when the *Standard* and the *Democrat and Journal* were consolidated.

The *Ohio Freeman* was established at Georgetown by John Duffy March 8, 1839. It was neutral in politics, and, after the publication of the thirteenth number, it was discontinued.

The *Western Wreath* sprang into existence September 6, 1845, with C. W. Blair, G. B. White and J. G. Marshall, editors, and Will Tomlinson, publisher. After ten or twelve numbers were published, the paper was purchased by Tomlinson, who was at that time proprietor of the *Standard*.

The publication of the *Western Literary Journal* was commenced at Georgetown September 8, 1849, by W. P. Stewart and G. W. King, Jr., with D. W. C. Johnson as editor. After five or six numbers were issued, P. McGroarty became editor, and William Stewart, entire owner. After the publication of twenty-one numbers, Mr. Stewart became editor and proprietor, and continued its publication. In March, 1850, he changed its name to the *Democrat and Journal*. Soon after, D. W. Johnson purchased this paper, and, forming a partnership with Will Tomlinson, of the *Standard*, the two papers were consolidated, and the *Democratic Union* thereby formed. Its first issue was dated January 1, 1851. This firm published the paper one year, when Tomlinson sold his interest to W. P. Stewart, and the paper was continued in the name of Johnson & Stewart until May, 1852, when Stewart became the owner, and continued its publication until the close of the volume, when D. W. C. Loudon and Abraham Sallee became the owners of the *Union* office. The first number of the paper issued by them was in January, 1853; they continued until September of the same year, when Sallee retired, and Loudon continued to publish the paper until May, 1854. One-half of the establishment was then purchased by S. H. Cook. In October following, Loudon sold his interest to W. H. Sallyards, who also rented Cook's share. The *Union* soon ceased to ex-

ist. It was succeeded by the *Independent American,* the first number of which was issued from the *Union* material, November 9, 1854. After the first number, Dr. Thomas W. Gordon became editor, and continued in this capacity until the nineteenth number, when he retired, and William Sallyards took charge of it, and conducted it until June 28, 1855, when J. H. Brown purchased Mr. Cook's share in the office and became editor. Mr. Sallyards sold his interest to Brown in November, 1855. The paper was continued under the name of *True Jeffersonian,* and was conducted by J. H. Brown and W. W. Young.

W. P. Stewart sought to revive the *Union,* but, after the issue of a single number, sold his prospects to John Reed and A. P. Harrison. Reed & Harrison published the first number of the *Brown County Democrat* at Georgetown, May 3, 1855, with C. A. White and G. W. Hamer, editors. August 16, White retired, and, November 22, Reed disposed of his interest to Harrison and withdrew.

August 26, 1858, the *Democratic Standard* was revived by Sallyards & Taylor, edited by J. P. Fyffe and T. T. Taylor. It made its appearance March 31, 1859, under the name of T. T. Taylor. In May following, Taylor disposed of his interest to A. R. Vancleaf, and it was then published by Sallyards & Vancleaf until Septemder 8, 1859, when Vancleaf retired. A week later, Taylor sold the paper to John G. Doren, who also purchased the *Brown County Democrat,* and consolidated them under the name of the *Southern Ohio Argus.* April 6, 1864, Doren sold the *Argus* to L. B. Leeds, who, in the fall of the same year, changed the name to the *Brown County News.* In 1868, he associated with him in its publication his son, Thomas J. Leeds, who retired in May, 1874, and since then L. B. Leeds has published the paper. Its politics are Democratic.

The publication of the *Union,* a Republican organ, was begun late in the year 1860, and continued for several years. W. H. H. Sallyards and William A. Evans were the publishers, and the former, editor.

The Georgetown *Sentinel* was started as an independent Democratic organ during the summer of 1874, by T. J. Leeds, publisher. Col. John G. Marshall was editor from its first issue until his death, when, for a time, the editorial department was managed by the publisher, and under him the paper supported R. B. Hayes for the Presidency. In April, 1877, Charles N. McGroarty purchased the *Sentinel,* and has since been its editor and proprietor. Since it has come into his possession, it has been unwaveringly Democratic.

The Georgetown *Gazette* issued its first number September 11, 1880. W. H. P. Denny was its founder, and is still its editor and publisher. It is the only Republican paper at Georgetown.

SCHOOLS.

Of the early schools of Georgetown, a great deal cannot be said; but, soon after the village was started, the usual subscription school was organized, and those parents who could afford it sent their children to obtain the meager rudiments of knowledge attainable. It is related that one of the earliest village pedagogues, who was of an experimental turn of mind, constructed a flue under the floor of his school cabin for heating purposes. The value of the invention could scarcely be said to be thoroughly tested, for it burned the schoolhouse very shortly after it was set in operation. This school building stood near where the Union Schools now are. John D. White, the father of Chilton A. White, was for many years the village schoolmaster. He came to Georgetown about 1825, from Mason County, Ky. His first schools he held in a little log cabin on his own lot, and, after the little brick schoolhouse was built—on Lot 35, Water street—he held sway there for a long time. Mr. White was also a practical surveyor, and his services in that business were frequently sought. It encroached so much upon his time that he finally gave up his school. He was elected County Surveyor, and served for thirteen years. Baldwin Summers, then instructed the Georgetown youth. He, too, came directly from Mason County, Ky., and remained in charge of the school till his death. Shepherd F. Norris, a New Hampshire lad, and a law student under Gen. Hamer, taught a term or two. When admitted, he began practice at Batavia, and was the first Common Pleas Judge elected from that district under the present constitution. Maj. William Wall taught a select school about 1826. Joseph N. White taught in the little brick schoolhouse a number of terms. He was an Eastern man, and a graduate of Oberlin College. Within the little brick house on Water street—used for a period of nearly thirty years—most of the influential men of Georgetown and vicinity to-day, as well as many others who have gone to other places, received their education. Among the latter were Gen. Grant, Gen. A. V. Kautz, Rev. Ezra Boring (a distinguished Methodist Episcopal divine), Gen. Jacob Ammen and Com. Daniel Ammen. It has not been attempted to give a complete list of the teachers. In the old schoolhouse, one room only was occupied, but in later years, during the winter, two were found to be necessary.

Soon after the passage of the new school laws, the people of Georgetown began to agitate the question of building a new schoolhouse. The enterprise was bitterly opposed by a faction, but a School Board, consisting of Chilton A. White, George D. Evans and Hanson L. Penn, favoring the new schools, was elected, and by a popular vote it was authorized to purchase a lot and erect a building at a cost not exceeding $6,000 Under this management, the present beautiful school building was erected. It contains six apartments, besides a large assembly room, for chapel exercises and other general meetings. The building, when completed, with the grounds, cost about $10,000. C. B. White was the first Superintendent. He opened the school in the fall of 1856. His successors have been, with perhaps several others, J. R. C. Brown, E. C. Ellis, William Wilson, D. W. Fite, R. C. Mitchell, Dr. Y. Stephenson, T. C. H. Vance, Miss Lizzie Barnett, O. P. Richards, James R. Conner, and T J. Curry, the present Superintendent, who has now entered upon his fifth year of service. The present School Board consists of D. V. Pearson, P. S. Moore and Christian Single. The schools are divided into six departments—first, second and third primary, intermediate, grammar and high. The last department has a three-years' course, including, reading, writing, arithmetic, English grammar, physical geography, drawing, algebra, geometry, astronomy, natural philosophy, United States history, universal history, Latin, composition and rhetoric. During the last three years, classes have graduated from the high school. A few years ago, a colored school was organized It is held in the old church building on Lot 30, Water street. The school enumeration of the district for 1882 is as follows:

White—Male, 183; female, 188; total, 371.
Colored—Male, 31; female, 29; total, 60.
Grand total, 431.

CHURCHES.

The Georgetown Methodist Episcopal Church was organized within a few years of the location of the county seat here. The earliest preaching was held in a dwelling house of Abel Rees, standing on Main Cross street, just below the C. Hurst Block. The first church, which was also the first in the village, was a small brick edifice, which stood on Outlot 16, Water street. It was erected about 1827. Among the prominent early members may be mentioned

Abel Rees and wife, Joseph Stableton and wife, John Purdum and wife, Hugh P. Payne and wife, and Thomas H. Lynch and wife. The present commodious brick house of worship was erected in 1846, and dedicated the following year by Rev. Joseph M. Trimble. Its architect was Hubbard Baker. The cupola of the new building was considered in its day a model of symmetry and beauty. The total cost of the chruch was about $6,000. Thomas L. Hamer and Hanson L. Penn were the heaviest contributors to its erection. Other members and friends of the church who subscribed liberally were David G. Devore, George W. King, Benjamin Penn, John Kay, D. J. Steward, Zaccheus Kay, William Jennings and Benjamin Sells. The membership at this time was about one hundred, and the ministers in charge during the construction of the church were Revs. Wesley Roe and Oliver Peoples. The church then formed a part of a circuit, but soon after Georgetown was made a station. In the old church, Revs. John W. Clark, James B. Finley, John Meek, John Stewart and George W. Maley were noted preachers. The last named was a peculiarly gifted divine, and, about 1837, held a revival at the Georgetown Church, which was remarkably successful. Some of the most prominent citizens of the vicinity, as well as many hardened sinners, were brought into the church under his effective preaching. Among the former were Thomas L. Hamer and Dr. George B. Bailey. It is supposed that 150 converts united with the church before the protracted meetings closed. Rev. John Stewart's ministerial labors were also blessed with a large ingathering of souls. Since the erection of the new church, the ministers who have built up the numerical strength of the congregation most strongly were Revs. Wesley Roe, Charles Ferguson, and the present pastor, Rev. J. Verity. The present membership exceeds two hundred, fifty-five of whom were received at one time during the summer of 1882. A prosperous and highly interesting Sabbath school is regularly maintained.

Concerning the origin of the Georgetown Christian Church, Elder Matthew Gardner, in his autobiography, writes: "About this time (1822 or 1823), I began to preach regularly in Georgetown, Ohio. * * The meetings were for some time held in a small schoolhouse; but, as this would not hold the people, as soon as the court house was erected, I preached in it. There was much opposition from the Methodists and Presbyterians. They did not like to see the Christians taking a start with the town. But this did not prevent the people receiving that religion which has the Bible for its only rule of faith and practice, to the exclusion of all sectarian creeds. A church was soon organized, which grew rapidly. In a few years, we erected a brick chapel. I was one of the largest subscribers, as I was generally to houses built by churches, which, through divine grace, I had organized. I even went over and labored on the building. I assisted in putting on the roof, to secure the walls before winter came on. This church prospered for several years, increasing to the number of nearly two hundred members." The brick chapel erected is still standing, and is now occupied by the colored school.

When the "reformatory" movement of Alexander Campbell and his co-believers swept over the country, the majority of the members of this congregation became converted to the new faith, organized a society November 16, 1834, and carried over with them the property of the former Christian Church. The sixteen original members who formed this new society were John D. White, Nathan Sidwell, Robert Allen, Horace Jones, William Denniston, Sarah Denniston, James Baker, Anna Sidwell, Margaret Baker, Hannah Shepherd, Mary Bentley, Elisha Mount, Sarah Mount, Lucretia Marshall, Margaret R. White and Mary Allen. January 1, 1836, the membership had increased to sixty-six; seven years later, it reached ninety. March 8, 1835, the first church election resulted in the choice of Robert Allen, Nathan Sidwell and

John D. White for Elders, and William T. McConaughy, James Baker, Ezekiel Miner and Abraham Ellis, Deacons. Elder Richard C. Ricketts was the first regular pastor, entering upon his labors October 24, 1835. In 1855, the membership was greatly reduced through church differences, and, after a time, regular preaching was suspended, and the organization almost destroyed. The old church was finally sold, and the society became almost extinct.

After the disintegration of this society, a few years elapsed without any services, but, early in 1876, the members who still lived at Georgetown secured the ministerial services of Elder J. H. Lockwood, who preached to them in the Georgetown Schoolhouse. During the summer and fall of 1877, these members erected a house of worship on North Main street. It is a frame structure, about 46x60 feet, surmounted by a belfry and bell, and costing, in the aggregate, about $2,000. The building was dedicated November 25, 1877, the services being conducted by Elders Isaac Errett, of Cincinnati; Dr. John Shockey and J. H. Lockwood. The day following, Elders Lockwood and J. Irvin West began a series of meetings, which resulted in numerous accessions, and an entire re-organization was effected December 6, 1877, at which time the following officers: J. W. Laycock, Thomas J. Brown and C. Phillips, Trustees; Conrad Wright and John Haslem, Elders; Thomas J. Brown and C. Phillips, Deacons. The membership at the time of organization was fifty-four; it has now reached eighty-two. Elder Lockwood remained pastor of the church until the spring of 1882, when he was succeeded by J. W. B. Smythe. A Sabbath school was instituted cotemporaneously with the church, with Lee Laycock as Superintendent. It has an average attendance of fifty pupils, and is an interesting and well-conducted school.

The Georgetown Presbyterian Church, as mentioned elsewhere in this chapter, had its origin in the Straight Creek Church, about three miles south of Georgetown. The first preaching in town was held at the court house. September 14, 1829, it was resolved that the Presbytery of Chillicothe be petitioned to change the name of the church to the Presbyterian Church of Georgetown, that the church be incorporated, and that the Trustees, Victor King, James Campbell, James Thompson, James Parker and John Maklem, be authorized to obtain a charter of incorporation. This was not effected until December 21, 1830, at which time the Trustees were James Thompson, James W. Campbell, Duncan Evans, Garret Snedaker and George Blair. It was about this time that the first church was built at Georgetown, a brick, occupying the site of the present Presbyterian Church. The earliest pastors divided their time equally between the Georgetown Church and the old Straight Creek Church for awhile, but as the Georgetown congregation increased proportionately much faster than the other, it soon secured three-fourths of the ministers' labors, and finally all. The earliest preaching at Georgetown was probably conducted by Rev. John Rankin. He was pastor of the Straight Creek Church for a number of years prior to 1829. In that year, Rev. R. B. Dobens was called, and remained with the church one year. January 9, 1830, Rev. Hervey O. Higby was engaged to preach for a year, and, in October, 1831, Rev. Robert J. Hall was called to the pastorate of the church, and continued in charge until 1836, when Rev. James H. Gass was installed minister. He remained several years. In 1837, the membership was 163; in 1841, it had increased to 197. In 1840, Rev. Moses H. Wilder was called to the church, and remained two years. Rev. L. G. Bingham then preached a year, and was succeeded by Rev. David Gould, who was pastor of the church until 1850. Revs. James G. Hopkins, J. Bole and J. Delamater supplied the pulpit for short periods, and Robert Young also preached awhile. Rev. C. Merwin was installed as regular pastor in 1856, but remained only a year or two. H. V.

Warren became pastor in 1858, and continued as such until 1866. The membership in 1861 had decreased to seventy-seven. After Rev. Warren's pastorate, the church was supplied for awhile by Revs. Joseph Swindt, Alexander Parker, W. H. Rogers, D. E. Bierce and H. W. Guthrie; and Rev. Erwin Caton became the next regular pastor. He was succeeded by the present minister, Rev. S. A. Vandyke, in 1873. The present church edifice was erected in 1853, at a total cost of about $7,000. The present membership is 114. A flourishing Sabbath school is regularly conducted. It at present is under the superintendency of George N. Woodward, and has a membership of 118.

The Ruling Elders of the church have been John Evans, Jonathan Moore, James Thompson, William King, James Campbell, Duncan Evans, Victor King, Garret Snedaker, William Buckner, William Griffin, Philip J. Buckner, John Donaldson, Samuel Martin, C. Snedaker, John Salisbury, R. A. Bower, S. W. Evans, Newton Parker, J. M. Barnes, W. P. Maklem, W. R. Parker, G. E. Matthews, J. H. Wills and W. J. Evans. The last five constitute the present session.

A Regular Baptist Church was founded at Georgetown in 1837. In that year, a brick edifice was erected on Market street, just east of the cemetery. Elder Aaron Sargent was the first minister, and the pastoral relation continued between him and this congregation for more than twenty years. The earliest influential members were Job Egbert, Walter Leach, Thomas Jennings, Basil Norris, their families, Henrietta Baker and others. Though organized with a small membership, the church grew steadily for awhile, at one time attaining a membership of about one hundred and fifty. Subsequent to Aaron Sargent, his son, James Sargent, H. H. B. Spencer, B. Y. Seigfried, Wenham Kidder, A. White, Rev. Mason and Rev. Lindsey have had charge of the church. Many members removed from this vicinity to other localities, and others were removed by death, till finally the membership became too greatly reduced to maintain a pastor regularly, and, about 1874, regular services ceased. Occasional meetings were held, however, until early in 1881, when, by order of the remnant of the once flourishing congregation, the Trustees, C. G. Turner and B. Ramsy, sold the church building, thus completely extinguishing the organization.

The Second Baptist Church (colored) was organized July 7, 1868, as the Anti-Slavery Baptist Church of Georgetown, by Elders S. D. Fox and Triplet, and Licentiates R. Burr and George Davis. The name was afterward changed for its present one. At its origin, there were scarcely more than half a dozen members, but the church books now enroll about seventy. The first Deacons elected were Amos Young and John Sharkelford. The pastors and their terms of service have been R. Burr, eight years; E. E. Burr, one year; D. B. Green, two years; G. W. Burr, six months; W. H. Steward, present pastor, entered upon his duties in the spring of 1882. There have been a few times of brief duration when the church was without a minister. The organization was effected and services held for about three years in the Union School building, then for several year the preaching was conducted in the dwellings of the members, and, since 1874, the schoolhouse for colored pupils, on Water street, has been occupied by them. The congregation is now engaged in constructing a frame house of worship, 28x38, at the extreme south end of Water street. A successful Sabbath school is in operation.

SOCIETIES.

Georgetown Lodge, No. 72, F. & A. M., was first chartered in 1824, and, on the 24th of June, 1825, Rev. John Rankin delivered an address before the members, which was well received, the lodge paying him $10 for the lecture.

In 1827, Thomas L. Hamer was Master of this lodge, and Jesse R. Grant held the same position in 1830. In 1832, the charter was surrendered and the lodge discontinued. Seven years later, however, in 1839, a new charter was granted, under the old name and number, and the lodge thus organized has continued to the present. As originally instituted in 1824, the lodge was officered as follows: Robert Allen, W. M.; Jesse R. Grant, S. W.; John Lindsey, J. W.; Joseph Davidson, Treasurer; George B. Bailey, Secretary; William V. Powell, S. D.; Samuel G. Sperry, J. D.; Francis Myers and Franklin Shaler, Stewards. In addition to the foregoing officers, the following members subscribed to the by-laws of 1824: Levin Hurley, T. L. Hamer, Joseph Stableton, John Wylie, John Dunn, John J. Higgins, John Ferrier, Charles White, John H. Shepherd, William Hill, Horace Bayles, Terry Wamacks, James Loudon, William K. Byrne, John W. Odell, Thomas Middleton, James Baker, John A. Wills, Enoch Ellsberry, William Shepherd and John D. White. The meetings of this lodge were held in the tavern, where the American House now stands, on the northwest corner of the square. The charter was surrendered because of the bitter opposition to Masonry which prevailed so extensively just after the disappearance of Morgan, and the accusation of his murder against this order. The excitement ran high at Georgetown, as elsewhere, and anti-Masonic officers were nominated and elected in Pleasant Township. A Mason was a doomed man, politically, and, under the pressure, the lodge succumbed. It was re-organized September 3, 1838, by the installation of the following officers: John D. White, W. M.; Terry Wamacks, S. W.; James Loudon, J. W.; William Blanchard, Treasurer; George B. Bailey, Secretary; Russell Shaw, S. D.; John Allen, J. D.; James Baker, Tiler. P. L. Wilson was the first member elected and received into the lodge. The first meetings were held in the old court house, then in the second story of the old brick house on the south side of the square, now occupied by Mrs. Carr B. White. About 1849, the Masonic Block, on the east side of the square, was erected by a number of stockholders, who were members, and the lodge has since had its home there. The present officers are: John Lefabre, W. M.; L. B. Leeds, S. W.; Louis F. Roth, J. W.; R. W. Evans, Secretary; Henry Brunner, Treasurer; I. L. Ronsheim, S. D.; Charles McKibben, J. D.; Jacob Fley, Tiler; Henry Brunner, Steward. The lodge meets every Thursday, on or before the full moon.

Georgetown Chapter, No. 52, Royal Arch Masons, was granted a warrant of dispensation October 22, 1852. The original members were Peter L. Wilson, John D. White, John Allen, Gideon Dunham, Hanson L. Penn, John J. Higgins, W. M. Gates, Robert Allen, H. Barr, David Barr, B. F. Sallee and W. B. McCormick. Its present membership is fifty-four. Its regular meetings are held on Thursday, after the full moon. P. L. Wilson, one of the charter members, has been elected Grand King of the Grand Chapter of Ohio. He has also been Deputy Grand Puissant of the Grand Council. The present officers of the chapter are: George M. Wood, H. P.; L. B. Leeds, Sr., King; D. B. Thompson, Scribe; C. B. Fee, Captain of H.; A. Armstrong, R. A. C.; Marsh Patton, G. M. of Third Vail; F. D. Blair, G. M. of Second Vail; Ford Rish, G. M. of First Vail; N. J. Thompson, Treasurer; I. L. Ronsheim, Secretary; Henry Brunner, Steward.

Barrere Council, No. 25, was granted a charter October 12, 1867. Its original membership comprised the names of A. Sallee, H. L. Penn, S. G. Boyd, R. C. Sallee, David Barr, John P. Biehn, F. J. Phillips, John J. Higgins, John Allen, A. Mehaffey and P. L. Wilson. The corps of officers now serving are: David Tarbell, Thr. Ill. M.; Fred Risch. Dep. Ill. M.; John Lafabre, Prin. Con. W.; A. Armstrong, Captain Guard; Henry Brunner, Treasurer; L.

B. Leeds, Recorder; Henry Brunner, Sentinel. The membership is now thirty-three; the time of meeting, every Monday night previous to full moon.

Confidence Lodge, No. 307, I. O. O. F., was instituted June 25, 1856. The charter members were William Shields, David Thomas, W H. Sly, Benjamin Sells, John C. Shepherd, J. H. King, Jeremiah Laycock and John Brockhaus. In 1859, the lodge was meeting in the now residence of Judge J. P. Biehn, on the east side of the square. Later, it occupied the west room of the second story of the Evans building, southwest corner Main and Main Cross streets. In 1866 or 1867, it removed to room it now owns, in the Arn Block, southwest corner of the square. W. H. Sly, one of the first members, has since been Grand Master of the State Lodge. In April, 1873, the lodge purchased ten and one-half acres of land a mile north of Georgetown, and converted it into a beautiful cemetery, which is becoming the final resting-place for many of the silent dead for miles around. Seventy-four lots have been sold up to September, 1882. The purchase was not made as a business venture, but because of the need at Georgetown of a new cemetery. Quite a considerable tract has been sold to the Pleasant Township Trustees. The revenues in excess of the actual expenses are used in improving and adorning the grounds. There are now about sixty-five active members in the lodge. Its officers at this date are: Cyrus Edwards, N. G.; J. W. Lawwill, V. G.; T. J. Leeds, Secretary; I. L. Ronsheim, Treasurer.

Georgetown Encampment of Patriarchs, No. 194, I. O. O. F., was instituted August 10, 1875, with the following members: George P. Tyler, L. B. Leeds, S. J. Murray, F. M. Wardlow, S. S. Brooks, W. L. Shidler and John A. Tweed. It is now officered by William Wills, C. P.; J. M. Thompson, S. W.; D. B. Thompson, J. W.; D. V. Pearson, H. P.; L. Arzeno, Scribe. Its condition is flourishing.

Georgetown Lodge, No. 98, Knights of Pythias, was instituted May 24, 1876. Its first officers were: E. F. Blair, P. C.; J. R. Moore, C. C.; R. L. Fite, V. C.; W. W. Young, Prelate; L. B. Leeds, Jr., K. of R. and S.; E. E. Roney, M. of F.; C. D. Thompson, M. of E.; M. J. Thompson, M. at A.; David Thompson, I. G.; U. G. Rees, O. G. Besides these, the original members included Dr. T. W. Gordon, Dr. Y. Stephenson, Adam Stephen, W. A Snedaker, Dr. W. W. Ellsberry, J. T. Brady and J. J. Lewis. Meetings are held every Monday evening, at the Odd Fellows Hall. The lodge is in excellent working order, and is equipped with complete regalia. The officers who are serving at this date are: John A. Jennings, C. C.; F. D. Blair, V. C.; U. G. Rees, Prelate; I. L. Ronsheim, M. F.; C. B. Fee, M. at A.; George N. Becker, M. of Ex.; J. H. Lawwill, K. of R. and S.; L. B. Leeds, I. G.; B. F. Woods, O. G.

Carr B. White Post, No. 232, G. A. R., received its charter June 3, 1882. Its first officers were: Charles D. Thompson, Post Com.; John A. Tweed, Sr. V. Com.; J. T. Brady, Jr. V. Com.; Thomas J. Leeds, Quartermaster; G. M. Zeigler, Adjutant; J. W. Gordon, Surgeon; Josiah Edwards, Chaplain. The remaining charter members were D. W. C. Loudon, Preston Carberry, B. F. Woods, J. B. Burgett, T. C. Smiley, W. W. McKnight, George P. Tyler, D. B. Thompson, John Wills, B. F. Tatman, W. H. H. Vance, A. W. Rees, George Slack, H. C. Louden, Rev. J. W. B. Smith and Samuel Cochran.

A lodge of Good Templars was instituted at Georgetown March 15, 1875, by P. M. Weddell, G. W. C. T., and Jay Pinney, G. W. S. E. The charter members were P. P. Ellis, Carr N. Waterman, Lizzie Kearns, Lee Markley, Emma Blair, Anna Campbell, Lizzie Marshall, Lu Miles, Henry Higgins, Sallie Matthews, B. C. Boude, Mrs. Boude, C. D. Miles, Charles Blair and

W. H. Blair. Charter officers: Mrs. D. V. Pearson, C. T.; Jennie Matthews, V. T.; W. H. Hannah, Chaplain; Charles Perkins, R. S.; S. D. Waterman, A. R. S.; Charles Crouch, F. S.; Mrs. H. C. Miles, Treasurer; W. B. McGroarty, W. M.; Nettie Kearns, D. M.; Sallie Devore, I. G.; John Rilea, O. G.; Mrs. Baker, R. H. S.; Mrs. Kearns, L. H. S.; Milton Baker, P W. C. T. The present officers are C. A. Blair, C. T.; Hassie Turner, V. T.; Mrs. Eva Pearson, Chaplain; Minnie L. Rees, R. S.; David Thomas, Jr., A. R. S.; Henry Hannah, F. S.; J. N. Harmon, Treasurer; Carey Slack, W. M.; Ida Markley, D. M.; Charles Hoehn, I. G.; H. C. Stewart, O. G.; Zoe Arzeno, R. H. S.; Bessie Higgins, L. H. S., Dott C. Rilea, P. W. C. T. Meetings are held every Monday evening, in the Presbyterian Church. The membership now numbers eighty-four.

A lodge of the A. O. U. W. was organized at Georgetown March 24, 1875, with a membership of fifteen. Its first officers were H. C. Loudon, M. W.; Michael Brunner, G. F.; E. E. Roney, Overseer; David Tarbell, P. M. W.; Jacob Risch, Recorder; J. R. Moore, Financier; Dr. Y. Stephenson, Receiver; W. A. Snedaker, Guide; John G. Rose, Watchman; L. Arzeno, J. W. Evans and Matthias Arn, Trustees. The lodge enjoyed a prosperous reign of several years, when it surrendered its charter and passed into nonentity.

HOTELS.

The American Hotel was built by different parties. Allen Woods erected the corner portion probably in 1820. It was a brick structure, containing two rooms, and north of it was a vacant space twenty feet in width, beyond which John Smith and James Crawford had erected a small brick building, which subsequently became a part of the hotel. The space between the two buildings was afterward built over by Crawford for Allen Woods, and the three parts were united in one, constituting the front of the present building. The property passed into the hands of Peter L. Wilson (Mr. Woods' son-in-law), piece by piece, and he built the entire rear portion. Mr. Wilson had located in Lewis Township in 1818, but removed across the river to Augusta, Ky., from which point he came to Georgetown in the winter of 1821-22. He commenced as landlord of the American in 1827, and continued to administer the affairs of that well-known hostelry until 1847, when he rented it, and finally, after several parties had occupied it, sold it to John McColgin in the fall of 1851. The latter gentleman repaired and refitted it, the building, about that time, suffered some damage by fire. The next proprietor was Artus Pepper, who was succeeded, about the 1st of November, 1862, by Esq. John Jenkins, after whom the building was called the "Jenkins House." In February, 1866, John Dillen became proprietor. and was followed by William Norris, who assumed charge December 2, 1867. Dillen was succeeded by George Shields, and he by B. F. Stump. The next and present proprietor is W. N. Bingamon, who uses only a portion of the building for hotel purposes.

Another building used as a hotel in early times, and, until within a year or two, stood on the south side of the square, where the bakery is now located. James Vandyke was host at this stand prior to 1827. Other proprietors who succeeded him were Thomas Kirker, Osmus Johnson, David Crawford and Richard Bingamon.

The National Union Hotel, at the northwest corner of Pleasant and Main Cross streets, was erected by Edward Lewis in 1863. The roof had just been placed on at the time of Morgan's raid. Mr. Lewis died in 1868, and his son, J. J. Lewis, became proprietor of the house, continuing until 1878. His mother, Mrs. M. M. Lewis, then had the management of the house until the fall of 1882, when she sold it to John M. Richards, who took possession No-

vember 15. A one-story hotel was kept at this place by Mr. Dowdney before the present house was built.

Since 1877, a portion of the Biehn House, on the north side of the square, has been used for hotel purposes. The first proprietor here was Michael Brunner, who remained in charge about a year and a half, and was succeeded by John Pierce. His successor, Albert Kautz, the present proprietor, assumed control in the spring of 1882.

BUSINESS INTERESTS.

The first bank of Georgetown, and the only one prior to the First National, was opened by Penn & Phillips in January, 1856. John W. King soon secured an interest in the business. A general banking business was carried on until November 15, 1878, when, under the name of F. J. Phillips & Co., the bank suspended.

The First National Bank of Georgetown was chartered May 23, 1882, with a capital of $50,000. The first stockholders were John Markley, James H. Dunn, H. C. Loudon, John A. Tweed, Joseph Cochran, W. S. Whiteman, James C. Dunn, J. P. Biehn, E. B. Fee, R. L. Fite, C. P. O'Hara, P. L. Wilson, John M. Markley, John M. Thompson, John Jennings, J. P. Helbling, Adam Stephen, W. J. Thompson, Robert Conn, L. G. Fee, H. B. Higgins, and W. J. Jacobs. Joseph Cochran was elected President; W. S. Whiteman, Cashier; and James C. Dunn, Teller. The bank owns a neat business room on North Main street, and is rapidly gaining a successful and extensive banking business. A large number of deposits have already been made, and the amount is constantly increasing.

The woolen factory on East Main Cross street—Outlot 15—was erected in 1863 by Warner & Ramey. Very soon after, J. B. Thomas owned an interest, and, during its existence of nearly twenty years, it has frequently changed hands. Thomas and William A. Pepper, W. N. Ramey and Dr. James Sidwell, each for a time owned a share of the factory; W. T. Gilbreath, assignee of W. N. Ramey & Co., sold it to Alfred Jacobs and J. N. Henning. Since then the different members of the firm have been William Jacobs, W. J. Jacobs, Robert Young, E. W. West, T. J. Brown, George Inskeep, W. A. Dudley. Since 1875, the firm name has been R. Young & Co., composed at present of Robert Young, W. A. Dudley and W. A. Young. The building is a large four-story frame, equipped with all the modern machinery necessary to manufacture yarns, jeans, blankets and flannels. It is, perhaps, the leading industry of Georgetown at present, and gives employment to eighteen hands.

The grist-mill, standing nearly opposite the woolen factory, on Outlot 14, the site of Jesse R. Grant's tannery, was built in 1873 by F. F. Steinman and Christian Single. Two years later, Mr. Single purchased the interest of his partner, and has operated the mill since.

The Georgetown Building and Loan Association was incorporated February 22, 1879, the articles of incorporation being recorded on the 24th of March following. The association was organized under legislative acts of May 1, 1852, and May 9, 1868; capital stock, $100,000. The incorporators were L. B. Leeds, Sr., John Lafabre, Henry Brunner, G. Pickard, L. B. Miles, B. F. Woods, E. B. Fee, A. Armstrong, S. P. King, A. D. Crouch and Michael Brunner. The institution is yet in existence.

POSTMASTERS.

William Butt is supposed to have been the first Postmaster of Georgetown. He settled here in 1821. Peter L. Wilson filled the office several years in Jackson's administration, and was succeeded by John Blair. B. C. Baker,

David Crawford, James Allen, John G. Brose, George D. Evans and James T. Morgan each held the position after Blair. Alfred Armstrong was Postmaster under Buchanan; George Kearns was appointed in 1860, and retained the position till 1872. Since then, Mrs. J. M. Bailey, Mrs. L. B. Powers, Mrs. Jane Crute, Charles F. King and Irving McKibben successively held the office until 1879, when George Kearns, the present Postmaster, again received the appointment.

The growth of Georgetown has been slow but steady since the date of its foundation. It is pleasantly located upon an elevated, rolling table land. Its population in 1870 was 1,037; in 1880, 1,293.

CHAPTER II.

UNION TOWNSHIP.

BY F. F. SHAW.

'Tis a great fault in a chronologer
To turn parasite ; an absolute historian
Should be in fear of none ; neither should he
Write anything more than truth for friendship,
Or else for hate. —*Lingua*.

'Tis in books the chief
Of all perfections to be plain and brief.
—*Butler*.

AS the historian for Union Township, we acknowledge our inability to perform that complete duty with the justice which the subject so interesting in its scope demands. Our township is large, populous, and the oldest settled in the county. Ripley, the largest village and the most important commercial point in it.

Imperfect as this history may be, we rely upon the general reader for that measure of charity which he would have meted out to him under similar circumstances. The writer would like to excuse the mention of his own name so often in the several matters treated of, but for thirty years he has filled many official positions in the township, and not to do so would leave the subject incomplete. Where it could be avoided it has been.

Union is bounded on the north by Jefferson and Byrd; on the east by Huntington Township; on the south by the Ohio River, and on the west by Lewis and Pleasant Townships. It lies in the easterly portion of the county. Its length on the Ohio River, by its manderings, is nearly seven and one-eight miles; its average width is about five and one-half miles, and it contains over forty square miles.

It is watered by Straight Creek, a good-sized and lengthy stream on the northwest; Eagle Creek, of about the same size, on the southeast; the Ohio River on the southwest, and through the center by Red Oak Creek. The last is a short stream, but, owing to the great hill surface some four miles back of its mouth, the quantity of water flowing through its channel is at times very great; it rises quickly, and is soon emptied into the beautiful Ohio.

The soil is formed upon alternating strata of clay and limestone, and partakes chiefly of these two earths. The river and creek bottoms are composed of sandy soil, largely impregnated with rich clay, forming most productive land for general farming. Nearly the entire river portion of the township, say one-half or more of the area, though hilly, has always been considered the best farming lands in this part of the county, if not the best in the county. It was originally heavily covered with the finest of timber—walnut, poplar, ash and other sure marks of rich land. The last mile or so of the northeast is good land, more level, and commands high prices in the market. It is easier farmed than the hill portion, makes pretty farms, and to-day is among the most valuable farm land in the county. Within the last year, a farm of 210 acres, four miles from Ripley, with rather poor improvements, sold for $100 per acre.

Along the river and throughout the southern portion of the township, are high ranges of hills, and from those along the river an extensive prospect of the Mason County, Ky., hills, valleys and surrounding country on both sides of the river is afforded, and some of the most beautiful sunsets are here seen; but we fear that the grandeur will soon be lessened by reason of the sad havoc made in the shearing of these hills and valleys of the grand old monarchs of the forest to make way for the vile, yet profitable, crop of tobacco.

Mr. Thomas Smith, one of the early settlers, moved from Kentucky to this township in 1815. He was a blacksmith, and at once set up shop on Cormick's Run, near Ripley (on the present Ripley & Georgetown Free Turnpike). Mr. John Thompson, present in our office to-day (July, 1882), aged seventy-eight years, in good health, informs us that he learned said trade under Mr. Smith, and while with him he and Mr. Smith frequently went to Maysville, Ky., ten miles up the river, for iron and steel in summer season in skiff, and in winter by sled over a path, there being no regular roads laid out. Mr. Thompson ironed a wagon for Mr. David Flaugher in 1827, which now belongs to Marion Stephenson. Mr. Thompson says he saw it in town the other day, a pretty good wagon yet. Mr. Thompson invented and patented over thirty years ago a wrought iron and steel plow—one of the best ever used in this section of country. Had he been furnished with sufficient means and an energetic managing partner, he could have been worth many thousands of dollars to-day. His son, George W. Thompson, now deceased, invented and patented also an improved hillside plow, which has given great satisfaction.

EARLY SETTLEMENTS.

Upon the soil of Union Township were made some of the first settlements of Brown County, if not the first. While the border Indian warfare along the Ohio River was aggressive and bitter, and the feuds between the races raged at their intensest pitch, there were doubtless many stirring adventures and probably tragedies enacted within the present limits of our township, which are now forgotten. The bottom lands of Eagle Creek, a noted stream in those early times, for a mile or two from its mouth lie wholly within its territory, Red Oak courses through its center, and Straight Creek bounds it on the west; both streams, had they tongues with which to speak, could reveal whole chapters from the great unwritten history of the past. Cabins were doubtless built for hunting purposes by adventurous spirits, who dared to face Indian hatred and hostility before the treaty of peace was declared in 1795. Mention is made that Cornelius Washburn and William Dixon, in 1793, crossed the river from Kentucky at Logan's Gap, and built a hut on Eagle Creek, one mile from the river, where Mr. Dixon continued to live for some time.

The first permanent settlement in the township is believed to have been made by Belteshazer Dragoo in 1794 or 1795. He was a Virginian, but, like most of the earliest pioneers of Brown County, had lived for a few years prior to his emigration to Ohio in Kentucky. Mr. Dragoo had tarried for awhile in Mason County Ky., then crossed the river and erected his primitive cabin on the waters of Eagle Creek, where E. M. Fitch now resides. He purchased a farm of 300 acres here, and spent the next few years in the ceaseless activity which the successful pioneer must assume in order to improve and develop his home. When the great Shaker excitement spread over this county, he became a convert to the faith, and joined the community. He sold his farm, and lived the remainder of his life with the Shakers near Cincinnati. His wife, Hannah, three daughters and a minor son, Benjamin, accompanied him, the latter under protest. As soon as Benjamin attained his majority, he returned to Union Township, and here lived and died. Of Mr. Dragoo's other three sons, Andrew and Belteshazer removed to Indiana, but Daniel maintained a life-long residence in Union Township.

William Kinkead was perhaps the next settler. He came in 1796. He was born in Augusta County, Va., and came with his father, William Kinkead, Sr., to Woodford County, Ky., in a very early time. William, Jr., married Anna Dunlap in Kentucky, and her brother, William Dunlap, accompanied them to this township. They built their cabin near where Scott Kinkead now resides, on the J. Harris Survey, several miles north of Ripley. Alexander Dunlap, the father of William, owned a large tract of land near Chillicothe, and in 1797, William and William Kinkead made a journey overland to it, and concluded to settle there; returning after the harvest was gathered, they packed their goods and sent them by keel-boat to Chillicothe, while they drove the stock across through the woods. The Indians were troublesome in that vicinity, and not liking the situation they returned to Union Township without unloading the goods from the boat. Mr. Kinkead remained a resident of this township for life, and died at a good old age. He had nine children, two of whom died young. The others were Nancy (Gilliland), William, Anna (Hopkins), Robert, James, Guy and Scott. Mr. Kinkead brought with him from Kentucky fifty cows, the property of himself and his father-in-law, Alexander Dunlap, and the products of his dairy, butter and cheese, he boated to Cincinnati, and sold there. From the proceeds he paid for the farm he had purchased.

William Dunlap, after living a year or two with the Kinkeads, married Polly Shepherd, and began housekeeping for himself just north of them. His family consisted of eight children--Amanda (Corruthers); James, a minister at Springfield, Ohio; Milton, a Greenfield physician; Nancy (Campbell); William; Alexander, a physician of Springfield, Ohio; Shepherd and Elizabeth Ann.

The Shepherds were also among the earliest settlers of Red Oak. John Shepherd emigrated to where William Gilliland now lives, near Red Oak Presbyterian Church, with a family of grown children. He was a Virginian, and died upon the place he settled in this township. One of the oldest boys, Isaac, was a cabinet-maker by trade, and an old bachelor. Jacob was a farmer, an occupied the home place at his father's death. John removed West. Abraham received a liberal education, and was a surveyor and miller. He built the first steam mill on Red Oak, at the "Buckeye Mills," and traded extensively in pork. He was portly and gentlemanly in bearing, and quite popular in the county, filling several offices of responsibility and honor. He was an early and prominent Mason. In his business transactions, he met with reverses, and finally moved to Putnam County, Ill. None of the Shepherds now reside in this vicinity.

Jeptha Beasley came about the same time, probably in 1798. He was from Spottsylvania County, Va., and born August 20, 1769. He had emigrated to Limestone, now Maysville, Ky., years before, and in times when Indian ravages were imminent. He served as a spy to watch the movements of the savages across the river. When he came to Union Township, he possessed but few worldly goods. He purchased the farm his son, Jeptha, now occupies, in the northeastern part of the township, and for a number of years engaged in farming and boating. He then removed to Ripley, and was the village inn-keeper for a while, but, tiring of this life, he returned again to the farm. He was Justice of the Peace for many years, and County Commissioner. His children were Sally, William, John, Elizabeth, Levi, Jeptha and Nancy.

Matthew McClung was an early settler about three-fourths of a mile east of this, on the present M. Germann place. He died from the effects of a fall from a horse. David Devore settled on Red Oak, about six miles from Ripley in 1800.

Rev. John Dunlavy resided on what is now the R. Mannon place, about a mile southwest from Red Oak Presbyterian Church, early in the present century. This church was organized in 1798 or 1799, and was the first in the county. During the first summer of its existence, prayer meetings were held in a thicket north of Ripley at the forks of the pike, where Spence Spears' tobacco warehouse now is; then a round log house was built near where the present church stands. It was soon replaced by a hewed-log church, which was burned. A stone house of worship was erected in 1817. Rev. Dunlavy is said to have been the first stated minister. He remained with the church not quite two years. His ministrations became tainted with the heresy of Shakerism, with which faith he afterward affiliated, and the congregation forbade his farther use of the church. He at first disregarded the prohibition, but at the second meeting afterward was met at the door by Jacob Shepherd, the sexton, who denied him admission. Rev. Dunlavy drew with him to the Shakers, it is said, nearly one-half the membership of this church. Rev. James Gilliland settled on Red Oak, and became pastor of the church in 1805, and continued in that relation until within a short time of his death, which occurred in 1854. A Latin school was held in this church for a long time; Alexander Gilliland and afterward Adam Gilliland were the teachers.

Col. Mills Stephenson was one of the earliest settlers on Eagle Creek, coming several years prior to the close of the last century. He was born in Delaware, and in his youth was filled with a passion for a life on the ocean wave. He embarked on a vessel as cabin boy, and was soon disenchanted from the rosy visions that had filled his mind. The drudgery he was compelled to perform on Sunday while the sailors played cards and indulged in other profanation of the Sabbath, did not accord with his notions of propriety, and he quickly abandoned his early love. He removed with his parents to Pennsylvania, and afterward came to Mason County, Ky. After his arrival i this township, he engaged in farming. He entered the war of 1812 as Colonel of a batallion, and served throughout. Fort Stephenson was named in his honor. His wife, Jane (Kilpatrick), died soon after the close of the war, and he removed to Ripley. Afterward he was one of a company who purchased the Buckeye Mills, but the investment proved disastrous. The death of Col. Stephenson occurred June 16, 1822, in Louisiana, while he was on a trip down the Mississippi. His children were Ephraim, Mary (Stephenson), Robert P., Isabel, Elizabeth (Wallace), Young and Lemuel.

On what was know as Bradford's Bottom, near the mouth of Eagle Creek, was quite a little settlement in very early times. The land then belonged to Ignatius Mitchell, of Kentucky. Jacob Middleswart was an early settler here. He was a renter only, and moved afterward with his family back into the interior of the county. Robert Savage, from Pennsylvania, settled in the same vicinity. He was well advanced in life when he came, and lived here till he died. Sophia McFadden, a widow, with her children, Hugh, Charlie and Sophia, lived close by. They afterward moved to Auglaize County. James Stephenson, a half-brother of Col. Mills, settled just east of Ripley, where some of his descendants still live.

Amongst the earliest settlers farther up Eagle Creek, were Thomas and Henry Bayne. They were of Scotch-Irish nationality, and came from Pennsylvania. Both died in this township, and their posterity are widely scattered. Richard Rollison, a Revolutionary soldier, was another. He afterward moved with the Hardestys and others to the Mad River. John and James Espy, were natives of Tyrone County, Ireland, and early residents here. The latter was drowned about three-fourths of a mile east of Ripley.

Fogus McClain was another of Eagle Creek's foremost settlers. He was from Western Pennsylvania; was implicated in the whisky insurrection there, and when matters came to a crisis took French leave, and hurried off down the

UNION TOWNSHIP.

Ohio in a boat, landing on Eagle Creek. He here bought a farm from Mitchell, and remained through life. He had been a Revolutionary soldier and was a Mason. He had but one child, John. Abner Howard built his cabin very early on the same stream. He erected a little mill about three and a half miles from the mouth of the creek. Robert Hopkins settled farther north.

The Ellis family was among the first to settle in the western part of Union Township. In 1798, Amos Ellis and Mary (McConnell) Ellis, his wife, located three miles north of Ripley, on the head-waters of Cormick Run. Two years before, they had left Pennsylvania with Thomas McConnell, her brother, and come to Washington, Ky., where they located temporarily. In the fall of 1797, Ellis and McConnell crossed the river and built huts on the land to which they moved their families the ensuing spring. Mr. McConnell remained on the farm he then settled for life, and his son, Milford, now occupies it. He was a zealous Baptist. In 1822, Amos Ellis was appointed County Treasurer, and the following year was elected to the same office. He was also elected a member of the Legislature in 1803 and again in 1809. He died in 1832 at the age of sixty-two years. His wife survived him seventeen years. Isaac Ellis, a brother of Amos, also came to the township in the spring of 1798, and settled on a farm adjoining his brother's. He had two sons, Elias and John, and several daughters. Both sons moved to Illinois.

Thomas Cormick, in 1797, settled on Cormick Run, about a mile northwest from Ripley. He was born in Nova Scotia, but had lived in Virginia and Kentucky before emigrating hither. He was a good specimen of the rough frontiersman, and raised a large family of children. When he came, two settlers, William and James Prigett Long, were living in this vicinity. James Henry was an early settler on "Pisgah Ridge." He lived on the farm now occupied by James Myers, and died December 4, 1834, in his seventy-sixth year. William Bowers, an Irishman, settled about three-fourths of a mile west of the Buckeye Mills, on Red Oak. He followed weaving, and remained on this place through life. Henry Martin was one of the first settlers in the region of Straight Creek. He was Justice of the Peace for many years, and Associate Judge of the county. John Mefford was one of the earliest near Levanna.

Col. James Poage owned a one-thousand-acre tract, including the site of Ripley, and settled on it with his family. In former times he had been wealthy, but he came west with broken fortunes. He is remembered as a quiet, unassuming gentleman, strictly honorable in all his transactions. He was well advanced in life when he arrived, and had a family of children, most of whom were men and women. He died April 9, 1820, in his sixty-fifth year. His wife, Mary, survived him ten years. Of their children, John, James, Robert, Thomas, George, Patsy, Elizabeth and Polly are remembered. Most of them died of consumption in early manhood and womanhood, and the few who escaped the dread disease have long since gone to other climes.

Archibald Tweed was one of the foremost pioneers of the township. He came prior to the present century. His family was large. He died December 24, 1830, aged eighty-four years. His wife, Jannet, preceded him to the grave five years. Alexander Jolly, from Maryland, was another original settler, who lived here through life. He was a prominent Baptist. William Campbell in 1800 moved to the township from Kentucky. He was originally from Virginia. William Humphries, Peter Shaw, Christian Wiles, John Redman, John Forsythe, Dr. Alexander Campbell, Thomas Dickens, John Laughlin, John Baird, Nathaniel Collins, Andrew Carr and William Colter were other early settlers.

RIPLEY.

Ripley was laid out about the period of the war of 1812 by Col. James

Poage, of Virginia, on a part of his 1,000-acre tract, No. 418. It was first called Staunton, from Staunton, Va. The name was afterward changed to Ripley in honor of Gen. Ripley, a distinguished officer in the war of 1812. The town is located on the east side of the Ohio River, about fifty miles above Cincinnati.

Among the early business men of Ripley was Thomas Myers, who is said to have been the first man engaged in merchandising in the village. Mr. Myers was followed by William Humphries and Dr. Campbell in the same business. George Poage, John Evans and Joseph N. Campbell were also early business men of Ripley. Thomas Hopkins, Peter Shaw, J. A. Hughes, Archibald Liggett, Silas Palmer, S. S. Campbell, Nathaniel Collins and Thomas McCague were also prominent men in the building of the town, and in augmenting its business interests. The county seat was located here in the latter part of the year 1818. The following is a list of the Mayors of Ripley from 1826 to 1882:

Nathaniel Collins (the first), Archibald Liggett, George W. King, S. S. Campbell, John Gaddis, Alexander Campbell, Sr., Silas Palmer, C. F. Campbell, John Gaddis, O. F. Shaw, C. Baird, A. P. Lewis, C. Baird, R. N. Jenkins, M. M. Murphy, David Gaddis, C. F. Campbell, David Gaddis, J. M. Bell, J. P. Johnson, David Gaddis, J. McCague, A. C. Collins, M. M. Murphy, W. H. Sly and W. D. Young. The following are the officers of Ripley: Mayor, W. D. Young; Police Justice, F. F. Shaw; Clerk, Stanley Merrill; Treasurer, Henry Fleig; Council, J. C. Liggett, Fred Fleig, J. S. Atwood, M. M. Murphy, Robert Campbell, Michael Linn.

There have been two additions made to the town of Ripley, to wit: "Poage's," in 1837, and "Poage Williamson's," February, 1852.

The first court held in Brown County was at the house of Dr. Alexander Campbell, in Ripley, in April, 1818, Judge Joshua Collett presiding. In 1819, a site for the county seat was purchased (now the Charles Abbott farm, on Straight Creek, about the nearest geographical point in the county), and the town of Bridgewater laid out. Two terms of court were held there during that year. The title being imperfect, the site was abandoned, and the county seat located at Ripley in the latter part of 1819. The citizens of Union Township raised by donation a considerable sum to aid in the construction of the new court house. Before its completion, the Legislature appointed Commissioners to again locate the county seat, who located the same at Georgetown, the present seat of justice. Afterward, by an act of the General Assembly, passed February 6, 1824, relief was granted James Poage by the County Commissioners, "allowing him for the building of a court house in the town of Ripley."

LEVANNA.

John Liggett was the first man to make any improvement on the present site of Levanna by making a clearing and building a log cabin in 1799. Thomas Cornack, Alexander Martin and Henry Tupper were also early settlers in this vicinity. George and Christian Shultz were the first men of business in the village, they being engaged in merchandising. These were succeeded by Butt & Shultz, who operated for a short time, when the name of the firm was changed to that of Waters, Butt & Co. Waters also kept the first ferry in the county at this point. These men were engaged in business here as early as 1810. Following these, were Myers & Evans, merchants, who are said to have accumulated considerable property while engaged in business here. Evans subsequently moved to Ripley, and Myers to Augusta, Ky.

The first school was taught here in a log cabin on the land of Matthew Davidson, now owned by John Pangburn, during the latter part of the year

Yours Truly,
John C. Waldron.

1800 by Henry Miller. In 1820, the first newspaper (the *Benefactor*) published in the county was issued at this place by Louden, Butt & Co. The paper was discontinued at the end of a year.

In the year 1849, C. W. Boyd located here, and was engaged as clerk in the store of Samuel Horn. During the year previous (1848), Joseph Ramsey had built a saw-mill, the same being purchased by D. G. Stillman in consequence of the death of Ramsey. Stillman continued to operate until the year 1856, at which time he sold the mill to C. W. and S. G. Boyd, who continued the business until 1866, when they rebuilt the mill, adding also a planing-mill, increasing their business from $10,000 to $200,000 per annum. In 1873, a store was opened in connection with their lumber business. The cooper shop in connection with the planing-mill manufactures between eight and nine thousand tobacco hogsheads annually.

The firm of C. W. & S. G. Boyd has been changed to the Boyd Manufacturing Company, and is an incorporated joint-stock company, doing business at Ripley, Levanna and Higginsport, in the county. The company is driving an extensive trade, and to-day, July 1, 1882, has virtually monopolized the trade in their line in the county.

The village contains one graded school, an organization of Good Templars, one adjunct church organization, blacksmith shop, post office, has daily communication with Georgetown, Ripley, Cincinnati, and all points on the Upper Ohio River.

For many years, dating back to 1849, the hills back of Levanna and for several miles below were set in the Catawba grape, and these vineyards produced large quantities of the very best of native wine, commanding the highest market price; but of late years these vineyards, as well as those in other parts of the township, have proved a failure. Other varieties have been substituted, but the wine is not so good, and many of the old vineyards have been abandoned, and other crops raised instead, so that the wine crop is less in quantity and something less in value per gallon.

HESTORIA.

Hestoria was laid out by Nicholas F. Devore, and the plat thereof recorded June 18, 1860, and contains twenty-six inlots of various sizes, most of them 132x264 feet; besides in the limits of the hamlet are several acres not laid out in lots. A part of the Ripley fair ground is within the limits of the corporation. There are many substantial and handsome dwelling houses here, mostly owned and occupied by merchants and others doing business in Ripley, which adjoins Hestoria, and is connected with it by a very fine iron bridge with ample foot walks on either side, crossing Red Oak Creek at the end of Second street in Ripley, and Empire street in Hestoria. The name Hestoria is made up from portions of the name of Mr. Devore's wife, "Hester," and daughter, "Victoria." Mr. Devore is in very poor health, and has been a great sufferer from pain for eleven years, and is now seventy-six years of age. His wife is also alive at the ripe age of seventy-one. They reside in a large, very neat and substantial brick dwelling on the river bank, within the limits of Hestoria. Mr. Devore is one of the oldest inhabitants of this county who were born here and continuously from birth resided in the county. He is one of our wealthiest men, and is largely interested in the Farmers' National Bank.

An addition was laid out by J. E. D. Ward, a printer, and also a member of the Twelfth Ohio Volunteer Infantry in the rebellion. He married a daughter of Mr. David and Mrs. Sarah E. Espy, and upon a division of the estate, Mr. Ward laid out his wife's portion in lots; had it surveyed and platted, which was recorded on the 15th day of July, 1867. Seventy lots were laid out, those fronting on Pike street being 66x125 feet; those back of the front tier to Extension street, are 66x120 feet, and those back of these 66x110 feet.

About six acres in the northwest corner of the Ward tract was sold to Jacob Stamm, and from the day of sale up to this year, early vegetables were cultivated on it in hot-house and otherwise. The Town Council of Ripley recently purchased this lot of ground for cemetery purposes, and it is now being handsomely laid out and improved. It is separated from the other cemetery lot laid out in 1832, now filled up, by a twenty-foot street called Debrose's street, which will be annulled, and the two tracts thrown into one.

There has been but little improvement in Ward's Addition. A great number of the lots were sold to poor colored people, who had no means to erect more than a "shanty," but peace and contentment reign here.

CHURCHES.

Presbyterian Church (Ripley).—This church was organized in the spring of 1816 by the Presbytery of Chillicothe. The original members, twenty-four in number, were all connected with the church at Red Oak, except two, viz., Dr. and Mrs. Adam Wylie, who had certificates in transfer from a church in Pennsylvania. During the two years succeeding its organization, the services of the church were held in private houses generally, and sometimes in the schoolhouse. Arrangements were made for the building of a church in 1817, and a lot was donated by James Poage for that purpose. A brick house, 45x45 feet, was erected, which was used until 1854, when another was erected and used until 1867, when it was sold and a new building erected. A very handsome little church was torn down to give place to the present elegant edifice, which was erected at a cost of $26,000. It was built on the old site, corner of Third and Mulberry streets. Rev. James Ross was the first regular preacher, commencing his labors in 1818, and continuing three years, leaving in 1821. In 1822, Rev. John Rankin was installed pastor. For twenty-three years he labored zealously, and became known throughout the country as an earnest anti-slavery man, and among the foremost in the temperance cause. In 1836, Mr. Rankin accepted the agency for the American Anti-Slavery Society for one year, during which time his place was supplied by Rev. James Dunlap. In 1838, a division in the General Assembly took place; this church decided to adhere to the New School branch connected with the Cincinnati Presbytery. After a few years, Rankin returned, and was given permission by the Presbytery to dissolve the pastoral relation.

In 1845, he organized another church, to which he ministered until the re-union of the churches in 1865. By the personal efforts of Robert McMillin, James Reynolds, Sr., Theodore W. Collins and others this church was erected in Ripley on Third street (now owned by the Disciples' Church.)

Christian Church.—In 1842, an effort was made to organize a society. During the summer, Rev. Mr. Baker by invitation preached occasionally. After one year, the congregation fitted up the second story of the warehouse belonging to a member of the church. The membership continued to increase until 1845, when it numbered 170. During the year 1846, a church building was erected at a cost of $7,000. The late Elder Matthew Gardner assisted in the dedicatory services.

Disciples' Church.—About the 1st of January, 1863, J. Z. Taylor, by invitation of J. P. Dougherty, began a series of meetings in the old Christian meeting-house in the town of Ripley. After some days of co-operation, it was proposed to unite the fragments of the two people, which proved a failure. A few persons then resolved to form themselves into a church, which they did near the middle of January, 1863, and employed J. Z. Taylor to preach for them.

During the first year, the society occupied the old Christian Church, and the second year they occupied Liggett Chapel, on Second street. At the close of the second year, it was ascertained that they were not able to pay rent for a building in addition to paying a minister, consequently the meetings ceased for want of available means and some place in which to worship. The society remained in a dormant state until the spring of 1867, at which time they purchased the Second Presbyterian Church on Third street for the sum of $4,000, when the regular meetings were resumed, and have continued to the present time.

Methodist Episcopal Church (Ripley).—This church stands intimately connected with the pioneer operations of the county. The Brush Creek Circuit was organized early in 1811, and its third quarterly meeting was held at Eagle Creek camp grounds. The next was held at Alexander Mehaffey's house, on Eagle Creek, September 12, 1812. Solomon Langdon was Presiding Elder, and Isaac Pavey preacher in charge of the circuit. At Eagle Creek camp ground, August 9, 1813, the following entry was made on the records of the quarterly conference:

Henry Bascom is recommended to the annual conference for a circuit to have and preach; obtained it.
(Signed) ROBERT FINLEY, *President pro tem.*

Thus emerged from our very midst that matchless orator whose fame has filled the world, and of whom Henry Clay, when urging his appointment as Chaplain to Congress, for which the noblest names of nearly all the churches were placed before Congress, and competition ran higher than ever before or since, rising to his full height, as an advocate, said: "Why, Mr. Speaker, Henry Bascom will preach you all to hell and half-way back again while the other aspirants are getting ready." Bascom was promptly elected Chaplain to Congress over all opposition, and thus from Eagle Creek we sent to the highest crag of the rock of our national glory the orator of Brown County, who was amongst preachers as the eagle among birds. In 1816, Brush Creek Circuit embraced Brown and three or four other counties, numbering thirty societies, fifteen local, beside the regular itinerant preachers. In 1812, Rev. Isaac Parry formed the class at "Fitch's," and Bishop Bascom appointed class leader at the age of sixteen. The following names appear on the records of the beginning of Methodism in this vicinity in 1812: H. B. Bascom, Alpheus Bascom, Hannah Bascom, Mrs. Parent, Hugh Allen, Mrs. Brown, Mrs. Staten, Henry Hardesty, Henry Morris, George Coates.

The first Methodist sermon was preached by Rev. John Collins at the first burial among the villagers of Staunton (now Ripley), it being the wife of Barnard Jackson, afterward one of the Township Trustees. This branch of the church was early organized in Ripley. A class of a few members was formed at the residence of Samuel Fitch, on Eagle Creek, in 1812. In 1818, Rev. John Gaddis was appointed class leader in Ripley by Rev. William Dixon, in charge of an adjoining circuit. The names of the principal members were John Ashbaugh, Sophia Ashbaugh, Ann and William Tupman, Rachel, Sophia and Anna Hardin, Mr. and Mrs. McDaniel, William Creekbaum and John Cauffman. The house of John Rhodes was the place of preaching, and afterward alternately the houses of Ashbaugh, Hardin and Jackson. The congregation in 1867 erected a new church building on Second street, at a cost of $35,000, including the furnishing of this handsome building in the best of style. The steeple is a model for symmetry and beauty. The auditorium will seat 600 persons.

A history of St. Michael's Church (Catholic) will be found in another part of this volume.

Baptist (Colored) Church (Ripley).—Until the year 1855, what few religiously inclined colored people lived in Ripley attended the Presbyterian Church. In August of that year, an organization was effected, and Rev. George Grayson, a colored man, became the preacher for this little band of poor, but well-meaning, people, and the church was then established. Jane Marshall, John Hughes, Adeline Hughes and Granny Brown were among the first members. By donations from friends, they were enabled to buy a little property, the old brick warehouse on Second street, where Mr. Devore's new two-story brick building stands, where, with rough benches and cheap lights, day and night services were held for some time; the congregation soon gained in numbers. Afterward this lot was deeded to Mrs. E. F. Liggett, holding the interest of her husband, one of the Trustees of the Methodist Episcopal Church, in part payment for the old Methodist Episcopal Church on Third street, now occupied by this congregation. This people have worked incessantly and to-day are out of debt, having paid $4,000 for the church building, which is large, well constructed and in good repair. The present membership is about one hundred and seventy-five. Present preacher in charge is Rev. J. M. Meek, to whom the congregation is very much indebted for his financial management of their affairs, bringing them out of debt in a few years' labor. Trustees, B. Spurlock, Joseph Bulger and Cupid Strander; Deacons, Joseph Washington, Charles Washington, Joseph Bulger, Harry Hawkins and Benjamin Spurlock.

Wesleyan (African) Church was organized at the house of Merritt Durgaw about thirty years ago. The first recollection of your historian, and it seems that it is about the oldest, as compared with those living, is that the first meetings were held in the second story of the J. D. Evans estate property on Third street, near corner of Main street on Second (now the saloon property of Atwood).

Afterward, the society perfected its organization, and met from time to time at the residence of Henry Hord and other good brethren.

The friends of the church saw that these good people were in earnest and determined in their efforts to build up a church, and they then lent them their aid, and the result was that the society soon completed a suitable building for public worship, and to-day occupies the same, free from debt. Rev. C. W. Clemens was instrumental in organizing the church. He was followed by his brother, R. J. Clemens, who superintended the building of the present church edifice, corner of Third and Cherry streets. The church afterward got into a difficulty about the minister in charge, Rev. J. Henderson, who, it is claimed, endeavored to carry them over to the African Methodist Church. He succeeded in winning over some twenty or thirty of the membership. In that weakened condition the church sent for Bro. T. H. Clinton, who possessed more than ordinary ability and who succeeded in uniting and building up the church, and remained as its faithful pastor for over ten years.

THE PRESS OF RIPLEY.

The first printing establishment brought to this county was purchased by Louden, Butt & Co., of Morgan, Lodge & Co., in Cincinnati, and a paper published on it entitled the *Benefactor*, in June, 1820, in the village of Levanna, two miles below Ripley, on the Ohio River, in this (Union) Township. It continued one year at that place, when a dissolution took place, and Mr. Louden sold his interest to William Middleton, of Ripley.

The second paper published in the county was the *Political Censor*. This paper was first established at Williamsburg, at that time the county seat of

UNION TOWNSHIP.

Clermont County, by Thomas S. Foot and Robert Tweed. The first number was issued in March, 1812. It strenuously opposed the last war with Great Britain, that being the bone of contention with the then contending parties in the United States. Foot & Tweed continued its publication until some time in 1814, when they sold the establishment to James Finley, who continued to publish the paper at Williamsburg one year, when he removed to West Union, Adams County, and continued its publication until March, 1822, at which time he removed to Ripley. In 1823, the establishment was purchased by John and James Carnahan, who published the paper until some time in 1824, when it was discontinued. Size of the paper was 17x22 inches; terms, $1.50 per annum in advance.

The third paper published in the county was the *Castigator*, the first number of which was issued at Ripley on the 11th day of June, 1824, by David Ammen.

The material on which the *Castigator* was printed, afterward printed the *Examiner*, the Ripley *Telegraph*, and still later *Freedom's Casket*, by Will Tomlinson, who removed the material to Piketon, Pike Co., Ohio, and published the *Hickory Sprout* upon it. After issuing eleven numbers of the *Sprout*, commencing July 24, 1844, the material was burned.

The first number of the *Farmers' Chronicle and Ripley Advertiser* was issued at Ripley on the 25th of August, 1830. It was edited by G. W. King, and published by Patterson. Mr. King had purchased the material for the office with the hope of assisting Mr. Patterson to obtain a livelihood for himself and family, but, finding that Mr. Patterson's propensity for alcoholic drinks was almost insatiable, he disposed of the press, type, etc., after keeping up the paper for nearly a year.

The *Ohio Whig*, C. F. Campbell, editor, issued its first number at Ripley August 4, 1834. The printing material had been purchased by Mr. Campbell from Isaac N. Morris, who had just ceased editing a short-lived paper at Georgetown.

The *Whig* was continued until some time in 1836, when Mr. Campbell sold the establishment to Robert B. Harlan, of Wilmington, Clinton Co., Ohio.

The next paper was the *Political Examiner*, the first number of which was issued at Georgetown by John Duffee and Thomas H. Lynch, on the 21st of June, 1837. After the publication of a few numbers, the paper was issued by Duffee & Pollock until after the returns of the election of 1838, when the publication of the *Examiner* was discontinued. At that time, Preston Sellers owned a share in the press, and he taking charge of the paper published it until the next August, when Lynch sold the material to C. Edwards, of Ripley. Mr. Sellers then procured new material, and continued to publish the *Examiner* until August, 1843, when he sold out to Isaac N. Walters, who removed the press and fixtures to Clark County, Ohio. Sellers then purchased the material upon which the *Free Press* had been printed at Xenia, Ohio, and removed it to Georgetown, where he continued to publish the *Examiner* until March, 1845, when it was removed to Ripley, and there published until August, when it was transferred by the Sheriff to G. W. and Oscar F. Shaw, who commenced the publication of the Ripley *Bee* upon the material. In August, 1839, as mentioned above, C. E. Edwards purchased the material of a Georgetown paper, the *Political Examiner*, and, removed it to Ripley, issued the first number of the Ripley *Telegraph* on the 7th of September, 1839. Mr. Edwards continued to publish it until January 8, 1842, when he sold to Morrison H. Burns, who published it until May, 1843, when he sold it to Will Tomlinson, who published *Freedom's Casket* on the same material.

The Ripley *Bee* succeeded the *Examiner*. It was published by George

W. and Oscar F. Shaw. The first number of the *Bee* was issued on the 23d day of August, 1845. The paper was continued under this firm until May 1, 1848, when L. G. Jenkins purchased G. W. Shaw's interest in the paper, which was then conducted by the firm of Shaw & Jenkins, until May, 1849, when Oscar F. Shaw sold his interest to C. F. Campbell. Campbell & Jenkins enlarged the paper, and continued the publication of the paper until the 19th of August, 1850, when Jenkins sold his interest to C. F. Campbell and T. F. Sniffin.

Among the graduates of the *Bee* office while it was under Campbell & Sniffin's control may be named Frank T. Campbell, ex-Lieutenant Governor of Iowa; Angus K. Campbell, a practicing lawyer at Newton, Iowa; J. Q. A. Campbell, editor of the *Republican*, a widely-circulated newspaper at Bellefontaine, Ohio; two other sons of Mr. Campbell, Archie and Charles, who have been connected with newspapers at other places; Henry R. Boss, a well-known printer and writer, now residing in Chicago; Capt. William Parker, editor and publisher of various papers in Amboy and Mendota, Ill., and in Kansas.

The next Ripley newspaper was the *Taylor Battery*, published by Isaac D. Shaw. The *Battery* was a Whig campaign paper and published only during the campaign of 1848.

The Ripley *Herald*, published by Will Tomlinson, the material being owned by a company of Spiritualists. The first number was issued on the 13th of May, 1852. The *Herald* advocated the doctrine of Spiritualism. After nineteen numbers of the paper had been issued, Mr. Tomlinson sold his interest to Oliver Baker and others, who changed its name to *Spiritual Era* and continued its publication until January, 1854.

A Pierce campaign paper called the *Granite Rock* was published in 1852 by Will Tomlinson in Ripley, edited by A. P. Lewis and N. A. Devore. After the first few numbers were published, the paper was conducted by Mr. Tomlinson alone. Next in the list was the *Scott Battery*, a Scott campaign paper for the campaign of 1852, published in the *Bee* office in Ripley, and edited by Isaac D. Shaw.

The *Loyal Scout*, another campaign paper, was published in Ripley during the campaign of 1860 by Will Tomlinson.

In June, 1867, the *Independent Press* made its appearance in Ripley, published by Ward & Sellers. At the expiration of eight months, the same was sold to Thomas Gliddon, who published it for a period of three or four months, when it was consolidated with the Ripley *Bee*. In January, 1870, Mr. Tomlinson began the publication of a paper in Ripley entitled the *Lunch Basket*. At the expiration of the third month, Mr. Tomlinson purchased an interest in the Ripley *Bee*, and discontinued the publication of the *Lunch Basket*. In the spring of 1870, began the publication of the *Reform*, the paper being published in the town of Ripley by a stock company, the publication of which terminated at the close of the sixth month.

On the 15th of July, 1874, S. J. Housh purchased of Reynolds & Baird the Ripley *Bee*, and the name of the paper was changed to the Ripley *Independent*, the same being published six months, when it was sold to M. J. Chase & Co., who again changed the name to the *Ohio Valley Times*. On the 20th of July, 1875, W. B. Tomlinson purchased the paper, resuming the old name, Ripley *Bee*.

The *Ohio Valley Times* was, in March, 1876, published by W. P. Reynolds. Afterward, November 25, 1878, J. C. Newcomb and W. P. Reynolds published the Ripley *Times* upon new material furnished by Newcomb and the old owned by W. P. Reynolds. The publication of this paper was continued until May, 1880, when W. W. Gilliland entered into copartnership with J. C..

Newcomb, buying out Reynolds' interest in the paper. The Ripley *Bee*, by W. B. Tomlinson, had continued on up to this time; then Mr. Tomlinson sold his subscription list to Gilliland & Newcomb, and the name was changed to the *Bee and Times*, Mr. Tomlinson removing his press and material to Ironton, Ohio, where he has ever since published a weekly paper called the Ironton *Busy Bee*. In August, 1881, Mr. W. W. Gilliland sold out to Newcomb, and the latter has continued to publish the *Bee and Times* to this date. The Chase publication was neutral in politics; the others were Republican.

H. J. Menaugh & Co. purchased material, and the Ripley *Saturday Budget* made its appearance on the 11th day of June, 1881, neutral in politics, and it has appeared regularly every Saturday since to the present time. This is the last paper started in Ripley or within the county; size, 26x40 at this date, July, 1882.

We are indebted to Dr. T. W. Gordon, in the Brown County Atlas, for copious extracts therefrom on the subject of the press, using his text as far as it will apply to Union Township.

THE SCHOOLS, EARLY TEACHERS, ETC.

It is quite difficult to give strictly accurate dates as to the early schools and teachers of our public scools; the following, however, will be found nearly so. The first teacher was Zaccheus Martin in 1816, Peter Wiles following him. Between 1820 and 1830, Rev. Mr. Reuben White, Nathaniel Brockway and others taught more or less. Between 1830 and 1853, the latter date being the year the new school system in Ohio went into operation, among others the following teachers were engaged: C. F. Campbell, Esq., Nathaniel Cradit, John McCague, M. P. Gaddis, George Palmer, David Abbot, M. and Mrs. Bissell, Mr. and Mrs. Henderson, Mr. and Mrs. Bowen, Joseph Hughes, W. G. Kephart, Horace Norton, Mr. Whittemore, Jonathan Taft, Capt. George W. Shaw, W. S. Humphreys, Andrew Coons, Elijah Warner, a Mr. Conkling and Mr. Earhart, of Pennsylvania. The latter taught in about 1825, and was the founder of the first Sabbath school in Ripley. In 1828, a college was founded, with Rev. John Rankin as President; James Simpson, Professor of Languages, and Nathaniel Brockawy, Professor of Mathematics. The school was continued to 1832. Mr. Brockway died of cholera that year, which was a sad and is a memorable year to our people.

In 1832, a female seminary was established by Rev. J. Rankin, with Miss Riley (afterward a missionary to India) First Assistant, Miss Ervin, second, and Miss Murray, third.

A college was founded in 1840 with Rev. J. Rankin, President, W. S. Humphreys and James Frazier, Assistants. Rev. Jonathan Taylor succeeding Mr. Rankin, this school continuing until 1849.

Among the distinguished personages who received their first instruction in the schools of Ripley were President U. S. Grant, Admiral David Ammen, Gen. Jacob Ammen, Gen. Robert Allen, C. Q. M. U. S. A., and a long list of eminent divines, editors, lawyers, physicians, missionaries, teachers and artists.

Under what is known as the "old school district system," or "free schools," but little benefit was derived from the limited public funds. The text-books used were the Explanatory Monitor, Pike's Arithmetic ("tare and tret made us boys swear and sweat"), Olney's Geography, Kirkham's Grammar and the English Reader. In February, 1853, the General Assembly of Ohio enacted substantially the present excellent system, which was published in the county papers, and the masses read and re-read its provisions. The justness of the principle, "That the property of the State should educate the children of the State," had the right "ring" to the poor man, and the far-seeing capitalist saw that as ignorance gave way to the intelligence of the whole people, his means were more safe—that theft, arson, murder and misdemeanors of all kinds were greater where ignorance prevailed; so, band in hand, the poor man and the rich one set the great school system of Ohio in motion. The results show the wisdom of our law-makers, and how easy it is to enforce law when the people want it.

The first Board of Education of Ripley under the new law was elected in April, 1853, and was composed of Archibald Liggett, Nathaniel Cradit and David Gaddis, Directors, and F. F. Shaw, Recorder of the town, *ex officio* Clerk of the Board. Mr. Liggett served many years, and died in 1877. His son, J. C. Liggett, is a member of the present School Board; Mr. Cradit and Mr. Gaddis are still living at advanced ages. Mr. Cradit has a son, and the said Clerk a daughter, teachers in the present schools, May, 1882. The present Superintendent, Prof. J. C. Shumaker, has filled that responsible position since 1871, and has proved "the right man in the right place."

The last report of the Superintendent is as follows:

TO THE BOARD OF EDUCATION:

Gentlemen—According to Section 6, of Rules and Regulations, I have the honor to submit this report of the Ripley Union Schools for the year commencing September 5, 1881, and ending June 1, 1882:

Number of teachers, 16; number of children of school age, 896; number of pupils enrolled—boys, 359; girls, 424; total, 783; average monthly enrollment—boys, 294; girls, 350; total, 644; average daily attendance—boys, 262; girls, 322; total, 584; number of days schools were in session, 186; per cent of attendance, 91; cost, per pupil, of the year's tuition, $7.90.

BRANCHES OF STUDY, WITH THE NUMBER OF PUPILS IN EACH BRANCH.

Alphabet, 80; reading, 700; spelling, 700; writing, 700; arithmetic, 534; geography, 418; English grammar, 377; oral lessons, 496; composition, 379; algebra, 58; American literature, 14; natural philosophy, 44; physiology, 22; physical geography, 26; Latin, 45; geometry, 28; science of government, 14; rhetoric, 14; trigonometry, 14; astronomy, 14; history, 48; German, 113; French, 10; number in graduating class of 1882, 14; whole number of graduates, 96.

TEACHERS' MEETINGS.

Monthly Teachers' Meetings were held during the year. Papers were read as follows:

"History of Education, and New Methods of Instruction," J. C. Shumaker.
"Practical Phonetics," Carrie Evans.
"Morals and Manners in School," J. T. Whitson.
"Use of Slates in Primary Schools," Julia Lowry.
"Some of the Results of Education," Lizzie Liggett.
"Flowers and Children." Ella Biehn.
"We Must Educate," Charles Young.
"Teaching Composition," Kate Shaw.
"Beginnings of Knowledge," Kate McClintick.
"Concert Exercises in School," Anna Creekbaum.
"What Children Learn out of School," N. Becker.
"The Right Use of Text-books," Anna Snifflin.
"Scylla and Charybdis," Sarah A. Perry.
"Literary Culture," Sallie Pierce.
"The Ideal School," S. B. Cradit.

AUTHORS' DAYS.

A few days during the year were devoted, by the higher grades, to the study of the works and characters of some of America's most eminent authors.

One day was devoted to the memory of the life, services and death of the lamented Garfield, and to the history of the American Republic.

These memorial exercises are full of interest and instruction to the pupils. They arrest the monotony and humdrum of school life.

They cause the pupils to study the very best gems of American literature.

They cause them to investigate the lives and characters of some of the best and purest men of the Republic.

If we could devote more time to the study of literature and the elegant arts—to the True, the Beautiful and the Good, I believe it would result in arousing in our young men and young women higher aspirations and nobler purposes. The study of good literature is refining, elevating, purifying.

DECEASED.

UNION TOWNSHIP.

THE HIGH SCHOOL.

The work in this department has been the best that could be done under the circumstances. I have been compelled, for the want of room in the Grammar Schools, to promote pupils to the High School who were not prepared for that grade.

I respectfully call the attention of the board to the fact that we must either lower the present good standing of the High School, or make some provision for maintaining its high character.

I respectfully suggest that all the grades of the High School be required to study the common branches next year, with such High School branches as they can take in addition thereto; and that there be no graduating class of 1884, or if there be any, only a few of the very best in the class; and that there be no promotions to the High School next year.

THE GERMAN DEPARTMENT.

This department, as in former years, has had entirely too many pupils for one teacher. I suggest for your consideration the propriety of permitting none but the children of German parents to pursue this study until they get into the Senior Grammar School. The teacher then to teach German in *German*. English pupils from the Senior Grammar and High Schools may study the German as a dead language, for the purpose of obtaining a better knowledge of language in general. I believe, as a general rule, English children will not learn to speak the German language from the study of German text-books.

THE COLORED SCHOOLS.

These schools are taking a higher ground every year. The attendance has been larger and better this year than ever before. There is a growing sentiment among these people in favor of a liberal education. I have been urging the pupils of this high school for years to persevere to the end and graduate. Three of them creditably completed the course, and have graduated with high honor. One of them taught in our schools during the past year with great credit to himself, and, from what I can learn, to the entire satisfaction of his patrons.

I am heartily glad that your Honorable Body has employed two of them to teach during the coming year. It will be an incentive to others to complete the course of study, and prepare themselves for usefulness, and for positions of honor.

PENMANSHIP.

During the few months that Mr. Wright was engaged as teacher of penmanship, the most marked improvement was made in the writing of the pupils.

I hope, now that we have a regular teacher of penmanship, that the improvement in this direction will be still more flattering. I suggest that the teacher of penmanship give at least one lesson a week in each department in mechanical drawing. I believe the results will justify the experiment.

GENERAL REMARKS.

The rudiments of music should be taught in our schools.

The text-book on English grammar should be changed, if it can be done without extra expense.

The course of study should be revised.

I hereby extend to the Board of Education, teachers and all, my heartfelt thanks for the cordial and generous support given me in the discharge of my duties.

I have the honor to be, gentlemen,
Yours very respectfully,
RIPLEY, Ohio, June 26, 1882.   J. C. SHUMAKER, *Superintendent*.

There are twelve whole subdistricts in the township, exclusive of Ripley, and four joint sub districts, the whole number of sixteen for the education of the white youth, and two additional districts, with good buildings, for colored youth. The school in Levanna, one in No. 6 and one in No. 7, require an assistant teacher in each. The average wages paid is about $40 per month. The buildings are neat, in good repair and supplied with improved desks and other school furniture.

STEAMBOAT BUILDING AT RIPLEY.

A number of years ago, there were built at Ripley several steamboats. The following is a list of those constructed here, as near as we can ascertain. There being no record kept, so far as known, we rely solely on the memory of some of our oldest citizens:

The "Paragon," built in 1826-27 by Capt. John Moore; the "Companion," built in 1831 by Peter aud Russel Shaw and Eli Collins; Eli Collins, Captain; Salem Shaw, Clerk.

The "William Parsons," by Archibald Knight and Y. Stephenson; the "Banner," built in 1828 by William Humphries and Dr. Carey A. Campbell; the "Messenger," by McMillin & Reynolds; the "Cavalier," by Capt. J. Patterson and Hayden Thompson; the "Ajax," built in 1835 by Peter and Russel Shaw; the "Fox," built in 1834 by Russel and Peter Shaw; the "Caledonia," by Capt. John Moore; the "Joan of Arc," built in 1836 by Porter, Collins & Evans, of Ripley, and Capt. C. B. Church, of Aberdeen; the "Conqueror" (six boiler), built in 1837-38 by Capt. John Moore; the "Shepherdess," by John Patterson; the "Fair Play," built in 1836 by Capt. John Moore; name not known, by Esq. Doty, of Cincinnati; the "Caledonia No. 2," by Capt. John Moore; the "Veteran," built in 1833 by Capt. John Rice; the "Shoal-Water," the hull of which was built in sections like vats—the boys called her the "Tanyard"—by a gentleman of Pennsylvania, Capt. Emery, an incessant smoker. It was said of him that he fell overboard from his boat into the river, and came up out of it smoking his cigar. This boat was built at the lower yard.

A great deal of repairing and altering of steamboats, such as splicing out, adding to length of hulls, etc., was done at the two boat yards here. The upper yard was owned by Porter, Collins & Evans, and the lower by the Turneys. A general superintendent by the name of William Gordon, of Cincinnati, was usually employed to plan and superintend the construction of these boats and the work at these yards.

When the "Ajax" was built, one of her owners, Russel Shaw, got out timbers for the boat in his woodland at Russellville, ten miles northeast of Ripley. His son Merritt, then a youth, with his brother Eli, hauled these timbers to Ripley by wagon and two yoke of oxen, through the mud roads, taking back six barrels of salt, all the team could pull through. Timber, of course, was plenty near the river; but Mr. Shaw desired to select the right kind, and did it.

In addition to what was done here long ago, the Boyd Manufacturing Company, having an office and some material at Ripley, a mill, lumber yard and store at Levanna, and the same at Higginsport in this county, does an immense business in building wharf-boats, barges, flat-boats, etc., etc., in addition to the general saw and planing mill business.

SOCIETIES.

Masonic.—A lodge of dispensation was granted to work in the first three degrees of Masonry, in 1818. Abram Shepherd as W. M., Phillip Roupe and Christian Wiles, Sr., as Wardens; Asa Shaw, Secretary. The first degrees were conferred in the Asa Shaw Building, on Market street, in Ripley, now burned down. In this building, the late Gen. James Louden was ballotted for, and elected, and the degrees were afterward conferred in Abram Shepherd's residence, on Front street, afterward owned by Thomas McCague, and now by a granddaughter of his, Mrs. M. L. Kirkpatrick.

The Grand Lodge of the most Ancient and Honorable Society of Free and Accepted Masons, of the State of Ohio, convened and assembled in the town of Lancaster, send greeting: Whereas a petition has been presented to us from Daniel H. Murphy, Amos Grantham, Thomas Middleton, Francis Coburn, John S. Beasley, William K. Burt, Zaddock Hook and William T. Tarble, all Free and Accepted Masons. * * * * Therefore a charter is granted to said brothers and their associates known as Union Lodge, No. 71, F. & A. M. Dated this 15th day of September, A. D. 1840.

Grand Lodge of Ohio.
SEAL.
F. & A. M.

W. B. HUBBARD, M. W. G. M.,
A. D. BIGELOW, R. W. D. G. M.,
W. B. DODDS, R. W. S. G. W.,
L. BERA, R. W. J. W.

Attest: G. F. SMITH, R. W. G. Secretary.

UNION TOWNSHIP.

The lodge room used was the third story of the brick building owned by D. H. Murphy, corner of Front and Main (or Ferry street as then known), where the lodge continued to work up to November 9, 1850, when the entire building, with all the paraphernalia, furniture, records and effects of the lodge, were destroyed by a fire, together with a considerable portion of the stock of general merchandise then in the lower and second stories, belonging to Daniel H. Murphy.

"Ripley, November 18, 1850, A. L. 5850.—At a regular meeting of Union Lodge, No. 71, A., F. & A. M., at their hall, in the third story of the brick building, corner of Main and Third streets, owned by Hayden Thompson, held this evening. Officers present, Jonathan Kelly, W. M.; Amos Grantham, S. W.; A. B. Martin, J. W.; D. H. Murphy, Treasurer; B. F. Johnson, Secretary; G. K. Snider, S. D.; Silas Huron, J. D.; Z. Hook, T. Members present, A. P. Hensley, Thomas Ren, W. S. Lane, J. Herzog. R. N. Jenkins, S. Martin, Isaac Moore, Samuel A. Dawson. D. G. Sellman, George McElwee, C. Ridgway, F. G. Shaw, L. G. Palmer, E. Flaugher; visitors, H. Johnson and L. Friedley.

"The W. M. announced to the lodge the destruction of the charter, by-laws, and effects of the lodge, when Bro. D. H. Murphy produced a dispensation from the M. W. Grand Master, William B. Hubbard, Esq., authorizing and empowering Union Lodge, No. 71, to work until the next meeting of the Grand Lodge."

The lodge continued to work in the Thompson Hall until the completion of the new Masonic Hall, which was in 1855, at the old corner of Front and Main, where it still continues. This new hall (the upper or third story, with a five-foot entrance on Front street), belongs to Union Lodge, No. 71. It was built by members of the lodge by stock subscribed and paid out from time to time by Robert Fulton, until its completion, in 1855, when the same was turned over to the lodge, and all stock assumed by it, bearing interest, but now all canceled by donation and payment.

The lodge rooms were handsomely frescoed and ornamented in design, and were elegantly refitted in November, 1876, at a cost of $1,200. A tornado occurring on Sunday after the completion of the work, unroofed the building, and the heavy rains following damaged the ceiling and walls so as to require nearly all this costly work to be done over again, amounting to some $400, which was promptly executed, and is now (1882) one of the most pleasant lodge rooms in Southern Ohio.

The present officers of Union Lodge, No. 71, are R. C. Rankin, W. M.; J. C. Liggett, S. W.; D. W. Shedd, J. W.; W. A. Dixon, Treasurer; Secretary, W. H. Armstrong; S. D., J. C. Shumaker; J. D., George Sheer; Tiler, G. W. Shaw; Chaplain, David Gaddis.

Lodge meets Monday evening, on or before the full moon.

Ripley Chapter, No. 84..—A warrant of dispensation was granted, dated October 17, 1858, to D. H. Murphy, L. G. Palmer, C. Ridgway, Robert Fulton, William Parker, Zaddock Hook, A. B. Martin, Samuel Martin, John Thompson and Sherry Moore, to confer the Chapter degrees. The officers were D. H. Murphy, H. P.; A. B. Martin, King; S. Moore, Secretary.

A charter was granted this Chapter October 15, 1859, A. L. 5859, signed by George Rex, G. H. P.; John M. Barrere, D. G. H. P.; P. Thatcher, Grand King; J. A. Riddle, Grand Scribe. Attest: John D. Caldwell, Grand Secretary.

This Chapter occupied the hall of Union Lodge, and meets on the first Monday after the full moon.

The present officers are J. L. Armstrong, H. P.; J. L. Wylie, King; D.

W. Shedd, Scribe; W. H. Armstrong, Secretary; J. C. Liggett, Treasurer; David Gaddis, Chaplain; R. C. Rankin, Captain of the Host; W. A. Dixon, Principal Sojourner; M. of 1st Vail, Al. White; 2d, Peter Benna; 3d, H. Lokey; R. A. Captain, John Hindman; Guard, George W. Shaw; Chaplain, David Gaddis.

The lodge and chapter memberships are large, and comprise some of our best citizens.

Lamartine Lodge, No. 118, I. O. O. F., was instituted at Ripley, Brown Co., Ohio, September 25, 1848, with the following charter members: Alexander P. Lewis, Isaac W. Parker, John W. Gue, James H. Smith and Mark Senier. A. P. Lewis died at Ripley in 1855; J. H. Smith died at Columbus in about the year 1856 to 1857.

The Grand Master gave our lodge the name of Lamartine, in honor of the renowned and revered patriot of the French Revolution.

Upon its organization and up to the fire of November 9, 1850, it occupied the third story of D. H. Murphy's brick building, corner of Main and Front streets. This fire consumed all the furniture, paraphernalia, charter and records of the lodge. The lodge then rented Hayden Thompson's third story, corner Third and Main, and continued therein until John Bennington's new building on Second street, corner of Liggett's alley, was completed in the spring of 1851, when the lodge then found a home fitted up especially for its use, and where it has remained until this day. The membership is now eighty-two. W. H. Sly. Esq., of Ripley, is one of our honored Past Grand Masters of the State. Two hundred and thirty-five members have taken the degrees of Odd Fellowship since its organization, many taking final cards upon their departure for their Western homes, and many have died. The following is a list of those who were members, and who have crossed the river of death to meet their Grand Master above, to wit: Robert R. Rice, died in October, 1850; Daniel Abers, died in California in 1851; Jacob H. Baker, at Ripley, Ohio, March 27, 1851; Past Grand Jacob De Bolt, at Ripley, Ohio, March 10, 1853; John Sentenney, at Ripley, Ohio, April 27, 1854; Past Grand A. P. Lewis, at Ripley, May 6, 1855; James Sparks, at Ripley, Ohio, June 10, 1858. Thomas M. Tweed, at North Liberty, Adams Co., Ohio, June 17, 1858; Past Grand R. N. Jenkins, at Ripley, Ohio, February, 1861; W. W. Liggett, killed in battle at South Mountain, September 15, 1862; A. S. Liggett, killed in battle at Stone River, December 31, 1862; W. F. Shedd, died on board steamer near Louisville, Ky., on his way home on sick furlough, May, 1862; George F. De Long. died a soldier in Virginia, July, 1864; Hilarius Spaelty, at Ripley, Ohio, December, 1864; W. B. Carey, at Florence, S. C., from starvation whilst a prisoner. February 26, 1865; James Carr, in Illinois, December, 1866; Past Grand W. S. Osbon, at Ripley, Ohio, November 28, 1867; Thomas O. Adkins, Jr., at Walnut Hills, Cincinnati, Ohio, January 8, 1868; Past Grand D. H. Murphy, killed near Cincinnati, Ohio, by explosion of steamer "Magnolia," March 18, 1868; Past Grand Jacob Herzog, at Ripley, Ohio, January 2, 1872; Past Grand John Bennington, at Ripley, February 20, 1873; Charles Hensel, drowned off steamer Fleetwood, September 10, 1873.

Lafayette Encampment, No. 51, I. O. O. F., was instituted in the town hall, for the reason that the Masonic hall (also used by Lamartine Lodge, No. 118, I. O. O. F.) was burned down, and no other suitable place could be had, June 2, 1851, with the following charter members, Grand Chief Patriarch, Alexander E. Glenn, of Columbus, performing the ceremony of institution: Jacob Herzog, George K. Snider, Archibald P. Hensley, Jacob De Bolt, Alexander P. Lewis, D. H. Murphy, Fr. Taylor Liggett and Campbell Howard. The first officers were: C. P., D. H. Murphy; H. P., Jacob De Bolt; S.

UNION TOWNSHIP.

W. George K. Snider; J. W., Adam N. Wylie; Treasurer, Campbell Howard: Scribe, Fr. Taylor Liggett. Propositions were received from the following applicants, and a dispensation granted by the Grand C. P., and the applicants elected and all the degrees conferred on the same evening, to wit: John Bennington, David Friedman, John J. Caldwell, Robert Lewers, Thompson F. Loyd, Horace F. Kellogg, Alexander Jolly, Harvey Palmer, L. G. Palmer, E. M. Fitch and John C. Carey.

At a meeting held June 5, at Odd Fellows Hall, the following appointments were made: Guide, Horace Kellogg; First Watch, L. G. Palmer; Second, T. F. Loyd; Third, Alexander Jolly; Fourth, A. P. Lewis, and Guards to the Tent, Jacob Herzog and J. J. Caldwell.

On motion of Patriarch De Bolt, it was ordered that the regular meeting nights of this encampment be the second and fourth Fridays of each month, which has so continued to this day, June, 1882.

The present officers are: C. P., James McMillin; H. P., W. H. Gilliland; S. W., C. D. Criswell; J. W., D. T. Cockerill; Scribe, F. F. Shaw; Treasurer, C. Zaumseil; Guide, W. D. Young; First Watch, J. M. Cochran; Second Watch, P. D. Newcomb; Third Watch, S. McDonald; Fourth Watch, S. Merrill; I. S., W. J. Mefford, and O. S., R. F. Gaddis.

The number of members July, 1882, fifty. The encampment occupies the hall of Lamartine Lodge, on Second street. Of the charter members, the following are deceased; Jacob Herzog, Archibald P. Hensley, Jacob De Bolt, Alexander P. Lewis, D. H. Murphy, F. T. Liggett. But one of the number survives—Mr. Campbell Howard.

Ripley Lodge, No. 32, A. O. U. W., of Brown Co., Ohio, was instituted at Ripley by D. D. G. M. W. G. C. Forsinger, November 20, 1874, with the following charter members: J. M. Justus, Isaac Broadhurst, J. R. Vance, T. M. Thompson, R. A. Thompson, Henry Fisher, Henry Fleig, Charles Hough, Joseph Shoulter, Robert Carr, L. W. Ross, R. F. Gaddis, A. B. Mefford, Joseph K. Vance, D T. Cockerill, S. P. Paul, William Hodapp, H. Denzelman, Jacob Miller, Ernst Gerth. The first officers were Charles Hough, P. M. W.; J. M. Justus, M. W.; J. K. Vance, General Foreman; Robert Carr, Overseer; Henry Fisher, Recorder; D. T. Cockerill, Financier; James R. Vance, Receiver; Isaac Broadhurst, I. W.; R. F. Gaddis, O. W.; A. B. Mefford, Guide; H. Fleig, R. E. Thompson and S. P. Paul, Trustees; Charles Hough, Representative to Grand Lodge; W. A. Dixon, M. D., Examining Physician.

The present officers are E. M. Chapman, P. M. W.; W. W. Kirkatrick, M. W.; George Frank, Foreman; M. Byersdolfer, Overseer; Stanley Merrill, Recorder; D. T. Cockerill, Financier; Joseph Scholter, Receiver; Jacob Stoody, Guide; R. L. Stephenson, I. W.; Adam Groppenbacher, O. W.; J. M. Hughes, M. Byersdoelfer, H. Fleig, Trustees; Joseph Scholter, Representative to Grand Lodge; Dr. J. L. Wylie, Examining Physician.

Ripley Lodge, No. 84, K. P., was instituted at Ripley in Odd Fellows' Hall, on Second street, on the 8th day of April, 1875. The following were the charter members: M. Creckbaum, L. Grim, Jr., W. C. Byersdolfer, C. Barrer, W. W. Hughes, Joseph Scholter, George P. Tyler, F. F. Shaw, George A. Stuess, Dyase Gilbert, M. Byersdolfer, R. Schneider, V. Roemer, J. M. Hughes, C. A. Linn, Jr., George W. Shaw, Charles Linn, Jacob Stamm, A. A. McPherson, George Klein and L. H. Williams.

The first officers were M. Creekbaum, P. C.; L. Grim, Jr., C .C.; Conrad Bauer, V. C.; C. A. Linn, Jr., Prelate; Michael Byersdolfer, K. of R. & S.; W. W. Hughes, M. of F.; George A. Stivers, N. of E.; G. W. Shaw. M. at A.; Joseph Scholter, I. G.; J. M. Hughes, O. G.; F. F. Shaw, A. A. McPherson and M. Byersdolfer, Trustees.

The officers for 1882 are P. C., W. H. Power; C. C., R. F. Gaddis; Prelate, George H. Schneider; K. of R. & S., L. Grim, Jr.; M. of F., J. M. Hughes; M. of E., Charles Linn; M. at A., Albert H. Grim; I. G., H. J. Menaught; O. G., Philip Linn; Representative to the Grand Lodge, F. F. Shaw.

Number of members at last report, fifty-one.

W. Wirt Liggett Post, No. 145, of the Department of the Ohio, Grand Army of the Republic, was instituted at Ripley on the 22d of September, A. D. 1881. A code of by-laws was enacted, which were approved by the Department Commander, George S. Canfield, A. A. G. Toledo, October 30, 1881.

The following is a list of the charter members: L. H. Williams, G. W. Early, George A. Stivers, Thomas Caster, Samuel Yeaton, G. Bambach, Jr., D. T. Cockerill, Jacob Miller, J. H. Bloom, William Wills, Joseph Fritz, Henry W. Rockwell, William Koot, L. Reichmann, Albert White, J. M. Hughes, John W. Adkins, George Monroe, M. Creekbaum, Fred Rutz, J. C. Shumaker, J. A. Steen, Elijah Martin, Orange Sutton, Jacob Kapp, A. Ludwig, T. H. B. Norris, Samuel Lemons, William H. Sutherland, William Pistner, D W. Johns, Thomas M. Hafer, A. M. Dale, C. C. Torrence, George Hanstein, Alfred Monroe, Byron Jones.

The following were the first officers of the post: M. Creekbaum, Commander; J. C. Shumaker, Senior Vice Commander; J. A. Steen, Junior Vice Commander; A. Ludwig, Adjutant; George A. Stivers, Q. M.; T. H. B. Norris, Surgeon; J. H. Bloom, Chaplain: L. H. Williams, Officer of the Day; Thomas Culter, Officer of the Guard; Elijah Martin, Sergeant Major; S. Yeaton, Q, M. Sergeant; Fred Rutz, Inspector, and George W. Early, Aid.

THE FLOODS IN THE OHIO RIVER.

The greatest overflow of the Ohio River at this place, of which we have an accurate account, was in 1832, which spread over its banks and over the entire bottom lands of the river and the tributary rivers and creek bottom lands near their mouths for many miles back of the river in places, and at this point covering the whole upper part of Ripley from Market street to Red Oak Creek (the southern boundary line of the corporate limits). The only visible mark of the height of this flood here is in the rear end of Hayden Thompson's brick building, on the northeast corner of Main and Third streets, where it stopped rising, as measured from the floor, at four feet two and one-half inches. Old settlers inform us that many frame and log houses, stables, sheds and pig pens with animals alive in and upon these structures passed by afloat on this broad and swift stream. Great damage was done in the loss of stock, fences, buildings and crops.

The next great high water was in the winter of 1847. From another mark in the Thompson building, referred to above, it stood on the floor three feet four and one-half inches. Both floods covered a great portion of Ripley. The damage was not quite so great, generally, as in 1832.

In 1862, and at other times since, the river has been over its banks. We have nearly every year what is called a "June freshet," coming sometimes sooner and sometimes later in the season, but those of 1862, 1875 and other dates not now remembered were unusually high, covering several times Second street between Main and the bridge over the creek. On these occasions, nearly all the property above Main street from Front to the old cemetery was under water, the inhabitants staying as long as the floor was to be seen, then moving to higher localities—into the churches and other places as opportunity offered. Occasionally, where there were two stories, the families would move "up stairs," and get to their homes by skiff.

UNION TOWNSHIP.

FIRE COMPANY AND NOTED FIRES.

"A common danger is a common interest." A fireman's fair was held in John Bennington's warehouse, on Easton street, in the year 1846 or 1847 (the old record book is lost), and proved a grand success, securing funds to buy the "Cumberland" engine and some hose. Previous to this, the only apparatus we had, in addition to what was known as the "bucket brigade," was a small affair called the "Tamer," a little hand engine worked by a crank, made something like the hand engines of this day, but, as compared with the useful and handsome apparatus of this time, it was an extremely insignificant affair, and of but little use. 'Twould be a curiosity to the present generation.

D. H. Murphy was President of the first organization, as we find from the first meeting recorded in the only record book we can find, where, "January 12, 1848, the company met pursuant to adjournment, D. H. Murphy, President, in the chair." Then was held the annual election of officers for the company, now composed of two divisions, with the following result: President, D. H. Murphy; Vice President, Samuel Hemphill; Secretary, W. B. Campbell; Treasurer, Dr. A. Beasley; Axmen, William Gaddis, A. M. Hoyt, Thomas Kirker, Charles Ridgway and David Gaddis. The first division was the "Cumberland," and the second division the "Amazon."

Officers of First Division.—First Director, John Thompson; Second, Isaac D. Shaw; Third, M. M. Murphy; First Engineer, A. Jolly; Second, A. B. Burt; Third, Thomas O. Adkins; Scribe, W. S. Humphreys.

Officers of Second Division —First Director, J. Kelly; Second, Dr. Alexander Dunlap; Third, A. P. Lewis; First Engineer, James A. Campbell; Second, Robert Lewers; Third, O. C. Ross; Scribe, W. B. Campbell.

Officers of Hook and Ladder Company.—First Foreman, D. G. Sellman; Second, James Harden.

Sixty-five names are enrolled as members of the first division for engine duty, and thirty for the hose. Sixty-two members are enrolled for second division engine, and twenty-nine for the hose.

Out of 186 members in all, we count so far as personally known ninety-eight deceased. W. B. Campbell served efficiently as Secretary from the first organization to June, 1852, resigning then, when F. F. Shaw was elected, and served till January, 1859, then John McCague from 1859 to 1865.

This organization remained as originally chartered under its own constitution and by-laws, with the two divisions under one head; one President, who was Commander in Chief, and directed the chief officers of each division at a fire until 1865, the last record being May 19. Since then, there have been two separate companies, the engines purchased since 1865 being the "Sherman" (name since changed to the "Murphy") and the "Hemphill," both good engines, and supplied with ample hose and hose carriages.

There are thirteen fire cisterns distributed throughout the town at intersections of streets. It is a notable fact that our fire companies have managed fires here with remarkable success. As long ago as February 25, 1851, Mr. C. Baird, then agent of the Columbus Insurance Company, presented a check for $25 from the company to the fire company as a recognition of the valuable services rendered at fires in Ripley in saving property.

The fire company had its friends. The ladies of Ripley held a fair for its benefit in February, 1851, netting over $450, and the "Ripley Sax Horn Band" gave a Christmas concert and fair in 1855 for its benefit, and presented the company with $170.

The present officers of the "Murphy" Company are as follows: Captain, H. Biehn; First Lieutenant, R. Campbell; Second Lieutenant, William Culter; Third Lieutenant, J. M. Cochran; Treasurer, William Maddox; Secretary, J. C. Liggett; Trustees, John Maddox, W. H. Armstrong and W. T. Thompson.

Officers of the "Hemphill:" Captain, L. Reinert; First Lieutenant, H. Fleig; Second Lieutenant, Conrad Bauer; Third Lieutenant, H. J. Menaugh; Secretary, N. Becker; Treasurer, A. Groppembacher; First Engineer, John Blatter; Second, Jordan Braun.

Noted fires.—The largest fire, and the one causing the greatest alarm for the safety of the town occurred July 20, 1847, at 12 o'clock midnight. It was first discovered in the warehouse and stable of Mr. P. D. Evans, on Easton street, and spread so rapidly that several times during the fire the citizens almost despaired of conquering the flames. Some fourteen buildings were burned, and as many more were on fire at different times. The principal sufferers were D. P. Evans, William Patterson, A. Liggett, R. Crozier, Eli Collins, L. G. Palmer, William Armstrong, John Bennington, George Easton, J. C. Campbell, William Parker and Shadford Easton. It destroyed so many buildings that one looking over the burnt district would exclaim, "How was it possible to save the balance of the town with no greater fire engine force?" Simply by every citizen doing something to arrest the flames. A writer for the *Herald* at that time said: "I must not close without one tribute of respect to the fair ladies. They fought the flames with such energy that the fiery elements could do nothing more than yield, either in admiration of their charms, or the deluge of water that kept up from the line of buckets that their delicate hands brought up from the river—no wonder so much was accomplished."

The Murphy corner fire, November 9, 1850, was also one that looked frightful for awhile. By the prompt arrival of the fire engines it was soon under control The "Cumberland" at the river kept the fire from spreading down Front street, the "Amazon," stationed at corner of Second and Main streets, prevented its spread up Main. It occurred at 11 o'clock in the daytime; had it occurred at that hour in the night, doubtless a very great conflagration would have been the result.

February 24, 1854, Boyle's Foundry and Finishing Shop was burnt; considerable loss.

A fire occurred December 4, 1854, in the two-story frame building erected by O. Baker, corner of Pawpaw (or Fifth) and Cherry streets. It originated in the room where a woman of dethroned reason was confined, and it was supposed to have been fired by her. She was so badly burned before being rescued that she died in a very few minutes.

September 5, 1856, at 2:30 A. M., the foundry and finishing shop of William H. McCague, on Front street, was afire, and extinguished in one and a half hours, but not until it had consumed the entire foundry and finishing establishment, and also the rear of Mr. McCague's dwelling, and a brick dwelling on the opposite side of the alley. Loss, $8,000; no insurance.

October 8, 1856, the Lowry & Carey Champion Saw-Mill burned down, with other loss. Their loss was $4,000; no insurance.

December 19, 1857, the saw-mill of Evans & Blair was entirely consumed; nothing saved except the lumber near the mill by aid of the fire department. This mill stood on the river bank just above Poage's Addition to Ripley. Loss, $1,000; no insurance.

May 12, 1863, a fire originated on the property belonging to the heirs of C. Ridgway, on Main near Front street (now Ronsheim). The wind being strong, the flames spread rapidly, and the fire was not extinguished until the building with Mr. Kountz's, east of it, and Mrs. Hardin's, across the street, was nearly destroyed. Total loss, $3,000.

UNION TOWNSHIP.

February 24, 1864, the Mrs. Ellen Shaw property, a two-story frame on Market street, was totally consumed. Loss, $1,000.

August 24, 1864, the stable of Ridgway's heirs and the two-story brick dwelling of Capt. L. G. Palmer burned; the stable entirely. A three-fourths damage resulted to Palmer's house. Total loss, about $2,500.

May 19, 1865, the large stable of the heirs of John Porter, on Fifth street, was set in flames by lightning, and entirely consumed. Dr. C. N. Woodward lost a valuable horse in this fire. Building insured.

There were many smaller fires during the period from 1847 to 1865, and many alarms; many fires extinguished by timely aid from neighbors; but space will not admit of their mention.

On the 26th of March, 1872, a large fire occurred in the brick block corner of Main and Second streets, east side. By skillful management of the fire department, the loss was confined mostly to the block.

On May 12th, 1874, Adam Hensel & Co.'s shoe store was fired, and the building, and that of Mr. Lokey, adjoining, considerably damaged.

One of the great fires of interest to the people of Ripley was that of the 10th day of May, 1876, which, originating in the heart of the town, bid fair to reduce to ashes all that portion lying between Second and Third streets, and between Liggett's alley and Main street. It is known as the "Reinert fire." This, like most fires in Ripley, was so well managed that the result was less disastrous than seemed possible.

Another great fire was that on Second street, originating in the frame machine shop of J. P. Parker, corner of Liggett's alley. The flames were not extinguished until the warehouse, its contents and the dwelling of J. J. Cochran, on same lot, Mr. F. Rutz's dwelling and shoe-shop adjoining, as well as a portion of A. Bodmir's, on the south of the alley, were burned, threatening at one time the large brick rows on the west of Second street. This occurred on the 2d of April, 1880.

POLITICS.

From the earliest elections down to the present, the town of Ripley and the township of Union, as well, have been Whig and Republican by varying majorities in the whole township from 1848 to 1882 of from two hundred to four hundred and fifty.

The old township record book found dates back to March 7, 1825. We find the following record: "The Township Trustees met; present, Barnard Jackson and Jeptha Beasley, Trustees, and John C. Poage, Clerk. The commission of Joseph McCarty as Justice of the Peace bears date the 18th of December, 1824, as appears from the face of the commission, it being presented this day " Also the following order: "Asa Shaw presented his bill for $1 for use of room to count ballots, etc., at the Presidential election, October 29, 1824, and allowed." The record nowhere states the vote for the several Presidential candidates.

We find no record of Justices from then to 1836, when C. E. Campbell certifies as Justice of the Peace to administering an oath of office to a Supervisor of Roads. From thence on we have Justices as follows: John Beasley, 1837 to 1849; Samuel T. McConaughy, 1838 to 1841; William Dixon, 1839 to 1860; Lemuel Lindsey, 1840 to 1846; C. F. Campbell, 1846 to 1849; W. F Wylie, 1852 to 1855; James Culter, 1855 to 1858; John Jenkins was elected in June, 1857, to fill the vacancy ocasioned by the resignation of A. M. Clark. Jenkins resigned in April, 1858, and John McCague was elected and held the office up to his death, October, 1879, when L. H. Williams was elected in his stead. F. F. Shaw was elected in April, 1860, and served continuously to the present date, his commission expiring April, 1884, excepting from 1866 to 1869 J. M. Bell served as Justice. David Tarbell was elected Justice of the Peace in 1858.

HISTORY OF BROWN COUNTY.

In April, 1845, is first mentioned the number of votes polled, there being that year 474 votes. The largest number polled was 1,285, November 7, 1876. The number of votes polled October, 1845, was 393. September, 1845, the Assessor returned: "Number of persons liable to do military duty, 289; number not liable, fifty-five. June 17, 1851—Vote on the new constitution: for, 98; against, 478.

October, 1871—Vote for Constitutional Convention, 696; against, 178.

August, 1874—Votes cast for new constitution, 298; against, 350; for minority representation, 183; against, 391; for railroad aid, 355; against, 274; for license, 352; against, 296.

The vote for Governor has been as follows:

1844—Mordecai Bartley, Whig, 369; David Tod, Democrat, 166; L. King, Liberty, 67.

1846—William Bebb, Whig, 377: David Tod, Democrat, 199; Samuel Lewis, Liberty, 74.

1848—Seabury Ford, Whig, 516; John B. Weller, Democrat, 199.

1850—William Johnston, Whig, 431; Reuben Wood, Democrat, 147; Edward Smith, Free Soil, 10.

1851—Samuel F. Vinton, Whig, 325; Reuben Wood, Democrat, 179; Samuel Lewis, Free Soil, 69.

1853—Nelson Barrere, Whig, 230; Samuel Lewis, Free Soil, 217; William Medill, Democrat, 173.

1855—S. P. Chase, Republican, 477; William Medill, Democrat, 169; Allen Trimble, American, 49.

1857—S. P. Chase, Republican, 473; H. B. Payne, Democrat, 201; P. Vantrump, 14.

1859—William Dennison, Republican, 459; Rufus P. Ranney, Democrat, 268.

1861—David Tod, Republican, 506; H. J. Jewett, Democrat, 169.

1863—John Brough, Republican, 719; C. L. Vallandigham, Democrat, 197.

1865—J. D. Cox, Republican, 695; George W. Morgan, Democrat, 264.

1867—R. B. Hayes, Republican, 650; Allen G. Thurman, Democrat, 315.

1869—R. B. Hayes, Republican, 537; George H. Pendleton, Democrat, 357.

1871—E. F. Noyes, Republican, 535; George W. McCook, Democrat, 302.

1873—E F. Noyes, Republican, 502; William Allen, Democrat, 299.

1875—R. B. Hayes, Republican, 642; William Allen, Democrat, 462; J. O'Dell, 12.

1877—William H. West, Republican, 624; R. M. Bishop, Democrat, 372; H. A. Thompson, 14.

1879—Charles Foster, Republican, 776; Thomas Ewing, Democrat, 441.

1881—Charles Foster, Republican, 721; J. W. Bookwalter, Democrat, 342; A. Ludlow, 6.

Of the Presidential elections, our records do not give the vote for electors until the year 1848, and the year 1852 is not recorded; otherwise it is complete from 1848 to 1880.

1848—Z. Taylor, Whig, 412; Lewis Cass, Democrat, 223; M. Van Buren, Free-Soil, 139.

1856—J. C. Fremont, Republican, 507; James Buchanan, Democrat, 235; Millard Fillmore, American, 63.

1860—Abraham Lincoln, Republican, 628; S. A. Douglass, Democrat, 343; J. C. Breckinridge, Democrat, ——; John Bell, Union, 45.

1864—Abraham Lincoln, Republican, 657; George B. McClellan, Democrat, 253.

UNION TOWNSHIP.

1868—U. S. Grant, Republican, 774; Horatio Seymour, Democrat, 284.
1872—U. S. Grant, Republican, 695; Horace Greeley, Liberal, 400.
1876—R. B. Hayes, Republican, 853; Samuel J. Tilden, Democrat, 428.
1880—James A. Garfield, Republican, 836; W. S. Hancock, Democrat, 423.

Of the Republican vote, there are about two hundred and seventy-five colored votes. So far as known, but one of these colored votes is other than Republican. Many of these colored citizens served in the Union army, and made good soldiers, the greater number moving into this township from different Southern States, mostly from Kentucky, during the war and since its close.

Our town and township has always been noted for its peaceable, quiet and orderly elections, notwithstanding the excitement ran high during the war and for some time afterward.

The *Political Examiner*, a Georgetown paper, under date September 24, 1840, contains the following announcement: " Once more unto the breach, once more! Grand rally at Ripley, Ohio, on the 30th instant. Preparation is already made to keep thousands of freemen—yea, all that may come—' without money and without price.' Gen. Harrison will most positively be there, among other invited guests, life and health permitting."

Gen. Harrison came to Ripley as advertised, and one of the largest conventions ever held in the county was the result. They came from every quarter—from Hillsboro and Highland County, from Clermont County, from every nook and corner of Brown County, and thousands from Kentucky—they came in large canoes on wheels, with casks representing hard cider barrels, and, in short, the people were ablaze.

PORK PACKING.

Ripley was second in the number of hogs packed in the State in 1846 Cincinnati being the first. At the time referred to and for some time thereafter, most of the pork packed there went South in barrels, by flat-boats, known as " broad-horns." These boats carried about ten to twelve hundred barrels, and as many as ten to fifteen boats would leave here in a season for the cotton and sugar plantations of the South. All this trade is now changed. Steamboats and railroads carry most of such freight, and the bulk of the hog trade of Ohio for the Southern market centers in Cincinnati. Uncle James Carr, now living, aged eighty-seven and a half years, in full possession of all his faculties, and to-day (June 5, 1882), making out his pension papers as a soldier of the war of 1812, says he helped build some of these " broad horns" at Ripley. It was hard work, the sawing mostly done by hand. Sometimes a little " jower " occurred, only when some " extra " whisky was aboard.

There were from as early as 1826 up to the present time, engaged in the pork trade here, the following-named gentlemen, as well as others not now remembered: Bartlett, from Chillicothe, Thomas McCague, Archibald Liggett, Eli Collins, H. Thompson, Samuel Hemphill, John, Henry, Joseph William and R. P. Bennington, Josiah Frost, Charles Ridgway, D. H. Murphy, John Snedaker, Joseph Wiles, Sr., James Stephenson, Silas Bayne, Campbell Howard.

In 1847–48, Mr. Eli Collins, then and for many years before a sagacious and prominent business man of Ripley, engaged in the pork trade in addition to his large dry goods trade, the writer, then seventeen years of age, taking charge of the pork business as chief clerk. Hogs were very low that year; Mr. Collins bought largely; the great flood came on, and a large lot of pork, lard and other effects were lost in the river by reason of the floor of the building (where a great deal of pork, lard, etc., was stored) giving way, the building being built out upon the public landing, and at this time surrounded by water up to within two feet of the upper floor. Mr. Collins and myself were in this story; I was weighing keg lard and marking it for shipment on the packet that day. The color getting too thick, I came out by a skiff used to get to and from the building for turpentine to thin the color, and while out the floor gave way like a mill hopper. Mr. Collins, with great difficulty, clambered up to a window sill, and was soon rescued. He lost heavily that year, and the depression of values, together with losses sustained in establishing a cottton factory at this place, forced him to succumb. Yet, no doubt, this grand and honorable business man would have arisen from the difficulties surrounding him if his former friends had supported him as they had done before. He was a public-spirited man, and died of a broken heart and shattered nerves.

Among the most successful pork merchants was Archibald Liggett, Esq. Bred a lawyer, skilled in general merchandising, and a close calculator, and above all an honest business man, he went upon the principle to sell at a reasonable profit. He was not like many who dealt in pork at this place, who, when the article advanced to a handsome margin, held on for more, and as it raised wanted more; finally, when it went down, down and down, held on till they were forced to sell for less than what their purchases amounted to.

Mr. Samuel Hemphill, now deceased, was generally conceded to be one of the best, if not the best, business man in Brown County. He engaged at different times during his long business career at this place in the pork trade, and was generally successful. He was seldom found with the losing party, for he kept well posted, and managed to get out before much loss was sustained. He was a public-spirited man, ever ready and foremost in any enterprise looking to the advancement of the town's interest and that of the public. He filled with honor official positions, never shrinking a duty; prompt, honest and pleasant, he died mourned by every true friend of our town.

THE HORSE TRADE.

We are informed by Mr. Robert Fulton that he and his brother, Andrew Fulton, now deceased, engaged in buying and selling horses from 1841 to the death of Mr. A. Fulton in 1873, and Robert Fulton to the present date (July, 1882). From 1842 to 1855, thirteen years, they bought stallions and mares, and transported them to Cuba, selling them there at fine prices. They made usually three trips in a year, sometimes four. From that time (1855), Cubans came here and made large purchases through the Fultons of horses suitable for omnibuses, volantes and carriages in their country. Mr. A. Fulton and his brother Robert made many trips to Mexico with horses—principally matched pairs. They sold a Canadian horse, "Smuggler," for $1,665. These men were splendid judges of horseflesh. Mr. Robert Fulton lately returned from Philadelphia, where he disposed of a lot of sixteen fine horses at very fair prices. These were selected in our own county and Kentucky.

Mr. Edmund Martin, of Eagle Creek, has been for many years engaged in buying up for the Eastern market the best specimens of draft horses, and at times harness horses for the same market.

Our people pay a great deal more attention now than years ago to breeding, not only horses, but all kinds of stock. They have found out that it pays to breed from the best specimens, and a little time spent in handling horses is not lost.

For the past two years, monthly stock sales have been held at Ripley, and a great number of horses and other stock disposed of by our farmers and dealers in stock to buyers from Cincinnati, New York and other points. These sales are held on the last Saturday of each month, bringing a great throng of people to our town, and consequently resulting in an increase of business.

STATISTICS.

The following levies have been made by the Trustees of the township, by the Board of Education of the township. by the Town Council of Ripley and by the School Board of Ripley, from 1853 to 1882, to wit:

By Township Trustees—In 1853-54-55 each, $\frac{1}{4}$ mill on the dollar valuation of all the taxable property of the township; in 1856, no levy, having funds left over sufficient; in 1857, $\frac{1}{4}$; 1858, $\frac{1}{2}$; 1859-60, $\frac{1}{4}$; 1861-62, $\frac{1}{2}$; 1863, 1; 1864, $5\frac{1}{4}$; 1865, $3\frac{3}{4}$; 1866, $4\frac{1}{4}$; 1867, $3\frac{1}{4}$; 1868, $1\frac{1}{2}$; 1869, $2\frac{1}{4}$; 1870, $3\frac{1}{4}$; 1871, $1\frac{1}{2}$; 1872, 1; 1873, $1\frac{17}{20}$; 1874, $4\frac{3}{4}$; 1875, $\frac{3}{4}$; 1876, $2\frac{3}{4}$; 1877, $1\frac{1}{8}$; 1878, $1\frac{1}{4}$; 1879, $\frac{3}{4}$; 1880, 1; 1881, $\frac{3}{4}$; 1882, $1\frac{1}{4}$ mills.

By Township School Board—In 1853, $\frac{1}{4}$; 1854, 1; 1855, $1\frac{1}{2}$; 1856, 3; 1857, $1\frac{3}{4}$; 1858, $2\frac{1}{2}$; 1859, 1860 and 1862, each $2\frac{1}{4}$; 1863, 1864 and 1865, $1\frac{1}{4}$; 1866, $1\frac{3}{4}$; 1867, $2\frac{3}{4}$; 1868-69, each, 3; 1870-71, $4\frac{1}{2}$; 1872, $6\frac{1}{4}$; 1873-74, each $3\frac{3}{4}$; 1875, $3\frac{1}{2}$; 1876, $3\frac{3}{4}$; 1877, 6; 1878, 5; 1879, $4\frac{3}{4}$; 1880-81, $5\frac{1}{2}$; 1882, $4\frac{1}{2}$ mills on all taxable property in the township, exclusive of Ripley and Hestoria School District.

By School Board of Ripley—In 1854, $3\frac{1}{2}$; 1855, $2\frac{1}{2}$; 1856, 3; 1857, $3\frac{1}{2}$; 1858, $3\frac{3}{4}$; 1859 and 1860, 4; 1861, 3; 1862, $2\frac{1}{2}$; 1863, 2; 1864, $3\frac{1}{2}$; 1865, 3; 1866, 4; 1867-68, 5; 1869, 6; 1870, 7; 1871-72-73-74-75, each 6; 1876, $5\frac{1}{2}$; 1877, 6; 1878, $5\frac{1}{2}$; 1879, 6; 1880, $5\frac{1}{2}$; 1881 and 1882, each $6\frac{1}{2}$ mills on the taxable property included within the corporate limits of Ripley and Hestoria School District.

By the Town Council of Ripley—In 1848-49, $5\frac{1}{2}$; 1850, 6; 1851-52-53, 8; 1854-55, 7; 1856, 8; 1857-58, $6\frac{1}{4}$; 1859-60, 7; 1861, 8; 1862, 5; 1863, 6; 1864, 7; 1865, 8; 1866, $8\frac{3}{4}$; 1867, $7\frac{3}{4}$; 1868, $7\frac{1}{4}$; 1870-71-72, 6; 1873, $6\frac{1}{2}$; 1874, $5\frac{1}{2}$; 1875, $6\frac{1}{2}$; 1876-77, 7; 1878, 6; 1879, $7\frac{1}{4}$; 1880-81-82, each 6 mills on all the taxable property, real and personal, within the corporate limits of Ripley.

We notice that in 1848 and 1849 the Council set apart for fire purposes one-half of 1 mill.

In 1856, a poll tax of 50 cents on each dog, and $1 on each female dog was levied by the Council, but our recollection is that it was easier to levy than to collect. The experiment has not been again tried by the town authorities, but all must admit that the State dog tax law works well; worthless curs are becoming scarce, and so far a great nuisance abated, and many dollars saved in sheep.

The following is taken from the returns made by W. W. Kirkpatrick, the Township Assessor of Union Township, to the Auditor of said county, May, 1882:

Number of horses, 971; value	$50,470
Number of cattle, 1,166; value	21,366
Mules, 16; value	845
Sheep, 355; value	910
Hogs, 2,333; value	7,578
Carriages, 382; value	12,846
Tobacco, household goods, etc	104,723
Watches, 246; value	5,021
Pianos and organs, 140; value	9,910
Value of merchandising	99,167
Value of tools and machinery	22,377
Moneys	85,323
Credits (notes, accounts, etc.), over and above indebtedness	185,660
Money in bonds	14,880
Value of dogs listed by owner	135
Number of sheep killed by dogs during the past year, 10; value	50
The number of births in the township the past year was	87
The number of deaths in the township the past year was	45

Number of acres of arable and plow-land...... 15,336
Number of acres of meadow and pasture....... 5,413
Number of acres of uncultivated and woodland...... 2,898

Total...... 23,647

Whole number of acres in township, exclusive of Ripley...... 24,109
Value of lands, excluding buildings...... $643,975
Value of houses...... 65,250
Value of mills...... 4,500
Value of other buildings...... 43,800

Total...... $757,525

RIPLEY CORPORATION.

Number of acres of arable land...... 139
Number of acres of meadow and pasture...... 20
Number of acres of uncultivated and woodland...... 10

Total in corporation...... 169

Value of lands, excluding buildings...... $16,605
Value of houses...... 35,550
Value of mills...... 3,500
Value of other buildings...... 3,020

Total...... $58,665

Value of lots, exclusive of buildings...... $134,666
Value of houses...... 338,030
Value of mills...... 3,000
Value of other buildings...... 8,950

Total and value of all...... $484,646

HESTORIA SCHOOL DISTRICT.

Number of acres of arable land...... 238
Number of acres of meadow and pasture...... 23
Number of acres uncultivated...... 32

Total...... 293

Value of lands, exclusive of buildings...... $12,313
Value of houses...... 7,420
Value of other buildings...... 1,300

Total...... $21,033

Value of lots, exclusive of buildings...... $10,000
Value of houses...... 20,500
Value of other buildings...... 360

Total...... $30,860

LEVANNA.

Value of lots, exclusive of buildings...... $1,765
Value of houses...... 7,600
Value of mills...... 4,000
Value of other buildings...... 700

Total...... $14,065

RECAPITULATION.

Value of Union Township lands and buildings...... $760,525
Value of Ripley corporation lands and buildings...... 58,675
Value of Ripley corporation lots and buildings...... 384,636
Value of Hestoria School District lands...... 21,033
Value of Hestoria buildings and lots...... 30,860
Value of Levanna lots and buildings...... 14,065

Total...... $1,469,784

UNION TOWNSHIP.

Value of churches in Union Township, exclusive of Ripley	$ 3,525
In Ripley	66,690
Total	$70,215
Value of public buildings, town of Ripley	$ 8,200
Value of public buildings, town of Ripley (schools)	11,350
Value of buildings, township school	6,765
Value of cemeteries, township and Ripley	2,540
Value of monuments	38,542
Total	$67,397

FOSSIL REMAINS AND OTHER CURIOSITIES.

In the year 1869, Mr. W. H. Dunn, owner of a sand bank on the south side of Red Oak Creek, some 300 yards from its mouth, found imbedded in this bank some fifteen feet below the surface, what proved to be a mammoth tusk, probably that of a mastodon. It was unfortunately broken in three pieces in its removal, and measured at its thickest point seven inches, and was doubtless originally fourteen feet long. On being exposed to the air, it became soft and crumbly. Correspondence was had with the great showman, P. T. Barnum, and a bargain made for its shipment to him at New York, which was done, he sending a draft in favor of Mr Dunn for $50 on its receipt.

Mr. Benjamin Sidwell, living within three miles of Ripley, has in his possession a molar tooth, found in Eagle Creek bottom, measuring ten inches long, four inches thick and nine inches wide, and which when found weighed twelve and one-half pounds, and, in all probability, was a grinder in the ponderous jaw of the mastodon to which the wonderful tusk belonged. There was also found at what was the old ford over Red Oak Creek, at now the east end of Third street, on the Ripley and Aberdeen County road, a scapula or shoulder blade or bone of what was believed to be one of the parts of the monster referred to. This and other valuable relics were collected by Mrs. Elizabeth Allen (now deceased), and kept as a museum at the corner of Second and Market street for a number of years. At her death, occurring about fifteen years ago, these curiosities, and there were many, some very rare and valuable, were distributed here and there, and doubtless a great number are now destroyed. Many of the most valuable were presented by Mrs. Allen's son, Lieut. L. C. Allen, to the university at Delaware, Ohio.

There was found several years ago on the farm of Mr. Benjamin Sidwell, in this township, a large stone pipe made of solid granite, which was nine inches long, bowl and stem to where it was formed for reed or mouth piece; the bowl was nearly two inches in diameter, and was in a good state of preservation when found. Mr. Sidwell parted with it to a curiosity seeker some years since.

Many Indian darts, stone hammers, axes and the like have been found in various parts of the township, mostly on Eagle Creek. Between the mouths of Eagle Creek and Red Oak Creek the river bank on the Ohio side has been washing away at a rapid rate, and has now reached a point in the wide and fertile valley land where the ancient dead were buried. Skeletons, pottery and other pre-historic remains are being constantly washed out into the river. Whose skeletons and by whose hands were formed this pottery must ever remain unknown. Doubtless the sacred and hallowed spot was nearly a quarter mile from the Ohio River at ordinary stage of water.

CEMETERIES.

There are several of these hallowed grounds in Union Township. One at Pisgah, on the hill back of Levanna; one known as "Howard's," east of Ripley about two miles; one at "Red Oak;" one at "Fitch's Chapel," on Eagle Creek, and several other church and private graveyards and lots. Besides these, there was laid out by the Town Council of Ripley a beautiful cemetery of grounds adjoining the fair grounds, purchased of Mr. David Espy in 1855, containing six acres; the lots having been disposed of, necessitated the purchase of additional grounds, which was made the present year (1882), consisting of six acres adjoining the other, now being improved after a beautiful plan in a most handsome manner. The "old graveyards," as they were known, above spoken of, are kept in repair by the township authorities from funds raised by taxation upon the real and personal property of the township. The Ripley Cemetery was and is the property of the village of Ripley, and is kept up and controlled by it. The revenues derived from sale of lots are used in protecting the grounds and beautifying the same. The remains of many interred in the old burying-ground at Ripley have been removed to the new cemetery. In the old lot and in country yards are buried the remains of many of our earliest settlers.

These old grounds are inclosed by substantial fences, but the untrimmed trees and undergrowth, with the moss-covered tablets and leaning stones, bring sad recollections of how many die and are soon forgotten.

BANKS IN RIPLEY.

The "Farmers' Branch of the State Bank of Ohio" was organized at Ripley, Ohio, being the first bank in Brown County, in August, 1847, capital stock, $100,000, and continued to transact business about eighteen years. The first President was A. Leggett, and its first Cashier D. P. Evans, who so continued until the closing up of the bank's business. A. J. Stivers was first clerk and teller, and served during all of the time of the bank. Mr. A. Leggett, Mr. Thomas McCague and Mr. James Gilliland severally served this bank as its honored Presidents. It was ably managed, and had the confidence of the public. The writer has many times seen Peter Kinney, then of Portsmouth, Ohio, come off the packet with his black carpet sack, and wend his way to this bank with large bundles of its issue, and go away with his sack filled with gold and silver, then at a small premium. Sometimes he had it hauled away by dray in half-barrel, boxes and bags of silver. Once as high as $20,000 of its paper was presented, and that sum in gold and New York exchange promptly paid over its counter.

The First National Bank of Ripley, Ohio, was organized in February, 1864; capital $100,000; afterward increased to $150,000; since then, in April 1879, reduced to $100,000. Its first President was Hon. John T. Wilson, who has continued in that position until the present time. Its first Cashier was Mr. John Bennington, a man highly esteemed for his integrity; he served until his failing health made it impossible to remain longer, and he gave up the position in 1869. He died February 20, 1873. Mr. W. T. Galbreath, its present Cashier, was chosen May 12, 1869. This corporation owns its banking building, a handsome and safe structure with fire-proof vault, double combination lock and burglar-proof safe. The charter expires February 24, 1883. It has enjoyed from the beginning every confidence of the public, and its affairs have been exceptionally well managed, particularly so since Mr. Galbreath's connection with the bank.

The Farmers' National Bank of Ripley, Ohio, was organized February, 1865, and chartered for twenty years, expiring February, 1885; capital $200,000, since reduced to $100,000. Dr. Alfred Beasley, now deceased, was its first President; Daniel P. Evans, Cashier, who continued to serve in that capacity until his death, January 1, 1877. Since then, Dr. E. R. Bell has been its Cashier. James

Gilliland became its President on the death of A. Beasley, and from death of Mr. Gilliland Hon. Chambers Baird has filled that honorable and responsible position. All its first officers are dead. Mr. A. J. Stivers officiated as teller from the organization up to his election as Assistant Cashier, and is now filling that honorable station. This bank has been well managed.

Savings Bank.—McMillen & Reynolds, dry goods merchants, together with some of the farmers on Red Oak, organized a private bank in the year 1852, and continued with divers changes in the management and in stockholders till June, 1876, at which time it suspended, and its affairs were administered upon by officers under assignment laws of the State of Ohio, but afterward closed up under the general bankrupt laws of the United States. The loss to the depositors in Brown County and Adams County, as well as those of Mason County, Ky. (opposite Ripley), was great, and a general shock thrilled the community.

UNDERGROUND RAILROAD.

Ripley has yet no railroad, but we have fair prospects for an early connection by rail with the outside world. It is confidently believed that work will soon be commenced on a standard gauge road connecting Huntington and Cincinnati through this county, along the Ohio River bank. But the town of Ripley was and is known far and wide as the place where the Underground Railroad had its mouth or entrance. On the high hill some 300 feet above the level overlooking the quiet village stands as of yore the old residence of Rev. John Rankin, who is still living at the ripe age of eighty-nine years. This building, if it could speak, could tell many adventures and hair-breadth escapes. At a window from dark to daybreak was ever the beacon light, easily seen from the Kentucky hills and the river bank, to which star of hope the fugitive's eye rested with delight—once here all was safe. Hundreds of escaped slaves have been fed, secreted and ticketed at and from this depot for Canada. There were plenty of stations along the route through Brown County, where aid and comfort was never denied. Mrs. Stowe, in " Uncle Tom's Cabin," draws upon facts transpiring at this place for that thrilling passage in relation to Eliza's flight, pursuit and perilous escape across the Ohio River. As an evidence of the truth of the statement, a member of Rev. John Rankin's family, his son, Capt. Richard C. Rankin, informs the writer that the river had been frozen over for some time, and people crossing on it. She, coming to the Kentucky bank through the snow at what is known as " Stony Point" (near the Asa Anderson farm, just opposite the Red Oak Creek mouth), and knowing the river to be frozen over, at once stepped into the slush and snow covering the ice, and crossed over safely to Crosby's Point; here she dropped the child's petticoat, which was picked up by the Crosbys the next day. Her pursurers tracked her to where she went into the river, as they supposed, for the weather changed suddenly warm, and the ice melted so that none was to be seen the next day on the arrival of the fiends who were hunting her down.

THE WAR OF THE REBELLION.

The following commands, as near as we can ascertain, were actively engaged during the rebellion: Company H, Twelfth Ohio Volunteer Infantry, was almost entirely made up of the youth and middle-aged men of Union Township. At a meeting of the citizens, held at the old Methodist Episcopal Church on Third street, to discuss and prepare for duty under the exciting situation, Fort Sumter having been fired upon by the enemy, a courier came hastily into the church and announced a telegram, saying that Col. Anderson had surrendered the fort! The meeting then adjourned to Armstrong's hall, where speeches and appeals were made, resulting in the formation of a company (afterward Company H, Twelfth Regiment), with Gen. Ammen, then a resident of Ripley, as its Captain. The next day he went to Columbus, and tendered to the Governor the company, which was accepted. On his return, the company proceeded to Camp Dennison, and on the formation of the regiment, Capt. Ammen was made its Lieutenant Colonel. Soon after, he was transferred, and became the Colonel of the Twenty-fourth Ohio Volunteer Infantry. Company B, Thirty-fourth Ohio Volunteer Infantry, was mainly made up of our best citizens. Also Battery F, First Ohio Light Artillery, and Company E, Seventh Ohio Volunteer Cavalry. Quite a number were in the Eighty-ninth Ohio Volunteer Infantry, the Fifty-ninth, Ninety-first and Seventieth, and Company K, One Hundred and Eighty-eighth Infantry. A number also were in the gunboat service, and in the Tenth and Sixteenth Kentucky Infantry, and a large number in the One Hundredth Massachusetts and other colored regiments, as also in other commands, many going into regiments where largest bounty was offered. An active home guard was regularly organized under the militia laws of the State, and did much valuable duty on the border; in addition, there was formed a company of old gray-headed sires known as the "Silver Grays;" the United States musket was altered to raised sight and long range; equipped and with ammunition to match, these old soldiers drilled, stood picket and served in raids when called out, which was frequently the case, not flinching, but eager for the fray. Many amusing incidents might be related, showing how ignorant bankers, clerks, lawyers and many mechanics and others were in the modus operandi of loading and firing their arms.

As regiment after regiment ascended the Ohio River on their way to Virginia, the loyal ladies, men and children thronged River street, with flags, booming cannon and music, cheering on the gallant defenders of our dear old flag. The reputation of Ripley's people for loyalty, liberality and hospitality and sacrifices during this long and painful struggle in the cause of right is well and favorably known throughout all this section of the county, and many officers and soldiers of the grand old Union army, not only hereabouts, but now in other States, would gladly say amen to all that we have said in this behalf. A long list of officers and soldiers from this township might be here inserted, who lost their lives on the tented field, but the history of the war is the proper place for details. We, however, give the list, so far as we can, of those whose remains were moved here from the field of battle, and those who have died since, and are buried in the beautiful Ripley Cemetery. It is as follows: Hiram Palmer, John Dawson, Isadore Schneider, W. W. Liggett, C. P. Evans, Thomas Evans, Dufore Young, Harry Patterson, John Derstine, William Shedd, William Devore, A. S. Liggett, Henry Butler, Harvey McNish, Saylem Mayfield, John McNish, Oliver Carr, Henry Sacker, Samuel Stallcup, Henry Zeller, Robert Wright, Nelson Mayfield, Wendell Mischler, Thomas O. Adkins, Samuel Horton, George W. Ross, John Fox, R. Keith, Daniel Fox, G. W. Shaw, William Tomlinson, R. C. Peters, William Lynch, A. M. Ridgway, James Guy, J. Turney, Fred Lewring, Ed Crosby, S. Thompson, James Thompson, Abe Williams, B. F. Crosby, C. S Bradford, E. J. Ramsy, Joe M. Johns, Ira Shaw, John Butts, Alfred Bartlett, Thomas Crawford, N. Wright. R. Easterby, Charles Stacy, Henry Moore, Theodore Cook, Marion Helmet, Ed Fields, William De Pugh, John Woodward, James Wanumser, Jerry Young, Lewis Cook, John Evans, James Hedges, John Dunham, S. B. Coleman, H. C. Lane. In addition to the above, of soldiers in the war of 1812, we find monuments to the memory of Robert Conn, Lieut. Peter Shaw, St. Clair Ross and William Sparks.

RIPLEY FAIR.

The late Mr. Alexander Campbell, of this county, was the pioneer in Brown County agricultural fairs. He, with Mr. Reason Shepherd, George Snedaker and others of Red Oak, received their first lessons at the Ohio State Fair, held at Cincinnati in September, 1850, and the following winter plans were made to organize a Brown County Agricultural Society, and an adjunct to the State Board. The first fair was held in the town hall (now school building) of Ripley for the show of fruits, flowers, domestic manufactures and light mechanical work, etc., whilst the exhibition of stock took place in what was known as the "horseshoe bend" in Red Oak Creek, adjoining Ripley. This fair proved a success, both as to finances and as an organization. According to previous understanding among the friends of the enterprise, the fairs were to be held alternately at Ripley, Russellville and Georgetown. The next fair was held at Russellville; but at the Ripley fair previous it was suggested that the election for officers ought to be held at Georgetown, in order, as a speaker said, to interest the people up there in the fair; it was so ordered, and at that election (an unusually bitter cold day) very few persons were enabled to attend from this part of the county, and the result was that a Board of Directors was chosen in favor of locating permanently the fair at Georgetown.

The fair at Russellville proved a success, and being compelled to either submit to a total disregard of the founders of the institution in relation to what was considered an element of strength, to wit: the migratory feature, or set up for themselves, the real workers and friends of the enterprise called a meeting to be held at the town hall in Ripley on February 17, 1853. At this meeting, the following preamble to the constitution afterward adopted appears of record:

WHEREAS, Agriculture, horticulture and the mechanic arts are the oldest, the most honorable, profitable and healthful employments in which man can engage, and are essential to our happiness, prosperity and independence as a community; therefore, for the purpose of improvement in these arts and sciences, and for our own elevation and improvement in knowledge as agriculturists and mechanics, we associate ourselves together and adopt the following constitution.

Then follows a constitution and by-laws, which remains the same, except such slight changes as experience dictated.

Under this arrangement, horticultural and annual fairs were held up to 1854. Then is was that our public-spirited men, A. Leggett, S. Hemphill, D. P. Evans, C. Baird, C. Ridgway, A. B. Martin, David Dixon, H. Kellogg, George Sibbald, Alexander Campbell, John Porter, B. E. Tweed, J. A. Campbell, F. F. Shaw, A. Dunlap, J. Kelley, R. N. Jenkins, C. F. Campbell, David Gaddis, W. B. Campbell, R. P. Bennington, Robert Fulton, Samuel Martin, A. Fulton, J. Bennington and others, saw the importance of the fair to the town and vicinity and to the community at large, and grounds were purchased adjoining Ripley (the present beautiful grounds (and August 4, 1855, a joint-stock company was formed. stock subscribed, 50 per cent called in at once, and contracts let for fencing, erecting buildings, etc., all of which was accomplished, and the first fair under the new organization held October 8, 9, 10 and 11, 1855. With the exception of the years 1861, 1862 and 1863, when from our border position during the rebellion it was thought not advisable to hold fairs, the association has held annually these exhibitions, and has kept pace with the growing interest of the same, increasing the premiums, and offering additional inducements and beautifying the grounds, until now this ranks among the foremost in Southern Ohio. This fair may now be styled an Ohio and Kentucky fair. Some of the stockholders and officers reside in Kentucky, and, as is well known, much of the fine stock and many handsome articles exhibited at this fair come from that State.

These grounds comprise twelve acres lying in the beautiful valley of the Ohio River above Ripley. A growth of twenty-one years in maple, cherry, locust and other shade trees adorn the premises. A floral hall, octagon, eighty feet in diameter, in the handsomest style of architecture; a mechanical hall, large, airy and well arranged; a dining hall, with kitchen and other arrangements in hotel style; a lady's dressing room; over one hundred stalls for horses and cattle, besides pens, etc., for sheep and hogs; booths, officers' quarters, etc., all in artistic beauty, and "the airy, fairy and most beautifully arranged band and Judges' stand, the finest in Southern Ohio. All combined make this one of the most attractive fair grounds in Ohio.

All this has been accomplished, not in a day, but by the untiring energy of the farmer, stock-raiser, artisan, mechanic, and lover of the fine arts during the long period of a score or more years, and by the efficiency of the Board of Managers, most of whom have had charge of its interests for years, and therefore justly entitled to the honors.

Much of the above information is obtained by an examination of the records kept by F. F. Shaw, the present Secretary, who, with the exception of two years, has officiated in that capacity since 1853.

RIPLEY GAS LIGHT AND COKE COMPANY.

This company was organized in the spring of 1860, and work commenced at once. A gentleman by the name of Runyan, a practical gas-works man, came here and superintended the construction of the works, assisted by Mr. Nathaniel Cradit, the present efficient Superintendent. On the 27th day of September, 1860, the gas works buildings were completed, and seventy-five dwelling houses and sixteen village street lamps lighted by gas.

The first officers were Chambers Baird, James Reynolds, Mr. Runyan, Daniel P. Evans and N. Cradit, Directors. Of these, C. Baird was chosen President; N. Cradit, Secretary, Treasurer and Superintendent of the works.

The present officers are Chambers Baird, President; J. C. Leggett, Secretary and N. Cradit, Treasurer and Superintendent.

Gas is now furnished to private consumers at $2.50 per thousand feet. A special contract is made between the company and the Town Council of Ripley for gas at a specified price per post for a given number of nights in the month, and certain hours of the several days of the month when gas is used. This contract is only by the year, and changes as different persons compose each succeeding Council, and price of coal changes.

RIPLEY BUILDING AND SAVINGS ASSOCIATION.

Copy of incorporation papers:

We, the undersigned citizens of Brown County, Ohio, do hereby associate ourselves together to become a body corporate under the sixty-third, sixty-fourth and sixty-fifth sections of "An act to provide for the creation and regulation of incorporated companies in the State of Ohio," passed May 1, 1852, for the purpose of raising money to be loaned among the members and depositors, for use in buying lots or houses, building and repairing houses, and for other purposes, under the provision of an act passed May 9, 1868.

The name and style of this association shall be the "Ripley Building and Savings Association."

The association shall be located in the town of Ripley, county of Brown and State of Ohio, where its business shall be transacted.

The capital stock of this association shall be $300,000, which shall be divided into shares of $200 each.

In testimony whereof, we have hereunto set our hands and seals, this 17th day of March, A. D. 1873. Signed: Samuel Gregg, M. J. Chase, J. T. Creekbaum, B. S. Norris, John K. Greenhow, Harvey Palmer, J. K. Vance, F. M. Green, J. P. Parker. Then follows a certificate of F. F. Shaw, Justice of the Peace, of the acknowledgment of these persons, etc., of same date. Then follows the certificate of R. H. Higgins, Clerk of Court of Common Pleas of Brown County, as to commission and signature of said Justice. This

UNION TOWNSHIP.   453

is followed by certificate of Secretary of State, which is as follows: "United States of America, Ohio, Office of Secretary of State. I, A. T. Wikoff, do hereby certify that the above and foregoing is a true copy of the certificate of incorporation of the "Ripley Building and Savings Association," filed in this office on the 28th day of March, A. D. 1873. In testimony whereof, I have hereunto subscribed my name, and affixed the great seal of the State of Ohio, at Columbus, the 28th day of March, A. D. 1873.
[SEAL.]   A. T. WIKOFF, *Secretary of State.*

The first officers of the association were S. Gregg, President; Dr. E. R. Bell, Vice President; F. F. Shaw, Secretary; J. Reynolds, Treasurer; Directors, W. L. Mockbee, William Maddox, B. S. Norris, J. K. Vance and J. K. Greenhow. The first meeting was held April 14, 1873. There were 517 shares actually subscribed, making $103,400. The amount paid weekly is 25 cents upon each share, and 10 cents monthly on each share. By the accumulation of these small sums, which were weekly loaned out; the small sums not otherwise loanable were put out upon interest, this not only being safely deposited, but drawing a small interest. By this means many poor sewing women and the wise young men of the place have now a small sum saved which would otherwise have been spent foolishly in all probability. The last annual report shows that the association will dissolve within a few months. The President and Secretary have continued in their respective offices from the beginning to the present time. The present Board is composed as follows: President, S. Gregg; Vice President, J. Kelly; Secretary, F. F. Shaw; Directors, C. Zaumsiel, J. C. Shumaker, J. K. Greenhow, John Maddox, J. M. Justice and L. Grim, Jr.

TRADES AND PROFESSIONS.

Drugs, medicines, etc.—Robert Fulton, William Maddox, Hunser & Co. and M. W. Beyersdoerfer.

Dry goods and general merchandise—H. N. Wiles, Wm Schæhfer, Anderson & Co., Snedaker & Co., W. H. Gilliland, W. H. Armstrong, M. Linn & Co., Mrs. P. Paebst, Mrs. Belle Mischler, Mrs. S. Shaefer.

Hardware—J. C. Leggett, Andrew King & Co.

Queensware, etc.—N. S. Devore, and small stocks in other stores.

Hats, boots and shoes—J. J. Caldwell W. H. McClain, N. Becker.

Clothing and tailors—A. Groppenbacher, Linn & Co., H. Ronsheim, L. Ronsheim, Peter Benua.

Boot and shoe makers—F. Rutz, P. Paebst, Hensel & Co., J. H. O'Connell, Joseph Reirer, John Pfeiffer, Peter Fahnert, Joseph Bulger, John C. Campbell.

Marble work—W. H. Harrison, Andrew Ludwig, L. Reichmann.

Carriages, wagons, etc.—R. M. Criswell, J. M. Hughes, Greene & Cochran.

Pianos—The Ohio Piano Company.

Foundry and finishing—John P. Parker.

Dentists—C. N. Woodward, J. A. Steen, C. B. Stephenson.

Physicians—A. N. Wylie, W. A. Dixon, L. M. Early, F. Smith, J. L. Wylie, L. F. Preston, J. C. Winters.

Lawyers—W. H. Sly, W. D. Young, C. Baird, G. Bambach, Jr., W. W. Gilliland, L. H. Williams.

Livery stables—R. Fulton, J. H. Woods, Ronsheim & Atwood.

Undertakers—John Maddox, L. Grim, Jr., & Bro.

Sewing machines—Cochran & Co., L. C. Hockett.

Stoves and tinware—Hindman Bros., Thompson & Lewis, A. O. Scholter & Co.

Hotels—Bank Hotel, Latona House, Ross House, Sherman House.

Saddlery and harness—W. Lokey, D. O. Evans, R. M. Johnson.

Blacksmiths—Greene & Cochran, J. M. Hughes, Daniel Miller, Jacob White, William Norris.

Gunsmiths—John Blatter, T. H. B. Norris.

Agricultural implement makers and dealers—J. C. Carey, A. Belchambers, S. Coggswell, J. C. Leggett, A. King & Co.

Bakers—L. Reinert, A. C. Bodmer, Joseph Kiehl.

Millinery—Mrs. P. Crawford, Mrs. N. Becker.

Insurance agents—W. H. Armstrong, McClintick & Co., J. C. Winters, Charles Linn, W. W. Gilliland, W. A. Moore, Robert Campbell, F. F. Shaw.

Carpenters—J. T. Creekbaum, W. F. Gaddis, George Collins, George Crane, D. T. Cockrill, John Bartholemew, L. G. Palmer, David Gaddis, R. F. Gaddis, George and D. Bartley.

Furniture makers and dealers—L. Grim & Bro., John Maddox, August Knochel.

Jewlers—Charles Zaumsil, Harry Eveslage.

Coopers—L. Ladenberger & Co., A. M. Dale, Jordan Braun, John Culter.

Painters—J. K. Greenhow, Henry Fisher, Lewis Boyd.

Coal dealers—J. McMillin, Reinert & Buchanan, Hollis Downing.

Tobacco merchants—McCormick Bros. & Co., Alonzo F. Ellis, Joseph A. Moore, H. N. Wiles & Co., G. F. Young, E. Stephenson, Frank Young, E. M. Fitch, F. M. Stephenson, Pangbam & Moore, Scott Mann, A. J. Stivers, S. Spears & Sons, Joseph Reiser, Kirkpatrick Bros., N. C. Ridgway, O. Edwards & Son, W. N. Masterson.

Meat dealers—Helbling & Keowler, George Frank, John Schwallie, Jacob Geiger, Martin Wetzel. There are cattle and stock dealers not included in the above.

Photographers—Harry Bischel, George Gabler.

Brick masons—Milton Conley, George Hartsell, B. S. Norris.

Barbers—Jackson Bros., J. W. Wheeler, R. Schneider.

Newspaper and job offices—*Bee and Times*, *Saturday Budget*, George W. Biehn.

Lumber dealers—The Boyd Manufacturing Company.

Flour and grist mills—Schilling & Scheer. Coslett Bros., J. W. Tweed.

Grocers—Henry Fleig, Belle Mischler, Mrs. S. Shaefer, W. H. Armstrong, R. Fulton, M. Linn, Al White, Bloom & Campbell, L. King, F. X. Frebis, H. N. Wiles, W. H. Gilliland, J. H. Snedaker & Co., Vorhees & Son, A. F. Smith.

Cigar manufacturies—C. Bauer, M. Beyersdoerfer.

Books, newspapers and notions—J. F. Frederick, N. Becker, and T. J. Cochran.

Confectioners, etc—Jacob Schmidt, L. Remist, A. C. Bodener and Joseph Kiehl.

Gas fixtures, pumps, etc.—N. Cradit.

Banks—First National and Farmers' National.

Notaries Public—W. H. Sly, G. Bambach, W. D. Young, W. W. Gilliland L. H. Williams, F. F. Shaw.

Saloons—Total number in the township, nineteen.

CHAPTER III.

LEWIS TOWNSHIP.

LEWIS TOWNSHIP, one of the largest into which Brown County is divided, is located in the southwest corner of the county, and is bounded on the north by Clark Township, on the east by Pleasant Township, on the south by the Ohio River, and on the west by Clermont County. Prior to the formation of Brown County, it constituted one of the subdivisions of Clermont, but then embraced a much greater scope of territory than at present. It was organized from Washington Township, by the Commissioners of Clermont County, June 2, 1807. It is said to have received its name from one of its earliest pioneers, who settled near its western boundary, but subsequently moved to Batavia, Clermont County.

The township has an area of more than twenty-six thousand acres. Originally there was but one voing-place—at Barr's Schoolhouse, District No. 8—but afterward, through the efforts of Higginsport, two precincts were formed, and the elections are now held at Higginsport and Feesburg.

The surface is greatly diversified with hill and dale, and renders artificial drainage unnecessary. White Oak Creek, forming the eastern boundary of the township, drains the eastern part, and Bullskin Creek, with its little tributaries, the central and western. Bullskin Creek was so named by one Richardson, an early settler, from the fact that, near the mouth of the stream, in early pioneer times, he discovered a bovine integument dangling from the branches of a tree. He supposed that the body of the animal had lodged there during a freshet.

Narrow, fertile valleys skirt the Ohio and the streams of the township, and from them hills rise to an altitude of 400 to 500 feet, in many instances very abruptly. At short intervals, these hills are traversed upward and backward from the stream by deep and precipitous ravines, reaching their source two or three miles inland, where the land becomes rolling. A fine growth of timber, comprising poplar, ash, walnut, beech and other varieties covered this territory originally, but the more valuable varieties have been almost entirely felled to satisfy the demands of commerce.

The soil consists chiefly of alternate strata of clay and limestone, and is highly productive. The land is very valuable, is under cultivation generally, except where the hillsides are too steep.

The first crops raised were corn and wheat, but, about 1840, the attention of the farming community was directed to tobacco-growing, and that article has now become the leading crop. Corn and wheat, however, are still raised in quantities sufficient for home consumption. About two million pounds of tobacco are annually produced in this township, which, in point of quality, is unsurpassed. It commands an average price of 12 to 13 cents per pound.

Gushing springs abound in all parts of the township, and furnish generous supplies of pure water. Deep wells are bored in places, but on the highest bluffs sometimes they have a depth of from eight to twelve feet only.

Blue limestone is the principal mineral, and is usually found beneath a stratum of gray limestone. The blue variety, when properly burned, produces a good quality of lime, while the gray is valuable only for building purposes. Beds of gravel are interspersed between the layers of stone, and, underneath the lowest, at the base of the hill, is a compact soapstone or blue clay, impervious to water. Few bowlders are to be seen in this region, but many flat stones, of a sandy, gray limestone nature, lie scattered over the surface. They are removed by the farmers and placed in large heaps, and in many instances are utilized for fencing.

Iron ore is of minor value. On the farm of William W. Clark, near the Shinkle's Ridge Church, an ore is found which, upon analysis, is found to contain 10 per centum iron.

Evidences of the pre-historic race are found here, generally in mounds. One of the largest, on the farm of Lewis Bolender, conical in shape, has an altitude of about fifteen feet, and a diameter at its base of sixty-five or seventy feet. Several of the smaller ones have been excavated, and the internal structure found to be homogeneous in character. A few stone implements were discovered in them.

PIONEER SETTLEMENT.

The history of the first white settlement of a township is not always indicated by the records of the first resident landholders. The first little clearings were often made by hunters and backwoodsmen, who preceded the purchasers of the soil in their occupancy of the land. Vestiges of these pioneers seldom remain, and their fame is usually unsung and their names unknown.

Alexander Hamilton is believed to have been the first settler in Lewis Township. He was a native of County Tyrone, Ireland, and is thought to have emigrated to America about the close of the Revolution, and to this township early in the last decade of the eighteenth century. He took a "squatter's claim" about two miles from the ferry, on the farm now owned by Joseph Clark. In 1795, he sold his claim to Joseph Clark, Sr., but remained in the vicinity until 1803. He then settled in Ross County, where he died in 1800. He had a family of five children, and a grandson, George Richardson, still lives at Feesburg.

Joseph Clark, Sr., to whom Hamilton sold his squatter's title, was the second known settler. He emigrated, with his wife and six children, from Pennsylvania, in 1795. It seems that Hamilton had lived mostly by hunting, and had made few, if any, improvements. It became necessary for Mr. Clark, on his arrival, to erect a substantial log cabin, which he proceeded forthwith to do, with the aid of his boys. It was small, and built of round logs, and still exists as a part of the residence of Joseph Clark, Jr., the grandson of the builder. Pioneer life began in earnest in this forest cabin, and the dense wilderness surrounding it gradually disappeared under the sturdy blows of the emigrant's ax, and was replaced by fields of golden grain. Wild game and hominy was the usual bill of fare. The corn-cracker and hominy-block were two of the chief instruments in use. In about five years, a grist-mill was placed in operation on White Oak Creek, where the corn for the family was ground until 1807, when Mr. Clark built one on Bullskin. He also built a copper still about this time, the second one in the township. Here Mr. Clark remained till his death, which occurred soon after the close of the war of 1812. He possessed winning business qualities, and was respected and esteemed by all who knew him. His hospitality was always open to those who stood in need of it. Mrs. Clark survived him only a few years.

John Clark, his oldest son, was born in Pennsylvania February 22, 1785, and was consequently ten years old when he came to Ohio with his father. As the oldest child, he became his father's chief assistant in developing the farm, and performed most of the manual labor in digging the mill-race in 1807. He was married, March 17, 1807, to Nellie Ryan, who was born in Kentucky November 28, 1787. Eleven children were born unto them. Mr. Clark followed

Very Respectfully,
Samuel Evans.

farming through life, and both he and his wife were shining lights in the Presbyterian Church. He died April 19, 1853, and his wife survived until December 12, 1869.

William W. Clark, Sr., another son of Joseph Clark, was born in Northumberland County, Penn., in September, 1789. In his pioneer home, he developed a liking for the art of grinding, and became a successful miller, and, with his energy and industry, a prominent citizen and business man. He was repeatedly elected County Commissioner. He was an ardent worker in the Presbyterian Church, and for a score of years served his church as Elder. He was called hence March 3, 1877. Mr. Clark was thrice married; first, to Rebecca Commons, of Virginia; consumption caused her death, and six children were left as the fruits of this union. His second wife, Martha Mofford, survived her nuptials only eighteen months. He was married, in 1845, to his third wife, Elizabeth McKee, whose maiden name was Ryan. She is still living at this writing, an active lady of eighty-four years.

In 1797, George Richardson, his wife and five children, Margaret, Sarah, Nancy, Lemuel and Mary, joined the Lewis Township settlement. In 1794, they left the Potomac in Maryland for the West, and reached Manchester Island, Adams Co., Ohio, by a flat-boat. Here the daughter Mary was born. The following year, they pressed on to the mouth of Bullskin Creek, and, two years later, came to this township, and purchased land in Graham's Survey. Mr. Richardson died here a few years later, and his widow subsequently married John Simms.

Lemuel Richardson, the only son of George, was born in Maryland July 4, 1785, came to Ohio with his father, and died here February 22, 1865. When eighteen years old, he married Nancy, daughter of Alexander Hamilton, and by her had nine children. For a second wife he chose Mary Lapole, the marriage resulting in a family of seven children. His third and last matrimonial engagement was consummated with Elizabeth Shaw, and eight children blessed this union. Mr. Richardson was through life a farmer. He was a patriot in the war of 1812, and participated in the battles of Tippecanoe and Lower Sandusky. In the latter he was wounded, and his wife went to him on horseback from her home at Feesburg, and brought him home. By religious faith he was a Presbyterian.

Prior to 1800, John Corothers, with his family, consisting of wife and two children, John and Mary, came from Pennsylvania and took up a squatter's abode on the D. Stephenson Survey. They were of German extraction, and subsisted mainly from the products of the rifle. About 1812, they migrated to Indiana.

In 1798 came Peter Emery and Charles Baum, with their families, from Pennsylvania, both settling on the farm now owned by John Heizer. They leased the land and remained until 1804, when Emery settled below Batavia, Clermont County, where he died. Baum, about the same time, purchased the farm now owned by William Tolin, in the forks of the Bullskin Creek, and there spent the remainder of his life. Both were natives of Germany, and both Lutherans.

The same year, Conrad Metzger entered the township, with his wife and two children, Samuel and Barbara. He was the son of Jacob Metzger, a native of Germany, who emigrated to America when a youth, and served in the Revolution, afterward, about 1800, settling near Chillicothe, where he died. Conrad was born in New Jersey in 1772, and raised in Pennsylvania, where he married Margaret, daughter of Charles Baum. On coming to Ohio, he first settled on the farm now owned by John W. Hook, where he cleared, in two years, twenty acres of land. In 1800, he purchased 100 acres of unbroken timber land, a part of the farm now owned by Joseph Metzger, and soon had a little cabin erected and corn patch cleared. Buck-skin was the chief article of raiment until deer became scarce, when flax was introduced as a substitute. Mr. Metzger accumulated property until he had 600 acres, earned by severe toil and strict economy. Both he and his wife were members of the Christian Church. He died in 1864, aged ninety-two years; she, in 1853, aged seventy-nine years. Of their nine children, three are now living.

About 1799 or 1800, Nehemiah Mathews, a widower, of English extraction but Virginian birth, came to the township with five children—Sally, Nehemiah, Mary, John and Nancy. He settled in D. Stephenson's Survey, about a mile and a half west of the ferry, and, soon after, married Nancy Bonaville. Their only child was Henry. Nehemiah, Sr., and wife, about 1830, moved near the present site of Eden Church, where both died, he in 1867, aged about ninety years.

Nehemiah Mathews, Jr., was reared in this township, and served sixty days in the war of 1812, in the Detroit and Toledo campaign. In 1821, he married Rebecca Floral, who died, leaving him four children. In 1835, he married Sarah, daughter of Peter Barr.

Col. Robert Higgins was one of the earliest and one of the most prominent public-spirited men of Lewis Township and of Brown County. He was born in Westmoreland County, Penn., about the middle of the last century. His father, Robert Higgins, was a native of Dublin, Ireland, and, at the age of ten years, entered a vessel as cabin boy; afterward married the Captain's daughter, Hannah Vanzant, and obtained command of the ship. In after years, he settled in New York, later in Pennsylvania, where he died. Young Robert grew to manhood in his native State, and moved to Virginia, where he married a Miss Wright. When the Revolutionary war opened, he raised a company, and soon rose to the rank of Colonel. At the battle of Germantown, he was taken prisoner and confined in New York Harbor, and subsequently at Long Island. He returned to his home on the Potomac, in Virginia, about the time of Cornwallis' surrender, and there married his second wife, Mary Jolliffe, who was born and raised near Winchester, that State. In 1798, they moved West, lived a year in Kentucky, opposite his survey in Lewis Township; then, in the spring of 1799, he crossed the river, and occupied a rude cabin on the site of Higginsport. Here, in the year 1800, was born to them a son, John J., father of Robert Higgins, for many years Clerk of the Court of Brown County. Col. Higgins was eminently identified with the interests of Lewis Township for many years. During the first few years, he was engaged in clearing his farm. His wife died in 1806, leaving three children—Robert, who died in the West; John J., who died at Georgetown; and Lydia, who was the wife of Gen. Thomas L. Hamer. Col. Higgins died in 1825.

Stephen Bolender, his wife and their nine children—Peter, Henry, Barbara, Catharine, Jacob, Elizabeth, Christian, Stephen and Joseph—settled in the township in 1800. He was of German descent, and born in Pennsylvania about 1750. He purchased 200 acres near the ferry, and, soon after, lost his wife. Both he and his wife were blacksmiths, and were perhaps the first to follow the trade here. He afterward married Elizabeth Fetterman, a native of Maryland, and, in a few years, moved to Taylor's Survey, buying first 1,342 acres and afterward adding 600 more. He was a local minister of the Dunkard faith and labored zealously for his church. He possessed a strong mind, will and constitution, and had a special admiration for a truthful man. His death occurred about 1821, and his wife survived him several years. By his two marriages he had fourteen children. Before death, he divided his extensive real estate by lot among his children. They all settled in this vicinity, though some in Clermont County.

Stephen Bolender, Jr., son of the above pioneer, was born June 6, 1800. At the age of nineteen, he married Rebecca Hancock. He was a life-long farmer and resident of Brown County. He was a man of unquestioned principle and integrity, and in manner was unostentatious and unassuming. His death occurred December 12, 1871, his wife surviving him. Both adhered to the Christian Church. Nine of their children are now living.

With the advent of the new century, the settlements increased more rapidly. John York settled about this time on White Oak Creek, in Col. Higgins' Survey. He remained here till his death, in 1832.

Samuel Tatman, with his wife and son James, came about 1800 or 1801, from Kentucky, and settled in E. Taylor's Survey, No. 1,659, but, in 1812 or thereabouts, moved near the site of Feesburg. He is said to have served in the war of 1812. Jacob Miller, Henry Wise, Sr., Henry Wise, Jr., and James Roney were also among the early arrivals.

John Boude was a widely known and kindly remembered character of early times. He was born near Lancaster, Penn., November 20, 1765, of Irish and French extraction. He married Ann Thame in 1793, and, three years later, they, with their son Samuel, came down the Ohio in a flat-boat from Pittsburgh to Maysville, then Limestone, Ky. Four years of pioneer toil were spent in that State, and in 1800 Boude purchased 400 acres in Lewis Township and moved thither. A modest little cabin was constructed about two hundred feet west of the present ferry landing, but it has long since been washed away by the waters of the Ohio. A brick edifice succeeded it in 1817, the first residence of the kind in this region. As early as 1800, Boude opened a ferry from the present site of Augusta, Ky., to the Ohio side, and landed many pioneers on Brown County soil. As early as 1820, he erected a warehouse at this point, and purchased grain, bacon, flour and whisky, boating them down the river. He superintended agricultural pursuits through life, possessed a vigorous constitution and keen eyesight, and was one of Brown County's most enterprising citizens, always ready to assist in any public improvements. He was appointed the first Sheriff of Clermont County. In religious belief he was a Presbyterian. He died July 21, 1841, and his wife survived him fourteen years. Their descendants are widely scattered. One grandson is Judge J. H. Boude, of Augusta, Ky.

Toward the close of the last century, William Park and family emigrated from Ireland to America, locating in Pennsylvania. About 1800, he came to this township, settling on Shinkle's Ridge, in Graham's Survey. They had twelve children in all, the last born while they were en route for Brown County, but only eight came with them here from Pennsylvania. He died in 1836, aged ninety-five years. He was a member of the Masonic order, and for many years Justice of the Peace. John Park, a son, came from Pennsylvania in 1819, and settled near his father. He held the post office at his residence for some time.

Leonard Metzger, brother of Conrad, emigrated from Pennsylvania about 1802; leased the farm now owned by William Sargent; married Barbara, daughter of Charles Baum, and a few years later, purchased a home near Felicity, in Clermont County, and removed there. In 1828, he purchased 168 acres in E. Stevens' Survey, and returned to this township, where he died November 20, 1861.

Charles Canary was born near Linningen, Germany, in 1744. Prior to 1776, he came to America, and served under Washington throughout the entire struggle for American independence. He married Margaret Swyer, at Philadelphia, March 31, 1777, and in 1790 they settled in Washington, Ky. March 16, 1804, he brought his family to Lewis Township, purchasing the farm now owned by John W. Hook, where both he and his wife died. He was among the early Justices, and, though he possessed some peculiar traits, was honored and esteemed. His son William, born in Washington, Ky., May 27, 1797, married Elizabeth Ross July 20, 1820, succeeded his father in the old homestead, and died March 2, 1865, leaving a large family.

James Cahall, another pioneer, and a native of Ireland, settled on James Herron's Survey. He was a weaver by trade.

In 1805, Christian Shinkle and family moved to the township. Henry Mohn, who had married the oldest daughter, accompanied them. Mr. Shinkle was of German descent, and was born and raised near Philadelphia. Though a mere youth when the Revolution began, he enlisted and served in his country's defense. He purchased 1,000 acres in the R. C. Jacobs Survey, when it was yet untouched by the woodman's ax, and spent his life here in wresting it from its native wildness. His wife died in 1814, and he remarried Elizabeth Stayton. Early in life he united with the Presbyterian Church, and was an upright and liberal man. His death occurred in 1833. Henry Mohn died in 1838; his wife, ten years later.

In 1805, Alexander Love arrived. He was born in Ireland in 1776, and in 1794 embarked for America, and soon after reached Cincinnati, where he worked at odd jobs, lived frugally and saved his earnings. In 1806, he purchased a little home in this township. now owned by George Love, and, with his young wife, Ellen, daughter of Charles Canary, moved on it. Both were members of the Christian Church. Their family consisted of seven children.

The same year, James and Aquilla Norris, two brothers, moved to Ohio. They were originally from Maryland, but immediately from Kentucky. James settled near Dayton, and Aquilla came to this township, accompanied by Abraham Norris, his nephew, the son of another brother, Thomas. Aquilla remained a citizen of the township till his death, which occurred soon after the war of 1812. A large family of children survived him. Abraham Norris was one of a family of sixteen children. In 1793, he located near Washington, Ky., and, three years later, married Anna Lamb. When he came to Lewis Township, he purchased 125 acres in Lawson's Survey, and there spent a life of useful, earnest toil. Bazil Norris, the oldest of his thirteen children, is at this writing still living. He was born November 28, 1796, and has lived in Lewis Township almost fourscore years.

In 1807, Joshua Davidson and family became residents of the township. Mr. Davidson was of Scotch ancestry, his father, William, having emigrated to America from Scotland. Joshua was an officer during the Revolution. Soon after the close of the war, he married, and, in 1790, settled in Bracken County, Ky., where he remained till his removal to Lewis Township. He settled on White Oak Creek, and died there in 1839. Of his eight children, William was the eldest, born in Pennsylvania in 1784. He early learned millwrighting, and followed that pursuit. He died at the age of fifty-five, leaving a family of ten children.

William Trout, in 1809, emigrated to the township, with his wife and one child, John. He was born in Tennessee, but learned the blacksmith's trade in North Carolina, and there married Sarah, daughter of Christian Hoss. He lived temporarily on the place David Barr now occupies, but subsequently moved to Knox's Survey. He died in 1879, his wife the year following. When Mr. Trout first set up his forge, he was of great service to the new settlement in pursuing his trade. In disposition, he was inclined to be peaceable and attentive to business.

In 1810 came Christian Hoss and wife, from Lincoln County, N. C. They were of German extraction, and have left many descendants in this township.

The same year, John Jackson brought his family from Kentucky, and settled in J. Graham's Survey, No. 2,338. He was engaged in the Indian struggles in 1812. His wife is remembered as a noble, self-sacrificing woman, whose services as a nurse were always ready when needed by any of her neighbors.

The year 1811 brought from South Carolina Christopher Barr, who was born on the Rhine, and had emigrated to America prior to the Revolution, and served in it as a patriot. He and his wife died in Lewis Township, at advanced ages. Peter Barr, their son, came from North Carolina in 1811, with his wife and three children—David, Margaret and Anna. He had married Barbary, daughter of Christian Huss, in 1806. On coming to Lewis Township, he bought fifty acres of land where John Richey now lives. His rude and yet frail pole cabin here was successively replaced by a solid hewed-log house, and a substantial brick, still standing. He was a pronounced Jacksonian in politics, and died August 13, 1852; his wife's decease occurred eleven years later.

Jesse Printy, another pioneer, was born in Trenton, N. J., in 1784, and, in 1796, settled in Mason County, Ky. Fourteen years later, he moved to this township.

John Hancock was another early settler. He subsequently moved to Kentucky. A daughter, Rebecca, widow of Stephen Bolender, Jr., is still living in the township, at the age of eighty-two.

John Bartley came from North Carolina and settled in Lewis Township, Graham's Survey, but, in 1835, moved to Illinois. The Logans, Wellses, John Sargent, Ephraim Minor and others were also early settlers. The war of 1812 momentarily checked the increasing tide of emigration, but it soon set in again, with greater vigor than before, and the township's wilderness became rapidly converted into pleasant farms and happy homes.

SCHOOLS.

As the first settlements of the township were made on the ridge in the vicinity of Union Church, it is highly probable that the first schools were also held here. It is said that a cabin for school purposes was erected here as early as 1802. One of the earliest teachers was Thomas Bonwell. Some time later, a rude house was built about one-fourth of a mile north of the present residence of George Love. The teacher's furniture in this school consisted of a small block of wood to sit on, a small table to pound on, and last, but not least, several beech withes, not small, the use of which needs no particularization. A "Hard-Shell" Baptist minister, Rev. Mann, taught the school six months in the year by subscription, accepting, for the scant tuition allowed, grain, fruit, homespun goods, etc. Among the pupils who attended this school may be mentioned Robert Cahall, William Young and Lydia Higgins.

It was not long before schools were started in other sections of the township. One stood near the Mt. Zion Methodist Episcopal Church; another near the old homestead of Benjamin Sells.

There are at present fourteen subdistricts in the township, besides several fractional districts. The school buildings are mostly frame, well furnished, and surrounded with pleasant yards.

Until 1870, the colored children had not access to the schools, and in that year the Board of Education established a colored district, including the entire township, and built a schoolhouse one and three-fourths miles from Higginsport, on the pike near George Love's place. The first teacher here was E. H. Jamison, colored.

The school enumeration of the township in September, 1881, was as follows:

Number of white males, 344; number of white females, 286; total, 630; number of colored males, 14; number of colored females, 13; total, 27; grand total, 657.

There are fifteen schoolhouses in the township, and the aggregate value of school property is $8,650. The school year averages twenty-seven weeks. The average daily attendance during the year closing September, 1881, was 298.

SCHOOLS OF HIGGINSPORT.

For many years, Higginsport has formed a special school district. The first schoolhouse in the place was a log cabin, built about 1807. It stood near the present residence of George Love. Another school was held about 1822, in Robert Higgins' warehouse, which stood just east of Lot No. 1 of the present town. The growth of the village warranted the erection of a log schoolhouse on the public square in 1828, which also served for a number of years as a meeting-house. A school was also taught once or twice in the currying room of a tannery which stood on the corner of Samuel Waterfield's lot.

As nearly as can be ascertained, a brick building was erected in 1845, on Lot No. 89. The school here was graded, and contained four departments. May 6, 1854, the subdistrict was made a special or village district, and T. J. Stafford was elected the first Superintendent, at a salary of $40 per month. Other Superintendents of these schools have been John Pattison, now of Cincinnati, Dr. Y. Stephenson, T. J. Curry, T. J. Mitchell, L. C. Dunham and E. B. Stivers.

As early as 1868, active measures were taken looking to the erection of a new building, owing to the insecurity of the old brick schoolhouse and its lack of room, but nothing was accomplished until the spring of 1880, when an election held for the purpose resulted in favoring the erection of a $15,000 house. The Board of Directors then in office were Dr. Wesley Love, Taylor Manchester and A. Nestor. The house, as now completed, has cost about $18,000. It is modeled after the school building of Maysville, Ky., but is a much handsomer and more commodious structure. The village now has a schoolhouse second to none in the county. It is constructed of brick, is 63x66 feet in size, two stories high, contains six rooms, each 33x26 feet and thirteen feet high. On the second floor is also a lecture hall, 56x33 feet, with a sixteen-foot ceiling. In the corner-stone was deposited a copy of each newspaper published in the county, a brief sketch of the schools from an early date by Prof. Wilber Smith, coins, and portraits of county officials and Presidents of the United States.

The enumeration of September, 1881, shows, of white males between the ages of six and twenty-one years, 161; white females between the ages of six and twenty-one, 175; total, 336; colored males between the ages of six and twenty-one, 8; colored females between the ages of six and twenty-one, 9; total, 17; grand total, 353.

The attendance is about two hundred and fifty pupils. Six teachers are employed. For the colored children, school is held in a rented building, where one teacher is employed. The departments are the high, grammar, first and second intermediate and first and second primary. E. B. Stivers was the first Superintendent in the new schools.

CHURCHES.

In the spring of 1818, Elder Matthew Gardner, a newly installed minister of the Christian Church, visited the settlement on Shinkle's Ridge, and there organized the Union Church. This was the first religious society in the township, though there had previously been occasional preaching by ministers of different denominations. In 1819, the congregation included over two hundred members. The first meetings were held in the woods, where Henry Mohn, John Young and John B. Shinkle were elected Deacons. In 1821, a stone chapel was erected, 44x64 feet. In 1852, it gave way to the present brick structure, 36x50 feet, costing about $1,500. There are now 122 members, served by Elder J. P. Daugherty, of Higginsport. The present Board of Trustees are Samuel Meranda, Michael Shinkle and William M. Gardner. The Deacons are J. M. Gardner and Walter L. Shinkle.

The Higginsport Christian Church was organized in 1839, by Elder John Phillips, and, for some reason, re-organized in 1841 by Elder Matthew Gardner. Under his care, a brick church was built (now used as a town hall). The society met with reverses, and was again re-organized in 1851 by Elder P. M. Devore and Namon Dawson. In 1874, the church decided to erect a new church, and appointed the necessary committees. It was finished at a cost of about $2,500, and dedicated November 7, 1875. Numerous accessions were made, and the congregation now numbers 215 members. The officers of 1882 are: Pastor, J. P. Daugherty; Trustees, B. F. Drake, W. E. Ellis and D. S. Guthrie; Deacons, George N. Evans, William Yearsley and John Pribble; Clerk, Ettie Martin; Treasurer, Dr. Guthrie. Sabbath school is held every Sabbath morning, and is superintended by William Yearsley.

The Christian Church at Feesburg, the second outgrowth of Union Church, was organized May 3, 1854, by Elder C. C. Phillips. The following is a list of its early members: Christian Shinkle, Sr., Susan Shinkle, Joseph Bolender, Sr., Elizabeth Bolender, John D. King, Mary King, William Norris, Gilbert Norris, Barbara Barr, Sarah Norris, Mary Mofford, Elizabeth Powell, Stephen Bolender, Rebecca Bolender, Celia Norris, John M. Miller, Celia Shinkle, Sarah Lindsey, Lydia Lindsey, Kizza Norris, Lydia Shinkle, Joseph Bolender, Jr., Sophia Irwin, Elizabeth Powell, Jr., N. B. Mofford, Maria Mofford, Sarah Barr, Daniel Shinkle, Jane Stewart, Margaret Cochran, Catharine J. Dudley, Elizabeth Shinkle, Margaret Speece, Susan Moyers, America Tatman, Rachel Wilson, Eliza D. Shinkle, Pelina Bashford, Minerva Bashford, William A. Wilson, Elizabeth Tatman, Harriet Coffman, Phœbe A. Boots, Ruth Speece, Christian Shinkle, Jr., Mary Judd, Sarah A. Norris, Emeline Norris, Nancy White and Mary E. White. The present membership is about three hundred. A house of worship was completed in 1855 at a cost of $2,033. It is a neat gothic brick, 58x34 feet, and sixteen-foot story, and well finished. The ground on which the building stands was donated by Mrs. J. W. Stayton and Mrs. John D. King. The first Trustees were Joseph Bolender, Sr., John D. King, William Norris, Daniel Shinkle and Joseph Bolender, Jr., elected October 2, 1854; the first Deacons were Joseph Bolender, Sr., and John D. King. The pastors, with their terms of service, have been C. C. Phillips, two years; Noah Michael, two years; O. J. Wait, two years; J. P. Daugherty, one year; S. A. Hutchinson, three years; Charles Manchester, one year; S. S. Newhouse, present incumbent, seventeen years.

Mt. Zion Methodist Episcopal Church was organized as a class at the residence of Benjamin Sells, about 1820. It is believed that Rev. Benjamin Lawrence officiated, and took into the class as members Benjamin Sells and wife, Jeremiah Plummer and wife, Jeremiah Joslin and wife, Thomas Yates and wife, Mrs. Molly Tatman, Namon Chapman and wife, William Plummer and wife, John Jackson and wife, and a few others. Namon Chapman was elected Class-Leader. The early meetings were conducted in private dwellings and the schoolhouse near Benjamin Sells' place. About 1825, the membership had attained sufficient strength to build a church, and a brick structure was reared about seventy-five yards south of the present church building. It was not entirely completed until about 1835. Namon Chapman, Jeremiah Plummer and Benjamin Sells were chiefly instrumental in its erection. The present commodious brick church was built nearly twenty-five years ago. Among the early ministers in charge of this church were Benjamin Lakin, William Thompson. Burrows Weslick, William Burke, James B. Finley, Henry B. Bascom and Rev. John Everhart.

Eden Methodist Episcopal Church is located in R. Lawson's Survey, No. 1,716. The class was organized soon after Mt. Zion. In 1837, the present brick structure was erected, but it has since been extended. The Trustees of the church are Joseph Cochran, George M. Wood, J. P. Richards, Alexander Martin and George Roselot; Stewards, George M. Wood and J. P. Richards; Class-Leaders, J. P. Richards, J. P. Martin and Ellen Norris. The present membership is about seventy. Rev. E. M. Cole is the minister.

A Methodist Episcopal organization was effected at Feesburg, by Rev. Jones, at the residence of George Richardson, in 1842. The following year their present comfortable church was begun, but, for some reason, not completed until 1846. An interesting Sabbath school has been maintained for many years in connection with the church work. With it O. H. Higgins has been prominently identified. Among the early ministers were Revs. Parish, Dimmett, Fee, Morrow, Wharton and Curry. The circuit was divided in 1877. From that date until 1880, Rev. H. Stokes supplied the pulpit. Rev. E. M. Cole ministers to it now.

In 1839, a class of the Methodist Episcopal faith was organized at Higginsport, in which Messrs. Patterson and Dennis Cassett were prominent. It included few members and little wealth, but a house of worship was erected just east of the town park, on Lot 52, where the little band met for several years, and then dissolved, in spite of the strenuous efforts of a few to maintain it.

The Wesley Chapel Methodist Church (German) at Higginsport seems to have been partially the outgrowth of the above class. It was organized in the spring of 1856, with a membership of fifteen, under the management of Rev. John W. Fishbach, and under his charge, a frame house, 26x38 feet, was erected in 1857, with Frederick Daum, Philip Prelzinger, Dennis Cassett, Ferdinand Martin and Dr. Smith as Board of Directors. Including the ground, it cost $900. Frederick Held was first Class-Leader; G. P. Moeller, first Steward. The present Steward is Charles Miller; the present Class-Leader, John Messersmith. The membership is twenty-eight at present, and Rev. William E. Nocka officiates.

Rev. John Rankin, a noted pioneer minister, organized the first Presbyterian congregation in the township, at the dwelling of John Clark, about 1820. It was originally small, but grew and prospered under an efficient ministry, and was known as the Ebenezer Church. A meeting-house was erected in a few years on Bullskin Creek, near J. N. Tolin's blacksmith shop. About twenty-five years ago, further services were abandoned.

The Presbyterian Church at Feesburg dates its origin from July 24, 1841, and within a short time, the present brick building, 40x50 feet, was completed, the Building Committee consisting of Daniel Trout and William Bucher. The original members were John McMerchey, James McKinney, William McMerchey, John Trout, David Trout, Daniel Trout, Joseph McKee, Samuel McBeth, Peter McMerchey, William Buckner, Mrs. William Baker and her two daughters, together with the wives of most of the male members—in all, about thirty

members. The congregation now numbers about eighty. It has been regularly supplied most of the time, but at present is without an installed pastor.

The Higginsport Presbyterian Church was organized March 18, 1848, by Rev. D. H. Allen, of the Cincinnati Presbytery, and Rev. D. Gould, of Georgetown, with the following members: William Maxwell, Esther Maxwell, Jacob Vandyke, Isabella Vandyke, Jane, Julia and Mary Pollock, William Tolin, Nancy Tolin, Charles McLain, Nancy Wiley, Ellen Strouble, Mary J. Davis, and James and Mary Miller. The original Elders were William Maxwell, Jacob Vandyke and James Miller; the present ones are Orin Doty and A. Schillings. The present Trustees are W. A. Maxwell, Orin Doty, C. E. Harrison and F. M. Park. Services were conducted in the Methodist Church until 1853, when the brick church now in use, 32x55, was erected. With the bell that surmounts it, the total cost was $2,500. The removal of families and death have reduced the membership to twenty-four, but, under the present ministrations of Rev. R. Valentine, of Augusta, Ky., it is recovering its former strength. This denomination also conducts services occasionally at Boude's Chapel, near the ferry, a small but neat frame building.

The German Reformed Church at Higginsport was dedicated October 20, 1872, by O. F. Accola, of Dayton, Ohio. The building is a small frame, and the membership seventy-two. The Trustees of the society are Henry Schaaf and Low Mohr. Otto Berz and Val Amstett are the Deacons.

Nearly fifty years ago, a congregation of Universalists was organized by Rev. Gillmore, of Cincinnati. Jesse Dugan, Samuel Yearsley, Isaac Roe, William Dugan, Samuel Collahan and a few others comprised the original membership. Rev. Schoonover served them for a number of years, but the congregation has long since ceased to exist.

EARLY ROADS.

During the first decade of this century, a road was cut through the woods from Boude's Ferry to Williamsport, the then seat of justice of Clermont County. It started from the river, just below the Sunnyside Garden, winding up the hill along the ravine through Stephenson's Survey, No. 630, then through J. Graham's Survey, and on as nearly as possible a straight line to its terminus. About the same time, one was built from Clark's grist-mill to the river. There are now several free pikes in the township—one from Higginsport to Georgetown and north; one between Higginsport and Feesburg; and a third from Higginsport west along the river into Clermont County.

CEMETERIES.

The custom prevailed generally in early pioneer times of interring the dead in private burial-grounds on the farms where they had lived; but, as the country improved, the quiet country churchyard became the repository of the silent dead. At Mt. Zion, the Old Ebenezer, Shinkle's Ridge, at the Union Christian Church and Eden Church, they are found. One has recently been laid out near Feesburg.

The wife of Stephen Bolender was among the first of death's victims in Lewis Township. She died in 1802, and was buried near Boude's Ferry. The earliest interments at Mt. Zion were those of Mr. Foster, Mr. Joslin, Mr. Symms, and Samuel, son of Lemuel Richardson. Mrs. Col. Higgins was probably the first person buried in the Higginsport Cemetery. Her death occurred in 1806, and subsequently the grounds that had received her body were donated by Col. Higgins for a public cemetery.

TOWNSHIP TREASURERS.

The earliest township records have been lost, but from 1838 the Township Treasurers have been: Dent Thomas, 1838–44; James C. Wells, 1844–45; Jesse Dugan, 1845–52; Columbus McKee, 1852–55; P. Ellis, 1855–56; Robert Anderson, 1856–63; J. C. Dugan, 1863–69; O. M. Beck, 1869-71; J. D. Winters, 1871–75; J. E. White, 1875–77; F. Schubort, 1877–80; H. Kennedy, 1880–82; W. W. Quinn, incumbent.

The following is a complete, or almost complete, list of the Justices of the Peace for this township: William Park, William Canary, James Wells, Jesse Printy, John Cann, John Ross, John Williams, John McGrew, Christian Simons, William Buckner, George Richardson, Joseph Richards, Daniel Trout, Charles Williams, James Tatman, David Barr, E. Hemphill, George Jennings, Nathan Kite, Harvey McKibben, William Swope, William Doty, Edward Thompson, R. C. Dugan, John Evans, Thomas Evans, Abraham F. Ellis, A. W. Norris, Elijah Warner, William Martin, Andrew Early, G. W. Early, E. K. Early, John A. Meherry, Thomas Hicks, James Norris, Luis F. Walther and Thomas C. Yates.

EARLY INCIDENTS, MANNERS, ETC.

Two kinds of forest-clearing were made in pioneer days, known as "smack-smooth" and "eighteen inches and under." The former designated the felling and burning of all timber, leaving no obstructions to the plow save the stumps; the latter indicated that only timber eighteen inches in diameter or under should be removed, larger trees being deadened. The pioneers deemed the latter preferable. Ten dollars an acre was the usual price paid for clearing "smack-smooth," but the other method commanded only $1.50 or $2 per acre.

The expression "Canary treat," so frequently heard, has this origin: More than half a century ago, at Higginsport, Squire Canary was elected in a crowd to "set up" the drinks. The men filed into an adjoining saloon and took their places along the bar, when Canary said, "Order what you want." Each called for his favorite beverage, Canary with the rest. All drank, and Canary paid for his own drink, remarking, "Each man ordered his own, and let him settle the bill." It is hoped that, to avoid embarrassment, each fellow had at least a little change.

Sheep-raising was for awhile impossible on account of the innumerable wolves that infested this region. Our dogs, the kind usually kept by the settlers, were of no value against the fierce sheep-destroyers, and all attempts to keep a flock of sheep were futile until a mass meeting of the whole township was held, where a resolution was passed requiring each householder to procure at least one hound, and as many more as possible. The yelp of the hound was soon heard at every farmhouse, and the wolves betook themselves forthwith to a more congenial clime, and sheep-raising became possible.

A tornado of February, 1858, swept away the first brick house in the township, erected by John Boude in 1817. It was rebuilt, however, on the same spot, and with the same brick, by its then owner, Lewis Lerch.

Among the earliest births of the township were two daughters of Leonard Metzger, both of whom became the wives of Jacob Waterfield; John J., the son of Col. Higgins; Samuel Richardson, who died in infancy; and Joseph Bolender.

The earliest marriage, the date of which is known, was that of Lemuel Richardson to Nancy, daughter of Alexander Hamilton, in 1803. William Miller early wedded Mary Richardson, and James Wells, Sallie Clark; also a sister of Sallie Clark about the same time married Maj. John Logan.

LEWIS TOWNSHIP.

MILLS.

In 1800, James Roney erected, on White Oak Creek, about eight miles from its mouth, the first mill in Lewis Township, and, it is believed, the first in the county. It was very rude in construction, with an overshot wheel, fifteen feet in diameter, and an old raccoon buhr, but ground out a satisfactory quality of flour. Edward Thompson succeeded Roney in the possession of the mill. A brick mill is still in operation at the same locality, known as Armleter's Mill.

Soon after this mill was set in operation, Col. Robert Higgins expended about $4,000 in erecting, near the mouth of White Oak Creek, a mill which was to compare with those in the East; but the site selected was unfortunate, as the back-water from the river during high water damaged the property greatly, and, though some flour of a superior quality was manufactured, the enterprise was abandoned.

Joseph Clark, Sr., and his son John, built a substantial frame mill on Bullskin in 1807, the latter operating it. It obtained a large custom, and, as the low water prevented its use throughout the entire year, the enterprising miller attached a steam-power in quite an early day. It was the first of the kind in this entire region, and attracted a large business. It was continued until about 1860.

The fourth grist-mill enterprise was undertaken by William Davidson, in 1818, on White Oak Creek, about three and a half miles from its mouth. The building he erected was a solid frame, still standing, and he operated the mill until about 1839. Since then it has passed through the hands of a number of owners, and was discontinued about 1860.

The Higginsport Grist-Mill was erected by Henry Davidson and William Dugan in 1855, and conducted by them until succeeded by the present firm, John Boyle & Co. The original firm added to their mill in 1861 the distillery, and, in 1863, the stone bonded warehouse, and consumed all the grain they could procure. Since the purchase by the present firm, machinery has been added to the mill for manufacturing the "patent process" flour, and it now has a capacity of forty barrels per day. The copper still consumes daily 200 bushels of grain.

This distillery was not the first at Higginsport. Joseph Shinkle and William L. Thomas, about 1842, commenced and operated one with success. Various owners successively possessed it until some time during the late war, when business was wholly abandoned. Only the one distillery exists now in the township, but in an early day there were from seventeen to twenty small stills in operation, among the earliest of which was Joseph Clark's.

TANNERIES.

A tannery built by John Miller about 1808, where the Ebenezer Church is now located, is believed to have been the first in operation. In 1836, one was started at Higginsport by John McGrew, and had an existence of about ten years, after which Charles Larimore taught several terms of school in the currying shop. Jonathan Cornell built one in 1847 at Leesburg, where the schoolhouse now stands. W. W. McKibben succeeded him, remodeled the tannery and did a good business for a number of years.

SAW-MILLS.

Three of these are now in operation in the township—one by water, two by steam. Stayton's water mill on Bullskin, was erected in an early day. Wm. W. White's is located near Feesburg. The first one here was erected in 1848; the present one, in 1868. The most extensive is the one at Higginsport, owned by a joint-stock company and operated by Boyd & Co. The company was organized Dec. 3, 1881, and the mill set in operation at a cost of $35,000.

It has a 200-horse steam-power, a capacity of 60,000 feet of lumber daily, and employs about eighty hands.

HIGGINSPORT.

Higginsport is a thriving village, situated in the southeastern part of the township, on the Ohio, close to the mouth of White Oak Creek. In 1880, it contained a population of 862. Two attempts were made here before the village was successfully started. September 1, 1804, the place was surveyed into lots, and, the same month, the town of White Haven platted and recorded at Williamsburg. It was substantially like the succeeding Higginsport in outline and arrangement. Notwithstanding Col. Robert Higgins, the founder, offered inducements to settlers, the village did not grow, and, a number of years later, the plat of White Haven was vacated, there being then but three families on its territory. February 28, 1816, it was replatted by Col. Higgins, and re-named Higginsport. The plat shows 114 lots, five by ten rods in size. The original streets, east and west, were Water, Washington, Columbia and Gains; north and south, beginning at the east, White Oak, Brown, Main and Jackson, the present John street being the western limit of the town. The streets were four rods in width; the alleys, one rod. The public square or park, 73x13 rods, was donated to the town by Col. Higgins in the following clause: "The public square for the purpose of building thereon a market house; a house of public worship, free for any worshiping society professing Christianity, and such other public buildings as may be necessary for the use of said town or county to which it does or may belong." He also made several other valuable donations to the town, one of which was a tract of about fifteen acres of land, lying in White Oak Bottom, which is now rented for about $80 per year. Bently and Overturf have made an addition to the town of forty-four lots.

About 1819, Stephen Colvin and family settled here, and found about half a dozen cabins, occupied by Col. Higgins, John Cochran, James Cochran, Mr. Arbuckle and James Norris, a colored man. Colvin was voluble in speech, and was employed to sell town lots at public auction. The town slowly improved, and, in 1828, a little store was opened by Sam Peil. He was soon succeeded by Nathan Kite and Benjamin Thresher. Jesse Dugan followed them in 1832, with an increased stock, and branched out into other business, continuing for about twenty years. He built the first brick house in 1835, still standing, at the corner of Water and Brown streets. A post office was established about 1830, and kept by Mr. Roberts, a tailor, crippled in the Revolution. B. F. Holden came from Maine and opened a store about 1835. Robert Anderson, a Virginian, came about 1833, and, in 1839, started a store. In 1849, he removed it from Water street, where all the business had been done, to Washington, then a back street. Time has shown the wisdom of this step. The present business may be summarized as follows: Five general stores, one clothing store, two drug stores, two tin shops, one hardware store, four millinery and fancy stores, one tobacco store and several groceries.

Isaac Pierce and Samuel Yearsley were early blacksmiths; Messrs. Vandyke and Maxwell, wagon-makers. In 1836, Amos Ellis kept a tavern. There are now two good hotels, the Pierce House and the Central. Five practicing physicians, one minister and several teachers are located here. There is a grist-mill and distillery, seventeen tobacco warehouses, and about thirty tobacco-buyers, who ship annually about two million pounds of the weed.

FEESBURG.

Feesburg, located in the north central part of the township, contains about two hundred inhabitants. It was laid out in 1835, by Thomas J. Fee. George Richardson, Wesley Tucker and William Martin were among the first

LEWIS TOWNSHIP.

purchasers of lots. Tucker and McKibben were the first merchants, Daniel Trout, then William Martin, following. William Matthews was the first blacksmith, succeeded by Jesse B. Dean. The first physician was Reuben Utter. Drs. J. T. Richardson and Stinson Barrott subsequently practiced, and Drs. O. M. Beck and Trout are located there now. Among the first settlers were Jacob Powell, Joseph Powell, Daniel Trout, Harvey McKibben, James Winder, John Wilson and William Swope. Joseph Barker taught the first school about 1844, in a frame house, which stood on land now owned by Mrs. Elizabeth Martin. In 1846, a frame schoolhouse was erected; subsequently, a two-story brick, a short distance west of town, and finally, a one-story brick, in 1869. There are now four merchants engaged in business here, two harness shops, and the usual number of other little industrial shops found in a country village. Feesburg is small, clean and very quiet. It contains no dram shop. It is built almost entirely on one street, which is a good gravel road passing through from Higginsport to Hamersville.

SOCIETIES.

Higginsport Lodge, No. 575, I. O. O. F., was organized June 22, 1874, with the following charter members: W. L. Shidler, J. H. Bolender, Hezekiah Barnum, Henry Schaaf, Thornton Thomas and Michael Brandt. Its membership has increased to forty-six, and the lodge is in prosperous condition. Not a single death has occurred since its organization.

Higginsport Lodge, No. 373, F. & A. M., was granted a dispensation October 17, 1867, the preliminary meeting having been held the preceding October 17. The first officers were: E. F. Blair, W. M.; Robert Drake, S. W.; Lewis Heizer, J. W.; William Dugan, Treasurer; James Hodkins, Secretary; Joseph Park, S. D.; George Fuenfgeld, J. D.; and Jackson Dugan, Tiler. They constituted all the charter members. The lodge has leased a good room, and is in a good, healthy condition, with a membership of forty-four. It has sustained the following losses by death: James Daugherty, March 18, 1868, by explosion of the steamer Magnolia; William Dugan, November 9, 1871; James H. Cahall, August 8, 1880.

The United Order of Foresters, No. 93, was organized October 26, 1878, fully instituted November 15, 1878, and chartered September 4, 1879, with this membership: C. T. Chambers, T. C. Yates, Louis Jones, James W. Ott, John Klein, Thomas Bilew, Henry Clundt, Peter Sanburn, Charles Walther, John F. Gardner, Henry Troutman, Henry Brunner, Charles Fretz, Louis F. Walther, Philip J. Daum, William Marshall, Robert Cahall, John Kautz, Philip Wolf, Frank Thomas, Joseph Betzer, Louis Lerch, Clark Bolender, John Shultz, M. S. Dillman, W. W. Quinn, William Marks, Lemon Thomas, John Brookbank, F. M. Blackburn, Henry Ehrenfels, John Fereno and L. S. Van Anda. The present membership is thirty. The first officers were: T. C. Yates, C. R.; Louis F. Walther, Secretary. Present officers: Frank Thomas, C. R.; Lemon Thomas, Secretary.

Higginsport Lodge, No 49, A. O U. W., was organized June 23, 1875, and the following enrolled as charter members: J. D. Winters, Alfred Loudon, Perry Drake, A. T. Chapman, J. W. Pinckard, S. S. Chapman, Eugene Van Briggle, W. L. Shideler, Louis Jones, Charles Reed, William F. Sallee, B. F. Lewis, H. G. Chapman, S. McDonald, John W. Hook, Wesley Love, Adam Seyler, John E. Ellis, Ferdinand Shubert, Frank Hite. The lodge at present numbers fifteen members. The first officers were: Alfred Loudon, P. M. W.; J. D. Winters, M. W.; A. T. Chapman, Overseer; Perry Drake, Foreman; William Sallee, Guide; Eugene Van Briggle, Recorder; Tolin Ellis, Receiver; W. L. Shideler, Financier. Their hall is in the Central Hotel building, and comfortably furnished.

HISTORY OF BROWN COUNTY.

Post of the Grand Army of the Republic, No. 210, at Higginsport, was organized May 20, 1882, and named in honor of Col. James P. Fyffe, of the Fifty-ninth Ohio Volunteer Infantry, and the following officers were duly elected, viz.: Post Commander, Capt. F R. Kantz; S. V. L., Alfred N. Young; J. V. C., T. C. Chambers; Surgeon, Dr. Wesley Love; Chaplain, Orin Doty; Adjutant, W. P. Cleveland; Inspector, T. C. Yates; Quartermaster, W. W. Quinn; Officer of the Day, Capt. C. E. Harrison.

In the memorable struggle between the North and the South, the heroic dead, in which it is in part the object of the above order to commemorate, Lewis Township was not remiss. Her citizens rushed to arms at the first call of the President for troops, and, throughout the four years' conflict that followed, she bore her full share of danger, suffering and loss. The following list of Lewis Township men, who enlisted and participated in the war, has been prepared with great care and pains, and it is hoped that but few names, if any, will be found missing:

Peter Acles,
Greene Anderson,
Isaac Beech,
David Boles,
John Burton,
Charles Blythe,
William G. Brookbank,
Thomas Bosley,
John Butts,
Gustavus A. Boehm,
James Bosley,
John W. Brookbank,
William Boles,
Joseph Cochran,
David Cann,
John B. Cann,
Robert Cann,
Kim Cropper,
James Cahall,
Charles Cook,
F. M. Cahall,
Samuel Cochran,
Leonard Downing,
William Dye,
Peter L. Devore,
Joseph Dugan,
John Dugan,
Norman Dugan,
Thornton Dugan,
George Dillman,
Orin Doty,
Augustus F. Day,
A. F. Ellis,
Franklin Fite,
Thomas D. Fitch,
Sidney A. Fitch,
Benjamin T. D. Fitch,
Charles Fitch,
Jacob Fraleich,
John F. Gardner,
William Halfhill,
John Henise,
Daniel Horn,
Jacob Hank,
Solomon Halfhill,
Capt. C. E. Harrison,
H. B. Harrison,
William Hodkins,
John Hicks,
Frank Hoover,

Abner Judd,
Irvin Johnson,
Henry Judd,
Jackson Johnson,
Benjamin Klincker,
Alfred Loudon,
John Lucas,
Sylvester Love,
James Lucas,
Carlo Lucas,
W. A. Maxwell,
William McConaughy,
Wesley McConaughy,
John McConaughy,
George Moore,
Thomas Moore,
J. P. Moeller,
Wilson Moore,
Devall Metzger,
John W. Metzger,
Jonas Metzger,
Wesley Metzger,
David Metzger,
Andrew Metzger,
Whalon T. Metzger,
H. D. Metzger,
George Metzger,
Lewis Mohn,
Lewis Myers,
George Myers,
James Mofford,
Robert Noftsger,
Peter Neu,
Harvy M. Overturf,
William K. Overturf,
Edward Ott,
Daniel O'Harra,
John N. Park,
F. M. Park,
A. J. Park,
R. A. Park,
Caleb Pierce,
R. C. Park,
Richard Penny,
Joseph Powell,
Allen Patterson,
William Richardson,
Fred Rhodes,
Madison Richardson,
Ruben Richardson,

Charles Reed,
Franklin Reed,
Peter Roth,
Salathiel M. Spencer,
John Spires,
John Scott,
William Shideler,
David Stout,
John Sneed,
Philip Shaffer,
T. S. Stafford,
Henry Smith,
J. L. Stayton,
Lewis Snyder,
W W Tolin,
J. N. Tolin,
Frank Thomas,
Jesse Thomas,
Charles Thomas,
William Woods,
John Workman,
James Weatherspoon,
Leander P. Wilks,
David Waters,
Joseph Waters,
Isaac Waters,
Charles West,
George Wilson,
James Wilson,
John Williams,
Earnest Whitmore,
Thornton White,
John White,
William M. White,
James C. White,
John E. White,
Edward White,
Richard White,
Alfred N. Young,
George S. Young,
William Yearseley,
Isaac Yearseley,
Thomas C. Yates,
Wyatt Yates,
Stephen Young,
William Young,
James Young,
Alison Young.

CHAPTER IV.

PERRY TOWNSHIP.

BY T. M. READE, M. D.

PERRY TOWNSHIP is situated in the extreme northern division of Brown County. It is bounded on the north by Clinton County, on the east by Highland, on the west by Clermont, and on the south by the townships of Sterling and Green. It is the largest township in the county, being eight and a half miles long by seven miles wide, and has an area of 35,816 acres. The surface of the land is level in its northwestern and southeastern portions, presenting an elevated plain, which is well drained by numerous brooks and rivulets. The soil in these sections is rich and capable of the highest cultivation. Water is found in abundance in all parts of the township, and hundreds of natural springs arise spontaneously from the rocky beds that underlie the upland and sloping plains. The East Fork of the Little Miami River enters the township at its northeast corner, pursuing a tortuous course as it flows through the interior, and makes its exit at the southeastern angle, close to the village of Marathon. The soil along its banks is rich in alluvial deposits, large tracts of bottom land spreading out and forming a valley of unusual richness and beauty. Gigantic trees line its course, which abound in rich and varied foliage.

The valley is relieved at intervals by high cliffs and gently sloping banks, which gives it a picturesque appearance, presenting in many situations beautiful and romantic scenery. About three thousand acres of woodland remains, or perhaps one-tenth of the whole area. Among the varieties of wood found here, the chief are several kinds of oak, the white being most numerous; black walnut, hickory, maple, beech and elm, with some cedar, locust, ash, dogwood, sycamore and wild cherry.

PRE-HISTORIC REMAINS.

Numerous mounds, the works of the pre-historic race known as Mound-Builders, afford curious and interesting relics to antiquarians. Curiously wrought implements in stone, evidently intended for various purposes in domestic life, as well as weapons of attack and defense in war, are discovered by the curious, such as pestles, hammers, mortars, flint arrow-heads, etc. Mastodonic remains are occasionally unearthed, and, from time to time, discoveries of the remains of Indian settlements are indicated by the appearance of gigantic skeletons, with the high cheek-bones, powerful jaws and massive frame peculiar of the red man, who left these as the only record with which to form a clew to the history of past ages.

GEOLOGY.

The geological structure is peculiar and interesting. The rocks belong to the Paleozoic era, Silurian age, or age of non-vertebratæ, and the foundations are a part of the Cincinnati group. The Paleozoic era is the second of the known geological eras of the world, and the Silurian is the first and oldest of its three ages; hence the fossils of the Silurian rocks are among the oldest of all fossils of which we have any knowledge. The fossils are identical with those found in and near Cincinnati. J. H. Cabel, of Urbana, who explored this region in 1880, found specimens of the following: Brachiopods, trilobites, crinoids, orthoceratites and coral. The Brachiopods are the usual square-shouldered varieties found in the Paleozoic age. Of the trilobites, the specimens of Isotelus Gigas are particularly fine. Specimens of crinoids are very rare, and are generally limited to broken fragments of stems. The drift deposits are the same as those found in the adjacent counties of Highland and Clermont. The most characteristic feature is the compact white clay that covers the flat lands. It is six to ten feet in thickness, and contains a great many scratched and glacially polished fragments of blue limestone, as well as representatives of the granitic series of the North.

There are but very few large bowlders found here. One of the most conspicuous is found in the immediate vicinity of Vera Cruz. Under the white clay is a seam of iron, which seems to mark the epoch of the forest bed of the drift. Geologists are certain that there was an advance of glaciers over this region, for they find the limestone well polished in places in the adjoining townships in Highland County. No bank gravel is found here except in the main valleys. It is of course abundant there in the usual terraces. It is often cemented in immense blocks, through the agency of the lime-water that percolates it.

Soil.—The soils of the township art of the usual character for these areas. The flat lands already referred to are covered with a considerable depth of clays, rich in all the elements of vegetable growth except organic matter. They are of course stubborn and intractable in certain seasons and under certain management, but they are rich in agricultural possibilities, and will, under wise culture, some day be transformed into gardens. What these possibilities are is often hinted at in the insulated portions of these white clay flats, where organic matter has accumulated; we find in such spots soils of the highest excellence and durability.

As the valley is approached, the native soils formed from the decomposition of Cincinnati shales and limestones are quite largely represented in the slopes of the hills. These slopes have all the excellence that belongs to such an origin. They constitute some of the strongest and most durable tobacco lands in the State. The valley itself is covered with an extensive deposit of organic matter, freely mixed with sand, constituting the sandy loam characteristic of the alluvial lands of the Ohio Valley.

PIONEERS.

"Can we forget that brave and hardy band,
Who made their home first in this Western land?
Their names should be enrolled on history's page,
To be preserved by each succeeding age.
They were the fathers of the mighty West;
Their arduous labors heaven above has blessed.
Before them fell the forest of the plain,
And peace and plenty followed in the train."

Abraham Claypool was born in Hampshire County, Va., April 7, 1762, and was married to Elizabeth Wilson in 1785, she inheriting two slaves. They moved to Randolph County, Va., in 1787. In 1790, he became a member of the Legislature of Virginia at Richmond, and there had the first insight into the miseries of the slave pen. Soon after, he commenced prospecting in the West, the field of his operations including Kentucky and the Northwest Territory. In June, 1796, he located, in company with Peter Hull, two 1,000-acre tracts in the territory now known as Perry Township, one on Solomon's Run and one on Glady Run. The same year, he was with Gen. Massie, laying out Chillicothe. The ordinance of 1787 having excluded slavery from the Northwest

SAMUEL WATERFIELD.

Territory—an institution which he disliked very much—he moved to near Chillicothe in 1799, taking his slaves with him and liberating them. Being a member of the first Ohio Legislature, he had an act passed for the establishment of a State road from Cincinnati to Chillicothe, afterward surveyed by R. C. Anderson through where Fayetteville now stands, hence called Anderson State Road. He died May 5, 1845, near Chillicothe.

Solomon Claypool, the son of Abraham Claypool, was born in Hardy County, Va., November 21, 1786. Soon after becoming of age, in 1807, he commenced opening his farm on Solomon's Run (named after him), about half a mile above Fayetteville (where Isaac Covalt resided in 1844), keeping "bachelor's hall." In April, 1816, he sold 397.34 acres to Cheniah Covalt, of Clermont County, having previously sold another tract to Erastus Atkins, including the present site of Fayetteville. He was without doubt the first permanent settler of Perry (then Stonelick) Township, of which he was Justice of the Peace. His nearest neighbor southwest was Hartman, and northeast was Van Meter (Stroup place, near Dodsonville). He was never married. He moved to Connersville, Ind., in 1816, where he died September 1, 1845.

Archibald Ballard, of Quaker parentage, was born in North Carolina. He moved to Highland County at an early day, and soon became guide and hunter for the surveyors in locating land warrants in the military district. In 1809, Mr. Ballard commenced improvement on his land on Glady Run (one of the Claypool and Hull tracts), and remained there until 1816. In that year, he moved to Dearborn County, Ind., where he died soon after. His son, Stephen, of age about 1814, remained with his father until his death; afterward settled on White River, below Indianapolis, and was there when last heard from. Aaron, another son, went into the army in 1816, and Amos died young, in 1817.

Nancy, daughter of Archibald Ballard, married Jacob Claypool in 1814. She died February, 1825, and was buried in Cramner's Graveyard. Her grave is now overshadowed by two large red cedar trees. Near by rest Jacob Fox and Obed Burnham. Jacob Claypool, son of Abraham Claypool, was born August 23, 1788, in Randolph County, Va. At the age of twenty-one (1809), he took possession of the 500-acre tract on Glady Run, and, leasing it to Archibald Ballard, the first cabin was built near the lower line, west of Glady, in December, 1809, and January and February, 1810. Jacob taught school in Union Township, Highland County, about the mouth of Dodson Creek, known in early days as the Mike Stroup place. His patrons, as appears from his schedule, were: The family of Joseph Van Meter, four scholars; the family of Peter Van Sant, three scholars; the family of Isaac Van Sant, three scholars; the family of Ebenezer Harmer, two scholars; the family of John Jones, two scholars; total, fourteen. After teaching this school, he made his headquarters at Ballard's, and paid a visit to Virginia. April 15, 1812, he entered the army at Franklinton, as Orderly Sergeant, in H. Ulry's rifle company, First Regiment Ohio Volunteers, Duncan McArthur commanding. They marched to Detroit; was in all of Hull's little fights; was paroled; returned home August 30 of the same year, and settled down to hard work on his land. He was married to Nancy Ballard in 1814. In 1822, he moved to Indianapolis, but, the following year, returned, with a full cargo of ague, and remained on his farm until 1833. He sold 240 acres to Peter O'Connor for $2,000, having previously sold small tracts to Ben and Joseph Rider, Joseph Doughty, M. L. Jinoways and others.

March 1, 1834, he started on a prospecting tour through Illinois, and settled at Morris, Grundy County, where Indians were then quite plenty, and only half a dozen white families thereabouts. William Brown and Jacob Robb and families, and William Robb and William Eubanks, accompanied him. The last two returned to Perry Township the following year. Mr. Claypool was well fitted for pioneer life, being hardy and robust, energetic and determined. He died August 17, 1876, at the age of eighty-eight years, leaving two sons, Perry A. and L. W. The former was born June 5, 1815; married Mary Halstead, youngest sister of A. A. Halstead, of Russel Station, in 1835, and died in Grundy County, Ill., October 15, 1846, leaving a widow and four children, all of whom are living there at present. The younger son, L. W., was born in Glady Run June 4, 1819, and removed with his father to Grundy County, Ill., where he has held several important official positions.

Casper Core came to the township in 1811, and, after remaining nine years, moved to Kentucky.

Asa Dunham came in 1813 and settled here, but died in a few years, leaving a widow, who afterward married Peter Lane. In the same year came James Puckett, Isaac Ruth and James Leonard.

Gideon Dunham was a native of Virginia, and, in 1814, settled on the land now owned by his son, Wilson. He purchased 286 acres from Walter Warfield, a land speculator. Mr. Dunham was married twice, and had a large family. Three children of the first marriage—Charles, Asa and Melinda—and nine of the second, viz.: Mary, Bowen, Sarah, Ruth, Gideon, David, Wilson and Elizabeth. Only two are living—David, who resides in Cincinnati; and Wilson, who occupies the old homestead. He was Justice of the Peace five terms subsequent to the formation of the township.

Ebenezer Davis came about this time. He soon after started a mill, which he ran successfully until 1822, when he sold it to Edward Boyle.

Edward and Nathan Bishop also came about this time. Edward held the office of Constable, and died in 1826. Nathan was also Constable for a number of years. He lived to an old age, and, at the time of his death, which occurred in 1876, was Mayor of the village of Fayetteville.

Isaac McCune, with his sons, Samuel and John, arrived about the same time. They moved afterward to Pike County, Ill.

Samuel McCulloch and Joshua Drake, also Samuel Ashton and his sons—Sam, Thomas, Zach, James and George—came during this year. Ephraim Granger and family settled on Glady Run, where Thurston Granger, his son, now resides.

Joseph W. Jinoways, a native of France, had offended a priest in Paris. To escape the church, he joined the army at eighteen; was sent to St. Domingo, under Le Clerc, to quell the negro insurrectionists, who had taken the fort before the troops landed, and murdered the garrison. It became too hot for Jinoways. He deserted and swam to an American merchantman, landed in Philadelphia, married Miss Johns and settled on Glady Run, where he died. He had seven sons—Joseph B., Augustus, Martin L. (who married Olive Bishop and removed to Illinois), Samuel, who married Charlotte Stanley July 21, 1838, moved to Missouri, and there died during the rebellion), Lewis (who, when last heard from, was in Peoria, Ill.), Alexander (died in Illinois) and Jackson, a boatman, whose place of residence is unknown). Mrs. Jinoways died in Woodford County, Ill., at an extreme old age. There were also a number of daughters in this family.

In 1815, Capt. William Lane was in the township. He was an early Constable. Adam Snell and William Curry were also here at this time. The latter was Justice of the Peace at the time of the first election of the township, and afterward moved to Highland County, where he was elected Sheriff. Joshua Drake was Constable of Perry Township in 1815.

In 1816, the following citizens were in the township—some of them may have come earlier: Russell Atkins, John Shackelford, Erastus Atkins, Thomas B. Bryan, John Mace, Vere Royse, Obed Burnham, Betsy Burnham, Daniel

Fox, William Eubanks, Jacob Sly, Ebenezer Hadley and Henry W. Royse. Thomas B. Bryan, well known as "Uncle Tommy," was a cooper and a widower. He had been a scout in Pennsylvania in the whisky insurrection. He lived on the Claypool place, and died about 1844. Vere Royse was a Constable in 1816. Obed Burnham was a chair-maker, and quite deaf. He died in this township. Obed Burnham, Jr., left the township early, and located at Jonesboro, Ill. Betsy Burnham married Abel Mossman. Daniel Fox was the proprietor of a saw-mill. Jacob Sly had been with Gen. Wayne in 1793. He had a great fancy for buckskin clothing, and donned it whenever he could procure it. His children were Joseph, David, Rebecca (married to L. Ashton), Cassie (married to James Ashton) and Clara. The son of Ebenezer Hadley, John Hadley, was residing near Streator, Ill., a short time ago.

The following are known to have been here in 1817: Valentine Fritz, Alexander Cahall, Matthew Leonard, Samuel Adkins, Nathan D. Lane, Charles McCoy, Jacob Fox, Jr., Silas Huntley, George Ranis, William Leonard, Thomas Hart, Neal McGindley, Stephen Adams, Tyre Smithson, Jacob Fox, Sr., Michael Snell, Chenial Covalt, Isaiah Hallsted, Moses Wood and Eben Hadley. Samuel Adkins had been a Revolutionary soldier, and died in this township. He was father-in-law to Isaiah Hallsted. Jacob Fox, Jr., was a good man; his first wife was Betsy Sly; he was buried in Cranmer's Graveyard. William Leonard was probably here with his father in 1814. Neal McGindley settled on Grassy Run. He once shot his son, Manasseh, accidentally, in a corn-field, mistaking him for a deer. His daughter Margery married Samuel Brown, and moved to Grundy County, Ill., in 1837; then to Iowa; both are dead; they raised a large family. Isaiah Hallsted came from Pennsylvania; he lived on Jacob Claypool's farm for years, then bought a tract on Glady Run; he had a large family of girls, and died here. Moses Wood afterward laid out Woodville, west of this township. Eben Hadley has long since moved to Lexington County, Ill., where, when last heard from, he was living at an extreme old age.

In mentioning the following settlers, we give the dates at which, from occurrences, they were known to be in the township. Their actual settlement may in some cases have been years earlier. In 1818, the settlement included William Rybolt, Joel Curliss (who was a New Jerseyman), Michael Fritz, John Miller (a noted character), William McCune, James Rush and John Smith. Samuel Cranmer was here before 1815; he was from New Jersey, and, in 1820, was Treasurer of the township; he donated the ground for Cranmer's Graveyard; his sons were Samuel, B. Doughty and Richard. John Pullman was a boatman, and died in Fulton. Phineas Allen, a Justice of the Peace, had probably been here long before this date. David Brown was living in the township in 1818; James and Abner were his sons; the latter married Martha Rider July 23, 1829, and both were living in Western Indiana in 1879.

In 1820, we have the following: William Boyle, a native of Ireland; was agent for Gen. Lytle; he had a son, William, and a daughter, Sarah, afterward Mrs. John Kelly. Edward Boyle settled near Fayetteville, and lived to the age of ninety; at the time of his death, in 1875, his descendants numbered eleven children and fifty-two grandchildren. Other settlers of 1820 were Patrick Morehead, Robert Alexander, William Brown, Charles Brooks, Joel Curliss, John Chamberlain, George Gearton, L. Ditto, Selby Huston, John Harmer, Mathias Pitzer, David Runyan, Charles Waits, Ellis Walling, Thomas Watson, John B. Mahan and James Leonard, Jr.

The dates of the advent of the following cannot be definitely ascertained, but were probably prior to 1820: Selby Hudson, William Hudson, Hugh McDinnell, William Parker, Patrick Savage, —— Kirtendal, John McManus, —— Thornhill, Andrew Kirskadden, —— Watson, Cranston Lowen, John

Beltz, William Bull, —— Bradley, John Hacklebender, Caleb Conklin, —— Shinkle, Thomas Ashton, Andrew McQuillan, William Benham, Benjamin Rider, Joseph Hallsted and Jonathan Hadley.

In 1821, these were in the township: Stephen Adams (Supervisor of Roads), John Hedges, Benjamin Doughty, Richard Applegate, John Lafarre, Daniel Hankins, Henry Hankins, Levi Tucker, Caleb Clark, W. L. Curliss, Heth Hart. In 1822: John Eichelberger, Abram Fox, Josiah Hobson, Joseph Curliss, C. M. Foster, Joseph Morseman, John Snowhill, Joseph Potter, Richard W. Ditto and John Eldridge. John Snowhill was a wagon-maker from Philadelphia; he died prior to 1840, leaving two sons, Andrew and Ben, and two daughters, Jane and Ellen. Joseph Potter had been a Revolutionary soldier; was under Gen. Wayne; he first settled on Sycamore, and died near Burnham's. Heth Hart was from Kentucky, and afterward moved to Highland County. W. S. and Joseph Curliss came from New Jersey; the former removed to Indiana.

After this period, immigration increased rapidly from the Eastern States and Europe. The identity of families and individuals was lost sight of, and, with the foundations which had been laid, the community advanced with the tide of progress which swept like magic throughout the entire State.

When the adventurous pioneer departed from the confines of civilization to seek a home in the unbroken wilderness, he brought with him his trusty rifle, to serve the double purpose of procuring the necessaries of life and defending himself against the wild denizens of the forest, or the more treacherous Indians, jealous of the white invader. The ax ranged next in importance, on account of its extended adaptability and varied powers of construction. With the addition of an auger, some powder, some lead, and the inevitable jack-knife, his outfit was complete. As he penetrated the woods, he marked his progress by cutting pieces of bark off the most prominent trees along the route, thus constituting the "blazed road" by which he was to return, and guide others in the same direction. Having selected a suitable location, his next care was the construction of a habitation, which was the usual log cabin, with its puncheon floor, clapboard roof and grating door, with the hospitable latch-string to welcome the weary traveler. The family was then removed. Other adventurous spirits soon followed. More cabins were built, and log-rollings were started. Ready help was given to all settlers. A new settlement was formed, and the foundations of civilized society were laid.

As a specimen of the customs of the early settlers of Perry Township, Mr. L. W. Claypool kindly furnishes from the private papers of his father a specimen of his exchanging work with his neighbors:

```
1813, February.  Boarding at Archibald Ballard's.
                 James Puckett, to rolling logs.................1 day.
                 Solomon Claypool, rolling logs................1 day.
                 — Dunham, rolling logs.......................1 day.
                 Solomon and others...........................4¼ days.
                 Solomon, hewing logs, etc....................4¼ days.
1814, January.   Dunham, rolling logs.........................1 day.
                 Dunham & Ruth, rolling logs..................1 day.
                 — Leonard....................................1 day.
                 Solomon, burning logs........................1 day.
                 — Puckett, rolling logs......................1 day.
                 — Dunham, rolling logs.......................1 day.
                 Asa Dunham, rolling logs.....................1 day.
                 G. Dunham, rolling logs......................1 day.
                 G. Dunham, building chimney..................1 day.
        April.   Solomon, sowing oats.........................1 day.
                 Bishop (Edward) building chimney.............1 day.
                 Isaac McCune, building chimney...............1 day.
                 Isaac McCune, raising stable.................1 day.
        July.    Solomon, harvesting..........................1 day.
```

One of the saddest incidents in pioneer times was the loss of little Lydia Osborne, of Williamsburg, July 13, 1804, and the long but fruitless search for her by many hundred men. Although her parents were not residents of this township or county, a thorough search was made over what is now the territory of Perry Township, and the last traces of her were seen here and in this vicinity. Lydia, aged eleven years, and Matilda, aged seven, the two daughters of Ebenezer Osborne, started, on the afternoon of the above day, to bring home their father's cows from the "big field" about a mile from the village. Finding them, the elder girl supposed, from the direction the cows took, that they were going from instead of toward home. Bidding her little sister remain where she was, Lydia started to head off the cattle, but, failing in this, and fearing that Matilda might become lost, she left the cattle and started to go to the place where she thought she had left her, but instead of finding her, she took the direction opposite from her home, and was soon hopelessly lost. The younger child, following the tinkling of the cow-bells, arrived safely at home. The following account of the search is principally from the graphic narration of the event written by Rev. James B. Finley, who participated in it. Night coming on, the parents of the unreturning Lydia grew anxious, and the alarm of "lost child" spread rapidly through the neighborhood. Bells were rung, horns blown and guns fired, and the woods and thickets beat and scoured all night, in vain. The news flew in every direction, and a constantly increasing crowd of frontiersmen gathered in and assisted in the search. On the third day, Cornelius Washburn arrived, with about five hundred others. Washburn was accompanied by his noted hunting dog, of which it was said he would follow any scent his master would put him on. The search was systematized, and continued by different companies in all directions. Perry Township was traversed, and the seventh night was passed on the head-waters of the East Fork of the Little Miami. Washburn had discovered traces of her—places where she had slept and gathered berries. The company grew, until a thousand men were believed to be in the field, many of them from Kentucky. An immense line was formed, the men being several rods apart, and the anxious, earnest search continued. On the morning of the fifteenth day, footprints of the wanderer were discovered on the banks of the North Fork of White Oak. Proceeding up a branch of the stream from this point, near a large blackberry patch was found a neat little house, built of sticks, with moss covering the cracks. On one side was a little door, and in the interior a bed of leaves, covered with moss and adorned with wild flowers. All could see at once that it was the work of a child, and the tears stole freely over the bronzed and manly cheeks of the pursuers, who gazed upon it, far from any human habitation, deep in the recesses of a vast wilderness. There were evidences that the child had been here several days, but the signs were believed to be three or four days old. It was at first believed that the child was near at hand, and renewed hope sprang up in the minds of all. The grief-stricken parents were present, and gave expression to mingled feelings of hope and despair. A quiet, thorough examination was made of the country around, but no fresh signs of her presence were discovered. Horse-tracks, however, were seen, and, two miles from "Lydia's Camp," as this place was called, her bonnet was found hanging on a bush, and, eight or ten miles farther off, an Indian camp was discovered. It was believed the Indians had carried her off, none knew whither. Further pursuit was abandoned, and the men returned home. The father, however, continued the search alone, and finally died of a broken heart. The child was never found.

L. W. Claypool, speaking of this occurrence, says of Cornelius Washburn that he engaged in it with the keen perceptive intelligence which only a noted hunter possesses, and that it was wonderful to see him, calm and thoughtful, walking slowly along, noting a leaf upturned, peavine, brush or anything disturbed, while others could see nothing, except at times he would point out to them tracks of the child on sand-bars, beds of leaves, or the like. Some of the searchers made so much noise, hallooing, blowing horns, etc., that Washburn begged of them to desist, and he would find the child, insisting that the child, after having been lost so long, would hide from man as quick as a wild animal. They would not heed him, but dashed ahead. Mr. Claypool continues: "I was once lost, when eight or nine years old, with Jake Ashton, a year younger, and can fully realize Washburn's assertion of fright. We went out early in the morning to hunt the cows; soon the path gave out, and we were lost in the flat beech swamps between Glady and Grassy Runs. We wandered about until nearly night, coming out at a new road recently underbrushed, just at the time an infair party of about a dozen couple on horseback were passing. Although knowing the most of them, we hid until they had passed.

"I have seen Mr. Washburn several times at our place on Glady—a peculiar looking man, large head, broad shoulders and chest, tapering down to small feet, out of proportion, as it seemed to me, his dress of hunting-shirt, leggings and moccasins adding to the illusion, perhaps. When last heard from, I believe he went on a trapping expedition to the Rocky Mountains, about 1830 or 1831, with one of the Hankinses, who came back without him. It was supposed the Indians killed him.

"I do not believe there were any Indians in Perry Township at the first settlement, perhaps not in the present century; at least, I never heard my father speak of it, but he would often allude to his experience with them in Virginia, in Chillicothe, Ohio, and other places. The township was rather an out-of-the-way place, or middle ground, only used at times by an occasional straggler. I have heard him talk of a few bears, but deer, wolves and wild turkeys were plenty, even in my day."

POLITICAL HISTORY.

Perry Township was formed by the Commissioners of Clermont County on June 6, 1815, and remained in that county until December 27, 1817, when the Legislature passed an act creating Brown County, and ceding the townships of Pleasant, Lewis, Clark and Perry, with certain portions of Adams, to the new county. The first election was held October 10, 1815, resulting as follows: For Senator, John Boggess, 16; Thomas Morris, 2; for Representatives (two to be elected), John Polloc, 6; William Fee, 5; Amos Ellis, 13; Samuel B. Kyle, 7; for Sheriff, Oliver Lindsey, 17; for Commissioner, John Shaw, 16; George C. Light, 2.

There were twenty three voters then in the township. Their names, as near as can be ascertained, were as follows: Solomon Claypool, Archibald Ballard, Jacob Claypool, Stephen Ballard, Casper Core, Asa Dunham, James Puckett, Isaac Ruth, Gideon Dunham, Sr., Ebenezer Davis, Isaac McCune, Martin Bishop, Samuel McCulloch, Joshua Drake, Samuel Ashton, Ephraim Granger, Joseph B. Jinoways, Edward Bishop, Joseph M. Jinoways, William Lane, William Curry, Joshua Drake, James Leonard, Sr.

In 1817, Perry voted in Clermont County for the last time, casting twenty-four votes for John Boggess, Representative, and six for Andrew Foote, Commissioner. The number of votes cast at the Presidential election of 1880 was 642—Republican, 74; Democratic, 568.

The following have been Justices of the Peace in and for this township: Jacob Claypool (1815), Isaac Ruth, Phineas Allen, Solomon Claypool, William Curry, Alanson H. Hallsted, Nicholas Halpin, Nathan Bishop, George Carrier,

Cheniah Covalt, William Conklin, William Davis, Richard Ditto, James Campbell, Joseph McDevitt, John Reeves, T. D. Pobst, Peter Vandervoort, James Kinkadden, Doughty Cranmer, Samuel Williams, Patrick Savage and Milton Fox.

Physicians: Dr. Samuel Anthony, Dr. —— Dart, Dr. W. B. Thompson, Dr. John Crew, Dr. Daniel Porter, Dr. John Magginni, Dr. Hugh Morgan, Dr. —— Edenfield, Dr. Komerus, Dr. W. C. Hall, Dr. F. Eichler, Dr. J. M. Hall, Dr. T. M. Reade.

The present township officers are: Trustees, Patrick McConn, Joseph Barbour, Bernard Berwanger; Assessor, Julius Gabet; Treasurer, Martin Berger; Clerk, James McCafferty.

The health of the community is generally good. Epidemics are very rare. The principal forms of disease occurring here are of malarial origin. Intermittent fevers of a mild type, bilious, and occasionally typhoid fever, present themselves. It is worthy of note here that the diseases mentioned are almost entirely confined to flat lands and undrained districts. The death rate is low.

The present population is about three thousand. The majority of the people are of European birth or immediate descent, the Irish and French prevailing. The French language is spoken to a considerable extent. Five-sixths of the citizens of this community belong to the Catholic Church, the remainder are mostly Methodists. Improvements are slowly made, but steady growth has been the rule in every department. The condition of public and private morals is truly remarkable. Crime is almost unknown—five years without a crime of any mention. A physician engaged in practice ten years can report over two hundred cases of birth, without a single case illegitimate.

The writer is indebted to Mr. L. W. Claypool, without whose assistance the early history of this township could not have been written. He also wishes to return thanks to those citizens of the township who have assisted in the work, to the reverend clergy of the different churches, to the Ursuline Convent authorities, to John and William Boyle, Henry McCarthy, and many others, whose co-operation he gratefully acknowledges.

MILLS.

In this, as in all other enterprises connected with the early history of Perry Township, the name of Claypool comes first. Solomon built the first mill and started the first distillery. Ephraim Granger came next in order. Both of these were the original "corn-cracker" mills, around whose departed shadows hang so many scenes of rural sport and pastime, dear to the memory of the hardy pioneers of those days.

These mills were situated on the respective farms of their owners. Thomas Bamber built a mill on the East Fork, which was afterward sold to Bevans & Snowhill. This was the first steam mill in the township. Joseph Hallsted built the Bank Mill, on the East Fork, near the Clinton County line. Ebenezer Davis, a very eccentric character, was a veteran miller of the olden time; he occupied the site of Boyle's Mill, on the East Fork, near St. Martin's. "Uncle 'Nezar" had an unhappy faculty of changing his religious convictions, and, whenever his brethren in the church refused to agree with him on points of doctrine, he would force them into concession by refusing them the use of his mill. He was a power in the land, and, when he declared he would "never grind another grist for a Baptist," the most disastrous results were likely to follow unless he was acknowledged "leader," with full power to instruct. He sold his mill and other property to Edward Boyle.

This location is now occupied by the extensive flouring-mills of John Boyle, complete in modern improvements.

Dillen & McConn built the Fayetteville Mills in 1870. The buildings, which were frame, were destroyed by fire in 1874. John Dillen rebuilt an elegant brick mill, with modern improvements, in the same year. It is still in operation. James Connally is the present proprietor.

CEMETERIES.

Cranmer's Graveyard is the oldest cemetery in the township. In this peaceful spot, after the toils and troubles of life, rest the mortal remains of the pioneers of Perry Township.

> "The breezy call of incense-breathing morn,
> The swallow twittering from the straw-built shed,
> The cocks shrill clarion, or the echoing horn,
> No more shall rouse them from their lowly bed."

The following names are found among those buried here:

Names.	Date of Burial.	Family Names.
James Ashton	1823	Granger, infant, 1821.
Samuel Cranmer	1827	Claypool.
Ephraim Granger	1839	Abernathy.
Samuel B. Granger	1839	Predmore.
John Snowhill	1838	Conklin.
Sarah Barnes	1835	Brown.
Benjamin E. Hadley	1844	Kimble.
Anton Sherwin	1856	Lake.
Obed Burnham	1846	Hallsted.
W. R. Jones	1853	Hankins.
Levi Moore	1845	Rogers.
John Gallagher	1856	Turner.
John Perrill	1854	Higgins.
John M. Sullivan		Mitchell.
Erastus Ireton		Van Horn.
John Ferguson		Curless.
— Dittoe		Black.
— Wood	1840	Reese.

The Vera Cruz (Catholic) Cemetery is the most beautiful and best-regulated cemetery in the township. The oldest name is that of Edward Bishop, who died in 1826. Patrick McConn donated this tract to the parish of Vera Cruz about 1860.

Fritt's Graveyard is situated on the Anderson State road, between Fayetteville and St. Martin's. It is at present but little used as a place of sepulture. The silent gravestones here tell the sad tale of the ravages of the epidemic cholera in 1851. Among the pioneer names found here are those of Covalt, Hallsted, Alexander, Tritts, Shingle, Dunham and Curless.

The ground for St. Patrick's (Catholic) Cemetery, Fayetteville, was donated by Cornelius McGroarty and Peter O'Conner. It contains more graves than any other in the township, and many beautiful tributes of love in enduring marble and granite add a melancholy beauty to this last resting-place of the sainted dead.

> "Perhaps in this neglected spot is laid
> Some heart once pregnant with celestial fire,
> Hands that the rod of empire might have swayed,
> Or waked to ecstasy the living lyre."

CHURCHES.

St. Martin's (Catholic) Cemetery is situated near St. Martin's Church. It is comparatively modern, and has some beautiful and appropriate monuments.

The majority of the first settlers were members of the Methodist Church. In the absence of a place of worship, they were wont to gather at a neighbor's house whenever the Word of God was preached. Ezekiel Hutchinson was the

first preacher of whom we have any record. He resided near Hartman's, below Pleasant Run. He was the pioneer preacher, having lived in the township several years prior to 1816.

Arthur W. Elliot, a celebrated pioneer and Methodist minister, began visiting this community as early as 1818. By his wise counsels he succeeded in uniting the few scattered families of the faithful into a regular church organization. A church was built near Cranmer's Graveyard, where regular services were held from 1828 to 1868, when it was abandoned, some of the congregation going to Marathon and some to the church at Fayetteville. Among the first Methodists were the following persons and families: Peter Lane, Samuel Cranmer, Christian Shinkle, Gideon Dunham, William Rybolt, Ephraim Granger, Ebenezer Davis.

The Fayetteville Methodist Episcopal Church was built in 1845. It is a neat brick building, pleasantly situated on the north side of Humber street, and is at present the only Methodist Church in the township. Many of the pioneers and their families were members of this congregation, among whom were the following: Gideon Dunham, William Ulrey, Calvin Smith, Valentine Fritz, Peter Lane, Mrs. Phœbe Harris, Richard Applegate, Dr. W. B. Thompson, Elias Long, William Rybolt, James Ashton, Thomas Ashton, Thomas Reeves, Reuben Clayton, Tab Lenmen, William Reeves, Dr. Crew, Alanson H. Hallsted. The church is in a prosperous condition at present, with forty members. Divine service is held semi-monthly, and conducted by Rev. Mr. Jackson.

THE CATHOLIC CHURCH.

[A full account of the Catholic institutions of this township is given in another portion of this work.]

EDUCATION.

There is perhaps no department so surrounded by the vail of obscurity as that of early education in new countries, and certainly no better guide can be found with which to measure the progress of a community than a comparison between the humble efforts of the early settlers in the cause of education, and the present admirable system of free schools, controlled and supported by the State.

The first attempts to teach were attended with the greatest difficulties, both to teachers and scholars. It is unnecessary here to detail the hardships, trials and adventures of the boys and girls of seventy years ago in Perry Township, who braved storm and flood, and wandered through woods and forded streams, without road or bridge to guide them, in search of the rude and cheerless cabin, provided with but few of the necessities and none of the comforts of a human habitation. Whoever learned to "read, write and cipher" in those days had to perform an amount of labor which would enable a youth of the present time to graduate with honors from any of our leading colleges.

But, in the face of all difficulties, the great majority of the "boys" now living who received their only education in these primitive schools have not only been successful in their respective avocations, but many of them have risen to eminence in the different departments of commercial, political and professional life.

The first school was taught by Jacob Claypool, commencing, as appears by an old copy-book used at the school, October 12, 1815. The school was kept in a log cabin, perhaps built for the purpose, on the bank of the East Fork, below the old State road, just where it leaves the stream to pass the Cranmer Graveyard. The patrons L. W. Claypool recollects having heard mentioned, were the Grangers, McCunes and Jinoways. There were perhaps others from below not now remembered. Jacob Claypool often mentioned, in after years, Clistie Granger, afterward wife of B. Doughty Cranmer, and sister of Thurston, as being a very apt scholar. The old log house stood there in after years, but its use is not remembered.

The next school known was taught in the summer of 1824, in a cabin on Jacob Claypool's lower line, east bank of Glady, afterward residence and cooper shop of "Uncle Tommy" (T. B. Bryan), until he died, soon after 1844. About the same time, Martin Bishop, Phineas Allen and Sam Ewing taught in the neighborhood at times.

John H. O'Connor kept school in a cabin adjoining his residence, on the north side of the State road, about one-third of a mile above Burnham's, or, say half way between Glady and Fayetteville. He commenced probably about 1827, and continued at intervals four or five years. Among the boys who attended school about this time who are still living are Joshua Fox, Thurston Granger, Wilson Dunham, John Boyle, Benjamin Snowhill, Andrew Snowhill and Andrew McQuillan, now of Perry Township; Joseph Leonard, of Clermont County; A. A. Hallsted, of Russell Station; S. W. Claypool, of Morris, Ill.; and James Kirskadden.

In 1835, the free school system was established by the State. Emerson Jester taught for a number of years near Ferristown. William Allen was a teacher in the township about 1840. James Sloane, Sr., taught at Cedarville from 1840 to 1850. He afterward moved to Highland County. James Sloane, Jr., taught at Campbell's Schoolhouse. He moved with his father to Hillsboro, and afterward became a distinguished lawyer. He was Judge of the Court of Common Pleas of Highland County, and died in Hillsboro about 1876. Michael Lyons came to Fayetteville in 1847. He taught in the township for twenty-seven years, his service embracing more time and more pupils than any of his predecessors. He is still living in Fayetteville.

The schools now in operation, and their condition for the year 1881, is expressed in the following statement, prepared by M. J. Clark:

District No. 1 is located in the northern part of the township. The building is of wood, and stands in the southeastern part of Section 612. The district enumerates—males, 22; females, 24; total, 46. David Murphy, teacher. Wages, $40 per month.

District No. 2 is located in the village of Fayetteville. The building is of brick, and contains two departments and employs two teachers. The district enumerates—males, 66; females, 61; total, 127; A. J. Bookmyer and Kitty Chaney, teachers. Wages, $50 and $35 respectively.

District No. 3 is located on the Georgetown & Fayetteville Free Turnpike, south of the village of Fayetteville. The building is of brick. The district enumerates—males, 47; females, 54; total, 101. Anderson McQuillin, teacher. Wages, $40 per month.

District No. 4 is situated in the eastern part of the township. The house is in Section 10,861, and is known as the Campbell Schoolhouse. The district enumerates—males, 20; females, 32; total, 52. Mary Carboy, teacher. Wages, $35 per month.

District No. 5 is situated in the southwestern part of the township, in Section 4,790; enumerates—males, 18; females, 23; total, 41. Teacher, Annie McCloskey. Wages, $30 per month.

District No. 6 is located in the southwestern part of the township, and is known by the name of Kirskadden District. The district enumerates—males, 25; females, 18; total, 43. Edward McQuillan, teacher. Wages, $40 per month.

District No. 7 is situated on the Cincinnati & Chillicothe Turnpike, between Fayetteville and Vera Cruz, in the western part of the township. The district enumerates—males, 21; females, 31; total, 52. Kate Carboy, teacher. Wages, $35 per month.

District No. 8 is situated in the western part of the township, and is known by the name of Glady District. The district enumerates—males, 68; females, 43; total, 111. Thomas M. Barry, teacher. Wages, $40 per month.

District No. 9 is located in the northwestern part of the township, in the eastern corner of Section 5,229; districte numerates—males, 33; females, 34; total, 67. A. J. Sever, teacher. Wages, $40 per month.

District No. 10 is situated in the northern part of the township, on the Blanchester pike. It is known as the Farristown Schoolhouse. The district enumerates—males, 37; females, 38; total, 75. Teacher, J. M. Edginton. Wages, $40 per month.

District No. 11 is located in the northeastern part of the township, in Section 2,790. It is known as the Aubry District. The district enumerates —males, 11; females, 15; total, 26. Teacher, M. J. Clark. Wages, $35 per month.

District No. 12 is situated northeast of St. Martin's, in Section 2,941. It is known as the St. Martin's Schoolhouse. The district enumerates—males, 31; females, 25; total, 56. C. C. Chaney, teacher. Wages, $40 per month.

District No. 13 is located in the southeastern part of the township It is known as the Huber Schoolhouse. The district enumerates—males, 33; females, 35; total, 68. Amanda Conrard, teacher. Wages, $35 per month.

District No. 14 is situated in the eastern part of the township, in Section 3,043, and is known as the Stringtown Schoolhouse. The district enumerates —males, 33; females, 35; total, 68. Bridget Campbell, teacher. Wages, $35 per month.

The following statements exhibit the condition of schools of Perry Township for the year ending August 31, 1881:

Total amount of school moneys received within the year	$4,356 33
Amount paid teachers	3,870 00
Fuel and contingent expenses	543 12
Grand total of expenditures	4,413 12
Balance on hand September 1, 1881	750 00
Whole number of schoolhouses in the township	14
Number of school rooms	15
Teachers employed	15
Average wages paid teachers	$40 00
Ladies	$35 00
Pupils enrolled during the year—girls, 455; boys, 458; total	913
Average daily attendance—boys, 275; girls, 255; total	530

Rate of school tax, three mills on the dollar.

FAYETTEVILLE.

Fayetteville is pleasantly situated on the south bank of the East Fork of the Little Miami, thirty-six miles from Cincinnati. It contains two churches, two schools, two hotels, several stores and saloons, two drug stores, and several other establishments for the different departments of trade, commerce and manufacture.

Erastus Atkins built the first house on the ground where Fayetteville now stands, in the year 1811. It was a double log house, and occupied the site of the present residence of T. S. Murray. In the same year, Thomas McCarthy bought a farm on the south of Atkins, which included the present corporate limits of the village. Russel Atkins, brother of Erastus, bought land north of this locality. He lived on his farm many years, and had a large family. He sold to Patrick McClosky in 1845, and moved to Newtown, Ohio, where he died in 1859. Cheniah Covalt owned the land on the east, including the present farm of John Cushing. He raised a large family, and lived here until his death. Mr. —— Hackelbander came about 1814. He had three sons—David,

Moses and John. He died here, after which his family moved to Illinois. Nathan Bishop came here from Virginia about 1811. He was a salt-manufacturer. He bought the farm on the west of the East Fork, from Erastus Atkins. He kept his farm, but ran a huckster wagon between here and Cincinnati; afterward became Constable, Justice of the Peace, and practiced law for many years. He was Mayor of Fayetteville at the time of his death, in 1876 He was married three times, and left a large family. He was a native of Vermont.

Cornelius McGroarty bought the present site of Fayetteville in 1818. He was a native of Ireland; came here from Cincinnati. He had several children. His son, Stephen J., was Colonel of an Ohio regiment in the war of the rebellion. He was a brave and gallant soldier, and died in Cincinnati a few years ago. His son Patrick, the able lawyer and distinguished orator, is a prominent member of the Brown County bar, and resides at Georgetown. Cornelius McGroarty removed with his family to Cincinnati and died there. He donated the land upon which St. Patrick's Church and Cemetery were built. Alpheus White came in 1820. He was a carpenter; raised a large family, and died here in 1838. John Ballard came about 1830. He was a remarkable man. When a boy, he was engaged in the rebellion of 1798 in Ireland. He was a soldier in Napoleon's army, and survived the terrors of the bloody field of Waterloo. He served as a soldier in the United States Army; became Captain of a company; received a land grant from the United States Government, but refused to accept it. He was Postmaster of Fayetteville many years, and died in 1874, aged ninety-four years. Thomas McKittrick came in 1830. He had nine children. His death occurred in 1868, at the age of ninety-six. Dr. W. B. Thompson came about 1835. He was first Postmaster of Fayetteville; lived here many years, and was successful in practice. He died in 1878, in Cincinnati. Patrick McClosky came in 1845, and William Nugent in 1850.

Fayetteville was incorporated in 1868, the petitioners being W. C. Hall, S. Bavouset, John C. Kelly, A. Mosset, C. A. Sourd, Frank Jacquemin, John Dillen, James Connally. The first officials were: Mayor, Patrick Savage; Marshal, James Busey; Clerk, P. K. Martin.

The present officers are: Mayor, Milton Fox; Marshal, James Busey; Clerk, T. S. Murray. Council: S. J. Fitzpatrick, J. M. Hall, James Connally, James McCafferty, John McConn, James McCaffrey. Constable, Henry McCarthy.

The present population is 400.

The professions at Fayetteville are to-day represented as follows: Attorneys at law, Milton Fox, Patrick Savage and J. A. Murray; physicians, F. Eichler, J. M. Hall and T. M. Reade; clergyman, Rev. John Bowe.

SOCIETIES.

Fayetteville Lodge, No. 172, F. & A. M., was established in 1851, and removed to Marathon in 1856. The following persons were charter members: D. G. Porter, J. G. Hilton, W. Boyle, E. C. Hartman, S. J. Bivans, John Reeves, Leonidas Mitchell and Peter Lane. The lodge holds meetings on Friday evenings of each month after moon, at their hall in Marathon.

Literary.—The Dickens Club was organized in 1880. Weekly meetings were held at the office of Dr. T. M. Reade until the spring of 1882, when the schoolhouse was selected as the place of meeting. It embraces thirty members. It was organized by D. G. Campbell, A. J. Bookmeyer, T. M. Barry and T. M. Reade.

Temperance.—The Fayetteville Total Abstinence Society was organized in 1879. The officers were as follows: President, Thomas Barry; Vice President, Cornelius Carboy; Secretary, T. M. Reade; Treasurer, John Boyle, Jr.; Chaplain, Rev. John Bowe. The membership is sixty.

CHAPTER V.

HUNTINGTON TOWNSHIP.

BY SAMUEL EVANS.

THE township bearing the above name is situated in the southeastern corner of the county and is bounded on the north by Byrd Township, on the east by Adams County, on the south by the Ohio River and on the west by Union Township. It was organized prior to the erection of Brown County, and was named in honor of Samuel Huntington, one of the signers of the Declaration of Independence. Its greatest length is from the Ohio River at the line between Adams and Brown Counties north to the Byrd Township line a distance of eight and three-eighth miles; the greatest width is about five and seven-tenths miles, being from the center of the east line to a point a few rods north of Logan's Gap. It contains nearly thirty two and three-quarter square miles, or 21,000 acres. The real estate value of the township as assessed in 1880 was $444,910; the village of Aberdeen, $55,629; total value, $500,539. The value of chattel property as returned at same time was $202,904, making a total valuation for taxation of $756,139; this being the assessed value, it will be understood that the real value would exceed $1,000,000.

The township ranks fifth in wealth as well as in area in the county, and is second to none in fertility of soil. The surface of the county is diversified by hills and narrow valleys. The southern part of the township has some very fine bottom land; the interior and northern is hilly, especially along the streams, and nearly the entire township is naturally well drained. The river hills and hills along some of the streams are steep and rugged, and generally very rocky. Along the river, there are some very fine stone quarries, where a good quality of building stone is obtained in abundance; the stone obtained is blue and gray limestone, with some fine grained sandstone or rather grindstone grit. The ancient drift of the bottoms along the Ohio River has at the bottom blue clay gravel or sandstones, and near the top yellow clay and black loam; the lower layers often contain logs, leaves, sticks and vines. There are no natural curiosities of importance in the township. Numerous evidences of the work of the Mound-Builders are found.

The principal agricultural products are corn, tobacco, wheat, oats, barley, rye and Irish potatoes. The soil and climate are well adapted to raising corn; the township, previous to the introduction of tobacco, produced about as much corn as any township in the county, and, in consequence of the abundance of corn, hog-raising was a flourishing business for years, but is not now so extensive.

STREAMS.

The principal streams are Eagle Creek, Big Three-Mile, Little East Fork of Eagle Creek, Brushy Fork, Suck Run and Fishing Gut Run. Eagle Creek is a large and rapid stream, running a little southwest; it rises in Adams County, washes the western border of the township nearly the entire length, and years ago furnished good power for mills. Little East Fork of Eagle Creek was a good mill stream, being very rapid; it is not now very valuable for water-power; it has its rise in Adams County, enters this township about two and one-half miles from the Byrd Township line, and flowing southwest empties into Eagle Creek near Logan's Gap. Big Three-Mile was a good mill stream till within the last twenty years, when it began to fail; it also rises in Adams County, enters this township from the east about three and one-half miles from the Ohio, and bearing west-southwest empties into the Ohio River two miles below Aberdeen. Fishing Gut Run is a small creek in the southeast part of the township. Brushy Fork and Suck Run are in the northern part, their course being nearly due west; they are rapid, and were once used for driving grist and saw mills.

TIMBER.

Formerly the whole township was covered with a dense growth of timber. The principal trees were black walnut, white walnut, oak (five species), blue and white ash, poplar, hickory (three varieties), soft and hard maple, locust (three species), two of buckeye, beech, coffee-nut, linn, mulberry, two kinds of elm, hackberry, and, along the streams, sycamore. Underneath these was a thick growth of small trees, viz., dogwood, two varieties of haw, persimmon, crab apple, box alder, ironwood, wild cherry, cedar, red bud and papaw. There were some chestnut, whitewood and blackgum, and perhaps some other varieties; in the shade of these was a heavy growth of vines and shrubs, viz., blackberry, raspberry, huckleberry and hazel, while the grape vine entwined its graceful arms from the hazel bush to the uppermost branches of the mighty oak; the wild strawberry grew luxuriantly in many places. It was there that the pioneers' swine were allowed to roam upon receiving a mark by which they could be known; they often strayed away from the settlements, and became as wild as the deer. In addition to furnishing food for the pioneers' stock, the forest also furnished many delicacies for himself and his family; wild honey was abundant, and one of the main articles of diet for the pioneer's table as well as one of their delicacies.

PIONEERS.

The men and women who supplanted the native red men, and planted civilization where the wild, untutored savage roamed, were of a noble type. While we owe a debt of gratitude to our fathers, who freed our beloved country from the British yoke of tyranny and the oppressive chains of despotism, should we not revere and honor the memory of the hardy pioneers, who, taking this now rich, noble and happy country from a state of nature, by their enterprise and muscle made it what it is?

Ellis Palmer was without doubt the first settler in Huntington Township. Shortly after Wayne's treaty, he settled near the mouth of Big Three-Mile Creek, and built a cabin, where he remained until about the year 1804. He then built a cabin near Evan's mill dam, on land now owned by Dyas Gilbert. He was a great hunter, both of the red man and of all kinds of game, and cleared several leases, but never was the owner of any real estate; after leaving the township, he moved into Adams County, Ohio, where he died at an advanced age, the father of three sons and four daughters, viz., James, Ellis, Joseph Lethia (wife of James Riggs), and three whose names cannot now be learned.

John Gunsaulus came to this township near the same time that Ellis Palmer did, but nothing is known of his first entrance into the township, except that, as early as 1803 or 1804, he erected a cabin and squatted on land now owned by Eliza and Arbelas Hiett, near the Ripley and Bradysville Turnpikes, on the Little East Fork of Eagle Creek. While here, he took a lease on Nathan Gilbert's land, now owned by E. Porter, about half a mile above Hiett Post Office. He was a man of great physical power, and did a vast amount of work in felling the mighty forest trees of this township. He was considered a good marksman, and often carried off the prize. About the year 1818, he moved into Jackson Township, where he died.

HUNTINGTON TOWNSHIP.

Benjamin Beasley, about the year 1797, built a cabin on the farm now owned by his grand-daughter, Mrs. Cord, about four miles north of where Aberdeen now stands. He planted an orchard of apple, peach and pear trees, and as soon as the peach trees came into bearing there was more fruit than could be used by the family or than could be sold; he erected a distillery, which he operated till his trees stopped bearing, and distilled the surplus fruit into peach and apple brandy. He was a soldier of the war of 1812, and a surveyor by profession. He was a native of Virginia, and moved to Kentucky about the year 1789; his wife Mary died about 1844, and he in 1846; both are buried in the family graveyard on the farm where he located. Nathan Ellis is believed to be about the second to make a fixed residence in this township. He located upon the present site of Aberdeen, and laid out the upper part of the village. Before the village was laid out, he established a ferry, the first one between Maysville, Ky., and this township; a short time after the ferry was established, a hotel was built by Evan Campbell. Ellis soon sold one-half of his ferry to Campbell, and Ellis became joint partner in the hotel. After the Evans ferry was established at the mouth of Fishing Gut Creek, Mr. Ellis bought five acres of land from James Edwards, next to the hill, on what is known as Gum street, for the purpose of making a public highway to the landing. He planted an orchard, which is supposed to be the first in the township. He was the first Justice of the Peace in the township, and died at an advanced age. His remains were interred on the top of the river hill back of Aberdeen on the farm belonging to A. J. Brookover's heirs. He was the father of a large and quite an intelligent and influential family. In politics, he was a Democrat.

Evan Campbell, a native of Redstone, Penn., emigrated to Kentucky about the year 1800, and settled three miles above Limestone (now Maysville) about 1801 or 1802. He purchased land opposite Maysville about the time Nathan Ellis established a ferry, and opened up a small hotel, it being the first in the township. Mr. Campbell owned a half-interest in the second steam ferry that plied between Aberdeen and Maysville. He died at a good old age, and left a large family, some of whom still live in Aberdeen.

John Gray and his wife, Mary (Stewart) Gray, moved from Nicholas County, Ky., to Huntington Township about the year 1799. They were the parents of a large family of children. They were both quite old when they were called from earth. Joseph Gray, their son, is now the owner of the real estate on which his father settled on locating in Ohio. Joseph Gray was born near where he now resides, on the Aberdeen and Zanesville pike in 1799. In 1817, he was married to Jane Kilgore, of Nicholas County, Ky., who died a few years ago. Mr. Gray is now the oldest person living in the township who was born within it.

William Hutchinson was born in Loudoun County, Va., about 1763, and about the year 1800 was married to Rebecca Cooper. He emigrated in the same year to Kentucky, and located at or near Washington, where he lived for eight years, when he bought sixty acres of land in this township about one and one-half miles from Aberdeen, where he lived till his death. They were the parents of eleven children, six sons and five daughters, all of whom lived to be grown. The family were all Democrats. He died January 7, 1847; his wife died January 15, 1853.

James Edwards and his brother were kidnaped in Scotland while small boys, and brought to America and sold into some servitude in Virginia at an early day. James was married to Sarah Jacobs, and in 1796 moved to Ohio, where he bought 1,000 acres of land of Col. P. Slaughter, who received the land for services in the Revolutionary war. Mr. Edwards built a cabin at the mouth of Fishing Gut at the lower end of Aberdeen. He paid $1,000 for 1,000 acres. He had three sons and three daughters, viz., George, James, William, Jane, Ellen and Nancy. Jane married William Rains, Ellen married John West and Nancy married John Rains. John Rains, son of William and Jane (Edwards) Rains, was born October 30, 1796, and was brought to Ohio by his parents when but six weeks old.

George Edwards, son of James Edwards, Sr., established a ferry at the mouth of Fishing Gut Run about seventy-five years ago, which was afterward owned and run by his nephew, John Rains, who ran it as a horseboat the last eight years it was used as a ferry. After the Aberdeen & Zanesville Turnpike was completed, this ferry was abandoned. There were at this time three ferries, viz., Campbell's, Powers' and Rains'.

John Evans was born in Maryland November 17, 1770, and died July 18, 1858. He was married in Pennsylvania to Mary Housh, daughter of John Housh, in the year 1792, and soon afterward moved to Blue Licks, Mason Co., Ky. In the fall of 1800, he came to Ohio, and purchased a tract of land about five and one-half miles north of Maysville on the waters of Little East Fork of Eagle Creek, near the center of Huntington Township, on which he built a small cabin. In March, 1801, he moved with his family into his cabin, near where he lived at the time of his death. Soon afterward he built a smith shop, which is believed to have been the first shop in the township. In 1827 and 1828, he erected a flouring mill, which he operated till within a short time of his death, when he sold it to his grandson, Samuel Evans. He was a hard worker, and so economical that in a short time he was in very easy circumstances. He was ever ready to lend a helping hand to the poor and needy, and was very liberal in public improvements, assisting in both money and labor. He was one of the first County Commissioners, his first term being for one year; he was re-elected for three years. He was a soldier in the war of 1812. He was the father of eleven children, nine sons and two daughters, viz., Abraham, Benjamin, John, William, Thomas, Hannah, Griffith, Andrew, Luban, Diana and Amos, of whom Griffith is the only one living, now nearly seventy-six years of age.

In the fall of 1807, John W. Games and William Gilbert left Virginia in a partnership wagon, each furnishing one horse. Games spent the first winter in a cabin near the center of Huntington Township on the farm now owned by Henry V. Martin. He shortly afterward took a lease, and sold it to William Hiett, and bought a tract of land from Samuel Daniels, where D. W. Games now lives. His first wife was Sarah Fryar, of Jefferson County, Va., by whom he had five children—William, John F., Gideon G., Mary and Ruth. His second wife was Sarah Haynes by whom he had two daughters, Josephine and one whose name is not known; she died young.

William Gilbert came to Huntington Township and settled on the farm near where Dyas Gilbert now resides, and cleared out and improved the most of his land. He married Margaret Fryar, a sister of John W. Games' wife, by whom he had the following children: Elizabeth, Ruth, Sarah, Rachel, Margaret, Nathan, John, William, A. B., Robert D. and Benjamin. His seecond wife was Elizabeth Anderson, by whom he had one son, Harvey A. His third wife was Elizabeth Ramey. He died in 1836, and is buried on the farm which he first settled in the township.

Thomas Cunningham, a Virginian, moved to this township about eighty years ago, and bought land adjoining John Evans', on the north. His children were John, James and Mary. The ashes of father, mother and sons lie sleeping in the old Evans' Graveyard. After the death of his father and mother, James became owner of his father's farm.

HUNTINGTON TOWNSHIP.   499

Ebenezer Davis and his wife, Catharine (Watterson) Davis, came to the township in 1809 or 1810, and settled on a farm west of the center of the township, now owned by Robert Stewart. He sold it, and bought a farm of John Cotton, adjoining John Evans on the west. In 1848, he sold it to James Hiett.

George Harrison married Mary Palmer, sister of Ellis Palmer, the first settler of the township, and settled on land now owned by James H. and Henry V. Martin; he was one of the first common school teachers of this township.

Flaughers, four brothers, Adam, Jacob, David and Henry, were Pennsylvanians; they came to this township and bought land in the southwest part of the township on the river hills; their farms joined, and lay in the following order, going west: David's, Adam's, Jacob's and Henry's, the last running nearly to Logan's Gap.

John Haush and Anna (Pentacost) Haush, his wife, were from Pennsylvania, and came to Huntington Township the same time that John Evans did. They lived and died on John Evans' land, where H. V. Martin now lives. John, and Mary, the wife of John Evans, were their only children. John Haush, Jr., married a Crusan, and came to this township in 1801. He afterward built a saw and grist mill about five miles southwest of Aberdeen on lands now owned by H. V. Martin and A. Evans' heirs.

John and Joseph Cochran came from Pennsylvania to Huntington Township about the year 1806 or 1807. They bought land where John Hawk's heirs and Joseph W. Shelton now live. John Cochran was married to Tamar Howard, daughter of Cyrus and Milly (Booze) Howard, about the year 1809, and lived where J. W. Shelton now lives. They had thirteen children—Joseph, John, Milly, William, Mary, Elizabeth, James, Tamar, Ellen, Thomas J., Sarah J., Malinda and Lydia. John Cochran was eighty-four years old at his death; he died September 19, 1864, being the same day of the month on which he was born. In 1833, he bought the farm now owned by Frank Schwallie, on Eagle Creek, five miles east of Ripley. He served in the State Legislature as follows: Representative, from 1824 to 1829; Senator, from 1829 to 1831. He was also Brigadier General of the State militia, and a soldier in the war of 1812. His and his wife's remains repose in the new cemetery at Ebenezer Church.

John Hawk was a Pennsylvanian, and in 1807 settled on the farm now owned by Owen Griffith. His wife's name was Susan Crabb, and by her he had the following children: Henry, Phillip, Jacob, Isaac (died young), John, Abram, William, Nathan, Susan, Sarah, Christena, Rebecca, Elizabeth and Catharine. Samuel Wilson married Christena Hawk about the year 1819, and settled on the farm owned by his son William, near the mouth of Three-Mile Creek. He was a fifer in the war of 1812, and died about twenty-five years ago; his widow is still living, eighty-three years old.

William Anderson was one of the pioneers who, with his wife, Isabella Daniels, came to this township as early as 1808. He was one of the Associate Judges of the Brown County Court. He owned the farm now belonging to William Shelton.

William and John Hiett came to Ohio about the same time as William Anderson, and settled in Huntington Township, six miles north of Aberdeen. William Hiett's wife was Mary Daniels.

It has been very difficult to obtain any very reliable information concerning a number of the pioneers; that they were here at a very early period is evident, but it may be thought that too much prominence has been given to some, too little to others very deserving, and no mention made of some meriting distinction; but, under the circumstances, the best has been done that could be at this late day. The following list contains the names of nearly all of the pioneers not mentioned heretofore: Jacob Swisher settled a little north of the present site of Hiett's Post Office, and died about twenty-five years ago; Timothy Shirly, Uriah White, James Parker, Jonathan Rees, Alexander Rees, Daniel Boone, Simon Reeder, John Scott, William Cooper, Ollie Kilgore, John Richmond, Samuel Haslam, a reed maker, Jonathan Ayres, Robert Covert, Gregory Glascock, first singing teacher of the township, Peter Glascock, John Blair, William Taylor, a soldier of the war of 1812, who died while in the service having a family of five small children, Thomas Shelton, James Howard, John Lack, James Higgins, Adam White, Richard Thomas, George Brown, —— —— Bascom, father of Rev. Henry Bascom, Daniel and John Moore, McKinney Burbage, Edward Veach, Henry Altic, Alexander Parker, Moses Race, John and James Stewart, brothers, who built a mill near the mouth of Little East Fork of Eagle Creek, Robert Taylor, Eli Hurin, father of Jeremiah and Silas and Samuel Hurin. Many of the men mentioned in the foregoing list were celebrated hunters, and some were "crack marksmen" with the rifle; John Gunsaulus is believed to have been as good as any of his day; he seldom missed his mark when the chances were favorable. It is related of him that he would bet on hitting a three-inch mark off-hand at a distance of 100 paces, and nearly always came off winner.

SCHOOLS.

The early settlers no doubt felt the great necessity of an education; they soon turned their attention to it, and began devising methods and providing means for educating their offspring. To this end, rude cabins were built by volunteer labor, and teachers paid by subscription, the rates paid per scholar for a term of thirteen weeks (sixty-five days) being from $1.50 to $2.50, owing to the number that could attend, making the wages of teachers from $8 to $10 per month. The books then used were Dilworth and Guthrie's arithmetics, Webster's and Cobb's spellers, English reader and American preceptor, Linley, Murray's and Kirham's grammars and Olney's atlas and geography. The Testament was also much used as a reader.

One of the oldest schoolhouses stood near the center of the township on land then owned by John Evans, now by H. V. Martin, and was built in 1805 or 1806. George Harrison, Adam Calduward, a Mr. Swan and Samuel Ewings were the first teachers, teaching in the order named, as near as can be ascertained. The house was abandoned about 1823. About the year 1812, a log schoolhouse was erected on the farm now owned by D. W. Earley, about three hundred yards northeast of Ebenezer Church. The first teachers were Levi D. Beverage and Isaac W. Gibson. In 1822, the house was moved to what is now the corner of the Ebenezer Churchyard.

In 1810 or 1811, a log cabin was built near Gilbert's mill-dam, about two hundred yards south of the junction of the Ripley and Bradysville and the Iron Bridge & Bradysville Turnpikes. James Said, a Mr. Goodwin, William McCalla, Silas Clark, John Coxet, Royal Tyler and Reuben Case were all primitive teachers there. This house was used for a schoolhouse till 1843, when a new house was built one-half mile below it on the farm now owned by Dyas Gilbert. This was the first frame house used for school purposes in the township, and was twenty feet wide by twenty-five feet long. It was built by subscription, and cost $250, seats and desks excepted. Nathan Gilbert, son of William Gilbert, taught the first school in the new house.

The whole number of districts in the township, except Aberdeen Special District, is thirteen, with three fractional of Union Township and two of Adams County.

HUNTINGTON TOWNSHIP.

No. 1 is at the head of Fishing Gut Creek, running to the county line. No. 2 is west of No. 1, and extends to the corporation of Aberdeen. No. 3 is west of Aberdeen, lying on the Ohio River to the west side of the Hamilton farm, below the mouth of Three-Mile Creek. No. 4 lies on the river hills north of No. 3, and extends to East Fork on the northwest, and to Howard's land on the east. No. 5 lies mostly north of Three-Mile Creek on Slickaway Run, and has a good frame house 26x30 feet, built in 1870. No. 6 lies in the center of the township on Little East Fork of Eagle Creek, and has a new frame house, built in 1878, which now occupies the place of the one built in 1843; size, 25x28 feet. No. 7, located on the Ripley & Iron Bridge Turnpike, northwest of the center of the township, has a good frame house. No. 8, situated in the north part of the township, has a good frame house, built, in 1872. No. 9, in the northeast part of the township, had lately part of its territory cut off, forming a joint subdistrict with a part of Sprigg Township, Adams Co. The house was built about 1847. No. 10, on Ellis Run, is known as Greerson's District, and has a new frame house, built in 1873. No. 11 lies along the Ohio River above Aberdeen, and has a good frame house, built in 1869. No. 12 (California District) is located at Taylorsville, and has a good frame house, erected in 1872. No. 14 lies near the center of this township, and was formed principally from District No. 6, and lies southeast of it.

The fractions of Union Township are No. 13, at Logan's Gap; No. 15, at Fitch Bridge, and No. 16, at Martin's Bridge. All the districts in the township have been furnished with improved school furniture. There is one colored school in the township. The house is located in Subdistrict No. 7; it is a box frame, and furnished with best school furniture. There is also a colored school in Aberdeen.

The scholars in the township are as follows: Number of white males, 326; females, 290; colored males, 16; females, 21; total number males and females, 651.

The tuition fund for the year, exclusive of the fractional districts, is $3,000; whole contingent fund, about $1,000; average wages paid teachers, nearly $38 per month. The educational interest, has increased very considerable in the last few years, and is still increasing, with prospects for a brighter future.

CHURCHES.

The first preaching in the township was by Rev. Waad, a Baptist, about the year 1806. A church organization soon began, and was in a short time completed, with preaching occasionally. There being no church houses, schoolhouses and family residences were occupied as such until about 1852, a good brick building was erected in Aberdeen, Rev. Baldwins, Pastor, and Rev. Mason occasional Pastor. A Mr. Hutchison, Hosea Paul, James Paul, Elizabeth Evans, Samuel Carpenter and family, William Ruggles and others were members. The first organization of the Methodist Episcopal Church in Aberdeen and vicinity was at the house of James Dennis.

The old schoolhouse in Aberdeen was used for a number of years. The McCallas, Campbells, Dennises and Kilgores were members of the organization. In 1845, the society erected a brick building on Main Cross street in the village of Aberdeen. The church is in a pretty good state of prosperity, having connected with it a flourishing Sabbath school, with all the other essential elements for church prosperity.

Huntington Presbyterian Church.—Some years previous to 1832, Rev. Rutter, Robert Rankin, Rev. James Gilliland and sometimes Rev. John Rankin, private houses, and schoolhouses, and a church was organized. The following persons were members: William Anderson and wife, Joseph

Daniels and wife, Robert Scott and wife, David Dunseth, Thomas Gibson and wife and James Mears. In 1832, a brick house was erected on the opposite side of the creek, and near where Hiett's Post Office now stands. The church stood for years, but about 1850 the brick walls became cracked and much damaged, so that it was unsafe, and it was taken down and rebuilt on a smaller scale on the same site. The church membership became much reduced in the course of a few years by the death of some and the removal of others. Services have not been kept up regularly, and consequently the church has become weak both numerically and otherwise.

Ebenezer Methodist Episcopal Church.—About 1815, Robert Dobbins, a local Methodist minister, owned the farm now owned by D. W. Early, and often held religious services in the neighborhood. Nathan Gilbert's house, where E. Porter now lives, became a religious preaching place, and a class was soon organized. In 1822, an old log schoolhouse was moved to the corner of the present church lot, a few rods south of the site of present house, which became a regular point in the circuit for preaching. About the year 1818, Robert Dobbins sold his farm to John Meek, another Methodist Episcopal minister. In 1834, Rev. John Meek, Elijah Reikerds, John Hook, John W. Game, Elias Painter and George Woods, who was class leader at that time, felt the need of a building suitable for holding their meetings. The site was donated, John Hook and John F. Games were appointed building committee, and a brick church 40x48 feet was erected. It was some years before the house was completed, and for some cause it was never dedicated. Besides the members named above, there were Arthur Vain, a licensed exhorter, and his wife, John Blair, wife and family, Mary Ann and Rachel Parker, John Cooper and wife, William Gilbert and wife, John Shelton and wife and some others. In 1878, the old brick was taken down, and a new frame erected on the same site, but a little smaller. It was dedicated by the Rev. William I. Fee, then Presiding Elder for the district. The Trustees of the church are Thompson Maddox, John F. Games, John R. Glasscock, D. W. Early, W. B. Games and Samuel Maddox. W. B. Games and Samuel Maddox, Stewards; W. H. Simpson, Samuel Maddox, John Eubanks, and W. E. Hook, class leaders. The society numbers about seventy members. There is a flourishing Sabbath school maintained at the church. D. W. Early is Superintendent of the Sunday school, and W. H. Simpson, Assistant Superintendent.

Fellowship Christian Church.—This society was formed several years previous to having a church building. The schoolhouse and private dwellings were used for holding religious services for a time, and a brick house was built, but did not prove to be a good structure. It was taken down about three years ago, and rebuilt on the same site and partly on the same foundation. For some years the church did not prosper, but now it appears to be in a promising condition.

Hiett Christian Chapel.—During the years 1867 and 1868, a number of members of Bethlehem and Fellowship, Churches, who lived at a distance from their churches, felt the necessity of a place of worship in their immediate neighborhood; prominent among the movers of this purpose were James Cochran, Dr. W. H. Evans, Rev. James Paul, Lewis Shelton and John K. Hiett. Meetings were first held at Buchanan's Schoolhouse; the interest increased rapidly, and on the 13th day of June, 1869, the church was organized with forty-eight members, Elder C. W. Garoutte, officiating. Measures were immediately taken to raise a subscription to build a church edifice; $2,200 was subscribed, and William Shelton donated half an acre for a church lot on the Ripley, Ironbridge & Bradysville Turnpike, a little north of the center of the township. On June 4, 1870, the name of the church was adopted, and a frame building 32x50 feet was erected on the above named lot. On the first Sabbath in September, the house was dedicated to the worship of God by Elder N. Summerbell, D. D., assisted by Elders Garrautte, Pangburn and Gardner. To Elder William Pangburn the church owes a debt of gratitude for his unceasing efforts; he was its first Pastor. John K. Hiett donated about one-half of the money raised toward building the chapel, and he, with Thomas Beck and Dr. W. H. Evans, were the first Trustees. James Cochran, Lewis Shelton, Hiram McDaniel and Lewis Swearingen were the first Deacons. Additions have been made to the membership from time to time until now it numbers 150. The Sabbath school which is under the guidance of the church is maintained about one-half of each year with an average attendance of forty. The church burial-place is Shelton's Cemetery, for a history of which the reader is referred elsewhere in this work.

Colored Church of Aberdeen.—About five years ago, the colored people of Aberdeen and vicinity felt keenly the necessity of a suitable house in which to hold their religious meetings. They took steps toward erecting a house of worship, and to this end subscriptions were raised, the white people assisting them liberally in this good enterprise. The house was shortly afterward built, being a neat frame, upon which at that time there was a debt, but the church has continued to reduce it, and now have their house nearly paid for. The church has a pastor, and holds religious meetings regularly.

Bethlehem Christian Church.—This church was organized by Elder Matthew Gardner, who commenced preaching in this vicinity about 1823. Elder Gardner writes: "After giving up preaching at the old stone meeting-house, on Lawrence Creek, in Kentucky, I began to preach once a month on the Ohio side of the river, opposite Maysville, some twelve miles from my home. I had occasionally preached there on my way to the Lawrence Creek Church. The neighborhood was famed for wickedness. Sabbath-breaking, by horse-racing and gambling, cock-fights and whisky-drinking, was common. I had a great desire to carry the Gospel there. There was no preaching on the Ohio side of the river within ten miles of them. A Methodist minister had sent an appointment, but when he rose to speak, the congregation, in concert, as previously arranged, arose and left the house and empty benches to preach to. They needed salvation. Could I reach them? I would try. I appointed meetings in their dwellings or log cabin schoolhouses, but the congregations soon became so large that, when the weather permitted, our meetings were in the woods. A church was soon organized. The revival continued. Many were added to the church, and, in a few years, Bethelehem Church numbered over four hundred members. We soon built a good brick chapel, and the church prospered. If ever the power of the Gospel was manifest to all, it was in that section of country."

The Bethlehem Church became the largest and most important Christian Church in the conference to which it belonged. Elder Gardner was its pastor for forty-five years. In 1829, the first brick house of worship was erected. This was destroyed by a storm in 1860, and a new frame edifice erected the same year, near the same site. On the third Sabbath in May each year, this church held a "big meeting," as it was termed. These annual meetings were attended by vast congregations. Some came a distance of twenty miles, and as many as three thousand persons were sometimes collected together. At some of the meetings, more than one hundred joined the church. The church now has a membership of over four hundred, and sustains a large Sabbath school.

THE GREAT STORM OF 1860.

A great storm swept over the West on Monday, May 21, 1860, destroying houses and barns, and blowing down forests. Elder Matthew Gardner gives a graphic description of the destruction of Bethlehem Christian Church by this storm:

"The third Lord's Day in May, 1860, was our communion meeting at Bethlehem Church. I was assisted at that communion by Brother William Pangburn and Brother Charles W. Garoutte, whose labors were blessed. We continued the meeting on Monday at 10 A. M., and met again at 3 P. M. The congregation was large. The house was of brick. It was 35x50 feet in size, and was nearly full. A few minutes before the hour for preaching, a heavy cloud appeared in the west, of a dark green color, attended with a roaring sound. The ministers had ascended the pulpit, which was at the side of the house, and I was sitting on a chair, leaning back against the pulpit. The men occupied the west end of the house. As the cloud approached, the storm gathered strength, the roaring becoming louder and louder. Trees were swept down, limbs and brush were driven along, all accompanied by deafening thunder. Great drops of rain began to fall. The preachers waited, for almost utter darkness prevailed. Suddenly a crash was heard; the cries and screams could be heard above the roaring of the storm. Half of the roof, commencing at the west end, had blown to a great distance. The west gable had blown in, down to the square, and came crashing through the ceiling upon the men, closely seated below. Then distinctly, above all the din of the storm, was heard the cry, 'What shall I do to be saved? What shall I do to be saved?' I did not at first leave my seat. Having my trust in God, I felt as safe there as anywhere else, and I knew not yet the end of the calamity. I supposed that a shaft of lightning had struck the house; and as I saw the mass that had fallen upon the men, I said to myself, 'There are six men killed.' None were killed. The rubbish was quickly removed, and the men were assisted out, bruised, but all living. A young man who had run from the house got out in time to be struck by a falling rafter, which broke his arm. His was the most serious injury. All started home with sad hearts."

CEMETERIES.

Many of the burial-places in the township seem to have been selected with a view to their peculiar fitness, while others are very inappropriately situated. The greater number of the burial-places are private. Some of the oldest are now turned out into the cultivated fields, and corn, wheat and other crops flourish where sleep the ashes of the venerable pioneer. These are called family "graveyards," but few are regularly laid out, and a great number are shamefully neglected.

The first regularly laid out cemetery in the township was Charter Oak Cemetery, in the river bottom, one and a half miles below Aberdeen.

The Odd Fellows of Charter Oak Lodge of Aberdeen bought and laid out about four acres in the year 1852. Its location is a beautiful one. It is well cared for, and is usually in fine trim, and is much the largest in the township. It is estimated that three hundred are already buried there.

Shelton Cemetery, on the Ripley & Iron Bridge Turnpike, about one mile north of the center of the township, was laid out into lots in 1870 or 1871, and, soon after, the company was incorporated. The cemetery is beautifully located, and is kept in good condition. The first person buried there was John B. Hawk. The lots, especially the choice ones, are already disposed of, but there are yet some very good ones for sale.

Martin's Graveyard has perhaps the largest number of graves in it of any other family graveyard in the township. Most of the graves are marked by marble monuments, or marble head and foot stones, while others are marked with freestone, and a few have only rough limestone, or no mark at all to designate them; the latter are very few. The Helms, Martins, McDowells, Lawwills and Coopers are mostly buried there.

Ebenezer Graveyard, at the Ebenezer Church, is a large country graveyard, and nearly all the ground that could be used is filled with graves. The site is not a pretty one, being too much inclined. The Gaines, Hooks, Earleys, Simpsons, Griersons and many others are here interred. D. W. Early, Sr., deeded to his sons a lot west of the Ebenezer Church, that might properly be called Early Addition, as it is regularly laid out into lots. There are buried there D. W. Earley, Sr., and wife, Hon. John Cochran and wife, Hon. Andrew Evans, two sons and one daughter, and other persons, nearly all being connected with those just mentioned.

Hiett's Graveyard, on Ephraim Martin's farm, has been well taken care of, and is on a fine site. The Hietts and their connections are the principal occupants of this burial-place. William Hiett and his wife, Mary, and John Hiett's wife, are buried here. They were among the early settlers of this part of the township.

Hickory Ridge Cemetery, at Fellowship Church, near the north end of the township, is now in a little better condition than it has been for years. It has a considerable number buried there. William Jenkins, Sr., an early settler of that neighborhood, is interred at this place.

Slickaway Graveyard is near the Bethlehem Church two miles north of Aberdeen. It is very badly cared for, although there are many persons buried here.

Beasley's Graveyard is on the farm of Mrs. Card, four miles north of Aberdeen. It is surrounded by a stone wall. Benjamin Beasley, Sr., his family and connections, are buried there. Benjamin Beasley was one of the very earliest pioneers of the township.

Evans' Graveyard is situated on the farm owned and cleared out by John Evans, who was one of the first settlers of the township. In it rest the ashes of John Evans and wife, John Housh and wife, Watty McDonald, Edward McDaniel and wife, Joseph Cochran and wife, John Housh, Jr., and James Cunningham and wife, all pioneers or early settlers, besides divers others. But few graves are marked so that a stranger could tell by passing whose remains are resting there. It is very much neglected.

Besides the cemeteries named above, there are several others that it is proper to mention, all of them being private or family, viz., McDaniels, Gilbert's, Maddox's, Anderson's, two Scott's, Griffith's, two Cooper's, Rain's, Veech's, Parker's, Flaugher's, Boone's, and perhaps some others, which have been left out unintentionally. The greater portion of these have been almost totally neglected for years.

MILLS.

Housh's Mill was built by John Housh, on the right bank of the Little East Fork of Eagle Creek, four miles from its mouth, about 1808. It was a small saw and grist mill combined, with one run of buhrs, with which corn, wheat and buckwheat were ground, the bolting being done by hand. It did the grinding well, and served the neighborhood for some time. The saw-mill was rebuilt about 1830, and operated till 1848.

Scott's saw-mill was built on the right bank of the same stream, one-half mile below Housh's mill.

Alfred and Evan Griffith built a saw-mill on the same stream, about two and a half miles from its mouth, but it never did much work. About the year 1870, Evan Griffith completed another saw-mill, half a mile below the former, but, like the first, it was not a success.

Gilbert's saw-mill, on the same stream, about five and a half miles from its mouth, was built about 1816, by William Gilbert, and operated till his death, in 1836, when it changed owners, A. B. Gilbert becoming the owner. He has owned and operated it ever since. It has done more work than any other water saw-mill in the township, and the work has always been of the best character.

In 1827, John Evans began to erect a flouring-mill on the right bank of the Little East Fork of Eagle Creek, five miles north of Aberdeen, and in 1828 it was completed. It was operated until 1858, when Samuel Evans became the owner. He remodeled it the next year, and operated it till March, 1876, when a severe flood washed away the dam and injured the races. When the mill was built, the stream afforded considerable power, but, as the timber was cut away along the stream, the power began to fail, and now the stream does not afford power for more than one-third of each year. The mill had a fine reputation for its work, and the flour commanded the best prices in its day. It is a three-story frame, 30x36 feet. It had two run of buhrs—one for corn and one for wheat—and did a general milling business. It was driven by an eighteen-foot overshot wheel.

Cochran's mill, near the mouth of the same stream, was built by Robert and James Stewart about 1816. John Cochran bought it about the year 1823, remodeled it, and operated it for about twenty years. The building was a two-story log, 24x28 feet, and had two run of buhrs—one for corn and one for wheat. It did a general milling business. It was driven by an overshot wheel.

Young's mill, on Eagle Creek, in the north end of the township, was built about sixty-five years ago. John Richmond then became the owner, and operated it for several years, and then sold it to James Baldwin. It was then a log building. Baldwin and Dr. Hamilton rebuilt it, enlarging it and putting in new machinery, costing them a large sum of money. John Ellis became the next owner, and he operated it till his death, in 1848. Milo Melvin then bought it, and ran it about ten years, when John K. Hiett became the owner, and, in 1869, sold it to Thomas Young, the present owner, who put in a new turbine water-wheel and otherwise repaired it. It has two run of buhrs, but never did a great deal of work.

Sharondale Mill was built by Daniel Boone. The building was log, and stood on the right bank of Big Three Creek, two miles north of Aberdeen, near the old stone still-house, a little below where William Bradford's residence now stands. Hickson bought out Boone in 1832, and Parker & Wright bought out Hickson, rebuilt the mill, applied steam-power, and operated it till 1835. William Carpenter then bought out Parker & Wright, and operated it till 1844, when Dr. Moore bought it, and, a short time after, T. B. Fulton went in as a partner. In 1857, T. B. Fulton bought out Dr. Moore, and operated it very successfully till 1874, when he sold it to Jacob Pimm, who operated it till 1876, and then A. R. Brookover became a partner. In March, 1878, Brookover became a bankrupt, and, in the same fall, his interest was sold to William Bradford, who also bought Pimm's interest, and operated the mill till in May, 1882, when it was burned down.

Reeder's mill was a small log mill, standing on the same side of the same stream as Sharondale, a little higher up the stream. It was built by Simon Reeder about 1820. I. H. Warstell owned and operated it for several years.

About 1855, a company bought the Reeder Still-house, which was built for a distillery, but never used. It was fitted up for a mill, and operated for a year or two. I. H. Warstell bought out the company, remodeled the mill and ran it occasionally till after the war, when he converted it into a distillery. It stands on the opposite bank of the creek from Reeder's mill.

Shelton's, or Scott's mill, stands on the same stream, half a mile above Reeder's mill. It is a small log mill, and is now quite old.

Parker & Carpenter's mill was built in 1844 by William Parker and William Carpenter. It was a large frame steam mill, on the river bank, below Market street, in Aberdeen. It did not prove to be very remunerative to its owners, and it was only operated a few years, when it was taken down and moved to Kentucky.

The Ohio Valley Mill was built in the fall of 1881, by T. B. Fulton and Elijah Davis. It is a steam flouring-mill, on the west side of Market street, in Aberdeen. The building is a frame, three stories, of wood, and a basement of stone, and cost $12,000. It has four run of buhrs and all the modern improvements in the way of mill machinery. It has a good reputation for its work, and, without doubt, is one of the finest mills of its size in the State.

TURNPIKE ROADS.

The township is pretty well supplied with regular laid out macadamized pikes, running in different directions. The Aberdeen & Zanesville pike was the first built, and has been much the best in the township. Its direction is northeast from the Ohio River, at Aberdeen, to Zanesville, leaving the township and passing into Adams County about three and a half miles from Aberdeen. It was built in 1840, 1841 and 1842.

The Ripley & Bradysville Turnpike was built in 1860 and 1861, by a company. It enters the township two miles northeast of Logan's Gap, and runs nearly east to the county line, one and a half miles above Ebenezer Church. The road lies between Ripley and Manchester, and six and a half miles are in the township.

The Ripley & Iron Bridge Turnpike enters the township at Eagle Creek, two miles above the last named, and bears a little southwest till it intersects the Ripley & Bradysville pike at East Fork, one mile below Hiett's Post Office. The distance in the township is about four miles. It was built in 1860 and 1861.

The Aberdeen & Huntington Free Turnpike was built, or commenced, in 1868, and completed in 1870. It was built under what is called the two-mile law. Its direction is nearly north, commencing at the old Aberdeen & Zanesville road, two miles north of Aberdeen, and intersecting the Ripley & Bradysville road one-fourth of a mile below Hiett's Post Office. Length in township, four and one-third miles.

The Huntington & Maysville Free Turnpike begins at the Ripley & Bradysville road, at Evan Griffith's farm, and, bearing southeast, intersects the Aberdeen & Huntington pike at J. C. Waldron's farm, three and a half miles north of Aberdeen. Length, two and one-fourth miles. It was built during the years 1880 and 1881.

Hiett's Post Office and Neel's store road was laid out in 1880, and is now nearly completed. Twenty per cent was raised by subscription, and the county furnished the balance of the money to build it. Its direction is nearly north, beginning at Hiett's Post Office and passing out of the township at Neel's Store, on Eagle Creek, thence up Eagle Creek to Decatur; whole distance, about seven miles; nearly four miles of it are in this township.

PROMINENT MEN OF THE TOWNSHIP.

Henry B. Bascom was the most noted of any man who ever resided in this township. At one period, he was perhaps second to none in popular pulpit oratory in the United States.

He was born in the State of New York May 27, 1796, and died at Louisville, Ky., in September, 1850. He united with the Methodist Episcopal

Church in the western part of Pennsylvania in 1811. Two years after, he was licensed to preach, and was received on trial in the Ohio Conference. At the age of sixteen, he moved into this township, and settled about three miles northwest of Aberdeen, where Conrad Eppensteiner's widow now lives. While he lived there, he devoted his time to study and laboring for his church. In 1823, he was elected Chaplain to Congress. In 1827, he was elected President of Madison College, Pennsylvania, which position he filled until 1829, when he became agent for the American Colonization Society. In 1832, he was elected Professor of Moral Science in Augusta College, Kentucky, and in 1842 he became the President of Transylvania University. He was a delegate to every general conference from 1828 to 1844. At this latter date, he wrote the famous "Protest of the Minority," in the general conference, and the report on organization at the formation of the Methodist Church South. When the agitation of the slavery question began to disturb the Methodist Episcopal Church, he attached himself to the South Branch, and edited the *Southern Quarterly Review* from 1846 to 1850, when he was elected Bishop, in which capacity he was serving at his death. He published several works.

An early Justice of the Peace, and a very prominent and well-known citizen, was Thomas Shelton. The Maysville (Ky.) *Bulletin* of February 17, 1870, contains the following personal sketch of him: "Death of Esq. Thomas Shelton, at Aberdeen, on Tuesday last, at the age of ninety-four years. He was born in Stafford County, Va., in 1776, and in about 1812, emigrated to this county. In 1816, he was elected a Justice of the Peace, which office he held without interruption to the day of his death. He was perhaps the most remarkable man of his section, from the fact that he has officiated at the solemnization of more marriages than any person in the United States. It has been estimated that he has united in the bonds of wedlock over four thousand couples, or eight thousand persons. Hundreds of young people from this State, whose parents were unfavorable to their plans, have flown to the old 'Squire,' and found his services an efficient remedy for their misfortune. He always claimed that the majority of his marriages were happily made, and, if they turned out to be contrary, he consoled himself with the reflection that his own part was well done, and he was not to blame. The old gentleman for many years previous to his death, had a peculiar passion for buying and trading watches. and it was said of him that he seldom made a good trade. He has purchased as many as six watches in one week, and has traded them off for other watches within the next week. He was a zealous and life-long Democrat, taking great interest in the progress and prosperity of his party, and never voting any other ticket. He had many generous impulses, and the members of his family and his neighbors were much attached to him."

Shelton was succeeded by Massie Beasley, who has solemnized more than three thousand marriages since 1870, a large proportion of them being without the authority of a license. Aberdeen has thus become as famous in Ohio and Kentucky for its irregular marriages as Gretna Green in England and Scotland. The following is the form of marriage certificate given by Esq. Beasley in cases of marriages without license, which is similar to one used by the officiating blacksmith of Gretna Green:

TO ALL WHOM IT MAY CONCERN.

ABERDEEN, O..........................188..
THIS CERTIFIES, That by virtue of a Marriage Contract by and between Mr.........
.................and Miss...of the County of
...................and State of........................ They have this day, in the presence of the undersigned witnesses, acknowledged themselves as Man and Wife.
....} Witnesses.
....
MASSIE BEASLEY, ESQUIRE.

HUNTINGTON TOWNSHIP.

John Cochran was a Senator and Representative to the Ohio Legislature. The reader is referred to pioneers of this township for further information of him.

Benjamin Evans, son of John and Mary (Housh) Evans, was born January 17, 1796, at Blue Licks, Mason Co., Ky., and died July, 1861. He was married twice. His first wife was Ruth, a daughter of William and Margaret (Fryar) Gilbert. They were married in 1818, and Ruth died about 1826. There were four children born to them—Mary, Margaret, Hannah, and a small child, whose name is unknown. Elizabeth Allison, his second wife, was a daughter of Joseph Allison, born April, 1806, died June, 1863. They were married about 1829. The fruits of this marriage were four sons and five daughters—W. G., Andrew J., Ruth, Thomas, Diana, Angeline, Matilda, Tacy and John; last two named died young. Benjamin held the offices of Land Appraiser, County Auditor from 1829 to 1831, and was elected Associate Judge shortly after his term of office as Auditor expired. He served two terms in the Ohio Senate, from 1847 to 1849, and also served two or three terms as Justice of the Peace.

John F. Games was born March 11, 1810, educated in the common school of his day, and taught school several terms. He served one term as Justice of the Peace in this township, and was elected Representative to the Ohio Legislature in 1854, but was not a candidate for re-election.

Andrew Evans, son of John and Mary (Housh) Evans, was born December 12, 1809, and died September, 1879. He held the office of Justice of the Peace of this township for twelve years, and represented Brown County in the Ohio Legislature from 1864 to 1866. He was a candidate for re-election, but was defeated by a small majority. He was elected as a War Democrat.

John C. Waldron was born in Adams County, Ohio, and emigrated to Huntington Township in 1829. He served as Township Constable fifteen years, as Justice of the Peace, and was elected Representative to the Ohio Legislature two terms—from 1870 to 1874. Politically, he is a Democrat.

Andrew J. Evans, son of Hon. Benjamin Evans, represented his county in the Kansas Legislature.

John W. Games, son of Hon. John F. Games, represented his county in the Kansas Legislature for two terms.

MILITARY.

Huntington Township bore an honorable part in the great war for the supremacy and perpetuity of the Union, and her soldiers have a record of which her people may justly be proud. From that memorable day of April, 1861, when the glorious old flag was struck with traitorous hands, and when the rebel batteries centered their fire on Sumter, until the grand and lasting victory at Appomattox, the sons of Huntington Towns ip, with their lives and all they held dear, were at the service of their country and on the side of the Union. In victory as well as defeat, in camp and field, in bivouac or on the march, at the cannon's mouth or around the quiet camp-fire, they showed themselves worthy sons of worthy sires. At the beginning of the war, their response to their country's call was prompt and cheerful. As months and years rolled on, the decimated ranks were filled by fresh and determined troops; and when the end came, there were but few families that had not laid on the country's altar some costly sacrifice. Of those who slumber in unknown and unmarked graves, upon fields exposed to the parching rays of a Southern sun, are sons of Huntington Township. There they wait the reveille for the brave and honored dead. But they have left the memory of their heroic deeds impressed upon the hearts of a grateful people, who will, to the latest generation, call them blessed. Those who were fortunately permitted to return feel a just pride in the war record of their township. There were tears and sorrows; their ranks and files had been fearfully thinned; the human sacrifice in behalf of the nation had been intensely severe; but better this sacrifice than a divided country.

While the men of the township contested the question of secession in the field, there was also an army of noble women at home, who bore an exalted part in the great contest. They never wearied in their efforts to supply to the soldiers at the front many tokens of remembrance; the sick were supplied with innumerable delicacies, and their fervent petitions were almost continuous to the God of battles for the cause of the Union; that right might triumph, and that the country might emerge from the great contest purified by defeat and disaster, till it be worthy of its founders and its defenders. The following list embraces nearly all who enlisted from this township; it is as near correct as can be obtained, since no record of enlistments was kept in the township. This list has been prepared with great care and labor. If any names have been omitted, it is to be regretted. It is possible that some names are recorded that do not properly belong to this township; if so, it is not for the purpose of over-estimating the township's honor, or encroaching upon the honor of any other portion of our great country. They served in nearly all the great battles of the rebellion; first, in Western Virginia, and, as the war progressed, they were scattered to almost every portion of the South, though the greatest number, perhaps, were engaged in Kentucky, Tennessee, Mississippi and Virginia. The following were commissioned officers from this township: George B. Bailey, Captain, Twelfth Ohio Volunteer Infantry; Joseph Blackburn, Captain Company F, Seventieth Ohio Volunteer Infantry; James Drennan, Captain Company F, Seventieth Ohio Volunteer Infantry; I. W. Adams, Second Lieutenant Company F, Seventieth Ohio Volunteer Infantry; D. A. Dodds, Captain Company F, Seventieth Ohio Veteran Volunteer Infantry; John Redman, Second Lieutenant, Eighty-ninth Ohio Veteran Volunteer Infantry; John Moore, Lieutenant in Tenth Kentucky Cavalry; Samuel Evans, First Lieutenant, Fifty-ninth United States Colored Infantry; John E. Carpenter, First Lieutenant, One Hundred and Seventy-fifth Ohio Volunteer Infantry; William Hubbert, First Lieutenant Company H, Seventieth Ohio Volunteer Infantry; Frank Harding, First Lieutenant Company H, Ohio Veteran Volunteer Infantry.

The enlisted men of Company F, Seventieth Ohio Volunteer Infantry, were: William Anderson, I. W. Adams, Benjamin Abrams, D. B. Brown, William Case, Henry Campbell, Dyans Campbell, Robert Campbell, D. A. Dodds, Joseph Dodds, Allen Dodds, Darius Dodds, Lawson Dragoo, Daniel Dragoo, Phillip Dragoo, J. B. Evans, Samuel Evans, John Flemming, Thomas Grier, James Galbraith, William Geddis, Paul Geddis, Oliver Gray, Caleb Glasscock, D. W. Games, W. T. Hook, William Hart, Henry Harding, Samuel Hiett, Griffith Hiett, John Hiett, William M. Haynes, Phillip Henderhand, B. F. Jacobs, George Jamison, Joseph Kilgore, P. J. Lane, Samuel Lyons, Ed Morgan, John McDaniel, Joseph McDaniel, D. E. Maddox, William Mills, John McDaniel, Jr., John Midghall, Alex Neil, John Newman, Daniel Reader, Alex Rains, Benjamin Reeder, John Sibbald, James Sibbald, J. W. Shelton, Alfred Shelton, Lewis Shelton, James Scott, John Swisher, N. B. Thompson, James Waldron, G. H. White.

Those of Company H, Seventieth Ohio Volunteer Infantry, were: W. C. Buck, James Bradford, William Brooks, James Fryar, William Hubbert, Silas Hurin, John Hurin, Charles Jumper, Darius Kilgore, James Kilgore, James M. Lawwill, Jeremiah Mahanna, C. Mahanna, John Mahanna, Jesse McKinley, Samuel Reed, S. N. Sawyer, Thomas Simons, Charles Walker, J. M. Sutton, Mark O. Neal, William McCune, Michael O. Neal, Andrew Smalley.

HUNTINGTON TOWNSHIP. 513

Members of Companies E and G, Seventieth Ohio Volunteer Infantry: James Brooks, C. Cook (E), Frank Harding (G).

Members of Company H, Twelfth Ohio Volunteer Infantry: Charles Case, J. E. Carpenter, J. B. Campbell, William Campbell, G. D. Evans, James Frame, T. F. Hill, Ephraim Helm, Luther Hall, William Hall, Sr., William Hall, Jr., Alex Hall, George Hall, Frank Hall, John Jones, Aaron Jones, Moses Paul, William Riggs, Thomas Sutton.

Members of Company E, Eighty-ninth Ohio Volunteer Infantry: Richard Bailey, E. Bowman, Amos Evans, W. H. Evans, G. W. Earley, Samuel Flaugher, John McNulty, J. W. McDaniel, William McDaniel, Alfred McNulty, John Redman, J. W. Swisher, G. A. Shelton, Jacob Scott, Samuel Scott.

Members of the Tenth Kentucky Cavalry: George Brookover, Joseph Carpenter, Power Campbell, W. R. Ellis, Thomas Carpenter, Thomas Harding, John Moore, Lieut. Joseph Power, F. P. Waldron, S. R. Worstell, T. J. Worstell, J. C. Sutton.

Members of Company B, Thirty-third Ohio Volunteer Infantry: J. W. Grierson, William Grierson, Robert Grierson.

Members of the Fourth Independent Cavalry were: William Bowman, John W. Scott, James Brittingham.

In the Seventh Ohio Volunteer Cavalry: J. W. Games, J. H. House.

In the One Hundred and Seventy-fifth Ohio Volunteer Infantry: B. F. Botts, William Crabtree, Daniel Hare, James Madigan, J. Paul, L. Schlitz.

In the One Hundred and Eighty-second Ohio Volunteer Infantry: John Carrigan, G. W. Davidson, M. B. Glasscock, S. McDaniel, Joseph Paul, H. Palmer, Lewis Paul, Harvey Teeters, James Payne, A. White, Lewis Shelton.

In Company C, One Hundred and Eighty-eighth Ohio Volunteer Infantry: William Gray, W. D. Grierson, Simon Reeder, J. W. Stewart.

The following list contains the names of soldiers whose company and regiment could not be definitely ascertained: George Anderson, William Atherton, John Brittingham, James Brittingham, T. Bennett, James Campbell, William Carroll, Ed Cunningham, John Daulton, Benjamin Campbell, Thomas Daulton, George Daulton, Ely Frame (Seventeenth Kentucky), T. H. Glasscock, L. Grimes, Marion Harover, James D. Howard, S. J. Housh, S. R. Hutchison, Smith Howland, Lewis Jones, Aaron Jones, D. C. Kerr, William Little, B. B. Lawwill, George McDaniel, James McDaniel, James McKinley, Jesse McDaniel, —— Mafferty, John Newman, Aristus Norris, Isaac Payne, John Rains, William Richmond, William Ruggles, John Rist, Permenius Ryan, P. Roush, John Ruggles, W. H. Sutherland, Powell Simpson, Henry Stafford, A. M. Shelton, J. W. Scott, William Shelton, Lewis Swearingen, William Savage, George Scott, Robert Taylor, P. W. Waldron, —— Young.

Soldiers of the war of 1812, residents of the township, all of whom are now dead: Nelson Austin, Richard Brown, George Brown, William Burnett, John Cochran, John Ellis (Captain), Jesse Ellis, Samuel Ellis, John Evans, Adam Flaugher, Jacob Flaugher, David Flaugher, Henry Flaugher, Mason Griffith, John W. Games, James Higgins, William Harding, Thomas Leechman, James Leechman, William Little, Arthur Mitchell, Hosea Paul, Alex Rains, William Taylor, Samuel Wilson.

VILLAGES.

Aberdeen is the only incorporated village in the township. It was originally laid out by Nathan Ellis, July 5, 1816. A. Woodough, Surveyor of Adams County, surveyed it. The plat was recorded July 12, 1816, by J. Darlington, Recorder of Adams County. James Power's Addition was laid out in 1832. John Beasley's First Addition was laid out in 1841, his second in 1845, and his third in 1850, at which time the village became incorporated. Arthur Mitchell was the first to engage in the mercantile business. His store, a frame building, stood just below Pike street on the river bank. The ground on which it stood is nearly all washed into the river. Andrew Scott was the second business man. His store was about where John O. Herron's grocery now is, on Ferry and Front streets. Nathan Hodges, William Parker and Shelby Campbell were pioneers in the grocery business, and following them were Ely Davison, James G. Lane, Morgan and Thomas Sharp, I. H. Warstell, James C. Power, J. S. Acklin and Moses Lamb. The first settlers were Nathan Ellis, James Edwards, Evan Campbell and James Power, all business men. James Helm was also one of Aberdeen's early business men, and was engaged in the dry goods business, hotel, ferry, and coal and lumber trade. William Parker and William Carpenter, about the year 1845, erected a large steam flouring-mill on the river bank, just below Market street, and operated it for a few years, but it did not prove profitable. It stood idle for several years, and then was torn down. The tannery now owned by Martin Rudle has been operated successfully for many years. It was built by Samuel McDaniel, and sold to Henry Grimes. Benjamin Bradford owned it for several years, then Martin & Cole became the owners, and enlarged it considerably, and operated it successfully till about the commencement of the late civil war, when L. C. A. Rudle became a partner. Since then, they have enlarged the buildings, added a fine steam engine and a great amount of machinery, and employ from forty to sixty hands. The first steam ferry that plied between Aberdeen and Maysville was owned by Maysville men, and was only operated about a year, when it was sold and went out of the trade. Campbell & Helm put in the second ferry-boat in the Aberdeen and Maysville trade, and ran it for a few years. James Helm owned the third, and ran it till after the rebellion, when William Linton bought him out, and put in the trade another boat. During 1879, James C. Power had a large double-engine boat built, and placed it in the same trade. Soon after, William Linton had his boat rebuilt, and named it Frank S. Owens, and in 1882 James C. Power bought and sold it. His boat, the Gretna Green, is still in the trade, and is a very fine ferry-boat.

In 1856 or 1857, Aberdeen built a large schoolhouse on Mountain street, below Main Cross street, in which there are now employed four teachers, besides the colored school. The number of white scholars is about three hundred and ten. The school is in a very good condition. The population of Aberdeen in 1880 was 883, being a slight increase in the last decade.

The Methodist Episcopal Church, on Main Cross street, was built in 1845. A good Sabbath school is connected with the church.

The Baptist Church was built in 1852, on Mountain, between Market and Locust streets. The Baptist Sabbath school is in a flourishing condition.

The Colored Methodist Episcopal Church, below Market street, was erected a few years ago. It is a small frame church, and the society is in good working order.

The Ohio Valley Mill, built by T. B. Fulton and Elijah Davis, is one of the finest mills of its size in the State, and is a very valuable addition to Aberdeen and vicinity. It was erected in 1881, at a cost of about $12,000.

H. S. True & Son, O. B. Spears and W. S. Spears are dealers in leaf tobacco, which is a new enterprise, and has given new life to Aberdeen through the tobacco season.

Campbell's saw-mill, built by Campbell & McCalla, on the corner of Front and Walnut streets, is a good mill, and worthy of notice. There are now in the town two dry goods stores, two drug stores, five groceries, two restaurants, two hotels, three blacksmith shops, three saloons, and two coal and lumber

HUNTINGTON TOWNSHIP.

dealers. Taylorsville, on the Aberdeen & Zanesville pike, three miles from the Ohio River, was laid out by William Lawwill, Sr., in 1850, and contains two stores, two smith shops, a school building and wood shop. It has a population of eighty-three.

Hiett is situated about six and a half miles north of Aberdeen, on the Ripley & Bradyville Turnpike, and contains a post office, dry goods and grocery store, one church (Presbyterian), one doctor (W. H. Evans) and stock scales. W. D. Grierson is Postmaster, and also runs the store. A few years ago, a Granger Lodge and another store existed here. The mail is semi-weekly. The Post Office Department has granted a tri-weekly mail, but as yet nothing further has been done to establish the new route.

LODGES.

Aberdeen Lodge, No. 149, F. & A. M., was chartered October 20, 1847. The first meeting after dispensation was granted was held April 23, 1845. The first officers were: Caleb Atherton, M.; Marshall McKinley, S. W.; Thomas Mills, J. W.; T. H. Worstess, Treasurer; James Dennis, Secretary; T. M. Moore, S. D.; Jesse Ellis, J. D.; James Helm, Tiler. These were also charter members. The officers for the year 1882 are: T. Heaton, M.; T. M. Martin, S. W.; Samuel Evans, J. W.; John Brookover, Treasurer; S. C. Bradford, Secretary; James Drennin, S. D.; G. Sorries, J. D.; W. R. Ellis, Tiler. The lodge is in fair working order, and has at present about sixty members.

Charter Oak Lodge, No. 137, I. O. O. F., was instituted October 12, 1849, with the following charter members: James C. Power, W. C. Clift, John McCalla, James S. Scott, Dyas Power, John Lepage, Thomas Sharp, James Bricker and John Stevens. James C. Power is the only charter member now belonging to the lodge, and Dyas Power, John McCalla and J. C. Power are the only charter members now living. The present officers are: A. B. Gray, N. G.; W. R. Brittingham, V. G.; A. H. Porter, Secretary; L. Schlitz, Treasurer. This lodge is in a good condition, has a good, comfortable hall, a large cemetery below Aberdeen, and a surplus fund of more than $1,000. The present number of members is seventy-five.

Magnolia Encampment, No. 186, I. O. O. F., of Aberdeen, was instituted June 17, 1875, with the following charter members: Dyas Gilbert, Daniel Pence, A. H. Porter, W. R. Flaugher, Thomas Sharp, J. W. Cheesman, P. W. Waldron, J. C. Waldron, J. W. Stewart, L. Schlitz and G. H. Wheeler. The present officers are: M. Jones, C. P.; John Curtiss, S. W.; John Sutton, H. P.; L. Schlitz, Treasurer; and A. H. Porter, Scribe. The present number of members is sixty-five. This is a flourishing society, many of its members being leading citizens of the township.

Gretna Green Lodge, No. 99, K. of P., of Aberdeen, was instituted, under a charter of the Grand Lodge of Ohio, May 18, 1876. The charter members were: G. H. Wheeler, Dyas Gilbert, Lawrence Schlitz, S. C. Bradford, F. W. Sharp, E. M. Flaugher, F. H Miller, C. B. Sutton, P. J. Neeper, John Crane, John Enis, Moses Jones, A. B. Jones, G. W. Schlitz, A. R. Brookover and Julius Clames. The present number of members is sixty-five. The officers for 1882 are: N. J. Sutton, C. C.; W. A. Rist, V. C.; Robert Helm, Prelate; Dyas Gilbert, Representative to Grand Lodge. This is a flourishing society, and bids fair to become the largest in the township.

GENERAL.

This township, on a full vote, could poll about seven hundred votes. The largest vote ever polled in the township was in 1880, at the Presidential election, viz.: W. S. Hancock, 394; James A. Garfield, 281; Neal Dow, 2; total, 677. The Democratic majority is strong. At a general election, it does not vary much; yet a nomination for township officers does not always insure an election. The best of feeling generally prevails between contending parties, and the contests are nearly always good-humored.

Tradition says Nathan Ellis was the first Justice of the Peace in the township. Thomas Shelton succeeded him in 1816, and held the office for forty-four years without intermission. James Parker, John F. Games, William Gilbert, Benjamin Evans, Henry Vane, Massie Beasley, Andrew Evans, Alex Grierson, John C. Waldron, William Riggs and Samuel Evans all served as Justices.

The present township board of officers is as follows: Justices of the Peace, Massie Beasley and Samuel Evans; Township Trustees, P. N. Bradford, Samuel Riggs and F. M. Stephenson; J. W. Guthrie, Treasurer; T. C. Carr, Clerk; Harrison Bradford, Constable.

Louis N. A. Riedle.

CHAPTER VI.

CLARK TOWNSHIP.

BY O. P. RALSTON.

THE township of Clark was one of the original townships of the county, and before the organization of Brown County was a township of Clermont County. It was created by the Commissioners of Clermont County October 18, 1808, and the boundaries established as follows: Beginning where the State road from Denhamstown to West Union crosses White Oak; thence running with the State road to the Adams County line; thence north with said line to Highland County; thence west with said county line to the corner of Highland County, and continuing west so far as to include Aaron Leonard and Moses Moss; thence south to the Lewis Township line; thence with the same to the place of beginning. The township originally included nearly one hundred square miles of territory, but it was reduced December 2, 1822, by the formation of Washington and Franklin Townships; March 23, 1823, by the formation of Pike Township, and December 1, 1828, by the formation of Scott Township. This left it in its present dimensions, containing 18,223 acres.

There are no streams of any magnitude in the township; the head-waters of Cloverlick drain the western part, Bullskin the southern, and several small tributaries of White Oak the eastern part. These streams are all too small to afford good water power for machinery.

The township lies on an elevated ridge, dividing the waters of White Oak Creek from the waters of the East Fork of the Little Miami River. It consists mostly of level table-lands, somewhat broken in the eastern and western part, but all susceptible of easy drainage. The soil consists of a heavy limestone clay, which was formerly very heavily timbered with oak, beech and sugar in the dry part, soft maple in the wet parts, poplar, walnut, hickory, some white and red elm, hackberry, buckeye, linn, blue and white ash, mulberry, black and red locust, sycamore, willow and dogwood. There are now 5,116 acres of woodland, 6,515 acres of plowed land and 6,592 acres of pasturage. The total value of real estate in the township is $367,870, which includes $8,409 of village lots. The population at the census of 1880 was 780 white males and 799 white females. The chief products of the township are corn, tobacco, wheat and oats. Grasses do not grow as well here as in the country farther north, and the land is not well adapted to stock-raising, though a goodly number of cattle and sheep are raised in small herds. The fruit crops become more uncertain and the yield poorer as the forests disappear; in the early settlement of the township, peaches were abundant, and the crop rarely failed, but now they are scarce, and of a poor and small character, and a crop is rarely yielded. Apples do not grow as large and fine or in as great abundance as they did in the virgin soil. Pears, plums and the smaller fruits are not extensively grown, but blackberries grow spontaneously in great abundance.

POLITICAL.

The first regular election held in the township was on the 8th day of November, 1808, when Jonathan Liming, James Liming and Christian Smith were Judges, and Jacob Bradberry, Clerk, and the following township officers were elected: Robert Wardlow, Christian Smith and Samuel Liming, Trustees; William Still and John Pitzer, Constables; Christian Smith, Clerk; Henry Zumalt, Treasurer; Thomas Liming and George Washburn, Supervisors; John Hill and Benjamin Smith, Overseers of the Poor; Thomas Liming, John Fiscus and Francis Myers, Sr., Fence Viewers; number of votes cast, eighty.

The first mention of a Justice of the Peace in the records is on April 3, 1809, when Alexander McBeth, Justice of the Peace, administered the oath to the Judges and Clerks of the second election. At this election, only twenty-seven votes were cast, and the following officers were elected: Alexander McBeth, James Thompson and Phillip Lindsey, Trustees; William Morecraft and William Hill, Listers and Constables; Christian Smith, Clerk; Henry Zumalt, Treasurer.

The first order drawn on the treasury of the township was on March 15, 1809, in favor of William Still for $1 for township services. On January 11, 1809, James McKinny took the oath of office as Justice of the Peace for Clermont County. On January 12, 1809, Alexander McBeth was sworn as a Justice. In March, 1810, the township was divided into four road districts instead of two, as before. The first jurors, returned March 4, 1811, were as follows: John Allen, James McCall, Samuel Liming, John Lindsey, Samuel Wardlow and George Little. By the year 1812, the wealth of the township must have materially increased, as the records show the following large sums to have been paid to the Supervisors—probably the first money paid from the treasury to those officers: William Still, $1.50; Abram Liming, $1.50; Robert Davidson, $1.50; Nicholas Devore, $1.50. October 11, 1811, James McKinny and William White were commissioned as Justices of the Peace. In 1812, the number of road districts was increased to six by the board, which then consisted of Joseph Foor, Christian Smith and Robert Allen, Trustees, and Francis Myers, Clerk. From the records it appears that up to the close of the year 1816 only thirty orders were drawn on the treasury, the total amount of which was $41.08. In 1820, although the township was reduced in size, the number of voters had increased to 132, and the following officers were elected: Robert Kennedy, John Lindsey and Christian Smith, Trustees; Francis Myers, Clerk; William White, Treasurer; A. Gibson, Constable and Lister. In the year 1819, soon after the organization of the county, Nathaniel Gist, by his trustees, purchased about one thousand two hundred acres of land on the east side of White Oak Creek, on which he settled thirty-four families (200 persons) of colored people, who were all legally warned to depart from the township, lest they should become a township charge.

An amusing incident is related by one of the old citizens of the township, explaining why Henry Clay received no votes in the township at the election in 1824. The election was held in a log schoolhouse on the farm of John Wilks, and Robert Kennedy, Lot Stratton and William Gould were Judges, and Joseph Ralston, Clerk. One of the Judges, who was also one of the four Whigs in the township, brought with him to the polls a roll of Clay's tickets, and laid them on the writing bench; they rolled back into a crack between the logs, and another of the Judges, who was not one of Clay's supporters, pushed the ballot-box back against them in such a way as to effectually hide them till the polls were closed; as these were the only tickets to be had, and as the voters were unable to remember the names on the tickets, they were not able to vote for their candidate.

In 1840, the number of electors in the township had increased to 232; of these, William Shannon had 175 for Governor, and Thomas Corwin had fifty-seven. In 1880, Hancock received 297 votes for President, and Garfield received 106, showing a Democratic majority of 191. The township has been

CLARK TOWNSHIP.   521

strongly Democratic since the days of Jefferson; this may be because it is settled principally by people from Kentucky and Pennsylvania.

JUSTICES OF THE PEACE.

The following is a list of the Justices of the Peace of the township with the dates of their election, the two previously mentioned being excepted: William White, 1812; William Chapman, January 3, 1815; John Lindsey, 1817; Francis Myers, January, 1818; Robert Allen, January 17, 1818; William White, 1821; Robert Kennedy, 1824; James Rounds, 1826; William Gould, April 7, 1828; Robert Kennedy, December 1, 1828; William Neal, April 4, 1831, served twelve years; William H. Kennedy, April 6, 1840; James Lindsey, April 3, 1843; James Ross, October 10, 1845; S. M. Blair, October 14, 1834; James Ross, October, 1846; George C. Moore, April, 1849; Jonas Murphy, October, 1849; William H. Kennedy, October, 1855; William Neal, Jr., October, 1858; R. M. Wilson, October, 1859; O. P. Ralston, April, 1864; James Redmon, April, 1865; J. P. McBeth, April, 1867; J. W. Lucas, April, 1870; Asher Brooks, April, 1876; T. B. McChesney, October, 1879; James O. Liming, April, 1882.

SETTLEMENT.

The first settlement was made in the northwestern corner of the township in 1802 by John Colthar and his sons, Mathey, Isaac, James and John, and John Frazee and family. In the latter part of the same year, or in the year following, Thomas Liming, James Liming and Samuel Liming settled on the creek in the eastern part of the township on R. Gamble's Survey, No. 3,024. In March, 1804, Christian Smith settled on Survey No. 3,062. From 1805 until 1808, the settlement seems to have been rapid. James and Lemuel Rounds, two soldiers of the Revolutionary war, settled on Survey No. 2,937; Aaron Leonard and Joseph, on the same survey; Henry Vandament, on Survey No. 3,859; Rasonna Roney and Thomas Allen, on Survey No. 3,862; George Wresler and John Pitzer, on Survey No. 3,862; Elijah Hall and John Springer, on Survey No. 2,937.

The central or more level portion of the township was not settled until 1810 or 1812, when William Kennedy came down the river in a "broad-horn" with two married sons, John and Robert, and a son-in-law, George Flick, and settled on Survey No. 3,779; a little later, James and Joseph Liming settled on Survey No. 2,936; James Thompson purchased Survey No. 2,737, on which he settled with his sons, William, John and Jesse P., and his son-in-law, Henry Whiteman. Jacob Kylander settled in the southern part on Survey No. 3,627. William Neal settled in the year 1820 on No. 573; Asa Dutton settled on the west end of Survey No. 573, about 1820, and erected the first saw-mill within the present boundaries of the township; it was built in 1822, and continued to cut lumber until 1836 or 1838, when it fell into disuse, and now no trace of where it stood is visible. John Brooks settled on Survey No. 2,939 as early as 1807 or 1808. William Gould and Daniel Gould, sons of Joseph Gould, and William C. Goff settled on No. 3,869.

The northeastern corner was not settled until after 1820; John Derry settled on Survey No. 10,658; Levi Wilson settled on Survey No. 12,012; Lewis Perry, on the east end of No. 573. John Wilks, James Kennedy and Hugh Kennedy settled on Survey No. 3,781; David Ogden and Samuel Price settled on No. 2,940; Michael Holman, on No. 4,857; William Jacobs, on No. 3,628; Lewis Shick, on No. 3,606 ; Moses Moss, on the northern corner of No. 3,627.

PIONEER BIOGRAPHIES.

John Colthar, Sr., was the first white settler in the present limits of the township. He and his sons, Matthew, Isaac, James and John, were natives of New Jersey, and settled in the northwestern part of the township on William Lytle's Survey, No 2,939, in the fall of 1801 or spring of 1802. The father was a good type of the hardy pioneer farmer, straightforward, honest and industrious; many of his descendants are still citizens of the township. Matthew Colthar, son of the above, was born in Essex County N. J., in 1777; he married Mary Church in 1816, and by her had the following children: Harrison, Rebecca, Jonathan, Harriet, Eliza, Sarah John P. and Sophia. Mr. Colthar mysteriously disappeared November 9, 1831. He was serving on the jury at Georgetown, and, on being dismissed Saturday, was seen to leave the court house just at dusk as if going home, but he was never heard of afterward. The country was scoured in every direction, but not a trace of him could be found.

John Frazee was one of the first settlers of the township. He located on Survey No. 2,939 in 1803 or 1804, and raised a large family. He was killed by the falling of a tree in 1822. As all of his decendants have left the county, no further account of him can now be learned.

John Brooks came to the township in 1805, and located on Survey No. 2,939, where he remained until his death in 1833. He raised a family of twelve children—three boys and nine girls: Jane, the eldest, was born in 1801, and is now the widow of William Neal, Sr.; John and Elizabeth, twins, were born in April, 1803; John is still a resident of the township, a member of the Methodist Protestant Church, and a highly respected citizen; William, born in 1805, resides on the old homestead; he was for many years a minister in the Baptist Church, and is characterized by his honesty and piety.

William Neal, Sr., was born in 1800, and came to the township when ten years of age, and when twenty years of age married Jane Brooks. He bought his first piece of land of William Duncanson in 1818, and by industry and strict economy he amassed nearly one thousand acres during his lifetime. He raised a family of eight children, five boys and three girls, most of whom still live in the township. His eldest child, Elizabeth, married Jonas Murphy; Julia Ann married John Colthar, and resides in Pike Township; Lewis, the oldest son, married and lives on Survey No. 10,717; John married Sarah J. Kennedy, and lives in Pike Township; William married Miss Dean, and is a farmer and storekeeper; Sarah married Stephen Kennedy; Sanford lives in the old homestead, and Randolph lives just south of the old homestead.

Christian Smith, who settled in the eastern part of the township on Survey No. 3,962, on Miranda's Fork of White Oak, was born in Holland in 1748; his parents died while he was small, and he was placed in a Catholic school to be educated for a priest, but on reaching his majority and finding the church had absorbed all his property, a comfortable patrimony left him by his father, he concluded to embark for the New World. He spent a few years in the coast trade from New York, and in 1790 married Elizabeth McDuffy, of New Jersey, with whom he emigrated to the backwoods of Kentucky, settling at Washington, where he remained a few years. In 1797 or 1798, he located on Robert Lawson's Entry, No. 2,523, near Georgetown, but a few years later, being disturbed by a still-house that was built near him, he traded his land for a farm in this township, on which he moved in 1804, and where he remained until his death in 1832. Joseph Ralston, the veteran school-teacher, who married Mr. Smith's only daughter, Eleanor, in 1813, got most of his education from his father-in-law, who in education was far in advance of his neighbors. Mr. Smith brought the first sheep to this section of the country, and for some years was obliged to keep them in a pen winter and summer to protect them from wolves.

Joseph Ralston was born at Pittsburgh December 6, 1793, and in 1794 came with his father (who was a blacksmith in Wayne's army) to Manchester, where he remained until 1807, when he removed to White Oak, and settled at the mouth of Miranda's Fork, on the northwest corner of Entry No. 901. There he resided until his marriage with Eleanor Smith, September 5, 1813, after which he resided on the Smith farm until his death, February 18, 1869. When twenty-eight or thirty years of age, his back was injured at a log rolling, and he was afterward unable to do hard work; he taught school with eminent success for forty years. He had three sons and seven daughters, but three of the latter died while small. The sons were Christian Smith, Andrew Jackson and Oliver Perry, and the girls were Orphia, Zorilda, Almira and Matilda Jane. Christian was born November 4, 1814, married Sarah Martin in 1836, removed to Ripley County, Ind., in January, 1842, and died September 27, 1869. Andrew was born September 8, 1818, married Nancy J. Perry in 1839, moved to Fulton County. Ill., in 1848 and died in February, 1875.

Samuel M. Blair was born near Knoxville, Tenn., October 24, 1798, and at the age of eleven years removed to Brown County, Ohio, with his father, who settled on the farm now owned by W. P. Macklem, two miles north of Georgetown. In 1821, when twenty-three years old, Mr. Blair settled on J. Watts' Entry. No. 3,781, one mile northeast of Hamersville. He was twice married, first to Matilda Tweed. by whom he had three children—Amanda, Jane and Matilda. Amanda is the widow of Samuel Wilkes, and still lives in Hamersville, the "good Samaritan" of the village. Mr. Blair's second wife was Mary Ann Davis, by whom he had ten children—four boys and six girls, viz., Marcus, Lafayette and Leander, who live in Illinois; C. Columbus, the Clerk of the Court of Brown County; Samuel Warren, the ticket agent at Hamersville; America, Martha, Almira, Minerva, Eliza and Sarah, the three eldest girls being dead. Mr. Blair, after filling most of the township offices, including six years as Justice of the Peace, was in 1857 elected County Commissioner, which position he creditably filled six years. He was a consistent Christian, and for many years was an Elder of the church. He died in 1871, and was buried in the cemetery at Unity Church; his wife survived him ten years, dying July 24, 1881.

Henry Van Deman settled on Survey No. 3,024 about the year 1806. He had a large family; Jacob settled on Survey No. 3,862, and when Scott Township was formed his house was in that township, although the larger part of his farm was in Clark. He was a farmer, but also preached for a number of years, first as a New Light, then as a Methodist, and lastly as a Campbellite. Benjamin married Susan Shick in 1842, and settled on Survey No. 3,781, where he raised four children—Daniel, who now occupies the old homestead; John, Mary and Barton S. George settled south of Benjamin, on the same survey. He was a preacher of the Campbellite Church, and raised a large family, who, after his death, emigrated to Illinois.

Robert Kennedy was born in Butler County, Penn., and settled just north of Hamersville in Brown County, Ohio, in 1811, where he remained until his death. He was a man of strict integrity and more than ordinary ability. He took an active interest in the early politics of the township, and for many years was a Justice of the Peace. He raised five children, viz., Thomas, who was three times married, and died of cholera at the old homestead at the age of forty years. He and his wife were found dead in the morning, having died alone during the night; James, a retired physician of Clermont County; John C., a retired physician, now residing at Felicity; Ella, the wife of S. B. Smith, and William H., who raised a large family, all of whom are dead.

George Flick was born in Butler County, Penn., June 11, 1785, and in 1806 married Jane Kennedy. They came to Ohio in 1811, and settled where

Hamersville now stands, where he remained until his death, October 7, 1861, his wife having died October 11, 1848. Their children were William K., born June 28, 1807; Catharine, born February 29, 1809; Jacob, born August 17, 1810; Margaret Jane, born in 1812, and George Wayland, born in 1815. William K. was a painter and chairmaker, and for eight years was Postmaster at Hamersville. He married Nancy A. Ford, August 9, 1832, and by her had seven children—Pauline J., Fernandes W., Martin V. B., William Benton, John K , Joseph S. and Martha M.; most of them are still residents of the township.

Nathaniel Moore was born in Pennsylvania in 1770, and spent his boyhood days in the Susquehanna Valley. When quite young, he made his way across the mountains to Pittsburgh, and engaged in boating and rafting on the Ohio River. From Pittsburgh he went to Limestone (now Maysville), and in 1799 he married Nancy Welch; in the following year, he moved to Ohio, and located on Eagle Creek. On his farm the first church in that region was built; it stood on the site of Moore's Chapel of to-day. In 1821, he moved to Brown County, where Hamersville now stands, his son Henry having cleared some land and built a cabin during the year previous. The house was the first one in this settlement that had stairs, hewed plank floor and doors. It was the meeting house for years, and in it such pioneers of the pulpit as Quinn, Findley, Collins, Westlake and others were entertained. As soon as he had his farm in shape, Mr. Moore commenced sawing lumber with which to supply the country for miles around. In 1828, he, with several others, contracted to carry the mails from Cincinnati to Portsmouth, and in this he was engaged twelve years. In 1844, he lost his wife, and went to live with his youngest son in Indiana, where he died in 1861.

Joseph Liming was born and raised near Philadelphia, Penn. He was a soldier in the Revolutionary war, and served in several severe battles. In 1799, he moved to the West, and settled near Lexington, Ky., where he remained four years; he then moved to Ohio, and after a three years' residence there he moved to Clark Township, and settled on White Oak in 1806. At the same time, his father, Henry, and two other sons came from Pennsylvania, and settled on White Oak. Joseph raised a large family of children. viz., Jonathan, Abraham, Samuel, Sarah, Joseph, William, James and Ahira Dellaplane. Samuel fought the Indians under Wayne, and Abraham, Joseph and James served in the war of 1812 until James was taken sick in the swamps near Detroit, and his two brothers were left to nurse him. James Liming was born in Pennsylvania, and in 1815 he married Christina Wrestler, and located on Survey No. 2,936. She died in 1829, leaving seven children, and he married Eunice Leonard, by whom he had seven children. He kept a nursery, and supplied many orchards of Ohio and Indiana. He died in 1847. The number of the descendants of this name in the township is very large, and the family have figured very extensively in the religious, political and agricultural growth of the township.

The practices of the first settlers were nearly uniform. They would build a rude log cabin, clear a few acres of ground for corn to supply their families with bread, potatoes and garden vegetables, trusting to their rifles to supply the table with meat other than pork, which was afforded by the few hogs they owned and allowed to run wild in the woods. For several years, little if any wheat was raised, as there were no mills at that day to make flour. The only sugar and molasses they had was that procured from the sugar trees of the forest. Their few wants were at all times supplied out of the abundance of the forest, which also furnished them with fuel, timber for building, and the tender shoots of the trees formed good pasturage for their cattle. They were a sturdy, honest, hardy race, on whose memory too much honor cannot be bestowed.

SCHOOLS.

Clark Township has always been characterized for the interest taken in the cause of education by its citizens, and by the great number of teachers that received their primary education in its schools. The early history of the schools of the township is almost lost; the first schoolhouse was the little round log pen that has been so often described elsewhere as to make it unnecessary to mention it here. The first schools were taught in private houses, and sometimes in huts that had been built and vacated by squatters who had been in the neighborhood some years prior to the first settlement. The first schoolhouse built in the present limits of the township was located near the east line of the township on the land of Jacob Vandeman; it was built about the year 1812. Near the same time, another was built near the northwest corner of the township on the land now owned by Thornton. The first teachers were William I. Bowler, the poet, known in the early newspapers as the "Backwoodsman," John Duly, John Morgan and John Derry. The first regular division of the townships into school districts was made by the Trustees June 6, 1826, when it was divided into nine districts, including the territory from Clermont County to White Oak Creek. The first district contained twenty-seven house-holders; the second twenty-two; the whole township contained 145 families. After the reduction of the township to its present size, it was divided into seven districts, each about two miles square, and each district was supplied with a good schoolhouse. After Hamersville became a village, it was made a special district, designated as No. 8, being in the northwestern corner of District No. 4. Each district is supplied with a neat and substantial schoolhouse of frame or brick, seated with the most improved desks, and in each, school is taught eight months in the year. The prominent teachers after the organization of Brown County were Joseph Ralston, William Fite, ------ Lawson, William H. Stephenson, Frederick Morgan, Mary A. Moore, Morgan Victoria Moore, D. W. Fite and C. C. Blair. The township has furnished and sent out into the world more well-qualified teachers according to its population, perhaps, than any other township in this part of the State. They are found in all grades here and in the Western States nobly teaching "the young idea how to shoot." The school fund of the township is as follows: Teachers' fund, State, $1,321.49; Virginia military, $53.50; township, $802.20; total, $2,177.19.

CHURCHES.

The first church society was a small class of New Lights or Christians that was organized in the southeastern corner of the township. The Protestant Methodists formed a class in the northern part, and a Methodist Episcopal class was formed in the west and central part of the township.

The first church built was a log structure on the State road on the lands of Lemuel Rounds that was built by the Methodists about 1835.

Mt. Nebo Methodist Church, a log building, near the Newhope and Bethel road, on the lands of John Brooks, was erected in 1838. In 1866, it was replaced by a good and substantial frame building that was burned down in the winter of 1881. The society is now building a new and still better house of worship.

The Disciples or Campbellites built a frame building in the west side of Scott Township about 1835; most of the members were from Clark Township. They worshiped at Unity, as the church was called, about ten years, when they organized at Hamersville, and, in 1860, built a brick church. They are the strongest society in the township, and still meet at Hamersville.

The Methodist society built a log church in Hamersville in 1848, which they used for fifteen or twenty years, but the class was always rather weak, and the lot and house were abandoned and finally sold.

A class of the Christian Union Church was organized soon after the war, in Brownsville, and in 1876 they built a nice frame building.

The early preachers of the township were George Vandeman (Disciples), Peter Shiek, Sr. (Disciples), Rev. Lawson and Sanford Ewing. The church denominations are Campbellite, New Light, Methodist Protestant, Methodist Episcopal, Christian Union and a few people of almost every other belief. The present ministers are Rev. S. B. Smith, Methodist; residence, Hamersville. He has been in the ministry nearly forty years, and has occupied all the offices of honor in the church, including Presiding Eldership. Rev. Bagby, New Light; residence, Hamersville; he has been in the ministry but a few years. James E. West, Disciples, has been six or eight years in the ministry, and now has a charge in Kentucky; William Brooks, Baptist, residence in the northern part of the township, superannuated and nearly eighty years old. P. S. Honaker, Christian, residence east end of the township; he has only been licensed a few years.

MILLS.

During the first few years of the early settlement, corn was reduced to meal in hand mills, consisting of two large stones about two feet in diameter dressed as millstones, between which the corn was crushed. In 1806, James Roney built a mill, a corn-cracker, where the old Thompson Mill, now owned by Mrs. Armstrong, stands. This was in Lewis Township, but served the people of Clark Township for a long time. Henry Zumalt built the mill in what is now Scott Township, on the site now occupied by Henry Young's mill, in 1808. A water saw-mill was built by Asa Dutton on Clover Creek in 1822, and Dilaplane Liming built one on Indian Run about 1830; both were on small streams, and were only operated while the creeks were very high, and when steam began to be generally used they were abandoned.

The first steam saw-mill was built in Hamersville by Eliakim and Nathaniel Moore and W. H. Kennedy in 1838; after being run by them a few years, it was sold to J. W. Prather, in whose hands it was twice burned down and rebuilt. It was afterward sold to C. P. Fite and Peter Kellum, who still operate it. Thornton Bros. are operating a steam saw-mill that was built originally by Thornton & Crooks, but burned down and was rebuilt by the present firm. A great deal of lumber is cut by portable mills. There is no grist-mill in the township, nor has there been one since the days of corn-crackers.

ROADS AND RAILROADS.

The first public road laid out in the township was known as the "Waters road," from Levanna to Williamsburg, then the county seat of Clermont County; it was laid out by Josephus Waters, and crosses the township diagonally, entering it on the eastern side near the middle, and leaving it near the northwest corner. The next road laid out was the Georgetown & Cincinnati State road, which crosses the township in nearly the same direction, entering on the southern line about one and a half miles from the southeast corner, and, passing through Hamersville, leaves near the middle of the western line. The next road is the Augusta & New Market road, which crosses the southeast corner of the township in a southwesterly direction. These and the New Hope & Bethel road are the leading throughfares. The Georgetown & Bethel and the New Hope & Bethel roads are piked across the township; the Hamersville & Higginsport is piked from the State road to Higginsport.

The Cincinnati & Portsmouth Railroad was graded across the township in

the fall of 1868, and the first train of cars was run into Hamersville in December, 1881, which place seems likely to be the terminus for some time. A trip from Hamersville to Cincinnati and return, that used to occupy three or four days by wagon, can now easily be accomplished in a few hours.

HAMERSVILLE.

The village of Hamersville was laid out by Nathaniel Moore, Sr., and George Flick in the year 1838. It was named in honor of Thomas L. Hamer, then a Member of Congress from this district, who was instrumental in having a post office located at that place. William C. Doudney, who kept the first store, was also the first Postmaster. A few years afterward, the post office passed into the hands of William H. Flick, a chair-maker and painter, who held the position during his life; at his death, his wife took charge of the office, and retained the position until her death, when her oldest daughter, Pauline J. Perkins took the office, and continued it until 1880, when it was placed in the hands of Dr. J. C. Stires. The village now contains two dry goods stores, three groceries, one drug store, one tobacco warehouse, one steam saw-mill, three blacksmith shops, two shoe shops, two physicians, two lawyers, and about two hundred inhabitants.

De Soto Lodge, No. 374, I. O. O. F., was instituted in the hall at Hamersville June 14, 1866. The charter members were O. P. Ralston, I. N. Ellsberry, C. Oursler, S. H. Ellis, T. J. Lindsey, W. F. Landon, D. S. Dean, W. O. Perkins, A. R. Gillet, Harvey Snider, R. F. Bryant, W. P. Landon, W. J. Thompson, Peter Dean and Dr. W. H. Langstaff. Only three of these now remain, viz., Messrs. Ralston, Perkins and Snider; the rest have taken cards and gone elsewhere. The first officers were: I. N. Ellsberry, N. G.; Charles Oursler, V. G.; S. H. Ellis, Secretary; T. J. Lindsey, Treasurer. Sixty-four have been initiated, sixteen admitted on card and four have died, making the present membership forty-two. The present officers are: J. H. Love, N. G.; C. W. Jordan, V. G.; M. V. Flick, Secretary; Cyrus Fite, Treasurer.

Clark Grange, No. 382, was instituted January 13, 1874, with O. P. Ralston, W. M., and J. S. Salsbury, Secretary. In 1876, they built a good hall, in which they now meet. The present officers are: Frank Devore, W. M., and O. M. Swope, Secretary. They kept a supply store in the first floor room of their building for three or four years, but discontinued it in 1880, and since then the room has been rented to William West for a store room.

An organization of the Good Templars was effected in 1874, but it has only maintained a fitful existence, and the meetings are held very irregularly.

CHAPTER VII.

FRANKLIN TOWNSHIP.

S. C. GORDON, M. D.

FRANKLIN TOWNSHIP was formed by order of the County Commissioners December 2, 1822, and is bounded and described as follows: "Beginning in the southern boundary line of Highland County dividing in part Highland and Brown, five and one-half miles from the corner or connection of the said line with Adams County, and running from thence due south to the township line dividing the townships of Eagle and Byrd; thence westerly with the line dividing Eagle, Pleasant and Clark Townships, six miles; thence north five and one-half miles to a point, from which point a line shall be run at right angles to the first line, forming one entire township, to be called Franklin Township." It was also ordered "that an election be held on the first Saturday in January next, at the house of Henry Dunn, in said township, for the necessary officers." March 3, 1823, a petition was made to the County Commissioners by a number of the inhabitants of that part of the county, "praying that the north and south lines or boundaries of Franklin and Washington Townships be so changed as to make White Oak Creek the line between the said townships of Franklin and Washington, thereby attaching all the territory between the said White Oak Creek and the said original north and south boundaries of Franklin and Washington Townships, to the said townships respectively, agreeable to the east and west line dividing said townships of Washington and Franklin; and the said application having been duly considered, it is ordered by the Commissioners that the alteration be made accordingly, and that White Oak Creek to the fork, and thence with the North Fork thereof, shall be the westerly boundary of the aforesaid townships of Franklin and Washington, thereby including all the territory east of the said White Oak Creek in and to the townships of Franklin and Washington." On the same day, a petition to change the line dividing Franklin and Pleasant was presented, "and the same having been duly considered, it is ordered by the Commissioners that the alteration be made accordingly, and that the Williamsburg road, so far as connected with the territory of the said townships, be the boundary line east and westwardly between the said townships of Pleasant and Franklin, thereby attaching all the territory south of the said Williamsburg road to the township of Pleasant." Afterward, Richard and Robert Blair (the latter owning the farm now owned by W. P. Maklem) were, upon their petition, stricken from Franklin into Pleasant Township.

When Scott Township was formed (January 1, 1828), that part of it east of White Oak Creek, and as far north as the southern line of Washington, was taken from Franklin Township. There was no other important change in the boundary of Franklin until June 25, 1853, when Jefferson was formed from Byrd, Jackson and the southeastern corner of Franklin Townships, the portion from this township including the Abbott mill.

On petition of B. W. Whiteman (then owning the farm now owned by Frederick Elschlager) and A. D. Ellis (then owning where Ephraim Brown now lives), the line was so changed as to throw them, together with those now owned by Mat Elschlager and William Ellis and Ephraim Brown, into Scott Township. This line is not straight, and there is some controversy about it. Franklin Township is bounded on the north by Washington, on the east by

FRANKLIN TOWNSHIP.

Jackson, on the south by Jefferson and Pleasant, and on the west by Pleasant and Scott Townships.

When the township was formed, Hosea Bunner was appointed by the Commissioners to enumerate the white male citizens, and to list the taxable property of the township. He was allowed for said service $8.

This township is watered, or rather drained, by Straight Creek (so called because it is straight the distance of half a mile or so from where it empties into the Ohio River), the West Fork of the same, which is generally spoken of as West Fork, and the West Fork of Eagle Creek, with their tributaries. Straight Creek enters the northeastern part of the township, flows in a westerly direction until it reaches Arnheim, where it trends to the south, and emerges from the south central part of the township into Jefferson, soon, however, to pass into Pleasant. West Fork flows through the western part of the township in a southerly direction, trending somewhat to the east, and empties into Straight Creek, about one and a half miles from the southern boundary of the township. The West Fork of Eagle Creek rises in the southeastern part of the township, and passes out near the southeastern corner into Jackson Township.

The surface of Franklin Township is generally level, but along the streams it is somewhat broken. The soil is generally fertile, yet there is considerable land that is badly worn. It has literally been "corned to death."

Originally, the land was heavily timbered with the different varieties of oak (the majestic white oak predominating), beech, hickory, maple, sweet gum, and, along the streams, walnut, poplar, ash, hard maple or sugar tree, elm and wild cherry, and, although there has been almost reckless destruction of the timber, there is still enough, with the exceptions of cherry, walnut and poplar, for local demands. Blue limestone for building purposes, as well as for roads, and for burning into lime, is abundant, and is easily obtained along the streams, where it crops out, but back from the streams it is deeply covered by clay drift.

The residents of Franklin are generally engaged in agriculture, manufactures of any kind having received but little attention. The principal crops for many years were corn, wheat, oats and hay. After the German element was added to the population, there was some barley raised, and a few vineyards planted, but the manufacture of wine has been abandoned, and at the present time there is not a vineyard in the township. Of late years, tobacco has been raised quite extensively, and can now be ranked as one of the principal crops. Last year (1881), the crops of the township were materially shortened by the drouth, but this year there has probably been raised the largest crop of corn, wheat, hay and tobacco ever produced in the township. The favorable weather of last fall gave an opportunity of putting in a larger acreage of wheat than usual, and the mild winter prevented it from freezing out. The hay was mostly put up in good condition, but some cut later was somewhat injured by wet weather The crop of oats was poor, being badly injured by rust. The corn on wet land is light, as is also tobacco, but, taken as a whole, they are up to the average—tobacco above, as a larger acreage was planted this year. Potatoes and sweet potatoes are raised in abundance for home consumption, as well as for market, and the same may be said of sorghum. The culture of flax, once so necessary for home wear, is a product of the past, and only remembered by the older citizens of the township.

EARLY SETTLEMENT.

Among the first settlers in what is now Franklin Township were Joseph Long, Robinson Lucas, Uriah Springer, Job Springer, Jacob Springer, John

Springer, George Washburne, Uriah Washburne, James Prickett, John Prickett, John Lindsey, Phillip Lindsey, Thomas Pindell, John Pindell, Reuben Bunner, Joseph Abbott, John Abbottt, Silas Abbott, Joseph Abbott, Jr., Greer Brown, John Carbery, James Dunn, Henry Dunn, Ferrel Dunn, Benjamin Hays, Charles B. Smith, McCord Brady, James Ball, Jacob Lucas, John Stansberry, Thomas Stansberry, Isaac Stansberry, Benjamin Wells, Josiah Stansberry, David Thorp, Terry Womacker and David Newman. They came mostly from Virginia, Kentucky and Pennsylvania, and, on their way, crossed mountains, rivers and forests, and fought their way through hardships, dangers and privations. They and their children were familiar with the alarms and dangers of a frontier life. There being no market within easy access for the products of the soil, there was little grain raised, and that little mostly Indian corn. The forests abounded in game of all kinds, deer and turkeys being abundant for many years, and, when the first settlers arrived, bears were plentiful, especially among the hills near the Ohio River. The wild bee had stored its honey in the hollow trees, and, when the hardy pioneers wished honey for their "johnny-cake," they felled a "bee tree," and carried the honey home in the fresh skin of a deer, the legs being tied together over a pole, which was placed on their shoulders, and stored in troughs hewn from the trunks of fallen trees, such things as jars and cans being unknown in the settlements, and even buckets were few. They were all expert in the use of the rifle (it being their almost constant companion), and were familiar with the habits of the bear, wolf, deer, turkey, etc.

As the country became more thickly settled, there was developed a propensity for horse-racing, horse-trading, and, occasionally, getting on a "spree," as whisky was considered "legal tender," and was easily obtained, as stillhouses were numerous, and a gallon of whisky was exchanged for a bushel of corn, or its equivalent. The hardy pioneer was brave and generous, but without the polish and formality of the present day, and the occasional traveler who entered his rude cabin was freely entertained, the fare simple, but being pressed upon him with genuine hospitality.

William Long and his wife, Mary (Evans) Long, came to the United States from Ireland, and, as early as 1798, if not before, they came from Kentucky, and settled on Cornick's Run, near the present site of Ripley, where the husband died and was buried, leaving his widow and six children—Nancy Jane, Margaret, Sarah, Joseph and Mary.

About 1800 or 1801, Mary Long and her children, who were not married, came to what is now Franklin Township, and settled on what is known as the Joseph Long farm, where Henry Miller now lives. Nancy married Uriah Springer. Jane married John Bunner, who was a cooper, and the son of Reuben Bunner, and they settled on his father's farm, now owned by L. Spencer. Margaret married Isaiah Lucas, son of Robinson Lucas. Sarah married Benjamin Purdum a tanner, who established a tan-yard, the first in the township, on his father-in-law's farm, where he lived for some years. Joseph (born January 22, 1784), married Charlotte Bunner; he lived on the home farm, his wife died May 17, 1855. In February, 1865, he went to Illinois, and, on October 23 of the same year, died, aged eighty-one years, eight months and one day. He was brought back to Franklin Township and buried by his wife in the old Baptist Churchyard.

Robinson Lucas moved from Virginia to Kentucky, came from Kentucky and settled near the Ohio River, at Cornick's Run, with William Long, Uriah Springer and James Prickett. We are informed that his sons, William and John, came over about a week before the rest of the family, and built the first shanty ever built at the mouth of Red Oak Creek, and, when the family arrived, they had twenty-one bears killed and hung to the trees around the shanty. After living here a short time, Mr. Lucas came up Straight Creek and settled on the farm now owned by Huston Rhoten, where he died and is buried. There were born to Robinson Lucas and wife nineteen children, fifteen living to grow up, viz., Temperance, Elizabeth, William, John, Jacob, Drucilla, Mary, Cynthia, Anna, Isaiah, Isaac, Sarah, Robert, Rhoda and James—the last two born after their parents came here. Temperance married William Arnold; lived for awhile north of the present site of Arnheim; afterward moved one mile east of Arnheim, where she died. Elizabeth married John Lindsey. William married Mary Hickembottom; settled on the farm now owned by the widow of Jacob Biery; they removed to Indiana in 1830, where the wife died; he came back, and died on West Fork. John married Margaret Harper, and settled on the farm adjoining his brother William; the farm is now owned by H. F. Pindell; he sold and went to Illinois. Jacob remained in Virginia when his parents moved to Kentucky; he married the widow of Moses Stansberry, and, about 1810, came to Ohio and settled on Straight Creek. Drucilla married Phillip Lindsey. Mary married Edward Pindell, son of Thomas Pindell. Cynthia married James Robins, and settled on Brown's Run, in Washington Township, where he died; she afterward married John Jacobs; they lived and died near Arnheim. Anna married Isaac Bunner; lived on West Fork, where they died; their son, Isaac Bunner, now owns the farm. Isaiah married Margaret Long, daughter of William Long; lived for some years on the east side of Straight Creek, on land now owned by B. W. Gordon; he sold to John Ernst and moved to Indiana, where he died. Isaac married Euphemia Harper, and settled on Straight Creek, above Arnheim, and, while running on a keel-boat on the Ohio River, he died at Gallipolis. Sarah never married. Robert married Mary Grogan; settled on Straight Creek adjoining his brother William, and, later, moved to Indiana, and from there to Illinois, where he died. Rhoda married Thomas Arnold; lived on West Fork till he died; she lived at Phillip Lindsey's until her death. James inherited the home farm; he married —— Harris, who lived but a few years; he afterward married Sarah Smith; he sold his farm to Michael Pindell and went to Indiana, and from there to Illinois. John Lucas and Margaret (Harper) Lucas had born to them Lydia, Presley, Reason, Euphemia and John. Lydia married Nathan Springer, son of Uriah Springer; they moved to Illinois, where she still lives, her husband having died some eight years ago. Presley went to Illinois with his father, and married Louisa Prickett, daughter of James Prickett; he died in December, 1881; his widow is still living. Reason married Martha A. West in 1839, and lived on the West Fork of Eagle Creek for eight years, then moved to Russellville, where they still live. Euphemia went to Illinois with her father, and married Reuben Long, and is still living there. John went to Illinois with his father, and married Sarah Smith; is still living in that State.

Uriah Springer, when he first came to Ohio, settled near where Ripley now is. He married Nancy Long, daughter of William Long, and there were born to them Hannah, Nathan, William, Joseph, Zadoc, Levi, Drucilla, Nancy, Uriah, Theresa and Mahala. When he came to what is now Franklin Township, he settled on the farm where Isaac Waters now lives, where he lived for many years. After the close of the war of 1812, he made a trip across the State on horseback, after the late James Bunner, who had been discharged from the army, but, on account of ill health, was unable to reach home. Bunner worked for him afterward, and off-bore the brick for the house which he shortly afterward built. This and the house where M. A. Courts now lives, built by John Lindsey about the same time, were the first brick houses built in the township. Mr. Springer was elected Justice of the Peace in 1822, and served as such officer, and as one of the Township Trustees, for many years. He and all his family went to Illinois.

Jacob Springer, brother of Uriah, settled on the farm on which J. W. Barnes now lives. John Springer settled on the opposite side of the creek.

George Washburne and his wife, Azuba (Robins) Washburne, came from Kentucky to this township about 1799, and settled on the east side of Straight Creek, on what was called Cherry Bottom; the land is now owned by Adam Wells. They lived here for some years; moved above the present site of Sardinia, and, after living there three or four years, moved to a farm on Wardlow's Run, but, in a few years, sold this farm and moved to Indiana, where they died. There were born to them Jeremiah, Isaac, Cornelius, Sarah, Rebecca, Rachael, Azuba, Phœbe and Nancy—the last three after they came to Ohio. Jeremiah married Nancy McDaniel; moved away, but where to is not known. Isaac married Rachael Laycock; settled on part of the home farm, on the east side of Straight Creek. Cornelius married Susan Dunn, daughter of James Dunn, and settled on the west side of Straight Creek, and set out an orchard; the house was on land now owned by B. W. Gordon, but the orchard on land now owned by the writer; the last tree has been gone for some seven or eight years. Sarah married James Holmes and moved to Clermont County, but where to from there is not known. Rebecca married John Stansberry. Rachael married Samuel G. Sperry; settled on farm now owned by Jasper Leming, opposite White Oak Valley, where they lived for several years, and moved to Indiana, where she died. Azuba married James Haas; settled on White Oak Creek; he lived but a short time, dying at her father's house. Phœbe married William Grant; settled on White Oak, below Sardinia, where they lived for some years, and then moved to Indiana. Nancy married Andrew Lowderback; lived on Brown's Run, on what is known as the Gabriel Hays place, for several years, then moved to Indiana.

James Prickett, with his wife, Mary, after living a short time near the Ohio River, came to this township and settled on the farm just above the present site of Arnheim, now owned by Thomas Lindsey. When he came, he found the second bottom, on which the present house stands, covered with huts or wigwams, made of poles and bark, left by the Indians. Thinking the easiest method to get rid of them was to burn them, he acted accordingly, and, after clearing the ground, put out an orchard, some trees of which are still living, and apparently thrifty; others are nearly dead, some being merely large stumps, from which the bark is gone, a few small limbs on one side still showing signs of life. The writer measured some of these venerable trees, and found three of them eight feet and two inches in circumference at four feet from the ground. Mr. Lindsey says that, three years ago, while the bark was on them, they measured nine feet. Two of those still living measure seven feet and eight inches in circumference. The spring near the house is still called the "Old Indian Spring." After living on the above-named farm for many years, Mr. Prickett sold it and removed to Illinois. His children were Dudley, Hannah, Sabra, Basha, Louisa and Lexie. Dudley married Eda Washburne and moved to Illinois with his father. Sabra married John McDaniel, and they moved to Missouri. Hannah married Enoch Laycock, and, for many years, lived where Christian Kieffer now lives, and afterward went to Illinois. Basha, Louisa and Lexie went to Illinois with their father.

John Prickett married Elizabeth Hays in Virginia; came to Franklin Township about 1800, and settled on what is known as the Jacob Arn farm, between the Arnheim and Brownstown and the Arnheim and Sardinia roads. The village of Arnheim was laid out on part of this farm. There were born to them Phœbe, James, William, Zadoc, Henry and Benjamin in Virginia, and Presley, Susan, Nimrod, Amelia, Manerva and Eliza after they came here. Nimrod and Amelia were twins. Phœbe married Simeon Gardner, and both

FRANKLIN TOWNSHIP.   535

joined the Mormons; they went to Nauvoo, returned to Indiana, and there died. James married Lucy Rice and moved to Indiana and died. William married Catherine Rice (sister of Lucy); they also moved to Indiana and died. Zadoc married Mary Ross; moved to Indiana about 1830, and afterward died. Henry married Elizabeth Washburne, moved to Illinois, and has since died. Benjamin married Sarah Ann Fleming, moved to Missouri, and is now dead. Susan married Isaiah Carberry, moved to Indiana, and from there to Michigan, where she died; her husband is still living. Presley married Mary Pindell; moved to Indiana, and there died. Nimrod married Mary Fleming and moved to Missouri, where he died. Amelia, born July 7, 1805, married Jesse Lindsey in 1827; her husband died in 1871; she is still living, on West Fork, the last of her father's family. Manerva married Peter Fraze; moved to Indiana, and from there to Michigan, where they both died. Eliza went to Indiana with her father and mother, and died the year following.

John Lindsey was born in Pennsylvania February 28, 1774, and married Elizadeth Lucas, daughter of Robinson Lucas, but whether in Virginia or Kenturky, or after his father-in-law came to Ohio, we have been unable to learn. He came to the territory now constituting this township about 1801 or 1802, and settled on land now owned by Joseph List, and, with his brother Phillip, who lived with him, cleared a small field. He and his brother shortly afterward bought a tract of land on West Fork, he taking the farm now owned by M. A. Courts, and on which he lives, and Phillip taking where Charles Elschlager lives. The title, however, not being good, they bought it again, from Cadwallader Wallace. Upon the organization of the county of Brown, in 1818, John Lindsey was one of the Commissioners, and, at the first election after Franklin Township was formed, was elected one of the Trustees. The same year, he was also commissioned as Justice of the Peace, which office, as well as that of Township Trustee, he held for many years. In 1824, Franklin Township gave him seventy-nine votes for Sheriff; in 1825, it gave him ninety-one votes for Commissioner; in 1826, for Sheriff, the vote of Franklin stood: John Lindsey, seventy-four; James Loudon, fifteen; John W. Odell, eighteen; and John Walker, three. In 1830, he was again a candidate for Sheriff, the vote of Franklin standing: Jeremiah Purdum, thirty-one; Robert Allen, four; Moses Laycock, twenty-four; and John Lindsey, thirty-seven. September 12, 1844, he deeded one acre of land for a burying-ground, and upon which to build West Fork Church. He died April 9, 1847, aged seventy-three years one month and twelve days, and is buried in the above-named churchyard, as is also his wife. There were born to them William, Hezekiah, James, Sarah, Rhoda, Rachel, Emma, Mary, Dorcas and Grant. William, born about 1797 or 1798, married Elizabeth Harris, and lived on the farm now owned by William Ellis, in Scott Township, for many years; he then went to Missouri, where he was living when last heard from. Hezekiah, born in December, 1799, married Nancy Wells, and lived for some years on West Fork, then moved to the farm now owned by Rev. S. A. Vandyke, in Scott Township. He was the first Clerk of Franklin Township, and held the office until 1828. He was elected County Auditor, and moved to Georgetown, and afterward left there, but where he went is not known to the writer. James married Mary Rich; lived near Hamersville for some years, and, on the death of his father, he bought the home farm, where he lived until his death. Sarah married John Rich, and they lived where Frederick Elschlager now lives, then moved near Hamersville, where she died. Rhoda married Henry Spires; moved to Indiana, where she died. Rachel married Enoch Smith, and they lived near New Richmond, where she died. Emma married Joseph Smith (brother of Enoch), and they lived at Chilo, in Clermont County, where they both died—

the former in the winter of 1881-82, and the latter in the spring of 1882. Mary married Warford Jordon, and, soon afterward, hey moved to Spencer County, Ind., where she was living when last heard from. Dorcas went with her sister Mary to Indiana, where she died. Grant married America Dennis, and lived on his father's farm. He and Wilson Morrow engaged in a bowing match on West Fork, and, going in bathing while heated, he was taken sick, and died a day or two afterward.

Phillip Lindsey was born in Pennsylvania February 13, 1782; came to this township with his brother John, and lived with him until he was married. He married Drucilla Lucas, and settled on the farm where Charles Elschlager now lives. His house burning down, he moved into the house where he and his brother John first settled until he could rebuild. He lived for many years on West Fork, and then moved to the James Prickett farm, above Arnheim, where he died May 22, 1866, in the eighty-fifth year of his age. There were born to Phillip and Drucilla Lindsey, Jesse, Delilah, Elizabeth, Preston, Thomas, Elijah and Drucilla. Jesse, born August 6, 1805, married Amelia Prickett in 1827, daughter of John Prickett, and bought forty-five acres of land where J. L. Carberry now lives. He cleared part of it, and, after some years, sold, and bought on West Fork, on the Arnheim & New Hope road, where he lived until his death, June 22, 1871. His widow is still living. Delilah married Valentine D. Carberry; her father gave them the farm on the Georgetown & Sardinia road, where F. W. Hanselman lives; he exchanged with Josiah Carberry for the farm on Sycamore Run, where they lived for many years, when he and Thomas Lindsey exchanged farms, they moving to where G. B. Carberry now lives, where he died. She afterward married Henry Dunn, and lived near Brownstown until her death. Elizabeth married Simon Kratzer, and they lived on her father's farm for some years, when they moved to the farm now owned by the writer, purchasing it from George Bohrer; after the death of her husband, she married Lemuel Rachford, and sold the interest in the farm, and bought property above Arnheim, where she died October 16, 1878. Preston died when about seventeeen years of age. Thomas was born November 23, 1813; married Mary Pindell; lived two or three years on his father's place, and then moved to the Carberry farm, on Sycamore Run, where he lived for about twenty years; he then moved to Arnheim, where he lived for nine years; from there he moved to the James Pickett farm, where he is still living. Elijah married Susan Pindell, daughter of Jacob Pindell; lived a few years on the home farm, when he bought the Uriah Springer farm, where he lived until his death.

Thomas Pindell married Elizabeth Mills, and came to this township among the first settlers, and settled on the farm now owned by Magdalene and Dorothy Biehn. There were born to them Sarah, Jacob, Nancy, Edward, Thomas, Gabriel, Samuel, Michael and Davis. Sarah married Benjamin Hays, and settled on Straight Creek, on the farm now owned by Conrad Kattein, opposite where he now resides. They lived there for some time, and moved to the farm on Brown's Run, in Washington Township, known as the Gabriel Hays farm. Jacob married Susannah Hays, sister of Benjamin Hays; settled on Straight Creek, on the farm now owned by Huston Rhoten, where his wife died; he afterward married Sarah Carbery, daughter of John Carbery, and died August 10, 1825; at the time of his death, was one of the Township Trustees; his widow afterward married Josiah Wolcott. Thomas married Marie Brady, daughter of McCord Brady, and settled on the farm now owned by Simon P. Berry, where he lived until his death. Gabriel married Elizabeth Pindell, daughter of John Pindell; settled on the farm now owned by J. M. Pindell, and there died. Samuel married Sarah McCollister, and settled on

FRANKLIN TOWNSHIP. 539

the farm above named, which he sold to his brother Gabriel, and moved to Washington Township. Michael married Jane Brady, daughter of McCord Brady, and settled on the farm on which Huston Rhoten now lives, where he died. Davis married Mary Springer, daughter of Uriah Springer, and remained on the home farm for some years, when he sold to George Biehn and moved to Illinois.

Joseph Abbott was born May 29, 1739, and his wife, Esther Abbott, September 17, 1746, and there were born to them eight children, as follows: Mary, born September 7, 1767; Chloe, February 5, 1769; John, November 22, 1770; Rebecca, November 22, 1774; Eunice, September 11, 1777; Silas, June 28, 1779; Jane, November 28, 1781; and Joseph, June 2, 1784. Joseph Abbott, Sr., moved from New Jersey to Virginia; served in the Continental army during the Revolution, and, shortly after the war, in company with Greer Brown (who had also been a soldier), came to Straight Creek and located 1,000 acres of Virginia Military land, in one body, each taking 500 acres. This land lies in the south central part of Franklin Township, on both sides of Straight Creek, and embraces some of the best land in Brown County. Mr. Abbott went back to Virginia and worked at his trade (being a millwright) for some years, then moved to Kentucky, and about 1804, came back to Straight Creek (where his son John already was) with the rest of the family (except Eunice, who had married a Mr. Lake, and moved to Northern Ohio), and settled where John E. Brown now lives, where he remained until his death. He is buried in what is known as the Abbott Graveyard.

John Abbott was born in New Jersey November 22, 1770; went, when a boy, with his parents to Virginia; there he learned the trade of millwright with his father, and, after he became of age, for helping him build a mill in Virginia, his father gave him 250 acres of the land he had located on Straight Creek. He came and picked out the land about 1792, and returned to Virginia, and went with his father to Kentucky, where he remained until about 1800, when he came back to Straight Creek, built a cabin on his land, and for four years lived here by himself. March 1, 1804, he married Hannah, daughter of Joseph and Experience Reynolds, who came and settled in what is now Jackson Township about 1802. The cabin which John Abbott first built, and in which he raised his family, is still standing. When he built the brick house (about 1836), he moved the cabin back, as it stood in front of the new one. John and Hannah (Reynolds) Abbott had borne to them eleven children, viz.: Lewis, December 1, 1804; Amanda, May 28, 1806; Eliza, September 15, 1807; Charles, July 15, 1809; Esther, March 20, 1811; Roxie, June 9, 1813; George, May 30, 1815; Elias, December 9, 1817; John M., February 6, 1820; Elizabeth, March 9, 1822; and Lucy J., June 29, 1827. Lewis married Deborah Jennings; lived one year at his father's mill, on Straight Creek, and moved to his father-in-law's farm, on Camp Run, in Pleasant Township, where he lived until his death, some years ago. Eliza married David D. Brown, son of John Brown and grandson of Greer Brown, and lived on Straight Creek for a number of years, then moved to Clark Township, near Hamersville, where she still lives; her husband died a few years ago. Charles married Sarah Brown, sister of David D. Brown, in 1830; moved to the mill, where he lived until 1838, when he bought and moved to the farm in Pleasant Township where he still resides; his wife dying in 1856, in September, 1864, he married Mrs. Frances Earhart, nee Winter. Esther married Thomas Silman; they moved to Eagle Township, where they lived for several years, and, while there, he built the mill at Fincastle, and afterward moved to McLain County, Ill., where his wife died; he went from there to Kansas, and lived but a short time. Roxie married James, son of John Brown, and moved to Cincinnati, where they lived for some years; she died about 1837 or 1838. George married Melinda, daughter of Michael Pindell; lived a year on the Pindell farm, and moved to Eagle Township, where he still lives. Elias inherited the home farm on Straight Creek, where he lived until his death, January 7, 1881; he never married. John M. married Lettie, daughter of David Newman; settled on Straight Creek, where Joel Martin now lives, where he lived for five or six years, and went to Indiana in 1850, where he still lives; his wife died several years since. Elizabeth married Caleb Shreves; lived for a year or two on the Richard Hewitt farm, then moved to near Russellville, where she died a year or two afterward. Lucy J. married J. F. Abbott, son of Joseph Abbott; they lived on Straight Creek, part of the time on the home farm, then bought of J. M. Abbott and lived there some years, where she died. Her husband sold this farm to Joel Martin, and is now living in Clermont County.

Silas Abbott, son of Joseph and Esther Abbott, and brother of John Abbott, married Lettie, daughter of Greer Brown, and settled where Abraham Berry now lives, between Straight Creek and West Fork, where he lived until his death. His wife lived there for some years afterward, when she died. Jane, sister of Silas, married Joseph Reynolds; moved to a farm near Carlisle, where they lived until their death.

Joseph, youngest son of Joseph and Esther Abbott, married Rhoda Masterson in Bracken County, Ky.; lived on the home farm on Straight Creek (now owned by John E. Brown) until his death. His widow lived there for several years afterward, and died in Missouri while on a visit to her children.

Greer Brown came with Joseph Abbott, after the Revolutionary war, and located his claim with him on the waters of Straight Creek, and came and settled on the farm where William Flaugher now lives, where he died, and was buried in the Abbott Burying-Ground. His wife died in Kentucky. Lettie, daughter of Greer Brown, married Silas Abbott, and Ann, sister to Lettie, married David, son of Joseph Newman, and lived at the home place, where they died.

James Dunn came from Virginia about 1800, and settled on the west bank of Straight Creek, about one mile below the present site of Arnheim. Henry Dunn, son of James Dunn, was born in Monongalia County, Va., January 6, 1779. He married Nancy Pindell, and came to Franklin Township at the same time as his father, and settled on land now owned by Adam Bauer, opposite where Christian Bauer now lives. After the formation of Franklin Township, the first election was held at his house. He lived here until the spring of 1832, when he sold out and moved to Illinois with ox teams, but, not being satisfied, he returned in September of the same year, and bought of Dennis Springer, of Virginia, 533 acres of land in Washington Township (the present village of Brownstown being on a part of it). The land was divided into tracts, and prices fixed on each tract. He paid $1.25 per acre for the whole. His son Rolla took one tract (116 acres) at 75 cents per acre, and Levi 112 acres at the same price. His wife dying, he married the widow of V. D. Carbery, and they lived there during the rest of their lives. There were born to Henry and Nancy (Pindell) Dunn twelve children, viz.: Roanna, Maria, Wilson, Rolla, Levi, Sarah, Elizabeth, Pindell, Nancy, Henry and Jane. Roanna married Henry Straight, and they moved to Illinois, and there died. Maria married Gardner Curtis, and they lived on east side of Straight Creek, and, about 1832, joined the Mormons and went to Nauvoo; after the Mormon war at that place, they came back to Ohio, then went to Utah, and are both now dead. Wilson Dunn married Rachel Parker, and lived in Georgetown and worked for Thomas Jennings (being a tanner) in the old Grant Tannery. He went from there to Illinois, where he now lives. Rolla, married Paulina Lucas; lived in Washington Township; laid out Brownstown, and, some years ago, moved to Illinois, where he now lives. Levi was born in 1813, and went with his father to Illinois in 1832, driving two yoke of oxen to a wagon; while there, he enlisted in Capt. Payne's company, in the Black Hawk war; he was with the command for a day or two, but his father, wishing to come back to Ohio, induced a man named Brown to take his place, and he was allowed to return. A short time afterward, Brown, while out with a team, was killed by the Indians, who took the horses and escaped. In 1834, Levi married Margaret Lucas; bought 112 acres of land of his father (where Robert Dunn now lives) and cleared up this farm, where he lived until 1856, when he bought where he now resides (288 acres), of George Bohrer, and has lived there ever since; his wife died while in Washington Township, and he married Mrs. Rebecca Kratzer. About 1833, he hewed a set of house-logs for Jesse R. Grant, the house being for Mr. Grant's sister, Mrs. Margaret Marshall, and was built in Georgetown, where Andrew Armstrong now lives; he boarded with Mrs. Marshall, who, at that time, lived in what is known as German Row. About 1836, he took the job of hewing for J. R. Grant the timbers for lining the jail then about to be erected, boarding with Noah Ellis, who lived about a mile north of Georgetown, on the farm now owned by F. M. Tracy; before he completed the job, however, he cut his foot badly, and had to give it up; he was taken home on a horse, loaned for the purpose by the late Gen. Thomas L. Hamer. Eli married Mary Parker; moved to Iowa in 1856, where they still live. Sarah married William M. Straight, and moved to Iowa in 1856. Elizabeth married Stephen Parker (brother of Rachel and Mary); lived in Jackson Township until the death of her husband; she afterward married Allen Hendrixson, and they are still living in this township, on the Ripley & Arnheim Turnpike. Pindell married Ann Owens, and lived at Brownstown for some years, where his wife died; he afterward married Catherine Padgett, and now lives in Warren County, but is about to move to Colorado, where he has two sons. Nancy married Uriah Lowderback, and moved to Brazil, Ind., where they now live. Henry married Lydia, daughter of Aaron Purdum, and lived on a farm in Washington Township; his wife died, and he married Amelia Lowderback and moved to Sardinia, where he formed a partnership with the late James McIntyre in merchandising, and died about 1876. Jane married James Prine, and is now living in Eagle Township, near South Fincastle.

Ferrel Dunn, son of James Dunn, settled on Straight Creek, just above his father, on the farm where Conrad Kattein now lives.

Benjamin Hays settled on the farm on the opposite side of the creek, which is also owned by Conrad Kattein.

Rev. Charles B. Smith, or, as he is more familiarly spoken of by those who remember him, "Uncle Charlie Smith," was born in Maryland November 25, 1765, and married his cousin, Lucy Burgess. His father gave him some twenty negroes, and also some three or four hundred acres of land in Kentucky. He, however, did not believe that slavery was right, and acted according to his convictions and gave his negroes their freedom. He did nothing with his land in Kentucky, never going near it, but came to the free territory which now constitutes the proud State of Ohio. Here he settled on the farm just west of Arnheim, known as the James Ball farm, and lived about where George Yockey now lives. (This farm is now divided, Joseph List owning a part of it.) How long he remained here we have not been able to ascertain. James Ball owned and lived on it afterward, and it is probable that he sold to Ball. He bought the farm now owned by Matthias Arn in 1818, fifty acres of Jesse Wood in March, and, in June of the same year, fifty acres of Ezekiel Thorp and Hannah Reed, administrator and administratrix of Luther Reed, deceased.

Here he lived until he sold to Balthazer Yecko, in 1831, and removed to New Market, Highland County, and died November 25, 1844. His remains were brought back to the field of his labors, and buried among his congregation, in the old Baptist Churchyard on Straight Creek. His tombstone bears this inscription:

"Sacred to the Memory of
"Charles Burgess Smith,
"Who was Born November the 25th,
"1765,
"and after serving his generation as a Regular Baptist preacher of the Gospel of Jesus Christ for nearly fifty years,
"Died November 25, 1844, aged seventy-nine years."

His widow died in Russellville, at the residence of her son William, about January 1, 1852.

There were born to Charles B. Smith and wife fourteen children, nine of whom lived to grow up—Walter, Mary, William, Lucy, Abraham, Hays, Sarah Ann, George and Charles. William married Patience Lawson in Kentucky, and lived in Russellville for many years, where he kept a store; his wife died February 18, 1848, aged forty-seven years five months and three days, and was buried in the old Baptist Graveyard, by the side of Charles B. Smith; William married again, and, after some years, went to Illinois, where he died. Lucy married Peter Runyon. McCord Brady settled on Straight Creek, opposite the present village of Arnheim. The farm is now divided, part owned by George Snider, part by the Lutheran Church and part by Conrad Kattein.

James Ball came to Ohio from North Carolina in 1808, and settled on the North Fork of White Oak, where he lived for some years. He afterward bought the farm west of Arnheim, part of which is now owned by Joseph List, but at that time it extended to what is Main street of the village. Here he remained until his death, which occurred May 27, 1849, in the seventy-fifth year of his age. He was one of the leading members of the Straight Creek Baptist society, and took an active part in building the old brick church above Arnheim, in the yard of which he and his wife are buried. His wife lived until August 20, 1855, when she died, in the seventy-eighth year of her age.

Joseph Stansberry married Sarah Lavorce in New Jersey, and moved to Virginia, and there were born to them Josiah, John, Thomas, Isaac and Mary. The father died in Virginia, and his widow married Jacob Lucas, and to them were born Asahel and Amelia. The Stansberry family (with the exception of Josiah) and Jacob Lucas, came to Ohio and settled on the east side of Straight Creek. John Stansberry was born November 18, 1792, and came to Franklin Township with his mother and step-father, Jacob Lucas, about 1810. He enlisted in the army in 1812, and was one of the command surrendered to the British by Gen. Hull in August of that year. He came home, and, July 4, 1813, married Rebecca, daughter of George Washburne. She was born February 20, 1794. They built a house and went to housekeeping on the east side of the creek, on her father's farm, and there lived for several years, and then moved to the farm on Wardlow's Run, where they resided until the death of Mr. Stansberry, January 3, 1880. His widow is still living, with her son, E. A. Stansberry, in Scott Township, near White Oak Valley. Thomas Stansberry came at the same time and married Margaret Lowderback. He lived and died on his farm on West Fork. (The farm is now owned by Christian Kieffer.) Isaac Stansberry, born December 15, 1799, came with his brothers, and, in August, 1817, married Anna Harris, who was born March 7, 1799. They settled on a farm owned by Thomas Harris (his father-in-law) on West Fork, and, in a few years, he bought the part east of the creek, and on which

FRANKLIN TOWNSHIP.

they moved (fifty-two and a half acres), and have ever since lived there. Mary Stansberry came with her mother and brothers. She married Adam Srofe, who bought a farm near Buford, Highland County, where they lived and died. Josiah Stansberry married Elizabeth Sheerer in Virginia, and came to Franklin Township about 1817, and settled where Frederick Stoehr now lives, and afterward moved to the west side of the creek, on part of the land known as the Lewis Ball farm, now owned by Adam Wells, where he died. Asahel Lucas, son of Jacob Lucas, married Jane Lucas, and died about three years ago. His widow is still living. Amelia Lucas married James Brady, and both died in 1876.

Benjamin Wells was born in Wales, and came with his father, Charles Wells, to the United States while they were colonies of Great Britain, and settled in Maryland, and there married Miss Rice, and, in the Revolution, served the colonies on shipboard, and had one hand disabled. After the death of his wife, he went to Virginia and married Mary Aultz, and lived there some years, where their children—Nancy, Jacob, Sallie, Henry and Adam—were born. They came down the river on a raft, and landed at the mouth of Red Oak Creek in 1810; rented of John Mann, near the "Beech Woods," where they lived for about five years, and bought 100 acres of land of John Springer, on the east side of Straight Creek, where they moved the year following. (Part of this land is now owned by M. B. Smith, and part by J. W. Barnes.) After they came to Ohio, Catherine, Jane, Diademia, Elizabeth and Mary were born. Nancy was married three times. Her first husband was Hezekiah Lindsey; the second, William Dye, who was killed by a fall from his wagon between Georgetown and Higginsport; and the third was Allen Jones. She moved to Higginsport, and died in 1880. Jacob married Jemima Rice, moved to Indiana and died in 1866. Sallie married Andrew Newman and moved to Illinois. Henry married Elsie Devore and moved to Washington Township, and there died. Adam was born in 1805, and, in 1829, married Elizabeth Rice, who died in 1842, and in 1844 he married Rhoda, youngest daughter of Josiah Stansberry. They are living on West Fork, where they have lived for many years. Catherine married David Rich, and they moved to the farm north of Arnheim now owned by Rudolph Kress, where she died. Jane married Samuel Smith, and lived for some years on the West Fork of Eagle Creek, then moved to Indiana, where her husband died. She and her children came back to Franklin Township, where she married David Day, and, after some years, went to Missouri, and there her second husband died. Diademia married Cecil Shaw, and moved to Russellville, where she died. Elizabeth died when about eighteen years of age, and Mary died when a child.

Terry Womacks was born in Virginia in 1789, and came to Ohio in 1806, and, in 1815, married Roxie, youngest daughter of Joseph Reynolds, who settled in Jackson Township in 1802. They settled on what is known as the Womacks farm, in Franklin Township, and here lived and died. There were born to them William H., Marinda D., Willshire, Wesley, Willis, Peter S., Jefferson, Ulysses G., Ellen, Lemuel and Francis M. William H. married Elizabeth Doty, and moved to Ripley, where he lived a short time, and moved to Rock Island County, Ill., where he still lives. Marinda married John Milligan, and moved to Byrd Township, where they are now residing. Willshire married Ellen Inskeep, who died in 1855, and he afterward married Mrs. Roush. They moved to Missouri, and he enlisted in the Confederate army. He was in the battle of Pea Ridge, and died from disease while in the Confederate service; his widow returned to Ohio, and is now living in Adams County. Wesley and Willis died when quite young. Peter S. married Amanda Heaton in 1848, and she died in 1870, and, in 1874, he married Jennie

Hunter. They live near Russellville, on the Russel Shaw farm. Jefferson was accidentally killed by a gun when seventeen. Ulysses G. married a Miss Moore, and lives in Missouri. Lemuel served three years in the Fourth Ohio Independent Cavalry Company during the war of the rebellion, and is now living in Des Moines, Iowa. Francis M. married Miss Rees and moved to Iowa, where they were living when last heard from.

Since 1825, there has been added a large German element to the population of Franklin Township, who, with their descendants, form a large proportion of the present inhabitants.

George Bohrer, born in Germany, came to this township in 1826, and bought of Hugh Meharry about five hundred acres of land, including the farm on which Levi Dunn now lives, and afterward bought the rest of the survey (1,500 acres). He also bought the Mosely Survey (850 acres), and between 800 and 900 acres of the Fox Survey, but lost about two hundred acres of the latter, as he missed one heir, who afterward sold his interest to Luther Reed. He built the house where Levi Dunn lives, Basil Waters, then of Georgetown, building the brick work, and Samuel Tucker doing the carpenter work. He built a horse mill on the run below his house, for grinding corn and wheat; also put up a still-house, and, on the farm now owned by his son Jacob, he built a steam saw-mill. In 1856, he sold out and moved to Illinois; bought a farm near Bloomington, but afterward gave it to his son Lewis and moved into the city, where he died in December, 1879.

Frederic Faul came with George Bohrer, and lived on the farm now owned by Frederic Stoehr.

About 1828, Michael Ziegler, Philip Faul and George Kloeckner came with their families and about 1830, Frederic Neu, Jacob Arn, John Kautz, with their families, Mrs. Kautz, with her sons George and Sebastian, and three daughters.

George A. Kress, John A. Kress, Phillip Miller, Balthazer Yecko, George Bohl and Peter Schatzman, with their families, settled in the township about 1831. Peter Biery and John Lauth, with their families, the same year; also Jacob Gross, with Valentine Dahl and family, Conrad Bauer and family, Lewis Weaver and Francis Hauck.

In 1832, Christian Wahl and Adam Bahl, with their families. Succeeding these came Frederic Gwinner, Joseph Weber, John J. Stephen, Christian Reisinger, George Biehn, Charles Hanselman, Matthias Arn, John Weisbrodt, Christopher Steinmann, Lewis Braun, Frederic Henges, John Ferdinand, Frederic Handman, Jacob Hook, Christian Kieffer and many others.

Frederic Gwinner came about 1833, and started a brewery on Straight Creek. He sold out to Conrad Kattein, who, for many years, manufactured the well-known Arnheim beer, which had a reputation far and wide. About three years ago, Kattein sold to his son Lewis, who built a brewery in the village of Arnheim, put in an engine and added a pair of buhrs for grinding corn. The brewery is not now in operation.

ARNHEIM.

Arnheim, the only village in the township, was laid out on land owned by Jacob Arn, for whom the village was named (Arn's Home), by John D. White, County Surveyor, November 4, 1837, John A. Kress and Frederick Handman being chain-carriers. On July 5, 1838, the addition to Arnheim comprising that portion north of and including Jackson street was laid out; Josiah Wolcott and Elijah Lindsey, chain-carriers. The harvest before, Thomas Lindsey cradled a crop of wheat for Mr. Arn on the site of the village. Francis Feike came from Austria and started a tan-yard where Kautz's store

FRANKLIN TOWNSHIP.

now is about 1831. He bought the land of James Ball (whose daughter he married), and, in a few years, sold to John Lauth and went to Cincinnati. He afterward went to Sardinia, where he established a tan-yard. Hill D. Stayton had a tan-yard on Sycamore Run about the same time, and for some years afterward.

Lewis Ball started a store where G. C. Reisinger now lives, and Wilson Ball one where the stable of Frederic Kautz now stands. William Cappe built where Charles Miller lives, and kept hotel, groceries and liquors. After Arnheim was laid out, Frederick Handman bought the lot and built the house where John J. Bohrer lives. Jacob S. Campbell built a log house opposite Kautz's store, and a blacksmith shop north of his house. He was the first Postmaster of the village. Augustus Straight built the house on the hill where Martin List now lives (where Lewis Braun lived for many years), and Miller Straight built the house where Conrad Hagins lives; he also kept a drinking saloon, but soon sold out. Frederick Henges built the house now owned by Stephen Bohrer, at the corner of Water street and the Sardinia road, and John Ferdinand the one where his widow now lives. Dr. Joseph T. Richardson built where Henry Bohl lives, and sold it to members of the German Reformed Church for a parsonage, and built where E. A. Lindsey lives, and there resided for several years. He was the first physician who settled in Arnheim, and was a member of the Fifty-third General Assembly, 1858-60, elected on the Democratic ticket. He sold his property to John Haas and moved to Higginsport. John Haas built an addition to the house for a store, and lived here until his death. E. A. Lindsey then bought the property, where he still lives, and keeps a general variety store, and is Postmaster. John Lauth sold to A. C. H. Cotterill, who kept a store and whisky saloon; he afterward bought the house where Charles Miller now lives, kept store there for several years, sold out and went to New Hope. Lewis Ball sold his store to Messrs. Allen & Davis, Davis building the house where John Mueller now lives. They remained in partnership until the death of Allen, after which W. C. Davis continued the business, and, when Campbell left Arnheim, was appointed Postmaster. He sold out, and Frederick Handman opened a store in the same building, and bought the John Lauth property, remodeled it, building an addition for a dwelling, where he lived and kept store for many years, doing a large business. He was Postmaster and Notary Public. In 1873, he made an assignment, and shortly moved to Kentucky, and died in Germany while on a visit.

In 1875, Frederic Kautz and P. W. Gross started a store at Handman's old stand, under the firm name of Kautz & Gross, and, after about three years, Gross retired, and the business is still carried on by Kautz. Thomas Lindsey bought out A C. H. Cotterill; lived there for nine years, keeping groceries and liquors, and sold to R. B. Dunn, who continued the business for several years He was also appointed Postmaster, and, when he left Arnheim, G. C. Reisenger became his successor, and was Postmaster until 1881, when he resigned, and E. A. Lindsey was appointed. There are at present in Arnheim two stores, one blacksmith shop, one wagon shop, one cabinet-maker and undertaker, one tailor, one house carpenter, one carpenter and plasterer, one hotel and saloon, one brewery (but not in operation), one tobacco warehouse (owned by E. A. Lindsey, but O. B. Moore, of Sardinia, is now there prizing tobacco), one Catholic Church, and schoolhouse of Subdistrict No. 5, the Lutheran and German Reformed Churches being just outside of the village. The population by the census of 1880 was ninety-eight.

MILLS.

What is known as the Abbott Mill, now owned by James Martin, was, until 1853, in Franklin Township. The first mill was built at a very early day, by Jesse Thompson, and, after his death, his sons, James and Samuel, operated it for some years, and sold to John Abbott, who afterward built the present mill, some fifty or more years ago.

George Schultz built a mill on Straight Creek, on the farm now owned by the writer, not far from 1820, but it did little good; when the creek was low, there would not be sufficient water come into the mill-race, and when it was high, the water would back up on the wheel, there not being sufficient fall just below the mill; some parts of this one were used in the present Abbott Mill.

Jacob Newman built a log horse mill on the farm now owned by Allen Hendrixson, every one taking a grist furnishing the horses and doing his own grinding. Wheat was ground the same as corn, and sifted by hand. Charles Abbott says he once stayed two days and one night at this mill, going home occasionally for something to eat, and feed for his horses, not daring to take them away, for by so doing he would lose his turn. Thomas Harris bought this mill, moved it to his farm on West Fork, and, after his death, James Dennis bought and operated it for several years.

John Carbery also built a mill above the present site of Arnheim, on Sycamore Run.

George Bohrer built a mill with tread-wheel. In dry times, this mill was kept going day and night. He sold it to Frederic Haudman, who moved it to Arnheim, and changed it so the horses were hitched to levers. It was used occasionally for grinding corn as late as 1865. There are three steam saw-mills now owned in the township, two stationary and one portable.

In 1832, George Bohrer built a steam saw-mill on the farm now owned by Jacob Bohrer. He sold half of his interest to Samuel G. Moore, and, about 1836 or 1847, they moved it to where Inskeep's Mill now stands. Moore sold his half to Lemuel Postlewaite, and, in 1845, Job and Fountain Inskeep bought Postlewaite's interest, and ran the mill, in company with Bohrer, until 1847, when they bought his half. They ran it in company until 1867, when Job bought his brother's interest. In 1872, he put in a spoke-lathe, felloe-benders, planer, etc., and in 1881 he put in a new engine, boiler and circular saws, and has a pair of French buhrs on which to grind corn.

Tracy's steam saw-mill, in the northeastern part of the township, was built by Daniel Markley about 1853. He sold to M. D. Barngrover about 1870. In 1874, Barngrover sold to Tracy & Waters, and, about 1879, Waters sold his interest to Martin Tracy, and afterward Ira Tracy sold his interest to his son Frank. It is now owned by Martin and Frank Tracy, but is rented by Randolph Waters, who is now running it. There is a pair of buhrs in this mill on which corn is ground every Tuesday and Friday.

G. C. Reisinger & Co. have a large portable steam saw-mill in the township. It was purchased new in 1881, and is owned by G. C. Reisinger, Lewis Kattein and Adam and Jacob Bohrer.

CHURCHES.*

The first church built in the township, and probably in the county, was the Straight Creek Baptist Church, built of round logs at a very early day, on Straight Creek, just above the present village of Arnheim, on ground given by James Prickett. This society was organized by Rev. Charles B. Smith, who preached at the cabins of the settlers and in the woods until the log church was built. As the church became old and the members more numerous, they built (not far from 1820) the brick church which is now in ruins. The water for making the brick was hauled in an ox-cart by William Long, now of Eagle Township, when a small boy, and the brick made by Woodbeck Low, the clay

---

*The sketch of St. Mary's Catholic Church will be found in the general history of the county.

F. M. Wardlow

being tramped by oxen; the pits where this was done still remain in the churchyard. We have tried to find some record of the members of this church and the date of its organization, and, although we've searched most diligently in six townships, the search has been unavailing. Stout Drake, who died in Pleasant Township some four years since, was for many years Secretary, and had the records, but we find no trace of them since his death.

Lutheran Church.—This church was organized in 1832, by Rev. Gerhardt. The members bought three-quarters of an acre of ground of Louis Weaver, and on it erected a log building. Among the members were Peter Schatzman, George Bohl, Peter Biery, Michael Ziegler, Phillip Faul, Frederic Neu, Adam Bohl, Louis Weaver, Valentine Bauer, Jacob Arn, John Kautz and Sebastian Kautz. In 1846, a division occurred in the church, and some eleven or welve families withdrew and organized the German Reformed Church. The present brick church was built A. D. 1852, Henry Kress doing the brick work and plastering.

German Reformed Church.—This church was organized in 1845, by Rev. F. Wahl. Among the members at that time were Jacob Gross, George P. Biery, Christopher Steinmann, Valentine Schaeffer, Peter Bauer, Adam Bauer, Adam Bohl, Frederic Ringeiser, Peter Mattell, Jacob Bohrer and Francis Hauck. They built the church A. D. 1847, on half an acre of ground bought of James Ball, and united with the German Reformed Synod of Ohio, which now belongs to the Cincinnati Classes of the Central Ohio Synod. The same pastor is in charge of this congregation and the one at Higginsport.

The late L. S. Van Anda, then of Sardinia, built the church, and it was plastered by P. R. Kinkead.

West Fork Church.—This society was first organized September 17, 1842, by Elder N. Dawson, on Middle Run, in Washington Township, at the house of Charles Thompson, where Charles C. Miller now lives, with fourteen members. June 27. 1846, " the church met at the new meeting-house on West Fork." December 25, 1854, a division occurred, part of the members continuing as the church of Christ at West Fork (or, as it is known in the proceedings, at Republican), and part uniting with the society at Immanuel's Chapel, in Jackson Township.

The church went down in 1862. In 1864, it was re-organized, with seventeen members, and continued as such organization until, under the charge of Elder W. H. Robinson. In 1867, it joined the Christian Union Conference, and has since been known as the Christian Union Church. There has been no regular service since 1879.

CEMETERIES.

There are six burying-grounds in the township—the Catholic Cemetery, where the old Catholic Church was built; one at each of the others; the old Straight Creek Baptist, the Lutheran, the German Reformed, and the West Fork, or Christian Union Churches, and the one on the farm owned by Benjamin Wardlow, known as the Abbott Burying-Ground. The latter, and those at the old Baptist and West Fork Churches, are public burying-grounds, and in them are buried most of the pioneers of the township. Here " the multitude comes, like the flower or the weed, that withers away to let others succeed." In the others, only the families of those connected with the respective churches are buried.

SCHOOLS.

Franklin Township for many years was divided into six school districts, but the house of Subdistrict No. 4 burned down in the winter of 1872-73, and in the spring that subdistrict was divided, and at the present time there are seven subdistricts in the township. All the schoolhouses in the township are frame, with the exception of the one in Arnheim (Subdistrict No. 5), which is of brick. The latter and the one in Subdistrict No. 2 are old houses; the others have been built since the spring of 1873. The negroes in the western part of the township are, for school purposes, attached to Scott Township, in which the schoolhouse is situated.

FRANKLIN GRANGE.

Franklin Grange, of the Patrons of Husbandry, was organized January 2, 1874, the charter members being E. T. Reed, M. G. Ziegler, C. F. Schatzman, Joseph Schatzman, J. T. Schatzman, Allen Hendrixson, W. M. Hendrixson, L. M. Wolcott, Levi Myers, Joseph Lucas, Daily Kratzer, Jacob Miller, Louisa Wolcott, M. A. Hendrixson, Elvira Reed and Mary Miller. The same year, they built a neat and commodious hall, with a storeroom in the first story, on the Ripley & Arnheim Turnpike, on ground bought of Joseph Lucas. At the present time, the officers are: C. F. Schatzman, Master; Levi Myers, Overseer; B. W. Gordon, Lecturer; W. M. Hendrixson, Steward; William Bauer, Assistant Steward; Allen Hendrixson, Chaplain; Joseph Schatzman, Treasurer; M. A. Hendrixson, Secretary; M. B. Smith, Gate-Keeper; Luella Schatzman, Ceres; Mary Miller, Pomona; Abigail Smith, Flora; and Louisa Wolcott, Lady Assistant Steward.

The Georgetown & Sardinia Railroad, now in course of construction, passes through the western part of the township across its entire width. The Ripley & Arnheim Turnpike is the only macadamized road in the township. This enters it at the south central part, and extends in a northerly direction, to Arnheim, three-fourths of the distance across the township.

TOWNSHIP OFFICERS.

In the Township Clerk's books there is no account of the election held at the house of Henry Dunn in January, 1823, but we find that John McBeath, Jacob Pindell and John Lindsey were elected Trustees, and Hezekiah Lindsey, Township Clerk. March 3, 1823, the Trustees met and agreed that the next election for township officers should be held at the house of Jacob Springer, on the first Monday of April next. At this meeting, they selected for Grand Jurors, Phillip Lindsey, Enoch Laycock, Henry Dunn and David Thorp; for Petit Jurors, Gabriel Pindell, James Jacobs and Andrew Moore; and laid off four road districts. On April 26, the additional part of the township was divided into two districts, making Shotpouch Run the dividing line. At this meeting, the schoolhouse near John Lindsey's was selected for holding the elections for the township. This schoolhouse stood about where West Fork Church now stands. The Supervisors for the several road districts were John Fowler, Richard Hewitt, Ezekiel Roddy, John Bunner, James McFadden and Lemuel Monahan. On Monday, March 1, 1824, at a meeting of the Trustees, they settled with the Supervisors, James McFadden reporting that all hands in his district had worked, but made no charge for his services; the others were each allowed $1.50 for their services, except Ezekiel Roddy, John Bunner and Richard Hewitt; they reported that all hands had worked in their respective districts except one day in each; this was deducted from their allowance, and an order for 50 cents each drawn.

In 1825, township officers were: Trustees, John Brown, Benjamin Smith and Jacob Pindell; Constables, H. Lindsey, Joseph Newman and James McFadden; Lister, H. Lindsey; Overseers of Poor, G. Anderson and Isaac Stansberry; Fence Viewers, James Lucas and Henry Prickett; Supervisors, D. Reynolds, G. Anderson, William Brown, Richard Hewitt, Sr., G. Pindell, J. Herron, Joel Martin and William Lindsey. " October 11, Uriah Springer sworn to office of Trustee to fill vacancy caused by death of J. Pindell."

FRANKLIN TOWNSHIP.

1826—Trustees, John Lindsey, William Brown and Uriah Springer; Clerk, H. Lindsey; Lister, H. Lindsey; Constables, James Lindsey, E. C. Sellenberger and James Prickett; Overseers of Poor, E. Roddy and Seth Flowers; Supervisors, James Prickett, Sr., Michael Pindell, Davis Pindell, Hiram Higgins, Silas Abbott, Enoch Laycock, John Rich, John T. Wills, Ezra Pool and Jacob Kratzer; Fence Viewers, John Clark and Dudley Prickett.

1827—Trustees, Uriah Springer, Lawrence Rose and William Brown; Constables, James Robins, James Lindsey and Thomas Grogan; Clerk, H. Lindsey; Treasurer, Joseph Rich; Supervisors, J. Pitzer, L. Remely, T. Silman, D. Reynolds, J. Woods, D. Newman, J. Carbery, R. Bunner and D. Johns; Overseers of Poor, P. Lindsey and Martin Gatts.

1828—Trustees, John Lindsey, U. Springer and E. C. Sellenberger; Constables, Henry Straight, T. Silman and James McFadden; Treasurer, Nicholas Smith; Overseers of Poor, Martin Gatts and Everett D. Smith; Fence Viewers, Josiah Carbery and S. Pindell; Supervisors, John Forsythe, D. D. Brown, John T. Wills, John Fields, Asahel Lucas, Silas Abbott and Henry Young.

1829—Trustees, John Lindsey, Uriah Springer and William Brown; Clerk, Michael Pindell; Treasurer, Benjamin Hays; Supervisors, Josiah Lucas, Samuel Pindell, Enoch Laycock, Thomas Pindell, Jr., Ferrel Dunn, John Lafabre, Joseph Abbott and James Gilman; Fence Viewers, Augustus Straight and Williaw Evans; Overseers of Poor, James Ball and Phillip Lindsey; Treasurer, Terry Womacks.

1830—Trustees, Uriah Springer, John Lindsey and Terry Womacks; Clerk, Greer Abbott; Constables, Henry Straight and Isaiah Lucas; Overseers of Poor, Uriah Springer and John Brown; Supervisors, John Brady, V. D. Carbery, David M. Pindell, Henry Young, Ferrel Dunn, Richard Brown, William Masterson and Peter Runyon; Treasurer, Gabriel Pindell; Fence Viewers, Henry Straight and Silas Abbott.

1831—Trustees, Terry Womacks, Uriah Springer and John Lindsey; Clerk, Greer Abbott; Constables, Thompson Lindsey and Isaiah Carbery; Overseers of Poor, Basil McLefresh and John Lafabre; Supervisors, Robert Morrow, Robert Elder, Eli Hewitt, George Reynolds, David Rogers, Augustus Straight, Joseph Long and James Ball; Treasurer, Gabriel Pindell.

1832—Trustees, John Lindsey, Terry Womacks and Uriah Springer; Clerk, Samuel Work; Constables, Thomas Lindsey and Lemuel Rachford; Treasurer, Gabriel Pindell; Supervisors, Basil McLefresh, Charles Abbott, Asahel Lucas, Issac Bunner, James Pindell, Uriah Springer, V. D. Carbery and Terry Womacks; Overseers of Poor, John Bunner and David Newman; Fence Viewers, John Lafabre, David Rogers and Nathaniel C. Heaton.

The dates of Commissions of Justices of the Peace for Franklin Township for the above time are as follows: Uriah Springer, May 13, 1822; John Lindsey, January 13, 1823; Joseph Newman, January 13, 1823; Uriah Springer, April 20, 1825; Lawrence Rose, January 7, 1826; John Lindsey, January 7, 1826; Marin Gatts, January 14, 1828; John Lindsey, January 12, 1829; John Lindsey, December 31, 1831; Uriah Springer, April 13, 1832. This is the last record of this kind until 1853, and, with the exception of Township Clerk, we find no record of the officers until 1858.

Justices of the Peace since 1853, with dates of commission, are as follows: Thompson Lindsey, May 2, 1853; Samuel Myers, June 16, 1854; William C. Davis, April 28, 1856; James T. Erwin, October 28, 1858; Joseph Newman, April 12, 1859; James T. Erwin, October 21, 1861; W. S. Campbell, April 23, 1862; Jacob Hanselman, May 11, 1864; Joseph Ward, November 17, 1864; Jacob Hanselman, April 15, 1867; Joseph Ward, October 12, 1867; H. L. Vance, April 12, 1870; Joseph List, October 18, 1870; J. T. Erwin,

April 15, 1871; Joseph List, April 18, 1873; J. T. Erwin, April 8, 1874; G. C. Reisinger, October 21, 1876; James T. Erwin, April 17, 1877; G. C. Reisinger, October 27, 1879; and Isaac Waters, April 17, 1880; G. C. Reisinger, re-elected October 10, 1882.

We find that the following persons were Township Clerk prior to 1868, viz.: John H. Hallam, in 1838, 1838 and 1840; William Myers, in 1841 and 1842; C. W. Reed, in 1843, 1844 and 1845; Thompson Lindsey, in 1852 and 1853; J. R. Lindsey, in 1854, 1855 and 1856; W. H. Wells, in 1857; W. C. Davis, in 1858, 1859 and 1860; R. B. Dunn, in 1861; W. H. Wells, in 1862; W. S. Campbell, in 1863; E. T. Reed, in 1864; D. W. Sharp, in 1865; R. B. Dunn, in 1866 and 1867. From this time, the records have been more fully kept. The township officers since 1867 have been:

1868—Trustees, M. A. Courts, A. J. Jacobs and Job Inskeep; Clerk, G. C. Reisinger; Treasurer, Joseph List; Assessor, Enoch E. Roney; Constable, Valentine Kaufman; Supervisors, Joseph Schatzman, G. W. Hanselman, A. J. Jacobs, A. Lucas, Adam Bauer, Phillip Kautz and Isaac Waters.

1869—Trustees, M. A. Courts, Joseph Schatzman and Huston Rhoten; Treasurer, Joseph List; Assessor, E. E. Roney; Constable, J. W. Morrow; Clerk, G. C. Reisinger; Supervisors, Reason Schatzman, G. W. West, A. Shaw, L. Bier, W. A. Waterman, Jacob Weber, C. Arn, Phillip Kautz and Isaac Waters.

1870—Trustees, M. A. Courts, Huston Rhoten and Joseph Schatzman; Treasurer, Joseph List; Clerk, G. C. Reisinger; Assessor, E. E. Roney; Constable, J. W. Morrow; Supervisors, Jonathan Hanselman, W. M. Hendrixson, William Hanselman, L. Bier, John Wells, Jacob Weber, Jacob Bohrer, Grant Lowderback and Christian Keller.

1871—Trustees, M. A. Courts, Huston Rhoten and Joseph Schatzman: Treasurer, Peter Bohrer; Clerk, G. C. Reisinger; Assessor, M. G. Ziegler; Constable, J. W. Morrow; Supervisors, A. Shaub, Phillip Dunn, Ed Inskeep, C. Sullivan, Charles Elschlager, John Weisbradt, Jacob Bohrer, John Davis and H. A. Palmer.

1872—Trustees, M. A. Courts, Huston Rhoten and Joseph Schatzman; Treasurer, Peter Bohrer; Clerk, G. C. Reisinger; Assessor, M. G. Ziegler; Constable, Stephen Myers; Supervisors, Stephen Myers, L. M. Wolcott, S. P. Berry, Harvey Wills, Henry Weber, A. Wells, A. Bauer, William Shaub and C. Keller.

1873—Trustees, Joseph Schatzman, M. A. Courts and Huston Rhoten; Treasurer, Peter Bohrer; Clerk, G. C. Reisinger; Assessor, L. M. Wolcott; Constable, Stephen Myers; Superintendent Free Turnpike, Allen Hendrixson; Supervisors, Jacob Miller, W. M. Hendrixson, W. W. Young, L. Bier, A. Wells, G. Hauck, F. Hanselman, William Shaub and James T. Erwin.

1874—Trustees, M. A. Courts, Huston Rhoten and Joseph Schatzman; Clerk, G. C. Reisinger; Assessor, L. M. Wolcott; Treasurer, P. Bohrer; Constable, J. W. Morrow; Supervisors, L. Bier, Hugh Wardlow, Rudolph Kress, S. P. Berry, William Ramsey, Peter Forthoffer, Isaac Waters, Adam Wells, Adam Bauer and Levi Myers.

1875—Trustees, M. A. Courts, Huston Rhoten and Joseph Schatzman; Clerk, G. C. Reisinger; Treasurer, Peter Bohrer; Assessor, W. H. Wells; Constable, J. W. Morrow; Supervisors, Stephen Myers, Hugh Wardlow, W. W. Young, L. Bier, Joseph List, Jacob Bohrer, Rudolph Kress and Fred Yochem.

1876—Trustees, G. W. Laycock, A. J. Jacobs and Phillip Stephen; Clerk, G. C. Reisinger; Treasurer, S. P. Berry; Assessor, H. F. Pindell; Constable, Stephen Myers; Supervisors, Jacob Miller, G. C. Mannon, William Hansel-

FRANKLIN TOWNSHIP.

man, Levi Jacobs, John Wells, Jacob Weber, C. F. Hanselman, J. P. Kautz and Phillip Stephen.

1877—Trustees, Phillip Stephen, A. J. Jacobs and G. W. Laycock; Treasurer, S. P. Berry; Clerk, Joseph List; Assessor, H. F. Pindell; Constable, William Shaub; Supervisors, Jacob Miller, Ira Hendrixson, S. P. Berry, L. Bier, John Wells, George Snider, C. F. Hanselman, R. Kress and P. Faul.

1878—Trustees, A. J. Jacobs, Phillip Stephen and Milford Lowderback; Treasurer, S. P. Berry; Clerk, Joseph List; Assessor, Samuel Kautz; Constable, J. W. Morrow; Supervisors, Peter Shaub, Ira Hendrixson, James Sullivan, John Wells, Frederick Kautz, F. W. Hanselman, Peter Berry and Phillip Stephen

1879—Trustees, H. F. Pindell, Phillip Stephen and Joseph Schatzman; Clerk, M. B. Smith; Treasurer, S. P. Berry; Assessor, C. F. Schatzman; Constable, J. W. Morrow: Supervisors, Phillip Dunn, F. W. Hanselman, M. A. Courts, Henry Bohl, Christian Bauer, H. F. Pindell, Phillip Stephen, Peter Shaub and John Wells.

1880—Trustees, Phillip Stephen, H. F. Pindell, Joseph Schatzman; Treasurer, H. F. Pindell; Clerk, Joseph List; Assessor, C. F. Schatzman; Constable, Joseph Weber; Supervisors, Peter Faul, W. W. Young, Peter Berry, Peter Shaub, A. J. Jacobs, Amos Bunner, George W. Hendrixson, C. F. Schatzman and H. F. Pindell.

1881—Trustees, H. F. Pindell, Phillip Stephen and F. W. Hanselman; Clerk, Joseph List; Treasurer, H. F. Pindell; Assessor, Samuel Kautz; Constable, Joseph Weber; Supervisors, J. T. Schatzman, Isaac W. Dunn, W. W. Young, A. D. Ellis, Amos Bunner, Jacob Arn, William Bauer, Peter Berry and Phillip Schweighart.

1882—Trustees, H. F. Pindell, Phillip Stephen and F. W. Hanselman; Clerk, Joseph List; Treasurer, H. F. Pindell; Assessor, Samuel Kautz; Constable, Joseph Weber; Supervisors, J. T. Schatzman, W. M. Hendrixson, W. W. Young, A. D. Ellis, Charles Elschlager, George F. Yockey, William Bauer, Phillip Kautz and Phillip Stephen.

Politically, Franklin Township is strongly Democratic, but in local elections there is no party spirit manifested; but in county, State and Presidential elections, although the people are strictly divided by party lines, good feeling and harmony generally prevail. Some of the votes cast in the township have been as follows:

1824—For Governor, Allen Trimble, 22; Jeremiah Morrow, 99; President, Jackson, 65; Adams, 4; Clay, 7.

1826—For Governor, Alexander Campbell, 51; Trimble, 44; John Bigger, 8; Benjamin Tappin, 1.

1828—Governor, John W. Campbell, 143; Allen Trimble, 1.

1830—Governor, Duncan McArthur, 11; Robert Lucas, 87.

1844—Governor, David Tod, 158; William Bebb, 13; Samuel Lewis, 2.

1876—President, S. J. Tilden, 227; R. B. Hayes, 43.

1877—Governor, R. M. Bishop, 166; William H. West, 31.

1880—Secretary of State, Lang, 225; Townsend, 34.

1880—President, W. S. Hancock, 230; J. A. Garfield, 44.

1881—Governor, J. W. Bookwalter, 168; Charles Foster, 33.

1882—Secretary of State, James W. Newman, 216; Charles Townsend, 27.

POPULATION.

The census returns show that Franklin Township had a less number of inhabitants in 1880 than in 1870, as follows: Population in 1870, 1,225; in 1880, 1,195; showing a loss of sixty in the ten years.

CHAPTER VIII.

PIKE TOWNSHIP.

BY C. C. DONLEY.

PIKE contains about twenty-three square miles, or 14,720 acres; its extreme length from east to west is eight and three-quarter miles; extreme width, about three and one-fourth miles. It is in the western part of the county, occupying the middle position in the western tier of townships. It is bounded on the north by Sterling and Green Townships and Highland County, on the east by Washington and Scott, on the south by Scott and Clark, on the west by Clermont County. The boundary lines were established in 1823, the survey being made by John McBeth. This was originally a part of Clark Township. Its topography is not very marked, as the land is mostly level or rolling. White Oak Creek on the eastern boundary causes some broken land in that portion, and Sterling Creek, crossing the township from north to south, a short distance east of the center, is bounded by low hills; some slight depressions are in the western part, through which small streams take their meandering courses.

Agriculture and stock-raising are the chief pursuits of the people; wool growing receives considerable attention. The principal agricultural products are wheat, rye, corn, oats, potatoes and tobacco. Many varieties of timber which have been planted by nature grow on our soil, the principal of which are oaks, beech, maple, elm, ash, gum, dogwood, locust and hickory.

The township is drained by the branches of White Oak Creek and the East Fork of the Little Miami River. Although the locality is not adapted to fruit-growing to any desirable extent, yet enough is generally gathered to supply the home demand.

IMPROVEMENTS.

Less than half a century ago, most of Pike Township was a dense wilderness; blazed roads and bridle paths constituted the principal thoroughfares for public travel; churches, commodious school buildings, cozy dwellings, roomy barns and easy vehicles were only pictured in the fancy of the sturdy pioneers of the forest; but subsequent energy and perseverance have caused the forests to give way to beautiful meadows, vast fields of growing grain and rich pasturage. The rude huts have given place to more comfortable dwellings and spacious barns. Temples have taken the place of private dwellings for religious homage; the old-time log schoolhouses, with slab benches without backs or desks, have ceased to be the dread of the youthful mind in his intellectual pursuits; the meandering tracks without their guides, and with but few evidences of civilization, have been straightened and improved until we have a system of roads over which a traveler may pass with the satisfaction of knowing from whence he came and whither he is going.

A large portion of this section of the county is almost level, and before the forests were broken the land was covered with water almost the year round, but the ever patient and persevering tiller of the soil has demonstrated the fact that this element cannot stop the wheels of agricultural development. In early times, this level portion was considered as almost worthless property, but since the clearing and draining of the land has been accomplished to a great extent, this has proved one of the most productive portions of the township. Many of the water courses have been enlarged by the regulation of the ditch law, and improvement in this line is still going on, and in time the swampy section will have a network of ditches which will carry away the surplus water before it can have time to damage the crops. One of the first and most noted drains thus established and improved is that known as the head-waters of one of the branches of Clover Creek.

The spirit of improving the public highways still moves on. In the summer of 1881, the citizens near the central part of the township improved the road, beginning at the top of the hill south of the residence of James Blair, and completing to the bridge across Sterling Creek at Blair's Crossing. This was done by grading the road, bridging and covering with gravel, and is said to be one of the best jobs of public road improvements by individual donations in the county. The Mount Orab & Georgetown Free Turnpike passes from north to south through the township, and was built in 1867–68 on the two-mile system. Artus Pepper, who lived on the road at that time, was the principal contractor.

Through the northeastern part of the township passes the Cincinnati & Eastern Railway. The only mill built in the township was erected by Christian Drum in 1856, in the hamlet now known as Gorgonia. The chief articles of commerce manufactured and sold at this mill were lumber and chair material. It has ceased to be used as a mill, the machinery being out of order and the building being old and almost ready to fall.

New Harmony, a small village in the northwestern part of the township, was laid out by E. B. Whorton in 1847, and probably at this day the population does not exceed 100 persons. David Wade kept a store here in 1848. Delos Laughlan was engaged in store business in 1850; after Laughlan, Luther Lyons and Test & Heming were in the goods business; later, Colthar & Long; McLain & Reynolds succeeded by Calvin Owens. Louis Thompson is at present in the mercantile business in the place; also small grocery stores by Maggie Thompson and Daniel Frazee. Jared E. Winter and Daniel Long are blacksmiths at this point.

Locust Ridge, another hamlet containing probably less than threescore inhabitants, is located to the southwestern part of the township. The first buildings were erected in the place probably in 1835. Adam Earheart was among the first who was in the mercantile business at this point. Henry H. Jones was for twenty years in the goods business here. Andrew Earheart was also in business here for several years previous to his death in 1860. Alonzo Earheart sold goods here for several years. The only merchants of the place at the present time are Jones & Vaughan, partners in general store. Dr. W. H. Langstaff lives at this place, and is the only physician living in the township. The blacksmiths are Charles M. Zollers and Robert Duncanson; boot and shoe manufacturer, John Vandelph; marble works, Charles Hancock.

Surryville consists of a store and post office, kept by C. C. Donley; blacksmith and repair shops of Wilber O. Robinson; church, school building and a few dwellings.

White Oak, a station on the Cincinnati & Eastern Railway, consists of a store and post office, kept by Perry Hoss; blacksmith shop by Mr. Stump, and several dwellings.

EARLY SETTLERS.

Henry Moyer, Sr., born in 1767, came to Brown County, Ohio, in the year 1816; lived on the land now owned by his sons and heirs in the western part of the township, near Locust Ridge, making that his residence until his death in 1829, aged sixty-two years. Henry was father of John and George F. Moyer, pioneer boys of the township whose names appear further on. He was a native of Chester County, Penn. The father of Henry came with him to Ohio; died in earlier days, and of his history not much can be gathered except he was a native of Germany.

Thomas Foster came to the township prior to the arrival of Henry Moyer and lived at that time on the farm which is now occupied by Wesley Thompson; he died in Williamsburg, Clermont Co., Ohio, about 1878.

William Thompson came from Greenbrier County, Va., in pioneer days, and settled on the farm now owned by Elijah McGohan. William was the father of Alexander, Isaac, James, John, William, Andrew and Felix, who were well known by many of the present citizens of Brown County as worthy and good men.

Charles Hunt was among the earliest who sought the unbroken forests of this part of the State. Of him, tradition can give but little account, as none of his posterity are here to give us the genealogy of the Hunt family. He lived on the farm now owned and occupied by George F. Moyer.

Jonathan Hunt was among the first comers to this section, and located on the farm which is now the home of Adam Earhart. His history, like that of Charles Hunt, is obscured in the mist of the past.

Jasper Shotwell flourished in the days in which it tried men's hearts to cope with the inhabitants of the dense forests, and resided subsequent to the settlement of Charles Hunt on the Moyer farm.

James McIntire lived in 1830 on the farm now owned and occupied by Theodore Knabe.

George F. Moyer, one of the eldest pioneers now living in the township, was born in Chester County, Penn., January 10, 1810; came with his father, Henry, and settled on the Moyer land, and has been a resident of the township ever since. He recollects distinctly the howl of the wolf, the wail of the wild cat, the fleet-footed deer and flocks of wild turkeys. He used to attend the musters of militia on the Allen farm (now Blair's farm).

John Moyer, born in Chester County, Penn., June 24, 1805, came to Ohio with his father, Henry, in 1816, and was a resident until his death, which occurred in 1880. His son, William H. Moyer, is a citizen of the township at this time.

Elijah Winter was born in Virginia in 1798, came here in 1817, and first lived in the vicinity of Locust Ridge, but during the latter part of his life, lived on the land now owned by Henry Seirs, near the New Harmony Cemetery; he died in 1844. Jared, James and William, sons of Elijah, have long been residents of the township. James died on his farm in 1876. The estate after his death was purchased by W. H. Holmes, of Maysville, Ky., and is now the home of his family. Jared and William are still living here, the latter a farmer by occupation, and the former a blacksmith, residing in New Harmony. During the year 1869, he was subjected to the misfortune of losing his dwelling and its contents by fire.

John Earhart, born October 11, 1777, in the State of Pennsylvania, came here in the spring of 1815, and purchased the farm on which he ever afterward lived, located southwest of Locust Ridge, now the property of George F. Moyer, and present residence of Lydia Thompson. Although he spent much of his time on his farm tilling the soil, he was a cooper by trade, and timber being plenty and of little value until manufactured into implements of utility, the profits of his labor were such as to enable him to live comfortably and happily. He died in February, 1851, and was laid to rest in the little family graveyard on the farm. His sons—Adam, David, John and William—are still living, Adam and William being present residents of the township. The former was born in

Isaac Waters

Lancaster County, Penn.; came with his father to Ohio when a boy not yet four years old, and lived at home until he married and moved on the farm on which he now lives; he also purchased part of the homestead of his father, which joined his first purchase. He is in his seventy-first year, and has always made farming his occupation. William was born five years after his father settled at the old home He, like his father, is a cooper, but does not work much at his trade of late.

Vincent Applegate was born in Mason County, Ky., in 1795; came here in 1836, and settled on the land now in possession of his heirs on the Williamsburg & New Hope road. He was among the first settlers in that portion of the township, and one who had a full realization of the inconveniences and disadvantages of settling in the woods, and having to clear and improve his lands, and at the same time provide a competence for a large family. He served as Justice of the Peace six years. His wife, originally Anna Lemon, whom he married in 1824, was a native of Maryland, born in 1808. Vincent died in the fall of 1869; Anna survived him twelve years, and died in the spring of 1881 at the old home. They had four sons and three daughters, namely, Milton, Frank, Mahlon, Newton, Amanda, Cordelia and Eliza. Eliza, Cordelia and Milton are dead; the rest, though living, are non-residents.

John Allen was probably the first man who settled in the eastern part of the township. He located on the farm now in the possession of Jerome Allen in 1810; was born in Westmoreland County, Penn., October 15, 1785. He was Colonel of the militia, which mustered on his farm in pioneer days. He lived in the township several years; the latter part of his life he spent in Georgetown, Ohio, where he died in 1879. He served in the capacity of Justice of the Peace for several years. He had three sons and four daughters —Sanford (who was probably the first white person born in the township), William, John, Eliza, Melinda, Rhoda and Nancy.

Vincent Brown was born in Kentucky in 1786; came to this township in 1801, and was married soon after his arrival here to Martha Ann Allen, thus being the first marriage ceremony performed in the township. He resided for a number of years on the old Brown homestead, now in possession of the heirs of Elliott Brown, prior to his death, January 7, 1853. Martha A., wife of Vincent Brown, was born in Kentucky in 1793, and died at the old homestead October 17, 1857.

James Young, born in 1811 in Bracken County, Ky., settled in 1856 on the land now occupied by his heirs in the southeastern part of the township; he was a lawyer by profession. Mary Young, wife of James, and daughter of Vincent Brown, was born in this township April 6, 1814, and is still living on the home property.

John B. Stump, born in 1796 in Hampshire County, W. Va., came here in 1828, and settled in the eastern part of the township on the farm now occupied by his son James, and lived there until his death in September, 1877. Mary C., his wife, is still living at the old home.

Joseph Keethler, born in October, 1780, was a native of the glades of Pennsylvania; came to Brown County, Ohio, in 1810, and located on the farm which was long the home of Christopher Day, Sr., and remained there about ten years, removing thence to Green Township, where he died.

James Brown, a native of Kentucky, born in 1795, came to this township in 1812; was married in 1814, and built a cabin on the land where George W. Watson now lives, and began to clear away the timber in order that the arrows from the eternal quiver of the sun might smite the earth and cause vegetation to spring forth for his subsistence. He lived in the township until 1855, when his career ended, and his remains were deposited in the Hendrickson Graveyard. His wife, Mary, in her eighty-fifth year, still lives in the township with her daughter, Maria Higgins, and is the oldest of the early pioneers of the central part of the township who are now living. Well can she recollect when the wolves and bears and deer were as plentiful throughout the township as the timid hare which gambols over the meadows now.

Henry Gates was the first who settled where James Liming now lives, and out of a family of ten, six died in 1848 with the cholera, three of whom lay dead in the house at the same time.

One Gennings occupied the land where Hampton Wardlow now lives for several years from 1812, being the first settler who built there.

Abram Fiscus in 1812 lived on the land now owned by Perry T. Dunn, being the first who occupied the premises.

Nicholas Peddicord first settled on the land where Reuben Wilson now lives, and was for several years thereafter a resident of the township.

Isaiah Wells, born in Wales in 1777, came to Pike Township in 1826, and built him a cabin on the land he purchased near New Harmony. The house stood on the land now owned by John Simpkins. He, like the other early settlers, located in the timber, and began to clear off the land, on the products of which he depended for subsistence. He continued a laborer on his farm until 1842, when he departed this life, and was taken to his last resting place in the New Harmony Cemetery. His sons, James and Daniel, came with their father, and the latter is still living on part of the old homestead, and drinking in the quiet enjoyment of rural life; he is now in his sixty-seventh year.

During the same year came Daniel Newberry, who purchased a farm on the New Harmony & Williamsburg road, on which he built a cabin, and commenced to exercise his strength and ingenuity by making less forest in the vicinity of his new home. He labored on his farm during the summer, and in the winter season was employed in going from house to house making shoes for the different families in the neighborhood. He continued to perform the duties devolving upon him until the year 1851, when he died from the effects of a stroke of paralysis at the age of eighty-five. Smallwood, son of Daniel Newberry, is still living on the old home place, and, although seventy-one years of age, he is still engaged in tilling the soil.

William Lewis Kinner was born August 14, 1759, in Westmoreland County, Va.; his real name was William Lewis, but at the age of six years he was kidnaped while playing near the coast, and carried away by a seaman. He was taught by his new friend, whose name was Kinner, to call himself William L. Kinner, which name he adopted. He was married to Nancy Becham in 1784, and emigrated to Adams County, Ohio, in 1796; thence to Ross County in 1800; from there to Clermont County, and finally to Brown County on the 23d day of February, 1815. He settled on the farm now owned by Elizabeth Strain, and there lived until his death, which was only a few years later.

Richard L. Kinner, son of W. L. Kinner, was born in Highland County, Ohio, December 23, 1805; came with his father in 1815 to Brown County, and has lived in sight of the place where his father first settled ever since. Although in his seventy-seventh year, he has a very correct recollection of the early events of his life.

James Hughs, a native of England, settled near Augusta, Ky., but soon left the State and came to Ohio. He married Sarah Cochran in 1819, and in 1823 purchased the farm on which William Hancock now lives, near the Pleasant Hill Schoolhouse, and there resided until his death in 1856.

William Hughs, son of James Hughs, born in 1822, came with his father, and has lived in the township ever since; now lives on his farm near where his father died.

PIKE TOWNSHIP. 561

James D. Higgins was among the earlier settlers, having come to the township in 1818. He taught a school the first year he was here on the Allen farm. He was a native of North Carolina, and was married in 1822 to Nancy Fiscus. He settled on the farm now the property of Elizabeth Strain; died in 1837, and his remains were interred in the old Allen Graveyard, on the land now owned by Charlotte Carr. Nancy survived him many years, and died in 1877. They had nine children—Robert, Mary, Dow, Sarah, William, Andrew, Nancy, John and James, all of whom are still living, five being residents of the township.

James Allen was born October 20, 1806, in Pennsylvania; was married in 1827; came to this township in 1837, and settled on the farm which is now the property of his son Jerome. He served for sixteen years as Justice of the Peace; died on his farm in 1858, and was buried in the Hendrickson grounds in Scott Township. The children of James were Milton, Martha, Robert, one child which died in infancy and Jerome.

John Allen, Jr., lived in the township several years from 1830; settled on the land now the property of Robert Boyd (part of the Blair farm).

Nicholas Allen was a resident in 1846, and occupied the property now owned by James Blair.

Smith J. Cowdrey, a native of Connecticut, was among the first settlers in the northwestern part of the township. He was born in 1785; went from his native State to New York; thence to Indiana; from there to Kentucky, where he was married in 1817 to Mary Brush (originally Beatty), and during the same year came to Pike Township, and settled on the farm now owned by Matthew Dyer. He lived in the township most of the time thereafter until his death; he died in 1860 at the age of seventy-five, and he was taken to his final resting-place near New Harmony. Although twenty-two years have elapsed since Mr. Cowdrey's death, his wife is still living among her children here; she is now in her ninety-second year, but has a vigorous mind and good recollection of early events. Her first remembrance of Ohio was when she was but four years old, living with her uncle, Gen. Lytle, where Williamsburg now stands, in Clermont County. In the year 1795, one Snider killed an Indian belonging to one of the neighboring tribes. The red men sought revenge, and came to the settlement, which stood on the present town plat of Williamsburg, and made known their intentions to have the scalp of the pale face who did the deed or spare none; but Lytle, fully awake to the value of strategy, so common to frontier life, gave them a feast of good things, many presents, and promised that the life of the offender should pay the forfeit, which quieted the savages, and they returned to their wigwams without further hostile demonstrations. William, James, Clara (now Brooks), Joseph, Achsah, Mary and Olive are the children of Smith and Mary Cowdrey; the first three are residents. The third and fourth generations being very numerous, give them a large posterity among us.

Daniel Kain is reputed to have been the first white man who settled in the western part of the township, none of whose posterity are here to narrate anything interesting concerning him and his pioneer home, only that he was a settler on the land now in possession of W. H. Holmes, adjoining New Harmony, and came here about 1811 or 1812.

Ramus Raper lived also on part of the Kain land during the first settlements.

Thomas E. McLain came here as early as 1834, and purchased the land now belonging to David Wilson in the northern part of the township. He was born in the county on the old homestead in Sterling Township, which is now the property of his brother, Archibald, and was married in 1833 to Mary

A. Hiles; he lived on the farm which he purchased here until his death, which occurred in 1863.

William P. Taylor, a native of Ireland, was born in 1808; came to Pike Township in 1845, and settled on the farm now owned by Daniel Long, after which he purchased the farm now owned by John Day. He was a cooper and manufacturer of chair stuff in connection with farming. He died in 1855 at his last-mentioned home, and was laid to rest in the burial-grounds at New Harmony. There were four sons and two daughters—Robert, John, James, William, Mary and Sarah. Robert only is a present resident.

In 1845, Reuben Wilson, Sr., came, and purchased a farm and built a house thereon in the midst of the thick forest. The house which he built is now the home of Elizabeth Buchanan. He was a native of Vermont; was born in 1795, and lived in the township until 1848, in which year he died of the cholera.

Huchins Allen was an early settler, locating on the land now owned by Andrew Higgins.

Samuel Wardlow was one of the early settlers in the eastern part of the township, when all the modes of egress and ingress were to follow blazed roads through the woods for miles. He, like most of the other pioneers, lives no more to watch the march of civilization and improvement.

Jonathan Church came to his present farm as early as 1840.

Isaac Penny was among the early settlers, and was the first person who lived on the farm where Lafayette now lives. He has been dead several years.

David H. Carpenter, born in Highland County, Ohio, in 1816, settled on the farm on which he now lives in 1847, on the Georgetown & Mount Orab pike.

Daniel Keethler, born in the township August 24, 1812, has always lived here, and now resides on his farm in the northern part of the township. He at present keeps his bed, being the victim of a stroke of paralysis.

Gideon Lowe, born in 1810 in Clermont County, Ohio, came to this township and located on the farm where he now lives in 1853.

James D. Day, born January 11, 1818, on Straight Creek, Brown Co., Ohio, came with his father and setlted in this township in 1824, and has since resided here. By occupation he is a farmer and stone mason.

Robert L. Alexander, born in Virginia in 1805, came to his present home in 1850, and has lived here ever since.

James Fry, Sr., was born in Bourbon County, Ky., in October, 1806; came from there to Clermont County, Ohio, in 1812, and from thence to Pike Township, locating on his present farm in 1848.

Alexander Holten, a native of Virginia, came in 1812, and located on the land now the property of Robert Boyd, where the old orchard used to stand, being part of the old Blair farm.

John Brown was the first who settled on the land where Elliot Brown spent the latter part of his life.

RELIGIOUS.

Tradition gives John Srofe and Joshua Archer the praise of being the first whose voices were heard proclaiming "the glad tidings of great joy" to the hardy pioneers of the eastern part of Pike Township. They held services at private houses along Sterling Creek, and the first house built exclusively for religious exercises was erected on the land now owned by William Hughs, south of his residence and west of the county road. Those who worshiped here were of the New Light persuasion. Peter Shick, Sr., and George Vandament were the pastors in those days.

In the western part of the township, services were held at the residences of John Earhart and others as early as 1824, by Rev. Beck, a Protestant Methodist.

Otho Parrell, a minister in the Christian Church, was among the early expounders of the Scriptures; he left the township and moved to Illinois in 1858.

In 1827, services were held at the residence of Isaiah Wells, near New Harmony. Hector Sanford was the first preacher in that locality, and a Methodist Protestant in belief. David Hannah and Sanford Evans were among the pioneer preachers in the northwestern part of the township, and the first church built in that section was on the land now belonging to Caroline Long. It was known as the Providence Meeting-House, and was built by the Methodist Episcopal Church organization in 1841. In 1846, a frame church was built in the graveyard by the Methodist Protestant society. Jonathan Flood preached the dedicatory sermon. The members of the original society were Isaiah Wells, Joseph Brower, James Wells, Elias Newberry, Daniel Wells, John Philipps, William Taylor, Smith J. Cowdrey and the wife of each.

The Methodist Episcopal society built a frame church in town in 1853, but it has ceased to be used, and the house and lot have been sold.

In 1856, the Methodist Protestant society erected the present church building in New Harmony.

Shiloh Methodist Episcopal Church Society was organized in 1853 by Revs. Bennett and Gossard, and held its meetings first in a cabin which stood near the present residence of Eliza Rush; during the next year, a schoolhouse being built on the present site, the society was permitted to use that and the subsequent building until 1877, when the Shiloh Chapel was erected, and the organization with its paraphernalia moved to a more spacious and lasting home. Shiloh Chapel was built at a cost of $1,400, Joseph Doughty having the contract.

The dedication services were conducted by Rev. Boyer, and were held in November of the same year in which the house was built.

The only pioneer members still connected with the society are Elizabeth J. Donley and Sarah Stuart (now Ogden), the rest having either withdrawn, moved away or died. The ministers who have had charge of the flock at this point are Revs. Wheat, Wolf, Philipps, Morrow, Middleton, Bodkin, Zink, Schultz, Green, Jackson, Armstrong, James, Head, Calhoon, Stokes, Callender, Goudey, Boltin, Nine, Gregg, Smith, Euel, Boyer, Eastman, Ross, McColm, McLaughlan, Edmondson and Fee.

SCHOOLS.

The first school taught in the township was by James Higgins in 1818, on the farm of Jerome W. Allen (present possessor), between where his residence stands and Sterling Creek. The pupils of that school were Sanford Allen, Rhoda Allen, Malinda Allen (children of John), Nancy, Andrew and Thomas Fiscus (children of John Fiscus), Mary and Rhoda Brown (daughters of Vincent), William and Louis Keethler (sons of Joseph). The next was taught in a schoolhouse on the same farm, north of his residence, in 1820; the next in a cabin on the land now belonging to Robert Higgins, in the field opposite the residence of Chambers Brown, in 1821.

The wages in those days were from $5 to $10 per month, paid by the patrons.

The first school taught in the vicinity of Locust Ridge was kept in a vacant cabin on the Jasper Shotwell farm by John Dooly; the first building erected exclusively for school purposes was on the farm of Theodore Knabe. Subsequent to that was a frame building on the old site, opposite the present one; afterward two brick buildings were erected on the same grounds at different times, and when in time it became necessary to change to a new site, on account of the unfitness of the old one, the present building was erected south of the old one on the land purchased of Adam Earhart.

In 1834, Thomas Anderson taught a school in a house which stood on the land where Robert Taylor now lives, back from the road in what was then a hazel thicket. This seems to have been the first school taught in the New Harmony District. Subsequent to this, school was kept in the old Providence Church, and in 1842 a log building was erected on a site purchased off the Bolar farm near the residence of Daniel Wells. In 1865, a frame building was erected on the same site, and in 1881 a lot was purchased in town, and the present building erected.

Cade McGouldric was the first who taught in the Shiloh District. The session was held in an old log schoolhouse which stood on the land now owned by James W. Donley, in the year 1846. In 1853, J. W. Donley deeded to the district a site off the southeast corner of his land, to be held as long as it is used for schoolhouse lot, and the second building was erected thereon, and in 1866 the present house was built on the same ground.

The first school building in the district, known as Areopagus, stood on the land belonging to the heirs of Martin Bavis, a few rods east of where the present house stands; the building, like the rest of those built in pioneers days, was a log structure. Fairview District originally used a log building, which stood south of the present one, near Shawnee Run.

The first School Board in the township met April 18, 1853, at the Pleasant Hill Schoolhouse. Elliott Brown was elected Chairman, and William Neff, Clerk. The other members were Nelson Applegate, John B. Stump, Gideon Lowe, William Sammons, James W. Donley and James M. Winter.

The resident teachers of the township are Joseph Young, Absalom B. Brooks, Nannie Donley, V. B. Young, Rufus Johnson, Harvey Hoss and Charles C. Donley.

SECRET SOCIETIES.

Lodge No. 618, I. O. O. F., at Locust Ridge, was established August 5, 1875. The Noble Grand who first presided was John W. McMahan; charter members, J. W. McMahan, Samuel S. Brooks, Samuel J. Meeker, Charles M. Zollers, Dr. W. H. Langstaff, William H. Jones, J. H. Campbell, Benjamin F. Applegate, Charles Ousler, Edward Duncanson, Absalom B. Brooks and William S. Emmons. Lodge rooms in second story over Jones & Vaughn's store.

New Harmony Lodge No. 435, F. & A. M., was established October 20, 1869, in the town of New Harmony, H. S. Reynolds, First Master; charter members, H. S. Reynolds, G. Patton, D. C. Wells, James W. Winter, J. E. Winter, D. Wilson, L. T. Mattox, W. A. Colthar, William Sammons, L. T. Earhart, W. T. Winter. Lodge room second story over Louis Thompson's store.

Pike Grange, No. 448, was organized in 1874, First Master, Robert Duncanson. The charter members were Robert Duncanson, Sylvanus and Ellen Patten, William and Levanche Chatterton, Clay and Ellen Patton, Newton and Marinda Jacobs, James and Lorinda Cowdrey, Alexander and Martha Henning, Shannon and Nancy Alexander, John and Alonzo Colthar, William Ogden, William Mayer, George Earhart and David Wilson. Sessions are held in the school building in Subdistrict No. 5.

POST OFFICES.

Pike Township contains four post offices. New Harmony, the oldest, was established in 1850. Mails were carried from Williamsburg, in Clermont County, to this place. The first Postmaster was Delos Laughlin, and in 1856 the route was extended through Locust Ridge and Clover Valley to New Hope, Locust Ridge being the second in order established, and H. H. Jones being the first Postmaster at that place. The other two points, one in Clark, the other in Scott Township, did not long continue on the route, after which Locust Ridge became the terminus until 1874, when the route was again extended to Surryville, William Surry being the first Postmaster at that point.

White Oak, on the Cincinnati & Eastern Railway, was the fourth and last, established in 1878, in the extreme northeastern part of the township, George Dunn having charge thereof. Originally the route to Locust Ridge from Williamsburg had only a weekly mail, then in time two mails, on Tuesdays and Fridays, and in 1880 changed to three mails each week—Tuesdays, Thursdays and Saturdays. White Oak has a daily mail.

New Harmony Cemetery contained originally one acre, deeded in 1845 to the Protestant Church, and one-half an acre was added in 1866. This continued in the possession of the church until 1880, when it was deeded to the Trustees of the township, who purchased two acres more, making three and one-half acres. The first who was laid to rest here was a small child of James Wells, in 1832.

JUSTICES OF THE PEACE.

The docket of John Allen (Uncle Jack) is the earliest record preserved relative to the office of Justice of the Peace. On this docket are transcripts (in 1824) of cases from the dockets of Francis Meyers and William White, late Justices, showing that Meyers and White, if they are of the township, were the earliest we have any exact account of in this capacity. On Allen's docket is a transcript from the docket of James D. Higgins in 1828, showing him to have been in office prior to that time. Allen held the office for several terms, probably until 1838. Nicholas Srofe held the office from 1838 to 1844; Samuel Wardlow, from 1842 to 1848; William Thompson, from 1842 to 1845; James Allen, from 1843 to 1858; Adam Earhart, from 1845 to 1851; John B. Stump, from 1851 to 1860; Jared E. Winter, from 1854 to 1857; F. B. Goll, from 1858 to 1861; V. C. Brown, from 1858 to 1861; Vincent Applegate, six years, dates not of record; also Isaac Dean, whose record we have not; James L. Irvin, from 1861 to 1866; Abraham Boler, from 1861 to 1864; Thomas E. McLain, from 1862 part of term, died in office; J. E. Derril, from 1867 to 1870; Henry H. Jones, from 1864 to 1879; Robert A. Higgins, from 1870 to 1879; F. S. Stevens, from 1879 to 1882. V. C. Brown, elected in 1879, one of the present Justices; Absalom B. Brooks, elected in 1882, one of the present Justices.

SOLDIERS OF THE LATE WAR.

During the civil war which agitated our nation from 1861 to 1865, our citizens responded to the calls of the Government promptly, leaving their homes in squads, hastening to the scene of action until the last year of the rebellion, when there were less than half a dozen men subject to military duty remaining on their farms. Their wives and children had to take their places on the farms, feeling that the cause for which the husband and father fought was as sacred as their homes. The hard-fought battles of Shiloh, Mission Ridge, Lookout Mountain, Stone River, Murfreesboro, Vicksburg, the siege of Corinth, Chickamauga, Franklin and Nashville and many others found them contending with the foe, and protecting the tattered banners which represented the principles for which our Revolutionary fathers had pledged their lives, their property and their sacred honor. Andersonville, Belle Isle, Camp Ford and other prison pens of the South were not without the presence of some of our brave and true. Sherman was not without some of them in his famous "march to the sea." And when the contest was over, and the returning braves came marching home, comrades there were who with them went, but homeward with them never came. They had sealed the pledge of eternal fidelity by sacrificing their lives to protect their country's honor.

Jordan Brooks, private, Company A, One Hundred and Seventy-fifth Ohio Volunteer Infantry; served nine months.

Abel Frazee, Fourth Independent Company, Ohio Volunteer Cavalry, private; served two years and nine months.

Warren Carr, Company I, Eleventh Ohio Volunteer Cavalry; served three months; also Company A, Fifth Ohio Veteran Volunteer service, two years and ten months.

Timothy Srofe, Fourth Independent Ohio Volunteer Cavalry, private; time of service, nine months.

William H. Russell, Fourth Independent Company of Ohio Volunteer Cavalry; served nine months.

Benjamin G. Kimball, Company A, Sixty-first Ohio Volunteer Infantry; served eight months; discharged for disability.

Benjamin F. Young, private, Company G, First Ohio Volunteer Cavalry; served three years.

Charles M. Pask, private, Fifth Ohio Volunteer Cavalry; discharged for disability—palpitation of the heart.

Allen Thompson, private, Fourth Independent Company Ohio Volunteer Cavalry; time of service, nine months.

Capt. William H. Langstaff, commissioned Second Lieutenant of Company —, One Hundred and Seventy-eighth Ohio Volunteer Infantry, September 1, 1864, by John Brough, Governor of Ohio; October 10, 1864, commissioned First Lieutenant of Company E, One Hundred and Seventy-fifth Ohio Volunteer Infantry, and on June 1, 1865, by request of his company, and meritorious conduct at the battle of Franklin and during the Hood campaign, was promoted to Captain of his company.

Robert H. Duncanson, private, Company A, One Hundred and Seventy-fifth Ohio Volunteer Infantry; time of service, nine months.

Frederic S. Stevens, private in Company E, Twenty-second Ohio Volunteer Infantry, served four months; also Company I, Forty-eighth Ohio Volunteer Infantry three years, and was veteranized; was a prisoner six months and fifteen days at Camp Ford, Tex.; rank, Sergeant.

John M. Colthar, private, Company H, One Hundred and Seventy-fifth Ohio Volunteer Infantry; time of service, one year.

James Srofe, private, Company D, Seventieth Ohio Veteran Volunteer Infantry; time of service, three years and seven months.

George Wilson, a private in Company H, One Hundred and Seventy-fifth Ohio Volunteer Infantry; time of service, nine months.

William F. Rush, Company G, Twenty-ninth Ohio Veteran Volunteer Infantry; served eight months and six days; rank, private.

Andrew F. Higgins, a private in Fourth Independent Company of Ohio Volunteer Cavalry; served one year.

James Liming, Company H, One Hundred and Eighty-ninth Ohio Volunteer Infantry; served nine months; a private.

John C. Kimball, rank, Corporal, Company A, Sixty-first Ohio Veteran Volunteer Infantry, served three years and three and one-half months.

Thomas B. Young, Company H, First Ohio Volunteer Cavalry; time of service, one year and seven months; a private.

Noah Kinner, private, Company F, One Hundred and Seventy-fifth Ohio Volunteer Infantry; served nine months.

Otho P. Stephenson, Second Ohio Veteran Volunteer Infantry, private, Company M; time of service, three years and four months.

PIKE TOWNSHIP.

Alexander Fox, private, Company A, Sixty-first Ohio Volunteer Infantry; served three years and six months.

Charles W. Hancock, Company B, Twelfth Ohio Volunteer Infantry; served three months; and Company L, Fifth Ohio Volunteer Cavalry; eighteen months, a private; also One Hundred and Fifty-third Ohio National Guards, 100 days; Corporal.

Byard H. Church, Company A, Fifth Ohio Volunteer Cavalry; time of service, three years and four months; private.

James F. Church, private, Company A, Fifth Ohio Volunteer Cavalry; served three years and four months.

George W. Church, Company A, Fifth Ohio Volunteer Cavalry; private; time of service, three years and four months.

Leondus Morue Church, private, Company A, Fifth Ohio Volunteer Cavalry; served three years and four months.

Jonathan Church, private, Company A, Fifth Ohio Volunteer Cavalry; served three years and four months.

William H. Moyer, Company F, Seventh Ohio National Guards; served 100 days; rank, a private. Also Company A, One Hundred and Seventy-fifth Ohio Volunteer Infantry; time of service, nine months; rank, Sergeant.

Lafayette Penny, Company E, Eleventh Independent Volunteer Infantry; rank, a private; served three years; lost a limb in a skirmish at New Middleton, Tenn.

Granville Patten, Company B, Forty-eighth Ohio Volunteer Infantry; served six months, and regiment consolidated with Eighty-third Ohio Volunteer Infantry, in which he seved six months; whole time, one year; private.

Sylvanus A. Patten, Company B, Forty-eighth Ohio Volunteer Infantry; time, one year; last six months served in Eighty-third Ohio Volunteer Infantry.

George W. Richards, Company H, Fifty-ninth Ohio Volunteer Infantry; veteranized; time of service, three years and ten months; high private.

Henry Carter, private, Company G, One Hundred and Seventy-eighth Regiment; served eight months.

Thomas F. Young, private, Company G, One Hundred and Seventy-fifth Ohio Volunteer Infantry; time of service, ten months.

John Robins, Company G, Forty-eighth Ohio Volunteer Infantry; a private; served three years, and was a prisoner six months at Camp Ford, Tex.

Perry Hoss, Company G, One Hundred and Seventy-fifth Ohio Volunteer Infantry; a private; was a prisoner at Cohawba and Selma, Ala., three and one-half months; time of service, ten months.

Orange D. Louderback, Company D, Fifty-ninth Ohio Volunteer Infantry; private; served three years three and one-half months; also in the United States service, Company I, Twelfth Ohio Volunteer Infantry; time, three months.

Jacob Wardlow, Company G, One Hundred and Seventy-fifth Ohio Volunteer Infantry; time, ten months; rank. a private.

Enoch A. Wisby, Fifty-ninth Ohio Volunteer Infantry; a private; served one year and three months.

Henry H. Jones, Company E, One Hundred and Eighty-first Ohio Volunteer Infantry; nine months; was Assistant Commissary.

Lieut. Levett T. Earhart, Company A, Fifth Ohio Volunteer Cavalry; enlisted as a private, and was regularly promoted for good conduct to the rank of First Lieutenant; entire time of service, three years and five months.

Benjamin Earhart, Company A, Fifth Ohio Volunteer Cavalry; time of service, three years; rank, a private.

Andrew Fry, Company K, One Hundred and Sixtieth Ohio National

Guards; 100 days; also Company E, Fortieth Ohio National Guards, two years; a private.

William Augustus Day, Company E, One Hundred and Seventy-fifth Ohio Volunteer Infantry; served nine months; a private.

Martin V. Bavis, Company B, Eighty-third Ohio Volunteer Infantry; time of service, ten months; rank, a private.

Francis M. Alexander, Fifth Indiana Volunteer Cavalry; sixteen months; a private.

Isaac Penny, Jr., Company H, Fifty-ninth Ohio Volunteer Infantry; private; died in the hospital at Murfreesboro, Tenn., May 16, 1863.

O. P. Straight, Company A, Fifth Ohio Volunteer Cavalry; rank, Sergeant; was a prisoner on Belle Isle, Va., in 1862; served three years.

Frank M. Straight, Company A, Fifth Ohio Volunteer Cavalry; private; was wounded at Coffeeville, Miss.; served three years.

Charles L. Straight, Company F, Merrill's Cavalry; served one year; rank, a private.

Elijah McGohan, Company E, One Hundred and Seventy-fifth Ohio Volunteer Infantry; private; served ten months.

William R. Chatterton, Company G, One Hundred and Fifty-third Ohio Volunteer Infantry; 100 days; rank, a private.

William Hancock, Company E, One Hundred and Seventy-fifth Ohio Volunteer Infantry; rank, private; served ten months.

John Hancock, Company F, Merrill's Cavalry; served one year; rank, a private.

Henry J. Hancock, Company F, One Hundred and Seventy-fifth Ohio Volunteer Infantry; a private; time of service, ten months.

Jeremiah Stuart, Company B, Forty-eighth Ohio Volunteer Infantry; time of service, three years; rank, a private.

David Hancock, Company F, One Hundred and Seventy-fifth Ohio Volunteer Infantry; rank, a private; time of service, ten months.

Taylor Montgomery, Company B, One Hundred and Seventy-fifth Ohio Volunteer Infantry; private; was a prisoner, taken in a skirmish near Columbia, Tenn.

Henry J. Long, Corporal, Company I, Forty-eighth Ohio Volunteer Infantry; time, one year; also Company A, Thirty-fourth Zouave Ohio Volunteer Infantry; eighteen months; was a prisoner at Andersonville almost a year.

James B. Coudrey, Company B, Eighty-third Ohio Volunteer Infantry; ten months; a private.

Samuel Davidson, Company G, Seventy-eighth Ohio Volunteer Infantry; private; time of service, eight months.

Calvin Meeker, Company D, Seventh Ohio Volunteer Cavalry; a private; time of service, two years and ten months; was a prisoner at Andersonville two months.

David Wilson, Company B, Eighty-third Ohio Volunteer Infantry; served ten months; a private.

James W. Donley, Company A, One Hundred and Seventy-fifth Ohio Volunteer Infantry; private under Capt. Johnson; time of service, ten months.

John Neal, Company A, One Hundred and Seventy-fifth Ohio Volunteer Infantry; private under Capt. Johnson; served ten months.

Reuben Wilson, Company E, One Hundred and Seventy-fifth Ohio Volunteer Infantry; private under Capt. Langstaff; served ten months.

Alexander E. Henning, Company E, One Hundred and Seventy-fifth Ohio Volunteer Infantry; a private under Capt. Langstaff; served ten months.

Vincent C. Brown, member of Twenty-ninth Ohio Volunteer Infantry; rank, private; time of service, six months.

PIKE TOWNSHIP.

Harvy Kennett, Companies I and K, Forty-eighth Ohio Volunteer Infantry; private; time of service, four years and seven months.

Alonzo Earhart, member of Fourth Independent Cavalry under Capt. Foster; rank, private; time, one year; also Company G, Seventy-eighth Ohio Volunteer Infantry; a private, and served one year.

Smith Long, a private in Company B, Forty-eighth Ohio Volunteer Infantry; one year.

John Higgins, Company K, Forty-eighth Ohio Volunteer Infantry; time, one year.

Erasmus Boyd, a private, Company A, One Hundred and Seventy-fifth Ohio Volunteer Infantry; served one year.

David E. White, a Sergeant in Company K, Twelfth Ohio Volunteer Infantry under Capt. Sloan; served three years; also was a Sergeant in Company C, Twenty-third Ohio Volunteer Infantry; time of service, one year and two months.

James L. Irvin, private in Company K, One Hundred and Twenty-sixth Ohio Volunteer Infantry; served thirteen months.

Louis Windsor, private in Company B, Forty-eighth Ohio Veteran Volunteer Infantry; served five years.

Smith Newberry, Company B, Forty-eighth Ohio Volunteer Infantry; time of service, five years.

William Evans, a private in Company B, Forty-eighth Ohio Volunteer Infantry; served three years.

Henry Wells, Company B, Forty-eighth Ohio Volunteer Infantry; rank, a private; enlisted for three years, but died in the service.

John Fry, Company G, Seventy-eighth Ohio Volunteer Infantry; a private; out eight months.

William T. Winter, Company B, Forty-eighth Ohio Volunteer Infantry; regiment consolidated into the Eighty-third; served one year; rank, a private.

Abram Winter, Company B, Eighty-ninth Ohio Volunteer Infantry; enlisted for three years; died in hospital at Carthage, Tenn., before the completion of the first year's service.

Steven Winter, Company B, Forty-eighth Ohio Volunteer Infantry; was killed at the battle of Shiloh; rank, a private; enlisted for three years.

John Winter, private, record not known.

John Tatman, One Hundred and Fifty-third Ohio National Guard; private; 100 days.

Robert Fry, Company E, Fortieth Ohio National Guards; time, two years; a private.

James Higgins was a member of the Seventh Ohio Volunteer Cavalry; rank, a private; served three years.

William Thompson, Company E, One Hundred and Seventy-fifth Ohio Volunteer Infantry; rank, a private; served ten months.

Andrew J. Thompson, Fourth Independent Cavalry under Capt. Forster; rank, a private; prisoner at Andersonville nine months; served three years. Andrew was the only person present when Gen. McPherson was killed at the battle in front of Atlanta. He (Thompson) was captured here. He is now and has been for nine years Superintendent of the Brown County Infirmary.

TOWNSHIP OFFICERS.

The following is a list of the officers of the township since 1840, which is as far back as the records have been preserved:

1840--Trustees, Samuel Wardlow and Vincent Brown; Clerk, Abram Fiscus; Treasurer, Aaron E. Day.

1841—Trustees, Daniel White, Samuel Jones, Adam Earhart; Clerk, Nicholas Pedicord; Treasurer, John Allen.

1842—Trustees, Elijah Winter, Daniel White, Luman Kimberly; Clerk, Nicholas Pedicord; Assessor, James Allen; Treasurer, John Allen.

1843—Trustees, Aaron E. Day, Isaac Thompson, Louis Vance; Clerk, John Fiscus; Assessor, James Allen; Treasurer, John Allen.

1844—Trustees, David Brannen, James Allen, Samuel Jones; Clerk, Aaron Day; Assessor, Felix Thompson; Treasurer, John Allen.

1845—Trustees, Samuel Wardlow, James Stills, William Taylor; Clerk, Robert Higgins; Assessor, Thomas E. Brown; Treasurer, Daniel Keethler.

1846—Trustees, William Taylor, David Brannon, James Brown; Clerk, T. B. Mahan; Assessor, Felix Thompson; Treasurer, Daniel Keethler.

1847—Trustees, James Brown, David Brannen, James Winter; Clerk, Robert Higgins; Assessor, Felix Thompson; Treasurer, John Allen.

1848—Trustees, James Allen, James Winter, John Stump; Clerk, James Day; Assessor, Robert Higgins; Treasurer, John Allen.

1849—Trustees, James Allen, William Thompson, John Stump; Clerk, James Day; Assessor, Robert Higgins; Treasurer, Hiram Day.

1850—Trustees, John Stump, Daniel Keethler, William Thompson; Clerk, William Whorton; Assessor, John Allen; Treasurer, Hiram Day.

1851—Trustees—James Allen, N. P. Applegate, James Brown; Clerk, William Neff; Assessor, Robert Higgins; Treasurer, Thomas Brown.

1852—Trustees, N. P. Applegate, James Allen, James Brown; Clerk, Delos Laughlin; Assessor, Adam Earhart; Treasurer, Thomas E. Brown.

1853—Trustees, N. P. Applegate, James Allen, James Brown; Clerk, William Neff; Assessor, Robert Higgins; Treasurer, Thomas E. Brown.

1854—Trustees, James Brown, William Thompson, John Thompson; Clerk, Milton Allen; Assessor, Robert Higgins; Treasurer, Thomas Brown.

1855—Trustees, John Thompson, Thomas E. McLain, Vincent Robins; Clerk, William Sammons; Assessor, John Lawson; Treasurer, Adam Earhart.

1856—Trustees, Thomas McLain, Vincent Robins, John Moyer; Clerk, Henry Jones; Assessor, Adam Earhart.

1857—Trustees, John Moyer, Vincent Robins, John Moyer; Clerk, Chambers Brown; Assessor, Thomas E. Brown; Treasurer, James Allen.

1858—Trustees, John Moyer, Alexander Thompson, Sanford Stratton; Clerk, Henry Jones; Assessor, Jarred Winter; Treasurer, James Allen.

1859—Trustees, Sanford Stratton, Alexander Thompson, Granville Patten; Clerk, Henry Jones; Assessor, Willliam B. Cowdrey; Treasurer, Adam Earhart.

1860—Trustees, Granville Patten, Alexander Thompson, Sanford Stratton; Clerk, Henry Jones; Assessor, Chambers Brown; Treasurer, Adam Earhart.

1861—Trustees, Granville Patten, Daniel Keethler, John Moyer; Clerk, Henry H. Jones; Assessor, Alexander Thompson; Treasurer, Thomas McLain.

1862—Trustees, James L. Irwin, Granville Patten, John Moyer; Clerk, John R. C. Brown; Assessor, C. W. Dougherty; Treasurer, Daniel Keethler.

1863—Trustees. Alexander Thompson, Sanford Stratton, S. Wardlow; Clerk, H. H. Jones; Treasurer, Daniel Keethler; Assessor, J. B. Langstaff.

1864—Trustees, S. Stratton, J. E. Winter, Ira B. Dunn; Clerk, V. C. Brown; Treasurer, D. Keethler; Assessor, Alexander Thompson.

1865—Trustees, S. Stratton, J. E. Winter, I. B. Dunn; Clerk, Raphael Sapp; Treasurer, D. Keethler; Assessor, Alexander Thompson.

1866—Trustees, S. Wardlow, H. Carter, A. Jacobs; Clerk, V. C. Brown; Treasurer, D. Keethler; Assessor, A. F. Higgins.

PIKE TOWNSHIP.

1867—Trustees, I. B. Dunn, Alfred Jacobs, Henry Carter; Clerk, V. C. Brown; Treasurer, Gideon Lowe; Assessor, Alexander Thompson.

1868—Trustees, A. Jacobs, I. B. Dunn, Elmore Dean; Clerk, V. C. Brown; Treasurer, G. Lowe; Assessor, Alexander Thompson.

1869—Trustees, John B. Langstaff, Elmore Dean, Perry Hoss; Clerk, V. C. Brown; Treasurer, Hiram S. Day; Assessor, Henry Jones.

1870—Trustees, William B. Cowdrey, Elmore Dean, Robert A. Brown; Clerk, Albert M. Day; Treasurer, Gideon Lowe; Assessor, Albert N. Brown.

1871—Trustees, Robert A. Brown, William B. Cowdrey, Hiram S. Day; Clerk, Albert M. Day; Treasurer, Daniel Keethler; Assessor, J. E. Winter.

1872—Trustees, David Wilson, J. Wardlow, J. E. Winter; Clerk, Jerome W. Allen; Treasurer, Daniel Keethler; Assessor, Albert Brown.

1873—Records do not show for this year who were the officers.

1874—Trustees, G. M. Blair, J. E. Winter, John M. Colthar; Clerk, Albert M. Day; Treasurer, Perry T. Dunn; Assessor, Samuel Blair.

1875—Trustees, George M. Blair, George Wilson, John Sidwell; Clerk, Albert M. Day; Treasurer, Perry T. Dunn; Assessor, Samuel Blair.

1876—Records do not show.

1877—Trustees, Robert A. Brown, J. E. Winter, Elijah McGohan; Clerk, Albert M. Day; Treasurer, Perry T. Dunn; Assessor, J. M. Dyer.

1878—Trustees, Elijah McGohan, Elias Bolander, J. E. Winter; Clerk, Albert M. Day; Treasurer, David B. Trout; Assessor, J. M. Dyer.

1879—Trustees, Elias Bolander, George Wilson, Elmore Dean; Clerk, Albert M. Day; Treasurer, David B. Trout; Assessor, Robert Werner.

1880—Trustees, Elmore Dean, G. M. Blair (Thomas Young appointed; Blair resigned), George Wilson; Clerk, Christopher C. Day; Treasurer, Granville Patten; Assessor, William C. Hancock.

1881—Trustees, George Wilson, Elmore Dean, John Sidwell; Clerk, Christopher Day; Treasurer, Frederick Bauer; Assessor, Isaac N. Jacobs.

1882—Present officials: Trustees, G. Wilson, John Sidwell, William Rogers; Clerk, Christopher C. Day; Treasurer, Frederic Bauer; Assessor, Isaac N. Jacobs.

CHAPTER IX.

EAGLE TOWNSHIP.

BY E. B. STIVERS.

EAGLE is one of the original townships of Brown County, and was formed from territory stricken off from Adams County upon the erection of Brown, in 1817.

From the date of its organization until the year 1823, most of the territory now within the boundaries of Jackson Township belonged to Eagle. The present outline of this township is nearly that of a square, and its geographical location is in the extreme northeast corner of the county.

It is bounded on the north by a portion of the east and west line separating Highland County from Brown, while on the east it is limited by a part of the dividing line between Adams and Brown. On the south, it borders on Jackson Township, and on the west it is limited by Washington.

The surface is level in the west, and undulating in the north and south, the only hill land bordering the course of Brush Creek through the township. The soil is generally productive, being, for the greater portion, limestone land, and well adapted to the production of wheat and corn. The flat land in the western part of the township is mostly a compact white clay soil, rich in all the elements of vegetable growth, except organic matter, which is characteristic of the localities known as the black maple swamps. These white clay lands, under their present culture, are not abundantly productive, but will some day, under wise culture, become the most valuable lands of the township.

The township was formerly covered with a dense growth of timber, which differed in kind and quality in the two districts above mentioned. The forest trees of the flat lands are mostly white maple, beech, several species of the oak, elm and hickory, with a dense undergrowth of hazel-brush and grapevines. This locality is especially noted for a species of wild grapes, called the "Fox grape," from its peculiar odor. The timber of the upland is white oak, black maple, ash, black walnut and some poplar, scattered among which are the smaller growths, dogwood, mulberry and redwood.

The distinct geological formation is the Cincinnati group, the predominant one of the county, the very summit of which series is attained in the northeastern portion of Eagle Township.

The agricultural products of Eagle are the chief sources of wealth of the people. The principal grains are wheat, corn and oats. Tobacco, within the last five years, has become a favorite crop with quite a number of farmers, and the quality as well as the quantity of the yield is not discouraging to those who properly cultivate and handle the crop. A few individuals are engaged in stock-raising and trading in a general way, but the greater portion of the inhabitants depend upon the products of the soil for a livelihood.

The township is well drained by Brush Creek and its tributaries, with the exception, perhaps, of a part of the western portion; but those lands are now being tiled and drained by artificial means, which is enhancing their value a great deal.

The political complexion of the township is and always has been Democratic. With 1,250 inhabitants, Eagle has a voting population of 300, 128 of whom are Republicans, and the remainder Democrats. Twenty-seven of the Republican voters are colored.

EAGLE TOWNSHIP.

Most of the heads of families are descendants of the first settlers who began to locate here about 1805. They, as a class, are sober and industrious persons, after whom the rising generation may well example. Besides the three church organizations supported in the village of Fincastle, there are some four or five others located at different points of the township. Several large Sabbath schools are sustained at many of the schoolhouses by energetic Christian persons, and which have a vast influence for good among the people.

The educational advantages of the township are such as are furnished by the common school only, yet they compare favorably, we believe, with the schools of like character throughout the county. New houses have been lately built, and generally furnished with modern improvements in school furniture, and the people are awakening to the importance of devoting more time and money to the advancement of the public schools.

Although none of the noble sons of Eagle have enrolled their names alongside of those emblazoned on the immortal pages of history, yet several have attained a degree of eminence far above the mediocre. They are not wanting in patriotic principles, as has more than once been shown when the country demanded their services. In the war of 1812, the war with Mexico, and in the late rebellion, Eagle had her representatives. In the latter war, more than two-thirds of her voting population enlisted in the cause. Scarcely a family was there that did not send a father or a son to the front, many of whom now sleep beneath Southern skies.

EARLY SETTLERS.

Among the first families that settled in Eagle Township was that of —— Livingston, who settled on the farm now resided upon by William Rhoten. Here also lived the Darling family. In 1806, William Laycock located here and built a cabin near the spring west of the road. This was the only house on the road at that time between New Market and Ripley, excepting the "old Gardner residence," in what is now Jefferson Township. Laycock, shortly after his coming, built a still-house in the woods directly east of Rhoten's present residence, and dug a ditch from the spring at the house to the still, which furnished him with an ample supply of pure water. Here Capt. Abraham Shepherd halted and refreshed his men with Laycock's brandy, while on the march to Sandusky and Detroit in 1812.

Jonas Sams came from Westmoreland County, Penn., to Kentucky, and thence to Ohio in 1803. Two years later, he settled on the head-waters of Brush Creek, in Eagle Township, on lands now owned by Milton Scott. Sams was an old hunter and Indian fighter, an expert woodsman, thoroughly familiar with frontier life. He was with Col. Crawford at his defeat and capture near the Wyandot village in 1782, and experienced the horrors of that fearful retreat. He says, in an account of that disastrous undertaking, that he and his brother, Jonathan Sams, joined Crawford's men at the Mingo Bottoms, and that, after the defeat of Crawford, he and seven others started for the fort at Wheeling, but that, after a perilous journey of ten days, four of which they were closely pursued by Indians, only he and two of his companions arrived at the point of destination, the others having been killed by their pursuers. The same paper gives the date of his birth as November 18, 1756. Of his own family, one son, Nehemiah Sams, now in his ninetieth year, is still living.

In 1807, Robert Breckenridge, who had previously purchased 1,000 acres of land on the waters of the West Fork of Brush Creek, removed from Bourbon County, Ky., and built a house on said land, near the late residence of James Wilson. Breckenridge was of Irish descent, and was born in Virginia. He was one of the few who took an active part in the early history of Eagle

Township, and he was no less active in the affairs of the county. In 1823, he was one of the Board of Commissioners that contracted for the building of the first court house at Georgetown. He was also for several years one of the Associate Judges of this county. His wife's maiden name was Mary Wright, and they had born to them thirteen children—Alexander, Samuel, William, James, Mary (Mrs. Kincaid, still living), Merrill, Rodney, Lucinda, Eliza, Salina, Margaret, Preston and Anna. John C., a grandson of Robert Breckenridge, resides on a portion of the land formerly owned by him.

The Coulter family settled on the head-waters of the West Fork of Brush Creek about 1809. William Coulter and wife first came. They were of Scotch descent, and emigrated from Pennsylvania to this county. Coulter was a powder-maker by trade, and was quite a welcome comer to the Brush Creek settlement. He was one among those from Eagle Township that served in the war of 1812. Shortly after the war, his father, James Coulter, came to his son's new home, and built a cabin a short distance from his residence, in which he lived alone and taught school for several years. He had several hundred dollars in silver, which he buried somewhere near his home before his death, and which has caused many stones to be turned and holes dug, but as yet "Coulter's piggin of silver" is safe. He had a son, John Coulter. that served in the Lewis and Clark expedition in 1803–04.

John Baker, also a Pennsylvanian, located on the farm owned at present by his son George in the year 1807.

The first settler in the Baker neighborhood was Adam Erwin. He located on the farm adjoining the Baker land on the north in 1804. Erwin built a still-house on the branch near his house, which was in operation as late as 1834. In this neighborhood resided the Records family. Spencer Records, a man of moderate education and considerable genius, built the first water-mill in the township. The Records family were Irish by birth, and came to Eagle Township in 1807.

Abraham Edgington, the first Justice of the Peace for Eagle Township after the erection of Jackson from its territory, lived at that time on the farm now owned by John Stanforth. He located there about 1810 or 1812. Benjamin Gutridge settled on land near Edgington's in 1814. He came from Kentucky.

The Alexanders came to Brush Creek in 1811. There were two brothers, John and Andrew, with their families. They came from near Stanton, Augusta Co., Va. They have numerous descendants now living in and about Fincastle. Andrew Alexander, son of John Alexander, is the oldest man living in Eagle Township. In speaking of early days in Eagle, he said: "My father, John Alexander, came here in 1811. The following year, we moved on the farm now owned by William Burns. We had for neighbors Breckenridge on the east, Cowans, Hughes and Millers, on the creek below us, but none on the west. That year, McColister was teaching in an old log cabin on the branch running through the farm now owned by J. R. Carey, and he dismissed his school and volunteered in the war. There were a plenty of deer, wild turkeys and other game in this region then, and north of where we lived were favorite hunting-grounds, where my uncle, Andrew, Jonas Sams, the Reynolds boys and Neal Washburne have spent many days." Of the early settlers he said: "Old man Murphy lived then on the Vance farm, afterward on the Widow Cross farm, and he shortly sold to Jacob Marquis, who started a tannery there. Jeremiah Fenton lived on the Fenton farm. The others that I now recollect, and who resided near here, were John Cross, Joseph Edgington, Abraham Edgington, Thomas Heatherly, the Ramseys and John McCanlas," and the others who have been previously named.

EAGLE TOWNSHIP.

Isaac Carey built a house near where J. R. Carey resides, in 1817. He came with his father's family to near Emeral, Adams County, in 1801. He served with his brothers, John and William, in the war of 1812, and, after his return, worked at the old furnaces in Adams County. In 1818, he married Miss Catharine Eyler, and immediately moved in his new home, before named, where he resided until his death, in April, 1866. Isaac Carey was a man of some note in official circles of the township and county. He was elected Justice of the Peace of Eagle Township in 1834, which position he filled for six years; afterward served as one of the Associate Judges of the county until the new Constitution abolished the office and created a Probate Judge instead. Of his family, one son, Dr. S. E. Carey, rose to considerable distinction as a man of business and learning. He graduated in the Ohio Medical College in 1844, and afterward became one of its Professors. He afterward helped to found a medical college at Indianapolis, Ind., of which he was some time one of the faculty. He always took an active part in home enterprises, and was one of the leading men in getting the C. & E. R. R. through this county.

John Bradley came to Eagle Township with his father about 1814. Mr. Bradley has seen much of the early history of the township. He resided on his father's farm, known as the Bradley residence, until within a few years, when he located in Winchester, Adams County, where he yet resides. He built the first house in Fincastle for John Frierun, and was instrumental in organizing the Methodist Church at that place. He says he cast one of the four votes polled in Eagle Township for John Quincy Adams for President in 1828. His parents came from Lancaster County, Penn., to Ohio in 1808.

Among those that located in the township from 1812 to 1820, inclusive, may be mentioned William Lurgey, Robison Spears, Samuel Masters, Abijah Moore, the Kettermans, William Denney, John Burris and John Rice.

TOWNSHIP OFFICIALS.

No very reliable information can be had concerning the early officers of the township. Probably most of the names of the early Justices of the Peace are given below, but as to the exact date of election and the term served, we can get nothing very satisfactory.

At the time of the division of Eagle Township, Stephen Reynold and James Kindle were acting as Justices. After the division, in 1823, Abraham Edgington was the first Justice of the Peace. Robert Breckenridge served in the same capacity about this time. Among some old papers formerly belonging to Francis Alexander, I found a commission from Allen Trimble, then Governor of Ohio, to Alexander, empowering him to act as a Justice of the Peace in and for Eagle Township. The date of this commission is the 8th day of June, 1829.

In 1834, Isaac Carey was elected a Justice of the township. Eli Goldsbury and Adams Morrow served in the same capacity following Carey.

William Laycock was one of the Justices, probably at the time of Alexander's election.

Daniel McLaughlin and Zeb Ketterman, about 1840.
Eli Goldsbury, from 1841 to 1845.
Robert Dunn, from ―― to 1855.
L. S. Martin, from 1859 to 1871.
J. C. Breckenridge, from 1871 to 1880.
J. H. Brown, from 1880 to 188-.
Adams Morrow, from 1853 to 1856.
P. E. Hare, from 1856 to 1871.
A. R. Skinner, from 1871 to 1877.
Nelson Long, from 1877 to 188-.

1848—Clerk, John McColgin; Trustees, Jesse Cross, Joseph Heaton, Benjamin Gutridge; Treasurer, Abraham Edgington; Constable, William Bruce.

1849—Clerk, Peter Wamacks; Trustees, James Cowan, Jesse Cross and Benjamin Gutridge; Treasurer, Adams Morrow; Constables, John Hare and Oliver Edgington; Justice of the Peace, Daniel McLaughlin.

1850—Trustees, Jesse Cross, Daniel McLaughlin, James Cowan; Treasurer, Adams Morrow; Constable, William Bruce (appointed); Clerk, P. S. Wamacks.

1851—Clerk, P. S. Wamacks; Trustees, Henry Eyler, Daniel McLaughlin, James Cowan; Constable, W. E. Bruce.

1852—Clerk, S. N. Records; Treasurer, Adams Morrow; Constable, Joseph Edie; Trustee, Zebadee Ketterman; Justice of the Peace, Chris Holmes.

1853—Clerk, S. N. Records; Treasurer, Adams Morrow; Trustees, Isaac Carey, William Tomb, Daniel Hare; Assessor, Francis Alexander; Constable, Z. Ketterman.

1854—Clerk, J. H. Bradford; Treasurer, Adams Morrow; Assessor, Daniel McLaughlin; Constable, Wilson Maddox; Trustees, Jesse Cross, Jeremiah Wilson, Daniel Denny.

1855—Clerk, S. S. Cowan; Assessor, Jesse Cross; Trustees, S. N. Records, Hugh Miller; Constable, C. N. Page; Justices of the Peace, Adams Morrow, Robert Dunn.

1856—Clerk, James Wilson; Treasurer, J. C. Breckenridge; Assessor, Lilly Stivers; Constables, E. A. Sellmon (Milton Scott, appointed); Trustees, Jesse Cross, Beasley Stivers, J. N. Records.

1857—Clerk, James Wilson; Assessor, Lilley Stivers; Treasurer, John F. Searight; Constable, J. B. Hill.

1858—Clerk, James Wilson; Assessor, Jesse Cross; Treasurer, J. F. Searight; Constable, J. B. Hill; Trustees, L. W. Brouse, J. R. Hare, A. R. Skinner.

1859—Clerk, R. B. McClanahan; Assessor, Jesse Cross; Treasurer, J. F. Searight; Constable, John Demaris; Trustees, Henry Eyler, George Cornelius, Lewis Brouse.

1860—Clerk, Z. B. Winters; Assessor, Lilley Stivers; Treasurer, J. F. Searight; Constable, John Demaris; Trustees, H. Eyler, William Borden, George Cornelius.

1861—Clerk, Z. B. Winters; Assessor, Jesse Cross; Treasurer, William Alexander; Constable, N. P. Long; Trustees, William Borden, J. Reese, G. W. Cornelius.

1862—Clerk, Z. B. Winters; Assessor, Jesse Cross; Treasurer, William Alexander; Constable, John Demaris; Justices of the Peace, Lewis Martin and P. E. Hare.

1863—Clerk, Z. B. Winters; Treasurer, William Alexander; Constable, John Demaris; Trustees, Hugh Miller, W. A. Borden, Henry Eyler.

1864—Clerk, Z. B. Winters; Assessor, John Heaton; Treasurer, Jesse Cross; Constable, D. L. Robbins; Trustees, Kindle Bowen, W. M. Robbins, L. W. Brouse.

1865—Clerk, Z. B. Winters; Treasurer, Jesse Cross; Assessor, John Heaton; Constable, D. L. Robbins; Trustees, G. W. Shaw, J. R. Hare, L. W. Brouse.

1866—Clerk, Z. B. Winters; Treasurer, John Alexander; Assessor, Beasley Stivers; Constable, D. L. Robbins; Trustees, L. W. Brouse, C. C. Eyler, G. W. Shaw.

EAGLE TOWNSHIP. 531

EARLY MARRIAGES.

September 24, 1819, Jonathan Sams and Elizabeth Bratten, by Noah Sprenger.

Be it remembered that in this day, I the undersigned, a Justice of the Peace in and for Brown County, Ohio, joined Henry Edgington and Margaret Beard, both of Eagle Township, and county aforesaid, in the solemn bonds of matrimony.
This the 5th day of August, 1819.
STEPHEN REYNOLDS, *Justice of the Peace*.

April 17, 1820, Robert Kincade and Mary Breckenridge, by Robert Moore, Justice of the Peace.

July 2, 1820, John Selmon and Hannah Reynolds, by Robert Moore, Justice of the Peace.

January 4, 1819—This day a license is issued to join George Reynolds and Hannah and Middleswart together in the bonds of matrimony according to law.
ABRAHAM SHEPHERD, *Clerk*.

September 9, 1819—This day a license issued to join Nehemiah Sams and Sally Bratten together in the bonds of matrimony according to law.

MILLS.

The early settlers of that portion of Brown (then Adams) County comprised within the present limits of Eagle Township experienced not a little inconvenience from a want of mills suitable for preparing their corn and wheat for food.

The old-time hand-mill, with its oddly constructed buhr-stones, was, indeed, quite an improvement, in a labor-saving point of view, over the clumsy pestle and mortar, yet the laboriousness of that process of preparing meal was necessarily very great. There were some three or four of the above-mentioned hand-mills in as many different settlements within the boundaries of this township when Reynolds' mill was put in operation. It was driven by horse-power, and was said to be the second of the kind erected within the present limits of Brown County, the other having been built a short time previous at Levanna, on the Ohio River. Joseph Reynolds came to Limestone (Maysville), Ky., from New York State in 1799, and, in the spring of 1800, purchased 1,250 acres of land in what is now Jackson (formerly Eagle) Township, and began clearing out a farm the same season. In 1804–05, having a large family himself, and other settlers having arrived in the vicinity, the hand-mill was found to be inadequate for the grinding of the grain of the settlement, and, after some bother in getting suitable buhrs, the horse-mill was put in operation. This supplied the wants of the people on Red Oak and Eagle Creeks, as well as those of his own immediate neighborhood, then known as the "Yankee Settlement." This mill stood on a slight elevation, a few rods east of the residence of Eli Long. Esq. The farm now owned by Long was formerly the old Reynolds homestead. Here Joseph Reynolds settled in 1800.

Previous to the year 1809, there were no mills other than the above mentioned nearer the settlement on Brush Creek in this township, than one on Cherry Fork, in Adams County; Patterson's, near what is now Hillsboro, in Highland County, and Sutton's Mill, near Decatur, within the present limits of Brown County.

About the year 1809, Spencer Records erected a small water-mill on Brush Creek, at a point about two miles below the present village of Fincastle. This was the first mill of the kind in the township. It was of the pattern known as the "tub-wheel," had but one pair of buhr-stones, and, although so very insignificant in its construction, yet, in those days, it was considered an important improvement in the settlement. It is said that Records dressed the buhr-stones from a kind of quartz found in the Sunfish Hills, Adams County, and brought them to the above-named place.

In the year 1812, Robert Breckenridge, who had lately removed from Kentucky to a large tract of land lying on the waters of Brush Creek, in Eagle Township, built a saw and grist mill on the creek, above the site of Records, and about one mile below the town of Fincastle. This was also driven by water-power, being a decided improvement on Records' little "tub-wheel," and was for a time the best mill in the vicinity. It was finally torn down, however, on account of the great labor and expense of keeping the dam repaired, the situation not being suitable for a mill of the kind, and the buhr-stones and other fixtures were removed to Breckenridge's residence, north of the creek, where he had a horse-mill constructed from them.

The term "horse-mill" was applied to that kind of mills which were driven by horse-power. The were constructed of heavy timbers, posts and cross-ties, so framed together as to support a large upright shaft or cylinder, which rested its lower extremity in a socket, and which was connected above with a set of cog-wheels, that, in turn, gave motion to the buhr-stones. The frame-work of the mill was large enough to allow the extension of a sweep or lever some ten or twelve feet long from the upright central shaft; to the lever or sweep, one or more horses were hitched, and, while a boy below vigorously applied the lash to keep up power, the "jolly miller" stood on a platform above, and manipulated the hopper and his pipe with one hand, and the old-fashioned bolting-chest with the other.

Of these horse-mills there were several in the township. Among the first built was the Kincaid Mill. It was built in 1815, by Samuel Kincaid, on his farm near Brush Creek. Later, quite a good one was built by Jacob Borris, near his residence, in the northeastern portion of the township. This mill was afterward removed to Fincastle, and the frame of it is still standing on a lot near Dr. Carey's residence.

After the removal of Breckenridge's mill from the creek to his home, John McCormick, an old soldier of the Revolution, who came from Pennsylvania to Adams County, Ohio, about the year 1812, rebuilt and greatly improved the Records Mill. In addition to the water-power, a tread-wheel, or tramp-wheel, as it is usually termed, was attached to the machinery, so that, in times of drouths and low water, the mill would not have to remain idle. There was a saw-mill connected with the grist-mill also. The McCormick Mill was for many years one of the better class of mills throughout that region. It passed under the management of various parties, and assumed almost as many different names, the last of which was the Cameron Mill.

It was torn down several years ago.

The Shreaves Mill, situated on White Oak Creek, where it cuts the northwest portion of the township, was of some local notoriety from 1845 to 1860. About the last-named date, the "Swamp Fox," a large saw-mill that had been built in 1848, on the Sardinia & Fincastle road, about two miles from the former place, for the purpose of sawing material for the plank road then under construction from Williamsburg, Clermont County, to Fincastle, Brown County, had corn and wheat buhr-stones attached to its machinery, and did considerable grinding for several years. This mill stood near the line between Washington and Eagle Townships, on the Cress farm. Greene Rose put the first saw in this mill.

The first steam-mill in the township was built at Fincastle, by Thomas Selmon and J. T. Brown, in 1843-44. This was replaced with the present one, by D. M. Sayers and S. W. Swain, in 1868. It is a two and one-half story frame, furnished with modern improvements in machinery, and has the reputation of making an excellent grade of flour. It is under the control of William Peddicord, Esq., and is known as the Eagle Mill.

EAGLE TOWNSHIP.

SCHOOLS.

The educational advantages of this region in the days of our forefathers were very limited indeed. Comparatively few they were who possessed the ability to instruct in even the rudiments of those branches of learning essential to an English education. The schoolhouses were necessarily rude in construction and furniture. The duration of the school term was not more than sixteen weeks—usually but thirteen, as the boys and girls could not be spared from the duties of farm work longer than that time; and, as that was in the winter season, when the few bad roads were at their worst, and taking into consideration, also, that many families lived two and some three miles distant from the schoolhouse, we are surprised at the advance in learning these hardy boys and girls made.

But the master was a character suited to the times and surroundings. He thoroughly believed in all—whatever their abilities or desires--walking in the pathway of knowledge, and, having physical powers at least on a par with his mental capacity, he usually carried out his theory to the letter, as many a youth could testify with " streaming eyes and striped back."

The first schoolhouse in the township, from what we can learn from the oldest living inhabitants, stood on the farm belonging at present to Joshua Carey. It was situated on the " branch," just below his house, and was of course not a very costly structure. Andrew Alexander, who recollects this house, says it was simply a poor kind of log cabin, as were all the houses in those days, built of round logs, and covered with clapboards held in position by weight-poles. The fire-place occupied one end of the structure, and a huge door the other. Light was admitted through an opening made in the side of the building by cutting out one or more logs and fitting in a frame of cross-sticks, covered with greased paper, as glass was not a procurable commodity then. The floor was laid with puncheons hewn on the school-grounds, while the seats were split from saplings and supported by pins driven into them. Along the side of the house occupied by the window was a large slab, or puncheon, supported on pins driven into the wall, and which served as a writing-desk for the entire school. The branches taught were reading, spelling, arithmetic and writing, the master furnishing each pupil with suitable quill pens. The first teacher in this school was Samuel McCollister. Some of the scholars who attended here were the Alexanders, John Miller, Hugh Miller, David Cowan, James Cowan, Dumfield Rhodes, John Murphy, Abe and Reuben Laycock and Polly Rhoades. John Records also taught this school.

The second schoolhouse stood on brush Creek, on the Breckenridge farm; Francis Alexander and John Mahan, teachers. The third house was on the farm owned by Andrew Alexander, and later known as the John McClelahan farm; Josiah Records and Francis Alexander, teachers. The date of these houses is from 1807 to 1818.

Another of the earlier schoolhouses was situated on the farm of Abraham Edgington, now known as the McVay farm. The Bakers, Edgingtons, Breckenridges, Kirkpatricks and Gutridges attended school here. John Helms was the first teacher. And still another one stood on the hill, just east of the present residence of James and Jesse Cross, north of Fincastle. School was held here for several years. The above earlier schools were all supported by subscription. The person desiring to teach would circulate a subscription paper in the neighborhood, taking as pay wheat, corn, flax, or anything in way of barter, when money could not be had, and, if he could get subscriptions sufficient to realize $8 or $10 per month. he would open a school. The tuition was from $1.50 to $2 per scholar for a term of thirteen weeks. No examinations of teachers were held, and any one might teach who could " read, write and cipher." After the formation of school districts and election of local Directors, subscriptions were secured by them. About 1830, some public funds were added to the subscription. Until 1840, even schoolhouses were built by subscription. In 1852, township districts were divided into subdistricts, the tuition funds raised by taxation, and schools put on a better and more liberal basis.

About 1820, a schoolhouse was built in the northwestern portion of the township, near the present residence of William Borden, and known as the Ketterman Schoolhouse. In 1834, the first schoolhouse was erected on the present site of Fincastle. Saily McNeely and a Miss Wylie were among the first teachers. The house was built of hewn logs, covered with an oak-shingle roof, and stood on the lot now occupied by the Christian Church. The first frame school building in the township was built in Fincastle in 1847. It stood on the lot lying in the southeast angle, formed at the crossing of School and Cooper streets. This was occupied until 1881, when the present building, in the south end of town, and fronting the Hillsboro & Ripley Turnpike, was erected.

THE SUB-SCHOOL DISTRICTS.

The sub-school districts in Eagle Township number eight in all. District No. 1 is located in the northeastern portion of the township, near the residence of John Dunn. The house is a frame, in good repair and is known as the McVay Schoolhouse. The district enumerates—white males, 31; females, 18; total, 49; no colored pupils. Wages paid last school year, $30 per month for first quarter; $33.33⅓ for second quarter.

District No. 2 includes the town of Fincastle and vicinity. The house has been lately erected, and is furnished with patent desks and other improvements. The district enumerates—white males, 28; females, 38; colored, 1; total, 67. Wages paid, $25 per month for first quarter; $30 per month for second quarter. Nine months school, including summer term.

District No. 3 is located in the southeastern portion of the township. The house is on Peter Roselot's farm, and is in good repair. The district enumerates—males, 27; females, 26; colored, 2; total, 55. Wages paid last school year, $33.33⅓ per month.

District No. 4 is in the southwestern portion of the township. The house has been lately rebuilt and newly furnished. The enumeration of this district is—white males, 27; females, 18; total, 45. No colored pupils. Wages paid last school year, $35 per month.

District No. 5 is in the northwestern part of the township, and is one of the largest. The house is situated at the crossing of the Fincastle & Sardinia and Arnheim & Mowrytown roads, and is widely known as the Borden Schoolhouse. The district enumerates—males, 28; females, 27; total, 55. Wages paid last school year, $33.33⅓ per month.

District No. 6 is the colored school of the township. The district includes most of the territory known as "The Settlement," and, although somewhat extensive in scope, is comparatively meager in point of numbers. The enumeration is—males, 24; females, 19; total, 43. Wages, $33.33⅓ per month.

District No. 7 is one of the fractional districts of the township, including a portion of Highland County. It lies in the northwest portion, and is known as "Dixie." The district in this township enumerates—males, 13; females, 12. Draws from Highland County—males, 17; females, 15. Total number of pupils in the district, 57. Wages paid in 1881–82, $35 per month.

District No. 8 is the largest district in the township, and is located in the southern portion. The house was built in 1879, and is in good repair. It is situated near the residence of H. L. Vance, and is known as the South Fincastle Schoolhouse. The enumeration in 1881 was—males, 35; females, 41; total, 76. Wages paid teacher, $35 per month.

Eagle Township has sent forth many excellent teachers "to rear the tender thoughts" and "teach the young idea how to shoot." Among the present resident teachers may be mentioned M. L. Abbott, Waldo Hare, Lizzie Elliott, Carrie Laney, A. N. Overstake, C. B. Stratton, Amos Eyler, Elzaphin Sayers, the Misses Fenton and T. M. Hare.

CHURCHES.

United Brethren Church.—Meetings for worship were held at private houses until about 1820, when the United Brethren Association erected a log house near the present site of the Borden Schoolhouse. The building was used both for church and school purposes, and was generally known as the Ketterman Schoolhouse. The association met regularly at the schoolhouse at this point until within the last year, when, through the activity and liberality of some of the members, a new and commodious frame church has been erected. It stands near the school building, on a lot given by John Euvard, one of the oldest living members of the church at this place.

The first minister in charge of the church here was Rev. Bessie. Following him, Revs. Toppin, Harrison and Davis ministered to the spiritual welfare of the organization. Rev. George Hempleton is the minister in charge at present.

Some of the more active members of the church, those who have labored zealously for the growth of the society, are John Euvard, William Parish, T. A. Borden, John McFadden, William Scott and William McFadden.

Crum Chapel.—This church was organized by a body of Methodists in 1855. The church lot was donated by John Denny. The house is a frame, and is situated near Denny's residence, in the eastern portion of the township. Dedicated by Elder Crum.

Christian Chapel.—Elsewhere mention is made of the organization of the Christian Church in this township. The first church, as there stated, was built in 1842. This was a frame building, of very poor accommodations. In 1867, the members felt that a more commodious house was absolutely necessary for their accommodation, and accordingly their present neat and comfortable brick chapel was completed. Elder J. P. Daughtery delivered the dedicatory sermon, in the presence of a large audience, in September (we believe) of above given year. There were present on this occasion quite a number of noted ministers of the church, prominent among whom was Elder Mathew Gardner. The church was first organized at Fincastle, by Alexander McClain, a man of fair talents and of some notoriety forty years ago. Of the early members, Thomas Selmon, John Alexander, Sr., William Marsh and David Selmon may be named.

The Disciples' Church at Fincastle, as has been stated, was built in 1851. The minister in charge at that time was Rev. Daniel Dillon. Isaac Carey and family, Andrew and Spencer Records and their families, were among earliest members.

The Methodist Episcopal Church, built at Fincastle in 1841, and which is still in use, was dedicated by Presiding Elder W. H. Raper. J. W. Clark and Rev. Steward had charge of this organization in its infancy. Robert Shepherd, John McKnight, John Manker, David Denny and Orin Basset, early members.

There was at one time an Associate Reformed Church at Fincastle.

The Baptist Church (colored).—In 1818, a large tract of land was purchased in the western part of Eagle Township, by the agents of Samuel Gist, for homes for his slaves in Virginia, whom he had lately freed. Shortly after their coming here, a Baptist association was formed, and, soon after, a church was built, which is still standing. It is a log building, and stands near the C. & E. R. R., about one mile west of South Fincastle Station. Rev. Charles Smith took a prominent part in helping organize the church, baptizing fifty persons in one day. Most of the persons who settled these lands became members of this organization. Their names, with an account of the settlement, are given elsewhere.

The Methodist Episcopal Church (colored) was built some years after the Baptist Church. The present building is a very comfortable frame, situated on the Fincastle & Sardinia road, a short distance from Five Points Station, on C. & E. Ry.

CEMETERIES.

"All that tread
The globe are but a handful, to the tribes
That slumber in its bosom."

" The majestic and courtly roads which monarchs pass over, the way that the men of letters tread, the path the warrior traverses, the short and simple annals of the poor, all lead to the same place, all terminate, however varied in their routes, in that one enormous house which is appointed for all living."

However great the privations and self-denials of our pioneer forefathers, however successful in the conquest of their undertakings, they, like " all that tread the globe," have to meet one common enemy—Death, who conquers all.

The Aerl Cemetery.—The above " hallowed spot " is the oldest place of burial in the township. It is situated in the northeastern portion of the township, on the farm owned by the widow of James Wilson, lately deceased, and formerly known as the Aerl farm, originally a part of the Breckinridge purchase. It lies just a few rods east of the old Breckinridge home, which is still standing, and contains something over one acre of ground. It is in a state of neglect at present, although some fresh-made mounds met our eyes, the walks and many of the graves being overgrown with weeds and briars.

It was made a place of burial as early as the year 1809, Elias Boatman being the first person interred there. Shortly following, two women, named Davis and Miller respectively, were buried near Boatman, and from that time until the present it has been a place of public interment.

In looking through this " city of the dead," with its quaint old headstones, blackened by the storms of many winters, we find recorded thereon the names of many who took an active part in the pioneer history of Eagle Township.

The following are a few of them:

Adam Erwin, died March 30, 1844, aged eighty years eight months and twenty-seven days. Nancy, his wife, died in 1860, aged eighty-three years.

Jeremiah Fenton, died November 19, 1863, in his eighty-fifth year. Susan, his wife, died March 8, 1828, aged forty-seven years.

Stephen Carey, died February 29, 1832, in his sixty-seventh year.

Joseph Eyler, died July 29, 1839, in his eightieth year. Mary Ann, his wife, died March 13, 1841, in her seventy-fifth year.

Solomon McVay died March 3, 1875, in his ninetieth year.

Elder Charles Payne died May 24, 1857, aged eighty-five years.

William Butlar, born in 1771, near Boston, England, died November, 1875.

William Lurguy, died in 1862, in his eighty-ninth year.

John Alexander, died March 3, 1832, in his seventy-seventh year. Jannett, his wife, died September 19, 1836, in her seventieth year.

John Records, died October, 1872, aged eighty years.

Abraham Edgington, died August 2, 1848, aged sixty eight years three months and two days.

Isaac Aerl died February 23, 1851, in his sixty-ninth year.

Patrick McLaughlin died August 19, 1848, aged seventy-four years five months and seven days.

John Cuss, died April 11, 1849, in his eighty-fourth year.

Dr. John Buchanuan, died March 30, 1859, in his forty-second year.

Samuel King Stivers, died August 7, 1864, in his seventy-eighth year. Mary Creed Stivers, wife of above, died January 3, 1868, aged seventy-seven years.

Among those buried here who heroically sacrificed their lives in the struggle to maintain the Union, and whose resting-place should never be forgotten while the stars and stripes protect our homes, are Capt. La Fayette Hare, John Edgington, Jesse Breckenridge, William Breckenridge, Corwin Bell, John Sayers, Richard Cowan, Lawrence Smith, Amos Rees, Samuel Pursel, William Black, Thomas Wilson, William Tigart, Nelson Records and John Hare.

THE FINCASTLE CEMETERY.

As early as the year 1864, from a want of family lots in the old Aerl Cemetery, it was urgently demanded that a new burial-place be selected in a suitable and convenient part of the township. But it was not until the year 1866 that the present beautiful site occupied by the Fincastle Burying-Grounds was determined upon. The grounds occupy the northwestern corner of what was once the Fincastle Fair Grounds, and a more beautiful spot for the final resting-place of the dead could not have been found in the township.

The cemetery is surrounded by a substantial stone fence, and from the arrangement of the walks and shrubbery, presents a very neat appearance to the passer-by.

The first interment in this cemetery was the remains of Dr. Samuel Laney. His grave is just to the left of the gate fronting the Ripley & Hillsboro Turnpike. And strange to say, his was the only grave in the cemetery for more than one year after his interment. In thinking of this, we are reminded of the words of Prentice:

> "Thou sleepest here, all, all alone!
> No other grave is near thine own.
> 'Tis well, 'tis well; but oh, such fate
> Seems very, very desolate."

The Burris Cemetery is a family graveyard, and is situated on the farm of John Burris, in the northeastern portion of the township.

The colored people in "the settlement," in the western part of the township, have burial-grounds near the Baptist and Methodist churches.

ROADS.

The roads of this, like those of other portions of the West, at the time of first settlement, were mere paths traced by the deer, elk, buffalo and other wild animals, with an occasional well-beaten trail found by the Indians. One of these latter trails was formerly well defined in its course across Eagle Township, and was widely known as

YORK'S TRACE.

It crossed near the Stivers settlement, south through the James Wilson farm, thence near the old salt wells, on Eagle Creek, in Jackson Township, through to Logan's Gap, on the Ohio River. Tradition tells us that an old hunter and trapper named York, "blazed" the trees along this once Indian trail, whence it became known as York's Trace. Some of his bear-traps were still standing in the vicinity as late as 1818.

THE HILLSBORO & RIPLEY TURNPIKE.

This was surveyed about 1836 by Williams Bros., of Cincinnati, and Samuel K. Stivers. The general direction of this road is along the course of the old road that connected the above-named places, and which was the first public highway through this section. Although the necessary funds were raised by the people of Eagle Township to complete this turnpike through it, yet, by some "crookedness," or misapplication of the money, the people in this and Jackson Township, also those in White Oak and Concord Townships, in Highland County, were "left in the mud."

As proof of the wrong done the citizens of Eagle Township in the construction of the above-named turnpike, we give the following list of names of residents of the township, with amount subscribed and paid by each:

Joseph Heaton, $250; J. N. Records, $300; J. McKnight, $300; Tom Selmon, $250; Adams Morrow, $300; Moore Edgington, $200; Isaac Carey, $300; James Cowan, $200; David Cowan, $50; Joe Massie, $50; Brice Edgington, $50; Andrew Alexander, $50; John Alexander, $50; Charles Welsh, $50; Jesse Cross, $150; S. King Stivers, $300.

THE PLANK ROAD.

The plank road that was to connect Williamsburg, Clermont County, and Fincastle, of Brown County, was the next road scheme following the Hillsboro & Ripley pike, by which the people were again induced to subscribe liberally, and, as usual, were "left in the mire."

About the year 1850, some very prominent men of the county took up the plausible theory of building plank roads throughout the county, instead of turnpikes, as the former could be built much cheaper than the latter and were quite durable. And as that seemed a novel way of utilizing the extensive forests of this region, of course the people readily fell in with the plans of the agitators.

The proposed plan was to extend the plank road then under construction from Batavia to Williamsburg, Clermont County, from the latter point via Mt. Oreb and Sardinia, to Fincastle, of this township and county. This was an idea. Fincastle would be the terminus of the road, and having already the funds paid for the proposed turnpike aforementioned, the town would rapidly increase in wealth and population. Dr. Carey, believing in the wisdom of the scheme, urged the appointment of meetings for the discussion of the subject. Meetings were held. The people became enthusiastic over plank roads. They subscribed liberally to further its progress; the road-bed was graded; timber felled and sawed into planks, a few of which were laid between Sardinia and Fincastle; they (the planks, of course) curled and warped up in the sun, the trees ceased falling, the mills stopped for want of logs and—the plank road disappeared in the mud.

THE HILLSBORO & RIPLEY PIKE.

The Hillsboro & Ripley pike deserved attention again. Plank roads were not profitable investments. Besides, the wrong done the fathers in the matter of the turnpike deserved righting by the sons. The gap in the pike through this township should be completed. This subject was agitated frequently from 1850 to 1878. Then the proper plan for constructing the road was advocated, namely, the people interested in the road to raise 20 per cent of its estimated cost, the remainder to be raised on taxable property of the

EAGLE TOWNSHIP.

county, and secured by interest-bearing bonds. This ignored "stock companies," and was liberal enough in its general tenor.

Through the energy of the members of the State Legislature from this county, a special act to authorize the Commissioners of Brown County, Ohio, to construct a free turnpike road from the terminus of the Ripley & Hillsboro Turnpike to Highland County line, was passed April 17, 1878. Immediately after the passage of this act, the following paper was circulated among the people by several of the leading citizens:

> We, the undersigned, agree to pay the amount set opposite our respective names, at the time and in the manner prescribed by the Commissioners of Brown County, Ohio, to aid in constructing a free turnpike road, beginning at the Highland County line on the farm of Peter Overstake, and running on or near the line of the Ripley & Hillsboro State road; provided, and it is hereby understood and agreed, that all subscriptions made hereto *in work*, shall be paid at the time and rate fixed by said County Commissioners.

The subscriptions in work amounted to $500, and in cash to $1,700. The subscriptions being presented to the Board of County Commissioners, and the act of the Legislature relating to the turnpike, the board, on the 15th day of June, 1878, resolved to improve the road. Dr. S. E. Carey, James F. Cross and S. Y. Hamilton gave bond to the sum of $5,000 to secure the payment of the subscriptions, and in due time the road was completed.

THE CINCINNATI & EASTERN RAILWAY.

The Cincinnati & Eastern Railway was put in operation in 1877, the first train passing over the road through Eagle Township August 7 of that year.

The road is intended to connect the coal fields of Jackson County, Ohio, with the city of Cincinnati. It was first to extend only to Winchester, Adams County, but is at present building rapidly east of that point toward its destination. The people of Eagle Township labored energetically and subscribed liberally to the funds for grading the above road.

South Fincastle Station was created upon the completing of the road through the township, and William Peddicord was appointed first station agent.

THE "COLORED SETTLEMENT."

The colored settlement in Eagle Township was made in 1818, by a number of the former slaves of Samuel Gist, a wealthy banker, resident of London, England, and an extensive land-owner and slaveholder in the United States.

It is not known that Gist ever visited his plantation here, or that he ever saw a single slave that cultivated his lands, but all was left to the management of resident agents appointed by him. These lands lay in the counties of Hanover, Amherst, Goslin and Henrico, Va., and included some of the finest plantations in the "Old Dominion."

In 1808, desiring to make ample provision for the future happiness of those who had so abundantly filled his coffers by their servitude, Gist made a will, the intent of which was certainly benevolent, but which has been most wretchedly executed. This document, of fifty-eight closely written pages, is a study within itself. It begins: "This is the last will and testament of me, Samuel Gist, of Gower street, in the parish of St. Giles, in the city of London, of the county of Middlesex, England."

After bequeathing various valuable estates and large sums of money to his only daughter, he designates what property and sums of money shall fall to the numerous persons who have been in his employ, and most explicitly does he provide for his slaves in Virginia, who numbered nearly one thousand souls!

Relative to them, the will provides that at his death, his "slaves in Virginia shall be set free." That his lands there shall be sold, and comfortable homes in a free State be purchased for them with the proceeds. That the revenue from his plantations the last year of his life be applied in building schoolhouses and churches for their accommodation. That all money coming to him in Virginia be set aside for the employment of ministers and teachers to instruct them. That " care be taken to make them as comfortable and happy as possible."

In 1815, Samuel Gist died, and Wickham, of Richmond, Va. (in conjunction with his father-in-law, Page), who had been appointed Gist's agent, proceeded to execute his will. Accordingly, through parties in Hillsboro, Ohio, 1,122 acres of land near Georgetown, and 1,200 acres west of Fincastle, in Eagle Township, were purchased for homes for these slaves. These lands were covered with thickets of undergrowth and sloughs of stagnant water, and were almost valueless at that time for any purpose other than pasturage. Here in June, 1818, came nearly 900 persons, a part of whom located on the Georgetown lands, the remainder on the Fincastle purchase. Their "comfortable homes" lay in the wild region about them; the education they received was in the stern school of adversity. As a matter of course, they did not prosper. Some who were able returned to Virginia. Others built rude huts and began clearing away the forest. What little money they had was soon spent. Scheming white men planned to get their personal property. They became involved in numerous law suits among themselves, and so from various causes they were reduced almost to pauperism. In later years, their lands have been sold, so that at present but few families remain as relics of this once large settlement. Among the first families that settled in this township were the following persons, most of whom had families:

Jacob Cumberland, George Cumberland, Samuel Hudson, Gabriel York, James Gist, Gabriel Johnson, Joseph Locust, James Cluff, —— Davis, Sol Garrison, —— Parsons, —— Williams, Glascow Ellis and Tom Fox. "Old Sam Hudson," as he was familiarly known, was an odd character, and many anecdotes are yet related of him. At one time, he was sent to the State Prison at Columbus for making unlawful use of another man's horse, and it so happened that a white man named Demitt accompanied him for a like offense. Upon being interrogated as to his occupation, Sam answered, "Preacher ob de Gospel!" Turning to Demitt, the officer asked, "What's your occupation?" "I clerk for Sam," was the shrewd reply.

Richard Cumberland (" Blind Dick "), Meredith Cumberland, Taylor Davis, Moses Cumberland, Ephraim Johnson and Winston Cumberland were also born in Virginia.

FINCASTLE.

Fincastle is the oldest town in Eagle Township, having been laid out by John Alexander, Sr., in the year 1835. The town was platted by Col. S. K. Stivers, and named by him after Fincastle, Va.

The first house in the town was built for John Frierson, on Lot No. 6, by John Bradley in 1835. Frierson shortly afterward opened a dry goods and notion store in the building. It is still standing, and was for many years the office of Dr. S. E. Carey. Dr. Samuel McElhaney was the first resident physician, he having located in the village in the spring of 1838.

A hotel was opened by William Parish in tha fall of 1837, and about the same date Jesse Edgington and G. W. McClellan commenced smithing and horse-shoeing in the town. The M. E. Church was erected in 1841 and the New Light, or Christian, in 1842. The steam saw and grist mill was built by Selmon & Brown in 1844, and thus it was the town of Fincastle began that existence which it has maintained without any serious changes until the present day.

EAGLE TOWNSHIP.

The only industrial scheme of any note ever in operation in the village was the carriage and wagon shop opened by John Alexander, in 1858, and continued until a few years ago.

Cooper shops of some local note were operated rather extensively from 1850 to 1865 by William Bell, Lilly Stivers and Joseph E. Winters.

Thomas Selmon operated a tress-hoop factory for several years. He began operations here in 1837, and for eight or ten years employed forty or fifty workmen.

The village at present contains about 125 inhabitants. There is one hotel, the Cottage House, opened by the present proprietress, Mrs. J. E. Winters, in the year 1840.

Two of the three churches have been mentioned above. The other one is the Disciples, or what is better known, "Campbellite" Church, organized in 1851.

The town supports two dry goods and grocery stores, one of which is owned by W. T. Hicks, the other by Winters & Hare.

The one blacksmith shop is owned at present by E. W. Sanders. William Bell still continues the old cooper shop. The steam grist and flour mill has been noticed under the proper head. Dr. Jesse Baird is the resident physician. John Phist carries on a boot and shoe shop.

The merchants who have been located here since 1837 are Moore Edgington, who built the second house in town; Brice Edgington, John Thompson, Adams Morrow, Manker & Son, John and Joseph Eyler, Milton Robins, John Erwin, Leroy Marshall, R. H. Hilling, D. M. Sayers, Peddicord Bros., Richard Ewan, Gilbert & Williamson, J. F. Searight, John Alexander and the present ones, given above.

Physicians—Drs. Carey, Rogers, Field, Viers, Buchanan, Pettijohn, Heaton, Shelton, Beheymer, Wilkins and Page.

Inn-keepers—Adams Morrow, in the spring of 1838; Louis Van Winkle, Milton Robins, Milton Scott, James Thompson and D. M. Sayers, from 1840 to 1867.

THE FINCASTLE FAIRS.

In September, 1855, a meeting of the leading citizens of Fincastle and vicinity was held and arrangements perfected to hold an exhibition of the better grades of live stock of the locality. Fincastle was selected as the place for holding it, and the display was made in the streets of the village. The result of this was so gratifying to the projectors of the scheme, that it was determined to repeat the exhibition the following year. This was done. The Christian Church was used for the display of the floral department, and the stock was exhibited in the meadow north of Mrs. Hare's residence. The following year, the stock ring was formed in the field north of where the old Associate Reformed Church stood.

These fairs, which were held but one day each, proved a source of both pleasure and profit; so much so, indeed, that a joint-stock company was formed among the citizens, and measures taken to secure suitable grounds for holding the next annual exhibition. A beautiful woodland north of Fincastle was leased, and the grounds put in proper condition for the coming season.

P. E. Hare was elected President of the association; D. M. Sayers, Vice President; Dr. S. E. Carey, Treasurer, and John Duffey, Secretary. The first fair was held on these grounds in 1858. This and those of the years 1859 and 1860 were largely attended, and continued five days each. Extensive preparations were making for the season of 1861, but the breaking-out of the rebellion frustrated the undertaking, and so ended the Fincastle A. & M. Association. The grounds were sold in 1866, and the Fincastle Cemetery now occupies the northwest portion of them.

VANCEBURG.

The little village of Vanceburg, or South Fincastle* Station and Post Office, was laid out by H. L. P. Vance, County Surveyor, on the farm of H. L. Vance, June 15, 1879.

The village is situated on the Cincinnati & Easiern Railway, at the crossing of the Hillsboro & Ripley Turnpike, two miles south of Fincastle.

The streets north and south are Pike, Oak, High and Vine. Cross streets are Broadway, Gum and Maple. The town plat contains eight acres.

Jonathan Burris purchased the first lot, on the corner of Broadway and Pike, on which he erected storeroom and dwelling. J. H. Brown purchased Lot No. 2, and erected storeroom and dwelling in 1880. W. M. Brown purchased Lot No. 12 about the same date, and erected wareroom and dwelling.

Thus began the village of Vanceburg, which, in the course of three years, has gained in a business point of view what Fincastle has been nearly fifty in acquiring. So much for a railroad.

The town at present contains two dry goods stores, owned by F. M. Plank and J. H. Brown, respectively; one blacksmith shop, Fred Hienche, proprietor; one drug store, Lee Erwin, proprietor, and one saloon; also telegraph office, railway depot, express office and post office. William Peddicord was first Postmaster and station agent. John Haines was the first blacksmith, and W. M. Brown one of the first merchants.

BERNARD.

This is a railroad station and post office on the Cincinnati & Eastern Railway, about two miles west of Vanceburg. The place is better known as Five Points, so named from the intersection of that number of roads at this place. The village contains two dry goods stores, one blacksmith shop and a few dwellings. The African M. E. Church is near this point.

JOHN MORGAN'S RAID.

On the 7th of July, 1863, the successful rebel raider, John Morgan, with about 2,500 men, crossed the Ohio River at Brandenburg, over into Indiana, and after sacking Corydon and Salem, turned his line of pillage up the river. This threw the river towns into consternation. Ripley, in this county, from the strong Union sentiment that prevailed there, had long feared an attack, and now waited with "fear and trembling" for Morgan's coming. The militia of the interior towns and surrounding country were given notice to be ready at a moment's warning to go to her rescue. On the 14th of the month, the alarm was given that Morgan was approaching, and to hasten with all speed to Ripley. They went, but no Morgan came to Ripley. No; while the brave militiamen of old Eagle were waiting with clenched fists and drawn clubs for Morgan at Ripley, he and his raiders were spreading terror and consternation in their own dear homes. Such great excitement never prevailed here as at that time. The word came that Morgan was at Sardinia, destroying everything before him. Women would frantically seize bed-clothes or some piece of house furniture and run pell-mell for the woods, corn-fields, and one very well remembered old lady actually buried her parlor mirror. What men were at home were engaged in secreting their horses, and some were so thoughtful as to secrete themselves. One very prominent Unionist cheered the raiders with "Hurrah for Vallandigham!" So passed the ever memorable 24th of July, 1863.

The main body of Morgan's men passed through Eagle Township along the

---

*The railroad station was named "South Fincastle" by the railroad company, hence the village is *generally* so called.

road leading from Sardinia to Winchester. They took a few horses, but further than that did no serious damages. The next day, Hobson's men came along in hot pursuit of Morgan, but nevertheless took time to scour the surrounding county to take the better horses that had been brought in from "the brush."

TORNADO OF 1860.

On the 21st of May, 1860, occurred one of the most frightful storms that ever swept over this region within the recollection of the oldest inhabitants. The storm came from the southwest, and struck Fincastle about 4 o'clock and continued to rage without ceasing for one hour. There had been no indications of a storm that day further than an unusual calmness of the atmosphere, and people were taken by surprise at their work, many quite a distance from shelter. No lives were lost in this vicinity, but houses and barns were blown down and many persons escaped death as by a miracle. Many orchards were totally destroyed, and great damage was done the forests, particularly the maple groves.

ANCIENT REMAINS.

In the mounds and ancient fortifications which are scattered over that vast scope of country stretching from the Appalachian system to the base of the Rocky Mountains, the territory occupied within the limits of Ohio is the most prolific. It is stated by good authority that no fewer than 10,000 mounds and 1,500 inclosures or circumvallations of earth and stone are within its borders.

The origin of these ancient remains has been a problem of no small moment to the archæologist, but all agree that they are the work of a race of people pre-historic to even the ancestors of the Indians.

The purpose for which these mounds and other works were erected is also problematic. It is inferred from the outline and general structure of some of the inclosures that they were works of defense. A noted one of this character is "Fort Ancient," in Warren County, yet we are not to suppose that all the inclosures of the various forms, structure and sizes were used for that purpose.

The mounds seem to have been erected as the funeral piles of the dead. In proof of this, it is found upon making excavations from the sides to the center of a tumulus that human skeletons still in a degree of preservation exist therein, while unmistakable traces of human remains are found within a few feet of the surface. These facts have led to the supposition that many of the tumuli were generations in forming. The theory is that a mound was formed by a succession of burials, commencing with a layer first upon the ground, with a small tumulus of a few feet over the first body; then the next at its side raised to an equal height, and so on till the base was of proper dimensions. Then, by a succession of burials on this base, a second layer would be formed, and in like manner layer after layer may have been added, until after the lapse of a few generations the mound would be completed.

Some of the tumuli are supposed to have been altars used in the religious rites of those who erected them. Others again, from their situation, are thought by some to have been used as watch-towers. But for whatever purpose they may have been erected, they stand to-day durable records of a race of people, all other races of whom have long since perished.

A tumulus about which there has been considerable speculation at different times, stands on the James Wilson farm, in the northeastern portion of Eagle Township and something over one mile east of Fincastle. From its situation on the most elevated portion of the table-lands north of Brush Creek, quite an extensive view of the surrounding country can be had from its summit. It is conical shaped, and measures in circumference about its base 103 yards; its vertical height is about twenty-five feet. Its summit is covered with locust and coffee-nut trees, some of which are over two feet in diameter. Several borings have been made from the summit down in a vertical line, but as yet nothing worth mentioning has been discovered within it. On the north of this mound, and but a few rods from it, are several bowl-shaped excavations, while to the west a few hundred yards is another tumulus, but much smaller than the above described one.

In the field southeast of the large mound is a ring about twelve feet wide and two hundred and twenty-five yards in circumference. This was formerly two or three feet in height, but from being plowed over many years, is now nearly on a level with the surrounding surface, yet it is clearly discernible from the color of the clay of which it is formed. In the woods south of this is another figure of an elliptical form, and quite well defined.

Mr. Levi Williams found on his farm, in the extreme northwest corner of the township, in 1871, a relic that attracted the attention of a great many persons, although some of the more incredulous supposed it to be the production of Mr. Williams, he being a very clever artisan in stone.

The relic referred to was nothing more or less than an effigy pipe, having the form of a human being in a crouching position, with the elbows clasped against the sides of the chest, hands and forearms resting on the knees. The image has considerable obscure ornamentation on its different parts, and is considered modern, the work of the red man. It is formed from free stone, is about fifteen inches in longest diameter and four or five inches in the shortest. It is now in the collection of H. H. Hill, of Cincinnati, Ohio.

Alva Moon.

CHAPTER X.

JEFFERSON TOWNSHIP.

BY W. P. WILLIAMS.

JEFFERSON TOWNSHIP is situated in the eastern part of the county, the second township from the eastern boundary and third from the northern boundary of the county. It is bounded on the east by Byrd Township, on south by Union Township, on the west by Pleasant Township, and on the north by Franklin and Jackson Townships. From the organization of the county until June, 1853, what is now Jefferson Township was a part of Byrd Township, when a survey was made and the present limits established. We have appended the official action of the township authorities in the matter of the organization, as taken from the township records:

"A large number of the citizens of Byrd Township, Brown Co., Ohio, believing that it would be not only for the convenience of a large majority of the citizens of said township, but that, justice and mercy demanding that our citizens should be released from the hard task of wading in mud through rain, and standing on beech roots, on election days, it was absolutely necessary that a new township should be formed, had meetings called, consulted together in regard to the matter, and finally concluded to take the necessary steps for the accomplishment of the aforesaid object. Accordingly, notices were posted in three public places within the limits of the proposed new township, of which the following is a copy:

NOTICE.

There will be presented to the Commissioners of Brown County, Ohio, at their next June meeting, a petition praying for a new township to be composed of the surplus territory over the constitutional limits of Byrd, Jackson, Franklin and Pleasant Townships, to be called Jefferson, beginning on the limits of Byrd and Jackson Townships where Eagle Creek crosses the line of Jackson and Byrd above Cosslett's Mill, thence to the Union Township line at such point as will leave the statutory limits in Byrd; thence with said Union line to the line of Pleasant on Straight Creek, including that part of Pleasant lying on the east side of Straight Creek; thence with the Pleasant line or up said creek to the Franklin Township line; thence northeast to the Franklin and Jackson Township line, so far as by running a southeast line to the beginning, to include territory for the proposed Township of Jefferson.

May 7, 1853.

In pursuance of the above notice, a petition was presented to the Commissioners of Brown County, at their June meeting, praying for the establishment of a new township, as described in the notice. Whereupon, a survey was granted by the Commissioners, and, when Byrd Township was surveyed, it was found to contain territory sufficient for the constitutional limits of two townships, so that no territory was required from any of the three townships of Jackson, Franklin or Pleasant. So the Commissioners granted the new township, which consisted merely of a portion of Byrd Township, and gave it the name of Jefferson Township.

For the purpose of organizing the new township, the Commissioners caused the following notice to be posted in different parts of said township:

NOTICE.

To the Electors of Jefferson Township, Brown County, Ohio:

You are hereby notified to meet at the tavern of John C. Davis, at the cross-roads in said township, on the 16th day of August, A. D. 1853, between the hours of 6 o'clock and ten o'clock A. M. of said day, and then and there proceed to elect one Township Clerk, three Trustees, and one Treasurer for said Township of Jefferson.

July 27, 1853.
S. MOORE and
JOHN WRIGHT,
Commissioners.

At the election as above ordered W. B. Logan, Michael Benner and James Glaze were elected Trustees; John Glaze, Treasurer; and J. N. Salisbury, Clerk.

Running through the township from north to south by a zigzag course is a ridge, or water-shed, dividing the township about equally. Water flowing east of this is carried into Eagle Creek, and that flowing west of it joins the waters of Straight Creek. Near this ridge, some of the land is somewhat marshy and flat, but not too much so for agricultural purposes. On these lands considerable timothy grass is grown. After passing the grass lands, the country is diversified by hills and narrow valleys along small streams, which have their origin in the low lands adjacent to the water-shed.

The soil, especially along the streams, is generally fertile, producing fine crops of oats, corn, wheat and tobacco.

The area of timber is considerably reduced. The demand might be said to exceed the supply, many farmers having to go into adjoining townships for rails with which to inclose their farms. The principal kinds of timber in the low lands are beech, with a sprinkling of oak on the hills, and along the streams the timber is walnut, ash, oak, linn and sugar.

Thus far, manufacturing has received but little attention, excepting of a local character. The principal streams are Eagle Creek on the eastern, and Straight Creek on the western boundaries of the township. Eagle Creek rises in the adjoining county of Adams, and flows a short distance through Jackson Township, thence into Jefferson, sometimes forming the boundary line, and then flowing inside of the boundary, and finally out again, before finally reaching the southern boundary line. Straight Creek, on the west, flows a short distance along the western line, and then passes off into Pleasant Township.

ROADS.

The original roads were laid out regardless of section lines or the cardinal points of the compass, but, since the opening-up of the county, the roads as first laid out, have been almost extinguished. The present roads are comparatively straight.

The first turnpike road built in the township, and the first in the county, was commenced in 1839, under a charter granted by the State, the State paying one-half the cost of construction. The remaining half was paid by citizens along the line taking stock. It is a double-track road, well and substantially built, constructed by Brooks & Crayton, the latter having been appointed by the State to superintend the building of the road. In the charter it was called the Ripley & Hillsboro Turnpike Road. It began at Ripley, and, running in a northern direction through Union Township, continued through Jefferson, dividing the latter almost equally, and about three-fourths of a mile into Jackson Township, where it stopped. Nothing more was done to it until 1870, when it was finished through Jackson Township, under a State law taxing the county for the construction of turnpikes. The original road was kept up by tolls taken at gates on the road until the year 1870, when it passed from the hands of the company into the control of the County Commissioners. Since then, it has been a free road, and kept in a traveling condition by taxation.

The Russellville & Georgetown Turnpike was built in 1872, under an act of the Legislature authorizing County Commissioners to levy a tax on all lands and property lying and being within two miles of the proposed road. This

JEFFERSON TOWNSHIP.

road is a single track, well made, mostly of knapped rock and gravel, and is in charge of the County Commissioners, who appoint a Superintendent of Turnpikes to see that the roads are kept in good condition, all expense being paid out of the county treasury.

The Russellville & Winchester Turnpike was built in 1871, under an act of the Legislature authorizing the Commissioners of the county to pay half of the cost of constructing the road, and the remaining half by the citizens on the proposed line of road. This road, like almost all other roads in the county, is a single track, well and compactly built of rock and gravel.

SAW MILLS.

The first saw-mill in the township was built in 1807, by Abraham Shepherd, on Eagle Creek, and was run by water. He operated this mill until he removed from the county. The first steam saw-mill was built in 1834, in the south part of the township, by Southerland, Mann & Spencer who operated it for a few years. A difference then arose among the proprietors, which could be adjusted only by selling the mill. It was purchased by three brothers named Dunn, who removed it to a point one mile south of Russellville, where it was run for several years. Business gradually failed, and it was finally abandoned. In 1842, a steam saw-mill was built in Russellville by the Miller brothers. It is now operated and owned by Robert Conn.

OFFICERS.

1853—Trustees, Michael Benner, W. B. Logan and James Glaze; Treasurer, John Glaze; Clerk, J. N. Salisbury; Justices, John McMahon and George Brown.

1854—Trustees, M. Benner, W. B. Logan and L. J. Kendal; Clerk, J. N. Salisbury; Treasurer, John Glaze; Constable, W. A. Maffett; Assessor, P. O'Harra.

1855—Trustees, M. Benner, J. Williamson and A. Edwards; Clerk, Alex Wilson; Treasurer, R. Shaw; Constable, J. H. Smith; Assessor, Thomas Mitchell.

1856—Trustees, M. Benner, John Williamson and W. B. Logan; Clerk, Alex Wilson; Treasurer, John Glaze; Constable, J. H. Smith; Assessor, E. Drake; Justices, Thomas Mitchell and Samuel Glaze.

1857—Trustees, M. Benner, W. B. Logan and L. Ramey; Clerk, A. Wilson; Treasurer, John Glaze; Constable, John B. Clifton; Assessor, E. Work.

1858—Trustees, M. Benner, John Hedrick and John Williamson; Clerk, Alex Wilson; Treasurer, Samuel Glaze; Constable, John B. Clifton; Assessor, Enoch Drake.

1859—Trustees, M. Benner, John Hedrick and John Williamson; Clerk, J. F. Baird; Treasurer, J. N. Salisbury; Constable, John B. Clifton; Assessor, E. Drake; Justice, John C. Campbell.

1860—Trustees, W. N. Ramey, John Hedrick and M. Benner; Clerk, W. H. Wilson; Treasurer, J. N. Salisbury; Constable, John B. Clifton; Assessor, George P. Tyler.

1861—Trustees, James Glaze, W. N. Ramey and John Hedrick; Clerk, W. S. Baird; Treasurer, J. N. Salisbury; Constable, J. B. Clifton; Assessor, Enoch Drake.

1862—Trustees, W. N. Ramey, John Williamson and C. B. Woods; Clerk, W. S. Baird; Treasurer, J. N. Salisbury; Constable, John B. Clifton; Assessor, E. Drake; Justices, John C. Campbell and G. W. Woods.

1863—Trustees, J. M. Abbott, George W. Brown and C. B. Woods; Clerk, J. B. Hughey; Treasurer, James E. Brown; Constable, Hugh Evans; Assessor, J. B. Clifton.

HISTORY OF BROWN COUNTY.

1864—Trustees, L. J. Kendle, Samuel Mefford and John Williamson; Clerk, P. S. Wamacks; Treasurer, J. B. Brown; Assessor, W. N. Ramey; Constable, W. S. Baird.

1865—Trustees, John Williamson, S. F. Mefford and L. J. Kendal; Clerk, W. S. Work; Treasurer, John C. Brown; Constable, W. S. Baird; Assessor, James P. Mooney; Justice of the Peace, A. Wilson.

1866—Trustees, Thomas Parry, W. W. Francis and J. P. Cropper; Clerk, W. S. Work; Treasurer, J. C. Brown; Constable W. S. Baird; Assessor, J. P. Mooney; Justice, J. B. Thomas.

1867—Trustees, Thomas Parry, W. W. Francis and J. P. Cropper; Clerk, Samuel Edwards; Treasurer, J. C. Brown; Constable, W. S. Baird; Assessor, J. P. Mooney.

1868—Trustees, W. W. Francis, J. L. Pilson and Robert Mannon; Clerk, Samuel Edwards; Treasurer, W. P. Williams; Constable, Thomas Mooney; Assessor, James B. Porter.

1869—Trustees, Alex Salisbury, Robert Mannon and James Baird; Clerk, L. H. Williams; Treasurer, W. P. Williams; Constable, W. B. Jacobs; Assessor, J. M. Mann.

1873—Trustees, Samuel Williamson, James A. Porter and A. McCormick; Treasurer, W. P. Williams; Clerk, L. H. Williams; Assessor, A. Kendal; Constable, J. C. Drake; Superintendent of Free Turnpikes, W. J Williamson.

1874—Trustees, J. P. Richey, John Brown and S. A. Myers; Treasurer, W. P. Williams; Clerk, Albert Conn; Assessor, L. J. Evans; Constable, H. W. Johnson; Justice, L. H. Williams.

1875—Trustees, J. P. Richey, F. M. Woods and John Brown; Clerk, L. H. Williams, Treasurer, A. M. Williamson; Assessor, S. A. Myers; Constable, W. Ball.

1876—Trustees, W. W. Francis, John Brown and Robert Mannon; Clerk, L. H. Williams; Treasurer, A. M. Williamson; Assessor, John Shotwell; Constable, W. Ball.

1877—Trustees, S. A. Smith, George H. Blair and W. B. Woods; Clerk, Albert Conn; Treasurer, A. M. Williamson; Assessor, John Shotwell; Constable, W. Ball.

1878—Trustees, George H. Blair, S. A. Smith and W. B. Jacobs; Clerk, Albert Conn; Treasurer, A. M. Williamson; Assessor, John Shotwell; Constable, A. B. Woods.

1879—Trustees, George H. Blair, W. B. Jacobs and S. A. Myers; Clerk, H. L. Hedrick; Treasurer, R. T. Baird; Assessor, John M. Blair; Constable, A. B. Woods.

1880—Trustees, James A. Porter, John Shotwell and S. A. Myers; Clerk, George E. Sidwell; Treasurer, J. N. Salisbury; Assessor, A. D. Sidwell; Constable, W. H. Howard.

1881—Trustees, John Shotwell, S. W. Kinkead and James A. Porter; Clerk, George E. Sidwell; Treasurer, J. N. Salisbury; Assessor, A. D. Sidwell; Constable, Wilson Ball.

1882—Trustees, J. P. Richey, J. M. Blair and A. A. McCormick; Clerk, George E. Fennin; Treasurer, J. N. Salisbury; Assessor, R. O. Evans; Constable, R. J. Young.

EARLY SETTLERS.

John Stevenson was born in Pennsylvania in 1787; was married to Miss Sarah Porter in 1808; came to Ohio in 1816; lived in Byrd Township, on what is called Rattlesnake Creek, until 1821, when he purchased a farm of 176 acres on the waters of Eagle Creek, in Jefferson Township, near the north-

JEFFERSON TOWNSHIP.

east line of the township. There he lived until 1863, when he moved to Russellville. Three children were born to them—Robert, Eliza and James. Robert, in his day, was a physician of considerable note; Eliza was married to Mr. Evans, who died a number of years ago; Mrs. Evans survives him, and has removed with her family to Illinois. James is the sole owner of the farm, and is living in Russellville, in quiet and bachelor-like seclusion. Sarah Stevenson died in 1833, aged forty-nine years. John died in 1866, aged seventy-nine years. Robert is also now dead.

James Edwards, Sr., was born in Aberdeen, Ohio, January, 1800. He lived there the first six years of his life, then moved with his father to Byrd Township, and settled on a farm on Eagle Creek, now owned by Harrison Edwards, a descendant of the Edwards family. In August, 1821, he was married to Nancy Jacobs, and they moved to an adjoining farm. There were born to them thirteen children, all of whom lived to marry. Mr. Edwards was Justice of the Peace for a number of years. His wife died February 26, 1848. In the spring of 1850, he sold his farm and moved to Russellville, where he engaged in tanning for about fifteen years. His health becoming impaired, he then withdrew from business. December 1, 1859, he was married to Miss Rachel Linton, and both are still living.

Thomas Mefford was born in Mason County, Ky., in 1803. He came to Ohio in 1825, and, in July of the same year, married Ellen Hodkins, and settled on a farm in Union Township. Three years later, they came to Russellville, purchasing a forty-acre farm and Town Lot No. 12, on which was a small log house, the second one built in Russellville. They lived in it until 1840, when they erected a two-story brick. Mr. Mefford engaged sometimes in blacksmithing, and occasionally manufactured a rifle, for which there was always a ready sale. He filled various township offices, and was Postmaster for sixteen years. His salary as such was at first $15 per annum. He was in early life interested in horses, and introduced the Morgan stock in this community. Of late years he has been an invalid, but has written a work on the horse and its diseases.

Aaron Wilson was born in Brooke County, Va., in 1791. He was married to Esther Baird, a native of the same county, and, in April, 1815, moved to Byrd Township, and, the following November, to the northeast part of Jefferson, and purchased a farm of 160 acres on the West Fork of Eagle Creek, about one mile east of Russellville. Nine children were born to them—Alexander, Sarah, Nancy, John K., Eliza Jane, William, Milton, Margaret and Alfred—all of whom are yet living except Eliza Jane, William and Sarah. Mr. Wilson sold his farm to his son, Alexander, and went to Peoria County, Ill., where he died in April, 1853. Mrs. Wilson died in August, 1854.

William Baird was born in Virginia; was married to Miss Sarah Moore; came to Ohio in 1814, and settled on the farm now owned by Wilson Pickerill. His children were Margaret, John M., Wilson, Amanda and Caroline.

Benjamin Culter was born in Brooke County, Va.; was married to Miss Parkinson, and came to Ohio about the year 1817, and settled on a farm of 150 acres lying on the road leading from Russellville to Eagle Creek, about midway between them. He raised a large family of children, and lived on this farm until 1833, when he sold it to his brother John, and removed with his family to Illinois, where he died.

John Barrett was born in Pennsylvania, and came to Ohio at an early day with his father, who settled on a farm near New Market, in Highland County, in 1820. John came to Jefferson Township and settled on a farm of 150 acres that his father had purchased and given to him. It now is known at the Schwallie farm. He lived here a short time, and returned to his native neighborhood, there married Miss Morrow, and came with her to his farm in this township. Here he lived until the spring of 1849, when he sold his farm to John Williamson and moved to Iowa. After a few years, he went to Oregon, since which time there is no further trace of him.

George Berry was born in Pennsylvania, and came to Ohio about the year 1817. He lived at Ripley a short time, then moved to Jackson Township, and, in 1822, came to Jefferson Township; and settled on a farm on the West Fork of Eagle Creek. His children were Mary, Margaret, Catherine and Samuel. He died in 1830, his wife surviving him a few years.

Jeremiah Allen was born in Kentucky, and came to Jefferson Township about 1817, purchasing a farm on the West Fork, located partly in Jefferson and partly in Jackson Townships. In 1834, he sold it to Samuel Pickerill and removed to Peoria County, Ill., where he soon after died.

John Sanderson was born in Highland County, Ohio, and married Rebecca Barrett. In 1820, he settled on a farm of 100 acres adjoining Russellville on the east. His children were Thomas, Alexander, James, Mary and Sarah Jane. Mr. Sanderson died in 1834. His widow, in 1839, married David Henderson, who died in 1852, and, soon after, she moved to Illinois.

John C. Henry was born in Kentucky in 1796, and was married, in 1818, to Margaret Baird, who was born in Virginia in 1802. They moved to Union Township, and, in 1828, came to Jefferson, settling on a farm of 110 acres near the southeast corner of the township. The early part of Mr. Henry's life was devoted principally to the cultivation and clearing up of his farm. He obtained a knowledge of law by reading, and his services as an attorney were often in demand in the local trials of this and adjoining townships. The children of Mr. and Mrs. Henry were William B., Nancy Jane, Mary and Elizabeth (twins), and John W. Henry. Mr. Henry died in 1864, aged sixty-eight years. Mrs. Henry still survives, and is the sole owner of the farm.

James Morrow as born and married in Ireland; came to Ohio about the year 1800, and settled on a farm of 100 acres in the southwestern part of the township, now owned by John P. Cropper. They lived on the farm for thirty-five years, when Mrs. Morrow died, and James sold the farm and journeyed into one of the Western Territories. Their children were eight in number—Robert, James, John, Nathan, May, Elizabeth, Nancy and Hannah.

Robert Bowers was born in Pennsylvania; married Miss Sarah Smith; came to Ohio in 1816, and settled on a farm of 150 acres one mile east of Russellville, where he lived until 1830. He then sold his farm and moved to a farm in the northeast corner of the township, where he built a fine brick dwelling house. He soon after moved near Russellville, and again went to a small farm west of the village. Mr. Bowers was twice married. His children were William, James, Martha, Allen, Albert, Rebecca, Margaret and Hannah. His first wife died in 1856. He was married, in 1859, to Elizabeth Menaugh. Mr. Bowers died in 1862, and Elizabeth in 1868.

Samuel Miller was born in Pennsylvania in 1784; was married to Miss Elizabeth Baird, and came to Ohio in the year 1823. He lived for a few years on Straight Creek, Pleasant Township, and, while there, built what was known as the Huggins Mill. Shortly after, he came to Jefferson Township, and settled on a farm of 100 acres, now owned by Joseph Francis. Before leaving his native State, Mr. Miller had learned the art of millwrighting, at which he worked whenever the weather would permit. This made it necessary for Mrs. Miller to assume the duties of landlady, which she did to the satisfaction of every one concerned. Their children were nine—John, James, George, Wylie, Oliphant, Washington, Johnson, Wilson and Allen. Mr. Wilson died in 1854. His wife survived him only seven days.

JEFFERSON TOWNSHIP.

Levi Laycock was born in Virginia in 1793, and, in 1800, came with his father to Union Township. He was one of the soldiers in 1812 whom Gen. Hull surrendered to the British. In 1816, he married Mary Washburn, and has since resided in this township. He was twice married. His children were Joseph, Ann, Jeremiah, Nicholas, John, Elizabeth, Moses and Zeruah.

Stephen Pangburn was born in Pennsylvania in 1780; came to Ohio about 1800. In a short time, he settled on a farm of fifty acres, now owned by J. B. Clifton. He married Nancy Knox, by whom he had six children—Levi, Jemima, Elizabeth, William, James and Eli. After Mrs. Pangburn's death, he married May Morrow, whose death occurred soon after. For his third consort he chose Sarah Feeby, by who he had two children—Abby and Samuel. Mr. Pangburn lived here about forty years, then removed to the West.

Joseph Washburn was born in Pennsylvania, and came to this township about 1800, settling near the western border, on the farm now owned by William Williamson. His wife was Elizabeth Mann, who bore him four children—Cornelius, Mary, William and Elizabeth. After a period of about thirty-five years, Mr. Washburn removed to Indiana.

James Alexander was born in Pennsylvania; came to Ohio about 1814, and settled on the farm now owned by Alexander Bishforth, one mile south of Russellville. His wife was May Frazee. Their children were seven in number—Ellen, Margaret, James, John, Sarah, Elizabeth and Pathena. In 1835, they sold the farm and moved to Indiana.

Isaac Washburn was born in Pennsylvania, and came to this township about 1800. He purchased about five hundred acres of land, now owned by Wilson Pickerill, Samuel Mefford, and the heirs of Knight McGregor and Mary Wills. He married Miss Rachel Laycock. Their children were Nicholas, George, Phœbe, Moses and William. Mr. Washburn died about 1825.

John Snedaker was born in Virginia in 1770, and was there married to Miss Charity Harris. Emigrating to Ohio, they settled in the east part of the township, near Eagle Creek, on a farm of 200 acres. Mrs. Snedaker died in 1844. Mr. Snedaker, in 1834. Their children were Garrett, Warren, Levina, Anna, Christian, Samuel, John, William, Nancy, Jesse and Noah.

Silas Bartholomew was born in Vermont, and was married in that State to Miss Chloe Fancher. He came to Ohio about 1802, and purchased a farm of 100 acres, situated in the south part of the township, adjoining Union, and now owned by Newton Liggett. Their children were Fancher, Samuel, Chester, Sylvanus, Silas, Chloe Ann and Martha. Mr. Bartholomew was a true type of the Vermont Yankee, somewhat eccentric in his manner of living and doing business, but withal an excellent man. Mrs. Bartholomew also partook somewhat of the eccentricities of her husband. Both lived on the farm until called away by death, the exact date of which we have been unable to obtain.

Valentine Kennett was born in Pennsylvania about 1798, and settled on a farm of 100 acres, which is now owned by the heirs of Moses Moore. The wife of Mr. Kennett was Susan McConnell. Their children were twelve in number—Samuel, James, John, Thomas, Arthur, George, Levi, Valentine, May, Margaret, Elizabeth and Susan. Mr. and Mrs. Kennett both died on this farm, well advanced in life.

Abraham Shepherd was a native of Virginia. He emigrated to Ohio in 1802, and purchased a tract of land on Eagle Creek, near the eastern boundary of the township, which is now occupied by Bowers Woods. He was a man of great energy and perseverance. He had received a liberal education before leaving his native State, and speedily became a man of influence in his neighborhood. Under his guidance, his farm was rapidly improved. In 1815, he built a grist-mill on Eagle Creek, and on his farm. It was the first mill of any importance in the township. Soon after, he sold the mill and moved to Ripley. He was a member of the State Senate when Brown County was organized. In April, 1818, he received the appointment of Clerk of Brown County, from Joshua Collett, Presiding Judge, and was the first to hold this position. He retained it seven years, and, during his term of office, played a conspicuous part in the political affairs of the county. His love of adventure and pioneer life was great, and he disposed of his possessions here and emigrated to the distant West, where he spent the remainder of his life.

James Work was born in Ireland. About 1797, he settled in Pleasant Township, and, five years later, came to Jefferson, purchasing a farm of 165 acres in the southwest part of the township, now owned by his son George. He married Mary Evans. Their children were Elizabeth, Jemima, Sarah. Rachel, Lucinda, Mary Ann, Joseph, Elijah, William, George and John. Mr. and Mrs. Work lived to a good old age, and died on the farm.

Edward Evans was born in Pennsylvania in 1760, and was married to Miss Jemima Applegate, who was also born in Pennsylvania. He was a soldier in the Revolutionary army, and was with Gen. Washington at Germantown in 1777, and within hearing distance of the battle of Monmouth in 1778, but, being sick, was not permitted to engage in it. Mr. Evans came to Ohio about 1800, and settled on a farm of 109 acres in the southern part of the township, now occupied by Hugh Evans, a descendant of Edward. Their children were thirteen in number—Elijah, William, Joseph, Robert, John, Hugh, James, Mary, Sarah, Isabel, Elizabeth, Rachel and Margaret. Mr. Evans died in 1839, and Mrs. Evans in 1840.

Samuel Harlow was born in Virginia in 1765; was married to Elizabeth Washburn; came to Ohio about 1800, and settled in the south part of the township, on a farm now occupied by Nelson Fuller. Their children were John, Cornelius, Jeremiah, Lewis, Mary and Rebecca. In 1836, he sold his farm and moved to one of the Territories, since which there is no trace of him.

At an early date, a Mr. Boulle settled on a farm on Straight Creek, in the southwest part of the township, where he lived a few years, and died. The farm was then sold, and was purchased by John Mann, and is now occupied by his son Scott.

John W. Campbell was born in Virginia; came to Ohio at a very early day, and settled in the southern part of the county; lived there until 1825, when he came to Jefferson Township, and bought a farm of 250 acres in the southwest part of the township, being the farm now owned by John Chapman. The wife of Mr. Campbell was Miss Ellen Jane Lilley. Mr. Campbell received, before leaving his native State, a liberal education, and, during the first few years of his life in Ohio, he was engaged in the practice of law in Ripley. He was chosen to represent his district in Congress during the administration of Andrew Jackson, and was appointed by him to a Judgeship, and, to discharge the duties of his office, he sold his farm and moved to Columbus.

Jacob Dowers is said to have been the first occupant of the farm now owned by E. M. Drake. Nothing further is known of him.

William Moore, a Virginian, settled early in the southeast part of the township, on the farm W. T. Purden now occupies. He afterward moved West.

Levi Howland was born in Massachusetts in 1782. He emigrated with his father to Kentucky, and, after a residence there of four years, came to Byrd Township. In 1811, Levi was married to Margaret Beem, who was born in Pennsylvania in 1791. They immediately settled in the eastern part of Jefferson, on a little place of twenty-eight acres. Soon after, Mr. Howland was

Robert Mannon

JEFFERSON TOWNSHIP.

called out in the war of 1812. He was a member of Capt. Abraham Shepherd's company of riflemen, and served forty days. He was very industrious, often working all night, it is said. His children were Sarah, Ulysses, John, Jane, Nancy, Rochester, Margaret, Willis, Levi and George. Mr. Howland died in 1864. His wife still survives, and is now ninety-one years of age.

Thomas Jolly, a Virginian, emigrated to this township about 1800. He married Lucy Gardner. Little else is known of him.

William Thompson came from Pennsylvania, very early, to the southern part of the township, on the farm now owned by the John Donaldson heirs. He married Hannah Evans and had four children—Jefferson, Susan, Elizabeth and Hervey. While serving in the war of 1812, he was killed by the Indians. Mrs. Thompson reared her family in this township, but afterward moved away to parts unknown.

Stephen Porter was born in Pennsylvania in the year 1800, and came to Ohio in 1818. He was married to Rachel Dunlavy in 1821; came to Jefferson Township and bought a farm of 165 acres on the west side of the township, his son James being the owner of the farm at this time. To them ten children were born—Margaret A., Keziah J., Eliza B., Mary G., Harriet A., Martha W., James A., Stephen D., Rachel A. and John B. Stephen D., his son, was Lieutenant in the Fourth Ohio Independent Cavalry, under Capt. John S. Foster; was honorably discharged, and went to Nebraska, where he held the position of Judge of the Court for a term of years. John also served a time in the army, and was honorably discharged. Mr. Porter died in 1862, and Mrs. Porter in 1880.

John McCoy came to Ohio from Kentucky in 1811, and bought a farm of 150 acres one mile southeast of Russellville. He was of Scotch descent, and was married to Isabel Baird. Their children were Alexander, Jane, Eliza, John, James, Sarah and Everetts. John, Sr., also had a brother named George, who came to the farm with him. In 1843, they sold the farm and went to one of the Western States.

Gordon Hopkins was born in Union Township, and came to Jefferson Township as early, perhaps, as 1820, and settled on a farm in the southern part of the township, where he lived for many years, and then moved West.

Benjamin Shreves was born in Pennsylvania, and came to Ohio in 1820; was married to Miss Minerva Heaton, and settled on the farm now owned by W. W. Francis. John and Jonah were two of his children; the names of the other children we have been unable to obtain, Benjamin leaving this farm when they were quite young, and going to the State of Indiana.

Samuel Shreves was born in Pennsylvania, and came to Ohio about 1820. He married Rachel Fowler, and settled near to and west of Russellville, on the farm on which Johnson Miller now lives. Their children were George, Ruth, Nancy, Frank, Andrew and Samuel. Mr. Shreves lived on this farm a number of years, then emigrated to Iowa.

John Mann settled, about 1820, on the farm now owned by John Brown, and, after a number of years, moved to Indiana. His wife was Nellie Glaze.

Charles Pearson came to the township, as nearly as can be ascertained, about 1800, leasing the farm now owned by Samuel Kinkaid. At the expiration of the lease, he removed from the township.

Thomas McAlister emigrated from Ireland in 1798, and settled in the southern part of the township. In a few years, he departed from this neighborhood, and of his subsequent residence nothing is known.

John Lilley came to the township about 1810, purchasing a little place near the southwest corner. He did not remain here long.

Elihu Parker, a Pennsylvanian, settled at a very early period in the southwest part of the township. Mr. and Mrs. Parker both died here. They had no children.

Robert Shaw was born in Jackson Township in 1797; married Miss McGuffey, and came to Jefferson in 1819, settling on a farm in the extreme northeast corner of the township, in the year 1820. He built a large flouring-mill on the waters of Eagle Creek, which crossed his farm, and operated the mill for a number of years, then sold it to two of his neighbors, Matthew Potts and John Coslett. About this time, his wife died, leaving him with a family of ten children. He afterward married Miss Lucinda Stewart, then moved to one of the Western States. His children by his last marriage were twelve in number, which made him, at the time of his death, the father of twenty-two children.

James Black came to Ohio at a very early period, and settled on Eagle Creek, in the east side of the township, on a farm of 100 acres, where he lived to raise a family, and died.

John Jolliff came to Ohio from Virginia at an early period, and settled on the farm in the northwestern part of the township now owned by John D. Mefford.

Justice Brockway was born in New York in 1777, and was married to Miss Thankful Boss, who was born in 1779. They came to Ohio in 1816, and settled on a farm of 200 acres of land just south of and adjoining Russellville. When Mr. Brockway moved to this State, he traveled by land to Pittsburgh, where he shipped his goods and family on a keel-boat, and he journeyed on by land with his team to Jefferson Township, where he arrived in the autumn of 1816. On arriving at his new home, he found his farm of 200 acres an unbroken forest, but the sound of his ax was soon heard, and, in a short time, a small piece of ground was made ready for the pioneer cabin. He opened up a fine farm, and raised a large family of children, twelve in number, and named Serepta, Almariah, Sarah, Lucy, Washington, Mary, Lavina, Justice, Orry, Jesse and Julietta. Mr. Brockway died in 1830, and Mrs. Brockway a number of years later.

Peter Shaw was a native of the State of New York, born in 1779. He was united in marriage to Elizabeth Reynolds, and emigrated to the Northwest Territory, settling in what is now Jackson Township, where he lived a short time, and then purchased a tract of 300 acres of land in what is now Jefferson Township, lying south of and adjoining Russellville. Here he lived for a number of years, and removed to Ripley, and there resided until his death.

Russel Shaw was born in Rensselaer County, N. Y., in 1781. He married Johanna Reynolds, and emigrated to the Northwest Territory in 1802, and settled in what afterward became Jackson Township, Brown Co., Ohio. Here he effected a settlement among a little colony that had preceded him a short time, which was known as the Yankee Colony, and lived there fifteen years, and then settled in Jefferson Township, buying 200 acres of land near what is now the northern boundary. The children of this couple were Sylvester, Susan, Anthony, Calvin, Experience, Alfred, Philena, Barnbridge, Cecil, Elizabeth, Greenleaf, Merritt and Eli. The parents died in 1864.

CHURCHES.

The first church in the township was built on John Snedaker's farm, near Eagle Creek, in the east part of the township. It was a small building, 18x21, very unpretentious and rudely finished. The house was built through the united efforts of the different denominations. The Presbyterian denomination, being strongest in the neighborhood, was the principal occupant. The first preaching was by the Rev. Reuben White, of the Presbyterian persuasion. This church served for a place of worship until the neighboring villages were supplied with better.

The Baptist Church.—The doctrines of the Baptist Church were promulgated and preached in this township as early as 1810 by the Rev. Mr. Smith, who lived in Jackson Township. He preached at farmhouses, principally at that of Elihu Parker, who lived in the southern part of the township. The believers in this faith gradually increased until the year 1828, when they resolved themselves into an organized body to build a house in which to worship, at a meeting held at the house of Elihu Parker. The following were the first members of the organization: Elihu Parker and wife, Enoch Drake and wife, Stout Drake and wife, Jonathan Fuller and wife, Nelson Fuller and wife, William Kirkpatrick and wife, Jerry Green and wife, Joseph Bratton and wife, William Bratton and wife, Adam Bratton and wife, Thomas Pistole and wife, William Derrickson and wife, Daniel Reed and wife, Robert Reed and wife, and Isaac Wilson and wife. A church site was selected on the farm of Porter Shaw, three-fourths of a mile south of Russellville, and a small frame building erected, some of the members subscribing money, some labor and some material. Rev. Aaron Sargent, who lived at Bethel, Clermont County, was the first pastor in charge. He held services once in four weeks, and, at intervening times, preaching was conducted by Bros. Lyon, Morris, Riley, Griswold, Aaron Sargent, Jr., Cook, Wedge and others. The membership increased, but a schism arose in the church, one faction, known as the Ironside Baptists, following the leadership of Rev. Smith, and the other that of Rev. Sargent, who remained in charge till old age rendered him unfit for the work. The effects of the division were ruinous. The membership fell away gradually, many joining other churches. The closing scene in the history of this congregation was the burning of the church, in the spring of 1855, from an unknown cause.

A number of members of the Associate Reformed Church who had settled in this township, with the assistance of a few who lived in Byrd and Union Townships, banded together, and, in 1830, took steps for the erection of a church building, on a lot donated by Eli Collins, a spirited member, then living at Russellville. It was completed the next year.

The first minister employed was James Caskey, who preached one or two days per month. During his absence, the pulpit would sometimes be filled by ministers from other stations. The organization, however, was destined to a short life. Removals, deaths and changing of memberships to other points produced a speedy decline. The house was sold and the proceeds divided among the surviving members. The members in the first organization were Thomas MacCague and wife, Eli Collins and wife, John Barrett and wife, Samuel Kerr and wife, William Wright and wife, Samuel Bayne and wife.

The Presbyterian Church.—The first account we are able to find of a Presbyterian Church organization in Russellville was in 1817. At a meeting of Washington Presbytery, held in Buckskin Meeting-House (now Salem Church), a petition was presented from a people living on Eagle Creek, praying that they be known on the minutes as the Eagle Creek Congregation. The request was granted at this meeting, and James Gilliland appointed to preach one Sabbath and six days at Eagle Creek. At a meeting of the same presbytery in August, 1817, Rev. Gilliland was again appointed to spend eight days in missionary labor, and Mr. Andrew W. Poage was to preach one Sabbath each at White Oak, New Market, Straight Creek and Eagle Creek. There was preaching to the people in this vicinity at various times by Rev. Gilliland and Rev. Reuben White up to April, 1829. At a meeting of the Chillicothe Presbytery held at Ripley April 1, 1829, Rev. J. H. Lockhart, from French Broad Presbytery, appeared, and was invited to a seat as corresponding member. At a meeting of the Chillicothe Presbytery October 1, 1829, at West Union, he was appointed to perform eighty days' labor in Brown County. At a meeting of the above presbytery in Hillsboro, January 5, 1830, he was received as a member of the presbytery. At this meeting the congregation of Eagle Creek presented a call asking for the pastoral labors of Mr. Lockhart, but, after discussion, it was decided that it could not be presented to Mr. Lockhart, for the reason that the congregation had not made satisfactory statements of the means provided for his support. At a meeting of the presbytery in West Union, April 6, 1830, the call was again presented, but for only half of his time. The call was accepted.

Father Lockhart, as he was familiarly known by all, was born in Rockingham County, Va., December 23, 1799, and removed with his father to East Tennessee at the age of ten. He was educated at Danbridge and Marysville, and, after reading theology privately with Dr. McCampbell, was licensed to preach, and, soon after, was ordained as an evangelist, and engaged in missionary work in the mountains of East Tennessee and North Carolina for two years. Cherishing a desire to breathe the free air of the North, he turned his horse's head toward Ohio, and, after a long and tiresome journey, he reached Ripley, where he met his old friend, Rev. John Rankin, who had preceded him North a few years. After a brief rest, Mr. Lockhart again engaged in home missionary work. All the feeble churches in Brown, Adams and other adjoining counties heard from his lips the Gospel message of salvation. He fixed his headquarters at Russellville, then a small village in the woods. There, without a wife, home or house of worship, and without the promise of money, he began his life work. Soon after accepting the call here, he was married to Miss Margaret McIlvaine. Their children were four in number, two of whom survive—John and Amanda.

In 1829, the members of the Presbyterian Church in Russellville and vicinity resolved to build a house of worship. In the summer of 1830, a brick building, 40x70 feet, was erected on a lot in the east part of Russellville. The cost of the building was supposed to be about $1,100.

Prominent among the members of the church at that time were Aaron Wilson and wife, Benjamin Marshall and wife, John Parker, Edward Francis, Eleanor Ashenhurst, Margaret Scott, Margaret Robinson, Matthew Tomb, Fanny Tomb, Eleanor Inskeep, Robert Bower and wife, John C. Henry and wife, Samuel G. Moore, John Lafabre and wife, Dr. Beasley, John Snedaker and wife, William Evans, Thomas Culter and wife, George McIntire and wife, Hannah Potts, Isabella Howland, George McCoy, Stephen Porter, Samuel Miller and wife, Daniel Williamson, Joseph Orr, Robert Poage and others. The first Clerk of the session was Dr. A. Beasley. Clerks since were S. G. Moore, J. Francis, and present Clerk, Dr. J. N. Salisbury. The house that was built was finished in taste to correspond to the financial condition of the members at that time, and served them for a place of worship until 1870, when it became necessary to repair the old house. But the congregation concluded to build a new house instead, and a beautiful brick building, very substantially constructed and finished, stood in the place of the old house. It cost $9,000, and would be considered a credit to any community. Soon after the new building was erected, Father Lockhart offered his resignation as pastor, which, on account of his advanced age, was accepted, with the condition that he would fill the pulpit when vacant. Rev. Guthrie was then employed to preach one-half of his time. He was succeeded by Rev. John McClung, who ministered to the this people a few years, and then accepted a call from the West. During his pastorate, Rev. Lockhart removed with his family to Ecksmansville, Adams

County, and soon after died, in his eightieth year. The next minister was Rev. Walter Mitchell, who now officiates. The Elders of the church from its organization have been William Evans, Benjamin Marshall, Edward Francis, John Glendenning, Aaron Wilson, Garrett Snedaker, A. Beasley, George McCoy, Samuel G. Moore, Robert Poage, John Culter, Isaac Sutherland, William Griffin, Samuel Miller, James Baird, Joseph Francis, James Blair, J. N. Salisbury, Lawrence Ramey, W. J. Williamson, J. A. Porter, Samuel Kinkaid and A. M. Williamson.

The organization of the Disciple Church was due principally to the labors of Elder Lucas, who preached in Russellville and vicinity as early as 1840. In 1844, measures were adopted for the erection of a church. Thomas Mefford donated a lot for a church building, with the proviso that it should revert to the grantor when no longer used for church purposes. A plain, substantial frame building was erected in 1845, at a cost of about $700. This served as a place of worship until 1869, when it was found that a large amount of repair was needed on the house. It was thought best to build a new house, and the lot once occupied by the Old-School Presbyterian Church was purchased, and a neat and substantial frame building erected on it in 1870. It is neatly and plainly finished on the inside, and preaching is had in it one day in each month. The ministers officiating have been J. B. Lucas, David Thompson, Abram Solle, John Dillon, William Thompson, J. S. West, —— Darah, James West, Joseph S. West.

The doctrines of the Methodist Church were preached in this township as early as 1825, at first in dwelling houses, barns and groves. The pioneer ministers were Revs. Baxter, Clark, Manker, Quinn and others. In 1836, arrangements were completed to build a house of worship, and in 1837, a commodious little brick building was put up on a lot of ground in the north part of Russellville. The prominent members at that time were Lowry McKnight, John Bassett, Asher Wykoff, Emor Stalcup, Harry Sidwell and others. In 1872, a lot was purchased in the northwest part of the town, being the north half of Lots No. 19 and 20, on which was erected a large frame church, which was very tastefully and neatly finished, and furnished with good modern appliances. The church now has an active working membership of about one hundred. The Trustees at the building of the new church were W. Ball, D. C. Culter, Ellis Sidwell, R. W. Pittenger, George Ferris, Charles Boggs, Samuel A. Smith, James Johnson, W. L. Johnson. The ministers who have labored in the church were Revs. Hare, Allen, Gossard, E. H. Field, Tibbetts, McDonald, Zink, Edgar, Kugler, Bolton, Colahan, Witham, Heade, Emeston, Coole, Wilson, Verity, Gregg, Hitzler and many others.

The Old-School Presbyterian Church was built in 1842. The formation of this congregation was the outgrowth of a division in the Presbyterian Church proper of Russellville, from which the following persons withdrew and formed an independent organization called the Old-School: Aaron Wilson and wife, John Lafabre and wife, John C. Henry and wife, Samuel Miller and wife, D. McConnell and wife, William Evans and wife and William Wilson and wife. Their house was built, as all others were in early days, by contributions of lumber, rock, brick, shingles, nails, etc. It was rudely finished, and was occupied as a house of worship only a few years. Rev. James Dunlap was the first and only minister in the church. After a short stay, he removed to another field of labor, and soon after the organization dissolved.

Preaching in the Christian faith was held in this township as early as 1810. The pioneer ministers were Revs. Barton Stone and David Perviance, of Kentucky, who made frequent visits to this locality and held services during summer in groves, and in dwelling-houses through cold weather. Rev. Alexander McClain also labored here. The followers of this faith increased, and at a meeting held June 26, 1827, in a small log house which stood on the same lot the present church occupies, an organization was effected with the following membership: David Kendle and wife, John Stitt and wife, Basil Glaze and wife, Thomas Shreve and wife, Eli Hewitt and wife, John Abbott and wife, David Newman and wife, Mary Butt and Joanna Shaw. Meetings were continued at the homes of members, groves and schoolhouses until 1830, when they built a brick church in Russellville, some of the members furnishing timber, joist, rafters, etc., others furnishing rock for foundation, others shingles, which were made by hand from the trunk of the sturdy oak. The women exchanged rags, eggs, butter and such other articles as they could spare, for nails, which went into the construction of the building. The first seats were made from the trunks of small trees, with large pins for legs. The house was first heated by burning charcoal in two large iron kettles. In a short time, the congregation became able to furnish seats of more modern style; also, stoves took the place of kettles as heaters. In this condition, the house was used up to May, 1860, when a terrible tornado swept over the town, unroofed the church and demolished part of the wall of the house. It was, however, rebuilt and re-roofed in a short time, furnished with new seats, papered, repainted and furnished in good style, and is now one of the neatest churches of the place. The membership at this time is about 260. Rev. Alexander McClain, the first minister in charge, labored here twenty-five years. His successors have been Revs. Henry Phillips, Daugherty, George W. Mefford, Coan, Pangburn, Cook and Walter Mefford.

CEMETERIES.

Some of the cemetery grounds in the township seem not to have been selected from an adaptability for burial purposes, while others are most beautifully located. The cemetery known as the Baird Burial-Grounds was set apart for cemetery purposes by Abram Shepherd at an early day, from the best information we can obtain, about the year 1812. Some time afterward, Mr. Shepherd sold his farm to George Baird, and it has been since known as the Baird Burial-Grounds.

We append a list of those whose remains repose here and who were born prior to 1800:

NAMES.	Born	Died.	Age.
Samuel Benington	1768	1845	77
Robert McNoun	1781	1847	66
Mary Burns	1772	1847	75
John Burns	1763	1850	87
Andrew Frazier	1776	1823	47
Elenor Frazier	1779	1843	64
May Shaw	1794	1837	43

Whole number of interments in the grounds, 115.

In 1831, the Associate Reformed branch of the church built a house near the limits of Russellville, on the east side of the town, and a part of the grounds on which they built their church was set apart as a cemetery. A list of those born prior to 1800 who lie buried here is as follows:

JEFFERSON TOWNSHIP.

NAMES.	BORN.	DIED.	AGED.	NAMES.	BORN.	DIED.	AGED.
James B. Moore	1800	1868	68	Matilda Moore	1800	1833	33
William Evans	1787	1873	86	George Baird	1776	1838	67
John Smith	1766	1840	74	Jane Baird	1770	1820	50
Sarah Smith	1779	1855	76	John C. Henry	1794	1854	60
Robert Moore	1789	1833	44	Sarah Baird	1797	1873	76
Rhoda Pearson	1778	1835	57	Samuel A. Butt	1790	1870	80
Isaac Bostwick	1787	1855	68	David Kendle	1786	1858	72
May Calahan	1790	1863	73	Theodosia Kendle	1794	1875	81
S. W. Calahan	1792	1860	68	John Clark	1790	1870	80
Henry Ryner	1797	1853	56	Elizabeth Bower	1798	1868	70
Russell Shaw	1781	1864	83	Robert Bower	1781	1862	81
James McMillan	1789	1850	61	Sarah Bower	1788	1856	68
Thomas Butt	1795	1851	56	John Stephenson	1787	1866	79
Thomas Shreve	1785	1854	69	Sarah Stephenson	1784	1833	49
Nancy McElfresh	1784	1850	66	May Fuller	1789	1861	72
Basil McElfresh	1771	1847	76	William Johnson	1796	1871	75
Caleb Shreves	1754	1817	63	May Johnson	1785	1871	86

NOTE.—The number of interments in the grounds, as near as can be ascertained, is 295.

Linwood Cemetery is located one mile east of Russellville, on the Winchester pike, and was surveyed in the spring of 1861. It contains five acres, and was purchased by the township Trustees under an act of the Legislature, authorizing Township Trustees to levy a tax for the purchase and inclosing of a cemetery. The ground was bought of the heirs of Jacob Schwallie for $475. They are inclosed by a beautiful osage orange hedge, and for adaptability and beauty of location are not surpassed by any cemetery grounds in Southern Ohio. This cemetery, besides all others in the township, is under the care of George E. Sidwell, Trustee of Cemeteries, under whose efficient management it is beautifully and neatly kept. The first interment in this township was that of the remains of John A. Kendle, youngest son of Leroy J. and Mary J. Kendle, who was removed from the society of tender and loving parents and a large circle of acquaintances on the morning of his life.

SCHOOLS.

The means provided for the education of the children of the pioneer settlers were very scant and limited, and the first houses used for school purposes were cabins that chanced to be without a dweller. In these houses, homemade chairs and benches made from poles constituted the seats. The first houses, built for the special purpose of school were rude structures of logs, built on a very unpretentious plan. One end of the house was generally occupied by the fire-place, finished inside with slab seats and puncheon floors, with clapboard roof, held in place by weight-poles. The books in use were Webster's Speller, American Preceptor, Murray's and Kirkham's Grammar, Olney's Atlas and Geography. As the population increased in numbers and wealth, the desire for better houses began to develop, the different districts assumed a more desirable shape, and good frame houses took the place of the pioneer log schoolhouse. The wages paid to pioneer teachers were from $10 to $15 per month. The early teachers were Anderson, Vail, Fancher, Cooper, Brown, Spencer, Wilson, Robe, Peacock, McKnight, O'Hara and many others.

The present status of Jefferson Township in respect to common schools is not excelled by any of the surrounding townships. The township is divided into five school districts, besides Russellville, which forms an independent district. In each of the districts is a good and comfortable frame house, furnished with seats of modern manufacture, heated with coal, and well ventilated and furnished with desks, maps and blackboards. The attendance is from twenty-eight to fifty scholars. In each district, a term of from six to eight months is taught.

616 HISTORY OF BROWN COUNTY.

The books in use are McGuffey's Readers, Ray's Arithmetic and Algebra Holbrook and Harvey's Grammar, Eclectic Geographies, McGuffy's Speller and Barnes' United States History. The teachers receive from $28 to $37 per month for winter terms, and $18 to $28 for spring school.

In 1854, the town of Russellville was incorporated, and within its limits is embraced one square mile of territory. In 1855, a two-story brick school building was erected, divided into three departments—Primary, Intermediate and High. The Primary Department is composed of pupils from six to twelve years of age, the Intermediate from twelve to fifteen and the High above the latter age. In the Primary School is taught the alphabet, the first principles of spelling, mental arithmetic, writing and reading to McGuffy's Third Reader. In the Intermediate School, arithmetic, geography, grammar and writing. In the Higher Department, arithmetic, descriptive geography, higher arithmetic, algebra, grammar, physical geography, mathematical geography, United States History, geometry and physiology. There are in this district about 185 pupils. The average wages paid are: In the Primary Department, $26 per month; in the Intermediate, $40, and the Superintendent, $55 per month.

WAR RECORD.

That the men of Jefferson Township bore an honorable part in the great struggle with secession, during the four long, eventful years from 1861 to 1865, and performed deeds of loyalty and heroism, the hotly contested fields of Cheat Mountain, Green Brier, Chickamauga, Stone River, Shiloh, Lookout Mountain, Mission Ridge and many others bear ample evidence. Among those who slumber in unknown and unmarked graves beside the still waters of the South, lie a number of the sons of Jefferson Township, there to await the reveille of the heroic, when time shall be no more. But the memory of their heroic acts will be cherished in the hearts of a grateful people, who to the latest generation will call them blessed. We give herewith a list of those who entered the service of their country from Jefferson Township, and were honorably discharged by death or expiration of time of enlistment:

Fourth Ohio Independent Cavalry—Martin Hayes, J. N. Cox, Ferris Strait, S. D. Porter, Alfred Glaze, Hugh Evans, Harvey Evans, Peter Mitchell, Leonidas Bayne, John Bayne, George Bayne, Newton Long, Alfred Williamson, Ellis Kennett, Albert Lewis, Joseph Henderson, Edward Credit, Sanford Williams, Lewis Williams, Samuel Edwards, Albert Williamson, Hiram Kendle, Stephen Bohrer, Porter McKee.

Ohio Cavalry—William Ellis, Josiah Edwards, James Shaw, Byers Hughey, Francis Metz, Elymer Drake, William Tucker, Basile Glaze, G. H. Davidson, John L. Davidson, Russell McMannis, Thomas McElfresh, Caleb McElfresh, A. G. Shaw.

Thirty-fourth Ohio Infantry—Elymer Shaw, William Wills, John Wills, George Crest, William Lewis.

Fifth Virginia Infantry—S. A. Collins, E. P. Wilkins, J. T. Williams, J. A. Collins, W. P. Williams.

Fifty-ninth Ohio Infantry—J. W. Shinn, William Triplet, Samuel Wills, William Culter, Cephas Davis, William McGlaughlin, W. A. Work.

Seventieth Ohio Infantry—Robert Baird, Lewis Baird, Abraham Evans, Samuel Blair, Baker Woods, James Sidwell, Wilson Sidwell, Alex Sowards, John Ramey, Louis Love, A. S. Coale, N. W. Williams, James Dixon, Joseph Cox.

First Ohio Artillery—John Stephens, Matthew Harrington.
Thirty-ninth Ohio Infantry—John Sidwell.

Regiment unknown—J. C. Preston, William Moore, Jacob Cooke, Alex Leggett, James Porter, Samuel Day, Frank Fowler, Robert Moffett.

Robert Conn

JEFFERSON TOWNSHIP.   619

Fiftieth Ohio Infantry—Nathan Dunn.
Eighty-ninth Ohio Infantry—Frank Pittser, Tailor Evans, Anderson Harris, Alfred Kendle, Isom Hatfield, James Edwards, Jr., George Metz, Warren Work, George H. Culter, Jefferson Thomson, Lee Evans, Joseph Wright, Nathan Ellis.
Fifty-ninth Ohio Infantry—Samuel McElhanie, William Jacobs, L. D. Fowler, George P. Tyler, Johnson Jacobs.
Seventh Ohio Cavalry—John Brown, John Rankin, Jeremiah Ellis, James Blair, John Parry, Amos Willliams, John Baird, Charles Hook, Samuel Metz, Robert Work.
Tenth Kentucky Cavalry—Hiram Tyler, Oliver Carr, William L. Johnson, Amos McKinley, George Howland.
One Hundred and Ninety-fifth Ohio Infantry—John D. Seip, Wilson W. Young, John B. Porter.

SOCIETIES.

Russell Lodge, No. 573, I. O. O. F., was chartered May 16, 1874, and instituted June 20, 1874. It is an active lodge and has done a large amount of work since its organization. It now has a good amount of funds on hand, and is in a thriving condition. Its charter members were John Williamson, George P. Tyler, William Brady, Amos McKinley, L. H. Williams, Charles Kancher, George L. Johnson, Amos Myers, A. W. Williamson, Albert Conn, G. C. Risinger, McShaw Hiram Tyler, A. M. Williamson and James Johnson. The present membership is thirty-eight. The present officers: N. G., T. Prine; V. G., S. C. Glaze; Secretary, James Johnson; Treasurer, Amos McKinley.

Russellville Lodge, No. 166, A., F. & A. M., was chartered on the 27th day of September, 1848, and, with the exception of a short time during the war of the rebellion, it has always been in a prosperous condition. It has had a representation at every communication of the Grand body of the State since receiving its charter. The charter members were P. L. Wilson, Lambert Nowland, Louis Fridley, Wilshire Womax, Reason Fowler, Charles McClain, J. J. Green, William McColgin and others. Its present officers are: A. M. Williamson, W. M.; S. A. Myers, S. W.; C. B. Evans, J. W.; W. P. Williams, Secretary; Johnson Miller, Treasurer; T. N. Salisbury, S. D.; James Johnson, J. D.; W. Ball, Tiler.

Magnolia Lodge, No. 96, Knights of Pythias, was chartered May 24, 1876, and instituted the 7th day of June following. In the early days of this organization, it did a fair amount of work, but not so much of late. Its charter members were F. M. Woods, W. W. Ellsberry, Amos McKinley, George P. Tyler, James Johnson, L. H. Williams, J. K. McGregor, L. J. Evans, Johnson Miller, J. B. Clifton, John McGregor, William Brady, Samuel Pilson, Thomas Woods, L. C. Troutman, J. W. F. Melvin, J. W. Day, Jacob Schwallie, C. D. Thompson, J. J. Lewis and Lee Kendle. The officers at present are: C. C., Henry Williamson; V. G., A. B. Woods; Prelate, R. O. Evans; M. A., George P. Tyler; K. of R. and Seals, A. M. Williamson; Inside Guard, Wilson Prine.

THE FIRST FAIR.

The first fair in Brown County was held in Russellville in October, 1852, on a small lot adjoining the lot on which the Disciple Church now stands. The officers were: Alex Campbell, President; John Glaze, Secretary; Samuel Glaze, Treasurer. The Board of Directors were: John Williamson, of Jefferson Township; George Snedaker, of Union Township; Samuel Kerr, of Byrd Township; Absalom King, of Pleasant Township. The ring in which the stock was exhibited was made by encircling a small piece of ground with a strong rope, which was made fast to stakes driven deep into the ground. The display of vegetables, machinery and mechanical manufactures, etc., was made in the Presbyterian Church, which stood adjacent to the grounds in which the stock was shown.

The premiums paid were small, but they acted as a strong incentive to the people to make the fair a success. The next fair was held at Russellville, in October, 1853, in the lot now occupied by the steam flouring mills. This was the last Russellville fair. Since that time, they have been held at Georgetown.

RUSSELLVILLE.

The first and only town of Jefferson Township is Russellville. It was platted in 1817 by Russell Shaw, and named for him. It is situated on the southeast corner of a tract of land containing 200 acres, which he bought in 1816; it was then an unbroken forest, without a trace of civilization, except that a road passed near by in the direction of Ripley. The first sale of lots was in the autumn of 1817; the number sold was thirty-two, which brought the sum of $840. The first lot sold was purchased by Seth Gardner. The first house in the place was built by the founder of the town on Lot No. 29, and is yet standing. It is now occupied by and belongs to John D. Seip. A short distance to the north of the town, Mr. Shaw built a dwelling-house for himself, where he quietly lived and tilled his farm; he also was a blacksmith, having learned the trade in New York, and he worked at his trade here.

The first people here were obliged to go to Maysville, Ky., to do their trading, but about 1834, Mr. Shaw opened a small store at Russellville. He resigned his hammer and anvil to his son Anthony, and devoted himself exclusively to merchandising. He received his youngest son, G. N., as a partner in business, and in a few years financial disaster overtook the firm, and they retired from business. Succeeding merchants have been Seth Gardner, Porter Tomb, Thomas Culter, James Culter, William Smith, Eli Collins, Silas Thomas Nolance and Devore, Caleb Shreves, Kerr, Fowler, Tweed & Kirker, T. Mitchell, Womax McKnight and Prine, Henry Prine, John Seip, Hedrick, Richard Conn, Robert Conn, Conn & Mooney, C. C. Ball, Conn, Mingua & Co., Seip & Moore and others. Those now in business are T. H. Davis and Seip & Williamson.

A few of the blacksmiths who succeeded Mr. Shaw and his son Anthony were William Stephens, Franklin Pittser, Mowrer Bros., Wykoff, Wills, Tyler, Dawley, Jones, Johnson, Ewick & McKinley. The first tanner was Hill D. Stayton. He was succeeded by William Jones, Edwards, Brown, Kendle and others. There is no tannery in the village now. Early shoe-makers were Mathers, Menaugh, Wilson, McNown, Lucas, Gardner, Brown, Prine, Hatfield Edwards and Johnson. Among the early harness-makers were Fisher & Lane, succeeded by Snider, James Culter, Crute Bros., McMahon, Allen Culter and W. P. Williams. In 1835, Michael Benner came to Russellville from Pennsylvania, and commenced the manufacture of hats. He worked with considerable success at the business for a number of years, then purchased a farm in the southern part of the township, to which he moved and gave his attention to agricultural pursuits. Mr. Benner was a good mechanic, and it has been said of him that when a man bought one hat of him he never needed another.

The first hotel was kept by Calvin Shaw; the second by Seth Gardner. These proprietors were followed by Henry Prine from the time of the opening up of business in Ripley down to about 1848. The business of hotel-keeping in Russellville returned fair profits. All the wheat that was raised for fifteen or twenty miles north of Russellville, and sometimes farther, was wagoned to Ripley to find a market, and the pork also was driven to that town to be packed

JEFFERSON TOWNSHIP.

preparatory to shipment to foreign markets. Russellville was located midway between the producing section and the place of market, and a profitable hotel business was long maintained here. The hotels kept in late years were by Main, Conn and the present one by John Williamson.

The pioneer physicians were Hersy, Beasly, Sharp, Mathers, Lilly and Orr, succeeded by John Thompson, Stevenson, Shepherd, Thompson and Hayes. The present physicians are J. N. Salisbury and A. M. Williamson.

The first account we have of wagon-making was by James Curran, who came from Pennsylvania at an early day, settled in Russellville and engaged in the above business. He spoke the Hiberian dialect, and was somewhat eccentric in his ways and manners, yet a good mechanic. To him may be assigned the honor of making the first pleasure wagon or carriage in this part of the country. He worked here until 1854, when he sold his property and went to one of the Western States.

In the early days of Russellville, a large amount of coopering was carried on, there being then a large amount of the finest oak timber hereabouts. It was manufactured into flour barrels, pork barrels, lard tierces, whisky barrels, etc., which found a ready market in Ripley.

The first school building in Russellville was a small, round-log cabin, built on Lot No. 31, now owned by the heirs of C. A. Ewick; the floor was built of puncheons, the seats of small timber, split in two pieces, smoothed, and with large pins for legs. The windows were of oiled paper; the chimney was built of small sticks plastered with clay, which was held together by straw cut in short pieces.

The exact date of the establishment of the post office at Russellville is not known, but it is thought to have been between 1825 and 1828. Alfred Beasly was the first Postmaster; his successors have been Robert Tomb, Thomas Mefford, Caleb Shreves, and J. N. Salisbury, the present incumbent.

In 1866, a post office called Red Oak was established in the extreme southern part of the township. The first Postmaster was Mr. Warwick; he was followed by Messrs. Miller, McKnight and the present Postmaster, Mr. Hook. A dry goods store, blacksmith shop and wagon shop comprise the business of the place.

In closing this sketch, we desire to tender our especial thanks to Mrs. Rhoda Collins, John Menaugh, Alexander Wilson, Mrs. Lavina Shaw, John Williamson, J. N. Salisbury and many others for much information received.

CHAPTER XI.

SCOTT TOWNSHIP.

BY R. B. M'CALL, M. D.

THE first comers to a new country for certain reasons choose the fertile regions bordering water-courses as the most fitting for settlement. Here in abundance they find that most indispensable article of household and farm consumption—pure running water; animals of the neighboring forest which congregate here to slake their thirst, the game destined to recruit the table with meats; and to these may be added the hope or belief that others may likewise be attracted to the same spot. In the White Oak Valley, the hardy pioneer found much to be desired by the settler—a wealth of timber for fuel and building, a forest overflowing with choice game of nearly every mentionable species, a fine, large stream of water teeming with innumerable fish, and promising excellent facilities for future usefulness, and a climate that has ever been esteemed for its healthfulness. All these he received in his deed of purchase by paying a trifling sum for the land. Hardships and perils were encountered, many of them, indeed, for they were inseparable from the lot of the venturesome pioneer. He endured much, suffered much, may be, yet his insecure, wild life had a kind of fascination in it, sweetened, we may conjecture, by the inspiring thought that he is laying the foundation to a state of future greatness for posterity.

The Indian must have been friendly; the four-footed denizen of the forest harmless or unsuccessful in quest of prey, as there is recorded no mention of savage butchery or blood-curdling tragedy enacted in the darksome depths of the forest. He levied without let or hindrance his contributions on forest and stream; his bill of fare, consisting of fowl, fish and fruit, was something truly wonderful, calculated by its plentifulness, freshness and variety to kindle the liveliest emotions in the bosom of an epicure. Bountiful nature with lavish liberality scattered her gifts on every hand; game was had at the dooryard, wild fruits of various kinds and in wasteful profusion were convenient of access, and had without price for the trouble of gathering. Honey and maple sugar, obtained with little labor, supplied his table the year round with the most delicious of sweets, for the bee tree was an institution of the country, and royal camps of sugar tree and maple were early put into successful operation. No elaborate contrivance was needed to ensnare the finny treasures of White Oak. His dwelling place was a cabin of unhewn logs, a single room doing duty as kitchen, dining room and sleeping apartment; a few logs properly placed and joined together, a roof of clapboards, kept in place by long poles, a chimney of mud and sticks, a broad, deep fire-place, in some instances capable of taking in a good sized saw log, and a puncheon floor, such was his castle rude and simple. Something to wear, plenty to eat, the prospective treasures of an uncultivated soil, robust health, a resolute will and an unswerving determination to do, these were his stock in trade. The fur cap, buckskin garments, Indian moccasins and trusty flint-lock were a *ne plus ultra* to frontier life. Wife and daughters required the expensive services of no *modiste* to adorn their persons with the latest styles in fashion and fabric, one, or at most two, plainly made frocks fulfilling every need, and for the rest they were con-

SCOTT TOWNSHIP.

tent with nature's unlabored embellishments. No imposing church edifices were there, no humble meeting-house where he might go " to hear the parson preach and pray," but then there were around him "God's first temples," where, kneeling on a carpet of green and drinking in the sweet music of birds, he performed his simple devotions.

Every cabin was a schoolhouse, and children were almost universally taught to read, write and cast up accounts, and the specimens of proficiency in these branches that have escaped the hand of time conclusively attest the correctness and efficiency of early methods of instruction.

The hospitality and benevolence are proverbial; every man was his neighbor; no one went hungry from his door; he had a Spartan's inflexibility of purpose, and a Roman's devotion to honor; he was truth and candor embodied; his comforts were divided, his opinions shared and his sorrows confided.

The earliest settlements within the present limits of Scott Township were for the most part by adventurers from Virginia, Kentucky, Pennsylvania, New Jersey, New Hampshire and Vermont. Little more than a decade had elapsed since the close of the War of Independence when the army of emigration from the Atlantic States and from Kentucky took up its devious march through the trackless wilderness to the remote Northwestern Territory.

The column reached and halted on the banks of White Oak Creek in the spring of 1800. In this year, Robert Wardlow purchased and settled on a tract of about three hundred acres in William Moore's Survey, No. 1,053, on the east bank of White Oak, in the extreme northern part of the township.

The following year, Col. Henry Zumatt moved on a smaller piece of land located in J. Burton's Survey, No. 1,213, in the central part of the township; and two years later, that is to say in 1803, Lewis Shick bought and took possession of a considerable tract in the southern quarter.

To Robert Wardlow, Henry Zumatt and Lewis Shick belongs the distinction of the traditional founders of the early settlements on White Oak. From some old correspondence in the hands of Henry Kimball, it is learned that prior to 1800 Mr. Wardlow resided near Rockridge, Va. He must have been esteemed a man of consequence and possessed of much pecuniary means, as is witnessed by a letter from Charles Campbell, attorney of Rockbridge, Va., dated August, 1804, and addressed to Mr. Wardlow, which, after referring to some matters of a business character, alludes to many messages of affectionate inquiry and interest. At his decease, Mr. Wardlow left quite a numerous family of children, four of whom survive their father. Henry and Levi and another (name unknown to the writer) are living.

Col. Henry Zumatt was born in Harrison County, Ky., in 1771. His early life was passed in hunting and Indian fighting in the savage wilds of his native State. Having negotiated the purchase of a fine body of land on White Oak, in John Burton's sectional survey, as already noticed, he with his family crossed the Ohio River, and after a tedious journey of several days' duration reached his destination in the spring of 1801. Zumatt pitched his tent on the east bank of the creek at a point a mile south of New Hope. The land bought by Zumatt for $2 an acre, and now owned by Henry Kimball, a son of his widowed wife by a subsequent marriage, is considered one of the most valuable farms in Brown County.

In 1808, a grist-mill, which stood on the site of Henry Young's flouring mill, was erected by Zumatt, and this was the first of any kind in the township, if not in the county. Up to this time, the settler took his grist of corn to Levanna, a small town on the Ohio River, and if he wished to procure flour, had to cross the river, as none could be had nearer than Augusta, Ky. Zumatt was commissioned a Colonel of militia at the outbreak of the war of 1812, and served with distinction at the head of the Fourth Detachment of Ohio troops. He died in 1814 in the prime of useful life, his untimely end deplored as little less than a calamity.

Of Louis Shick not much can be said beyond the fact that he emigrated from Virginia and settled in the township on the land now owned by Jackson Pitzer. As nearly as may be ascertained, he came to Ohio in the year 1803. A few years later in the wake of Wardlow and Zumatt, came the Myers family, consisting of Francis Meyers and wife and three sons—Thomas, Francis, Jr., and William, then Joshua Davidson, Benjamin and Nicholas Smith, James McCall, the McBeth brothers—John and Robert—John Stansberry, John Pitzer, Jacob Fite, Jonathan Atwood and James Morris.

Three families, namely, Zumatt, the Myers and McBeth, purchased the whole of John Burton's Survey, No. 1,213, of 1,333 acres, Zumatt taking in the southeast, the Myers in the southwest, and the McBeths in the north. O. F. Dunn and John Samms own the Myers purchase; Henry Young, James J. Smith, Henry Wardlow and Jefferson Fite, the McBeth.

Francis Myers took possession of his purchase in the spring of 1804. In a few years he divided his farm equally among his three sons, Thomas and Francis, Jr., subsequently acquiring the whole by buying the other brother's share. Mr. Myers was a Kentuckian, of whose life little more is known than that he was a good neighbor, and lived to the remarkable age of 105 years. Thomas married, and began life on the farm of his inheritance. A few years of farming sufficing to give him a distaste for agricultural pursuits, he converted his ready means into cash, abandoned his home to a tenant, and removed to Levanna to begin the career of a very successful merchant. Becoming dissatisfied with small returns, after one year in Levanna he removed to Augusta, Ky., where in less than a quarter of a century he had built up a fortune of a quarter of a million dollars. Mr. Myers was married to Betsey Davidson, a daughter of Joshua Davidson, who bore him several sons and daughters, and made him a most exemplary wife. An old neighbor of Mr. Myers tells of that gentleman that his first venture as a merchant was a little affair kept in his cabin on the farm. Two shelves supported by pegs driven in the wall behind the only door, a bolt of jeans and a few simple articles beside, this was the first store. Mr. Myers had a business motto, and it ran thus: "Take care of the cents, and let the dollars take care of themselves." Francis remained a farmer, took an active and intelligent interest in the concerns of the little community wherein he dwelt, was prominent in the local politics of the township, and was elected its first Clerk, and subsequently twice chosen a Justice of the Peace. His amusing whimsicalities, droll ways and quaint sayings are remembered with immense satisfaction by his early acquaintances. He died in 1860, and was interred in the family burying ground on the farm. The year that witnessed the commencement of the Myers settlement, brought the McBeth brothers, John and Robert, in their hands a deed of gift from their father for 800 acres of land. They became the largest land-holders in the township, owning more than half of John Burton's large survey of more than 1,300 acres. Robert built on the land where Henry Young lives, and John built a cabin near where James J. Smith resides. In the following year, 1805, Lieut. Joshua Davidson and James McCall erected cabins on the west bank of White Oak, the former in John Brown's Survey, No. 1,795, at a point a little south of Zumatt's place of settlement, and the latter in Lewis Booker's Survey, in the southern quarter of the township. Henry Pickering lives where Davidson's cabin stood seventy-seven years ago. Lieut. Davidson had been an officer in the patriot army, serving through the seven years' struggle for American independence. He crossed the frozen Trenton with bleeding feet, starved with his

SCOTT TOWNSHIP.

beloved commander at Valley Forge, helped to make it hot for the red coats at Brandywine, and triumphed with Lafayette at Yorktown, where he had the satisfaction of seeing Cornwallis transformed into Cobwallis. He was with the hero of Stony Point, in his Indian campaigns, and one night in an altercation concerning some prisoners he was guarding, he raised a musket he had snatched from a soldier to shoot Wayne, who was approaching him with drawn sword. He was the father of nine children—John, Joseph, William, Joshua, Ruth, Mary, Ellen, Betsey and Nancy. Mary was married to Lot Stratton, Ellen to John Birngammon, Betsey to Thomas Myers and Nancy to More Ralstin. The children are all dead. Until his death, which took place in 1844, at the age of ninety years, any mention of the grand struggle through which he had passed would rekindle the martial fire in the old man's breast.

John McCall and Samuel McCall own and live on the land which their grandfather purchased in 1805. James McCall was an Irishman, whose parents came over to the colonies while the war of the Revolution was in progress. His father hated the British with religious fervor born of English persecution of the Irish; therefore, the vessel that bore him across the Atlantic had no sooner embarked its living freight than he sought his son and urged him to enlist in the cause of liberty. James enlisted, taking the bounty of $1, and served three years in the privateer navy of the infant Republic. After the expiration of the war, he settled in Pennsylvania, his father having purchased a farm of several hundred acres in that State. In 1785, he married Jane Ramsey, by whom he had six children—Margaret, John, Robert, James, Nancy and Samuel. None of the family save James emigrated to the Western country. A younger brother of his was the father the late Gen. George A. McCall, of Pennsylvania, who was a prominent Division Commander in the late war of the rebellion. Only James, John and Robert of all his family settled on White Oak. In 1816, Robert was married to Phœbe Kimball, the issue of which union was James, Albert, Mary, Samuel, John, Jane and Benjamin, of whom only James, Albert, John and Samuel are living.

All that is remembered of Mr. Morris is that he built a cabin somewhere on the land now owned by David Brannen; that he had occasion once to clear off ten acres of land and did so by felling all the timber so as to cross and interlace, and then set fire to the whole, making a magnificent bonfire. The Pitzer family settled in the western part of the township as early perhaps as 1805. John Pitzer was the patriarchal head of the family. To the writer's knowledge, only four children survive—Joseph, Matilda, John and Jackson, of a family of ten, namely, Eliza, Rebecca, Delilah, Matilda, Nancy, Martha, Joseph, John, Henry and Jackson. Joseph, John and Jackson are prosperous farmers, and have lived all their lives in Scott Township, where they were born.

Benjamin Kimball and family departed from Hopkinton, N. H., in 1801, with Wheeling, Va., as the objective point of their journey, where they arrived three months later. Subsequently he moved to Ohio, and, at the opening of the late war with Great Britain, joined a regiment of Ohio troops, and served till the treaty of Ghent put an end to the struggle. In 1816, he married the widow of Col. Zumatt, deceased, who bore him one child, Henry Kimball. Of the fruit of his first marriage, only Timothy and Hazen are known to be living.

Jacob Fite, the founder of the numerous family of that name, came to Ohio and settled in the western quarter of the township somewhere in the first decade after 1800. He chose a tract of land in the survey of D. Lambert, No. 2421. William and Charles, the two surviving descendants of Jacob Fite, have not wandered from the home of their father's adoption. All who know them respect their industry, honesty and temperate habits.

John Stansberry moved to White Oak about the time that the Myers and the McBeths did. He located in the eastern part of the township on an extensive tract of fine land, where he went resolutely to work to conquer, single-handed, the hardships that beset the path of the settler. In a few years, he had cleared off a good deal of land, established a fine sugar orchard and camp, and put things generally in good shape. When hostilities between Great Britain and the United States began in 1812, he volunteered in defense of his country's flag. He and John McCall and perhaps others from the same settlement were handed over to Gen. Brock in Hull's remarkable surrender at Detroit. Mr. Stansberry married early in life a very estimable lady. He died a few years since at an advanced age, having passed the allotted threescore and ten, and earned by a worthy life the commendation of "well done, good and faithful servant."

Samuel Gibson emigrated to Ohio, and settled on White Oak in the year 1814. Mr. Gibson reared a family of ten children—Andrew, Margaret, Jennie, William, Samuel, Sara, Robert, James, Agnes and Hugh. Hugh Gibson, the only living representative of the family, resides in New Hope. Andrew Gibson, recently deceased, who was the eldest son, was the father of several children. A daughter of his, Mrs. Martha Gibson Davy, was married to John R. Davy, a wealthy business man of Cincinnati. The youngest daughter, Drusilla, married Joseph L. Clemens; Margaret was married to Joseph Scott; Betsey to John Thompson, and Nancy twice, the last time to William Stratton, all of whom reside in New Hope or neighborhood.

Among the settlers who came after 1820 were James J. Smith, Henry Young and William Stratton.

William Stratton was born in Pennsylvania, and came to the settlement on White Oak about the year 1820. Soon after locating a farm in the western half of J. Brown's Survey, No. 3261, behind the west bank of the creek, he was offered employment on the canal, where he went and died. He left a family of eleven children—Lot, Lewis, Aaron, Christopher, John, Sandford, Bonde, Lavina, Nancie, Susie and America. Perhaps the only survivors of this large family are Lavina Holten and America Wisbey. Lot Stratton married Mary Davidson, and settled near the ancestral roof-tree. This union, like that of his father, was a prolific one, there being born ten children, who are all dead, except Marion and Nancy. Napoleon, a deceased son, was for many years a prominent and successful educator.

James J. Smith and Henry Young came to White Oak in 1835. Mr. Smith bought a part of the old McBeth purchase, and erected a dwelling east of New Hope, just in the outskirts of the village. Here he has lived for forty-seven years. Mr. Smith has filled offices of trust and profit, both in the township and county. He is now eighty years of age, has good health, and may live many years to come.

Like Mr. Smith, Henry Young settled on a part of the McBeth purchase. He has owned and operated for many years a flouring and grist mill on the site of the one built by Col. Zumatt. He has served the township and county in various official capacities. He has but one child living—Matilda, wife of James McKinly, and two sons and one daughter deceased—Robert, Richard and Lucinda. Mr. Young is over eighty years of age, is hale, and looks as if he might live a score of years yet.

Any sketch of the early settlements along White Oak would be incomplete without a mention of George Bingamon, James Boothby and Mr. Wills.

George Bingamon bought and settled on the west bank of White Oak in the northern part of L. Booker's Survey, No. 901, at a point opposite the McCall purchase, on the east bank, about the year 1812. By energy and pru-

Respectfully &c,
Fno. Smith.

SCOTT TOWNSHIP.

dent management, Mr. Bingamon succeeded in accumulating quite a competency before his death, which took place some eighteen years since. Several sons blessed Mr. Bingamon's happy wedlock—Solomon, Lewis, Harrison, Sanford, Richard and A. J. Bingamon. James Boothby bought in the southwestern quarter of J. Kerr's Survey, No. 6702, and Mr. Wills, the father of Howe, located in the western part of the same survey, probably as early as 1808.

Such is a brief and imperfect resumé of the facts in the history of the early settlement of Scott Township. One by one the old settlers dropped off, until two years ago the last of that venerable band closed his eyes on the fleeting scenes of the world. The chronological course of our summarized narrative now brings us down to the date of the organization of the township.

In 1828, detached parts of Clark and Franklin, two original townships, were united into one whole, and the new corporation called Scott Township. Scott is the smallest township but one in the county, comprising an area of twenty-one and one-eighth square miles, or 13,520 acres, valued in 1881 by the Board of Equalization at $208,752, or about $15.43 per acre. But what is lacking on the one hand in extent of territory is made up on the other in importance and advantage of location; for although not exactly in the center of the county, it may be said to be the most nearly central, as it has five other townships adjoining it, namely, Pike, Washington, Franklin, Pleasant and Clark, while extent, value and variety of productions, internal improvements, political strength and influence are about equally distributed on the four points of the compass. Scott Township is bounded on the north by Pike and Washington, on the east by Washington and Franklin, on the south by Pleasant and Franklin and on the west by Clark, and has an outline of twenty miles in length, made up on the south and west by two straight lines at right-angles, and on the north and east by a succession of short lines and angles forming one broken and extended boundary line. The general surface is undulating, broken here and there by ravine and vale, and traversed by a multitude of streams, principal among which are White Oak, Sterling and Miranda Creeks. White Oak is much the largest, and is the outlet of all the others; it flows from north to south the entire length of the township, being joined successively by Sterling and Miranda. Sterling and Miranda come in from the west and join White Oak, the former a quarter of a mile west of New Hope, and the latter north of the village of White Oak Valley. Along White Oak, and extending for perhaps half a mile back on either side to the higher or table land, is a belt of alluvial lands called bottoms, whose unvarying level is interrupted only by the small channels of tributary streams. Before the timber was stripped off, these bottoms were frequently inundated by the annual spring freshets, and received rich deposits of sediment from the receding waters. Though in the recollection of the oldest citizen they have been overflowed but once since the removal of the timber, yet their productiveness remains apparently undiminished. In the table-lands behind the bottoms a distinctive limestone clay, relieved in many places by strips of sandy loam along the smaller water-courses, is the prevailing character of the soil. No mineral wealth has been found, notwithstanding there have not been wanting enthusiastic visionaries who have diligently sought to find treasures of gold and silver, which they firmly believed to be hidden somewhere in the foundations of the hills. The economical and commercial importance of the timber of the White Oak region merits for it a particular mention. White Oak, from which the country derives its baptismal name, and beech predominate largely. Extensive bodies of white oak are met on every hand, notwithstanding the destructive warfare waged for forty years by the woodman's ax.

A stranger would find it hard to believe the considerable growth still to be seen is little more than a trace of the vast luxuriance of forty years ago. White oak has been the farmer's well nigh exclusive resource for material to build his fences, for boards and cooper stuff and for building material. Poplar was once plentiful, but at present barely one of those royal looking giants of the forests is left to greet us. Beech has always been abundant and valuable to the farmer, and in the future will be an object of solicitous care so long as he shall require wood for fuel. Black and white walnut, ash, elm, hickory, linn and sycamore are indigenous. Formerly, there was much black walnut growing both on the bottoms and upland; the trees were of the largest dimensions, affording a very fine quality of lumber, but recently large quantities have been cut off and sold, yielding handsome returns. There used to be much sugar tree and maple, and sugar orchards and camps were a legion, but the enterprising exactions of the farmer in his quest for rich newly-cleared lands have swept away about the last remnant of them. Hickory, with its toothsome fruit, has passed away. Slippery elm, red elm, ash, linn and wild cherry, the *prunus virginiana* of botany, have become scarce. The first has been much in quest for its bark, and both it and the last have been extensively used in domestic medicine. The tall sycamore that used to line both banks of White Oak, standing like giant sentinels with their leaning stems and towering tops meeting above the flood, have, too, well-nigh disappeared.

Grain, grass and tobacco are abundantly produced on bottom and upland. In quality and yield of wheat, corn and hay, Scott Township will doubtless compare favorably with similar equal areas in the same industry anywhere in the State.

Wheat and corn have ever been esteemed the leading products of the White Oak Valley. As has been stated, they are not now as formerly as much depended upon for revenue, or, more properly, general income, yet are largely grown, principally for local consumption. Previously wheat and corn were raised chiefly on the bottoms and second bottoms, but since underdrainage by means of tiling has been introduced, and the oak flat-lands adequately relieved of the cause of their former unproductiveness, no such superiority can be claimed. The yield of wheat per acre will vary perhaps from ten to twenty-five bushels, and that of corn from twenty-five to seventy-five bushels. Oats are raised to an inconsiderable extent; rye not at all, except for dressing. Timothy and red-top are harvested on a pretty large scale, but not to an extent that would give them any great prominence among the products of the country. Some clover is grown, chiefly for grazing and land dressing. Of the 5,023 acres of meadow and pasture land, four-fifths may be are in timothy and red-top and one-fifth in clover and all other grasses.

Tobacco since 1860 has been the staple, affording the farmer a large and ever-increasing revenue. Growing and fitting for market of large droves of sheep, cattle and hogs has hitherto been the chief industrial pursuit of the landed proprietor, but is now almost abandoned in favor of tobacco culture. Samples from a crop raised on the farm of Henry Kimball, Sr., and sold to Robert Young, tobacco merchant of Higginsport, received the first award at the Centennial in 1876. The principal growers of the weed have been Henry Kimball, F. M. Stratton, John McCall, George W. Stratton, O. F. Dunn, John Samms, D. M. Brannen and Jefferson Fite.

Scott Township began political life in 1828. December 28, 1828, the oath of office was administered by Martin Gatts, a Justice of the Peace to Dr. Enoch Ellsberry, James McCall and William Hilligoss, Trustees; Jacob Thomas, Treasurer; Francis Myers, Clerk; Andrew Gibson, Constable, and David M. Smith, Fence Viewer. This was the first official act performed in the name of the newly created township. The Trustees met March 2, 1829,

SCOTT TOWNSHIP.

for the purpose of laying out and establishing road districts, which they proceeded to do with suitable official dignity and deliberation, dividing the township into seven such districts. At the same meeting, Andrew Gibson, Constable, was directed to publish by written proclamation the next annual election for township officers, to be held at the house of Daniel Holloway April 6, 1829. At a meeting held March 9, 1829, to organize the township for educational purposes, it was agreed, after much wise legislating, to authorize the formation of six school subdistricts, but it was not, however, until after the ensuing April election that the new regimé was put into effective operation. According to a list in township book No. 1, dated May 3, 1829, Scott Township had 111 householders, among whose names appear the following: Abraham Forcyth, Jacob Hiler, William Hilligoss, Joseph Blair, Nicholas Peddicord, Daniel Vandament, Reuben Fite, Duncan McCoy, Samuel Liming, Robert McCall, Jonathan Atwood, Joseph Pitzer, John Palmer, Lot Stratton, More Ralstin, Thomas Cotterill, Robert Patton, Jacob Gatts, Samuel Gibson, Henry Gatts, James McFadden, Cyrus McGehey, George Bingamon, James Boothby, John Ross, James Allen, Abraham Remley, Hezekiah Lindsay, Abraham Smith, Nicholas Smith, Elijah Sollenberger, Benton Smith, Daniel Reynolds, Daniel Holloway, Joshua Davidson, George Courts, Thomas Young, Everett Smith, Thomas Sillman, John Stansberry, John Hoss, James Knight, Jacob Fox, Benjamin Kimball, Garland Anderson, John Hill, John T. Wills, Samuel McBeth, Henry Pickering, George Hendrixson, Abraham Foulk, John Hiler, Widow Fisher, Nancy Gotherman, John Fite, Jacob Vandament, Willis Bert, Samuel Glascock, John Whites, Catherine Stratton, James Johnson, James Brown, Francis Myers, Jr., Charles Fite, James McCoy, Andrew Gibson, Andrew G. Patton, John Barngroover, Matthew Buzby, Josiah Boothby, Alexander Hanna, John Pitzer, Daniel White, John Hening, Thomas Ross, John Fields, Rebecca Smith, Ebenezer Smith, Conley McFadden, Mary Davidson, William Lindsey, Benjamin Smith, Toliver Roglin, John Forsythe, Thomas Forsythe, Michael Landerback, Jasper Kimball, Nancy Robbins, Parmelia Ellsberry, Enoch M. Ellsberry, Wesley Ellsberry, John Fox, William M. Patton, Joseph McDannold, Martin Gatts, Nicholas Wallace, Enoch Hendrixson, Isaac Holloway, Aaron Stites, James Gibson, William Buzby, Lewis Stratton, John Bingamon, John Day, John Courts, James McCall, Alexander Patton, Jacob Hoss, John McKibben, Jacob Thomas, David Thomas.

In a statement of annual settlement made by the Trustees March, 1830, no charge for services has been made by any township officer. An exhibit of receipts and expenditures for 1831 has this quaint recital of facts: "receipts, nothing; orders drawn on the Treasurer in favor of Jacob Vandament, $4.62¼" following which is the stupendous showing for 1832, of nothing for receipts and a $20 promise in the shape of orders drawn on the Treasurer. We learn that in 1833 the Trustees devoted the proceeds of the sale of an estray horse, amounting to $45.50, and sold to Levi Samms, to township purposes, $36 of which was expended in the purchase of four plows for the use of Supervisors. For 1833, the receipts by the Treasurer aggregated $67.45, and the expenditures for public service amounted to $70.20. In 1835, the Treasurer's per centum was the handsome sum of 48 cents and no mills, while the compensation of Trustees was $2.25 each for two of them, and $1.50 for the other. Supervisors received from 75 cents to $1 presumably to make up losses against delinquents or for extra work.

In the annual settlement for 1840, the Trustees found in the Treasurer's hands 22 cents for township purposes, and $59.29¼ of road funds, and gave an order for 12¼ cents to be paid out of those funds, and at the same time caused John Ristine to give his bond for $1,500 as Treasurer. The subjoined statement of a settlement made with the township officers dated March 7, 1842, is added with the hope that it may be of interest to some: "Trustees, John Fiscus received for service $1.50, John Stansberry, $0; James Boothby $0; Treasurer, John Ristine, $1.50; Clerk, B. W. Whiteman, $2; Supervisors, Henry Young, $2.25; Vincent Robbins, $3.50; Jacob Hiler. $3; Amos Dawson, 75 cents; Joseph Bingamon, $1.50; Christopher Stratton, $1.35; Constable, G. W. Stayton, $1.35. Signed: B. W. Whiteman, Clerk of Scott Township."

In 1845, there were between the ages of twenty-one and forty-five, ninety, and between the ages of eighteen and twenty-one, forty-five, making a total enrollment fit for militia duty of 135 men, and there were, besides, twelve exemptions.

The first to fill the responsible office of Justice was Martin Gatts; the first Clerk was Francis Myers; the first Treasurer, Jacob Thomas; the first Board of Trustees, Dr. Enoch Ellsberry, James McCall and William Hilligoss; the first Constable, Andrew Gibson. The Justices of the township have been: Martin Gatts, Francis Myers, Reuben Fite, Garland Anderson, Hezekiah Lindsey, James J. Smith, George Hendrixson, Lyman Vanmeter, Amos Dawson, William Espey, W. S. Wharton, B. W. Whiteman, Hyson Moler, Henry Young, G. W. Stayton, A. E. Stansberry, Walter Gooden and W. N. Parker. The office of Clerk has been filled by Francis Myers, John Ross, John Fiscus, John Dorman, John Ristine, James J. Smith, Alfred Duncamon, B. W. Whiteman, N. B. Stratton, Amos Dawson, C. P. Myers, W. D. Courts, T. S. Kimball, W. S. Wharton, John Cook, A. J. Bingamon, J. K. P. Stevens. G. W. Stayton and J. H. Smith.

The township revenues have been entrusted successively to Jacob Thomas, John Ristine, John Ross, G. H. Wrestler, J. H. Thompson, R. R. Blair, William Blair, Joseph Scott, John Stansberry, Henry Young and W. A. Bivans. Among the Assessors elected for the township are found the names of James Thompson, Col. Butt, R. R. McKenzie, Thomas Moler, F. M. Patton, Christian Wahl, Peter Wahl, William Campbell.

According to the best information to be had, the first elections held in the township were held in the old log mill built by Henry Zumatt, and at the time of holding them owned by John Sollenberger. Afterward a house for the purpose was rented in New Hope, and ever since elections have been held in that village.

In politics, Scott takes rank among the most prominent of her sister townships. Hezekiah Lindsey, elected Auditor in 1833, and James J. Smith, his successor in office, elected in 1840, were both Scott Township men. More recently, in 1862, Dr. W. W. Ellsberry was elected Auditor, and subsequently re-elected. B. W. Whiteman and Alfred Parker were called to take charge of the Treasurer's office, the former for one and the latter for two terms. Henry Young had one term as Sheriff. Wall Applegate was chosen, but died before the time to assume his office. Scott has had two Commissioners, James McCall and Jefferson Fite, and two Representatives in the Legislature, Dr. Enos B. Fee and Eli B. Parker.

The town of New Hope and the hamlets of White Oak Valley and Wallsburg are the three villages of the township which vie with each other in friendly rivalry as centers of traffic and political wisdom.

To the prudent forethought of Daniel Holloway and Lawrence Rose the New Hoper is indebted for the choice of a site at once attractive and healthy. Seventy-five years ago, Daniel Holloway, with assistance of neighbors, laid the foundation of the first house in the embryo town, an unpretentious structure of

SCOTT TOWNSHIP.

unhewn logs, rough fashioned, of a single room, illuminated by one small window.

A few years Mr. Holloway's little dwelling stood alone on the slight plateau above White Oak; then came Lawrence Rose, and another house was added; and as the years came and went others sought and found homes, clustering around the first rude cabins of Holloway and Rose. Ere long a mill was added, then a blacksmith shop, to gladden the ears of the hamlet, hungering, so to speak, after the familiar sounds of industrial life. Early the merchant discovered the new field for enterprise. Above the entrance to a low-browed, rambling frame building that stood on the spot now occupied by F. M. Patton's residence, old inhabitants remember seeking the legend, Peter Kookis, the first store-keeper of New Hope. Peter was unquestionably the first dispenser of dry goods and groceries that beamed on the delighted town and country folk. His stock was small but ample; the business grew and prospered, and Peter did not fail to lay up the wherewithal to extend it.

Following Kookis next came George Bingamon, who displayed his wares in a frame which stood on the corner where John W. Young has his residence. At the expiration of a year or two, the business was disposed of to Lot Stratton and Morefield Patton. These gentlemen enlarged the stock and extended the trade until they made it one of the most prosperous in the county.

Kookis, Bingamon and Patton & Stratton, each in his way and unconsciously, labored for the same end—the building up of an interest which, in after years, grew into a marvelous structure of activity and wealth.

But the war came, and with it inflation and high prices. The war vanished, and with it the glory of the town as a commercial center.

Succeeding the last-named firms, the following gentlemen, at various times, were engaged in the dry goods business:

A. C. H. Cotterill, William Blair, William Creighead, James Young, James Walker, Joseph Steward, Benjamin Whiteman, Lewis Bingamon, William Keys, James McCall, Andrew Fox, W. W. Ellsbury, F. M. Patton, Doepka, Philip Krum, V. B. Smith and M. W. Fite.

A. C. H. Cotterill sold goods in the rooms occupied by F. M. Patton, and did a thriving business for many years. The firm of O. J. Steward, for the time and country, had an immense business, the annual sales being little, if any less, than those of the largest house in the county. The first inn in the town was a small affair, kept by John Fiscus. The first blacksmith shop was that of John Fox; the building had stood in the bottom, near what was called the "Sterling Fork of White Oak," was torn down, and put up on a spot nearly opposite to Mr. Fite's present residence.

The first tannery was operated by Nicholas Wallace; the next, by Benjamin Purdum, where Jonah Purdum now lives; and the third by James Heaton.

Dr. Enoch M. Ellsbury opened the first physician's office, and also kept the first post office in a small house about ten by twelve, still standing, an appurtenance to Jonah Purdum's dwelling.

This was the first post office established in the township. The appointment of Dr. Ellsberry was from John McLean, Postmaster General under John Quincy Adams, confirmed and dated at Washington December 15, 1828. After Ellsberry, Benjamin Purdum, O. J. Stewart, G. W. Stayton, W. P. Wharton and F. M. Patton, have successively kept the office, Purdum, Stewart and Stayton each having it for several years, and F. M. Patton, the present incumbent, for the last eighteen years. In this connection it may not be out of place to annex the following, addressed to Dr. Ellsberry from the Post Office Department:

POST OFFICE DEPARTMENT, WASHINGTON, April 30, 1834.

To Enoch Ellsberry, Postmaster of New Hope, Brown Co., Ohio:

SIR—To determine, with as much accuracy as possible, the relative position of the several post offices, and the courses of the post roads in the United States, so that they may be correctly designated on the maps of the Department, I am desirous of obtaining such information of the topography of the country in your vicinity, as you may be enabled to give.

You will, therefore, receive a series of questions, on the annexed leaf, from one to ten.

You will please to fill up the blank spaces left for your answers, and return the leaf, with all convenient dispatch, addressed to the "Post Office Department, care of D. H. Barr."

You are also especially requested to furnish a plat, or sketch, of the country in your vicinity, showing:

The courses of the post roads;
The sites of the post offices;
The distances along each post road, from office to office;
The courses of other roads than post roads, if any; and the distances along them to the post offices, or to places where mail roads join, or cross; and the
Bearings and distances, on straight lines, from your office to the other offices.

Early attention to this sketch, or plat, with a return of the replies and statements called for in the annexed inquiries, inclosed and directed as above, is desired.

Very respectfully,

W. T. BARRY,
Postmaster General.

In the summer of 1849, the cholera scourge made its appearance in New Hope, carrying terror, death and bereavement into every family. On the third day of its appearance, seven deaths occurred, the first victim being William Purdum. The total number of deaths in a population of 100 was twenty-two. The victims were William Purdum, Thomas Early, Martin Gatts, Sr., and wife, Martin Gatts, Jr., and wife and two children (all died in the same house), Cinderilla Lauderback, Andrew Young and daughter, Wilson Fox, wife of John Stills, wife of Andrew Fox, Nelson Fox and wife and child, wife of G. W. Cotterill, Perry Applegate, Robert Stills, Samuel Whiteman and Jacob Gatts—Jacob Gatts being the last victim.

Squire Henry Young relinquished his business and heroically devoted himself to the care of the sick and dying, never forsaking his post for a moment till the grim king of terrors was vanquished and the field won.

The date of the settlement of White Oak Valley is obscure, no reliable data being at hand. From the best information given, the settlement on the west bank was the oldest (past tense, because Rosstown no longer exists). It is said there was a mill built on the site of the present one in 1835, by Alexander Hanna and James Ross. However, it is known that Robert Blair and John Ross erected a carding-mill here, and afterward attached a grist-mill. These gentlemen probably built the excellent mill for many years known as Gatts' Mill, now owned by Robert McCall.

At one time, White Oak Valley was a thriving hamlet, possessing, besides the mill, two or three good stores, a post office, a blacksmith shop and a shoe shop. William Espey and Joseph Hills sold goods at different times. John Robbins has been the principal goods dealer for many years.

Wahlsburg Post Office, named in honor of Peter Wahl, is a youthful hamlet. It is located at the junction of the Georgetown & Mount Oreb Free Turnpike with the White Oak Valley & Arnheim road, at a point equidistant from Georgetown and New Hope. But a few years ago, two blacksmith shops, one of them John Lee Brown's, and two dwelling houses, were the only buildings. Ten years since, Peter Wahl erected a large building, storeroom and living house in one and opened the first and only dry goods trade in the place. About three years ago (1879), Wahlsburg was granted a post office, and Mr. Wahl was appointed Postmaster. After Mr. Wahl, Wilson Leonard, a blacksmith of the place, added another improvement to the place by building a handsome two-story frame residence. Not far from his new dwelling, Mr. Leonard has more recently erected a two-story blacksmith and wagon shop. In the past year, Christian Wahl has built an attractive cottage in the place. Wahlsburg is a thriving little burg, and promises to improve in the future.

Schools for the instruction and moral training of youth are so intimately connected with the interests and organic growth of the State that we are not surprised to learn that, away back in the eighth century, in the reign of Charlemagne, that monarch made a successful effort to popularize the instruction of all classes of people, by decreeing a public school to every parish in his empire. Later, Alfred the Great, of England, was inspired to the same good work, and, with the lapse of time, Germany became the acknowledged leader in the advancement of learning. The colonists of New England, New York, Pennsylvania, New Jersey and Virginia, English, Scotch, Irish and Germans, brought a love of learning with them to the New World, and a knowledge of the methods of imparting it to others. From such a source, our forefathers in the Northwest possessed the requisite rudiments of knowledge to enable them to educate their children in some degree, in the absence of schools and teachers.

Of the first schools of Scott Township, for the want of authentic records, not much is known. Tradition takes the place of record, and informs us that the few in operation anterior to the historical epoch of 1828 were maintained almost solely by subscription, and were kept in the most primitive of log structures. Teachers were paid from $5 to $15 per month, not in metallic or paper currency, as nowadays, but in the then no less current products of the soil and chase. When the teacher happened to be an unmarried man, or the school remote from his home, the patrons took turns in boarding him, receiving his labor morning and evening on the farm or extra instruction given the children, as adequate compensation. Reading, writing and arithmetic were the branches, and a teacher's reputed proficiency in them was considered a fair gauge of his usefulness. There are not wanting evidences to show that the pioneer teacher was successful in his noble calling. Indeed, many specimens that have been spared, in the writings as well as in the persons of pupils of the schools of that age, betray the fact that their methods were little if any inferior to those of the present day.

Zachariah Pettijohn, David Smith, Joseph Ralston, Reuben Fite and Jacob Peddicord were among the teachers of an early day. Zachariah Pettijohn is said to have taught the first subscription school in the township. David Smith, Joseph Ralston, Reuben Fite and Jacob Peddicord are the best remembered by persons living who were indebted to them for what education they received in early life.

The schoolhouses of the period were log cabins, with a single door, lighted by a long, narrow aperture in one side, filled in with oiled cloth or paper, and warmed by a fire-place of the most extraordinary dimensions. They were by no means numerous, and, as they were used only in the winter time, and the pupils in some instances had to trudge many miles in the cold, large fires of burning logs were kept, so it was not an unusual occurrence for teacher and pupils to be engaged in the praiseworthy effort to extinguish an incipient conflagration that somehow had started in the neighborhood of the fire-place. After the passage of the legislative act of January 28, 1825, relative to the better organization of the schools, the householders of Scott Township met in pursuance thereof and divided the township into eight school subdistricts. A committee of three, a Clerk and a Collector were selected for each district. By the law, a tax of half a mill was authorized, which, with private contributions for the same end, enabled each district to provide itself with a more suitable house. They who were too poor to defray the expenses of schooling their children were partially provided for by the same law, and partly by assessments imposed on their neighbors.

March 9, 1829, the Board of Township Trustees, composed of Enoch Ellsberry, James McCall and William Hilligoss, met and re-organized the township for educational purposes, replacing the eight subdistricts of the old administration by six new ones, making five white and one colored. The year 1854 dates the construction of the first accredited Board of Education in the township. The members were B. W. Whiteman, Chairman; Henry Palmer, Secretary; Dr. E. B. Fee, N. B. Stratton, Joseph Wills, G. H. Wrestler and Jacob Newman, and they met in Temperance Hall, New Hope. The enumeration of youth in 1854 was 373 whites and 63 colored.

The colored district was formed in behalf of a colony of blacks, which was settled half a century ago in the northern part of the township, under the auspices of a rich Virginia planter. Not many years ago, the spirit of improvement was engendered, and the result was that in a surprisingly short time each district had exchanged its old house for a handsome new frame structure that does much credit to the taste of its projectors.

Amount of money in hands of the Township Treasurer, for school purposes, in 1839, $327.59.8; in 1840, $337.89.4; in 1841, $362.87; in 1842, $270.67; in 1844, $353.55; in 1845, $314.81; in 1847, $499.93. The average annual cost of all the schools of Scott Township, for ten years, from 1870, has been $2,228.96. This amount includes the cost of two buildings and incidental expenses. And the average paid teachers for the ten years, commencing with the year 1871, is $1,637.62. It may be added that in the last eighteen years, District No. 1 has had a new schoolhouse, built in 1864, at a cost of $750; District No. 2 (Smoky Row), one built in 1866, at a cost of $700; District No. 3 (Goose Run), one built in 1869, at a cost of $650; District No. 4, one built in 1877, at a cost of $1,000, and District No. 5, one built in 1870, at a cost of about $1,200, with a recent annexation (in 1881), at a cost of $800, and one in the colored district, built in 1874, at a cost of $400.

To the schools is wedded the church, with its restraining and refining influences, the two united as one marching on and overthrowing the defenses of ignorance, sloth and bigotry. The settler carried to his wilderness home with his love of learning a profound reverence for the institutions of Christianity, and while he sought to instill in the minds of his children the light of intelligence, he did not forget to imbue their hearts with the Divine inspiration of truth.

The church that held the first divine services in the township was of the Methodist Episcopal denomination; the building in which the service was administered was an edifice of that primitive type never seen anywhere except in a new settlement. It stood on a spot nearly opposite the former residence of Dr. Enoch Ellsberry, where A. J. Bingamon now lives, in the town of New Hope. Here our fathers were wont to assemble, not in gawdy holiday garments, but attired in homespun and buckskin, and here they offered up their fervent prayers. For a quarter of a century there was no other place of worship; then, in 1849, Temperance Hall was placed at the disposal of the church, and service held in it till 1851, when the substantial brick that crowns the commons was erected at a cost of about $2,000.

The building fund was raised by subscription, the success of the enterprise being in a great measure due to the efforts of the Rev. Charles Ferguson.

The winter of 1850 witnessed the memorable revival, by which 140 accessions were made to the membership of the church. Mr. Ferguson's connection with the church as its pastor terminated in 1852.

A Sunday school was organized in 1852, and while nursed by the foster-

S. B. Sheldon M.D.

SCOTT TOWNSHIP.

ing care of the church, made an excellent record; but some years since the attendance began to decline, and continued to do so, notwithstanding the well-meant exertions of friends to stay its decay. Of late, successful efforts have been made to revive it, and it is believed with a fair prospect of success.

In 1867 or 1868, Rev. Henry Robison, of the Christian Union persuasion, by indefatigable endeavors, succeeded in uniting a congregation in every school district in the township. He held meetings at regular monthly intervals in all the schoolhouses, multitudes from the country round flocking to attend his ministrations. The New Lights have built a beautiful church edifice at Fair View, and given it the suggestive name of Fair View Chapel. The prospects of the church at Fair View are indeed flattering; besides having a membership scarcely exceeded by that of any other church in the county, its pastors are among the most talented and best workers. Fair View Chapel has a good working Sunday school, with a large and interested attendance.

White Oak Lodge, No. 292, I. O. O. F., was instituted at New Hope July 18, 1855, by Thomas J. McLain, Grand Master, with Brother G. W. Slayton, Brother Joseph R. Scott, Brother James L. Weaver, Brother William Blair and Brother O. J. Stewart as charter members.

Brother G. W. Stayton and Brother Joseph Scott still live near the scene of their early labors in the cause of Odd Fellowship, and watch with uncommon interest the ever increasing prosperity of the order. Brothers Weaver and Blair, many years ago, sought homes in the West, where, it is believed, they have continued to devote themselves to the good of the order. Brother O. J. Stewart, who was one of the most active and interested of workers, long since crossed the dark river to rejoin the Grand Lodge beyond.

Save a short period dating from the outbreak of the war of the rebellion, the history of White Oak Lodge has been one of encouraging prosperity. During that exceptional period, its affairs fell into neglect, its organization was broken and only the most strenuous efforts of friends obviated the impending forfeiture of the charter. The blow was a heavy one, and it was several years before the lodge entirely recovered its primitive vigor and activity. In the twenty-seven years of its existence, it has had 110 initiations and eight accessions on card. For the first year, there were twenty-five new members added; for the decennial period, from 1855 to 1865 inclusive, fifty-five; from 1865 to 1875, forty-six; from 1875 to 1882, nine. The whole number on card, eight; the number dropped, forty-six; the number of deaths, six. The benefits to date aggregate, in round numbers, $800. Value of assets, including stabling attached, amounts to $939.63.

The following list includes the names of all the Past Grands of White Oak Lodge: Brother O. J. Stewart, P. G.; Brother William Blair, P. G; Brother J. L. Cornell, P. G.; Brother William Hays, P. G. (Maj. Hays); Brother Andrew Gibson, P. G.; Brother H. C. Gibson, P. G.; Brother Joseph R. Scott, P. G.; Brother E. B. Fee, P. G.; Brother W. W. Ellsbury, P. G.; Brother G. W. Stayton, P. G.; Brother F. M. Patton, P. G.; Brother M. Patton, P. G.; Brother Jonah Purdum, P. G.; Brother A. J. Parker, P. G.; Brother Andrew Fox, P. G.; Brother John G. Thompson, P. G.; Brother Joseph Blair, P. O.; Brother Z. T. Peddicord, P. G.; Brother L. W. King, P. G. (Grand Representative); Brother O. P. Ralston, P. G. (Grand Representative); Brother William Shields, P. G.; Brother R. B. McCall, P. G.; Brother W. A. Bivans, P. G.; Brother A. J. Bingamon, P. G.; Brother D. M. Brannen, P. G.; Brother T. P. Dunn, P. G.; Brother Lewis Bingamon, P. G.; Brother Warren Carr, P. G.; Brother A. C. Wardlow, P. G.; Brother Isaac Atwood, P. G.; Brother A. F. Remley, P. G.; Brother V. C. Brown, P. G.; Brother W. S. Whorton, P. G.; Brother Aaron Leonard, P. G.; Brother John Bovis, P. G.; Brother H. W. Warner, P. G.; Brother O. F. Dunn, P. G.

HISTORY OF BROWN COUNTY.

From the firing of the first shot on Fort Sumter till the day the President issued his famous call for 75,000 men, April 15, 1861, the hearts of the people of this township throbbed with a single impulse, a desire to avenge the insult. Those who went forth to do battle in defense of their country's flag, were: In the Fifty-ninth Ohio Volunteer Infantry, William Applegate, Anthony Wallace, Jacob Wallace; in the Fourth Ohio, Foster's Independent Company, James Blair, Samuel Boyd, A. K. McGonedrick, Dr. G. W. Gordon, promoted Surgeon of Eighteenth Indiana, M. D. Thompson (died); in the First Ohio, Volunteer Cavalry, Cornelius Bingamon, Clinton Fiscus, Jacob Gatts, John McKenzie, M. D. L. McKenzie, Jerry Purdum, F. G. Smith, V. B. Smith, B. F. Young, Winters Young, T. B. Young, Francis M. Young, George Young, James Barnes (killed); of the Seventh Ohio Volunteer Cavalry, H. R. Craig, John Gatts (wounded), Walter Gooden, V. B. Purdum, E. C. Smith, J. E. Smith (died at Andersonville), J. V. Srofe, promoted Second Lieutenant January 1, 1863; T. L. H. Wardlow, G. W. Young, J. O. Young (died at Andersonville), Samuel Stephens (discharged), John Couther; in the Seventieth Ohio Volunteer Infantry, O. P. Cotterill, John Cotterill, Aaron Fiscus (killed), Martin Long (killed), Samuel Myers (killed), Henry White (discharged), Thomas L. Scott, promoted First Lieutenant; in the Twenty-seventh Ohio Volunteer Infantry, Eli Campbell, B. O. Morris, E. E. Roney, J. V. Srofe, Second Lieutenant (resigned), F. M. Young (killed), H. Couther, W. N. Barngroover, Samuel Doty (killed), S. A. Keys, John Hitesman (wounded), John McKenzie (wounded), Peter McKee, John C. Bingamon, W. F. Srofe, promoted Second Lieutenant (1863), commissioned First Lieutenant (1863), commissioned Captain (1865), J. W. B. Anderson; in the Thirty-ninth Ohio Volunteer Infantry, George W. Stratton (imprisoned in Libby); in the Twelfth Ohio Volunteer Infantry, A. K. McGonedrick, Winters Young, F. G. Smith, W. P. Srofe, Francis M. Young; in Forty-seventh Ohio Volunteer Infantry, Rudolph Neff; in the Sixty-first Ohio Volunteer Infantry, Benjamin Kimball, Greenbury Keyes, Alfred Radstin (killed); regiment unknown, B. F. Remley, W. B. Wrestler, William Lindsay, John Barnes, James Barnes, of Lieut. J. V. Srofe's command, was shot and killed while making a night sortie on the enemy's pickets. Alfred Ralstin was shot and killed at Antietam, the ball piercing his forehead. Samuel Doty was shot in the face while marching in the advance at the battle of Pittsburg Landing, and died in the hospital at Cincinnati. Aaron Fiscus and Martin Long were killed at the same time, by the explosion of a transportation boat on the Mississippi. Greenbury Keys, F. M. Young, M. D., L. McKenzie and Francis M. Young all died in their country's service.

The foregoing list was made up from information furnished by Lieut. Srofe, and may be imperfect as shown by the files, as that gentleman drew upon his memory for the facts.

The annexed congratulatory order, addressed to the First and Seventh Ohio, in which were many brave lads from Scott Township, as it meets the veteran's eye, will recall one of the most pleasing events of his experience:

HEADQUARTERS FOURTH DIVISION, CAVALRY CORPS, M. D. M.,
EDGEFIELD, TENN., June 10, 1865.

GENERAL ORDERS, NO. 21:

Before severing his connection with the command, the Brevet Major General commanding desires to express his high appreciation of the bravery, endurance and soldierly qualities displayed by the officers and men of his division in the late cavalry campaign. Leaving Chickasaw, Ala., on the 22d of March, as a new organization, and without status in the cavalry corps, you, in one month, traversed 600 miles, crossed six rivers, met and defeated the enemy at Montevallo, Ala., capturing 100 prisoners; routed Forrest, Buford and Rhoddy in their chosen position at Ebenezer Church, capturing two guns and 300 prisoners; carried the works in your front at Selma, capturing thirteen guns, 1,100 prisoners, and five battle flags, and finally crowned your successes by a night assault upon the enemies' intrenchments at

SCOTT TOWNSHIP.

Columbus, Ga., when you captured 1,500 prisoners, twenty-four guns, eight battle flags and vast munitions of war. April 21, you arrived at Macon, Ga., having captured on your march 3,000 prisoners, thirty-nine pieces of artillery and thirteen battle flags. Whether mounted with the sabre, or dismounted with the carbine, the brave men of the Third, Fourth and Fifth Iowa, First and Seventh Ohio and Tenth Missouri Cavalry, triumphed over the enemy in every conflict. With regiments led by brave Colonels, and brigades commanded with consummate skill and daring, the division, in thirty days, won a reputation unsurpassed in the service. Though many of you have not received the reward to which your gallantry has entitled you, you have, nevertheless, received the commendation of your superior officers, and won the admiration and gratitude of your countrymen. You will return to your homes with the proud consciousness of having defended the flag of your country in the hour of the greatest national perils, while through your instrumentality, liberty and civilization will have advanced the greatest strides recorded in history. The best wishes of your commanding General will ever attend you.

E. UPTON, *Brevet Major General Commanding.*

Official, JAMES W. LATTA, *Asst. Adjt. Gen.*
Official, CHARLES D. MITCHELL, *Lieut. A. A. A. G.*

The physicians of Scott Township have been among the most popular and successful in the county.

Dr. Enoch Matson Ellsberry came to Scott Township in 1824, and opened an office in the village of New Hope. Here was began a career of professional usefulness that extended over a period of twenty-eight years, and ended only with his life. Dr. Ellsberry is remembered by many who love to recall his fearless independence, candor and unostentatious benevolence of character. His deeds of charity and numberless acts of disinterested kindness, as well as his prompt and energetic punishment of insult and injustice, have ever been popular themes of fireside reminiscences. He was born in Tennessee December 29, 1797, one year after the admission of the State into the Union. When a boy, his parents emigrated to the State of Kentucky, and settled near Paris. Seven years later, or about the year 1810, they removed to Ohio, and settled at Bethel, Clermont County. Until he was sixteen years old, his habits and occupation were those of a farmer, but at that age, having profited by the slender advantages of the times for a good education, he became a teacher and a successful instructor. Unsatisfied with so unambitious a field and its unprofitable compensation, he left it at the age of twenty-one to begin the study of medicine in the office of Drs. Wayland & Hopkins, two eminent physicians of the day. After a thorough course of study, he opened an office in Bethel and commenced the practice, which was interrupted in 1822 by his marriage with Miss Eunice Morris, a daughter of Judge John Morris, of Tate Township, Clermont County, and a niece of the late distinguished Senator Tom Morris, who made his name famous by introducing in the Senate of the United States the first petition urging the non-extension of domestic slavery in the new States and Territories. The issue of this marriage were five sons and three daughters. John Rush Ellsberry was the oldest, and a physician whose promise of usefulness was broken by the decree of death. Isaac N. Ellsberry, like his eldest brother, died young, just when he was at the threshold of a brilliant career at the bar. Thomas Ellsberry, who was a farmer, died at the age of thirty-three. Dr. W. W. Ellsberry, like his oldest brother, embraced the profession of medicine, and by his splendid talents and devotion to his chosen art, has won for himself an enviable position. Benjamin, the youngest son, is a prominent business man, who, by tact and indomitable perseverance, has made a name in the business world. Dr. Enoch Ellsberry died November, 25, 1852, leaving behind him a name untarnished by a breath of reproach. He was once the Democratic nominee for Congress, but was defeated by his Whig opponent.

In the footsteps of Dr. Ellsberry came Dr. Enos B. Fee. These gentlemen formed a partnership in 1844, which lasted two years. On its dissolution, Dr. Fee began the practice on his own responsibility, and only ceased to be the beloved and universally respected medical adviser of the good people of Scott Township with his removal to Georgetown, the county seat, in 1870.

Dr. Fee, while a resident of Scott Township, was thrice chosen to represent the county in the Legislature, and declined a re-election for the fourth time. Since his removal, the Doctor has been twice elected Treasurer of Brown County, which office he found in a very unsatisfactory condition, but will leave perfectly rehabilitated. These two gentlemen were the pioneer physicians of the township.

Dr. William Gatts, Dr. James Weaver, Dr. George Gordon, Dr. W. W. Ellsberry, Dr. James Connell, Dr. W. A. Bivans, Dr. W. J. Srofe and Dr. R. B. McCall have at various times practiced at New Hope.

Drs. Weaver and Gatts were eclectics, and came to New Hope during the prevalence of the cholera in 1849. They were quite successful in combat with that dread scourge, and consequently acquired an extensive practice. Dr. Srofe at present resides in Lynchburg, Ohio, where he has acquired a lucrative business.

Dr. W. A. Bivans and Dr. R. B. McCall, are the only two physicians in New Hope. The former gentleman has resided there for twenty years, the latter since 1873. Both are well known to the profession of the county, and have, by a fair share of ability and a conscientious regard for the duties of their calling, deserved the respect and patronage of the community.

CHAPTER XII.

GREEN TOWNSHIP.

BY E. B. LANCASTER.

IN shape, this subdivision is rectangular. It is bounded on the north by Perry Township, on the east by Highland County, on the south by Pike Township and on the west by Sterling Township. It occupies a position in the boot leg of the county. The territory embraced within these boundaries formerly belonged to Sterling Township, and, on the 2d day of December, 1834, was set apart by the County Commissioners and formed into a new township, designated as Green. This name was given it by Joseph Kratzer, who was active in measures leading to its separation from Sterling, from the fact that the place where he was then residing was called Greenbush. At this place, there was a thicket of green bushes, and from this came the name of the village Greenbush and the township of Green. The first election was held at Mr. Kratzer's house, and thirty-three votes were polled, thirty-two of which are said to have been Democratic, Jacob Hare being the only Whig voter. Mr. Hare voted alone for two or three years, when he was re-enforced by Nicholas Smith. These men lived to see their principles triumphant. The surface of the township is level, and the lands are drained by the Sterling Fork of White Oak Creek, and by a portion of the main creek, which crosses the southeastern corner. Much artificial draining is done by means of ditches, conveying the water into these streams. The State road passes north and south through the western part of the township, and the old Chillicothe road passes through the center, east and west. The Cincinnati & Eastern Railroad crosses the extreme southern part, and forms for some distance almost the boundary line between Green and Pike Townships.

EARLY SETTLEMENT.

The lands of Green Township were level and swampy and uninviting to the early emigrants seeking homes in the North and West, and, in consequence, permanent settlements were not made, comparatively speaking, until a late day. There were probably no residents at all of the country now comprising the territory of Green prior to 1810, or even as late as the war of 1812. If so, tradition fails to give any account of them. The first to occupy the lands were squatters and the poorer classes of emigrants, who, driven from the better lands in the neighboring country by those coming in possession of them, were compelled to pitch their tents where they could. This class made little or no improvements, and lived almost entirely by hunting and trapping. For some years, this line of settlement continued, and those coming from the adjoining country were, in general, men of little or no means, and made temporary stops only. For this reason, and from the fact of the death of all of the pioneers who made permanent settlements, and the removal of their immediate descendants from this locality, but little can be given of Green's pioneers.

Prior to the year 1816, Joshua Archer, a man of family, settled in the southern part of the township. He emigrated from Kentucky, and had lived, before settling in Green, farther south, in what is now this county. He was an exhorter, and preached some, conducting the religious services of the neighborhood.

About one mile north of the village of Mt. Oreb, in 1816, there lived Mrs. McFarron, widow of George McFarron. Her family consisted of one son and several daughters, one of whom was the wife of Benjamin Frazier. Mr. Frazier lived in the same vicinity. Another son-in-law of Mrs. McFarron was Charles Dunham. His wife's name was Nellie, and among their children were Polly, John, Samuel, Nathaniel and Gideon. John Rhubart married another of the daughters of the widow mentioned above, and lived in the same neighborhood. These folks had previously lived in the vicinity of Georgetown.

George Laferre lived in the southern part of the township about the same time as the families above named. He was a man of family. The families thus far mentioned made few improvements, and did not remain long in this locality.

Prior to 1816, Joseph Kratzer and family settled in the vicinity of Greenbush, which village he afterward laid out. He emigrated from the State of Pennsylvania, and lived on Straight Creek, in this county, before coming up into Green Township. While living in the Straight Creek neighborhood, he married Polly Dunn. Their sons and daughters were Enos, Henry, Samuel, Benjamin, Simon, James, Rosa, Hannah and Dolly. The father improved land here, and lived in Green until his death. Most all of the sons improved land in the township. Samuel is a resident of this locality. Enos and James died in the township.

Thomas Harris, another pioneer of this locality, is a native of Pittsburgh, Penn., where he was born in 1802, and, in 1807, with his parents, removed to Clermont County, this State, and settled in the neighborhood of Bethel. In 1816, he removed to this vicinity. He has been twice married—first, to Sarah Fiscus, and second, to her sister, Matilda Fiscus. The children by the first marriage were Abram and Sapphira, and by the second, Rebecca, James, Lovina, Nancy, Martin V., Thomas, Sr., John E., Jeremiah, Cynthia, Henry, Thomas, Jr., Elizabeth and Mary A. Thomas Harris, our subject, has lived over fifty years with his present wife, and has celebrated his golden wedding, at Mt. Oreb, which was attended by eleven of his children and thirty grandchildren, and numerous others of his relatives and friends. When Harris moved to this township, Brown County was a part of Adams and Clermont Counties, and Green Township was part of Sterling. From our interviews with Harris, who is now eighty-two years of age, and who is corroborated by all of the old pioneers now living, we derive much of the information concerning the early settlement of Green Township.

In 1816, there was not a house between Mt. Oreb and Greenbush, if, perhaps, a hut is excepted that stood on what is now the Weaver farm. Where Jesse Day now resides, not far from the year 1816, there lived Robert Ellis.

Thomas Ross, about the year 1817, settled on the premises formerly occupied by Benjamin Frazier. His children were Israel, John, Thomas, Isaac, Margaret and Sarah, and perhaps others. Mr. Ross cleared considerable land, which he improved, and erected good buildings thereon. He lived in the township until his death, which occurred in 1849.

Joseph Keethler emigrated from Bracken County, Ky., and settled in what is now Pike Township in 1810. He had a large family of children, some of whom, later, settled in Green Township. Among them were James, Louis, William and Samuel, all of whom improved land in the township. James and Louis still reside here.

As early as 1817, Fred Bingamon was a resident of this locality. He improved the David Weaver farm.

Robert Hicks and Thomas Slade settled here about the time that Thomas Ross came. Elijah South removed into the township from near Bethel, in

Clermont County; cleared some land in the neighborhood of Mt. Oreb, but remained only a short time.

Among the second class of settlers coming into the township can be named the following: Praetor Mallott, who settled and made improvements in the vicinity of Greenbush not far from the year 1824; Samuel Day, whose parents and their family settled in the western part of Sterling Township at the close of the last century, an account of whom is given in the sketch of Sterling Township; Mr. Day improved a farm in the vicinity of Benton, and erected good buildings thereon; Nicholas Smith settled just west of Samuel Day; Hezekiah Stout settled on White Oak, improved land and became a permanent settler; he was one of the pioneer settlers in that locality; after Mr. Stout's death, George Bingamon became a resident of the land; in the same neighborhood, Samuel Garron settled and improved land.

The township was slow in being peopled and improved; the land from Greenbush up to the northern boundary line comprising fully one-half of its acreage, is very flat and level, and was for years very swampy, and, until 1840, was unoccupied, if, perhaps, is excepted one locality. This portion was then a dense forest and unimproved. Jacob Hare was perhaps the only resident in this section prior to the date given. He settled on Five-Mile Creek about the year 1836. In 1840, John Wallace removed from Huntington Township to the land now occupied by him, situated a little north of the center of the township, and made improvements. Jacob Hare was then, to his knowledge, the only neighbor of Green on his north, east or west.

About ten years later, the northeastern part of the township began to be settled by a class of foreigners, coming principally from Belgium, who, by frugality and industry, have made for themselves good homes, and are well-to-do farmers. Among the first families settling here were Peter Leonard, with wife and two children; Michael Pierre, France Cordie and Joseph Gillum, all men of families. The lands of Green have been ditched and drained, and now compare favorably in productive quality to any of Brown County. The old pioneer foreigners will leave a goodly heritage for their sons and daughters to enjoy. All honor is due to those horny-handed sons of toil, who left their native land and crossed the ocean, cast their lot in the swamp lands of Green Township, and, by hard labor and unceasing toil, have made it what it now is. It is true that our township has been looked upon as almost worthless by some people in other parts of the county. These persons must remember that we are just emerging from the backwoods, as it were. Wild deer were killed in this township as late as 1848. James Keethler killed a deer near where Mt. Oreb now stands in 1847. The last deer was killed by G. W. Stansberry. A few wild turkeys are yet found in the township.

CHURCHES.

The first religious services in the township were conducted in the settlement along Sterling Fork of White Oak, by Joshua Archer, as early as the year 1815 or 1816. The meetings in this locality were held in the cabins of the pioneers, and, when the weather permitted, in the groves—God's first temples. This region of country was, from the year 1808, continuing for many years, in White Oak Circuit, and was, from its earliest settlement, visited by the itinerant ministers of the Methodist Episcopal Church. The following named were the preachers who traveled the circuit from 1808 until 1824: 1808, David Young; 1809, John Johnson; 1810, Isaac Pavey; 1811, Benjamin Lakin, Eli Trent; 1812, W. Griffith, Reuben Rowe; 1813, Robert Finley, D. Sharp; 1815, John Strange, S. Cheneworth; 1816, John Strange, Isaac Pavey; 1817, W. Griffith, James Simmons; 1818, B. Westlake, S. T. Wells; 1819, F.

Landrum; 1820, William Page, L. Swormstedt; 1821, A. W. Elliott, Z. Connell; 1822, William Page, Benjamin Lawrence; 1823, D. D. Davidson, Samuel West; 1824, G. W. Maley, J. Everhart.

Methodist Episcopal Church at Mt. Oreb.—About the year 1824, the first regular church organization of the township was effected at Benton, by the Methodists of the neighborhood, among whom were John Thomas, Nathan Rust, William Weeks, David Vandyke, Thomas Ross, Thos. Kratzer, Nicholas Smith and Samuel Day. Their first meeting-house was built of logs, and stood on the farm now owned by E. Bratton. After some years, the building was destroyed by fire. It was thought to have been the work of an incendiary. This denomination soon rebuilt, but this time a frame structure was erected, which was occupied by the congregation as a place of worship until about 1875, when they again rebuilt, and the present neat frame church, with belfry and bell, at Mt Oreb, is the monument of their enterprise. The church has been on a number of different circuits, and attached to various stations, but, in the absence of records, we are unable to give them. At present, it is on the circuit designated Mt. Oreb and Sardinia, with Rev. G. W. Fee in charge. It is in a flourishing condition.

The first Sunday school of the church was organized about the year 1843 or 1844. Among those prominent at the organization were Samuel Day, Adam Shroufe, Nicholas Smith, Thomas Ross, Enos Kratzer, James Keethler and Ervin Huggins. The first Superintendent was Samuel Day. Among the teachers were Ervin Huggins, John Ross, Thomas G. Ross, G. W. Day and Dennis Callahan. The organization took place in the old log church building in the village of Benton. Among the first scholars were John C. Day, Mary E. Day, John Richards, W. B. Richards, A. Smith, Benjamin Smith, Mary Callahan, Nancy Callahan, Bennett Kratzer, Samuel Kratzer, Nancy Kratzer, Margaret Ross, Sarah Ross, Isaac Ross, Deborah Ross, James Ellis, Samuel Wright, William Wright, Amanda Truitt, Jane Truitt, Eliza Truitt. Samuel Day remained as Superintendent for eight or ten years, and was succeeded by James Campbell, who held the office about one year. William Weeks was Superintendent for a series of years, and was succeeded by H. W. Day. Mr. Day remained Superintendent for five or six years. The school averaged about sixty in attendance. Mr. Day was succeeded by F. M. Smith April 3, 1870. March 19, 1871, Mr. Smith was re-elected to the Superintendency. Previous to this year, school had only been conducted during the summer season. The average attendance up to this time was about sixty. April 7, 1872, the school was re-organized, and the average attendance for the year was over one hundred, there often being present from 150 to 175 scholars. Mr. Smith served as Superintendent until March 24, 1877, when he declined a renomination for re-election. His successor became D. L. Day, who continued in that capacity until September 21, 1879, and then resigned. The next Superintendent was H. W. Walker. In 1880, F. M. Smith was again elected Superintendent, and has since served the school. He is an earnest worker in the Sabbath school cause.

Christian Union Church.—In 1864, a church society by the name of Christian Union was organized at what was known as the " Gum Corner " Schoolhouse, located in the northwestern part of the township. The minister effecting the organization was Rev. Peter Wolf.

The congregation continued worshiping at this schoolhouse and at one called Maple Grove until the summer of 1881, when they erected the church building now standing in the northwestern part of the township. This house was dedicated to the service of God in September, 1881; sermon by Rev. Peter Wolf. Services are held twice a month. The present ministers in charge are Revs. George Slusher and T. J. Screetchfield.

NOAH HITE.
(Deceased)

GREEN TOWNSHIP.

Christian Union Church at Mt. Oreb.—This church was organized in 1867, by Rev. W. H. Robinson, with a large membership. Mr. Robinson was a very successful revivalist, and, under his earnest efforts, 159 accessions to the church were made during the winter of 1867-68. The writer of this history was present one night when seventeen persons joined the church, and the congregation was dismissed, the benediction had been pronounced, and the congregation were departing for their homes, when one of the new converts remarked: "Bro. Robinson, had you have held on a little while longer, my father and mother would have joined." Robinson recalled the congregation and renewed the invitation, and eleven persons united with the church afterward, making twenty-eight in all that joined the church that night.

Mr. Robinson continued as pastor of the church for several years. While a successful revivalist, he had not the modern power of converting the pocketbook, and, being poorly paid, had to resort to other means for the support of himself and family. Rev. Absalom Brooks succeeded Mr. Robinson to the pastorate of the church. These were the only regular ministers that the congregation have had. In 1870, the membership was seventy-four, and, three years later, numbered 130. Some time after the organization of the society, the present one-story frame church building was erected. It is the largest house of worship in the township, and is supplied with a belfry and bell. The church is not now in a flourishing condition; the membership seems not to have adopted the modern plan of keeping up churches. No church can exist in this day unless it has a good financial basis, which has been the case from the earliest ages.

SCHOOLS.

As nearly as can be ascertained, the first school held in the township was taught by Thomas Ross, in a cabin which stood in the immediate vicinity of where the hamlet of Benton now is. This was about the year 1820. The first house built for school purposes stood in the southern part of the township, on Sterling Fork of White Oak. There are now eight school districts in Green, with as many buildings, valued at $6,000. The report of the County Auditor to the State Commissioner of Schools for the year ending August 31, 1881, makes the following exhibit: Number of boys enrolled, 249; girls, 207; total, 456. Average monthly attendance, 383, of which number 210 were boys. Average number of weeks school was in session, 27. Average wages paid gentlemen teachers, $33 per month; average wages paid lady teachers, $24; number of teachers employed, 12, two of whom were ladies. Branches taught—alphabet, reading, spelling, writing, arithmetic, geography, English grammar, oral lessons and composition. Amount paid teachers during the year, $2,231.20; amount paid for fuel and other contingent expenses, $288.21; total expenses for carrying on the schools for the year, $3,544.41.

VILLAGES.

Mt. Oreb, the largest village in the township, is located on Sterling Fork of White Oak and the State road, twelve miles north of Georgetown. It was laid out by Daniel Keethler September 3, 1850, and the lots surveyed by William S. McLain. The original number of lots was nineteen. Before the village was laid out, a store was kept on the southwest corner of Hight street and Broadway, where the Lancaster building now stands, by Henry Dennis, who became the first merchant of the place. James McClure was another of the early merchants. Henry Varley and Charles Zeller were the first village smiths. The growth of the village was at first slow, and few improvements were made until after the completion of the Cincinnati & Eastern Railroad, when it began to assume a business air, and is now a thriving little village.

The post office was established here some years after the laying-out of the village, and among the Postmasters have been the following: William Weeks, Dr. M. Stroup, Samuel N. Weeks, F. M. Smith and A. C. Earhart, the present incumbent.

In 1877, an addition of thirty-one lots was made to the place by H. M. Smith. The name of Mt. Oreb was given to the village by the original proprietor, and, as there has been some controversy about its origin and the correct way of spelling the name, we have gone to some trouble to get at the facts in the matter. Mr. Keethler took the name from the Bible. The word "oreb" primarily means raven or crow, and is the name of the Midianite chieftain that invaded Israel, and was defeated and driven back by Gideon. It is but slightly touched upon in the narrative of Judges, but the terms in which Isaiah refers to it (x, 26) are such as to imply that it was a truly awful slaughter. It is placed in the same rank with the two most tremendous disasters recorded in the whole history of Israel—the destruction of the Egyptians in the Red Sea, and the army of Sennacherib. Some claim the name was Mt. Horeb, and that the H has been dropped. The word is frequently spelled Mt. Orab. which we think is without authority. It should be spelled with an *e*—Mt. Oreb. It is the name of a Midianite chieftain, and it is the name of a rock where Oreb was slain.

"And they slew Oreb upon the rock Oreb, * * * and brought the heads of Oreb and Zeeb to Gideon." (See Judges, vii, 25.)

Mt. Horeb and Mt. Oreb mean the same thing when speaking of a place.

The village now contains six dry goods stores and groceries, two drug stores, one tinshop and a large hardware and farming implement store, four blacksmith shops, one fine mill, one wagon shop, one barber shop, two churches, a nice schoolhouse, two shoe shops, a stave and hame factory, one livery stable, three millinery stores, four mantua maker shops, and is advancing in wealth and population rapidly in all respects; to illustrate, lands that were $30 per acre four years ago, cannot now be purchased for $125 per acre in ten-acre lots. The physicians of Oreb are Drs. M. Stroup, A. E. Earhart and J. R. Lancaster.

Greenbush, the second village in size, is situated in the western part of the township, at the intersection of the old Chillicothe and State roads. It was laid out May 28, 1838, by Joseph Kratzer. The surveying was done by John D. White. It contains two dry goods stores, one hotel, a schoolhouse, blacksmith shop and one tile factory. The village is improving. The most active man in the line of improvements in the village is E. A. Tissander, a native of France. He is the proprietor of the hotel and of one of the stores. This section is the most fertile of the lands of the township.

The little hamlet of Benton, situated on the State road, about a mile north of Mt. Oreb, is the oldest place in the township, it having been laid out January 26, 1838, by B. H. Gardner. Some ten years later, a post office was established here, with G. W. Day as Postmaster. In 1853, Mr. Day was succeeded by James McAfee. The office was discontinued in the course of a few years. The original number of lots was eighteen. The hamlet never improved much, and now to the passer-by there is scarcely any evidence of a place to be seen.

INDUSTRIES.

The manufacturing interests of Green have been very meager. About the year 1838, Benjamin Gardner erected and operated a saw and grist mill at Benton, with steam power.

A grist and saw mill was built in the northern part of the township about the year 1842, by Louis Weber and a Mr. Mahover. This mill was operated

GREEN TOWNSHIP.

until the close of the war, when it was destroyed by fire. It was soon afterward rebuilt by Mr. Weber. This was also a steam power mill, which was in operation until a year or two ago, when the machinery was taken out and put in the grist-mill now at Mt. Oreb.

Not long after the village of Mt. Oreb was laid out, a saw-mill was built on Sterling Fork, of White Oak, by Daniel Keethler. Soon afterward, a grist-mill was added by Calvin Rilea; the power of the mill was furnished by steam. About the beginning of the war of the rebellion, this mill was destroyed by fire, but was at once rebuilt and the grist-mill operated until about six or eight years ago, and the saw-mill until two or three years ago.

In the northern part of the township, there is in operation a steam grist and saw mill, carried on by Messrs Spice & Washburn. The mill was built about the close of the late war by Martin Miller.

In 1875, Granville Fiscus built a tile factory in the northern part of the township, which was carried on for five or six years.

The stave, hames and heading factory of John Richard's Sons, of Cincinnati, located at Mt. Oreb, was built by them in 1877, and has since been under the same management.

The grist-mill at Mt. Oreb under the proprietorship of John and Henry Waits (brothers), was erected in the summer of 1880. It is a modernly constructed mill, with steam power, and has a capacity of about eighteen or twenty barrels of flour per day.

JUSTICES OF THE PEACE.

The early records of the township have been destroyed, and only a partial list of the Justices of the Peace can be given. Some of the names of persons who served as such in the earlier years of its history as recalled by residents of the township, are James Garron, Nicholas Smith and Thomas Ross. The names contained in the following list are of record, and the dates given show when commissioned:

John H. Beckwith, April 12, 1855, resigned April 2, 1857.
Alva Moon, July 21, 1855, resigned September 26, 1857.
James McAfee, April 21, 1857, resigned February 20, 1858.
George W. Stansberry, October 29, 1857.
Samuel Day, April 21, 1858.
Gilead Bahan, October 27, 1860.
G. W. Day, April 23, 1862.
Joseph Stephens, April 15, 1864.
J. L. Irwin, April 7, 1865.
John F Black, December 8, 1865.
A. H. Cook, November 13, 1866.
Joseph Stephens, April 15, 1867.
H. C. Malott, November 24, 1869.
Joseph Stephens, April 11, 1870.
James E. Huggins, February 26, 1872.
A. Moon, April 21, 1873.
James E. Huggins, March 15, 1875.
J. M. Healion, April 13, 1878.
J. C. Glover, April 19, 1879.
H. H. Jones, April 18, 1881.
Absalom Brooks, April 17, 1882.

GREEN IN THE WAR OF THE REBELLION.

The people of Green Township are proud of their soldiery. So soon as the dread alarm of war had been echoed to her quiet homes and peaceful fields from the distant hills and woodland, her youth and middle-aged responded to the call "To arms! your country is in peril," and from her workshops, from the forge, the bench, the accountant's desk and the plow, went forth her sons and defended the Nation's honor. We regret exceedingly that in the small space here allotted us that more could not be said of the soldiers of the township whose names appear in the following list, which has been prepared with great care to omit no names and an effort to avoid mistakes:

Thomas Chambers, Forty-eighth Regiment Ohio Volunteer Infantry.

Simpson Chambers, Eighty-ninth Regiment Ohio Volunteer Infantry, died in prison.

John Robbins, Forty-eighth Regiment Ohio Volunteer Infantry.

Wesley Robbins, Forty-eighth Regiment Ohio Volunteer Infantry, wounded.

Martyn Robbins, Forty-eighth Regiment Ohio Volunteer Infantry, died in prison.

S. Conover, died in Andersonville Prison.

Daniel Tucker, Forty-eighth Regiment Ohio Volunteer Infantry.

R. W. Beard, Twelfth Regiment Ohio Volunteer Infantry.

George Mann, Twelfth Regiment Ohio Volunteer Infantry.

Thomas Kratzer, Twelfth Regiment Ohio Volunteer Infantry, wounded at the second battle of Bull Run.

B. F. Malott, Twelfth Regiment Ohio Volunteer Infantry.

Robert Moore, Sixtieth Regiment Ohio Volunteer Infantry.

William Smith, died in prison.

Benjamin Hodgson, missing on the skirmish line.

William Dean, Twelfth Regiment Ohio Volunteer Infantry.

George Conover, One Hundred and Seventy-fifth Regiment Ohio Volunteer Infantry.

John Morgan.

Richard Smith, Forty-eighth Regiment Ohio Volunteer Infantry, wounded, and missing.

Jacob Thomas, Forty-eighth Regiment Ohio Volunteer Infantry, killed.

S. Malott, Forty-eighth Regiment Ohio Volunteer Infantry, killed.

Lewis Kratzer.

Amos Kratzer, Eighty-ninth Regiment Ohio Volunteer Infantry.

Wilson Kratzer.

Reason Kratzer, Thirty-fourth Regiment Ohio Volunteer Infantry.

F. M. Kratzer, Eighty-ninth Regiment Ohio Volunteer Infantry.

Saul Hughes, Twelfth Regiment Ohio Volunteer Infantry, killed.

Joseph Hughes, Company R, Twelfth Regiment Ohio Volunteer Infantry.

Edward L. Hughes, Company R, Twelfth Regiment Ohio Volunteer Infantry, killed at South Mountain, Md., September 14, 1862.

William Jones, died in the service.

D. C. Malott.

J. C. Glover.

Henry Driver, Sixtieth Regiment Ohio Volunteer Infantry.

L. Malott, Forty-first Regiment Ohio Volunteer Infantry.

George Fryman.

Henry Fryman, died in the service.

Samuel Beard, Thirty-fourth Regiment Ohio Volunteer Infantry, killed.

William Workman, Forty-eighth Regiment Ohio Volunteer Infantry.

William Wilson, Forty-eighth Regiment Ohio Volunteer Infantry.

Henry Moore, Sixtieth Regiment Ohio Volunteer Infantry.

Jerry Priest.

GREEN TOWNSHIP.

Walter Chaffin, Forty-eighth Regiment Ohio Vounteer Infantry, killed.

S. Conover, One Hundred and Seventy-fifth Regiment Ohio Volunteer Infantry, died in prison.

Thomas Wallace, One Hundred and Seventy-fifth Regiment Ohio Volunteer Infantry.

John W. Wallace, Eighty-third Regiment Ohio Volunteer Infantry, died in service.

James H. Wallace, One Hundred and Seventy-fifth Regiment Ohio Volunteer Infantry, killed.

Lot Reynolds, Forty-eighth Regiment Ohio Volunteer Infantry.

James Donley, Twelfth Regiment Ohio Volunteer Infantry.

Jesse Callahan, Fifty-ninth Regiment Ohio Volunteer Infantry, wounded.

Andrew Sroufe, Forty-eighth Regiment Ohio Volunteer Infantry, died in service.

John Sroufe, Forty-eighth Regiment Ohio Volunteer Infantry.

Joseph Sroufe, Forty-eighth Regiment Ohio Volunteer Infantry, died in service.

R. H. Sroufe, Forty-eighth Regiment Ohio Volunteer Infantry.

Levi Waits, Daniel Wallace, John Dedrick.

G. W. Bayham, Twelfth Regiment Ohio Volunteer Infantry.

J. P. Shannon, Twelfth Regiment Ohio Volunteer Infantry.

Jefferson Waits, Twenty-seventh Regiment Ohio Volunteer Infantry.

William Webber, Eleventh Regiment Ohio Volunteer Infantry.

F Webber, Eleventh Regiment Ohio Volunteer Infantry.

W. W. White, Forty-eighth Regiment Ohio Volunteer Infantry.

J. D. Shannon, Forty-eighth Regiment Ohio Volunteer Infantry.

A. Scott, William Hill, G. Bayham, James Hare, Samuel Hare, John Wait, Henry Tucker, Joseph Nevitt, Jacob Leavertin.

John F. Reynolds, Forty-eighth Regiment Ohio Volunteer Infantry.

D. C. Hays, Thomas Sroufe, William Ellis, Porter Hays, A. G. Sroufe, R. Hays, C. W. Fiscus, P. W. Keethler, Wayne Keethler, Arthur Glaze, R. S. Grisham, John Grisham, James Grisham, G. W. Stratton, Frank Stratton, Enos B. Stratton, A. J. Kinnett, A. E. Day, Isaac Atkins, Wiley Watson, William Kinnett, Harvey Kinnett, Thomas Kinnett, Jr., J. G. Stansberry, C. M. Stansberry, Michael Hawkman, James Waters, Randolph Waters, William Fields, J. Fiscus, M. W. Channel, Samuel Channel, J. C. Vance, Marion Donley, D. E. White, John White, Columbus White, William White, S. H. Raper, Joseph Day, James Day, H. W. Day, S. A. Day, D. L. Day, George Weeks.

Samuel N. Weeks, Company I, Twelfth Regiment Ohio Volunteer Infantry; Company K, Twenty-seventh Regiment Ohio Volunteer Infantry, promoted to First Lieutenant Company C, Twenty-seventh Regiment Ohio Volunteer Infantry.

Lewis J. Weeks, Company K, Twenty-seventh Regiment Ohio Volunteer Infantry, killed in the battle at Corinth, Miss.

James Reynolds, Forty-eighth Regiment Ohio Volunteer Infantry.

Levit Conver, Wilson Watson, Job Conver, William Conover Israel Jennings, Lee Gray, James Richards.

Wright Wilson, Fifty-ninth Regiment Ohio Volunteer Infantry.

C. W. Lague, Henry Newkirk.

Samuel C. Wright, Sixtieth Regiment Ohio Volunteer Infantry.

James Newkirk.

John H. Morgan, Sixtieth Regiment Ohio Volunteer Infantry.

Charles Haven, Sixtieth Regiment Ohio Volunteer Infantry, died with disease in Virginia.

John C. Weaver, Sixtieth Regiment Ohio Volunteer Infantry.

Elish Jordan, Sixtieth Regiment Ohio Volunteer Infantry.

William Moore, Sixtieth Regiment Ohio Volunteer Infantry.

A. Newton Hirons, Company F, Sixtieth Regiment Ohio Volunteer Infantry.

John Hirons, Albert Fry.

CHAPTER XIII.

JACKSON TOWNSHIP.

THIS township was originally a part of Eagle Township, from which it was separated June 20, 1823, by the County Commissioners, who ordained that the line dividing Franklin from Washington Township be extended to the Adams County line, and that all that part of Eagle Township lying south of the line so extended shall constitute a new township, to be known as the township of Jackson. The land thus included contained 16,989½ acres, which now have an assessed value of $238,474, that being but about one-half of their real value. The population at the last enumeration (1880) was 966. The township in shape is nearly square, being about six miles long on either side. It is bounded on the north by Eagle Township, on the east by Adams County, on the south by Byrd and Jefferson Townships, on the west by Franklin Township. It is drained in the east, south and center by the West Fork of Eagle Creek and its tributaries, and in the northwest by a branch of Straight Creek and its tributaries. The land is so indented by the deep ravines, which mark the courses of these numerous streams, as to give it the appearance of being very hilly. The township lies in the Virginia Military District, and all the land was entered by holders of military warrants, who located tracts of fr m twenty to four thousand acres, the largest tract being 4,000 acres, surveyed for Thomas Fox by Arthur Fox, District Surveyor, February 22, 1792, and designated as Survey No. 700. The next survey in size was No. 1785, containing 2,666⅔ acres, entered by Lewis Lansford, heir at law of William Lansford, deceased, and surveyed by Arthur Fox February 23, 1792.

OFFICERS.

The first election held in the township was at the house of Stephen Reynolds on the third Saturday (19th) of July, 1823. At this election the following first officers of the township were elected: Edward Francis, William Greathouse and John Wright, Trustees; Matthew Campbell, Clerk; Thomas Brady, Treasurer; James Crute, Constable; Adam Sellman and William Donaldson, Overseers of the Poor; Henry Thomas and William Glendening, Fence Viewers.

On April 5, 1824, the officers elected were: William Greathouse, Ervin Cutter and Samuel Evans, Trustees; John Sellman, Clerk; Thomas Brady, Treasurer; James Wright and Samuel Pickerill, Overseers of the Poor; James Crute, Lister, and by appointment Constable; James Wright was appointed Trustee to fill the vacancy occasioned by the death of Ervin Cutter, in the latter part of May.

April 4, 1825—James Wright, Matthew Campbell and John Wright, Trustees; William Tomb, Clerk; Thomas Brady, Treasurer; John Newten and Thomas Sergent, Constables; William Davidson and David McBride, Overseers of the Poor; Robert D. Tomb, Lister.

April 3, 1826—Stephen Reynolds, Matthew Campbell and Thomas Brady, Trustees; William Tomb, Clerk; Thomas Brady, Treasurer; James Crute, Constable; Stephen Reynolds and Sylvanus Parker, Overseers of the Poor. Amos Evans was appointed Constable on April 15.

April 2, 1827—Thomas Brady, Thomas Rickey and Matthew Campbell, Trustees; John W. Reynolds, Clerk; Thomas Brady, Treasurer; John Gregg and James Crute, Constables; Samuel Bennington, Overseer of the Poor. James Crute did not serve as Constable.

April 7, 1828—William Greathouse, Kenneth Prine and Jacob Neal, Trustees; John W. Reynolds, Clerk; Thomas Brady, Treasurer; John Gregg, Constable; Samuel Evans and John Clark, Overseers of the Poor.

April 6, 1829—Edward West, Robert Pollen and William Davidson, Trustees; William Tomb, Clerk; Edward Francis, Treasurer; Thomas Sergent, Constable; Matthew Campbell and Jesse Morrow, Overseers of the Poor.

April 5, 1830—Edward Francis, John Wright and William Davidson, Trustees; William Henderson, Clerk; Edward Francis, Treasurer; Thomas Sergent, Constable; John McKnight and John Wright, Overseers of the Poor. James Mehary was appointed Constable on December 25, to fill vacancy occasioned by the resignation of Thomas Sergent.

April 4, 1831—Henry Sidwell, Kenneth Prine and Thomas Ricky, Trustees; David A. Henderson, Clerk; Edward Francis, Treasurer; James Crute, Constable; Henry Sidwell and Matthew Campbell, Overseers of the Poor.

April 2, 1832—Samuel Pickerill, Joseph Shaw and James Wright, Trustees; Samuel Bartholomew, Clerk; Edward Francis, Treasurer; James Crute, Constable; William Davidson and Robert Patton, Overseers of the Poor.

April 1, 1833—William Greathouse, Henry Young and James Wright, Trustees; Samuel Bartholomew, Clerk; Edward Francis, Treasurer; James Crute, Constable.

April 7, 1834—Samuel Pickerill, John Cox and William McColgen, Trustees; Samuel Bartholomew, Clerk; Edward Francis, Treasurer; J. C. Higinbotham, Constable.

April 6, 1835—William McColgen, Henry Young and Aaron Eyler, Trustees; Harris Sidwell, Clerk; Edward Francis, Treasurer; Thomas Sergent, Constable.

April 4, 1836—William McColgen, Henry Young and William Greathouse, Trustees; John Francis, Clerk; Edward Francis, Treasurer; John Gregg, Constable.

April 16, John Donaldson was appointed Constable, vice John Gregg, who failed to give bond.

April 3, 1837—William McColgen, Samuel Pickerill and Josiah Rhoten, Trustees; John Sellman, Clerk; Thomas Brady, Treasurer; William Lain, Constable.

April 2, 1838—William McColgen, Samuel Pickerill and Alexander Wilson, Trustees; John Anderson, Clerk; Edward Francis, Treasurer; William Lane, Constable; Robert Moore appointed Constable vice Lane, resigned.

April 1, 1839—William McColgen, William Greathouse and John Parker, Trustees; John Anderson, Clerk; Edward Francis, Treasurer; William Lane, Constable. William Lane resigned, and William Burns was appointed; he resigned, and John Sedwill was appointed; he resigned, and William Ball was appointed.

April 6, 1840—John Cox, James Wright and John Francis, Trustees; William Cox, Clerk; Edward Francis, Treasurer; John McGregor, Constable.

April 5, 1841—David Kendall, Henry Smith and John Parker, Trustees; John Sellman, Clerk; Edward West, Treasurer; John McGregor, Constable.

April 4, 1842—David Kendall, John Parker and William McColgen, Trustees; Robert McKnight, Clerk; Edward West, Treasurer; John McGregor and Stephen Parker, Constables; Edward Francis, Assessor.

Robert McKnight resigned, and Edward Francis, Jr., was appointed Clerk.

JACKSON TOWNSHIP.

April 3, 1843—David Kendall, John Parker and William McColgen, Trustees; John L. Beveridge, Clerk; Edwards West, Treasurer; Edward Francis, Assessor; John McGregor, Constable.

April 1, 1844—John Brady, Aaron Eyler and Samuel Pickerill, Trustees; John L. Beveridge, Clerk; Edwards West, Treasurer; S. P. Evans, Assessor; John Long, Constable.

April 7, 1845—John Brady, Aaron Eyler and William Cox, Trustees; Fountain Inskeep, Clerk; Edwards West, Treasurer; R. W. McKee, Assessor; William Wallis, Constable.

April 6, 1846—John Brady, Aaron Purdom and Jesse Kendall, Trustee; F. Inskeep, Clerk; Robert Moore, Treasurer; R. W. McKee, Assessor; McCord Brady, Constable. McCord Brady refused to serve, and Ellis Sidwell was appointed Constable. He in turn resigned, and Thomas Sergent was appointed.

April 5, 1847—John Brady, Aaron Purdom and David Thorp, Trustees; Fountain Inskeep, Clerk; Robert Moore, Treasurer; R. W. McKee, Assessor. Thomas Sergent, Constable, resigned, and Henry Streight was appointed.

April 3, 1848—Aaron Eyler, David Thorp and John Brady, Trustees; F. Inskeep, Clerk; Robert Moore, Treasurer; R. W. McKee, Assessor; Henry Streight, Constable. R. Moore died, and Edwards West was appointed Treasurer December 22.

April 2, 1849—Moses Moore, Jesse Kendall and George W. Mefford, Trustees; F. Inskeep, Clerk; E. West, Treasurer; Samuel Dixon, Assessor; Henry Streight, Constable; resigned, and J. McCallister was appointed.

April 1, 1850—Moses Moore, Aaron Eyler and James Wright, Trustees; F. Inskeep, Clerk; E. West, Treasurer; S. Dixon, Assessor; J. McCallister, Constable.

April 7, 1851—Benjamin Brady, Aaron Eyler and James Wright, Trustees; F. Inskeep, Clerk; E. West, Treasurer; Samuel Dixon, Assessor; Stephen Myers, Constable.

April 5, 1852—Josiah Rhoten, Isaac Waters and Samuel McNown, Trustees; Calvin Wright, Clerk; Aaron Eyler, Treasurer; S. Dixon, Assessor; S. Myers, Constable.

April 4, 1853—Isaac Waters, Jesse Kendall and E. West, Trustees; Robert Parker, Clerk; Aaron Eyler, Treasurer; S. Dixon, Assessor; J. N. Middleswart, Constable.

April 3, 1854—E. West, Jesse Kendall and John Brady, Trustees; R. Parker, Clerk; A. Potts, Treasurer; S. Dixon, Assessor; J. W. Sergent, Constable.

April 2, 1855—E. West, S. McNown and William McColgen, Trustees; R. Parker, Clerk; A. Potts, Treasurer; John Brady, Assessor; Andrew Henderson, Constable.

April 7, 1856—E. West, Aaron Eyler and Benjamin Brady, Trustees; R. Parker, Clerk; A. Potts, Treasurer; John Brady, Assessor; A. Henderson, Constable. R. Parker left the township, and F. Inskeep was appointed Clerk.

April 6, 1857—S. McNown, Oliver Reynolds and Anthony Shaw, Trustees; William Campbell, Clerk; A. Potts, Treasurer; Cornelius McColgen, Assessor; George M. Davis, Constable.

April 5, 1858—A. Shaw, B. Brady and O. Reynolds, Trustees; A. Henderson, Clerk; A. Potts, Treasurer; C. McColgen, Assessor; G. M. Davis, Constable. O. Reynolds refused to serve, and S. McNown was appointed Trustee.

April 4, 1859—A. Shaw, S. McNown and H. Parker, Trustees; A. Henderson, Clerk; A. Potts, Treasurer; Kenneth Rhoten, Assessor; G. M. Davis, Constable.

HISTORY OF BROWN COUNTY.

April 2, 1860—A. Shaw, S. McNown and H. Parker, Trustees; A. Henderson, Clerk; William Campbell, Treasurer; H. Rhoten, Assessor; G. M. Davis, Constable.

April 1, 1861—S. McNown, Eli Long and Valentine Wagner, Trustees; A. Henderson, Clerk; W. Campbell, Treasurer; C. P. Eyler, Assessor; G. W. West, Constable.

April 7, 1862—E. Long, V. Wagner and W. P. Custer, Trustees; E. A. Pindell, Clerk; W. Campbell, Treasurer; C. Reynolds, Assessor; G. M. Davis, Constable.

April 6, 1863—Officers same as in 1862. June, 1863, S. McNown, Trustee vice W. P. Custer, deceased.

April 4, 1864—S. McNown, M. Schwallie and S. Dixon, Trustees; A. Henderson, Clerk; W. Campbell, Treasurer; W. Parker, Assessor; G. M. Davis, Constable. January 12, 1865, Isaac Waters, Trustee, vice M. Schwallie, moved away.

April 3, 1865—S. Dixon, Jacob Reynolds and John Schwallie, Trustees; William Parker, Clerk; Aaron Eyler, Treasurer; S. Dixon Assessor; G. M. Davis, Constable.

April 2, 1866—J. Reynolds, J. Schwallie and Henry Parker, Trustees; John C. Marshall, Clerk; John L. Beveridge, Treasurer; S. Dixon, Assessor; C. C. Beveridge, Constable.

April 1, 1867—J. Reynolds, S. J. Campbell and B. Brady, Trustees; Cornelius McColgen, Clerk; J. L. Beveridge, Treasurer; M. H. Prine, Assessor; C. C. Beveridge, Constable.

April 6, 1868—N. Marshall, J. Laney and F. Inskeep, Trustees, C. McColgen, Clerk; J. L. Beveridge, Treasurer; H. Prine, Assessor; J. E. Edwards, Constable.

April 5, 1869—N. Marshall, J. Laney and F. Inskeep, Trustees; C. McColgen, Clerk; W. Parker, Treasurer; J. M. Campbell, Assessor; John E. Edwards, Constable.

April 4, 1870—N. Marshall, J. Schwallie and John Fiscus, Trustees; D. Trautwein, Clerk; W. Parker, Treasurer; J. S. Campbell, Assessor; E. W. Reed, Constable.

April 3, 1871—Trustees, Clerk and Treasurer as in 1870; C. Neu, Asessssor; G. W. West, Constable.

April 1, 1872—B Marshall, J. Reynolds and B. Brady, Trustees; D. Trautwein, Clerk; W. Parker, Treasurer; C. Neu, Assessor; G. W. West, Constable.

April 7, 1873—B. Marshall, J. Reynolds and P. Schreckler, Trustees; John T. McColgen, Clerk; J. M. Alexander, Treasurer; J. B. Prine, Assessor; W. J. Davis, Constable.

April 6, 1874—P. Schreckler, S. McNown and Henry Prine, Trustees; G. M. Campbell, Clerk; J. M. Alexander, Treasurer; Jacob B. Prine, Assessor; W. J. Davis, Constable.

April 5, 1875—S. McNown, H. Prine and J. Schwallie, Trustees; G. M. Campbell, Clerk; Michael Gunner, Treasurer; V. Bachmann, Assessor; E Reed, Constable.

April 3, 1876—Robert King, S. Dixon and J. Schwallie, Trustees; G. M. Campbell, Clerk; W. Campbell, Treasurer; V. Bachmann, Assessor; S. S. Potts, Constable.

April 2, 1877—W. Marshall, J. M. Alexander and Peter Snider, Trustees; W. R. Evans, Clerk; W. Campbell, Treasurer; A. Wagner, Assessor; E. B. Brown, Constable.

April 1, 1878—Trustees as in 1877; R. B. Dunn, Clerk; J. H. Fritts, Treasurer; A Wagner, Assessor; M. Henderson, Constable.

JACKSON TOWNSHIP.

April 7, 1879—G. M. Campbell, V. Bachmann and J. M. Reynolds, Trustees; R. B. Dunn, Clerk; J. H. Fritts, Treasurer; Kenneth Prine, Assessor; M. Henderson, Constable.

April 5, 1880—Trustees as in 1879; C. A. Kleinknecht, Clerk; J. A. Schwallie, Treasurer; R. B. Dunn, Assessor; Abner Reed, Constable.

April 4, 1881—F. Inskeep, Henry Wohlleber and John W. Eyler, Trustees; C. A. Kleinknecht, Clerk; J. A. Schwallie, Treasurer; R. B. Dunn, Assessor; A. Reed, Constable.

April 3, 1882—Trustees as in 1881; G. M.Campbell, Clerk; J. T. Potts, Treasurer; J. A. Schwallie, Assessor; W. Henderson, Constable.

JUSTICES OF THE PEACE.

The following is a complete list of the Justices, with the date of their commissions: Edward Francis, April 29, 1824; Stephen Reynolds, January 29, 1825; M. Greathouse, November 16, 1825, October 13, 1828, October 3, 1831, November 7, 1834; Thomas Brady, January 19, 1828; Thomas Sergent, January 1, 1831; James Wright, November 30, 1833, December 8, 1836, December 6, 1839, December 3, 1842; Robert McKnight, December 8, 1837; William Sellman, November 23, 1840; Alexander Wilson, November 11, 1843, November 7, 1846, December 1, 1849; Samuel E. Evans, elected May 3, 1845, —election was contested and set aside, and he was re-elected June 7, 1845, commission dated June 26, 1845; William Wallis, June 3, 1848, April 30, 1851, May 3, 1854; Fountain Inskeep, November 25, 1852, November 26, 1855, October 19, 1858, October 21, 1861; John Neill, April 21, 1857, April 10, 1860, April 13, 1863, resigned March 7, 1864; Ethan A. Pindell, April 15, 1864; A. Henderson, November 17, 1864; John H. Rees, November 29, 1867, November, 1870, resigned October 1, 1872; Andrew Henderson, November 30, 1872; William Campbell, April 15, 1867, April 11, 1870; Conrad Neu, April 21, 1873; William H. Middleswart, November 2, 1875, October 21, 1878; Andrew Henderson, April 15, 1876, April 19, 1879, April 20, 1882; W. W. Pennell, October 26, 1881, removed from the county, and was succeeded by R. B. Dunn, April 17, 1882.

STATISTICS.

In 1824, the real estate of Joseph Reynolds, deceased, was valued at $8 per acre, a cow at $7 and a mare at $50. At the Presidential election of 1832, 122 votes were cast—103 for Jackson and nineteen for Clay. At the Presidential election of 1836, seventy-seven votes were cast for Van Buren and sixty-nine for Harrison. At the October election, 1837, 119 votes were cast. In 1840, there were 483 youth of school age in the township. In 1845, there were 219 males in the township between the ages of eighteen and forty-five years, and 105 of them were liable for militia duty. The township now has a voting population of 174.

PIONEERS.

The following mention is made of a few of the early settlers who located in the township between the years 1801 and 1820. There may have been many others who merit mention in this place, but if such there were the most diligent inquiry has failed to discover even their names.

Stephen Reynolds, a native of New York State, emigrated to Ohio in 1801, and located about half mile south of where the village of Carlisle now stands, in Jackson Township, where he remained until his death in August, 1842. His son Oliver, who was born in 1794, married Zylpha Middleswart in May, 1810, and by her had ten children, eight of whom are now living. After his marriage, he removed to Ash Ridge, north of Carlisle, where he remained till 1854, when he moved to the extreme northern part of the township. He participated in the war of 1812, and for some time was a Trustee of his township. He died in 1866, leaving his widow, who still survives at the age of eighty-three years.

John Glendening came to Jackson Township about the year 1803 or 1804, and settled on over 100 acres of land in what is now the western part of the township, part of his farm being in Jackson, and part in Franklin Township. He was a native of Scotland, and emigrated to America at an early day. He located and for a number of years lived in Virginia, where he married Jenett Wilson, a native of Ireland. At the time of their emigration to Ohio, they had nine children—six girls and three sons—one son having died in Virginia. Their children are now all dead, and their sole representatives in the county are four grandsons and one grand-daughter. A grand-daughter also lives in Highland County and a grandson in Missouri.

James Inskeep was born in New Jersey in 1766 of English parents. He moved to Virginia, and there married Delila Delaney, who died leaving two children, and two preceded her to the grave. In 1805, Mr. Inskeep emigrated to Ohio, and settled in what is now Jackson Township, where he remained until his death. Shortly after settling here, he married Elenor, daughter of John Glendening. By this marriage he had eleven children, of whom seven are now living, viz., John, born in 1811, married Sarah Haynes and settled on part of the home farm, where he raised four children—girls; Joshua, born in 1812, married Nancy Reed and settled on the home farm, where he raised three boys and six girls; Joseph, born in 1813, settled on the home place, and married Martha Hill, by whom he had four boys and several girls; he now lives in Missouri; Job, born 1819, settled near the home farm, and married Susan Myers, who died without issue; Fountain, whose biography appears elsewhere in this work. The sons, with the exception of Joseph, all reside in Brown County. The father died in 1824 under the following circumstances: On the 24th of May, while returning from West Union, where he had been attending court, he attempted on horseback to ford Eagle Creek, which at that time was swollen by recent rains; but by some accident was thrown from his horse and drowned. His widow died in 1861.

Anthony Shaw was born in New York State near the borders of Massachusetts. He married Sarah Niles, by whom he had twelve children, the majority of whom are still living. In 1810, with his wife and two children, he emigrated to Brown County, Ohio, and settled about one mile southwest of Carlisle Village, where he remained perhaps eight years. After living in different portions of what are now known as Jackson and Franklin Townships, he finally settled in the southern portion of Franklin Township on Straight Creek, where he remained until his decease. He had served as Trustee of Franklin Township, and was by the community surrounding him highly respected. He died in June, 1840. His son, Andrew J., who was born in this township in 1816, is now living in the northern part of the township, where he moved with his family in 1859.

Sylvanus Parker, a native of Maryland, emigrated to Ohio with his parents, Peter and Rachel (Harper) Parker, and located in Jackson Township in 1812. They lived in Pennsylvania, Virginia and Kentucky before their emigration. Sylvanus married Nancy Feeley, by whom he had two children—John, who married Sarah Patton and had six children, and Elizabeth, the wife of Josiah Ross, the mother of two children, both surviving.

Terry Wormacks emigrated from Virginia to Ohio, and in 1813 located in Jackson Township, on part of the land owned by James Inskeep. He married Roxy Reynolds, and by her had a large family of children.

Thomas Brady came from Virginia with Wormacks, or about the same time, and located in Jackson Township. He married Anna Glendening, and had a family of nine or ten children, all of whom are now dead or have left this county.

Joseph McManis was born in Pennsylvania in 1796, and in 1815 emigrated to Ohio with his parents, Charles and Ellen McManis, who located in what is now Jackson Township. After living in Brown County several years, they removed to Adams County, where they resided until their deaths. Joseph was three times married—in March, 1819, to Jane Donaldson, by whom he had nine children; in May, 1840, to Mary Bishop, by whom he had three children, and in November, 1847, to Ruth Mathias, by whom he had seven children. He died in Livingston County, Ill., in November, 1872. A more extended sketch of him will be found among the biographies of this township.

Capt. John Rice emigrated to Ohio and located in Jackson Township in 1816. His father, James Rice, with his family emigrated from Ireland prior to the American Revolution. Capt. Rice was born in Philadelphia, where he married Jane McNight, who emigrated from Ireland with her parents at an early day. He had charge of a company of cavalry in the war of 1812, and also served on the frontiers of Ohio and Indiana and in the engagement at Tippecanoe. He had a family of thirteen children, some of whom are now living in Washington Township, to which he moved in 1820, and where he died in September, 1843.

Brice Rukey was born in New Jersey about the year 1809. About the year 1817, his parents, Thomas and Hester Rukey, emigrated to Brown County, Ohio, and settled near Eagle Creek, in the southern portion of what is now known as Jackson Township, near where Thomas B. Rukey at present resides. Brice was here reared amid the stirring scenes of pioneer life, and received but a rudimentary education. He married Elizabeth Greathouse, by whom he had nine children, five of whom are living, viz., Lucinda, Mary J., Ellen, William and Thomas B. Mr. Rukey was a member of the Methodist Episcopal Church, and died in October, 1877. His wife died some time before him.

Edward Francis was born in Ireland, and when three years of age came to America with his parents and located in Jackson Township, Brown County, near Ash Ridge. He married Elizabeth Plummer, of Adams County, by whom he had four children. After his marriage, he settled on the farm now occupied by his son James W., where he resided until his death in November, 1870.

Josiah Rhoten with his wife Mary (Prine) and three children emigrated from Kentucky to Ohio, and in 1814 located in Jackson Township. He purchased fifty acres of land where the village of Carlisle now stands. He died in 1865 and his wife in 1855. They had six children born to them after their settlement there. Of their nine children, Christopher, William, Huston, Hannah and Catharine live in Brown County, Thomas, Prine and Jane are dead, and Kenneth lives in the State of Illinois.

William McNown was born in Ireland, and at thirty years of age emigrated to America and settled in Pennsylvania. In 1818, he came to Jackson Township, and located on Eagle Creek. He brought with him his wife, Mary (McKnight), and five children and had one child born after his settlement. Of his children, one married S. L. Fenton, of this township; Robert is in Dexter, Iowa; William in this township, and the rest are dead.

William McColgen was another early settler, but we are unable to give the date of his settlement. He came from Virginia with his wife, Isabella, and several children. He died in this township, and his children have all left the county. He occupied several township offices during his life, and was a man of prominence in the community.

HISTORY OF BROWN COUNTY.

CHURCHES.

About the years 1815 or 1816, a Methodist class was organized with thirteen members in the western part of the township, in what was then called the Mahappy neighborhood, and class meetings and occasional church services were held at the houses of the members, but mostly in the house of Mr. Mahappy, whose house stood on Eagle Creek, in the edge of Adams County. Previous to the organization of this class, a class was formed at the house of Samuel Evans on Ash Ridge. Among the first members of this class were Samuel Evans and wife, Robert Patton and wife, Josiah Rhoten and Mary, his wife, John Crute and Elsie, his wife, and John Nelson and wife. Services were held in the houses of Robert Patton and Samuel Evans. In 1819, these two classes united and formed White Oak Station, more recently known as Ash Ridge Church. About 1824, ground having been obtained of Samuel Evans for that purpose, a log church was built by the people of the neighborhood. In this church the society worshiped until the fall of the year 1856, when they built a one-story frame church in Carlisle at a cost of $1,100, in which they still worship.

About the time of the breaking-out of the rebellion, a division of the church took place, and about fifty members withdrew, and formed the Christian Union Church. They took possession of the old log church, which had been deserted when the congregation moved to Carlisle, and worshiped in it until they built the present one-story frame building that stands on the ground near the old log which is still standing. The church building belongs to the society, and their preachers are employed by the congregation, as the church is independent of any conference or other higher court.

Mount Olivet Methodist Church is the outgrowth of meetings held on the border of the township at the houses of James Pendill, William Davis and others about the year 1832. The meeting place was afterward changed to a schoolhouse that stood near the site of the present church. In 1835, a half acre of ground was donated to the church by John Francis, and on it the society built a small log church, in which their services were held until it was replaced by the present frame structure.

Pleasant Hill Christian Church was organized by Alexander McClain, in the house of Daniel Robbins, in Adams County, in 1836, with nine members, among whom were Daniel Robbins and Sarah, his wife, Isaac Edgington and Sarah, his wife, and Emily Edgington. In 1843, they built a frame church on the hill above the present church on an acre of land procured of Nathaniel Glaze. In 1839, they purchased a half-acre of land of Dodridge Smith, on which they built the present church. Among the pastors who have served this congregation are John McMillan, Newman Dawson, Jackson Daugherty, Samuel Gray, Rufus McDaniel, Walker Mefford, Benton Sellman, Margaret Wallace, and since 1861, George W. Mefford.

Emanuel Chapel (Christian) was built about 1857 on land donated by J. Brady. The society was organized and services were held as early as 1850. The meetings until the church was built were held in a schoolhouse that stood near the site of the present church. The church was built by subscription. Soon after the war the zeal of the society flagged, and the services were for a time discontinued, but were commenced again about 1875, under the ministrations of Rev. Harrison Toll, and now they are having occasional preaching.

SCHOOLS.

In 1817, a small three-cornered schoolhouse was built on the branch of the creek above James McNown's residence, in which Samuel McKee and James Thompson taught school in early days. This is supposed to have been the first schoolhouse built in the township, schools that were held prior to that date being in private houses. There was also a log schoolhouse built on Ash Ridge at a very eary day, in which Stephen Morris, Samuel Swan and a teacher named May taught a number of schools. In 1820, a schoolhouse was built in the eastern part of the township on Eagle Creek, in which Isaac Gantz was the first teacher. Prior to this, he taught in the house of Mr. Mahappy, and in a little log church in Adams County, in the same neighborhood. In 1824, a school was taught in a log hut on Eagle Creek by William Brown. Another pioneer schoolhouse stood just north of the present site of Carlisle.

There are now in the township six districts, with a good schoolhouse in each and an enrollment of 107 boys and 122 girls. The total value of the school property in the township is assessed at $2,100 or $350 in each district. The amount expended annually for the support of these schools is about $2,000, of which $1,500 is for the salaries of teachers, and the balance for fuel, repairs and other contingencies.

CARLISLE.

The town of Carlisle was laid out by John Anderson and John Anderson, Jr., May 30, 1834. The plat, recorded June 16, 1834, contains thirty-one lots, eight poles long by four poles wide, two streets, Main street and Cross street, and fifteen cross alleys one pole wide. Main street is sixty-six feet wide and seventy-six poles long, and bears north 40 degrees east. Cross street is sixty-six feet wide and twenty poles long, and bears north fifty degrees west. The alleys run parallel to Cross street, and divide the lots into squares of two lots each. The town lies on the Ripley & Hillsboro pike, which runs through Main street.

The post office, which is called Ash Ridge, was established soon after the platting of the town. Among the Postmasters have been Ethan A. Pindell, who occupied the office in 1857, and for a number of years afterward, Andrew Potts, William Parker, Jacob S. Campbell. The present incumbent of the office is Mrs. Jane L. Campbell, who was appointed at the death of her husband in February, 1882.

The industries of the town are not extensive. Samuel Mitchell opened a tavern on Main street in 1853, and continued it several years, but finally sold out and left the town. Some time prior to 1850, a carding and fulling mill was built in the northeastern part of the town by David Ross. He sold it to Thomas Prine, and he to George Davis, in whose possession it was burned down, but was afterward rebuilt by him, and operated a number of years. The machinery was finally taken from it and sold, and the building left to decay. A saw-mill was built south of town by Addison Williamson in 1854, and operated by him several years. It is now owned by Job Inskeep. The enterprises of the town now are two saloons, two shoe shops, two blacksmith shops, three general stores, one hotel, Ætna House, and two secret societies.

Ash Ridge Lodge, No. 492, I. O O. F., was chartered May 10, 1871, and instituted August 19, 1871, with ten charter members. William Parker was the first N. G., and George P. Tyler the first Secretary. In 1875, the lodge built a second story on a large frame building at a cost of $700, and now occupy it as a lodge room. There are now twenty-four members.

Union Lodge, No. 127, K. of P., was instituted March 24, 1880, by Charles D. Iddings, Grand Chancellor, with fourteen charter members. The lodge now occupies a hall on Main street, over one of the stores. The first officers were: George M. Campbell, P. C.; Dr. A. Gilfillen, C. C.; L. B. Campbell, V. C.; J. M. Parker, P.; R. B. Dunn, K. of R. and S.

CHAPTER XIV.

WASHINGTON TOWNSHIP.

WASHINGTON TOWNSHIP was organized December 2, 1822, and the boundary lines then described were as follows: Beginning in the southern boundary line of Highland County, dividing in part Highland and Brown, at a point five and one-half miles from the corner or connection of the said line with Adams County, and running from thence due south to the township line dividing the townships of Eagle and Byrd, thence westwardly with the line dividing Eagle, Pleasant and Clark Townships; thence north five and one-half miles to a point (from which point a line shall be run at right angles to the first line run, forming one entire township, to be called Franklin Township), and from the said last-mentioned line to continue north to the line dividing the townships of Clark and Perry; from thence with the said line and its bearings to the Highland County line; thence with the said lines dividing the counties of Highland and Brown, with the bearings therof, to the point of beginning, forming one entire township, to be called Washington Township.

A portion of the above-described territory was used on the formation of Scott Township, December 1, 1828.

On the north of this subdivision is Highland County, on the east Eagle Township, on the south Franklin Township, and on the west Scott and Pike Townships. Generally speaking, its surface is level, there being some hills along the water-courses. The surface is well watered by the East Fork of White Oak Creek, Slab Camp, and smaller tributaries of the first-mentioned. The East Fork of White Oak flows through the northern part of the township from east to west, and joins the main stream of the same name, which forms the line separating this township and Pike, at the western boundary of the township. Slab Camp Creek, so named, as tradition gives it, after an Indian camp that was once pitched along its waters, and the remains of which were traceable to the pioneer settlers. The soil is fertile, and the products correspond with those of other sections of Brown County. Pikes are as yet unknown to this section, but in railroads it excels all other townships in the county, having direct communication with the outside world in three directions, and in the near future will be added the fourth. The Cincinnati & Eastern Railroad passes through the northern part of Washington, running in an easterly and westerly direction; the Hillsboro & Sardinia road terminates at Sardinia; and the Georgetown & Sardinia Railroad is in process of construction.

EARLY SETTLEMENT.

The first permanent settlement made in what is now Washington Township is credited to the Wardlaw family. Just prior to the dawn of the present century—in the early spring of 1800—Robert Wardlaw, with wife, Martha Downey, and a number of sons and daughters, some of whom were married and were parents themselves, emigrated from Kentucky and halted on the banks of White Oak and effected the Wardlaw settlement. The family had for some years resided in Kentucky, where the father owned considerable land, which, it is said, he traded for that on White Oak. Here he possessed 300 acres, in Survey No. 1,053, which lies on either side of White Oak Creek, in what is

WASHINGTON TOWNSHIP. 665

now the subdivisions of Washington, Scott and Pike, at a point where the three are close together. Robert's home was in Scott, but those of William and Samuel, who were men of families, were in Washington, along the North and East Forks of the creek. The family had, prior to going to Kentucky, resided in the State of Virginia. Further reference to the father will be found in the sketch of Scott Township. Other sons and daughters of Robert and wife were John, James, Josiah, Hugh, Mattie and Jane. William's wife was Isabel Nesbitt, and their children were James, Samuel, Philander, Robert, Jane, Mary and Matilda, the most of whom became permanent residents of Brown County, and the men folks assisted in the clearing and improvement of land. The father, William, was a soldier of the war of 1812, a member of Capt. Jacob Boerstler's company, and was engaged in battle with the company at Brownstown, where he was killed August 4, 1812. Samuel Wardlaw married Elizabeth Nesbitt, a sister to William's wife, and their sons were Allen, Preston, Levi, Rainey and Henry; and the daughters were Mary, Ann and Elizabeth. All remained permanent settlers in the county, and Levi and Rainey of the township, where both are now residing, on the original tract of their parents Samuel died May 6, 1848, in the seventy-fifth year of his age.

John Wardlaw married Elizabeth Lance, and settled in Washington Township. James married Nellie Irwin, and became a permanent settler of this township. Josiah's wife was Sarah Kimball, and they resided in Scott Township. Hugh married Rebecca Irons, and remained permanently in the township. He, too, went into the war of 1812, with his brother, enlisting in the same company and regiment. His death occurred January 24, 1864, aged seventy-two years; and that of his wife, March 19, 1871, in her seventy-ninth year. Jane became the wife of Joseph Calvin, a pioneer of this township.

Joseph Calvin, of whom we could learn but little, came to the White Oak region some time prior to 1805, as it appears of records in Clermont County, that he was married to Jane Wardlaw June 1, 1805, by William Hunter, a Justice of the Peace of that county. He settled on White Oak, just above the Wardlaw settlement. His children were Sophronia, Polly, James, Sally, Luther, Robert and another son, whose name is not recalled. Mr. Calvin hailed from Kentucky.

Vinson Calvin, a brother of the one above named, with his family, came from Kenton's Station, Ky., removing on Christmas Day, 1807, and effected a settlement on White Oak, near Joseph. He was a native of Kentucky, and was twice married. His second wife was Christina ———, and their children were Lewis, Ann, John and Elizabeth, all of whom were born in Kentucky. It is said that Simon Kenton, Jr., was a half-brother to these sons and daughters. Lewis married Zena Graham, and, in connection with Joseph McFadden, purchased 500 acres of land in Washington Township, which they improved. He removed from this vicinity some years ago to Clermont County, where he died in 1878. Ann married John Hineman, and lived in this neighborhood many years, then removed to the West. The others married and went West.

Among the first settlers in the vicinity of Sardinia, and the most prominent man in the community, was John Moore, a native of Madison County, N. J., born near Elizabethtown December 4, 1779. His parents were natives of England, and, in religious belief, were Friends, or Quakers. At the age of sixteen years, our subject left the parental roof and located in Monongalia County, W. Va., where he engaged in teaching. In 1799, he was united in marriage with Frances Graham, and, six years later, removed to Ohio and settled on Red Oak Creek, in the vicinity of Ripley. In 1807–08, he taught school on Straight Creek, and afterward at Red Oak. Mr. Moore settled near

Sardinia soon after his arrival in the Buckeye State, remaining on Red Oak not longer than a year or two. He spent the summers on his land in Washington Township, and was engaged in teaching during the winters, at the points named. This plan he continued until the winter of 1815-16, when he began teaching in what was afterward long known as the Moore Schoolhouse, near the present site of Sardinia, and continued teaching thereat until 1834. His wife died in 1832, and he afterward married Mrs. Fannie Pettijohn. Father Moore was an Elder in the Presbyterian Church from 1812 until the organization of the Congregational Church in Sardinia, in 1851. From an obituary notice written at his death, November 9, 1857, we quote as follows: "Exact in his intercourse with his fellow-men, honest in all the transactions of life, desirous of promoting the good of mankind, and possessing a Christian character worthy of imitation, he won the affection and esteem of the community in which he lived. Few live so exemplary. He had a taste for reading, which he did not fail to cultivate in the decline of life. The Bible was his daily companion. He was a constant attendant upon the services of the sanctuary. * * * * *" In politics, Mr. Moore was an Abolitionist, and afterward a Republican. He was a man of strong character, fixed principles and undaunted courage in advocating his principles. It is said by a venerable and highly respected citizen of Sardinia that John Moore molded the character of the community in which he lived. By his first marriage, Mr. Moore had ten children, only five of whom lived to the age of maturity. Jane married Amzi Huggins. Sarah married Rev. R. I. Huggins, and they now reside near Bethel, Clermont County. She is the only child that survived her father. The eldest son, Josiah, married Patsy Gilliland. settled in the vicinity of his father, and there became an enterprising and useful citizen, a sketch of whom appears elsewhere in this work. The next son, Ira, died in 1849, aged twenty-nine years; John B., the youngest son, died in 1845, at the age of twenty four years.

The Pettijohn families, five in number—namely, those of James, Edward, Richard, Amos and Thomas—emigrating from Monongalia County, W. Va., were among the earliest settlers of this locality. Just at what ime they came is not definitely fixed; however, it is certain that they were here early in the present century, and are to be classed with Washington's earliest pioneers. On the question of the time of their emigration, we give the date as fixed by the son of James, a resident of St. Louis, as two years before Ohio became a State. Now, as there is a question on this point, too, we leave the reader to his own opinion. It is thought, by one who has given the subject of pioneer history in the vicinity of Sardinia some attention, and is well versed in the history of the township, that the date of the Pettijohn settlement as given above is too early by several years. It appears of record that a deed for land lying in Survey 3,389 was made to Amos Pettijohn under date of November 28, 1809. Of these families our knowledge is limited, as none of the immediate descendants are in this locality, and therefore not a great deal of their family history can be given. Amos Pettijohn, whose wife's given name was Susan, and their children, so far as known, were Hannah, Nancy, William and Rachel, settled a little northeast of the present village of Sardinia. He was one of the first Elders of the Presbyterian Church, and a useful and influential citizen. Thomas Pettijohn settled north of Sardinia. His wife's given name was Ruth, and their children, so far as known, were Samuel, Boaz, Huldah, Ruth and Elias. Richard Pettijohn settled in the same vicinity. He raised a large family of children, and the survivors are all now in the West. He was one of the first Justices of the Peace in Washington Township. Of James and Edward we know nothing, save that the former's wife was Elizabeth Johnson, a native of Virginia, and that William, their son, was a soldier in the war of

1812. Abraham Pettijohn, of one of these families, married soon after their arrival, and remained in this vicinity for about thirty years, and became a man of some prominence in the township.

It is said that all of these families were noted Abolitionists, and instilled these principles into their children, who became noted for their devotion to this then unpopular and odious doctrine. From these families sprang twelve physicians, ten of whom are still living, and are engaged in active practice. In 1829, there were as many as a dozen Pettijohn families, who sprang from the pioneer settlement in and about Sardinia, residing in the township at one time.

In the fall of 1809, an addition was made to the White Oak settlements by the removal of David Graham from West Virginia to this section. Mr. Graham was a native of West Virginia, and, before his emigration to Ohio, had married Jane Dunn, of that State, and on his arrival his family consisted of wife and five children—one son and four daughters—and afterward were added to the family two sons and five daughters. By name, the children were Zena, Rebecca, Dortha, Susan, Cassandra, Elizabeth, Jane, Alice, Nancy, John, David and Henry. The father settled on a tract of land now situated on the road leading from Sardinia to Brownstown, about one mile southwest of Sardinia. This pioneer was one of the original members of White Oak Presbyterian Church, and a valuable man in the community in which his life was spent. He died August 7, 1845, in the seventy-second year of his age, his wife having preceded him nearly six years, aged sixty-seven years. Their remains rest in the graveyard at Sardinia. Zena, the eldest daughter of these parents, married Lewis Calvin. Rebecca married Joseph McFadden, now deceased; she is a resident of Sardinia. Dortha married S. D. Runyan, both of whom are dead. Susan married Jacob Davis, and both are dead. Cassandra is the wife of Dr. Isaac M. Beck, of Sardinia. Elizabeth married Oliver Shroufe, and is in Iowa. Jane married Shepherd Johnson, and is in Kansas. Alice married George Parks (deceased), and is a resident of the State of Illinois. Nancy became the wife of Andrew Raney, and died in Illinois. The sons are all in the West.

In 1808, John Vance and wife, Lydia Reiss, emigrated from Lexington, Ky., to Clermont County, stopping in the vicinity of Bethel, on Clover Creek, where the father rented land of Jasper and John Shotwell, upon which he resided until the year 1810, and then removed to a tract situated on the east side of White Oak, in the extreme northwestern part of the township, which he had purchased of the same men. Here Mr. Vance reared the little and rude log cabin, the home of the pioneer, and began the task incumbent upon all comers to a new country. He was a man of some family before coming to Ohio. While hailing, as he did, from the Blue Grass Region, he was not a native of that State, having formerly come from Virginia. He was the father of the following-named children: Margaret, William, Sarah, Reiss, Elizabeth, John, Patrick, James, Lewis A. and Morris. William is now residing on the homestead, and is the father of twenty children, all of whom were born on that farm. He has been twice married. His first wife was Sophronia, daughter of the pioneer, Joseph Calvin; and his present wife was Margaret Jane Moore. Margaret married John McCain. John married Mrs. Elizabeth (Bratton) Sands. Patrick married Rebecca Brannon. James married Jane Cumberland. Lewis married, first, Matilda Dey, and second, Jane Stanford. Morris married Nancy Calvin. Sarah married Thomas Schroufe. Elizabeth married Daniel Runnels, and Reiss died unmarried.

About the time that David Graham made his appearance in the township, there settled on the present site of the village of Sardinia Joseph Bratton, a man of family, who improved land, upon which he resided until the neighborhood of 1828, when he removed into Highland County.

A line of settlement along Slab Camp was made during the war of 1812-15, or about that time. The families emigrating thither were the Days, Hamiltons, Higinbothams and Nevinses. The Hamiltons, of whom Robert was the head, came from Virginia, and their land was on the stream named, situated about two miles southeast of Sardinia. Mr. Hamilton was a native of the State from whence he emigrated, born July 26, 1788, and his wife, Nancy Parish, was one year his senior. They were married in 1811, and, before settling in this locality, stopped a year or two in the vicinity of Georgetown. Their children were Sarah, Ellen, Ann, Joseph, Elizabeth, Amanda, Delilah, Joshua and Susannah. Mr. Hamilton was commissioned a Justice of the Peace of the township in 1826.

The Higinbothams, of whom some of the sons and daughters were Samuel, Elizabeth, Mary, Rebecca, Catherine, Sarah and John, settled across the creek from Hamilton's. They only remained in the township a few years.

Andrew Nevins was a Kentuckian, and emigrated to this State early in the present century, and stopped some time in the southern part of the county before making a permanent settlement on Slab Camp Creek. He was twice married, and had a number of children, among whom were Hugh, John and Andrew P. He was a pious man, and one of the early Methodists of this vicinity. It was greatly through his efforts that a society of that denomination was so soon organized in the Slab Camp settlement. It is said that it was on his invitation that Rev. John Strange, one of the old itinerant Methodist preachers, first came to hold services in this section of the country.

Of the family of Days we can give no information, the descendants having all removed from the neighborhood. A family by the name of Lyon settled along Slab Camp at about the same time the above-mentioned families came there. Later arrivals in Washington were the Kincaids. Matthew, the father, was a native of Pennsylvania, and emigrated with his father to the Northwest Territory in 1797, and effected a settlement in what afterward became Adams County. His father, Samuel Kincaid, was in the war of 1812, and lost his life at Fort Meigs, where he was killed by the Indians May 5, 1813. Matthew, too, was in that war. In 1817, he located in this township, settling in the vicinity of Sardinia. He was a tanner by trade, and carried on that business for twenty years. His death occurred January 9, 1871.

Two years later came to this locality the families of Thomas Purcell and Clarkson Dunn, both of Irish descent. Mr. Purcell hailed from Kentucky, and became a resident of the country around Sardinia. Mr. Dunn was a native of Maryland; also his wife, Elizabeth Hamilton. The former was a soldier in the war of 1812. In 1816, with his wife and three children, he descended the Ohio River in a flat-boat and landed at Ripley. He soon removed to Straight Creek, and, in 1817, located near Georgetown, and in 1819 made a permanent settlement above Sardinia. He was a prominent citizen of the township. His death occurred in September, 1852, and that of his wife some years later.

Among the pioneers of Washington of whom but little is now known other than that they resided in the township were Levi Estel, James Bell and John Kibler, all of whom carried on mills on White Oak.

The settlements along the water-courses grew rapidly, and it was but a few years from the beginning of the march of emigrants to this region until the lands were all taken up and the vicinity peopled. In 1825, among the names of householders other than those mentioned above were the following: Joseph Line, William Grant, Jeremiah Purdum James Little, Richard Rilea, Thomas Rilea, Joseph Wright, David McKee, Peter Shinkle, Benjamin Cornell, Simon

WASHINGTON TOWNSHIP.

Kenton, Adam Ewing, Daniel Reynolds, Vinson Robins, Everett Smith, John Bingman, John Hoss, William Reave, John Dey, James Bonner, George Washburn, John Stansberry, John Poe, Benjamin McDaniel, Hampton Pangburn, John Hindman, John Vansandt, John Gregory, John Oldum and James Bonner.

The land lying in the southwestern part of the township was not settled, comparatively speaking, until a late day—not until after 1830. A family of Germans by the name of Ernst settled on and improved land in that locality. Many other Germans settled throughout the southern part of the township, the first of whom were the Feiks and Biehms. The reader, as he proceeds, will notice, in connection with other subjects, the names of later arrivals. It is beyond our province to here further trace the line of settlement and speak of the hardy forefathers of many of the people of Washington, who, by their toil and privations, made possible the beautiful fields and highly cultivated farms of to-day.

JUSTICES OF THE PEACE.

The following are the names of persons commissioned to the office of Justice of the Peace in Washington Township, with the dates of their commissions: Richard Pettijohn, January —, 1823, December 20, 1831; John J. Gregory, May, 1826, May 1, 1829, April 13, 1832, April 29, 1835; Robert Hamilton, April 10, 1826; William K. Eskridge, January 12, 1829; Joseph Wright, November 29, 1834, January 19, 1838; Matthew Kincaid, April 12, 1838, April 4, 1856; Seth G. Wright, January 19, 1841; Henry Strait, May 24, 1841; Huston Bare, November 5, 1843, October 24, 1846, October 19, 1849, November 4, 1852, October 22, 1855, November 1, 1858, October 21, 1861, April 7, 1865; Eli Dunn, December 27, 1843, April 14, 1853; Levi Dunn (elected), April 7, 1845, May 20, 1848; Abiel Hayes, April 30, 1851; A. N. Nevin, May 3, 1854; R. Dunn, April 12, 1859; Thomas Davis, April 23, 1862; David Kinzer, November 17, 1864; William Vance, October 12, 1867; William F. Gregory, October 28, 1870, October 31, 1873; A. D. Marsh, April 15, 1871; P. R. Kincaid, April 18, 1874, April 17, 1877, April 17, 1880; Stephen Feike, October 21, 1876, October 27, 1879.

TOWNSHIP OFFICIALS.

1823—Trustees, Joseph Calvin, Jeremiah Purdum; Treasurer, John Hindman; Clerk, —— ———; Lister, William Grant; Overseers of the Poor, John Vinsandt, Matthew Day; Fence Viewer, Clarkson Dunn.

1824—Trustees, Jeremiah Purdum, Matthew Day, John Stansberry; Treasurer, Peter Shinkle; Clerk, Joseph Worstell; Lister, William Grant; Overseers of the Poor, James Dey, Levi Estel; Fence Viewers, Christopher Poe, James Robins.

1825—Trustees, Abraham Pettijohn, Peter Shinkle, Edward Pettijohn; Treasurer, Joseph Wright; Clerk, Matthew Kincaid; Overseers of the Poor, William Grant, Amos Pettijohn.

1826—Trustees, Abraham Pettijohn, Mark Day, Joseph Calvin; Treasurer, Thomas Rilea; Clerk, Matthew Kincaid; Overseers of the Poor, John Pettijohn, John Bratton; Fence Viewers, Andrew Nevin, Edward Dey.

1827—Trustees, David McKee, A. Starke, George Kauts; Treasurer, Clarkson Dunn; Clerk, John Moore; Overseers of the Poor, John Bingman, James Bell; Fence Viewers, Michael Hough, Lewis Calvin.

1828—Trustees, Hugh Gunnison, John Vansandt, Thomas Rilea; Treasurer, John Purdum; Clerk, John Moore; Overseers of the Poor, Thomas McGee, Matthew Kincaid; Fence Viewers, Richard Pettijohn, James Wardlow.

1829—Trustees, John Anderson, Hugh Nevin, Amos Pettijohn; Treasurer,

Abraham Pettijohn; Clerk, Matthew Kincaid; Overseers of the Poor, Philip Waters, James Bell; Fence Viewers, Robert Ewing, Edward Day.

1830—Trustees, John J. Gregory, Hugh Nevin, George Wright; Treasurer, Clarkson Dunn; Clerk, Matthew Kincaid; Overseers of the Poor, John Anderson, ————; Fence Viewers, ————.

1831—Trustees, Robert D. Lilley, Aaron Purdum, George Knight; Treasurer, Thomas Rilea; Clerk. Josiah Moore; Overseers of the Poor, Abiel Starke, Stephen Alexander; Fence Viewers, Richard Rilea, George Marsher.

1832—Trustees, Robert Graham, Aaron Purdum, John J. Gregory; Treasurer, John Moore; Clerk, Josiah Moore; Overseers of the Poor, P. R. Kincaid, James Wardlow; Fence Viewers, John Nevin, James Wardlow.

1833—Trustees, Joseph Wright, John J. Gregory, Robert Graham; Treasurer, Clarkson Dunn; Clerk, John Moore; Overseers of the Poor, James Bell, Ellis Dey; Fence Viewers, Robert Graham, Abraham Pettijohn, James Rilea.

1834—Trustees, Zachariah Pettijohn, John J. Gregory, Clarkson Dunn; Treasurer, Aaron Purdum; Clark, John Graham; Overseers of the Poor, John Nevin, ————; Fence Viewers, William B. Wills, Richard Pettijohn.

1835—Trustees, Thomas Rilea, Clarkson Dunn, John J. Gregory; Treasurer, ————; Clerk, John Graham; Overseers of the Poor, Thomas Rilea, Isaac M. Beck; Fence Viewers, Joseph Wright, William B. Lilley, Hugh Kennedy.

1836—Trustees, Clarkson Dunn, William Vance, Thomas Rilea; Treasurer, Aaron Dunn; Clerk, Robert Graham; Overseers of the Poor, John Gregory, George Wright and James Wardlow; Fence Viewers, John B. Mahan, Joseph Pettijohn.

1837—Trustees, Joseph Wright, Hugh Nevin, Levi Dunn; Treasurer, Aaron Purdum; Clerk, Robert Graham, Overseers of the Poor, Josiah Moore, William B. Lilley; Fence Viewers, John B. Mahan, Robert I. Huggins, Stephen W. Gilleland.

1838—Trustees, Clarkson Dunn, George Wright, Henry Strait; Treasurer, Aaron Purdum; Clerk, S. W. Gilleland; Overseers of the Poor, John Dey, Ellis Dey; Fence Viewers, James Cumberland, John B. Mahan, W. B. Lilley.

1839—Trustees, Clarkson Dunn, George Wright, Henry Strait; Treasurer, Aaron Purdum; Clerk, Robert Graham; Overseers of the Poor, John B. Mahan, William Wills; Fence Viewers, V. M. Diboll, Shepherd Johnson, Eli Wells.

1840—Trustees, Hugh Nevin, Ira Tracy, Clarkson Dunn; Treasurer, Aaron Purdum; Clerk, John Gaddis; Overseers of the Poor, John B. Mahan, Josiah Moore; Fence Viewers, Clarkson Dunn, A. P. Nevin, William Lilley.

1841—Trustees, Clarkson Dunn, Ira Tracy, John Wright; Treasurer, Aaron Purdum; Clerk, John Gaddis; Overseers of the Poor, John B. Mahan, J. W. Myers; Fence Viewers, Moses B. Briggs, A. P. Nevin, Clarkson Dunn.

1842—Trustees, Ira Tracy, John Wright, Clarkson Dunn; Treasurer, Aaron Purdum; Clerk, Joseph Hamilton; Overseers of the Poor, John B. Mahan, E. P. Evans; Fence Viewers, ————.

1843—Trustees, Hugh Nevin, Levi Dunn, Joseph Wright; Treasurer, Aaron Purdom; Clerk, John H. Hallam; Overseers of the Poor, A. P. Nevin Squire Purcell; Fence Viewers, Matthew Kincaid, Squire Purcell, William Wilson; Assessor, John Moore.

1844—Trustees, Joseph Wright, Hugh Nevin, Levi Dunn; Treasurer, M. B. Riggs; Clerk, John Moore; Assessor, George Wright; Overseers of the Poor, I. M. Beck, V. M. Diboll.

1845—Trustees, Henry Dunn, Joseph Wright, Samuel Wright; Treasurer,

WASHINGTON TOWNSHIP.

M. B. Riggs; Clerk, Joseph Hamilton; Assessor, John W. Evans; Overseers of the Poor, James McIntire, Imri Kirk.

1846—Trustees, Huston Bare, Samuel Wright, Henry Dunn; Treasurer, M. B. Riggs; Clerk, C. P. Evans; Assessor, A. Hays; Overseers of the Poor,

1847—Trustees, Huston Bare, Samuel Wright, Wilson Dunn; Treasurer, M. B. Riggs; Clerk, Robert Carter; Assessor, Abiel Hays.

1848—Trustees, Samuel P. Wright, Wilson Dunn, A. N. Nevin; Treasurer, O. P. Griffith; Clerk, John S. Kerr; Assessor, I. W. Evans.

1849—Trustees, J. P. Biehn, Eli Dunn, A. Hays; Treasurer, O. P. Griffith; Clerk, M. B. Riggs; Assessor, William B. Wills.

1850—Trustees, Joseph Hamilton, Joseph Wright, Ira Tracy; Treasurer, Huston Bare; Clerk, M. B. Riggs; Assessor, William Marshall, Jr.

1851—Trustees, Ira Tracy, Joseph Wright, Joseph Hamilton; Treasurer, Huston Bare; Clerk, M. B. Riggs; Assessor, William Marshall, Jr.

1852—Trustees, James Cumberland, Levi Dunn, A. N. Nevin; Treasurer, H. Bare; Clerk, M. B. Riggs; Assessor, William Marshall, Jr.

1853—Trustees, A. N. Nevin, Levi Dunn, Ira Calvin; Treasurer, Huston Bare; Clerk, M. B. Riggs; Assessor, J. R. Rilea.

1854—Trustees, Ira Tracy, H. W. Kennedy, Noah Hite; Treasurer, Huston Bare; Clerk, M. B. Riggs; Assessor, J. R. Rilea.

1855—Trustees, Henry Dunn, A. P. Nevin, Noah Hite; Treasurer, H. W. Kennedy; Clerk, J. C. Chapman; Assessor, P. N. Kincaid.

1856—Trustees, Henry Dunn, Jr., J. C. Dunn, Noah Hite; Treasurer, H. W. Kennedy; Clerk, R. G. Barber; Assessor, P. R. Kincaid.

1857—Trustees, Huston Bare, Noah Hite,, Henry Dunn, Jr.; Treasurer, H. W. Kennedy; Clerk, S. S. Pangburn; Assessor, P. R. Kincaid.

1858—Trustees, Noah Hite, Huston Bare, Conrad New; Treasurer, H. W. Kennedy; Clerk, T. J. Curry; Assessor, P. R. Kincaid.

1859—Trustees, Henry Dunn, Huston Bare, Ira Tracy; Treasurer, H. W. Kennedy; Clerk, S. S. Pangburn; Assessor, P. R. Kincaid.

1860—Trustees, Henry Hays, Huston Bare, Ira Tracy; Treasurer, H. W. Kennedy; Clerk, S. S. Pangburn; Assessor, A. M. Page.

1861—Trustees, Ira Tracy, William Henderson, Allen Henderson; Treasurer, Huston Bare; Clerk, Wesley Love; Assessor, A. M. Page.

1862—Trustees, Allen Henderson, Noah Hite, John Wright; Treasurer, Huston Bare; Clerk, S. S. Pangburn; Assessor, P. R. Kincaid.

1863—Trustees, John Wright, Allen Henderson, Henry Dunn; Treasurer, Huston Bare; Clerk, S. S. Pangburn; Assessor, P. R. Kincaid.

1864—Trustees, Noah Hite, John Wright, Allen Henderson; Treasurer, Huston Bare; Clerk, W. M. Davis; Assessor, John Wright.

1865—Trustees, Noah Hite, P. R. Kincaid, Valentine Sneeder; Treasurer, H. W. Kennedy; Clerk, S. S. Pangburn; Assessor, William Marshall, Jr.

1866—Trustees, F. W. Smith, William Henderson, Stephen Ball; Treasurer, John Wright; Clerk, C. C. Blair; Assessor, David Kinzer.

1867—Trustees, Stephen Ball, F. W. Smith, William Henderson; Treasurer, John Wright; Clerk, T. C. H. Vance; Assessor, D. Kinzer.

1868—Trustees, Ira Tracy, Stephen Ball, F. W. Smith; Treasurer, John Wright; Clerk, A. D. Marsh; Assessor, D. Kinzer.

1869—Trustees, Ira Tracy, Martin List, Jr., William F. Gregory; Treasurer, John Wright; Clerk, Eli Tracy; Assessor, David Kinzer.

1870—Trustees, W. F. Gregory, Martin List, John Smith; Treasurer, John Wright; Clerk, Eli Tracy; Assessor, David Kinzer.

1871—Trustees, W. F. Gregory, Martin List, J. L. Smith; Treasurer, John Wright; Clerk, Eli Tracy; Assessor, P. R. Kincaid.

1872—Trustees, W. F. Gregory, L. Ball, Henry Stephens; Treasurer, John Wright; Clerk, Eli Tracy; Assessor, P. R. Kincaid.

1873—Trustees. Stephen Ball, Henry Stephens, W. F. Gregory; Treasurer, John Wright; Clerk, R. L. Waters; Assessor, P. R Kincaid.

1874—Trustees, W. F. Gregory, John Tracy, Jacob Bohl; Treasurer, John Wright; Clerk, Eli Tracy; Assessor, N. S. Dunn.

1875—Trustees, Josiah McFadden, Henry Stephens, George Kress; Treasurer, John Wright; Clerk, Eli Tracy; Assessor, N. S. Dunn.

1876—Trustees, Henry Stephens, George Kress, Ellison Purdy; Treasurer, John Wright; Clerk, C. C. Hite; Assessor, N. S. Dunn.

1877—Trustees, Ira Tracy, James Knight, Stephen Rohrer; Treasurer, John Wright; Clerk, C. C. Hite; Assessor, George Wright.

1878—Trustees, Ira Tracy, James Knight, Stephen Rohrer; Treasurer, W. E. Deihl; Clerk, Eli Tracy; Assessor, N. S. Dunn.

1879—Trustees, Adam Bawer, Peter Ballein, John Corboy; Treasurer, Henry Stevens; Clerk, Eli Tracy; Assessor, George Wright.

1880—Trustees, Adam Bawer, Peter Ballein, John Corboy; Treasurer, Martin List; Clerk, J. B. McClain; Assessor, McCray Vance.

1881—Trustees, Adam Bawer, Peter Ballein, John Corboy; Treasurer, John Wright; Clerk, J. B. McLain; Assessor, McCray Vance.

1882—Trustees, Henry Stevens, C. C. Hite, James Ervin; Treasurer, John Wright; Clerk, A. M. Waters.

CHURCHES.

Sardinia Presbyterian Church.—Under date of November 1, 1811, in the records of White Oak Congregation, Presbyterian Church, there appears the following: "The Rev. John Boyd, having been previously invited, came to this congregation and took charge thereof. Although the people of this congregation had been favored with frequent supplies of a preached Gospel prior to this time, yet they were not organized until the following year, and, when Mr. Boyd came among them, it was on the invitation of the people, without any order of presbytery. Previous to Mr. Boyd's taking charge of the congregation, the Rev. James Gilliland had, by particular request, preached a number of times, and had baptized six children for Francis Pettijohn, namely, Deborah, Sally, Zachariah, Lewis, Barlow and Joseph; and one or two of Joseph Bratton's children. At this time, there were only nine professors or communicants in the congregation, namely, Isabel Bratton, Thomas Pettijohn and Ruth, his wife, David Graham, John Moore and Fanny, his wife, Joseph Bratton and Ann, his wife, Francis Pettijohn."

At the spring session of Washington Presbytery, held in April, 1812, a supplication was presented by White Oak Congregation, praying for one-fourth part of the ministerial labor of Rev. John Boyd, as a stated supply, which was granted. Some time in the summer of 1812, Thomas Pettijohn and John Moore were chosen to the office of Ruling Elders, and were ordained September 18 of that year. On the following day, the session met at the tent near the house of Mr. Bell. There were present Rev. John Boyd, Moderator; Thomas Pettijohn and John Moore, Elders; and John Davies, of New Market session, and John Evans, of Straight Creek. At this session, Mrs. Deborah Pettijohn and Amos Pettijohn made application for admission to the church on examination. On the evening of the same day, four of Amos Pettijohn's children were baptized, namely, Hannah, Nancy, William and Rachel. Some time during the year before a session was formed, the following-named children of Thomas and Ruth Pettijohn were baptized: Samuel, Boaz, Huldah, Ruth and Elias; also Francis Pettijohn's daughter Naomi. The annual report

WASHINGTON TOWNSHIP.

for the year 1812 exhibited ten baptismals, all of whom were children; members admitted on examination, two.

On the second Sabbath of 1813 were baptized Lena, Dorothy, Rebecca, Susannah and Cassandra, daughters of David Graham. The annual report for that year shows nine children baptized; number in communion, eleven (the same number communed in 1812), and none admitted on examination. August 13, 1814, Mrs. Jane Wardlow was admitted on certificate from Mt. Pleasant congregation, Kentucky. John Pettijohn and Susannah, wife of Amos Pettijohn, were admitted on examination. Two children were baptized during the year, and fourteen communed. The report for the year 1815 was as follows: One baptized, three admitted on examination and four on certificate; communicants, twenty-one.

The pastorate of the Rev. John Boyd continued with the church until about April 1, 1816, and the church was without a pastor until November, 1817, when the pulpit was supplied by Revs. James Gilliland and Robert B. Dobbins. During the year closing November 1, 1816, four were admitted on certificate and one on examination, and the number of communicants was twenty-six. Six children were baptized. The report of the following year showed a membership of twenty-seven.

Until the latter part of the year 1815 or the first of the year following, services were held at private houses, and perhaps in the groves when the weather permitted. This year, a rude log house was erected, which stood in Highland County, probably two miles northeast of the present village of Sardinia, just over the line separating the two counties. January 1, 1818, the church extended a regular call for one-quarter of the labor of Rev. Mr. White as a stated pastor. The call was accepted, and Mr. White was installed pastor of the united congregations of New Market and White Oak about June 3, 1818. The membership for the years 1818, 1819, 1820, 1821 and 1822 was thirty-two, thirty, thirty-two, thirty-six and thirty-nine, respectively. Mr. White remained the pastor of the congregation until December, 1823, and preached occasionally for them until March 7, 1824, when he delivered his farewell sermon. Rev. Robert Dobbins, as stated supply, succeeded Mr. White to the pastorate, and served from April 24, 1824, until 1833, when the Rev. Robert Rutherford's ministerial labor began with the congregation. Father Dobbins is said to have been an eccentric man, strong in his affections and positive in his hatreds. In 1829, the second church building was erected, on ground given to the congregation by Amos Pettijohn, located at the cemetery at Sardinia. It was constructed of brick, and served as a place of worship until about the year 1846, when the present frame building was erected at Sardinia. John Moore was very active in the interests of the church, and gave liberally toward the building of the new edifice. The membership of the church in 1830 was forty-five; in 1831, seventy-four; and in 1832, eighty-four. Mr. Rutherford was succeeded to the pastorate by Rev. Dyer Burgess in 1837, who served the church during that and the following year, when his successor was the Rev. James Shaw, who remained in charge until May, 1841. During the decade from 1830 to 1840, the records, as pertains to the pastors, is obscure, and it is possible that some of the names given were only supplies. During this period appears the names of Rev. George Pogue and James H. Dickey, and, in 1840, that of Rev. John Rankin. The latter year, the church membership was ninety-six. In 1841, the name of Rev. Dyer Burgess again appears.

October 1, 1841, Rev. Daniel Gilmore became pastor of the church, and continued in that relation until November 3, 1844. His successor was Rev. John Rankin, who was a supply only. In 1845, the membership was 126. April 26, 1846, Rev. Samuel Rankin was ordained as pastor of White Oak

Congregation, and served until December 3, 1850. In 1848, the congregation petitioned the Presbytery to change the name of the church from White Oak Congregation to that of Sardinia Church, which was done. Rev. Rankin was succeeded by Rev. John H. Byrd, whose pastorate commenced May 1, 1851, and ended in 1854. Under his ministry, the church, September 29, 1851, adopted new articles of faith, and was organized as a Congregational Church, which lasted only through his pastorate, then again became a Presbyterian Church. In 1852, the Beauford and Sardinia Churches were consolidated. Other pastors of the church have been as follows: Rev. S. A. Vandyke, December, 1854, to 1857; Rev. V. M. King, October 1, 1859, to 1868; Rev. H. W. Guthrie, June 1, 1868, to January, 1870. The church was then without a pastor for some years. Rev. S. A. Vandyke became the stated supply, and served the congregation in 1879, 1880 and 1881.

Methodist Episcopal Church at Sardinia.—Among the early settlers of what is now Washington Township, there were a number of Methodist families who had settled mainly along the stream known as Slab Camp, prominent among whom were the Nevins, Days and Hamiltons. For a number of years, the principal preaching-place of this denomination was at the house of Andrew Nevin. Private residences were freely thrown open for worship in the early days of the settlement along Slab Camp, and, later, schoolhouses were much used. At what time the first class or society was here organized we cannot state, as we can find no record on the subject. However, from tradition, there seems to have been a Methodist society along the stream named at a very early day. This section of the country was then in White Oak Circuit, the ministers of which, from 1808 to 1820, were the following named: 1808, David Young; 1809, John Johnson; 1810, Isaac Pavey; 1811, Benjamin Lakin, Eli Trent; 1812, W. Griffith, Reuben Rowe; 1813, Robert Finley, D. Sharp; 1815, John Strange, S. Chenoweth; 1816, John Strange, Isaac Pavey; 1817, W. Griffith James Simmons; 1818, B. Westlake, S. T. Wells; 1819, F. Landrum; 1820, William Page, L. Swormstedt. In about the year 1829, this congregation joined the township in the erection of a schoolhouse, paying so much money with the understanding that it was to be used in part by them as a place of worship. They here held meetings until 1840, when Andrew Nevin donated to the church about one acre of ground, located about one and a half miles southeast of Sardinia. That year, there was here erected a frame church, which was occupied by the congregation until 1860. This year, they purchased a lot in the village of Sardinia, of Huston Bare, and erected a neat one-story frame church building, in which they continue to worship. The church has long been known as the Mt. Carmel Methodist Episcopal Church. The charge is now on the Mt. Oreb and Sardinia Circuit, and Rev. G. W. Fee is the pastor. Membership, 115.

In 1840, a Baptist Church was organized at Sardinia, with a membership of twelve or fifteen. There had then, for some years, been living in the neighborhood the Rev. Hampton Pangburn, a minister of that denomination, and principally through his efforts the organization at this place was effected. The minister organizing the church was Rev. John Stearns. A meeting-house was built in 1841 or 1842. The society did not flourish, and only existed a few years.

Wesleyan Methodist Church.—There was organized in the village of Sardinia, about the year 1844 or 1845, a society known as the Wesleyan Methodist Church, by the Rev. Silas H. Chase. The organization was effected in the Baptist Meeting-House, with a membership of about twenty persons. In the absence of records, we cannot give the names of ministers who have served the charge. The congregation now meet for worship once a month, at what is

WASHINGTON TOWNSHIP. 675

known as the Oakleaf Schoolhouse, situated about one and one-quarter miles west of Sardinia. The minister in charge is Rev. Mr. Clayton.

GRAVEYARDS.

It was the custom of the early settlers to inter the dead on their own land, in what became family burying-grounds. Of these there are a number which dot the farms of Washington, some of which became public graveyards, as was the case of the one at Sardinia. This graveyard had its origin in the family burying-ground of Amos Pettijohn, who, prior to 1829, deeded two acres of land, including or adjoining the family yard, to the Presbyterian Church, with the view of a church being erected thereon and a public place of burial formed. It is beautifully located on the summit of a hill, and many neat marble slabs and columns mark the tombs of loved ones. Many of the pioneers were here interred. John B. Mahan, of whom reference is made elsewhere in this work, is buried in this yard, upon whose tombstone is the following inscription: "In memory of John B. Mahan, died December 15, 1844, aged forty-three years eight months and nine days. A victim to the slave power." Interments are still made here.

In the eastern part of the township is located what is known as the Biehn Graveyard. One-half acre of ground was donated by Henry Biehn, February 24, 1852, to the Trustees of the Evangelical Protestant Church, to be used for a public graveyard. Interments were made in it as early as 1840. It has been used exclusively by the Germans.

The Mt. Carmel Graveyard, located at the old site of that church, has a history similar to the church, so long as it stood there. The ground was given for a graveyard and for church purposes by Andrew Nevin, a zealous Methodist. It was quite extensively used until the church was removed, but of late years there have been but few interments made here, and the grounds have been allowed to grow up briars and weeds.

SCHOOLS.

Of the first schools of Washington Township but little can be given to the reader, from the fact that there was no record made of them, and from the few survivors who were of school age during the first and second decade of the present century, not much can be obtained. We learn from Mrs. McFadden, widow of the late Joseph McFadden, and daughter of the late David Graham, one of Washington's pioneers, that probably the first school was taught on the Amos Pettijohn land, adjoining Sardinia, by Jack Pettijohn, a son; the latter was a cripple, and could do no farm work; he was badly crippled—could not walk, and had little use of his hands and arms, hence was placed in charge of the children of the pioneers, to whose literary training he was to give his attention. This temple of learning consisted of a shed, open at one end, between two cribs, such as was designed for the threshing apartment. The teacher was known by the scholars as "Lame Jack," and his lameness, too, at times afforded for them some merriment, inasmuch as it was very difficult for him to use the rod, he being compelled to have the pupil under punishment directly at his side, and even then it required great exertion to accomplish the end. The location of this school was not far from the site of the cemetery at Sardinia. School was not long continued at this place, for soon the neighborhood built a schoolhouse just west of where Sardinia now is, on the present land of Squire Bare. The Pettijohn School was probably as early as 1812, and the house referred to built about the year 1815. John Moore was the first teacher at this house, and for nineteen consecutive years was the only master the youth of that vicinity knew.

It was generally understood that Mr. Moore, as soon as corn-husking was over with, was to enter the schoolroom, and there remain until sugar-making began, when school was discontinued until the following fall. The children for miles around attended the Moore School, and almost the entire neighborhood was educated under his instruction. Mr. Moore had previously taught several schools on Red Oak and Straight Creeks.

In the Wardlow neighborhood there was built a schoolhouse which stood a little south of the East Branch of White Oak, about the year 1812. The first master in this house was Thomas Clark. About the year 1820, in the Vance neighborhood, school was taught by Patrick Montgomery. Maj. Vance, now living in the same vicinity, was one of his pupils.

In 1825, the township was divided into four school districts, but, as a description of them all is not of record, we will refrain from giving any. On the 1st of December, 1828, the boundary lines of the township were changed, which made a redistricting of the township into school districts necessary. This occurred in the spring of 1829, when the following described districts were made: No. 1, including a part of the Fourth School District of Eagle Township, beginning so far east of the northeast corner of Washington Township that a line running south and parallel with the east line of the township will include John Hurst, Orange Hamilton, Widow McFadden and John Rice, out of Eagle Township; then on to the southeast corner of Washington Township; thence with the south line of the township so far that a line running north will include the house lately occupied by Samuel Willaims; thence in such a direction to James Bell's mill as to include Michael Huff and Ezra Wheeler; thence north to the Highland County line; thence with said line east to the beginning. List of householders: John Hurst, Widow McFadden, Orange Hamilton, John Rice, David Armstrong, Robert Butler, Daniel Williams, William K. Eskridge, Abraham Cline, Joseph Line, Widow Higinbotham, George Mick, Robert Hamilton, Edward Pettijohn, Abraham Hogles, Andrew Nevin, John Nevin, John Pettijohn, Hugh Nevin, Michael Huff, Ezra Wheeler, Abel Starke, Stout D. Runyan, James McFadden, Michael Conley, Samuel Ewing, Widow Gibler, Jonathan Sams, James L. Rilea and William Marshall.

District No. 2—Beginning at the northeast corner of No. 1, thence west with the Highland County line so far that a south line will strike the head of Vansandt's Run; thence down said run to the East Fork; thence down the East Fork to the mouth of Middle Run; thence up Middle Run to Kenton's improvement; thence to Slab Camp Run, at the place where the road leading from John Moore's to Straight Creek crosses said run; thence easterly to the west line of District No. 1 so as to include William Grant and Mark Day; thence with the line of District No. 1 to the beginning. List of householders: John Hindman, Thomas Purcell, William Hindman, Samuel Pangburn, John Pangburn, P. R. Kincaid, Matthew Kincaid, Amos Pettijohn, Peter Williams, Joseph Line, Mark Day, William Grant, Robert D. Lilly, Abraham Pettijohn, John Moore, David Graham, James Wardlow, James Bell, James Kennedy and Levi Estel.

District No. 3—Beginning at the southeast corner of District No. 2, thence with the line of said district westerly to Middle Run at Kenton's improvement; thence up Middle Run to Richard Pettijohn's so as to include Benjamin Cornell; thence south to the township line; thence east with the township line to the southwest corner of District No. 1; thence with the east line of said district to the beginning. List of householders: Peter Shinkle, James Rilea, Richard Pettijohn, John Purdum, Thomas McGee, David McKee, Richard Rilea, Jeremiah Purdum, Aaron Purdum, Philip Waters, Joseph Wright, Matthew Day, Thomas Rilea, Clarkson Dunn and Benjamin Cornell.

WASHINGTON TOWNSHIP.

District No. 4—Beginning at the Highland County line at the northwest corner of District No. 2; thence west to the North Fork of White Oak; thence down the same to its junction with the East Fork; thence up the East Fork to the mouth of Vansandt's Run; thence up said run and with the line of District No. 2 to the beginning. List of householders: George Wright, Joseph Calvin, Isabel Wardlow, Philander Wardlow, James Wardlow, William Vance, John Vance, John Anderson, John J. Gregory and George Oldum.

District No. 5—Beginning at the mouth of Middle Run, thence up said run to Richard Pettijohn's; thence south to the township line; thence west with the township line to the southwest corner of the township; thence with the township line to White Oak Creek, at the mouth of Blackwood's Run; thence up White Oak and the East Fork to the beginning. List of householders: Nancy Dey, Patrick Vance, Samuel Wardlow, Edward Day, Jackson Ewing, Alvin Newton, Hugh Gunnison, Lewis Calvin, Adam Ewing, Peter Lauderback, Richard Grissom, William Reeves, James Straight, Samuel Fleming, James D. Wilson, William Wilson and Nicholas Van Ness.

The School Directors for the above district, when formed, so far as is of record, are the following: District No. 1, Andrew Nevin, Sr., Edward Pettijohn and George Mick; District No. 2, D. Lilley, John Pangburn and John Moore.

January 15, 1831, at a meeting of the Trustees of Washington Township and the township of White Oak, in Highland County, District No. 4 was changed, a portion of it being added to White Oak Township, in the county named, for the convenience of the scholars thereof.

March 25, 1834, District No. 2 was divided, and District No. 6 formed therefrom. It was designated as follows: Beginning at the mouth of Middle Run, thence up said run to Kenton's improvement; thence to Slap Camp Run, at the place where the road leading from John Moore's to Straight Creek crosses said run; thence easterly to the west line of District No. 1 so as to include James Kennedy; thence with the line of District No. 1 to James Bell's (now Bingamon's) mill; thence down the center of the East Fork of White Oak to the beginning.

The number of white youth enrolled in the six districts in 1860 was as follows: District No. 1, 68; District No. 2, 69; District No. 3, 137; District No. 4, 51; District No. 5, 52; District No. 6, 108; total, 485. During that year, there were three colored children enrolled in District No. 1, and two in District No. 3. Grand total, 490.

Between the years 1860 and 1870, another district was formed, and the enrollment for the seven districts in 1870 was as follows: District No. 1, 40; District No. 2, 85 white and 6 colored; District No. 3, 126 white and 4 colored; District No. 4, 51; District No. 5, 53; District No. 6, 82; District No. 7, 84; total, 492.

During the next decade, two more districts were formed, and the enrollment in 1880 was as follows: District No. 1, 41 white and 3 colored; District No. 2, 65 white and 1 colored; District No. 3, 77; District No. 4, 70; District No. 5, 45; District No. 6, 53; District No. 7, 45; District No. 8, 67; District No. 9, 41 white and 4 colored; total, 509.

The annual report of the County Auditor on schools makes the following exhibit of the schools of Washington Township for the year ending August 31, 1881: Of the nine houses now in the nine school districts of the township, one was erected during the year at a cost of $1,500. Ten teachers were employed; average wages per month, $35.35; average term of school, twenty-four weeks; total enrollment within the year, 459, of which number 101 were studying the alphabet, 201 reading, 322 spelling, 226 writing, 247 arithmetic, 126 geography, 49 English grammar, 29 oral lessons and 1 composition. Total expenditures for school purposes, $3,212.41, of which sum $2,073 was paid teachers. The school property is valued at $4,500.

In this article on schools, we have not noted all of the changes in the boundary lines of the districts since the formation of the first four, but only those of earlier years.

The following were the members of the Board of Education in 1880 and 1881: Lewis Allmann, Gideon Kirk, O. B. Moore, Peter Ballein, Josiah McFadden, Ellsberry Hays, John Butts, Jacob Snider.

MILLS.

The first mill built in Washington Township was the Wardlow Grist-Mill, later known as the Levi Estel Mill. It stood on White Oak Creek, about two miles west of Sardinia, on land now owned by John Wright, and was erected by John Wardlow, and, after a few years, was sold to Levi Estel. As nearly as can be ascertained, the mill was erected about the year 1812 or 1813. It is said that it was never of much force, and did not stand many years.

Some years later, John Kibler, an enterprising man, erected a mill on the East Branch of White Oak, in the extreme northeastern part of the township, and there laid out a town. Mr. Kibler was a very popular and active man, and, had he lived, the town at the mill would very likely have been the Sardinia of to-day, but his death, occurring in 1829, put a stop to the growth of the place. This mill is now owned by John Sands, and, until the winter of 1881–82, was in operation, but at that time the dam was washed away, and the grinding has since been discontinued.

One mile east of Sardinia, on the same stream, some time after the Kibler Mill was built, a saw and grist mill was erected by James Bell, which was in operation until about the year 1847.

In 1831 or 1832, John B. Mahan and John Dunham built a saw-mill at the mouth of Slab Camp. This they ran some years as a saw-mill, when a grist-mill was added. The dam, however, washed out in a few years, and the mills were suffered to go down. Later, a steam saw-mill was built on this site by Calvin Rilea, who afterward added a grist-mill, when the machinery was removed to Brownstown, and is now in the mill at that place.

Another saw-mill stood on the old Vinson Calvin land, built by Joseph McFadden, but there not being sufficient water in the stream to run it successfully, it was soon abandoned.

VILLAGES.

The villages of the township are Sardinia and Brownstown. The former, the larger of the two, is a thriving little place of about three hundred inhabitants, pleasantly situated on the East Branch of White Oak Creek, and is one of the few railroad towns of Brown County, the Cincinnati & Eastern passing through it, and it being the terminus of the Hillsboro & Sardinia Railroad. The village was laid out by William B. Lilley and Josiah Moore, March 30, 1833, at which date the surveying was done by Jeptha Beasley, then County Surveyor. The original number of lots was sixteen. Additions were made by the same men August 12, 1836, and May 23, 1837. The first houses erected in the place were by Dr. I. M. Beck and Josiah Moore. Both were built on Main street, opposite to each other, and are yet standing. The frame of Mr. Moore's house was the first up, but the house of Dr. Beck was the first completed. The first merchant in the vicinity was Dr. Robert D. Lilley, who sold goods in 1828, and, in 1832 or 1833, sold his stock of goods to William B. Lilley and Josiah Moore, proprietors of the village, who carried on a store for some years, and then quit the business. In the latter part of 1833, a store was opened by George Salt, who was the merchant for about a year. Messrs. Cowan & Masters then opened a store in a little log building where all their

WASHINGTON TOWNSHIP.

predecessors had held forth. But finally this firm erected a two-story frame house, adjoining the house of Dr. Beck. The first tavern was kept by John B. Mahan, opened about the year 1835. The village smith was Willis Gilliland. His was the first hammer to rebound from the heavy anvil and break the quiet of the peaceful village. His shop was built in 1837, and stood on Winchester street, where now is the livery stable of Nathan Dunn. Among the early industries of the village may be mentioned the turning establishment and cabinet shop of Josiah Moore, who began the business as early as 1835. He patented a bed, and made a great deal of furniture, and supplied Hillsboro and other places of that region with articles of his manufacture. About the same time, Robert J. Huggins carried on quite an extensive wagon-making shop. Not far from the year 1847, a factory for the manufacture of wind-mills was started at Sardinia. It was an extensive affair, and the proprietors employed five or six workmen, and had as many traveling salesmen. Soon after Sardinia was laid out, a carding-machine and oil-mill was put in operation by John L. Pangburn, who was the proprietor until his death, which occurred in 1837. The mill then passed through several hands, and, in three or four years, was abandoned. Another of the early industries of the village was the tannery carried on by Franz Feike, who began business in 1836 or 1837, and continued operations until about 1856, when he removed to Missouri and the yard went down.

There was a post office at this point prior to the laying-out of the village, called "Lilley" Post Office, so styled after the first Postmaster, Dr. Robert D. Lilley. It was established in 1828 or 1829. Since Mr. Lilley ceased acting in that capacity, the Postmasters have been as follows: William Lilley, who served from 1832 until about the year 1837; Josiah Moore, Moses B. Riggs, Huston Bare, Thomas Davis, William Campbell and Stephen Feike. The latter is the present incumbent. After the town was laid out, the name of the office was changed to Sardinia.

The Campbell Bros.' Carriage Manufactory.—On the west side of Main street, near Broadway, is located the establishment above named. In 1855, A. F. Campbell, Sr., came to Sardinia and engaged in general blacksmithing. At his death, in 1863, a son, W. G. Campbell, carried on the work, and about the close of the war, he began the manufacture of wagons, and had a general repairing shop, situated on Graham street, employing from three to five hands. In 1870, his brothers, John and A. F. Campbell, became partners, and the three have since carried on the business. They commenced the manufacture of carriages and buggies, in addition to the other work, in 1874, and the following year built the two-story frame shop, in which the present business is done.

Cross Bros.' Establishment.—In 1861, the firm of Anderson, Huggins, Cross & Co. commenced the manufacture of plows and farm wagons. They erected a large two-story house on Graham and Winchester streets, and worked a force of about six men. In about a year, the firm changed to Anderson & Cross, and in 1868 it became Anderson, Cross & Co. Since 1870, it has been under the present management, with Cross Bros. as proprietors. They commenced manufacturing buggies in 1872, and quit in 1880, and are now selling ready-made work, dealing in agricultural implements and hardware.

In the spring of 1881, a mill, for the sawing and working of wood, was built by Messrs. H. Beck and Edward Huggins, and has since been leased and is now carried on by G. A. Canoly and James Ervin.

Sardinia Lodge. No. 683, I. O. O. F.—Was instituted in Moore's Hall, where it still meets, July 23, 1879, by Grand Master E. K. Wilcox, of Cleveland. The charter members were Peter Bauline, John T. Wilson, Martin Wilson, O. P. Kennedy, M. R. Ketterman, E. P. Keller, John Duncan and O. B. Moore. The lodge has now a membership of twenty-five. Present officers: E. H. Raney, N. G.; John Campbell, V. G.; O. B. Moore, P. S.; Z. C. Lewis, R. S.; A. N. Irvin, Treasurer.

Sardinia has for years been noted for the musical talent of its people, in which branch they have excelled the people of neighboring towns. This fact is said to be due to the efforts in that direction of the late John Moore, who for many years taught music in the village, and who, with his descendants, were concerned in every concert, band and choir of their time. There is at this writing a good brass band in the village.

The physicians of Sardinia have been Peter Williams, who settled in this vicinity about the year 1824; Robert D. Lilley, who came in February, 1828, and remained until November, 1832; Dr. I. M. Beck, now engaged in active practice, where for more than half a century he has administered to ailing humanity, having located where the town now is in July, 1829, and since remained, excepting a period of five years; Dr. John McIlhaney, who located at this place in 1836, and remained one year; Dr. Newkirk, who practiced from 1843 until 1845, and Dr. J. B. McClain, now a practitioner of the place, who came in 1866.

The village has ever been a temperance place. When it was laid out, it was with this understanding, and, while it has not ever been without saloons, they have been few in its history as compared with other places much less in population. The temperance movement was introduced in this vicinity by Rev. Robert Dobbins, and inaugurated in the year 1830. Dr. Isaac M. Beck was one of its warmest supporters in that early day, and has to this day cooled none in his ardor in the support of the cause. He, it is thought, was the first lay temperance lecturer in Southwestern Ohio. He delivered a lecture on this subject in this vicinity August 1, 1830. and repeated the same in the same vicinity in August, 1880, just fifty years afterward.

Brownstown, situated in the southern part of the township, on Brown's Run, is a small village of about fifty inhabitants. It was laid out by Rolly Dunn, August 26, 1848; number of lots, twenty-one. The post office was established here June 5, 1876, with J. G. Tracy, Postmaster, and there has been no change since. In September, 1881, E. A. & B. A. Thompson erected a steam saw-mill at this point, and in several months added a grist-mill, which is also operated by steam power.

TORANADO OF 1856.

On the 17th day of May, 1856, a severe storm passed through a portion of Washington Township, doing serious injury along its path. The first place any material injury was done was on the farm of Mr. J. H. Dunn. There were immense trees twisted off and torn up by the roots, fence rails and branches of timber were carried in every direction, and some dozen sheep, which were so unlucky as to be in its course, were killed; passing from here through the woodland of Mr. Ira Tracey, it laid waste everything before it, until reaching his barn, which was a very large frame building, the roof of which was nearly entirely carried away, shivering the rafters and sheeting into fragments, part of the roof being carried to the distance of from twenty to thirty rods from the barn. The roof of a brick building adjoining his dwelling was entirely blown off; also, the roof of his dwelling was very materially damaged. But Mr. Tracey sustained the greatest injury in the loss of his orchard, which was almost entirely destroyed, the trees being torn up by the roots, or broken off near the ground, a part of which was carried to the distance of from eighty to ninety poles. Mr. Tracey's loss was in the neighborhood of $500 or $600. Benjamin Wardlow was very considerably damaged, his dwelling house was carried off to the first story; also his orchard, together with the orchard of James Wardlow, was much damaged. Where the storm passed through the timber, it was nearly all either torn up by the roots or twisted off near the ground, the width being from fifteen to twenty rods.

CHAPTER XV.

STERLING TOWNSHIP.

STERLING is one of the border townships, Clermont County forming its western boundary; on the south is Pike Township; on the east, Green, and on the north is Perry. It is situated in what is known as the boot-leg of Brown County, and contains 17,272 acres of land. The general surface is level, but slightly broken along the streams, except in the western and southwestern parts on the larger water-courses, where there are some hills. Originally, the surface was heavily timbered with white oak, sugar, hickory, swamp elm and black and sweet gum. Although considerable of the forest growth has been removed, there still remains a great deal of timber. The predominating soil is clay, yet alluvial flats appear about the sources of the streams, which are of great richness. Five Mile Creek, Four Mile Creek, Crane Run and other tributaries of the East Fork of the Little Miami River have their sources in the township. The East Fork of the Little Miami River flows through the extreme northwestern corner of the township, and the southern part is crossed by the Cincinnati & Eastern Railroad.

LAND SURVEYS.

The original survey, entries, with dates, etc., of land comprising the townships of Sterling, as taken from the book of original surveys, in the office of the County Recorder, is exhibited in the following list:

No. 954, 1,000 acres (east part), surveyed by William Lytle May 14, 1795, for Timothy Peyton.

No. 968, 1,200 acres (south part), surveyed by William Lytle for Benjamin Temple.

No. 2,945, 100 acres (east part), surveyed by William Lytle March 27, 1797, for James Thompson (assignee).

No. 2,944, 444½ acres (east part), surveyed by William Lytle March 27, 1797, for Samuel Coleman.

No. 3,047, 260 acres, surveyed by William Lytle July 10, 1797, for John Breckenridge.

No. 3,048, 200 acres, surveyed by William Lytle July 10, 1797, for John Breckenridge.

No. 3,343, 2,000 acres, surveyed by William Lytle August 20, 1798, for John Harvie.

No. 3,344, 1,000 acres, surveyed by William Lytle August 29, 1798, for John Harvie.

No. 3,335, 300 acres (north part), surveyed by William Lytle October 1, 1798, for Charles Lee (assignee).

No. 3,336, 300 acres (north part) surveyed by William Lytle October 1, 1798, for Robert Campbell (assignee).

No. 3,622, 400 acres, surveyed by William Lytle April 8, 1799, for Archibald McIlvain (assignee).

No. 4,456, 466⅔ acres (north part), surveyed by William Lytle March 20, 1804, for Charles Bradford.

No. 4,247, 666⅔ acres (east part), surveyed by William Lytle September 1, 1804, for William Lytle (assignee).

No. 4,246, 600 acres, surveyed by William Lytle September 3, 1804, for Peter Thomas, John Southard and Nathaniel Dobbs.

No. 4,251, 600 acres, surveyed by William Lytle October 10, 1804, for James Morrison (assignee).

No. 4,451, 500 acres (west part), surveyed by William Lytle October 11, 1804, for James O'Hara and Nicholas Bowsman.

No. 4,252, 1,000 acres, surveyed by William Lytle September 5, 1805, for John Tibbs.

No. 4,792, 666⅔ acres (west part), surveyed by William Lytle November 9, 1805, for the representatives of Thomas Bowyer (deceased).

No. 4,793, 666⅔ acres (west part), surveyed by William Lytle November 11, 1805, for Robert Sayers and James Taylor (assignees).

No. 4,789, 1,000 acres, surveyed by William Lytle November 11, 1805, for William Buford

No. 4,785, 1,555⅔ acres, surveyed by William Lytle November 14, 1805, for Thomas Martin.

No. 4,787, 444⅔ acres (south part), surveyed by William Lytle November 14, 1805, for Henry Bowyer.

No. 4,798, 200 acres (south part), surveyed by William Lytle November 9, 1805, for James Bell.

No. 12,010, 318¼ acres, surveyed by George C. Light October 11, 1823, for Justus F. Randolph (assignee).

No. 12,381, 133½ acres, surveyed by George C Light October 11, 1823, for William M. P. Quinn.

No. 12,926, 1,266¾ acres (west part), surveyed by P. N. White January 22, 1830, for Leroy Jordan and Anderson Thompson (assignees).

Nos. 12,934 and 10,363, 300 acres, surveyed by A. Lotham August 5, 1830, for Timothy Kirby (assignee).

No. 12,935, 50 acres, surveyed by Timothy Kirby June 23, 1832, for Timothy Kirby (assignee).

No. 13,641, 233 acres, surveyed by C. Wallace January 19, 1835, for Cadwallader Wallace.

No. 13,614, 250 acres, surveyed by John Hill May 14, 1835, for Thomas L. Shields (assignee).

No. 13,950, 258 acres (north part), surveyed by C. Wallace November 7, 1837, for James Stallings.

Nos. 250 and 309, not described.

PIONEER SETTLERS.

From all accounts, it is thought that Hugh McLain and family were the first permanent settlers of the township. Hugh McLain was a native of Ireland and emigrated to America just previous to the Revolutionary war, and was for some years engaged in merchandising, buying trinkets in his native country and selling them in this, and in turn buying in this country and selling in Europe, which kept him crossing the ocean frequently. He continued in this line of business until the war between England and America made it dangerous to be on the sea, when he settled in the State of Pennsylvania and there married Mary Allison and became engaged in agricultural pursuits. He performed some service along the border against the Indians during the Revolutionary war, and in the latter part of 1796 emigrated to Ohio and stopped at Columbia, and remained in that vicinity for two years, then removed into the southern part of Survey No. 3,343, located in what is now Brown County, in which he had purchased a tract of 200 acres of land. His family consisted of wife and two sons—John, an imbecile, and Archibald. The father died in

1816, and the mother about the year 1825. Archibald was born in Lancaster County, Penn., August 17, 1779, and was married while residing in Hamilton County, this State, to Mary, daughter of William Shaw, who bore him the following sons and daughters—Nancy, born in 1800, and died at the age of eleven years; Jane, born October 18, 1802; Hugh, died in 1806; William S., born March 25, 1807; Archibald, born March 27, 1809; Thomas E., born March 15, 1811; Margaret, born December 5, 1813, and Robert, born January 10, 1818. Archibald, some years after settling in Brown County, purchased fifty acres of land adjoining the 200-acre tract before mentioned, the half of which his father had given him.

From the history of Clermont County, it appears that James Kain and his family were the first permanent settlers in Williamsburg Township; that in the year 1795 and the early part of 1796, the elder Kain had worked at this place, building a cabin in the village and clearing a considerable tract of land for Gen. Lytle on Kain Run, which was long afterward known as the "big field." The writer of the sketch of Williamsburg thus alludes to the pioneer, Archibald McLain, in the account given of the first settlement of that village: "In the summer of 1796, James Kain came here from Newtown, where he had settled several years previously, to build the first cabin, which was erected on Lot 43, where is now the residence of Adam C. Walker. He was accompanied by his daughter Mary, a young girl of a dozen years, and her companion, Mary Bunton, who did the cooking for the workmen employed on the cabin; and these, it is claimed, were the first white women who came to reside in the eastern part of the present county of Clermont. James Kain occupied his house in the fall of 1796, and his family was moved from Newtown in an old-fashioned Conestoga wagon, by Archibald McLain, who followed mere bridle-paths, which often made it necessary to form wider roads, so that the trip occupied several days. The king-bolt of this wagon, probably the first that was ever used in the county, is yet in the possession of the McLain family." Mr. McLain was an Elder in the Old-School Presbyterian Church in the village of Williamsburg. In 1806, he united with the Presbyterian Church in Felicity (then named Smyrna), and in 1808, when a Presbyterian Church was first organized at Williamsburg, he was ordained one of its first Elders. His death occurred October 19, 1855. He was a member of the church forty-nine years and an Elder forty-seven. During this long period, his walk and conversation were becoming the Gospel. He was a useful citizen, a kind, accommodating neighbor and an affectionate husband and father.

Of the sons of Archibald McLain, William S. married Sarah Everhart, of Clermont County, a daughter of Daniel Everhart, from Virginia, who settled at Williamsburg in 1809, and was in his day one of the most prominent business men of the village. William S. is a resident of that village and is well known throughout this region of the country, where he has done extensive surveying. Archibald married Phebe Ross, and resides on the home farm. A sketch of him appears elsewhere in this work. Thomas E. married Mary Hiles, and removed to Pike Township, this county, where he died in 1863. Robert married Ann Collins. Of the daughters, Jane married Thomas, son of John Kain, one of the first settlers of Williamsburg, and Margaret married B. Wharton. On the McLain farm are standing two thrifty apple trees that were set out by the pioneer Hugh McLain about the year 1800.

Absalom Day, a native of the State of New Jersey, was born April 7, 1773, and when a boy not out of his teens, came with his parents, Jeremiah and Sarah (Dod) Day, to Ohio, stopping for a time at Columbia, at the mouth of the Little Miami River, then removed to Williamsburg, arriving in 1796, and received one of the ten lots given by Gen. Lytle to the first ten settlers of the village. The father, Jeremiah Day, was a native of England. Absalom, while at Columbia, married Elizabeth, daughter of George Earhart, who was born in Chester County, Penn., May 30, 1776, and to them were born the following named children: Mary, born January 28, 1797; Sarah, born December 1, 1798; Elizabeth, born September 25, 1800; Samuel, born November 16, 1802; Susannah, born June 20, 1806; Katie Ann, born September 2, 1808; Joseph, born January 19, 1811; Aaron, born September 13, 1812; Sophia, born July 20, 1814; David E., born December 28, 1815; Absalom, born December 26, 1817, and Anna J., born June 20, 1822. Father Day, after residing at Williamsburg for two or three years, removed to a tract of land in the western part of what is now Sterling Township, Brown County (on the present site of the post office of De La Palma). He died February 17, 1839, aged sixty-five years ten months and ten days. His wife died September 4, 1843, in her sixty-eighth year. They were members of the Methodist Episcopal Church and worshiped at Clover, in what is now Clermont County, in the earliest existence of the society at that place; and later, the Day residence was the preaching point for years in that locality.

Of the seven daughters of this couple, Mary married William Day; Sarah married Daniel Ready; Elizabeth married Jacob Waits; Susaunah married John Coulter; Katie Ann married Benjamin Reed; Sophia married William Weeks, and Mary J. died unmarried. The sons were married as follows: Samuel to Miriam Hayward, a native of Virginia, both are now residing in Green Township, this county; Joseph to —— ——, Aaron to Julia Mowry; David died unmarried, and Absalom to Caroline Willey. Mary and Sarah Day were born at Williamsburg, the others in Brown County.

The families of John Anderson and Moses Leonard settled in what is now Sterling Township in 1799 or 1800, both purchasing land in the J. Harvie Survey, No. 3,344. They were brothers-in-law, and emigrated to Ohio together a year or two before settling as described. They came from New Jersey to Pittsburgh by land, and thence down the Ohio River by boat, and landed at the mouth of the Little Miami, where they remained until their removal to this vicinity. Mr. Anderson was a native of Maryland, born February 10, 1773. His wife was Martha Wood, a native of Greene County, Penn., and their children were Margaret, born May 16, 1797, and married Moses Warden; Eliza, born March 11, 1799, and married William Boyd; William, born February 8, 1801, and married Eliza Shannon, of Clermont County; Amelia, born September 20, 1804, and married Paul Stricklin, of Clermont County; Nancy, born September 17, 1806, and married Robert Justus; Thomas W., born March 12, 1809, and married Lovisa Pittser; Macajah, born July 24, 1811; John T., born September 30, 1813, and Hiram C., born May 16, 1815, and married Rebecca Black. The latter now resides on the homestead, where all the children were born and reared. The parents died, the father June 25, 1839, and the mother February 16, 1854, and were buried at Williamsburg.

Mr. Leonard was a Pennsylvanian by birth, and was married to Elizabeth Anderson. Their children were John, who was twice married—first, to Margaret Smith, and second, to Mrs. Sarah Smallwood, a widow; Elizabeth, who married Andrew Smith; Hannah, Casey, Aaron, Levi, George and Ellen. Hannah married Jacob Mason, of Williamsburg; Casey married Frances Holeman; Aaron married Elizabeth Perrine; Levi married Mary A. Hickey, of Clermont County, and died on the homestead December 14, 1872, in the sixty-sixth year of his age; George married Mary Amos, of Cincinnati, and Ellen married John Shotwell. The last two are the only survivors of the immediate family.

Moses Leonard was at the battle of Brandywine in the capacity of a wag-

STERLING TOWNSHIP.

oner. His death occurred January 9, 1844, aged eighty-four years, nine months and twenty-four days, and that of his wife July 11, 1834, in her sixty-first year. John Leonard served in the war of 1812.

In 1799 or 1800, George Earhart, a German, settled on land in the southern part of the township, south of the tract purchased by John Anderson. He, with his family, came from Pennsylvania, and landed with the Days at Columbia, and thence removed, as stated above, to the vicinity of the Andersons. His wife was Elizabeth Fanchon. The oldest son, John Earhart, stopped at Williamsburg, where he remained as a permanent settler, and proved himself a great addition to the settlement, as he became the plow-maker of the neighborhood. His skill in making wooden mold-boards was very great, and his work was in good demand. He was also a cooper and a handy and useful man generally. His sons—John, George and Samuel—became well-known citizens.

Other children of George Earhart were Huldah, Tryphena, Mary, Sanford, Sarah, Samuel and Peggie.

In the latter part of the eighteenth century, the Boyd family emigrated from Ireland and settled in Bucks County, Penn., but not content there, soon removed to land adjoining the city of Lexington, Ky. The parents were John and Mary. Samuel, a son, was married while in Pennsylvania to Abigail Stewart, and with a family of nine children, emigrated from his Kentucky home, in March, 1804, and settled in Survey No. 3,622. He had two years previously been here and made a purchase of 400 acres of land in the southern part of the survey named, of Archibald McIlvain. The sons and daughters were John, William, Robert, Samuel, James, Jane, Martha, Mary, Elizabeth and Nancy, of whom Jane was born on the Ohio River while en route to Kentucky, and James, the youngest, was born here; all the others were born in Kentucky. The father was a resident of the township until his death, which occurred suddenly by apoplexy, while in Clermont County, in May, 1825. He was identified with the Presbyterian Church at the neighboring village of Williamsburg. The daughter Jane was married to James McGavi, John to Shelamith Reece, William to Eliza Anderson (Robert died young), Martha to Ephraim McAdams, of Clermont County, whose family were very early settlers at Williamsburg. Mary was married three times, first, to John Hays; second, to Jacob Willis, and third, to William Cobb; Samuel to Margaret Everhart, Elizabeth to James McAdams (Nancy died single), and James was twice married; first, to Serena South, and second to Sarah McDonald, and is the only survivor of the Boyd family. He resides on the homestead, where nearly three-quarters of a century have been passed, and about which cluster the recollections of nearly as many years. William and John Boyd were both in the war of 1812; the latter served as a Lieutenant.

The Waits brothers, James and Charles, emigrating from the Redstone country in Pennsylvania, settled in Kentucky, on the North Fork of the Licking River, in the spring of 1794, and in 1802, removed to Ohio and made permanent settlements on Four Mile Creek, in the western part of Sterling, near what is now the Clermont County line. James farmed his land until about the year 1838, when he sold it to Ira Willey and passed the remainder of his life with his son Jacob, who resided near the center of the township. Other sons and daughters of James Waits were John, Charles, Peter, William, David, Richard, James and Nancy (twins), Sarah, Christina and Elizabeth. The father died March 2, 1855, aged ninety-five years, and the mother July 14, 1856, aged ninety-four years. Charles was a soldier of the Revolutionary war, and for services rendered drew a pension from the Government. Three of the sons, Charles, Peter and John were in the war of 1812; two of them, Charles and Peter, were members of Capt. Jacob Boerstler's company of riflemen, which was organized at Williamsburg, and it was in the service from April 24, 1812, to October 24, 1812. It was engaged at the battle of Brownstown, where four of its men, including the Captain, were killed, August 4, 1812, and another died afterward of wounds received in the same engagement.

Of the two brothers who settled on Four Mile Creek, Charles raised quite a family in that vicinity, and there lived and died. He, too, was a soldier of the Revolutionary war.

Hillery B. Walker and Adam Snell, of Pennsylvania, emigrated to this State together in 1806, and effected settlements in the northwestern part of the township. Mr. Walker was a native of the State from whence he emigrated, born March 25, 1782, and his wife Elizabeth was born May 1, 1789. They died February 21, 1845, and May 25, 1844, respectively. Their family consisted of the following named sons and daughters: John, Adam S., George, Michael, Thomas, Lurinda J., William, Susan, Ruth, Hillery B., Hillery J., Eliza E., Washington, Matilda, Hannah and Cyrus G. Mr. Snell's children were Michael, Daniel, Hannah, Rachel, Susan, Matilda, Polly and Elizabeth.

Thomas Ross, with family, settled on the William Buford Survey, No. 4789, located near the center of the township, in 1814. He was a native of Washington County, Penn., born in 1789. His parents were Ignatius and Mary (Jennings) Ross, who were among the earliest emigrants at Columbia, arriving in 1791. Ignatius died there in 1827. Mr. Ross was unfortunate in purchasing his land in this township, from the fact that he had to pay for it the second time. While at Columbia, he married Mary Dobbins, of Virginia, and there were born to them Mary, Albert, Eveline, Thomas, Malinda, Rhoda and two others who died young. He lived here until his death, which occurred February 14, 1861. He was one of the first settlers of the township, and for a term of years served as a Justice of the Peace, and in 1842–43 he was a Representative in the State Legislature. His wife died February 12, 1854.

George Levengood, Andrew Shearer, John and Morris Trout were among the pioneers.

These were the bulk of the pioneers of Sterling. The elevated and broken tracts of land lying adjacent to the East Fork of the Little Miami River and its larger tributaries were early taken up and occupied by the numerous home-seekers, who were continually landing at Columbia during the last decade of the past century. The old town of Williamsburg, laid out in 1795–96, with its mill a year later, was the center of attraction, and ere many years the choice land was gone, and arriving emigrants turned their course in other directions. The dreary and altogether uninviting aspect of much of the low, swampy land of what is now this township greatly impeded rapid settlement. The pioneers just named, with their families, the sons and daughters marrying and settling around them, improved and lived upon the land of the township best located then to suit their wants, and slow immigration followed. The major portion of the township was not settled and the lands improved until a late period in the history of Brown County. It will be noticed in the original entries that some of the land was not surveyed until 1837. An idea of the condition of the township in 1838 can be formed from the list of property-holders at that time, given further on.

TOWNSHIP ORGANIZATION—JUSTICES OF THE PEACE.

Sterling was organized as a civil township from Perry and Pike Townships December 7, 1824. Its boundary lines were then described as follows: Beginning at the southwest corner of Highland County, running from thence west to

STERLING TOWNSHIP.

the Brown County line; thence north with the same to where it crosses the East Fork; thence east to the Highland County line, and thence with the same to the beginning. It included what are now the townships of Sterling and Green. This territory was equally divided by the County Commissioners December 2, 1834, on the formation of Green Township, from the east half.

We are only able to give in the following a partial list of the names of those persons who served as Justices of the Peace of the township prior to 1854, and this from tradition:

John Boyd and Charles Waits were the first Justices of the Peace after the organization of Sterling. Each served for a period of nine years at least. John Leonard, Titus Hair and William Weeks were later Justices. Archibald McLain was first commissioned Justice of the Peace in 1836. From 1854, the names and dates of commissions are given from record:

Theophilus Simonton, November 10, 1854; Archibald McLain, October 26, 1854; Joseph R. Long, October 29, 1857; Theophilus Simonton, October 29, 1857; Archibald McLain, April 21, 1858; John S. Price, October 22, 1860; Archibald McLain, April 22, 1861; John S. Price, October 22, 1863; B. Britton, April 15, 1864; Archibald McLain, August 10, 1865; B. Britton, April 15, 1867; John C. Curry, October 5, 1868; Thomas Sheldon, April 12, 1869; Archibald McLain, December 9, 1869; Thomas Sheldon, April 15, 1872; Archibald McLain, December 19, 1872; V. B. Creager, April 19, 1875; John Wilson, January 5, 1876; V. B. Creager, April 13, 1878; John Wilson, January 7, 1879; Marion Wilson, March 24, 1881; V. B. Creager, April 18, 1881

PROPERTY-HOLDERS IN 1838.

The following list contains the names of those who held property in Sterling Township in 1838, together with the amount of land and the number of survey in which located:

William Arthur , 97 acres, No. 3,343; John Anderson, 121 acres, No. 3,344; George Arnold, 50 acres, No. 3,345; James Arthur, 50 acres, No. 3,344; ———— Addenbrook, 100 acres, No. 3,622; Joseph Arthur, 100 acres, No. 5,257; Samuel Boyd (heirs), 200 acres, No 3,622; George H. Bohrer, 74 acres, No. 4,578; Benjamin Cole, 144 acres, No. 3,344; Robert Chalfant, 200 acres, No. 3,343; James Crawford, 156 acres, No. 3,343; Ira Connor, 50 acres, No. 4,250; John Creamer, 86 acres; No. 954; Absalom Day, 50 acres, No. 3,344; John Davis, 136¼ acres, No. 4,787; Daniel Everhart, 200 acres, No. 3,335; Adam Everhart, 103 acres, No. 4,789; John and Samuel Everhart, 119 acres, No. 3,344; Erie Frazee, 50 acres, No. 3,344; John Fulk, 75 acres, No. 954; Francis Holeman, 47⅓ acres, No. 3,343; Holmes & Wilson, 301 acres, No. 4,251; William Hewitt, 221⅓ acres, No. 4,578; Robert Irvin, 50 acres, No. 4,246; Robert E. Irvin, 57 acres, No. 3,344; Timothy Kirby, 45 acres, No. 4,246; Timothy Kirby, 200 acres, No. 12,934; Timothy Kirby, 50 acres, No. 13,195; Timothy Kirby, 94 acres, No. 13,197; James Kelly, 343 acres, No. 3,344; John Leonard, 66¼ acres, No. 3,343; Moses Leonard, 50 acres. No. 3,344; Robert Laughlin, 200 acres, No. 3,343; William Lytle, 56¾ acres, No. 2,792; William Lytle, 50 acres, No. 4,252; George Livingood, 40 acres, No. 4,252; Levi Leonard, 50 acres, No. 3,344; George Lowe, 100 acres, No. 3,622; Nathan Livingood, 10 acres, No. 4,252; Archibald McLain, Jr., 138 acres, No. 3,344; Robert Means, 333⅓ acres, No. 4,788; B. J. Miller, 50 acres, No, 3,343; B. J. Miller, guardian for John Bruen, 50 acres, No. 4,246; Martin Thomas, 713⅓ acres, No. 4,785; David Malott, 100 acres, No. 3,343; William McLain, 50 acres, No. 3,343; Theodore Malott, 50 acres, No. 4,252; Samuel R. Malott, 170¼ acres, No. 4,252; John Morgan, 100 acres, No. 4,798; John Morgan, 100 acres, No. 4,799; John Morgan, 50 acres, No. 8,287; Archibald McLain, 100 acres, No. 5,257; Ocasler & Helm, 400 acres, No. 10,-421; William Porter, 100 acres, No. 3,343; John Porter, 100 acres, No 3,343; Benjamin Reed, 106 acres, No. 3,343; Benjamin Ross, 50 acres, No. 3,343; Thomas Ross, 500 acres, No. 4,789; Thomas Ross (one brick house, $915); George Smith, 52 acres, No. 3,343; John Savory, 70 acres, No. 4,257; Abraham Smith, 65½ acres, No. 3,343; Nathan Sidwell, 33⅓ acres, No. 4,792; John Simpkins, 124 acres, No. 3,336; Smith Simpkins, 100 acres, No. 3,336; William Shotwell, 220 acres, No. 4,789; John Shotwell, Jr., 212 acres, No. 4,789; Morris Trout, 25 acres, No. 3,343; Morris Trout, Sr., 24 acres, No. 3,344; John Trout, 75½ acres, No. 3,343; John Trout, 25 acres, No. 3,345; James Taylor, 246⅔ acres, No. 4,792; James Taylor, 50 acres, No. 4,792; James Taylor, 430 acres, No. 4,752; James Taylor and H. Bowyer, 197¼ acres, No. 4,787; James Taylor, Jr., 83¼ acres, No. 4,788; James Taylor, Jr., 803 acres, No. 909; James Taylor, Jr., 555⅓ acres, No. 4,785; James Taylor, Jr., 309 acres, No. 4,785; James Taylor, Jr., 666⅔ acres, No. 4,793; James Taylor, Jr., 197 acres, No. 909; Southard and Dobbs Thomas, 444 acres, No. 4,246; James Taylor, 200 acres, No. 4,252; United States Bank, 12 acres, No. 4,790; United States Bank, 62⅓ acres, No. 4,786; United States Bank, 40 acres, No. 4,792; United States Bank, 500 acres, No. 4,451; United States Bank, 199 acres, No. 4,251; unknown, 130 acres, No. 4,257; James Waits, 118 acres, No. 4,250; Charles Waits, Sr., 100 acres, No. 4,250; Charles Waits, Jr., 50 acres, No. 4,250; Curtis Wilson, 106 acres, No. 3,344; Ebenezer Wood, 160 acres, No. 12,010; H. B. Walker, 61 acres, No. 4,246; William Worrell, 89 acres, No. 968; Jacob Waits, 49 acres, No. 4,252; total number of acres, 14,854.

CHURCHES AND GRAVEYARDS.

The pioneer families of Sterling were Methodists and Presbyterians, and attended the societies of these denominations at Clover and Williamsburg, situated only a few miles from the main settlement, but in Clermont County. It may not be thought out of place to refer briefly to the early history of these societies, inasmuch as they were the pioneer church organizations for miles around, and families from this township constituted a part of the membership. From the history of Williamsburg Township, Clermont County, under the head of Clover Chapel of the Methodist Episcopal Church, is taken the following: "On the 29th of August, 1804, William Winters and Peter Light executed a deed for a lot for church purposes at Clover, to Amos Smith, Joshua Lambert, William Smith, Moses Rumsey, Ephraim Duke, Samuel Nelson, Samuel Nutt, Augustus Clark and Thomas Lemon as Trustees. These began a hewed-log house in the course of a few years, which was never wholly finished, yet preaching was held there several years, and ever since 1804, Methodist preaching has been maintained with more or less regularity in the Clover neighborhood." Among the early members of this society were the Days, Andersons, Trouts and Earharts. The first class leader was Amos Smith. The church then was on the White Oak and Moscow Circuit.

About the year 1813, prayer-meetings were inaugurated at the house of Absalom Day, and occasionally held there, and several years later a church organization was effected, it being the result of the outgrowth of a camp-meeting which had been in progress in the vicinity of Batavia, conducted by the Rev. John Collins. Some of the members of this society were the Days, Smiths, Charles Waits, Jr., and the Earharts. Andrew Smith was one of the class leaders.

The McLains and Boyds were members of the Presbyterian Church at Williamsburg, which was organized by the Rev. Dr. Hoge in the year 1808, and held meetings in the court house for more than twenty years, under the pastorate of Rev. R. B. Dobbins, who continued in charge until 1833. Their first church building was erected in 1830. Archibald McLain was one of the original members of this church and one of its first Elders, in which office he continued forty-seven years.

Salem Methodist Episcopal Church.—A church organization of Methodists existed for some years, beginning in about 1834, in the southern part of the township, where services were held in a schoolhouse on the farm of Archibald McLain, composed of the families of that persuasion in that vicinity. After a few years, the organization weakened, and finally "went out." It was, however, revived and meetings were held along from time to time until in 1854, when the society had recruited its membership and gained sufficient strength to erect a house of worship. Among the members at this period were John Newberry and wife, Mother Anderson, Thomas Anderson and wife, Archibald McLain and wife, James Long and wife, Ezra Willey and wife, Edward Collins and wife, John H. Daughterty and wife and Mrs. Overton. A half-acre of ground was donated by T. W. Anderson for the purpose of erecting a church thereon. The pastor of the church was Rev. Andrew Murphy, who appointed the following-named men as Trustees: A. McLain, J. R. Long, John Newberry, John H. Daugherty and Ezra Willey. In August, the Trustees contracted with C. L. Rilley to build a meeting-house, for which they were to pay him $550. The one-story frame building now standing there is the one then built. This appointment was in 1854, a part of the Williamsburg Circuit, and the Rev. Levi Thomas was the colleague of Mr. Murphy on the circuit. It is now attached to Williamsburg, and the pastor is Rev. Mr. Moler.

Burdsall Chapel is the name of a Methodist Episcopal Church located in the northern part of the township. The society was organized in what was known as the Morgan Schoolhouse in that vicinity, in November, 1843, with a membership of eleven, among whom were Charles Brown and sister Rebecca, A. E. Adams, L. D. Simonton and wife Maria, Samuel Simonton and wife Elizabeth. Other members of about that period were Rarrack Butt and wife Harriet, Harriet Stroub, John Shannon and wife Margaret and Thomas Shannon. It was made a part of Batavia Circuit, of which the ministers in charge were Revs. John W. Clark and William I. Fee, the latter of whom preached the first sermon to the class in the schoolhouse. Services were held in the Morgan Schoolhouse, at the residence of Charles Brown and at another schoolhouse in the neighborhood until the building of the present neat one-story brick edifice in 1854. The lot, one acre, upon which the building stands, was given to the society by Timothy Kirby, of Cincinnati. Not long after the church was organized, Edward Burdsall and family united with the little band, and the former became a zealous and hard-working member, active to the interests and prosperity of the church; he gave liberally in work and money, and was a leading factor in the construction of the edifice, from which fact the church was called Burdsall Chapel. The dedicatory sermon was preached in the summer of 1855 by Rev. W. E. Hines. The ministers in charge of Batavia Circuit from 1844 to 1852, are as follows: 1844, Revs. John W. Clark, O. P. Williams; 1845, Revs. Barton Lowe, Thomas K. Coleman; 1846, Revs. Barton Lowe, Andrew J. McLaughlin; 1847, Revs. H. Wharton, Enoch West; 1848-49, Rev. L. D. Harlan; 1850, Revs. David Whitman, John W. Ross; 1851, Revs. Levi P. Miller, G. C. Townsley. In September, 1851, or the year following, Williamsburg Circuit was formed, and Burdsall's Chapel became a part thereof, and the ministers in charge, from 1851 for some years, were as follows: Rev. L. P. Miller, Rev. B. P. Wheat; Revs. A. Murphy, John Smith; Revs. A Murphy, Levi Thomas; Revs. W. E. Hines, James H. Middleton; Revs. W. E. Hines, E. P. James; Revs. E. C. Merrick, James Kendall; Revs.

M. P. Zink, S. G. Griffith; Revs. W. E. Hines, S. G. Griffith; Revs. W. E. Hines, N. Green. In the absence of records, we cannot give the date that this appointment was made a part of the Marathon Circuit, to which it now belongs. Rev. William Jackson is now in charge. Present membership, between eighty and one hundred.

Five-Mile Christian Church.—This church, situated in the northeastern part of the township, on Five-Mile Creek, was organized in that vicinity by the Rev. Alexander McLain in 1842. The original membership consisted of Jacob Hair and wife Elizabeth, and two daughters, Savilla and Letta A. Hair. The Hair residence was the preaching place of this society for some years, when a hewed-log house was erected for a place of worship, which stood on the site of the present church. One-half acre of ground was given for church and burial purposes by A. Hair, and later one acre was purchased of Thomas Sheldon and added to the graveyard. The following in the order given have served the charge: Revs. Aexander McLain, John McMillen, Alexander Thompson, George Mefford, William Pangburn, John Sheldon, ——. Rapp, Rufus McDaniel, George C. Hill, and Lewis Shinkle, the present incumbent. The present edifice, a one-story brick, with belfry and bell, was erected in 1870 and 1871, and dedicated on the fourth Sunday of June, in the latter year, by the Rev. Namon Dawson. The membership is now about one hundred and forty. Interments were made in the graveyard about the date of the building of the log church.

Bloom Rose United Brethren Church.—Situated northwest of the center of the township, on Five-Mile Creek, was organized about the year 1845. Among the original members were Zelinda Brown, Reuben Harbaugh, Joseph Brown, Theophilus Simonton, Rolin Ireton, Nancy Simonton, Thomas Stewart, Nancy Stewart and Archibald and Maria Bracelin. The first pastor of the church was Rev. Mr. Heindricks. A neighboring schoolhouse answered as a place of worship until 1849, when, under the pastorate of Rev. John Walters, a small frame building was erected, which is yet used by this denomination. The lot was deeded by Joseph Brown to Thomas Prall, Archibald Bracelin and Theophilus Simonton, Trustees of the church, for burial and church purposes, dated February 2, 1849. Revs. McNeil, Cooper and Henry Tobey were among the first pastors of the church. February 20, 1856, Joseph Brown, in consideration of $72.93, deeded to Edmund Burdsall, John Junkins, Joseph Brown and Robert Forker, Trustees of the graveyard, about two acres of ground, which was added to that of the church. Burials were here made as early as 1845, the first interment being that of Joseph, son of Joseph and Zelinda Brown, who died July 9, 1845. The congregation are now erecting a neat one-story brick building, which will be completed yet this fall, at a cost of about $2,500. The membership is about sixty, and the pastor of the church Rev. W. R. Houlston.

Taylor Chapel.—A Methodist Episcopal Church, located in the center of the township, dates from the spring of 1874, when organized in the Ross Schoolhouse. The following summer, the congregation built a frame structure of medium size, in which they continue to worship. The constituent members, in 1874, were as follows: J. R. Long, John Hill and wife, E. C. Hill, George Hatton and wife, Susan Hill, Henry Runyan, G. P. Bishop and wife Elizabeth, Mary J. Conklin, Margaret Wedmeyer, Lucinda Wedmeyer, Barbara Ogden, Jane Bishop, Dora Ross, Enoch Simpkins, Ichabod Bishop, Alfred Bishop, Mary J. Bishop, W. Parcust, E. Wedmeyer, Kate Bishop, Barbara Hesler, Margaret E. Meyers, Olie Runyan, Bell Meyers, Nancy Stephens and Mary E. Waits. The ground upon which the church is built was donated by James Taylor. The edifice was dedicated in December, 1874; sermon by Rev.

Granville Moody. This appointment belongs to Marathon Circuit, and has a membership of twenty-seven. The ministers in charge have been Revs. William McMullen, Peter Wells, E. P. James, W. J. Baker, and William Jackson, present incumbent.

The graveyard across from the church had its origin in a small strip of ground appropriated by Thomas Ross for burial purposes. Some years later, to this was added about two acres given by James Taylor. Interments were made in this burial-ground as early as 1840.

Todd's Run Baptist Church (Colored).—Was organized by Elder Riley April 29, 1870, with twenty members, among whom were R. Willis and wife, H. Williams and wife, J. Cope and wife. They have erected a neat frame church building in the southern part of the township, which was dedicated August 20, 1882. Present membership, thirty-nine. Present pastor, Elder George Davis.

SCHOOLS.

In the absence of records, but a few fragments of school history can be given. The names of most of the early teachers have passed out of recollection, and only a few can be recalled. As early as 1814, there stood on the Samuel Boyd farm, in the southwestern part of what has since become Sterling Township, of Brown County, located about where now stands the blacksmith shop of George Bishop, a schoolhouse, in which school was taught by Leonard Raper, who was one of the earliest settlers in the Concord neighborhood, Clermont County, and one of the first teachers. Mr. Raper served as a soldier in the British Army during the Revolutionary war, and was among the men surrendered by Lord Cornwallis at Yorktown. He was the father of the distinguished Methodist divine, Rev. William H. Raper. He was a man of good qualities, and is remembered as a worthy and beloved instructor of the pioneer youth. He died March 18, 1833. Of the pupils of Mr. Leonard, Archibald McLain and James Boyd are still living, and in the immediate vicinity of the old schoolhouse. Moses Warden was Leonard's successor. He was a saddler by trade, and a Methodist local preacher; was one of the earliest citizens of Bethel, near which place he died in 1859. A Mr. Free and Amos Danberry were later teachers in the same house. About the year 1824 or 1825, Archibald McLain assisted in building a schoolhouse that stood a little northwest of the one just mentioned, where Polick's residence now is. Among the masters of this house were R. McLaughlin, Matthew Smith and A. McLain. In six or eight years, another schoolhouse of this neighborhood was built a little south of the present residence of Archibald McLain. One McCollough and A. McLain taught in this house. About the same time, another schoolhouse was erected, on the Hillsboro road, a little northeast of De La Palma. In 1835, Archibald McLain was the teacher here, and prior to this date James Lucas. In 1837-38, Mr. McLain taught in a schoolhouse on Five-Mile Creek, near the graveyard at the United Brethren Church.

In the Day neighborhood, as early as 1808 or 1809, a schoolhouse stood, in Clermont County, just across what is now the Brown County line. H. B. Walker was at this time the teacher. In the northern part of the township there was standing a schoolhouse in which school was kept in 1825 by John Skinner. Subsequent instructors were Charles McManaman and David Waits.

Under the old school law, a number of districts were formed and in each one a comfortable but rather rude house provided, but no statistics of value appear. There are now (1882) seven school districts in the township, with eight substantial schoolhouses, in which school is taught on an average of eight months in the year. The amount paid teachers within the year closing August 31, 1881, was $2,068.42. Total expenditure for school purposes, $2,555.07.

Balance on hand, $1,378.27. The value of the school property is $5,000. Ten gentlemen teachers were employed in 1881, and paid on an average of $32 per month; the total number of pupils enrolled for the same year was 422; average daily attendance, 343, 94 of whom were studying the alphabet; 376 reading; 397 spelling; 350 writing; 274 arithmetic; 99 geography; 65 English grammar; 20 oral lessons; 10 composition and 2 drawing. There are 26 colored pupils enrolled in the township, taught by a colored teacher.

POST OFFICES.

Sterling has no villages, yet there are in several places clusters of houses that might be termed hamlets, at some of which post offices have been established, namely:

De La Palma, established in 1852, with William Weeks, Postmaster. The office has since been filled with the following named: Swift Conner, Wesley Leonard, W. E. Conover, John W. Curry and Mrs. Margaret Malott. It is located in the western part of the township.

Eastwood is the name of the post office at Salem Station, on the Cincinnati & Eastern Railroad, located in the southern part of the township. It was established March 8, 1878, with George W. Smith as Postmaster, who is still in office.

The third post office is at Crosstown, in the western part of the township, near the line separating Brown and Clermont Counties. The office was established June 23, 1881, with W. N. Stewart as Postmaster.

INDUSTRIES.

The manufacturing interests of Sterling have been very meager indeed, which fact is due to the closeness to the old town of Williamsburg and the East Fork of the Little Miami River, which at an early day afforded excellent water-power.

Williamsburg was an early manufacturing town, and had in operation a grist-mill as early as 1798, if not prior to that date, as Gen. William Lytle, the proprietor of the town, in connection with Gen. Taylor, in July, 1797, employed Peter Wilson, of Kentucky, to come to the newly laid out town to build a small grist-mill. Not long after 1800, Gen. Lytle constructed the present mill there, which afforded all the conveniences of a good mill for the people living far and near. In 1802, a tannery was operated by Nicholas Sinks, and these, with later industries at that point, answered the wants of the early settlers of Sterling, and prevented a great demand for such at home.

About the year 1851, Archibald McLain and Curtis Wilson erected a sawmill, with water-power, on Todd's Run. At the same time, another such mill was built on the same branch, but farther up, by Hiram Anderson and John Smallwood. Neither of them, however, were operated very long, owing to the difficulty in keeping up the dam; it would wash out at each freshet.

In 1870, Stephen Waits built a saw-mill on Crane Run, which was destroyed by fire on the night of the 16th of August, 1871. Mr. Waits rebuilt the mill that fall, and connected with it grist machinery, which was used for grinding corn, but not for making flour.

At different times, a number of portable saw-mills have been in operation and other stationary mills.

In 1866, John Irwin built a chair factory on Five Mile Creek, near the United Brethren Church, where he was engaged in making all kinds of sitting chairs until his death, which occurred May 1, 1882.

CHAPTER XVI.

BYRD TOWNSHIP.

BY JOHN M. THOMPSON.

THE Commissioners' journal of Adams County, Ohio, contains the following relative to the organization of Byrd Township:

DECEMBER 2, 1806.

The Commissioners proceeded to divide the County of Adams into townships in the following manner, to wit:

NO. 3, BY THE NAME OF BYRD.

Beginning at the northwest corner of Huntington Township; thence with the north line thereof to the northeast corner of the said township; thence north with the line of Sprigg, and passing its corner to the north line of Adams County; thence with the said line west to the northwest corner of the county; thence south to the beginning.

JUNE 2, 1807.

The Commissioners proceed to divide Byrd Township by running line due west from the southwest corner of Wayne Township to the county line, and ordered that the new township or north part of the division be called by the name of Eagle, etc.

JUNE 3, 1807.

Upon examination, it is found that in dividing Byrd Township the north line was so far south that Byrd Township would not have the quantity of square miles allowed by law. Therefore, it is ordered that the line between Byrd and Eagle Townships be altered and established as follows, to wit: Beginning at the southwest corner of Wayne Township; thence north, with the line of Wayne Township, 320 poles; thence west to the west line of the county.

Thus, it is seen, it was one of the original townships of Brown County at the time of its organization. It was named in honor of Charles W. Byrd, Secretary of the Northwest Territory. It is bounded as follows: North by Jackson Township, west by Jefferson, south by Union and Huntington, and east by Adams County. It is six miles long north and south, and five miles wide east and west. It contains 20,000 acres of land. The surface of the township is neither flat nor hilly, but sufficiently rolling to insure good drainage. The higher points fall by easy descent to the lower lands, making nearly all suitable for an easy cultivation. The soil of the township is fertile. The principal productions are corn, wheat, oats, tobacco, potatoes and pork. Tobacco and wheat are the staple productions. This township is third in the county in the amount of tobacco produced. It is well watered by the East and West Forks of Eagle Creek and Rattlesnake Creek, which furnish considerable water-power. In a few places in the township it is hilly, and that is along the creeks, but as a whole the surface is level, covered at an early day with timber. Numerous springs of excellent water abound in the township, and in parts where springs are lacking water is obtained by digging to the depth of from twelve to forty feet.

Byrd Township contains no very valuable minerals. The most valuable is the blue limestone. It is used for building stone, or for burning into lime. In the upper portion of it are found marine shells, and on the hillsides it is found in detached pieces. Underneath the lowest strata or base of the hills is a compact soapstone, or blue clay, impervious to water. At the time the first white settlers appeared, the land was nearly all covered with timber, which they had to clear away to make their cultivated fields. Abundance of timber is still left, but not such a surplus that owners are anxious to clear off their farms. Walnut, which used to be abundant, has nearly all been cut out. At first it was of little value, and was used for various purposes, as rails, building timber, etc. Oak, hickory, ash, elm, beech and poplar compose the principal timber now, though there are small amounts of other kinds.

EARLY SETTLERS.

The earliest settlers of the township of whom we have any account were John Knox, Thomas Hatfield, John McLaughlin, Andrew Dragoo, Lawrence Ramey, George Fisher, John Wright, Nathaniel Beasley and Benjamin Sutton. Lawrence Ramey had a family of ten children—nine girls and one boy. He settled southwest from Decatur about one mile and a quarter. His only son, George, died while serving in the war of 1812. Lawrence Ramey died April 3, 1835, aged eighty-one years. These settlers came mostly from Virginia, prior to the year 1800, and effected a settlement when the whole country was in wilderness and abounded in all kinds of game.

The first settlement within the present limits of the township of which any definite account can be obtained was made by John Knox, who settled on the East Fork of Eagle Creek, about two miles from Decatur, on the lands where Hiram Foster now lives, in 1796. Knox was a native of Virginia. He had a family consisting of five sons and three daughters. Knox was a hard worker, and endured many hardships. Himself and family joined the Shaker community, but most of them afterward returned.

Henry Earhart came from Virginia to this township in 1801. Himself and wife traveled part of the long journey in a two-horse wagon. In descending the precipitous hills, it was necessary to check the vehicle. This was done by fastening small saplings to the wagon. They proceeded in this manner until they reached Wheeling, where they chartered a flat-boat and floated to Maysville. Here they stopped, and made their way to their new settlement. He assisted Nathaniel Beasley in the erection of the first house in Decatur, which was torn down in April, 1882. He devoted his time mostly to splitting rails, clearing timber, hunting, and the raising of houses. A few years later, he left, and went back to his native land. He went into the war of 1812, and was never heard of afterward.

Nathaniel Beasley was one of the earliest and most prominent settlers. Before settling here, he had been a member of several surveying parties in Southwestern Ohio, and been inured to the severest extremes of weather when far from the habitation of any white man. The surveying expeditions were attended with great risk of attack from Indians, and on several occasions the parties to which he was attached lost some of their men from savage assaults. The surveys were made right in the midst of deadly foes, and required great dispatch and secresy. After moving to Byrd Township, Mr. Beasley gave some attention to surveying, and laid off a number of roads, farms and villages. He was elected Surveyor of Adams County, and served many years, and was Captain, and afterward General, in the State militia. He ultimately became one of the wealthiest land-owners in the community, and one of the most intelligent and esteemed citizens of the county. He was born in Spottsylvania County, Va., May 19, 1774, and died March 27, 1835. His wife was Sarah Sutton, the daughter of one of the earliest settlers of Byrd Township.

William West was born in Fairfax County, Va., February 16, 1781, and, when eight years of age his father brought him to Mason County, Ky., settling at Kenton's Station, near where Washington now is. When sixteen years old, he came with his father across the river, and remained with him near Aberdeen until 1806, when, with his wife, whom he had married the year previous, and a child, he pushed forward to the farm near Decatur, which he occupied throughout the rest of his long, eventful life. When he arrived, the country about him was one vast wilderness, broken only here and there, at distant intervals, by small clearings. He died at the old homestead January 24, 1870, in his eighty-ninth year. At that time, he had six children living and four dead; forty-two grandchildren living and seventeen dead; thirty-five great-grandchildren living and eight dead—an aggregate posterity of 112. In politics, he has been an unflinching Democrat.

Thomas Hatfield, with his family, moved from Mason County, Ky., to the farm his son David now occupies, on West Fork, in 1804. It was then an unbroken wilderness. He was formerly from Pennsylvania. Mr. Hatfield remained on this place the rest of his life. He had a family of ten children—Thomas, Mary, John, Sarah, Martha, Jonas, Deborah, Elizabeth, Isom and David. One of the daughters, Martha, joined the Shakers, but, after a few years, returned to her father's house.

John Wright, his wife, Margaret (McKetrick), and their children, William, Margaret, Robert, John, Thomas, Samuel and Jane, settled one mile north of Decatur in 1801 or 1802. Mr. Wright had two children born unto him after his settlement here—Alexander and James. He came from near Lexington, Ky., and had previously lived in Virginia. He purchased 400 acres of land from Gen. Nathaniel Beasley, and lived and died on the place. His eldest son, William, settled on 200 acres of the farm, married Elizabeth Thomas December 25, 1805, and died on the home place. John Wright, Sr., represented Adams County in the State Legislature soon after his emigration hither, and while it met at Chillicothe. A Mr. Evans and family were living on the creek before 1802.

James Moore was one of the early settlers. He was from Pennsylvania, and was an early Justice of the Peace of Byrd Township. His son James is said to have been the first child born in the township, in 1800. Mr. Moore had two other sons—Robert and John—besides several daughters.

Benjamin Sutton was another early pioneer. He came from Maysville, Ky., and, for more than a score of years, was Justice of the Peace. His daughter Sally married Nathaniel Beasley. Mr. Sutton had but two sons. Of these, Othe never married, and boated on the Ohio and Mississippi extensively. Tingley married and reared a large family.

David Montgomery operated a little farm a short distance north of Decatur, and afterward carried on a little blacksmith shop in the village. He was well advanced in life when he came to this township, but it was at quite an early day.

Other early settlers were the Howlands, on Eagle Creek—John Howland and his family. His sons, Ichabod and John, served in Capt. Shepherd's company of riflemen during the war of 1812. Two other sons were Levi and Izatus. William Sparrs, who had settled in the northern part of the township, was one of the prisoners in Hull's surrender. Samuel Shaw and Mr. Kilpatrick, two other soldiers in the war of 1812 from this township, were killed by the Indians while on their way home from Fort Meigs. William Shields was an early settler some distance southwest from Decatur. He lived to a good old age. George Edwards, originally from Fairfax County, Va., but directly from the vicinity of Aberdeen, settled in the northwestern part of the township about 1806. His father, James, was an early settler at Aberdeen. David McBride settled early on Eagle Creek. He was of Irish extraction. Another Irish settler, somewhat later, was John Stitt. Samuel Pickerill, with his family, came to the township in 1810, and remained until his death, in 1850, at the advanced age of ninety-six years. He had been a drummer boy in the Amercian Revolution. About 1807, Joshua Grimes settled in this township, and spent the balance of his life here.

HISTORY OF BROWN COUNTY.

John West, Sr., is the oldest settler in the township now living, and resides about two miles from Decatur. He was the son of William West, and was born January 1, 1797. He was married to Louisa Steward, who reared a family of seven children. His wife died a few years since. Mr. West was a powerful man in his day, and a hard worker. During his son John's life, the farm was placed under his control, but since his death, the old man has again the supervision. Mr. West is a member of the Christian Church at Liberty Chapel. In politics, he holds strongly to the Democratic faith.

Joseph Stevenson, deceased (familiarly called "Uncle Joe"), was one of the late pioneers of this community. He was born in Washington County, Penn., in the year 1804, and came to this neighborhood in 1814, when he first engaged in the occupation of farming. He followed this for several years, when he removed to Decatur and took charge of the hotel business. He also engaged in mercantile business quite awhile. He has held many minor offices in the township, among which was Justice of the Peace. He was Postmaster from 1852 to 1877, when he gave up business and settled down to quiet life. He died August 24, 1882, in the seventy-ninth year of his age. He married Nancy Geeslin December 30, 1830, who reared him eleven children—nine sons and two daughters. His wife and six sons are living. Mr. Stevenson was a member of the Presbyterian Church of Decatur, and was much respected by all who knew him.

James Snedaker, deceased, may be classed with the pioneers. He was born in Brown County October 22, 1814; died in Decatur July 25, 1882, in the sixty-eighth year of his age. He first engaged in the occupation of a farmer, and spent his life in and near Decatur. He devoted his time principally to the mercantile business, and did a big business in Decatur at an early day. In 1877, he was appointed Postmaster, vice Joseph Stevenson, resigned, which he continued to keep until the day of his death. He was married to Susan Robb, who reared a family of eight children, seven of whom are living. Mr. Snedaker belonged to the Presbyterian Church, and held various offices of trust in the church. He was an honest man, and was much respected by all who knew him.

EARLY TIMES AND CUSTOMS.

In the earlier settlements of this section, ponds, marshes and swamps abounded, where to-day are found fertile and cultivated fields. The low and flat lands were avoided for the higher lands, not only on account of the wetness, but for sanitary reasons. The proximity of a spring also had much to do with the location of the cabin, but in the selection of places for the erection of other buildings, convenience was the ordinary test. The corn-crib, made of rails or poles, and covered with clapboards or hay, as convenience suggested, was as apt to be in close proximity to the front as at the rear of the building, or near the stable. The habitations of those days were the double log cabin, with an entry between the two rooms, clapboard roof, puncheon floors, with chimneys of split sticks and clay mortar, clapboard doors with wooden hinges and latches. A loom and a spinning-wheel were indispensable, as well as a hominy-block and pestle, and a hand-mill to manufacture meal and flour. The cabins were furnished in the same style of simplicity. The bedstead was home-made, and often consisted of forked sticks driven in the ground, with cross-poles to support the clapboards or the cord. One pot, kettle, frying-pan were the only articles considered indispensable, though some included the tea-kettle.

The distilleries afforded the best and almost the only market for the surplus grain, and usually paid several cents per bushel for corn more than could be obtained elsewhere.

The clothing of the early pioneers of this township was as plain and simple as their humble homes. The clothing taken to this new country was made to render a vast deal of service until a crop of flax or hemp could be grown out of which to manufacture the household apparel. The prairie wolves made it difficult to take sheep into the settlements, but, after the sheep had been introduced, and flax and hemp raised in sufficient quantities, it still remained an arduous task to spin, weave and make the wearing apparel for the entire family. In summer, nearly all persons, both male and female, went barefoot. Buckskin moccasins were commonly worn. Boys of twelve and fifteen years of age never thought of wearing anything on their feet, except during three or four months during the coldest weather. Boots were unknown until a later generation. After flax was raised in sufficient quantities, and sheep could be protected from the wolves, a better and more comfortable style of clothing prevailed. Flannel and linsey were woven and made into garments for the women and children, and jeans for the men. The wool for the jeans was colored from the bark of the walnut, and from this came the term butternut, still common throughout the West. The black and white wool mixed varied the color, and gave the pepper and salt color. As a matter of course, every family did its own spinning, weaving and sewing, and for years all the wool had to be carded by hand, on cards from four inches broad to eight to ten inches long. The picking of the wool and carding was work in which the little folks could help, and at the proper season, all the little hands were enlisted in the business. Every household had its big and little spinning-wheels, winding-blades and warping-bars and loom. In many of the households of Byrd Township there will still be found some of these relics. It involved a life of toil, hardship, and the lack of many comforts, but it was the life that made men of character.

This township contains no incorporated village. The first peach trees planted in the township were on the farm of S. W. Pickerill. The public square at Decatur was left for a court house when Adams and Brown were yet united, and it was confidently expected that Decatur would be made the county seat of Adams County. The first Freemason lodge was established in the county at Decatur in 1817. Benjamin Sutton is said to have been the first Justice of the Peace in the township, which office he held for the period of twenty-five or thirty years. The first voting-place in the township was in a frame building on the farm that John F. Pickerill now owns. It is now torn down. This was when Jefferson and Byrd Townships were united. It was removed to Decatur, and has remained there ever since. When they were combined, it made one of the largest townships in the county.

The first store in the township of which we have any account was kept near Baird's Mill, about the year 1800, in a log building. It was kept by Stephen Hoboken. He emigrated from near Hagerstown, Md. He carried on a good business, trading with the Indians and whites, and made himself quite a snug fortune. He disappeared rather suddenly one night, and nobody knew whither he went. His property was in ashes in the morning, and the supposition is that the Indians plundered the property, stole the goods, and then killed him for his money.

ROADS.

With the beginning of the century, there were no roads in Byrd Township, and for years what were called roads were little better than wagon-tracks through the forest. These were supposed to follow the Indian trails. The highway was wide enough for all necessary purposes, but, down to 1835 or later, the roads were execrable. The undrained country partly explains the cause. When the ground was frozen and worn smooth, or dry and solid, no roads were better. But the proceeds of the road taxes in money or labor were totally inadequate to keep them even in a tolerable condition at the time most wanted, and only within recent years has it been realized that drainage is essential to a good road-bed. Nearly all the roads in the township are now pike roads, except a few by-paths. The Ripley & Locust Grove Turnpike, which runs through the township, was once a toll road, but was made a county road in March, 1879.

The Decatur & Russellville Turnpike is a free road, built by a special act of the Legislature in 1880.

FIRST MILL.

The first mill in the township was built by John Austin, but it is hard to get the date of its erection. It was situated on Eagle Creek, just below the junction of the East and West Branches. Several mills were built in the township in after years, with all the modern improvements. The Decatur Mill, the Baird Mill and the Fitch Mill are the only mills in the township at the present time.

CEMETERIES.

There are five public graveyards in this township—the Decatur Cemetery; the old Eckman Burial-Ground, on the farm of George West, the Evans Burial-Ground, two and a half miles west of Decatur, on the Decatur & Russellville Turnpike; the Woods Graveyard, situated near Eagle Chapel, on Main Eagle Creek; and the Liberty Cemetery, at Liberty Chapel.

Distances from Decatur to various neighboring points in Brown and Adams Counties: Ripley, eleven miles; Aberdeen, thirteen miles; Red Oak, five miles; Russellville, six miles; Georgetown, thirteen miles; Arnheim, eleven miles; Brownstown, fourteen miles; Carlisle, eight miles; Fayetteville, thirty-three miles; Feesburg, eighteen and a half miles; Fincastle, fifteen miles; Levanna, thirteen miles; Greenbush, twenty-five miles; Hamersville, eighteen miles; Higginsport, eighteen miles; Locust Ridge, twenty-four and a half miles; Mt. Oreb, twenty-two miles; New Harmony, twenty-six miles; New Hope, seventeen miles; Sardinia, seventeen miles; St. Martin's, thirty-seven and a half miles; White Oak Valley, seventeen miles; in Adams County, Eckmansville, five miles; North Liberty, seven miles; Winchester, ten miles; Youngsville, twelve miles; Tranquility, seventeen miles; West Union, nine miles; Fairview, three miles; Bentonville, seven miles; Manchester, twelve miles; Bradyville, twelve miles; Jacktown, nineteen miles.

SCHOOLS.

In 1820 or 1821, the first log schoolhouse, with its rough puncheon floor and greased-paper windows, was erected one-half mile west of Decatur. Thomas Moore, who combined the duties of a pedagogue and farmer, was the first teacher. Judge Livingston wielded the birch a few terms afterward. Several log schoolhouses were soon after built in different parts of the township. In succeeding years, as people became able to incur the expense, they built better schoolhouses. The schoolhouses constructed during the last decade are in keeping with the progress of events in educational matters, and compare favorably with school buildings throughout the county. The early schoolhouses were structures of logs, without windows, the light being admitted through cracks between the logs, which were in the winter closed with oiled paper. Geographies, dictionaries and grammars were unknown, and teachers were usually able to teach only "reading, writing and arithmetic."

There are seven school districts in the township. All of them possess good substantial frame buildings. The schools are well attended, and are in charge of reliable, capable instructors.

The Ohio Valley Academy was an educational institution of an advanced grade, which its founder sought to establish and perpetuate at Decatur. Rev. J. A. R. Rodgers and others, about 1862, started it. Catalogues and views of the prospective buildings, including a dormitory for young men, a ladies' boarding hall and a fine academy building, a spacious assembly room, recitation rooms, library, etc., with all the appointments of a first-class institution, were widely circulated. The estimated cost of the building was $30,000. Students appeared from various parts of the State and from Kentucky, but, instead of the fine architectural structures anticipated, they found only a dilapidated building in which to recite.

The instructors for 1863 were: R. A. McCollough, Principal; Miss Sallie J. Embree, Assistant; Miss Lizzie Dugan, Assistant; Rev. J. A. R. Rodgers, Teacher of Languages; Rev. J. M. Waddle, Teacher of Elocution; Miss Mary Evans, Teacher of Instrumental Music. They continued as instructors until 1865, when the corps of teachers was changed. One hundred and twenty-four students attended from 1863 to 1865. The classical department contained nine; scientific department, thirty-five; and the English department, eighty. The instructors for 1865 were: C. A. Kenaston, A. M., Principal; Miss Elizabeth Kinney, Assistant, and Teacher of French; Rev. J. M. Waddle, Teacher of Elocution; William A. Dixon, Lecturer on Physiology; Miss N. Y. Montgomery, Teacher of Instrumental Music. The Examining Committee were Rev. James Porter, Rev. D. Vandyke, T. P. Sniffin, William A. Dixon. M. D., W. N. Pickerill and E. F. Moulton. The academy continued for a few years only. Want of support caused its decline.

CHURCHES.

Traveling missionaries visited this country in very early times, and brought the glad tidings of peace and good will to the inhabitants. But little is remembered of them. Camp-meetings at an early day supplied a recognized want and were generally attended in large numbers. Churches soon sprang up, the first of log, and then of better material as the people became able. The first religion established in the township was probably that of the Shakers. It was preached here as early as 1804, their first services being held in groves or private houses. Afterward, a structure was erected in which they worshiped. It is described as being a log pen of but five or six feet in height and divided into two departments, in one of which the men, and in the other the women worshiped. This building was afterward converted into a more suitable and convenient church. The continuance of the Shakers as a religious body in this township, covered a period of five or six years, when most of them removed elsewhere.

The Presbyterian Church is situated in Decatur, and was erected in 1838. It was a brick building, cost about $1,000, and stood a little west of the site of the present one. It was organized November 12, 1841, with twenty-two members—John Farris and James Blair were the first Ruling Elders, and were ordained by the Rev. John Rankin, November 13, 1841. The organization of this church and erection of the house were due to the exertions and self-sacrifice of John Farris, formerly of Cabin Creek, Ky., and Dr. Simeon Bearce, a young physician from the New England States. For a time previous to the organization of the church, the community about Decatur had been deeply agitated by the discussion of slavery, and the doors of the only church edifice for holding public meetings were closed against anti-slavery lectures. This fact, doubtless was one of the immediate causes which led to the organization of this church. In the year 1859, the brick building was torn down and the present house erected under the superintendence of Daniel Copple, Alexander Kirkpatrick and John West, Jr., at an expense of $1,200. When the Ripley Presbytery left the New School General Assembly, this church continued with the Presbytery and separated from the Assembly. The names of the ministers who have served this church since its organization are Rev. Jesse Lockhart, Rev. James R. Gibson, Rev. Victor M. King, Rev. William Lumsden, Rev. J. A. R. Rodgers, Rev. H. V. Warren, Rev. Henry Osborn, Rev. John Stewart, Rev. John N. McClung, Rev. S. C. Kerr.

The first Methodist Episcopal Church in the township was supposed to have been built about the year 1825. It was a log structure and was located on the Pittenger homestead. It still stands at the present date. The brick church in Decatur was supposed to have been built about that date. The brick structure was torn down in 1860 to make way for a frame building. The contractors were the Montgomery Bros., and it cost about $1,200. The names of the ministers since 1845 are: 1845-46, Revs. William H. Sutherland and M. G. Perkizer; 1846-47, Revs. Jacob Holmes and Philip Nation; 1847-48, Rev. Barton Lowe; 1848-49, Rev. De Witt Clinton Howard and Charles Fergason; 1849-50, Revs. M. P. Zink and E. H. Field; 1850-51, Revs. William B. Jackson and E. H. Field; 1851-52, Rev. Jesse M. D. Robertson; 1852-53, Revs. James Armstrong and George H. Reid; 1853-54, Revs. James Armstrong and George H. Reid; 1854-55, Revs. William Q. Shannon and A. P. Dunlap; 1855-56, Revs. B. P. Wheat and Thomas Head; 1856-57, Rev. Joseph Blackburn; 1858-59, Revs. M. T. Zink and Nathaniel Green; 1859-60, Revs. Edward Merrick and Edward Moscore; 1860-61, Revs. Thomas Head and T. A. Fiddler; 1861-62, Revs. J. M. Sullivan and H. E. Perkizer; 1862-63, Revs. William Ramsey and John Bloomhuff; 1863-64, Revs. William Ramsey and H. C. Middleton; 1864-65, Revs. William McMullen and H. C. Middleton; 1865-66, Revs. William McMuller and H. M. Keck; 1866-67, Revs. E. P. James and Isaac Ross; 1867-68, Revs. Isaac Ross and S. W. Edmiston; 1868-69, Rev. S. W. Edmiston; 1869-70, Revs. S. W. Edmiston and Lytle; 1870-71, Revs. De Witt Peak and Graham Kennedy; 1871-72, Revs. W. J. Quarry and Charles J. Wells; 1872-73, Revs. W. J. Quarry and D. Lee Aultman; 1873-74, Revs. W. J. Quarry and D. V. Ross; 1874-75, Revs. J. L. Gregg and William Gaddis; 1875-76, Revs. J. L. Gregg and W. P. Jackson; 1876-77, Revs. A. E. Higgins; 1877-78, Rev. A. E. Higgins; 1878-79, Rev. W. J. Baker; 1879-80, Rev. E. D. Keys; 1880-81, Rev. S. W. Edmiston; 1881-82, Rev. S. W. Edmiston; 1882-83, Rev. L. O. Deptuty.

The United Presbyterian Church is located in Decatur, and was built in the year 1849 by Daniel Bayless and William Kane. It is a frame building, 40x50, and cost about $1,000. At the time of its organization, the membership was small, and members from the Cherry Fork Church moved their membership here. Rev. Alexander McClennhan was the first minister. He departed this life in 1860, and was succeeded by Rev. J. M. Waddle. The congregation was without a pastor until 1875, when the Rev. Thomas Mercer received a call, which he accepted; he continued as their pastor until 1881, when he turned his attention to farming. The church has no pastor at the present day, and the organization is about broken up.

The Christian, or Disciple, congregation that worships at Liberty Chapel dates its origin back to 1810. In that year, Elder Archibald Alexander organized the church. The members at this time, or shortly afterward, included individuals from the Gardner, Devore, Pickerill, Ramey, Ristine, Hughs, Fisher, Reeves, Hatfield and Longley families. In 1812, John Longley began to preach for the church, and continued six years. In 1816, a great revival was held in the peach orchard, near the upper end of the present burying-grounds, and many conversions made. The following year, old Liberty Stone Meeting-House was built. Many of the neighbors, church members and others, turned out with teams and hauled the stone; others contributed money. The building committee consisted of David Devore, Jeptha Beasley and Samuel Pickerill. The masons who built the walls were Daniel Copple and Joseph Hughes. Matthew Gardner did at least part of the carpenter work. The walls are 44x34 feet, two feet in thickness and perhaps twelve feet to the square. About 1832, this organization united with a Disciple congregation which had formerly been a Baptist organization at Red Oak, but was won over in the reformatory movement by the followers of Alexander Campbell. The union of the two churches was harmonious and complete. John Ramey, Lovel Pickerill and Florence Shoafstall were among the first Elders of the church. After them came William N. Ramey, Ackles Geeslin, T. J. Pickerill, G. E. Hatfield, D. B. Hatfield, R. P. Fisher and Joseph Stitt. The ministers have been Jesse Holton, David Hathaway, John Ross, John Rogers, J. B. Lucas, John Young, David Thompson, B. F. Sallee, W. D. Moore and J. S. West. For about seventy years, the average membership has been about seventy-five. Two churches have sprung up under her influence, one at Russellville about 1843, and one at Bethlehem soon after. The change in the pike-road, which formerly ran in front of the old church, made the location undesirable, and the house needing repairs a new frame church was built at a cost of $1,200, and dedicated December 13, 1874, by Elder J. S. West.

Eagle Chapel Church is situated on main Eagle Creek, about two and a half miles south of Decatur. It is of the New Light denomination, and was erected in 1876 at a cost of $1,200. Rev. R. H. McDaniel was the first preacher; he continued in charge until 1881. Rev. J. F. Burnett succeeded him, and is their pastor at the present day. The church is growing in membership and great interest is being manifested.

SOCIETIES.

The Sons of Temperance, Grand Army of the Republic, Patrons of Husbandry and Freemasons each had an organization here, but they are now no more. The first Freemason Lodge in the county was instituted at St. Clairsville, now Decatur, about the year 1817. Capt. James Carr, now a member of Union Lodge, No. 71, of Ripley, was one of the charter members.

POLITICS.

This township has been Whig and Republican since its organization, and it is of little use for a Democrat to be a candidate for a township office. The Democrats have carried an office or two, but it has been by hard and persistent work. Byrd Township is one of the three Republican Townships in the county, and it generally polls a strong vote. The campaigns of 1840, 1863, 1876 and 1880 gave evidence of the very intense heat to which political feeling can be aroused, and many incidents might be recounted showing the extent of party enthusiasm in 1876 and 1880.

The vote of the township from 1875 to 1880: 1875, Governor, R. B. Hayes, Republican, 162; William Allen, Democrat, 103 votes; 1876, Secretary of State: Milton Barnes, Republican, 158; William Bell, Jr., Democrat, 102; 1876, President: R. B. Hayes, Republican, 174; Samuel J. Tilden, Democrat, 113; 1877, Governor: William H. West, Republican, 150; Richard Bishop, Democrat, 100; 1878, Secretary of State: Milton Barnes, Republican, 163; David R. Paige, Democrat, 101; 1879, Governor: Charles Foster, Republican, 179; Thomas Ewing, Democrat, 125; 1880, Secretary of State: Charles Townsend, Republican, 179; William Long, Democrat, 126; 1880, President: James A. Garfield, Republican, 184; W. S. Hancock, Democrat, 132; 1881, Governor: Charles Foster, Republican, 168; John W. Bookwalter, Democrat, 119; John Seitz, Prohibitionist, 3.

The present township officers are: Joseph Bayley, J. P. Moore and E. M.

Davidson, Trustees; A. F. Liggett, Clerk; George E. Howland, Treasurer; A. H. Mahaffey, Assessor; Morgan Hatfield, Constable.

The present Township Board of Education is composed as follows: District No. 1, J. P. Moore; District No. 2, William Rickey; District No. 3, John Stevenson; District No. 4, James Woods; District No. 5, Col. J. W. Henry; District No. 6, John McPherson; District No. 7, colored, in charge of the Board of Education. Average length of the school year is eight months. Average wages paid to teachers, $30. Population of Byrd Township, in 1860, 1,240; in 1870, 1,251; in 1880, 1,300.

James A. Stevenson, of this township, in 1865, was elected to the office of County Auditor by the Republican party; he served two years. William B. West, Democrat, was County Commissioner from 1874 to 1880, and in 1882, Samuel W. Pickerill was also elected County Commissioner from this township.

THE WAR RECORD.

The citizens of Byrd Township have reason to be proud of her soldiery during the great contest of 1861-65. In common, the men of this township gave a prompt response to the call at the outbreak of the war. The following is a list of the men who bore arms from Byrd Township, so far as the names could be obtained. It is not strange, however, if some have been overlooked. It was designed to be a complete list, but the means of information at command prevent it:

Amos Richmond, William Warren, Joseph Warren, John Warren, R. J. Smith, G. W. West, J. Q. Smith, William Kirkpatrick, Byron Swisher, Boone Funk, James Goff, James Stevenson, John Stevenson, William Stevenson, William Draper, Orvil Draper, W. B. Norton, John Norton, Bruce Moore, Edward Burbage, W. H. H. Edwards, John Thompson, A. P. Thompson, George Henderson, Richard Shofstall, Joseph Elefritz, Thomas McBride, John McBride, John White, George Pittinger, William Pittinger, Robert Kerr, Thomas Kerr, Green Pickerill, Samuel Pickerill, Norval Johnson, William Emerick, R. T. Fisher, L. McLaughlin, F. D. Sanders, James Thompson, John Thompson, Samuel Thompson, John Hughey, William Shofstall, George Thompson, Simon Reeves, W. W. Baird, Col. John W. Henry, George Henry, E. S. Kirkpatrick, William Milligan, Joseph Guyley, William Kirkpatrick, Lewis Brown, William Hughes, James Norton, James Hughey, James Purdin, J. H. Mann, John Edwards, H. N. Wallace, William Adamson, John P. Liggett, Thomas Dillinger, Thomas Robinson, Wesley Adamson, Jonah Hatfield, David Hatfield, Ferd Hatfield, Travis Reed, Green Norton, Nimon Ramey, Graham Kennedy, Peter Galbreath, Samuel Williams, George Caldwell, John Cox, George Mourer, Robert Menneaugh, Wilson Menneaugh, Samuel Porter, Thomas Montgomery, George Montgomery, William Burbage, John Howard.

NEAL.

This is a small village, situated three miles from Decatur, in the southeastern part of the township. It is on main Eagle Creek; also on the Decatur & Aberdeen Free Turnpike. It contains a store and post office, a blacksmith shop and a few dwellings. The population is about twenty-five. The post office was established in June, 1882. The present Postmaster is A. E. Neal. It is on the mail route from Decatur to Aberdeen. The mail is carried twice a week, Thursday and Saturday. This is a good trading point, and many goods are sold here; butter and eggs are the staple productions, and find ready sale in this market.

DECATUR.

This is a small village of 260 inhabitants, and is situated in the eastern part of Byrd Township. This village was laid out about the year 1802. It was named in the first place St. Clairsville, in honor of Gov. Arthur St. Clair, but there being another St. Clairsville in the State, it was changed. For awhile it was known as Hard Scrabble. The name Decatur as then agreed upon, and it so remains up to the present date. The first house in the village was built by Nathaniel Beasley, about the year 1802, or when the town was laid out. It was a double log cabin, with one entry, and covered with clapboards, but afterward weather-boarded and covered with shingles. It was said to have been the finest house in the country in its day. It remained as a dwelling until April, 1882, and was the property of Amelia Thompson, who sold it to George E. Howland to make way for a handsome storeroom. The first hotel in the township was kept in Decatur in a log cabin, where George E. Howland's dwelling stands. This building was built about the year 1804, and the hotel-keeper was Thomas Moore.

About the year 1830, Silas Thomas started a hotel in the village, and did quite a successful business. It was the usual stopping point with farmers in going to Maysville with their produce. Ripley was no market in those days. The public square would be crowded with teams several times during the year, going to market. This was the great thoroughfare to Washington City, and several of our Presidents and Congressmen have stopped here on their way there. The first schoolhouse known in the village was a log one, but in what year it was built and who taught is not known. Decatur contains two stores, two blacksmith shops, one woolen factory, one carpenter and wagon-maker shop, one hotel, one saddlery and harness-making shop, three churches, one schoolhouse, one paint shop, one butcher shop.

The Postmasters of Decatur since 1830 have been Silas Thomas, Wesley Pierce, Benjamin Eckman, Joseph Stevenson, W. W. Salsbury, Joseph Stevenson, James Snedaker and Eliza Snedaker. In 1841, a large carding and fulling mill was operated in Decatur by John Fearis. It burned down during the winter of 1846-47, and soon after a large woolen manufactory was erected by the citizens in this community and carried on until within several years. Jacob Zerker formerly owned and operated a carding-mill near Decatur. The village was once a station on the Underground Railway, and many negroes were here assisted onward on their way to freedom.

The Decatur business directory for 1882 is: John Sheeler, butcher; J. S. Smith, saddler; Dr. J. W. Frisler, physician; D. B. Hatfield, teacher; W. Scott Stevenson, salesman; H. N. Wallace, St. Cloud Hotel; H. G. West, farmer; G. W. Smith, painter; John M. Thompson, insurance agent; William Pittinger, carpenter; John D. Gordon, boot and shoe maker; John Sowers, cooper; Rebecca Campbell, milliner; J. P. & J. W. Thompson, blacksmiths; John Stevenson, Justice of the Peace; George Pittinger, carpenter; W. E. Moore, teacher; John Vanners, broker; Samuel Montgomery, carpenter; Joseph Kerr, Justice of the Peace; John Kirkpatrick, carpenter and wagon maker; Gen. Williams, blacksmith; R. J. Smith, harness-maker; Joseph Gayley, carpenter; John Wilson, barber; Miss Sallie Henderson, dress-maker; L. O. Depty, minister; Joseph Walters, brick and stone mason; William Emrick, grocer and confectioner; Miss Eliza Snedaker, Postmistress; William R. Snedaker, Assistant Postmaster; S. W. Evans, dealer in general merchandise; George E. Howland, dry goods, boots and shoes, hats, caps and hardware.

SURNAME INDEX

ABBOT, 425
ABBOTT, 285 380 381 384 416 532 539 540 546 551 585 601 614
ABERNATHY, 486
ABERS, 432
ABRAMS, 512
ACCOLA, 469
ACKLIN, 514
ACLES, 474
ADAMS, 312 316 344 346 395 481 482 512 553 579 633 689
ADAMSON, 702
ADDENBROOK, 687
ADKINS, 432 434 435 450 481
AERL, 589
ALEXANDER, 295 366 481 486 562 564 570 576 579 580 583 585 586 590 592 593 605 658 670 700
ALLEN, 346 356 361-363 365 392 393 396 401 404 410 421 425 440 445 469 481 484 490 520 521 535 545 556 559 561-563 565 572 573 604 613 631 701
ALLISON, 251 276 511 682
ALLMANN, 678
ALLOUEZ, 318
ALTIC, 500
AMMEN, 339 340 356 362 393 395 400 423 425 450
AMOS, 684
AMPUDIA, 350 351
AMSTETT, 469
ANDERSON, 241 251 281 292 340 363 449 453 470 472 474 479 496 499 501 505 512 513 550 564 615 631 632 640 656

ANDERSON (continued)
663 669 670 677 679 684 685 687-689 692
ANTHONY, 303 485
APPLEGATE, 341 374 482 489 559 564 565 572 606 632 634 640
ARBUCKLE, 472
ARCHER, 562 643 645
ARK, 254
ARMSTRONG, 249 404 409 410 431 432 436 453 454 526 541 563 676 700
ARN, 406 534 541 544 549 552 553
ARNBY, 333
ARNOLD, 533 687
ARTHUR, 687
ARZENO, 405 406
ASH, 254
ASHBAUGH, 421
ASHBURN, 363
ASHENHURST, 612
ASHTON, 282 480-482 484 486 489
ATHERTON, 513 515
ATKINS, 479 480 491 492 653
ATWOOD, 416 453 624 631 639
AULTMAN, 700
AULTZ, 543
AUSTIN, 513 698
AYRES, 375 500
BACHMANN, 658 659
BAGBY, 526
BAGLEY, 384
BAHAN, 651
BAHL, 544

BAILEY, 303 315 361 392 401 404 410 512 513
BAIRD, 301 365 415 416 424 435 449 451-453 593 601-604 609 613 614-616 619 702
BAKER, 291 386 389 392 401-404 406 409 420 424 432 436 466 576 583 691 700
BALDWIN, 365 501 506
BALL, 532 541-543 545 549 551 602 613 619 620 656 671 672
BALLARD, 322 479 482 484 492
BALLEIN, 672 678
BAMBACH, 434 453 454
BAMBER, 318 321 322 485
BARBER, 671
BARBOUR, 485
BARE, 362 669 671 674 675 679
BARKER, 362 473
BARNES, 322 380 403 486 534 543 640 701
BARNETT, 400
BARNEY, 301 313 396
BARNGROOVER, 631 640
BARNGROVER, 546
BARNUM, 445 473
BARR, 233 234 292 404 460 462 463 465 470 498 634
BARRER, 433
BARRERE, 317 364 366 431 440
BARRETT, 281 603 604 611
BARROTT, 473
BARRY, 491 492 634
BARTHOLEMEW, 454
BARTHOLOMEW, 605 656
BARTLETT, 382 441 450
BARTLEY, 316 440 454 463
BASCOM, 421 466 500 509
BASHFORD, 465
BASSET, 585
BASSETT, 613
BATES, 274
BAUER, 433 436 454 540 544 549 552 553 573
BAULINE, 679
BAUM, 459 461
BAUMGARTEN, 333
BAVIS, 564 570
BAVOUSET, 492

BAWER, 672
BAXTER, 613
BAYHAM, 653
BAYLES, 404
BAYLESS, 281 700
BAYLEY, 701
BAYNE, 414 441 611 616
BEACH, 306
BEARCE, 303 314 699
BEARD, 581 652
BEASLEY, 241-244 250 281 285 303 359 360 362-364 413 430 435 439 446 449 495 505 510 513 516 612 613 678 694 695 701 703
BEASLY, 251 505 621
BEATTY, 561
BEBB, 316 440 553
BECHAM, 560
BECK, 282 303 314 470 473 503 562 667 670 678-680
BECKCR, 405
BECKER, 426 436 453 454
BECKWITH, 651
BEECH, 474
BEEM, 606
BEHEYMER, 593
BELCHAMBERS, 454
BELL, 416 439 440 446 453 589 593 668-670 672 676-678 682 701
BELLI, 281
BELLINGER, 331
BELTZ, 481 482
BENHAM, 482
BENINGTON, 614
BENNA, 432
BENNER, 600 601 620
BENNETT, 361 513 563
BENNINGTON, 432 433 435 436 441 446 656
BENNNINGTON, 451
BENTLEY, 401
BENTON, 349
BENUA, 453
BERA, 430
BERGER, 332 485
BERKELEY, 279
BERRY, 374 375 381 536 540 552 553 604
BERT, 631

SURNAME INDEX.

BERWANGER, 485
BERZ, 469
BESSIE, 585
BETZER, 473
BEVANS, 485
BEVERAGE, 500
BEVERIDGE, 657 658
BEYERSDOERFER, 453 454
BICKING, 235
BIEHM, 669
BIEHN, 237 362 363 394 404 405 409 426 435 454 536 539 544 671 675
BIER, 552 553
BIERCE, 403
BIERY, 533 544 549
BIGELOW, 430
BIGGER, 316 553
BILEW, 473
BINGAMON, 406 626 629 631-633 636 639 640 644 645 677
BINGHAM, 402
BINGMAN, 669
BIRNGAMMON, 625
BISHFORTH, 605
BISHOP, 440 480 482 484 486 490 492 553 661 690 691 701
BISSELL, 425
BIVANS, 492 507 632 639 642
BLACK, 255 362 486 589 610 651 684
BLACKBURN, 341 473 512 700
BLAIR, 361 362 364 365 392 396 402 404-406 409 410 436 473 500 502 521 523 525 530 555 556 561 562 573 602 613 616 619 631-634 639 640 671 699
BLANCHARD, 404
BLATTER, 436 454
BLOCK, 251
BLOOM, 434 454
BLOOMHUFF, 700
BLYTHE, 474
BOATMAN, 586
BOBST, 333
BOCKER, 331 333
BODENER, 454
BODKIN, 563
BODMER, 454
BODMIR, 439
BOEHM, 474

BOERSTLER, 334 665 686
BOGGESS, 364 484
BOGGS, 613
BOHL, 544 545 549 553 672
BOHRER, 536 541 544-546 549 552 616 687
BOLANDER, 573
BOLE, 402
BOLENDER, 456 460 461 463 465 469 470 473
BOLER, 565
BOLES, 382 474
BOLTIN, 563
BOLTON, 613
BONAVILLE, 460
BONNER, 669
BONWELL, 384 463
BOOKER, 624 626
BOOKMEYER, 492
BOOKMYER, 490
BOOKWALTER, 440 553 701
BOONE, 226 230 233 249 318 500 505 506
BOOTHBY, 281 626 629 631 632
BOOTS, 465
BOOZE, 499
BORDEN, 580 584 585
BORING, 400
BORLANDO, 324
BORRIS, 582
BOSLEY, 474
BOSS, 424 610
BOSTWICK, 615
BOTETOURT, 279
BOTTS, 513
BOUDE, 282 405 461 469 470
BOULGER, 324 330
BOULLE, 606
BOVIS, 639
BOWE, 330 492
BOWEN, 425 580
BOWER, 362 392 403 612 615
BOWERS, 415 604
BOWLER, 525
BOWMAN, 295 384 513
BOWSMAN, 682
BOWYER, 682 688
BOYD, 288 340 404 419 454 471 561 562 571 640 672 673 684 685 687 688 691

BOYER, 563
BOYLE, 321 322 361 471 480 481 485 490 492
BRACELIN, 690
BRACKENRIDGE, 289
BRADBERRY, 519
BRADFORD, 450 506 512 514-516 580 681
BRADLEY, 482 579 592
BRADY, 341 362 375 384 405 532 536 539 542 543 551 619 655-660 662
BRANDT, 473
BRANNAN, 322
BRANNEN, 572 625 630 639
BRANNON, 572 667
BRATTEN, 581
BRATTON, 611 646 667 669
BRAUN, 436 454 544 545
BREASON, 322
BRECKENRIDGE, 362 363 575 576 579-583 589 681
BRECKINRIDGE, 440 586
BRESLIN, 321
BRIANT, 362
BRICKER, 269 515
BRIGGS, 670
BRINK, 332
BRISBOIS, 331
BRITTINGHAM, 513 515
BRITTON, 687
BROADHURST, 433
BROCK, 626
BROCKAWY, 425
BROCKHAUS, 405
BROCKWAY, 425 610
BROOKBANK, 473 474
BROOKOVER, 495 506 513 515
BROOKS, 405 481 512 513 521 522 525 526 561 564 565 566 600 649 651
BROSE, 410
BROUGH, 317 440 566
BROUSE, 580
BROWER, 563
BROWN, 280 281 303 309 316 318 341 354 362 372 386 399 400 402 409 421 422 479 481 486 500 512 513 530 532 539-541 550 551 559 562-565 570-573 579 582 592 594 601 602 609 615 619

BROWN (continued)
620 624 626 631 634 639 658 663 689 690 702
BRUCE, 580
BRUEN, 687
BRUMMER, 333
BRUNNER, 394 404-406 409 473
BRUNSON, 361
BRUSH, 561
BRUTE, 323
BRYAN, 364 480 481 490
BRYANT, 529
BUCHANAN, 364 410 440 454 562 593
BUCHANNAN, 589
BUCHANON, 281
BUCHER, 466
BUCK, 512
BUCKHANNON, 276
BUCKNER, 303 403 466 470
BUFORD, 682 686
BULGER, 422 453
BULL, 482
BUNNER, 531-533 550 551 553
BUNYON, 683
BURBAGE, 500 702
BURDSALL, 689 690
BURGER, 362
BURGESS, 541 673
BURGETT, 380 405
BURKE, 281 466
BURNET, 283 299 300
BURNETT, 513 701
BURNHAM, 479-481 486
BURNS, 423 576 614 656
BURR, 403
BURRIS, 579 589 594
BURT, 392 430 435
BURTON, 474 623 624
BUSEY, 492
BUTLAR, 586
BUTLER, 220 326 350 351 450 676
BUTT, 290 356 361 395 396 409 416 419 422 614 615 632 689
BUTTS, 361 450 474 678
BUZBY, 631
BYERSDOELFER, 433
BYERSDOLFER, 433
BYRD, 276 674 693

SURNAME INDEX.

BYRNE, 404
CABEL, 475
CADWELL, 283
CAHALL, 462 463 473 474 481
CAHILL, 324
CALAHAN, 615
CALDUWARD, 500
CALDWELL, 431 433 453 702
CALHOON, 563
CALLAHAN, 646 653
CALLENDER, 563
CALVIN, 233 274 376 379 665 667 669 671 677 678
CAMPBELL, 280 284 292 302 303 309 310 312 314 316 341 349 352 354 355 361-364 366 389 392 396 401-403 405 413 415 416 423-425 430 435 436 439 451 453 454 485 491 492 495 496 501 512-514 545 551-553 564 601 606 619 623 632 640 646 655-659 663 679-681 701 703
CANARY, 461 462 470
CANFIELD, 434
CANN, 470 474
CANOLY, 679
CAPPE, 545
CARBERRY, 405 535 536
CARBERY, 532 536 540 546 551
CARBOY, 490 491 492
CARD, 505
CAREY, 340 363 432 433 454 576 579 580 582 583 585 586 590-593
CARNAHAN, 423
CARPENTER, 501 506 509 512-514 562
CARR, 415 432 433 441 450 516 561 566 619 639 701
CARRIER, 484
CARRIGAN, 362 513
CARROLL, 513
CARTER, 569 572 573 671
CARTWRIGHT, 271
CARYON, 254
CASE, 500 512 513
CASKEY, 611
CASS, 334 349 440
CASSETT, 466
CASTER, 434
CATON, 403

CAUFFMAN, 421
CHAFFIN, 653
CHALFANT, 687
CHAMBERLAIN, 481
CHAMBERS, 473 474 652
CHAMPION, 436
CHAMPLAIN, 318
CHANEY, 490 491
CHANNEL, 653
CHAPMAN, 356 362 364 385 433 465 466 473 521 606 671
CHARLES, 281
CHASE, 317 424 440 452 674
CHATFIELD, 324
CHATTERTON, 564 570
CHEESMAN, 515
CHENEWORTH, 645
CHENOWETH, 674
CHEVALIER, 331
CHEYMOL, 322 323 325 327 333
CHINNETH, 384
CHURCH, 430 522 562 569
CLAMES, 515
CLARK, 226 229 230 251 281 362 365 392 401 439 456 459 466 469-471 482 490 491 500 551 576 585 613 615 656 676 688 689
CLARKE, 245 365 366
CLAY, 261 312 316 360 421 520 553 659
CLAYPOOL, 235 476 479-486 489 490
CLAYTON, 489 675
CLEMENS, 422 626
CLEMENTS, 241
CLEVELAND, 474
CLIFT, 515
CLIFTON, 601 605 619
CLINE, 676
CLINTON, 360 422
CLUFF, 592
CLUNDT, 473
COALE, 616
COAN, 614
COATES, 421
COBB, 685
COBURN, 252 430
COBWALLIS, 625
COCHRAN, 277 281 289 338 364 365 384 405 409 433 435 439 453 454 465 466

COCHRAN (continued)
  472 474 499 502 503 505 506 511 513 560
COCKERILL, 341 366 433 434
COCKRILL, 454
COFFMAN, 465
COGGSWELL, 454
COLAHAN, 613
COLE, 466 514 687
COLEMAN, 450 681 689
COLLAHAN, 469
COLLETT, 300 363 416 606
COLLINS, 295 363 415 416 420 421 430 436 441 442 454 524 611 616 620 621 683 688 689
COLTER, 415
COLTHAR, 281 521 522 555 564 566 573
COLVIN, 375 379 380
COMMONS, 459
CONKLIN, 482 485 486 690
CONKLING, 425
CONLEY, 454 676
CONLON, 324
CONN, 276 409 450 601 602 618-621
CONNALLY, 486 492
CONNELL, 642 646
CONNER, 400 692
CONNOR, 687
CONOVER, 652 653 692
CONRARD, 491
CONVER, 653
COOK, 284 285 396 399 450 611 614 632 651
COOKE, 616
COOLE, 613
COONS, 425
COOPER, 495 500 502 505 615 690
COPE, 691
COPPLE, 699 701
CORBOY, 672
CORD, 495
CORDIE, 645
CORE, 480 484
CORMICK, 415
CORNACK, 416
CORNELIUS, 580
CORNELL, 471 639 668 676
CORNSTALK, 230

CORNWALLIS, 460 625 691
COROTHERS, 459
CORRUTHERS, 413
CORWIN, 316 344 346 349 520
COSLETT, 454 610
COTTERAL, 281
COTTERILL, 545 631 633 634 640
COTTON, 499
COUDREY, 570
COULTER, 576 684
COURTNEY, 303
COURTS, 535 552 631 632
COUTHER, 640
COVALT, 479 481 485 486 491
COVERT, 500
COWAN, 576 580 583 589 590 678
COWDREY, 561 563 564 572 573
COWEN, 363
COX, 317 440 616 656 657 702
COXET, 500
CRAB, 375
CRABB, 499
CRABTREE, 513
CRADIT, 425 426 452 454
CRAIG, 373 640
CRANE, 363 454 515
CRANMER, 481 485 486 489 490
CRAWFORD, 312 362 392 406 410 450 454 575 687
CRAYTON, 600
CREAGER, 687
CREAMER, 687
CRECKBAUM, 433
CREDIT, 616
CREEKBAUM, 341 421 426 433 434 452 454
CREIGHEAD, 633
CREST, 616
CREW, 485 489
CRISWELL, 433 453
CRONE, 322
CROOKS, 526
CROPPER, 474 602 604
CROSBY, 449 450 587
CROSS, 576 580 583 590 591 679
CROSSON, 322
CROUCH, 406 409
CROZIER, 436

CRUIKENCAMP, 332
CRUM, 585
CRUSAN, 499
CRUTE, 410 620 655 656 662
CULTER, 434 435 439 454 603 612 613 616 619 620
CUMBERLAND, 383 592 667 670 671
CUMING, 259
CUNNINGHAM, 496 505 513
CURLESS, 486
CURLISS, 481 482
CURRAN, 621
CURRY, 359 375 400 464 466 480 484 671 687 692
CURTIS, 540
CURTISS, 515
CUSHING, 491
CUSS, 589
CUSTER, 658
CUTTER, 655
DABLON, 318
DAHL, 544
DALE, 434 454
DALY, 324 326 329 330
DANBERRY, 691
DANIELS, 496 499 501 502
DARAH, 613
DARLING, 575
DARLINGTON, 283 363 513
DART, 485
DAUGHERTY, 379 384 465 473 585 614 662 689
DAULTON, 513
DAUM, 466 473
DAVIDSON, 254 271 381 404 416 462 471 513 520 570 616 624 626 631 646 655 656 701 702
DAVIES, 672
DAVIS, 244 300 336 359 362 365 374-376 384 392 403 469 480 484 485 489 499 509 514 523 545 551 552 585 586 592 599 616 620 657 658 662 663 667 669 671 679 687 691
DAVISON, 514
DAVY, 626
DAWLEY, 620
DAWSON, 431 450 465 549 632 662 690

DAY, 281 379 474 543 559 562 570-573 616 619 644-646 650 651 653 668-670 674 676 677 683 684 687 688
DEAN, 473 522 529 565 573 652
DEBOLT, 341 432 433
DEDRICK, 653
DEIHL, 672
DELAMATER, 402
DELANEY, 660
DELONG, 432
DEMARIS, 580
DEMERIS, 580
DEMITT, 592
DENMAN, 364
DENNEY, 579
DENNING, 250 281
DENNIS, 501 515 536 546 649
DENNISON, 317 336 440
DENNISTON, 401
DENNY, 399 580 585
DENZELMAN, 433
DEPTUTY, 700
DEPTY, 703
DEPUGH, 450
DEQUELEN, 323
DEROUGH, 375
DERRICKSON, 611
DERRIL, 565
DERROUGH, 396
DERRY, 521 525
DERSTINE, 450
DEVORE, 301 309 310 315 340 361 365 392 401 406 413 419 422 424 450 453 465 474 520 529 543 620 700 701
DEY, 667 669 670 677
DIBALL, 303
DIBOLL, 670
DICKENS, 415
DICKEY, 253 366 673
DILLEN, 362 406 486 492
DILLINGER, 702
DILLMAN, 473 474
DILLON, 384 585 613
DIMMETT, 466
DISNEY, 351
DITTO, 362 481 482 485
DITTOE, 486

DIXON, 310 412 421 431-433 439 451 453 616 657 658 699
DOANE, 366
DOBBENS, 402
DOBBINS, 314 384 502 673 680 686 689
DOBBS, 682
DOD, 683
DODDS, 430 512
DOEPKA, 633
DONALDSON, 385 393 403 609 655 656 661
DONALSON, 283
DONLEY, 554 555 563 564 570 653
DOOLY, 563
DOREN, 399
DORMAN, 632
DORSEY, 392
DOTY, 430 469 470 474 543 640
DOUDNEY, 529
DOUGHERTY, 254 420 572
DOUGHTY, 479 482 563
DOUGLASS, 440
DOW, 516
DOWDNEY, 365 409
DOWERS, 606
DOWNEY, 392
DOWNING, 233 454 474
DRAGOO, 252 274 412 512 694
DRAKE, 234 239 266 341 361 465 473 480 484 549 601 602 606 611 616
DRAPER, 702
DRENNAN, 512
DRENNIN, 515
DREUILLETTES, 318
DRIVER, 652
DRUM, 555
DRYDEN, 341
DUDLEY, 409 465
DUFFEE, 423
DUFFEY, 593
DUFFY, 395 396
DUGAN, 362 380 381 469-474 699
DUKE, 252 340 688
DULY, 525
DUNCAMON, 632
DUNCAN, 679
DUNCANSON, 522 555 564 566

DUNHAM, 255 341 361 365 379 392 404 450 464 480 482 484 486 489 490 644 678
DUNLAP, 292 316 354 413 420 435 451 613 700
DUNLAVY, 262 271 273 274 283 286 299 363 413 414 609
DUNN, 404 409 445 530 532 534 536 540 541 544 545 550-553 560 565 572 573 579 580 584 601 619 624 630 639 644 659 663 667-672 676 679 680
DUNSETH, 502
DURGAW, 422
DUTTON, 323 521 526
DYE, 379 384 474 543
DYER, 378 561 573
EARHART, 425 539 556 563-565 569 571 572 650 684 685 688 694
EARHEART, 555
EARLEY, 500 505 513
EARLY, 434 453 470 502 505 634
EASTBURN, 281
EASTERBY, 450
EASTMAN, 563
EASTON, 436
EBENSTEINER, 331
ECKMAN, 703
EDENFIELD, 485
EDGAR, 613
EDGINGTON, 250 576 579-581 583 589 590 592 593 662
EDGINTON, 491
EDIE, 281 580
EDMISTON, 700
EDMONDSON, 563
EDWARDS, 284 334 364 395 405 423 454 495 496 514 601-603 616 619 620 658 695 702
EGBERT, 290 340 361 386 389 403
EHRENFELS, 473
EICHELBERGER, 482
EICHLER, 485 492
ELDER, 333 551
ELDRIDGE, 482
ELEFRITZ, 702
ELLIOT, 489
ELLIOTT, 585 646

SURNAME INDEX.

ELLIS, 254 260 281 290 341 361 362 364 371 372 381 400 402 405 415 454 465 470 472-474 484 495 506 513-516 529 530 535 541 553 616 619 644 646 653
ELLISON, 250 251 281 301 361 363-366
ELLSBERRY, 303 404 405 529 619 630-634 636 641 642
ELLSBURY, 633 639
ELSBERRY, 361
ELSCHLAGER, 530 535 536 552 553
EMBREE, 699
EMERICK, 702
EMERSON, 249
EMERY, 430 459
EMESTON, 613
EMMONS, 564
EMRICK, 703
EMRIE, 366
ENIS, 515
EPPENSTEINER, 510
ERNST, 331 332 533 669
ERRETT, 402
ERVIN, 425 672 679
ERWIN, 551 552 576 586 593 594
ESKRIDGE, 669 676
ESPEY, 632 634
ESPY, 264 291 341 414 419 446
ESTEL, 668 669 676 678
EUBANKS, 479 481 502
EUEL, 563
EUVARD, 585
EVANS, 254 292 340 361-363 365 367 376 382 383 394 399 400 402-404 406 410 416 422 426 430 436 446 450-453 458 465 470 493 496 499-503 505 506 511-513 515 516 532 551 563 571 601-603 606 609 612 613 615 616 619 655-659 662 670-672 695 699 703
EVERHART, 466 646 683 685 687
EVESLAGE, 454
EWAN, 593
EWICK, 620 621
EWING, 346 440 490 526 669 670 676 677 701
EWINGS, 500
EYLER, 579 580 585 586 593 656-659
FABIAN, 332 333
FAGINS, 379

FAHNERT, 453
FANCHER, 605 615
FANCHON, 685
FARRIS, 699
FAUL, 544 549 553
FEAGINS, 372-375
FEARING, 265
FEARIS, 703
FEE, 310 361 364 365 393 404 405 409 466 472 484 502 563 632 636 639 641 642 646 674 689
FEEBY, 605
FEELEY, 660
FEIK, 669
FEIKE, 544 669 679
FENNIN, 602
FENTON, 576 585 586 661
FENWICK, 321 323
FERDINAND, 333 544 545
FERENO, 473
FERGASON, 700
FERGUSON, 401 486 636
FERRIER, 362 392 404
FERRIS, 383 613
FETTERMAN, 460
FICHTER, 331
FIDDLER, 700
FIELD, 593 613 700
FIELDS, 450 551 631 653
FILLMORE, 440
FINDLAY, 299 316
FINDLEY, 524
FINLEY, 218 253 295 361 363 384 401 421 423 466 483 645 674
FINNIN, 331
FISCUS, 520 560 561 563 571 572 632 633 640 644 651 653 658
FISHBACH, 466
FISHBACK, 300 315 345 363
FISHER, 364 365 433 454 620 631 694 700-702
FITCH, 268 365 412 421 433 454 474
FITE, 362 400 405 409 474 525 526 529 624 625 630-633 635
FITZGERALD, 364
FITZPATRICK, 492
FLAUGHER, 365 387 412 431 499 505 513 515 540

FLEIG, 331 416 433 436 454
FLEMING, 535 677
FLEMMING, 512
FLEY, 404
FLICK, 521 523 529
FLOOD, 563
FLORAL, 460
FLORER, 375
FLOWERS, 551
FOOR, 376 384 520
FOOS, 356 365
FOOT, 423
FOOTE, 484
FORBES, 254
FORCYTH, 631
FORD, 316 440 524
FORE, 309
FORKER, 690
FORSINGER, 433
FORSTER, 571
FORSYTH, 380
FORSYTHE, 380 415 551 631
FORTHOFFER, 333 552
FOSTER, 341 362 440 469 482 553 556 571 609 694 701
FOULK, 631
FOWLER, 341 392 550 609 616 619 620
FOX, 241 274 403 450 479-482 485 490 492 569 631 633 634 639 655
FRALEICH, 474
FRAME, 513
FRANCIS, 602 604 609 612 613 655-657 659 661 662
FRANK, 433 454
FRAZE, 535
FRAZEE, 281 521 522 555 566 605 687
FRAZIER, 314 383 425 614 644
FREBIS, 454
FREDERICK, 454
FREE, 691
FREMONT, 440
FRETZ, 473
FRIDLEY, 619
FRIEDLEY, 431
FRIEDMAN, 433
FRIERSON, 592
FRIERUN, 579
FRISLER, 703

FRITT, 486
FRITTS, 659
FRITZ, 434 481 489
FROST, 379 385 441
FRY, 562 569 571 654
FRYAR, 496 511 512
FRYMAN, 652
FUCHS, 331 333
FUENFGELD, 473
FULK, 687
FULLER, 606 611 615
FULTON, 362 431 442 451 453 454 506 509 514
FUNK, 702
FYFFE, 335 340 363 399 474
GABBERDENN, 332
GABET, 485
GABLER, 454
GACON, 322 323 325 333
GADDIS, 416 421 425 426 431-435 451 454 670 700
GAINES, 505
GALBRAITH, 512
GALBREATH, 393 446 702
GALLAGHER, 486
GALLUP, 301
GAMBLE, 521
GAME, 502
GAMES, 365 496 502 511-513 516
GANTZ, 663
GARDNER, 256 295 343 352 353 354 401 420 464 465 473 474 503 534 575 585 620 650 700 701
GAREAU, 318
GARFIELD, 317 441 516 520 553 701
GARNER, 239
GAROUTTE, 384 502 504
GARRAUTTE, 503
GARRON, 645 651
GASS, 402
GATCH, 281 283 295
GATES, 404 560
GATTS, 551 630-632 634 640 642
GAYLEY, 703
GEARTON, 481
GEDDIS, 512
GEESLIN, 696 701
GEIGER, 454

SURNAME INDEX.

GENNINGS, 560
GERHARDT, 549
GERMAN, 392
GERMANN, 413
GERTH, 433
GEYER, 331-333
GIBLER, 676
GIBSON, 260 500 502 520 626 630-632 639 700
GIDDINGS, 352
GILBERT, 433 494 496 500 502 505 506 511 515 516 593
GILBREATH, 409
GILFILLEN, 663
GILLELAND, 670
GILLET, 529
GILLILAND, 314 361 383 413 414 424 425 433 446 449 453 454 501 611 666 672 673 679
GILLMORE, 469
GILLUM, 645
GILMAN, 551
GILMER, 309
GILMORE, 673
GIST, 520 586 591 592
GLASCOCK, 500 631
GLASSCOCK, 502 512 513
GLAZE, 309 310 361 393 600 601 609 614 616 619 653 662
GLENDENING, 655 660 661
GLENDENNING, 613
GLENN, 432
GLIDDON, 424
GLOVER, 364 651 652
GOFF, 521 702
GOFORTH, 300
GOLDSBURY, 579
GOLDTRAP, 235
GOLL, 565
GOOD, 284
GOODEN, 632 640
GOODENOW, 363
GOODIN, 281 333
GOODWIN, 500
GORDON, 341 394 399 405 425 430 530 533 534 550 640 642 703
GOSSARD, 563 613
GOTHERMAN, 631
GOUDEY, 563
GOULD, 402 469 520 521
GRAHAM, 463 469 665 667 670 672 673 675 676
GRANGE, 550
GRANGER, 480 484-486 489 490
GRANT, 290 313 317 335 393 394 400 404 409 425 441 534 541 668 669 676
GRANTHAM, 431
GRAY, 495 512 513 515 653 662
GRAYBILL, 384
GRAYSON, 422
GREATHOUSE, 314 655 656 659 661
GREELEY, 317 441
GREEN, 403 452 563 611 619 690 700
GREENE, 453 454
GREENHOW, 452-454
GREGG, 452 453 563 613 656 700
GREGORY, 669-672 677
GREINER, 331
GRIER, 512
GRIERSON, 505 513 515 516
GRIFFIN, 403 613
GRIFFITH, 499 505 509 513 645 671 674 690
GRIM, 433 434 453 454
GRIMES, 276 513 514 695
GRISHAM, 653
GRISSOM, 677
GRISWOLD, 611
GROGAN, 533 551
GROPPEMBACHER, 436
GROPPENBACHER, 433 453
GROSS, 544 545 549
GUE, 432
GUNNER, 658
GUNNISON, 669 677
GUNSAULUS, 494 500
GUTHRIE, 403 465 516 612 674
GUTRIDGE, 576 580 583
GUY, 450
GUYLEY, 702
GWINNER, 544
HAAS, 534 545
HACKELBANDER, 491
HACKLEBENDER, 482
HADLEY, 481 482 486
HAFER, 434

HAGINS, 545
HAINES, 335 594
HAIR, 687 690
HALFHILL, 474
HALL, 282 380 389 402 485 492 513 521
HALLAM, 552 670
HALLSTED, 481 482 484-486 489 490
HALPIN, 322 484
HALSTEAD, 480
HAMER, 244 286 290 301 312 313 315 335 343-346 349-352 364 366 389 392-395 399-401 404 460 529 541
HAMILTON, 240 312 379 456 459 470 501 506 591 668 669 671 674 676
HANCOCK, 317 441 461 463 516 520 553 555 560 569 570 573 701
HANDMAN, 544 545
HANK, 474
HANKINS, 482 484 486
HANNA, 631 634
HANNAH, 341 394 406 563
HANSELMAN, 536 544 551-553
HANSTEIN, 434
HARBAUGH, 690
HARDEN, 435
HARDESTY, 414 421
HARDIN, 421 436
HARDING, 512 513
HARE, 341 513 579 580 585 589 593 613 643 645 653
HARLAN, 365 423 689
HARLOW, 606
HARMAR, 222 223 230 249 250
HARMER, 479 481
HARMON, 341 406
HAROVER, 513
HARPER, 533 660
HARRINGTON, 616
HARRIS, 489 533 535 542 546 605 619 644
HARRISON, 220 222 224 316 341 355 399 441 453 469 474 499 500 585 659
HART, 251 481 482 512
HARTMAN, 479 492
HARTSELL, 454
HARVIE, 681 684
HASLAM, 500
HASLEM, 402
HATFIELD, 619 620 694 695 700-703

HATHAWAY, 701
HATTON, 690
HAUCK, 544 549 552
HAUDMAN, 546
HAUSH, 499
HAVEN, 654
HAWK, 384 499 504
HAWKINS, 422
HAWKMAN, 653
HAYES, 352 399 440 441 553 616 621 669 701
HAYNES, 496 512 660
HAYS, 336 341 362 393 532 534 536 541 551 639 653 671 678 685
HAYWARD, 684
HEAD, 563 700
HEADE, 613
HEALION, 651
HEATHERLY, 576
HEATON, 515 543 551 580 590 593 609 633
HEDGES, 450 482
HEDRICK, 601 602 620
HEINDRICKS, 690
HEISLER, 384
HEISS, 333
HEIZER, 376 381 459 473
HELBLING, 331 332 362 398 409 454
HELD, 466
HELM, 513-515 688
HELMET, 450
HELMS, 505 583
HEMING, 555
HEMPHILL, 435 441 442 451 470
HEMPLETON, 585
HENDERHAND, 512
HENDERSON, 422 425 604 616 656 657 658 659 671 702 703
HENDRIXSON, 541 546 550 552 553 631 632
HENGES, 544 545
HENGHOLD, 333
HENING, 631
HENISE, 474
HENNEPIN, 318
HENNING, 409 564 570
HENRY, 254 415 604 612 613 615 702
HENSEL, 432 439 453

SURNAME INDEX.

HENSLEY, 431-433
HERBERT, 303
HERRON, 462 514 550
HERSY, 621
HERZOG, 331 333 431-433
HESLER, 690
HETERICK, 303 361
HEWITT, 540 550 551 614 687
HICKEMBOTTOM, 533
HICKEY, 684
HICKS, 380 470 474 593 644
HICKSON, 506
HIENCHE, 594
HIETT, 494 496 499 500 502 503 505 506 509 512
HIGBY, 402
HIGGINS, 276 281 301 336 340 341 344 361-365 392 393 404-406 409 452 460 461 463 464 466 469-472 486 500 513 551 560-563 565 566 571 572 700
HIGINBOTHAM, 656 668 676
HILDRETH, 219
HILER, 631 632
HILES, 562 683
HILL, 321 384 404 513 520 580 596 631 653 660 682 690
HILLIGOSS, 630-632 636
HILLING, 593
HILLS, 634
HILMAN, 383
HILTON, 492
HINDMAN, 432 453 669 676
HINEMAN, 665
HINES, 689 690
HIRONS, 654
HITE, 473 647 671 672
HITESMAN, 640
HITZLER, 613
HOBOKEN, 697
HOBSON, 482 595
HOCKETT, 453
HODAPP, 433
HODGES, 514
HODGSON, 652
HODKINS, 473 474 603
HOEHN, 406
HOGE, 688
HOGLES, 676

HOLDEN, 472
HOLEMAN, 684 687
HOLLOWAY, 631-633
HOLMAN, 521
HOLMES, 382 534 556 561 580 687 700
HOLTEN, 562 626
HOLTON, 701
HONAKER, 526
HOOD, 566
HOOK, 430 431 459 462 473 502 505 512 544 619 621
HOOVER, 474
HOPKINS, 340 402 413 415 416 609 641
HORD, 422
HORN, 392 419 474
HORNE, 381
HORTON, 450
HOSS, 462 463 555 564 569 573 631 669
HOUGH, 433 669
HOULSTON, 690
HOUSE, 513
HOUSH, 424 496 505 511 513
HOWARD, 255 335 362 365 366 415 432 433 441 499-501 513 602 700 702
HOWE, 231 235 359
HOWLAND, 513 606 609 612 619 695 702 703
HOYT, 435
HUBBARD, 430 431
HUBBERT, 512
HUDSON, 314 481 592
HUEY, 379
HUFF, 676
HUGGINS, 380 646 651 666 670 679
HUGHES, 322 416 422 425 433 434 453 454 576 652 701 702
HUGHEY, 601 616 702
HUGHS, 256 560 562 700
HULL, 476 479 542 605 626 695
HUMPHREYS, 361 362 425 435
HUMPHRIES, 415 416 430
HUNSER, 453
HUNT, 282 556
HUNTER, 281 362 543 544 665
HUNTINGTON, 493
HUNTLEY, 481
HURIN, 500 512
HURLEY, 404

HURON, 431
HURST, 394 676
HUSTON, 481
HUTCHINSON, 235 465 486 495
HUTCHISON, 501 513
IDDINGS, 663
INDIAN, Battise 234 Black Hoof 224 Black Snake 234 Blue Jacket 224 Chinskau 234 Crane 224 Little Turtle 221 224 Sinnamatha 234 Tarhe 224 Tecumseh 222 232 234 235 Wolf 234
INNIS, 382
INSKEEP, 409 543 546 552 612 657 659 660 663
IRETON, 486 690
IRONS, 665
IRVIN, 316 565 571 680 687
IRWIN, 465 572 651 665 692
JACKSON, 312 313 316 344-346 395 409 421 439 454 463 465 489 553 563 606 659 690 691 700
JACOBS, 254 336 361 362 392 409 462 495 512 521 533 550 552 553 564 572 573 602 603 619
JACONET, 333
JACQUEMIN, 492
JAMES, 563 689 691 700
JAMESON, 335
JAMISON, 463 512
JANUARY, 281
JEFFERSON, 312 521
JENKINS, 406 416 424 431 432 439 451 505
JENNINGS, 254 340 362 379 382 384 386 401 403 405 409 470 539 540 653 686
JESTER, 490
JEWETT, 317 440
JINOWAY, 489
JINOWAYS, 479 480 484
JITTLE, 251
JOHNS, 434 450 480 551
JOHNSON, 244 290 363 386 392 396 406 416 431 453 474 564 570 592 602 613 615 619 620 631 645 666 667 670 674 702
JOHNSTON, 244 290 317 335 365 386 389 440
JOLIFF, 610

JOLIFFE, 244
JOLLEY, 341
JOLLIFFE, 315 460
JOLLY, 310 375 415 433 435 609
JONES, 384 401 434 466 473 479 486 513 515 543 555 564 565 569 572 573 620 651 652
JORDAN, 355 529 654 682
JORDON, 380 536
JOSLIN, 465 469
JUDD, 465 474
JUMPER, 512
JUNKINS, 690
JUSTUS, 433 684
KAIN, 281 561 683
KANCHER, 619
KANE, 700
KANTZ, 228 474
KAPP, 434
KATTEIN, 536 541 542 544 546
KAUFMAN, 552
KAUTS, 669
KAUTZ, 309 335 340 341 400 409 473 544 545 549 552 553
KAY, 363 392 401
KEARNEY, 324
KEARNS, 405 406 410
KECK, 700
KEETHLER, 559 562 563 572 573 644-646 649-651 653
KEITH, 302 450
KEITHLER, 362
KELLER, 332 552 679
KELLEY, 451
KELLOGG, 433 451
KELLUM, 526
KELLY, 322 393 431 435 453 481 492 687
KENASTON, 699
KENDAL, 601 602
KENDALL, 364 656 657 689
KENDLE, 602 614-616 619 620
KENNEDY, 470 520-523 526 670 671 676 677 679 700 702
KENNETT, 571 605 616
KENTON, 226 229 230 232-235 249 318 359 373 665 668 669
KEOWLER, 454
KEPHART, 425

SURNAME INDEX.

KER, 260
KERANS, 393
KERR, 241 309 362 365 427 513 611 619 620 629 671 700 702 703
KERWALD, 333
KETTERMAN, 579 580 679
KEYES, 640
KEYS, 633 640 700
KIBLER, 668 678
KIDDER, 403
KIEFFER, 534 542 544
KIEHL, 454
KIFFMEYER, 330
KILGORE, 495 500 501 512
KILPATRICK, 380 382 414 695
KIMBALL, 438 566 623 625 630-632 640 665
KIMBERLY, 572
KIMBLE, 486
KINCADE, 303 581
KINCAID, 365 576 582 668-670 672 676
KINDLE, 579
KING, 301 310 314 316 336 340 341 361 363 380 383 393 396 401 403 405 409 410 416 423 440 453 454 465 619 639 658 674 700
KINKADDEN, 485
KINKADE, 352
KINKAID, 609 613
KINKEAD, 413 549 602
KINNER, 560 566
KINNETT, 653
KINNEY, 446 699
KINZER, 669 671
KIRBY, 682 687 689
KIRK, 671 678
KIRKATRICK, 433
KIRKER, 281 283 363 364 406 435 620
KIRKPATRICK, 379 430 443 454 583 611 702 703
KIRPATRICK, 699
KIRSKADDEN, 481 490
KIRTENDAL, 481
KITE, 470 472
KLAWITTER, 332 333
KLEIN, 332 433 473
KLEINKNECHT, 659
KLINCKER, 474

KLOCKNER, 332
KLOECKNER, 544
KNABE, 556 563
KNIGHT, 430 631 670 672
KNOCHEL, 454
KNOX, 462 605 694
KOBLER, 295
KOMERUS, 485
KOOKIS, 633
KOOT, 434
KOSSUTH, 392
KOUNTZ, 436
KRATZER, 536 541 550 551 643 644 646 650 652
KRESS, 331 333 543 544 549 552 553 672
KRUM, 633
KUGLER, 613
KUNDIG, 321 322
KUPFER, 333
KYLANDER, 521
KYLE, 484
LACK, 500
LACOCK, 254 294
LADENBERGER, 454
LAFABRE, 361 404 409 551 612 613
LAFARRE, 482
LAFAYETTE, 562 625
LAFERRE, 644
LAGUE, 653
LAIN, 656
LAKE, 486 539
LAKIN, 341 466 645 674
LAMB, 462 514
LAMBERT, 281 625 688
LANCASTER, 643 650
LANCE, 665
LANDERBACK, 631
LANDON, 529
LANDRUM, 646 674
LANE, 431 450 480 481 484 489 492 512 514 620 656
LANEY, 585 589 658
LANG, 331 553
LANGDON, 421
LANGSTAFF, 529 555 564 566 570 572 573
LANSFORD, 655
LARIMORE, 471

LASALLE, 318
LATTA, 641
LAUDERBACK, 634 677
LAUGHLAN, 555
LAUGHLIN, 415 564 572 687
LAUTH, 331 332 544 545
LAVORCE, 542
LAWRENCE, 340 465 646
LAWSON, 374 375 385 389 466 522 525 526 542 572
LAWWILL, 405 505 512 513 515
LAYCOCK, 402 405 534 535 550-553 575 578 579 583 605
LEACH, 403
LEAVERTIN, 653
LECARON, 318
LECLERC, 480
LEDOM, 250
LEE, 232 243 274 681
LEECHMAN, 513
LEEDOM, 364 366
LEEDS, 365 396 399 404 405 409
LEGGETT, 446 451-454 616
LEGGITT, 362
LEMING, 374 534
LEMON, 559 688
LEMONS, 434
LENMEN, 489
LEONARD, 282 480-482 484 490 519 521 524 634 635 639 645 684 685 687 691 692
LEPAGE, 515
LERCH, 470 473
LEVENGOOD, 686
LEWCAS, 254
LEWERS, 433 435
LEWIS, 254 314 316 317 363 405 406 416 424 432 433 435 440 453 473 553 560 576 616 619 680
LEWRING, 450
LIGGETT, 292 301 340 380 416 422 426 431-434 436 441 442 450 605 702
LIGGITT, 361
LIGHT, 276 281 364 484 682 688
LILLEY, 606 609 670 677-680
LILLY, 621 676
LIMING, 519-521 524 526 560 566 631
LINCH, 301 361

LINCOLN, 336 440
LINDSAY, 631 640
LINDSEY, 251 343 361 362 403 404 439 465 484 520 521 529 532-536 543-545 550-552 631 632
LINE, 668 676
LINN, 361 362 416 433 434 453 454
LINTON, 514 603
LIST, 535 541 542 545 551-553 671 672
LISTER, 655
LITTLE, 513 520 668
LIVINGOOD, 687
LIVINGSTON, 575 698
LOCKE, 218
LOCKHART, 314 363 611 612 700
LOCKWOOD, 402
LOCUST, 592
LODGE, 395 422
LODWICK, 281
LOGAN, 222 230 243 362 463 470 600 601
LOKEY, 432 439 453
LONG, 254 415 489 531-533 546 551 555 562 563 570 571 579-581 616 640 657 658 687 689 690 701
LONGLEY, 700
LOTHAM, 682
LOUDEN, 395 405 419 422 430
LOUDERBACK, 569
LOUDON, 306 310 336 340 341 355 356 361 363-365 375 396 404-406 409 473 474 535
LOUISO, 361
LOVE, 341 462-464 473 474 529 616 671
LOW, 546
LOWDERBACK, 534 541 552 553
LOWE, 335 562 564 573 687 689 700
LOWEN, 481
LOWRY, 426
LOYD, 433
LUCAS, 284 316 344 356 363 474 521 531-533 535 536 540-543 550-553 613 620 691 701
LUDLOW, 283 440
LUDWIG, 434 453
LUERS, 324
LUMSDEN, 700
LURGEY, 579
LURGUY, 586

SURNAME INDEX.

LYNCH, 341 395 423 450
LYON, 372 381 611 668
LYONS, 490 512 555
LYTLE, 230 241 243 245 246 281 283 318 324 481 522 561 681-683 687 692 700
LYUCH, 401
M'ARTHUR, 280
M'CALL, 622
M'CLAIN, 254
M'CLURE, 254
M'CONNELL, 254
M'DANIEL, 254
M'KINNEY, 254
MACCAGUE, 611
MACE, 480
MACKLEM, 523
MADDOX, 435 436 453 454 502 505 512 580
MADIGAN, 513
MADISON, 240 312
MAFFERTY, 513
MAFFETT, 601
MAGGINNI, 485
MAHAFFEY, 702
MAHAN, 314 315 481 572 583 670 675 678 679
MAHANNA, 512
MAHAPPY, 662 663
MAHON, 314
MAHOVER, 650
MAIN, 621
MAKLEM, 376 383 402 403 530
MALEY, 401 646
MALLON, 330
MALLOTT, 645
MALOTT, 651 652 687 692
MANCHESTER, 464 465
MANKER, 585 593 613
MANN, 454 463 543 601 602 605 606 609 652 702
MANNON, 413 552 602 607
MARCH, 384
MARKLEY, 310 405 406 409 546
MARKS, 473
MARQUETTE, 318
MARQUIS, 576
MARSH, 585 669 671

MARSHALL, 300 301 303 315 336 341 361 363 365 386 392 393 396 399 401 405 422 473 541 593 612 613 658 671 676
MARSHER, 670
MARTIN, 254 276 281 335 363 380 383 385 392 393 403 415 416 425 431 434 442 451 465 466 470 472 473 492 496 499 500 504 505 514 515 523 527 538 540 545 550 579 580 682
MASON, 403 501 684
MASQUELETTE, 322
MASSIE, 241-243 250 251 281 283 359 360 476 590
MASTERS, 579 678
MASTERSON, 355 454 540 551
MATHERS, 620 621
MATHEWS, 460
MATHIAS, 661
MATTELL, 549
MATTHEWS, 303 383 403 405 406 473
MATTOX, 564
MAXWELL, 469 472 474
MAYER, 564
MAYFIELD, 450
MCADAMS, 282 685
MCAFEE, 650 651
MCALISTER, 609
MCARTHUR, 241 242 244 316 344 359 372 479 553
MCBEATH, 550
MCBETH, 466 520 521 554 624 626 631
MCBRIDE, 655 695 702
MCCAFFERTY, 485 492
MCCAFFREY, 322 492
MCCAGUE, 416 425 430 435 436 439 441 446
MCCAIN, 667
MCCALL, 362 520 624-626 630-634 636 639 642
MCCALLA, 500 514 515
MCCALLAS, 501
MCCALLIAN, 324
MCCALLISTER, 657
MCCAMPBELL, 612
MCCANLAS, 576
MCCARTHY, 485 491 492

MCCARTY, 362 439
MCCHESNEY, 521
MCCLAIN, 362 414 453 585 613 614 619 662 672 680
MCCLANAHAN, 365 580
MCCLELAHAN, 583
MCCLELLAN, 440 592
MCCLENNHAN, 700
MCCLINTICK, 426 454
MCCLOSKEY, 490
MCCLOSKY, 491 492
MCCLUNG, 413 612 700
MCCLURE, 649
MCCOLGEN, 656-658 661
MCCOLGIN, 341 361 392 406 580 619
MCCOLGINS, 361
MCCOLISTER, 576
MCCOLLISTER, 536 583
MCCOLLOUGH, 691 699
MCCOLM, 563
MCCONAUGHY, 402 439 474
MCCONN, 330 362 485 486 492
MCCONNELL, 254 303 415 605 613
MCCOOK, 440
MCCORMACK, 303
MCCORMICK, 255 295 404 454 582 602
MCCOY, 314 481 609 612 613 631
MCCULLOCH, 480 484
MCCUNE, 480-482 484 489 512
MCCURDY, 382
MCCUTHEON, 251
MCDANIEL, 254 384 421 503 505 512-514 534 662 669 690 701
MCDANNOLD, 631
MCDEVITT, 485
MCDINNELL, 481
MCDONALD, 226 231 235 241 242 244 250 322 359 433 473 505 613 685
MCDONOUGH, 343
MCDOWELL, 244 359 366 505
MCDUFFY, 522
MCELFRESH, 615 616
MCELHANEY, 592
MCELHANIE, 619
MCELWEE, 431
MCFADDEN, 414 550 551 585 631 665 667 672 675 676 678
MCFARLAND, 282 284 285

MCFARRON, 644
MCGAFFICK, 393
MCGAVI, 685
MCGEE, 669 676
MCGEHEY, 631
MCGINDLEY, 481
MCGLAUGHLIN, 616
MCGOHAN, 556 570 573
MCGONEDRICK, 640
MCGOULDRIC, 564
MCGREADY, 270
MCGREGOR, 605 619 656 657
MCGREW, 470 471
MCGROARTY, 396 399 406 486 492
MCGROTY, 322
MCGUFFEY, 610
MCHUGH, 384
MCILHANEY, 680
MCILVAIN, 681 685
MCILVAINE, 612
MCINTIRE, 556 612 671
MCINTYRE, 232-234 252 281 291 341 541
MCKEE, 380 459 466 470 616 640 657 662 668 669 676
MCKENZIE, 250 281 632 640
MCKETRICK, 695
MCKIBBEN, 361 362 394 404 410 470 471 473 631
MCKINLEY, 512 513 515 619 620
MCKINLY, 626
MCKINNEY, 380 466
MCKINNY, 389 520
MCKITTRICK, 492
MCKNIGHT, 341 361 405 585 590 613 615 620 621 656 659 661
MCLAIN, 469 555 561 565 572 639 649 682 683 687-692
MCLAUGHLAN, 563
MCLAUGHLIN, 579 580 589 689 691 694 702
MCLEAN, 300 349 633
MCLEFRESH, 551
MCMAHAN, 564
MCMAHON, 330 601 620
MCMANAMAN, 691
MCMANIS, 661
MCMANNIS, 616
MCMANUS, 481

MCMERCHEY, 466
MCMICHAEL, 376
MCMILLAN, 615 662
MCMILLEN, 449 690
MCMILLIN, 420 430 433 454
MCMULLEN, 326 691 700
MCNEELY, 584
MCNEIL, 690
MCNEMAR, 270-273
MCNIGHT, 661
MCNISH, 450
MCNOUN, 614
MCNOWN, 362 620 657 658 661 662
MCNULTY, 513
MCPHERSON, 433 571 702
MCQUILLAN, 330 482 490
MCQUILLIN, 490
MCVAY, 583 586
MEACHAM, 274
MEANS, 687
MEARS, 502
MEDILL, 317 440
MEEK, 401 422 502
MEEKER, 564 570
MEFFORD, 254 380 384 415 433 602 603 605 610 614 621 657 662 690
MEHAFFEY, 404 421
MEHARRY, 544
MEHARY, 656
MEHERRY, 470
MEIGS, 262
MELVIN, 506 619
MEMBRE, 318
MENAUGH, 341 425 436 604 620 621
MENAUGHT, 434
MENNEAUGH, 702
MENZONS, 249
MERANDA, 465
MERCER, 700
MERRICK, 689 700
MERRILL, 416 433 570
MERWIN, 402
MESNARD, 318
MESNER, 333
MESSERSMITH, 466
METZ, 616 619
METZGER, 459 460 461 470 474
MEYERS, 565 624 690

MICHAEL, 465
MICK, 676 677
MIDDLESWART, 414 581 657 659
MIDDLETON, 361 362 364 389 393 395 404 422 430 563 689 700
MIDGHALL, 512
MILES, 308 405 406 409
MILLER, 213 254 283 384 419 433 434 454 461 465 466 469-471 481 515 532 544 545 549 550 552 553 576 580 583 586 601 604 609 612 613 619 621 651 687 689
MILLIGAN, 543 702
MILLS, 414 512 515 536
MINER, 402
MINGUA, 620
MINOR, 364 463
MISCHLER, 450 453 454
MITCHEL, 385
MITCHELL, 361 380 400 414 464 486 492 513 514 601 613 616 620 641 663
MOCKBEE, 453
MOELLER, 466 474
MOFFETT, 616
MOFFORD, 459 465 474
MOHN, 462 465 474
MOHR, 469
MOLER, 632 689
MONAHAN, 550
MONROE, 312 355 360 385 434
MONTGOMERY, 226 229 570 676 695 699 700 702 703
MOODY, 690 691
MOON, 598 651
MOONEY, 620
MOORE, 254 303 309 310 314 360-363 375 376 381 383 400 403 405 406 429-431 450 454 474 486 500 506 512 513 515 521 524-526 529 544-546 550 579 581 600 603 605 606 612 613 615 616 620 623 652 654 656 657 665-667 669 670 672 675-680 695 698 701 702 703
MORECRAFT, 520
MOREHEAD, 481
MORGAN, 317 339 340 362 394 395 404 406 410 422 440 485 512 525 594 595 652 653 687
MORRIS, 281 300 301 313 315 343 345

MORRIS (continued)
  346 351 361 364 366 389 393 395 396
  421 423 484 611 624 625 640 641 663
MORRISON, 364 682
MORROW, 262 283 312 316 344 360 365
  466 536 551-553 563 579 580 590 593
  604 605 656
MORSEMAN, 482
MOSCORE, 700
MOSS, 282 519 521
MOSSET, 492
MOSSMAN, 481
MOULTON, 699
MOUNT, 401
MOURER, 702
MOWRER, 620
MOWRY, 684
MOYER, 555 556 569 572
MOYERS, 465
MUELLER, 322 545
MULLEN, 321
MURPHY, 336 416 431 432 433 435 441
  490 521 522 576 583 689
MURRAY, 322 352 405 425 491 492
MYERS, 293 392 404 415 416 474 520 521
  550-552 602 619 624-626 630-632 640
  657 660 670
NAGLE, 254
NATION, 700
NAVARRONN, 333
NAYLOR, 281
NEAL, 362 366 512 521 522 570 656 702
NEEL, 509
NEEPER, 515
NEFF, 306 564 572 640
NEIL, 512
NEILL, 322 659
NELSON, 251 281 662 688
NESBITT, 665
NESTOR, 464
NEU, 474 544 549 658 659
NEVIN, 669-671 674-677
NEVINS, 668
NEVITT, 653
NEW, 671
NEWBERRY, 217 560 563 571 689
NEWCOMB, 424 425 433
NEWHOUSE, 465
NEWKIRK, 290 385 386 389 394 653 680
NEWMAN, 512 513 532 540 543 546 550
  551 553 614 636
NEWTEN, 655
NEWTON, 239 303 677
NILES, 660
NINE, 563
NOCKA, 466
NOFTSGER, 474
NOLANCE, 620
NORRIS, 341 361-363 400 403 406 434
  452-454 462 465 466 470 472 513
NORTON, 303 425 702
NOWLAND, 619
NOYES, 440
NUGENT, 492
NUTT, 688
O'BANNON, 241
O'CONNELL, 453
O'CONNER, 341 486
O'CONNOR, 321 322 479 490
O'DELL, 440
O'HARA, 409 615 682
O'HARRA, 474 601
O'MALLEY, 324 326 333
OCASLER, 688
ODELL, 404 535
OGDEN, 521 563 564 690
OGLESBY, 295
OLDUM, 669 677
OMSLER, 393
ORR, 612 621
ORTON, 217
OSBON, 432
OSBORN, 281 341 700
OSBORNE, 483
OTT, 473 474
OURSLER, 362 529
OUSLER, 564
OVERSTAKE, 585 591
OVERTON, 689
OVERTURF, 474
OWENS, 514 541 555
PADGETT, 541
PAEBST, 453
PAGE, 580 592 593 646 671 674
PAIGE, 701
PAINTER, 502

SURNAME INDEX.

PALMER, 340 396 416 425 431 433 436 439 450 452 454 494 499 513 552 631 636
PANGBAM, 454
PANGBURN, 353 376 381 382 384 416 503 504 605 614 669 671 674 676 677 679 690
PARCUST, 690
PARENT, 421
PARISH, 466 585 592 668
PARK, 461 469 470 473 474
PARKER, 361 362 365 375 376 379 380 383 393 402 403 424 431 432 436 439 452 453 481 500 502 505 506 509 514 516 540 541 610-612 632 639 655-658 660 663
PARKINSON, 603
PARKS, 667
PARRELL, 563
PARRY, 421 602 619
PASK, 566
PASKINS, 392
PATCHOWSKI, 333
PATTEN, 564 569 572 573
PATTERSON, 230 364 423 430 436 450 466 474 581
PATTISON, 464
PATTON, 404 564 631-633 639 656 660 662
PAUL, 433 501 502 513
PAULDING, 221
PAVEY, 421 645 674
PAYNE, 317 363 401 440 513 541 586
PEACOCK, 615
PEAK, 700
PEARSON, 281 341 393 400 405 406 609 615
PEDDICORD, 560 582 593 594 631 635 639
PEDICORD, 572
PELL, 472
PENCE, 515
PENDILL, 662
PENDLETON, 440
PENN, 301 303 310 376 392 393 400 401 404 409
PENNELL, 659
PENNY, 474 562 569 570
PENTACOST, 499
PEOPLES, 401
PEPPER, 406 409 555
PERKINS, 406 529
PERKIZER, 700
PERRILL, 486
PERRINE, 684
PERRY, 276 384 426 521 523
PERVIANCE, 613
PETERS, 450
PETTIJOHN, 314 315 593 635 666 667 669 670 672 673 675-677
PEYTON, 681
PFEIFFER, 453
PHILIPPS, 563
PHILLIPS, 254 402 404 409 465 614
PHIST, 593
PIATT, 281
PICKARD, 409
PICKERILL, 393 603-605 655-657 695 697 699-702
PICKERING, 624 631
PICKETT, 536
PICKRELL, 362
PIERCE, 374 381 409 426 472 474 703
PIERRE, 645
PIKE, 396 423
PIKETON, 423
PILSON, 362 364 602 619
PIMM, 506
PINCKARD, 362 473
PINDELL, 362 532 533 535 536 540 550-553 658 659 663
PINKERTON, 286
PINNEY, 405
PISTNER, 434
PISTOLE, 611
PITTENGER, 613 700
PITTINGER, 702 703
PITTSER, 619 620 684
PITZER, 481 520 521 551 624 625 631
PLANK, 594
PLUMMER, 465 466 661
POAGE, 285 290 415 416 420 439 611-613
POBST, 485
POE, 669
POGUE, 673
POLICK, 691

POLK, 346 349 350
POLLEN, 656
POLLOC, 484
POLLOCK, 285 364 395 423 469
POMEROY, 393
POOL, 551
PORTER, 303 341 343 407 430 439 451 485 492 494 502 515 602 609 612 613 616 619 688 699 702
POSTLEWAITE, 546
POTTER, 482
POTTS, 610 612 657-659 663
POWELL, 404 465 473 474
POWER, 434 496 513-515
POWERS, 260 341 410 513
PRALL, 690
PRATHER, 526
PREDMORE, 486
PRELZINGER, 466
PRESTON, 453 616
PRIBBLE, 465
PRICE, 363 521 687
PRICKETT, 254 532-534 536 546 550 551
PRIEST, 652
PRINE, 541 619 620 656 658 659 661 663
PRINTY, 280 163 170
PUCKETT, 480 482 484
PULLMAN, 481
PURCELL, 319 322-324 330 331 668 670 676
PURDEN, 341 606
PURDIN, 702
PURDOM, 361 657 670
PURDUM, 361 384 393 401 532 535 541 633 634 639 640 668-670 676
PURDY, 672
PURSEL, 589
QUARRY, 700
QUINLAN, 361
QUINN, 470 473 474 524 613 682
RACE, 500
RACHFORD, 536 551
RADSTIN, 640
RAIN, 505
RAINS, 281 496 512 513
RALSTIN, 625 631 640
RALSTON, 297 362 375 392 519-522 525 529 635 639

RAMEY, 409 496 601 602 613 616 694 700-702
RAMSEY, 419 552 576 625 700
RAMSY, 403 450
RANDOLPH, 682
RANEY, 667 680
RANIS, 481
RANKIN, 314 341 402 403 420 425 431 432 449 466 501 612 619 673 674 699
RANNEY, 317 440
RAPER, 334 561 585 653 691
RAPP, 690
RAU, 219
READE, 318 475 485 492
READY, 684
REAVE, 669
RECORDS, 576 580-583 585 589 590
REDMAN, 415 512 513
REDMON, 254 521
REECE, 685
REED, 322 362 399 473 474 512 541 544 550 552 611 658-660 684 688 702
REEDER, 283 500 506 512 513
REES, 365 376 384 385 389 400 401 405 406 500 544 589 659
REESE, 290 386 486 580
REEVES, 340 393 485 489 492 677 700 702
REICHMANN, 434 453
REID, 315 341 700
REIKERDS, 502
REINERT, 436 454
REIRER, 453
REISENGER, 545
REISER, 454
REISINGER, 544-546 552
REISS, 667
REMELY, 551
REMIST, 454
REMLEY, 631 639 640
REN, 431
REX, 431
REYNOLD, 579
REYNOLDS, 420 424 425 430 449 452 453 539 540 543 550 551 555 564 576 581 610 631 653 655-660 669
RHOADES, 583
RHODES, 421 474 583

SURNAME INDEX.

RHOTEN, 533 536 539 552 575 656-658 661 662
RHUBART, 644
RIBOURDE, 318
RICE, 430 432 535 543 579 661 676
RICH, 535 543 551
RICHARDS, 310 400 406 466 470 569 646 651 653
RICHARDSON, 284 286 365 455 456 459 469 470 472-474 545
RICHEY, 463 602
RICHMOND, 500 506 513 702
RICKETTS, 402
RICKEY, 656 702
RICKY, 656
RIDDLE, 431
RIDER, 479 481 482
RIDGELY, 354
RIDGWAY, 340 431 435 436 441 450 451 454
RIEDLE, 518
RIEVES, 394
RIGGS, 364 494 513 516 670 671 679
RILEA, 406 651 668-671 676 678
RILEY, 393 425 611 691
RILLEY, 689
RINGEISER, 549
RIPLEY, 416
RISCH, 404 406
RISCHEL, 454
RISH, 404
RISINGER, 619
RIST, 513 515
RISTINE, 632 700
ROBB, 479 696
ROBBINS, 580 631 632 634 652 662
ROBE, 615
ROBERTS, 472
ROBERTSON, 700
ROBINS, 533 534 551 569 572 593 669
ROBINSON, 549 555 612 649 702
ROBISON, 254 639
ROCK, 322
ROCKWELL, 434
RODDY, 550 551
RODGERS, 380 699 700
ROE, 401 469
ROEMER, 433

ROESNER, 330
ROGERS, 254 302 322 364 383 403 486 551 573 593 701
ROGLIN, 631
ROHRER, 672
ROHSHEIM, 405
ROLLISON, 414
RONEY, 361 373-375 379 381 382 405 406 461 471 521 526 552 640
RONSHEIM, 404 405 453
ROSE, 406 551 582 632 633
ROSECRANS, 332
ROSELOT, 466
ROSS, 265 292 362 365 380 420 433 435 450 462 470 521 535 563 631 632 634 644 646 649 651 660 663 683 686 688-690 700 701
ROTH, 404 474
ROUDEBUSH, 365
ROUNDS, 521 525
ROUPE, 430
ROUSH, 513 543
ROWE, 645 674
ROYSE, 480 481
RUBENECKER, 331
RUDDELL, 234 235
RUDDLE, 234
RUDLE, 514
RUGGLES, 501 513
RUKEY, 661
RUMSEY, 688
RUNNELS, 667
RUNYAN, 452 481 667 676 690
RUNYON, 542 551
RUSH, 481 563 566
RUSSEL, 363
RUSSELL, 285 345 363 366 566
RUST, 646
RUTH, 480 482 484
RUTHERFORD, 673
RUTLAND, 332
RUTTER, 501
RUTZ, 434 439 453
RYAN, 456 459 513
RYBOLT, 481 489
RYNER, 615
SACKER, 450
SAID, 500

SAINTCLAIR, 254 265 275 276 280 283 284 300 703
SALE, 295
SALISBURY, 383 403 600-602 612 613 619 621
SALLEE, 362 396 404 473 701
SALLYARDS, 396 399
SALSBURY, 529 703
SALT, 678
SAMMONS, 564 572
SAMMS, 624 630 631
SAMPLE, 253 380
SAMS, 575 576 581 676
SANBURN, 473
SANDERS, 593 702
SANDERSON, 604
SANDS, 667 678
SANFORD, 563
SAPP, 572
SARGENT, 275 283 364 365 403 461 463 611
SAVAGE, 322 414 481 485 492 513
SAVORY, 688
SAWYER, 512
SAYERS, 582 585 589 593 682
SCANLAN, 322
SCHAAF, 469 473
SCHAEFFER, 549
SCHAEHFER, 453
SCHATZMAN, 544 549 550 552 553
SCHEER, 454
SCHILLING, 454
SCHILLINGS, 469
SCHLITZ, 513 515
SCHMIDT, 330 454
SCHMITZ, 331 333
SCHNEIDER, 433 434 450 454
SCHOLTER, 433 453
SCHONAT, 333
SCHOONOVER, 469
SCHRECKLER, 658
SCHREIBER, 331 333
SCHROUFE, 667
SCHUBORT, 470
SCHULTZ, 546 563
SCHWALLIE, 331 332 454 499 615 619 658 659
SCHWALM, 332

SCHWEIGHART, 553
SCOFIELD, 303
SCOTT, 230 281 318 363 379 474 500 502 505 509 512-515 575 580 585 593 612 626 632 639 640 653
SCREETCHFIELD, 646
SEARIGHT, 580 593
SEDWILL, 656
SEIGFRIED, 403
SEIP, 619 620
SEIRS, 556
SEITZ, 701
SELLENBERGER, 551
SELLERS, 341 395 423 424
SELLMAN, 431 435 655 656 659 662
SELLMON, 580
SELLS, 341 363 380 392 401 405 463 465 466
SELMON, 581 582 585 590 592 593
SENIER, 432
SENTENNEY, 432
SERGENT, 655-657 659
SERTEL, 331
SEVER, 491
SEWELL, 255
SEYLER, 473
SEYMOUR, 317 441
SHACKELFORD, 480
SHAEFER, 453 454
SHAFFER, 474
SHALER, 404
SHANE, 394
SHANKS, 251
SHANNON, 316 520 653 684 689 700
SHARKELFORD, 403
SHARP, 379 382 514 515 552 621 645 674
SHAUB, 552 553
SHAW, 310 340 347 364 396 404 411 415 416 423-426 430-435 439 450 452-454 459 484 543 544 552 580 601 610 611 614-616 620 621 656 658 660 673 683 695
SHAYSGREEN, 322
SHEARER, 686
SHEDD, 431 432 450
SHEEK, 254
SHEELER, 703
SHEER, 431

SURNAME INDEX.

SHEERER, 543
SHELDON, 638 687 690
SHELTON, 499 500 502-504 509 510 512
    513 516 593
SHEPARD, 280 379
SHEPHERD, 309 310 360 361 363 364 401
    404 405 413 414 430 451 575 581 585
    601 605 609 614 621 695
SHERMAN, 565
SHERWIN, 486
SHICK, 374 521 523 562 623 624
SHIDELER, 473 474
SHIDLER, 405 473
SHIEK, 526
SHIELDS, 362 405 406 639 682 695
SHINGLE, 486
SHINKLE, 462 465 471 482 489 668 669
    676 690
SHINN, 341 616
SHIRLY, 500
SHOAFSTALL, 701
SHOCKEY, 402
SHOFSTALL, 702
SHOTWELL, 281 556 563 602 667 684 688
SHOULTER, 433
SHREVE, 614 615
SHREVES, 540 609 615 620 621
SHROUFE, 646 667
SHUBERT, 473
SHULTZ, 416 473
SHUMAKER, 426 429 431 434 453
SHUMALT, 380
SHUSTER, 381
SIBBALD, 451 512
SIDWELL, 381 401 409 445 573 602 613
    615 616 656 657 688
SILLMAN, 631
SILMAN, 539 551
SIMMERAL, 251
SIMMONS, 470 645 674
SIMMS, 459
SIMONS, 512
SIMONTON, 687 689 690
SIMPKINS, 560 688 690
SIMPSON, 260 425 502 505 513
SINGLE, 400 409 567
SINKS, 692
SKINNER, 579 580 691

SLACK, 379 405 406
SLADE, 340 644
SLAUGHTER, 241 495
SLAYTON, 639
SLOAN, 571
SLOANE, 341 490
SLUSHER, 646
SLY, 336 361 393 405 416 432 453 454 481
SMALLEY, 512
SMALLWOOD, 684 692
SMILEY, 393 405
SMITH, 223 239 251 254 264 281 283 295
    300 317 334 361 365 366 375 395 396
    405 406 412 430 432 440 453 454 464
    466 474 481 489 519-523 526 532 533
    535 541-543 546 550 551 553 563 586
    589 601 602 604 611 613 615 620 624
    626 627 630-633 635 640 643 645 646
    650-652 656 662 669 671 684 688 689
    691 692 702 703
SMITHSON, 481
SMYTHE, 402
SNEDAKER, 310 402 403 405 406 441 451
    453 454 605 610 612 613 619 696 703
SNEED, 474
SNEEDER, 671
SNELL, 480 481 686
SNIDER, 392 431-433 529 542 553 561 620
    658 678
SNIFFIN, 424 426 699
SNOWHILL, 482 485 486 490
SNYDER, 393 474
SOLLE, 613
SOLLENBERGER, 631 632
SOLOMON, 482 485
SORRIES, 515
SOURD, 492
SOUTH, 644 685
SOUTHARD, 682
SOUTHERLAND, 601
SOWARDS, 616
SOWERS, 703
SPAELTY, 432
SPALDING, 350 351
SPARKS, 432 450
SPARRS, 695
SPEARS, 414 454 514 579
SPEECE, 465

SPENCER, 403 474 532 601 615
SPERRY, 404 534
SPICE, 651
SPILLER, 331
SPIRES, 474 535
SPRENGER, 581
SPRINGER, 254 521 531-534 536 539 540 543 550 551
SPURLOCK, 422
SROFE, 341 543 562 565 566 640 642
SROUFE, 653
STABLETON, 362 364 401 404
STACY, 450
STAFFORD, 464 474 513
STALCUP, 613
STALLCUP, 450
STALLINGS, 682
STAMM, 420 433
STANFORD, 667
STANFORTH, 576
STANLEY, 296 480
STANSBERRY, 532-534 542 543 550 624 626 631 632 645 651 653 669
STARKE, 669 670 676
STATEN, 421
STAYTON, 462 465 474 545 620 632 633 639
STEARNS, 674
STEEN, 434 453
STEHLE, 330
STEINMAN, 409
STEINMANN, 544 549
STEPHEN, 405 409 544 552 553
STEPHENS, 616 620 640 651 672 690
STEPHENSON, 334 393 400 405 406 412 414 430 433 441 453 454 459 460 464 469 516 525 566 615
STEVENS, 461 515 565 566 632 672
STEVENSON, 361 363 602 603 621 696 702 703
STEWARD, 401 403 585 633 696
STEWART, 361 376 392 396 399 401 406 465 495 499 500 506 513 515 610 633 639 685 690 692 700
STIGLER, 394
STILL, 375 520
STILLMAN, 419
STILLS, 572 634

STIRES, 529
STITES, 631
STITT, 614 695 701
STIVERS, 362 433 434 446 449 454 464 574 580 589 590 592 593
STOEHR, 543 544
STOKES, 466 563
STONE, 352 613
STOODY, 433
STOUT, 250 251 474 645
STOWE, 449
STRAIGHT, 540 541 545 551 570 677
STRAIN, 560 561
STRAIT, 616 669 670
STRANDER, 422
STRANGE, 645 668 674
STRATTON, 520 572 585 625 626 630-633 636 640 653
STREIGHT, 657
STRICKLIN, 684
STROUB, 689
STROUBLE, 469
STROUP, 479 650
STUART, 563 570
STUESS, 433
STUMP, 406 555 559 564 565 572
SULLIVAN, 341 486 552 553 700
SUMMERBELL, 354 503
SUMMERS, 400
SURRY, 565
SURVEY, 413
SUTHERLAND, 434 513 613 700
SUTTON, 360 434 512 513 515 694 695 697
SWAIN, 582
SWAN, 500 663
SWEARINGEN, 503 513
SWINDT, 383 403
SWISHER, 500 512 513 702
SWOPE, 470 473 529
SWORMSTEDT, 646 674
SWYER, 461
SYMMES, 253
SYMMS, 469
TAFT, 425
TAMME, 331
TAPPAN, 316
TAPPIN, 553

SURNAME INDEX.

TARBELL, 248 363 404 406 439
TARBLE, 430
TATMAN, 362 405 461 465 470 571
TAYLOR, 335 336 340 350 351 361 364 394 399 420 421 425 440 461 500 513 562-564 572 682 688 690-692
TEAL, 255
TEETERS, 513
TEMPLE, 681
TEST, 555
THAME, 461
THATCHER, 431
THEIS, 394
THIEN, 333
THIENPONT, 331
THOMAS, 341 355 405 406 409 470 471 473 474 500 602 630-632 646 652 655 682 687-689 695 703
THOMPSON, 282 290 302 303 341 361-363 365 373 379-383 402-405 409 412 430-436 440 441 450 453 466 470 471 485 489 492 512 520 521 529 546 549 555 556 564-566 571-573 593 609 613 619 621 626 632 639 640 662 680-682 690 693 701-703
THOMSON, 619
THORNHILL, 481
THORNTON, 362 525 526
THORP, 532 541 550 657
THRESHER, 472
THURMAN, 440
TIBBETTS, 613
TIBBS, 383 682
TIFFIN, 302 355
TIGART, 589
TILDEN, 441 553 701
TISSANDER, 650
TOBBE, 331 333
TOBEY, 690
TOD, 316 317 340 440 553
TODD, 281
TOLIN, 459 466 469 474
TOLL, 662
TOMB, 580 612 620 621 655 656
TOMLINSON, 396 423-425 450
TOPPIN, 585
TORRENCE, 363 434
TOWNSEND, 553 701

TOWNSLEY, 689
TRACEY, 680
TRACY, 541 546 670-672 680
TRAPP, 332
TRAUTWEIN, 658
TRENT, 645 674
TRIMBLE, 286 312 316 317 334 355 401 440 553 579
TRIPLET, 403 616
TRITTS, 486
TROUT, 281 340 462 466 470 473 573 686 688
TROUTMAN, 473 619
TRUE, 514
TRUITT, 646
TUCKER, 384 472 473 482 544 616 652 653
TUPMAN, 421
TUPPER, 416
TURNER, 403 406 486
TURNEY, 430 450
TWEED, 254 309 310 380 405 409 415 423 432 451 454 523 620
TYLER, 257 340 363 365 405 433 500 601 619 620 663
ULREY, 489
ULRY, 479
UPTON, 641
UTT, 250
UTTER, 365 473
VAIL, 615
VAIN, 502
VALENTINE, 469
VALLANDIGHAM, 317 440
VANANDA, 473 549
VANBRIGGLE, 473
VANBUREN, 316 395 440 659
VANCE, 276 314-316 356 362 400 405 433 452 453 551 572 576 585 594 653 667 669 671 672 676 677
VANCLEAF, 399
VANDAMENT, 521 562 631
VANDELPH, 555
VANDEMAN, 523 525 526
VANDYKE, 403 406 469 472 535 646 674 699
VANE, 516
VANEMON, 374

VANERVOORT, 485
VANHORN, 486
VANMETER, 373 479 632
VANNERS, 703
VANNESS, 677
VANSANDT, 669
VANSANT, 479
VANTRUMP, 317 440
VANWINKLE, 593
VANZANT, 460
VARLEY, 649
VAUGHAN, 555 564
VEACH, 500
VEECH, 505
VERITY, 384 401 613
VIERS, 593
VINSANDT, 669
VINTON, 239 317 440
VOGEL, 331
VOLNEY, 221
VORHEES, 454
WAAD, 501
WADDLE, 699 700
WADE, 250 251 281 555
WAGNER, 658 659
WAHL, 544 549 632 634 635
WAIT, 465 653
WAITS, 481 651 653 684 685 687 688 690-692
WALDRON, 281 365 418 509 511-513 515 516
WALKER, 253 290 389 392 512 535 633 646 683 686 688 691
WALL, 254 335 362 374 375 382 383 400
WALLACE, 305 384 414 535 631 633 640 645 653 662 682 702 703
WALLER, 363
WALLING, 481
WALLIS, 657 659
WALTERS, 395 423 690 703
WALTHER, 470 473
WAMACKS, 404 580 602
WANUMSER, 450
WARD, 233-235 419 424 551
WARDEN, 684 691
WARDLAW, 664 665
WARDLOW, 405 520 547 549 552 560 562

WARDLOW (continued)
565 569 571-573 623 624 639 640 669 670 673 676-678 680
WARFIELD, 480
WARING, 364
WARNER, 409 425 470 639
WARREN, 402 403 700 702
WARSTELL, 506 514
WARWICK, 621
WASHBURN, 226 231 232 235 242 250 281 318 355 412 483 484 520 605 606 651 669
WASHBURNE, 532 534 535 542 576
WASHINGTON, 224 312 355 422 461 606
WATERFIELD, 464 470 478
WATERMAN, 405 406 552
WATERS, 331 341 384 416 474 526 533 544 546 552 558 653 657 658 670 672 676
WATSON, 481 559 653
WATTERSON, 499
WATTS, 231 523
WAVERLY, 396
WAYLAND, 641
WAYNE, 221 223-225 232 243 251 252 355 359 481 482 524
WEATHERSPOON, 474
WEAVER, 286 290 394 544 549 639 642 644 654
WEBBER, 653
WEBER, 332 544 552 553 650 651
WEDDELL, 405
WEDGE, 611
WEDMEYER, 690
WEEKS, 646 650 653 684 687 692
WEGMAN, 332
WEISBRADT, 552
WEISBRODT, 333 544
WELCH, 524
WELLER, 316 440
WELLS, 362 463 470 532 534 535 543 552 553 560 563-565 571 645 670 674 691 700
WELSH, 590
WERNER, 573
WESLEY, 299
WESLICK, 466

SURNAME INDEX.

WEST, 362 365 383 402 409 440 447 474 496 526 529 533 552 553 613 646 656-658 689 694 696 698 699 701-703
WESTLAKE, 524 645 674
WETHERINGTON, 281
WETHINGTON, 251
WETZEL, 454
WHARTON, 384 466 632 633 683 689
WHEAT, 563 689 700
WHEELER, 454 515 676
WHITE, 282 283 290 335 336 339 340 361-366 373 380 386 392 393 396 399-404 425 432 434 454 465 470 471 474 492 500 512 513 520 521 544 565 571 572 611 631 640 650 653 673 682 702
WHITEMAN, 232-235 361 409 521 530 632-634 636
WHITES, 631
WHITFIELD, 323
WHITMAN, 689
WHITMORE, 474
WHITSON, 426
WHITTEMORE, 425
WHORTON, 555 572 639
WICKHAM, 592
WIESE, 331 333
WIKOFF, 453
WILCOX, 679
WILDER, 402
WILES, 415 425 430 441 453 454
WILEY, 382 469
WILKES, 523
WILKINS, 593 616
WILKS, 474 520 521
WILL, 223
WILLEY, 684 685 689
WILLIAMS, 303 433 434 439 450 453 454 470 474 485 590 596 599 602 616 620 676 680 689 691 702 703
WILLIAMSON, 303 310 593 601 602 604 605 612 613 616 619-621 663
WILLIS, 281 685 691
WILLLIAMS, 619
WILLS, 301 386 403-405 434 487 551 552 605 616 620 626 629 631 636 670 671
WILSON, 361 362 389 393 400 404 406 409 446 465 473 474 476 499 513 521 560-562 564 566 570 573 575 580 586

WILSON (continued) 589 595 601 603 604 611-613 615 619-621 652 653 656 659 660 670 677 679 687 688 692 703
WINDER, 473
WINDSOR, 571
WINTER, 539 555 556 564 565 571-573
WINTERS, 453 454 470 473 580 593 688
WIRT, 316
WISBEY, 626
WISBY, 569
WISE, 362 461
WITHAM, 613
WITTEMORE, 425
WOHLLEBER, 659
WOLCOTT, 536 544 550 552
WOLF, 222 473 563 646
WOMACKER, 532
WOMACKS, 543 551
WOMAX, 619
WOOD, 231 317 363 380 386 404 440 466 481 486 541 684 688
WOODRUFF, 254
WOODS, 290 374 376 379 385 389 393 405 406 409 453 474 502 551 601 602 616 619 702
WOODWARD, 394 403 439 450 453
WORK, 551 601 602 606 616 619
WORKMAN, 474 652
WORMACKS, 660
WORRELL, 688
WORSTELL, 513 669
WORSTESS, 515
WRESLER, 521
WRESTLER, 524 632 636 640
WRIGHT, 362 380 402 429 450 460 506 576 600 611 619 646 653 655 656 659 668-672 676-678 694 695
WYKOFF, 613 620
WYLIE, 303 361 404 420 431 433 439 453 584
YATES, 341 465 470 473 474
YEARSELEY, 474
YEARSLEY, 465 469 472
YEATON, 434
YECKO, 332 542 544
YOCHEM, 552
YOCKEY, 541 553

YORK, 461 589 592
YOUNG, 254 295 310 358 362 374 399 402
    403 405 409 416 426 433 450 453 454
    463 465 467 474 506 513 526 551-553
    559 564 566 569 573 602 619 623 624
    626 630-634 640 645 656 674 701
YOUNGS, 274
ZANE, 291 292
ZAUMSEIL, 394 433
ZAUMSIEL, 453
ZAUMSIL, 454
ZEIGLER, 405
ZELLER, 450 649
ZERKER, 703
ZIEGLER, 544 549 550 552
ZINK, 563 613 690 700
ZOLLERS, 555 564
ZUMALT, 520 526
ZUMATT, 623-626 632

www.ingramcontent.com/pod-product-compliance
Lightning Source LLC
Chambersburg PA
CBHW060908300426
44112CB00011B/1391